D1568224

Clarendon Lectures in English

BIBLIOPHOBIA

The End and the Beginning of the Book

BRIAN CUMMINGS

OXFORD
UNIVERSITY PRESS

Great Clarendon Street, Oxford, OX2 6DP,
United Kingdom

Oxford University Press is a department of the University of Oxford.
It furthers the University's objective of excellence in research, scholarship,
and education by publishing worldwide. Oxford is a registered trade mark of
Oxford University Press in the UK and in certain other countries

First Edition published in 2022

Impression: 1

Published in the United States of America by Oxford University Press
198 Madison Avenue, New York, NY 10016, United States of America

British Library Cataloguing in Publication Data

Data available

Library of Congress Control Number: 2021942603

ISBN 978–0–19–284731–7

Printed and bound in the UK by
TJ Books Limited

τὰ τῆς γε λήθης φάρμακ᾽ ὀρθώσας μόνος,
ἄφωνα καὶ φωνοῦντα, συλλαβὰς τιθείς,
ἐξηῦρον ἀνθρώποισι γράμματ᾽ εἰδέναι

Euripides, fr. 578 (from the lost play *Palamedes*)

All changed, changed utterly:
A terrible beauty is born
          W. B. Yeats, 'Easter, 1916'

Preface

I begin with an apology to myself as much as to my readers: books take a long time to write. At an exhibition in Cambridge in 1983 for the five-hundredth anniversary of Martin Luther's birth the final display was an old charred volume. Alongside was a description of how Luther burned books in 1520 to defy his own excommunication, and how his books were burned in turn to mark him as anathema. How, I wondered, had such an object of horror survived? To my astonishment, I found out the book was a changeling, some surplus nineteenth-century records of the Nottinghamshire Water Board, set alight by librarians for the occasion to provide a visual symbol. This, too, struck me as a strange kind of sacrilege. What is it, I asked myself, that makes a librarian burn a book? Or what keeps another safe as holy treasure? The book, it seemed, is *sacer*, as the Romans would say: both hallowed and cursed.

This idea has nagged in my mind ever since, like a scruple which will not go away. I chose book-hating as an appropriate subject for an inaugural professorial lecture at the University of Sussex in 2008, where I recalled famous instances of bibliophobia, alongside reflections on my first term as a teacher, long ago, during which a fatwa was declared against Salman Rushdie. To this day, none of my seminars has ever been so animated; a colleague knocked on the door to see if we were all right. To colleagues at Sussex in those years, who talked through my strange fascination with books and violence, I now offer penitence, especially Geoff Bennington (who knocked on the door), Homi Bhabha, Maggie Boden, Adriana Bontea, Peter Burke, Jackie Cassell, Tom Crow, Mat Dimmock, Andrew Hadfield, Maurice Howard, Rod Kedward, Jeremy Lane, Robin Milner-Gulland, Ambra Moroncini, Michael Morris, Claudia Nocentini, Michelle O'Malley, John Röhl, and Martin van Gelderen.

Later, I was asked to give the Clarendon Lectures at Oxford in 2012. It is to this invitation, and to many acts of friendship that it incurred, that a genesis proper of this book belongs. Over the course of several weeks, I was able to formulate an argument, and share ideas, with members of the university and other visitors, including Sharon Achinstein, Laura Ashe, Colin Burrow, Bart van Es, Kantik Ghosh, Vincent Gillespie, Anne Hudson, Paulina Kewes, Peter McCullough, Laura Marcus, Katie Murphy, David Norbrook, Bernard and Heather O'Donoghue, Seamus Perry, Will Poole, David Rundle, Emma Smith, Adam Smyth, Kathryn Sutherland, Dan Wakelin, Philip West, and David Womersley. At Christ Church, where I was a Visiting Fellow, I lingered over wine in company with Kate Bennett, Mishtooni Bose, Sarah Foot, Peter McDonald, Sara Mortimer, and especially mine host, Brian Young. My warm thanks go to the Faculty of English, and to the Dean and Students of Christ Church.

An added benefit of the Clarendon Lectures is that they bring with them the generous patronage of Oxford University Press. Jacqueline Norton and Ellie Collins have been patient guardians and muses throughout, over lunches in Berlin, London, and New York, as well as Oxford. They have kept faith with me and encouraged me, sharing an enormous knowledge of books, along with other colleagues at the Press such as Andrew McNeillie, Judith Luna, and Paul Luna. Not least, they also put me in touch with Karen Raith, Vasuki Ravichandran, Cailen Swain, and Aimee Wright, who have helped with editorial processes and picture research. Ellie also found me a blessed pair of readers, who not only did not scorn the project, but who perused it with learned sensitivity, ardour, and wit, making me laugh out loud and renew my toil. Leofranc Holford-Strevens has been an incomparable editor.

Over time an idea has grown from book-burning to a broader enquiry into the history of books as objects, and also the philosophical basis of writing in general. This research has been partly funded by the generous support of the Leverhulme Trust, the Arts and Humanities Research Council, and library fellowships in Wolfenbüttel, the Huntington, and the Folger. At an early stage, I realized that such a study needed to extend over the widest global reach and epochal time. The book ranges across six continents, seven religions, and five thousand years of writing, from Sumeria to the smartphone. It contains written examples from each of the last thirty centuries, and several before. This has challenged and defeated my expertise at every turn. It also means the book does not claim in any way to be comprehensive, and indeed I have willingly abandoned chronology and geography as structural devices. Instead, I adopt a more personal approach. My method borrows from the idea of the essay, and the artistic genre of the collage; at times, it has even strayed into the territory of the travelogue. I have therefore learned from friends who are masters in these arts, such as Anna Hollstein, Gabriel Josipovici, Adam Phillips, and Colin Thubron; and from others who have walked or talked with me round places or things I know too little about, such as Guillemette Bolens, Euan Cameron, Michele Campopiano, Terence Cave, Roger Chartier, Jenny Clement, Craig Clunas, Line Cottegnies, Jean Demerliac, Simon Ditchfield, Milad Douelhi, Eamon Duffy, Kathy Eden, Ziad Elmarsafy, Lukas Erne, Michael Fend, Kit Fan, Ken Fincham, Helen Fulton, Indira Ghose, Alice Goodman, Jan Graffius, Margreta de Grazia, Stephen Greenblatt, John Guy, Jon Haarberg, Tim Harrison, Hugh Haughton, Babette Hellemans, Andreas Höfele, Hyosik Hwang, Isabel Karremann, David Kastan, Matt Kavaler, Jim Kearney, Tamara van Kessel, Kevin Killeen, Gerard Kilroy, Stephan Laqué, Ceri Law, Edward Wilson Lee, Russ Leo, Amanda Lillie, Henk Looijesteijn, Monica Loup, César Lucas-Nuñez, Julia Lupton, Penny McCarthy, Jon McGovern, Peter Mack, Lynne Magnusson, Noriko Manabe, Peter Marshall, José Luis Martínez-Dueñas

Espejo, Jean-Christophe Mayer, Charlotte Methuen, Oliver Morgan, Joe Moshenska, Subha Mukherji, Lalage Neal, Jeanne Nuechterlein, Anne O'Donnell, Natalie Oeltjen, Claudia Ölk, Roger Pardo-Maurer, José María Pérez Fernández, Lino Pertile, Jason Peters, Claudia Portela, Burcht Pranger, Sameer Rahim, Jenny Richards, Claudia Richter, Karis Riley, Thomas Röske, Davide Sala, Regina Schwartz, Kirsti Sellevold, Bill Sheils, James Simpson, Helen Smith, Nigel Smith, Peter Stallybrass, Paul Stevens, Alan Stewart, Richard Strier, Céline Surprenant, Ramie Targoff, Margaret Tudeau, Elizabeth Tyler, Wyger Velema, Stefano Villani, Alex Walsham, Tamar Wang, Rowan Williams, George Younge, and Antoinina Bevan Zlatar. Asadour Guzelian shared with me his memories as well as his photography of the Rushdie book-burning in Bradford. Kit and Hugh in particular have mulled over the whole thing, read chapters, opened bottles, walked miles. Alex and I spent three years working closely together which has deepened everything here. To Eamon a special dedication is due, with a nod to his love of poetry as well as holy relics.

A book about books owes most of all to the people who devote their lives to them: I here archive my debt to curators at a host of institutions, including the Bibelmuseum and Rijksmuseum in Amsterdam; the Stadsarchief and Plantin-Moretus Museum in Antwerp; the Universitätsbibliothek in Basel; the Staatsbibliothek, Neues Museum, and Jewish Museum in Berlin; the University Library and the College libraries of Corpus Christi, King's, Magdalene, Queens', and Trinity in Cambridge; the Cathedrals of Canterbury and Chichester; the Library of the University of Virginia in Charlottesville; of Trinity College, the National Museum of Ireland, and the Chester Beatty, Dublin; of the Cathedral and the Old Palace in Durham; the Biblioteca Medicea Laurenziana in Florence; the Museum of the Alhambra in Granada; the Houghton Library at Harvard University; the Biblioteka Jagiellońska in Kraków; the British Library, the British Museum, the Institute of Historical Research, Lambeth Palace Library, the National Archives, St Paul's Cathedral Library, the Stationers' Company, the Warburg Library, and Dr Williams's Library in London; the Clark Library at the University of California in Los Angeles; the Musée de l'imprimerie and the Musée gallo-romain in Lyon; the Bayerische Staatsbibliothek and Glyptothek in Munich; the New York Public Library; the Museo Archeologico in Naples; the Germanisches Nationalmuseum in Nürnberg; the Bodleian, the Taylorian, and the College libraries of All Souls, Christ Church, Corpus Christi, Lincoln, Merton, and New College, Oxford; the Archives Nationales, the Bibliothèque nationale de France, the Bibliothèque de l'Arsenal, the Louvre, and the Société de l'histoire du Protestantisme in Paris; the Rosenbach Library and the University of Pennsylvania in Philadelphia; the epigraphic collection of the Museo Nazionale, the Vatican Museums, and Vatican Library in Rome; the Huntington Library in San Marino; the National Museum in Seoul, and the early printing museum in Cheongju; the Fisher Library, PIMS and CRRS at the University of Toronto; the

Library of Congress, the Folger Shakespeare Library, the Freer and Sackler Galleries, and the Smithsonian, in Washington, DC; the Herzog-August-Bibliothek in Wolfenbüttel; and York Minster Library. Among many companions of the book in those places and elsewhere I cherish John Barnard, Nicholas Bell, Peter Blayney, Karen Brayshaw, Hugh Cahill, James Carley, Emily Dourish, Caroline Duroselle-Melish, Liz Evenden, Guillaume Fau, Mirjam Foot, Alex Gillespie, Betty Hagerman, Christopher de Hamel, Arnold Hunt, Monika Jaglarz, Kristen Jensen, Elisabeth Leedham-Green, Deidre Lynch, Kathleen Lynch, Scott McKendrick, David McKitterick, Giles Mandelbrote, Arthur Moratti, Robin Myers, Eef Overgaauw, Andrew Pettegree, Ed Potten, James Raven, William St Clair, David Selwyn, Liam Sims, Michael Suarez, Abbie Weinberg, Margaret Willes, Heather Wolfe, and Georgianna Ziegler. Richard Ovenden and I agreed not to worry that we were writing similar books. An especially warm hug goes to Sarah Griffin and Steven Newman at York Minster Library, and to staff and students there on my long-running Religion and the Book Seminar. Most of all, I have learned more about books from Henry Woudhuysen than anyone. More than that, he has been a supportive critic and magus of my strangest ideas about them for two decades.

While I have ranged far and wide in the writing of the book, I have tried above all not to be phoney in my interests. As often as not, thoughts have come to me in travelling, by listening to new languages, and getting to know their strange scripts; in visiting exhibitions and art galleries. To curators of museums, temples, mosques, or churches all over Europe and the Americas, Australia, China, Morocco, Singapore, or South Korea, I make a silent blessing. For the dead who have left me: especially Margaret Aston, Irena Backus, Jean-François Gilmont, Eric Griffiths, Geoffrey Hill, Stephen Medcalf, Kevin Sharpe, and Tony Trott; and above all my parents, who first read to me and who left me their books, I say a little prayer. Within my family, my steadfast brother David, my marvellous aunt Melva, as also Archie, Helena, Marzenna, Anna, Cris, Evert, Marian, Molly, Charlie, Sophie, and Jamie, have humoured me as I burbled on. Above all, three people will recognize in these pages an odyssey of mind and heart. My children, Thomas Cummings, who is a molecular biologist, and Daniel Cummings, who is a musician, have shared their passions with me as well as mine; they will find their ideas or their favourite artists on almost every page. Finally, Freya Sierhuis has lived and journeyed every minute, in retrospect and prospect. She has taught me to feel with something of her intuitive grace, and every word I have written comes from conversation with her.

CONTENTS

V. THE BODY AND THE BOOK

VI. GHOST IN THE BOOK

Note On Texts

Classical Greek and Latin sources, including late-antique authors, whether in the original languages or English translation, are cited from the Loeb Classical Library; later Latin texts from Oxford Medieval Texts and the I Tatti Library. Translations of Hebrew scriptures, the Christian Bible (KJV), the Qur'an, and the Book of Common Prayer (unless otherwise noted) are from the Oxford World's Classics editions. For the Talmud and other Jewish texts, I have used the online collection at sefaria.org. For Buddhist texts, I have used the resources of the Pali Canon Online and the Buddhist Digital Resource Centre (BDRC). For Islamic texts I have used the Islamic Texts Society. Citations of Christian church fathers (unless otherwise noted) are from J.-P. Migne's *Patrologia Graeca* and *Patrologia Latina* (*PG* and *PL*). Shakespeare is quoted from the Oxford Shakespeare. All other references appear in footnotes. Transliterations from a myriad of world scripts comply as closely as possible to conventions used in my constant companion: *The World's Writing Systems*, edited by Peter T. Daniels and William Bright (Oxford: Oxford University Press, 1996). Non-English words in common use, where diacritics might be distracting, are left as they are. Proper names, similarly, are given in the source language except where common use prevails. Some words, sometimes for clarification, sometimes maybe as talismans, appear in the original scripts.

List of Figures

List of Plates

I

DEATH OF THE BOOK

tota enim philosophorum vita, ut ait Socrates, commentatio mortis est

Cicero, *Tusculan Disputations* (45 BCE)

1

Is There a Future for the Book?

Wonder is never far from terror. At first the internet presaged utopia, a brave new world of freedom. Of a sudden, chains on human knowledge evaporated into thin air. 'We cannot eliminate inequality or abuse of power, but through technological inclusion we can help transfer power into the hands of individual people and trust that they will take it from there', says *The New Digital Age* (2013), with clunky optimism, co-authored by Google's humanitarian Chairman.[1] As digital books coincided with a new millennium, iconoclasm met prognosis in latent triumphalism. The first-ever issue of *Wired* in 1993 boasted: 'Books once hoarded in subterranean stacks will be scanned into computers and made available to anyone, anywhere, almost instantly.'[2] In July 2010, Amazon declared Kindle digital books outsold print (hardcover and paperback combined). Paper and moving type, it appeared, would turn into memories, as if antiquarian pastimes, like codicology or calligraphy. Books in postmodernity are outdated. Most people gain most information from digital sources, from smartphones or social media even more than laptops. Young people especially, literate, sophisticated, and intelligent, may never have bought a newspaper, or rarely read a physical book all the way through. Information is gained, or constituted, by other means. Meanwhile in October 2004, ironically at the Frankfurt Book Fair (which dates back to 1454, just after Johannes Gutenberg built his press), *Wired*'s prophecy came to life in Google Books. The ambitions of this project are totalitarian: nothing less than a database of all the books in the world.

Today, the project appears less utopia than dystopia, as it shatters through copyright and property law, threatens public libraries with destruction, and reproduces error upon error in merciless transcription. Now we tell ourselves we live in an age of the death of the book. An early prophet of doom was Margaret Atwood, speaking in 2007 to the theme 'Digitize or Die'. She advocated damage limitation toward new technology.[3] An elegy for her beloved personal library met deterministic fatalism about the future. In the decades since Atwood, that minimal hope offered by the word 'or' has diminished: we are all digitized, and we are still dying. Even as Atwood promoted the need to digitize, digitization was sucking our souls. In that year, Shoshona Zuboff conducted research into Google now present in *The Age of Surveillance Capitalism* (2019).[4] If the book is a machine, Google owns the rights, and also the machine that reads it. We are deluded to call ourselves its readers. Artificial intelligence drives each end of the process.

Already by 2007, algorithms supposedly designed to search knowledge mirrored back onto our selves. Facebook reads us, not the other way around. It is difficult not to feel apocalyptic: fear of obsolescence fights hand in hand with fear of oblivion. Which will come first? Such sentiments are not new to the twenty-first century: they feature in early twentieth-century modernism. Filippo Marinetti prophesied that books were fated to disappear, along with cathedrals and museums; in a Futurist manifesto of 1913, he called for 'a typographic revolution directed against the idiotic and nauseating concepts of the outdated and conventional book'.[5] Marinetti's rebellion against the standard typeset page also beset Gertrude Stein, James Joyce, and Ezra Pound. In an opposite plane, tradition regrouped. F. Scott Fitzgerald in 1936 bemoaned the consequences of cinema for literary authors: 'the power of the written word subordinated to another power, a more glittering, grosser power'.[6] It is possible to feel, four generations later, that the predictions look antiquated, like 'the death of the novel' that Walter Benjamin proclaimed in his 1930 essay *Krisis des Romans*; or 'the death of the author', in Roland Barthes's enduring sally of 1967.[7] In comparison to climate change or surveillance capitalism, the survival of books in printed form appears perhaps a trivial matter.

Report of the death of the book is exaggerated. We should have known: the Torah foretold the false prophet as 'the dreamer of dreams'.[8] Abū Naṣr al-Fārābī, in the ninth-century *Treatise of the Intellect*, said prophecy is not about fact but imagination.[9] The front cover of *The Future of the Book in the Digital Age*, published in 2006, depicts a machine on top of a pile of hardbacks, in victory.[10] The machine is an iPod, a device nobody now uses. I first heard bloomsdoom prophesied as a sixteen-year-old schoolboy, by the City Librarian of Birmingham: strange how common *bibliophobia* is among librarians. Yet the technology she predicted would destroy the age of paper—the microfiche—is a thing of the past. Most people today have never seen the monstrous contraption of the microfiche reader. Such is the irony of technological change and desuetude. In the 1990s, in an early case of memes going viral, a spoof email went the rounds proposing a new device for storing and retrieving information, called BOOK 1.0.[11] The device, it was said, was environmentally friendly, requiring no power source other than a human hand. The email also advertised a new device PENCIL 2.0, a 'manual input device', now in development, with which a user could make notes into BOOK 1.0. The joke may yet be reversed, as digital technologies fight against newer technologies in the ever-expanding Matrix. Paper may be old-fashioned but its capacity to last is well proven. Indeed, twentieth-century paper is the least well-lasting; older books survive better than new ones; manuscripts on vellum better still. How email will be archived in the libraries of the future, including the one about BOOK 1.0, no one yet knows.

This book is not about the e-book. The Kindle is a passing phase, a parasitic substitute for existing formats. If a new technology is central to my argument it is the smartphone. It might be said that it is a not a 'book' at all, yet in addition to other functions it takes the place of a personal library of physical books. The Kindle *War and Peace* is not different in kind from an Oxford World's Classics paperback; but literature is not the only model for a book. Twenty-five years ago, any house in London, however indifferent to Tolstoy, would have contained a number of paperbacks: an *A to Z*, to navigate the local streets; a Yellow Pages to find a plumber or a new restaurant; a few cookbooks and travel guides. Somewhere would be a pile of newspapers and magazines. If you ran out of information you took a bus to a public library. Now all such things cohabit a smartphone inside the library of the World Wide Web. Everything about a smartphone is new-fangled, yet it performs functions forever old: a storage device for information. Like books, smartphones promise access to ideas: objects of desire, or a passage to free agency.

Prevailing argument in the last decades assumes the digital book is completely new, conceptualizing the relation of digital to physical as one of replacement. Yet this is not what has happened. So far, most people choose to use the two alongside each other. The same happens in music, where streaming coincides with a revival of vinyl, and new interaction between live and recorded performance. All the arts react to the energies of digital media. Yet alongside this is a curious fear, or paranoia. Digital media combine strange forms of intimacy and exchangeability, with almost unimaginable distance or loss. Where is your text? It is on my phone, but then again, it is not. I received it from you, but then, you are not there. I was reminded of this when I had the necessity of clearing my parents' home, a while ago. Loss combined with consolation, as I found my parents' and grandparents' letters and notes. The question struck: what will survive of me? For much of my life the telephone was the place where I spoke to my parents. Many significant moments of life are recorded on SMS or Skype, but I don't know where that is kept; some of my most important emails I can no longer access, even if the US government can. Anxiety of estrangement from the archive of daily life is pervasive.

As the digital age came into being it aroused euphoria and hostility, mixed with panic and experimentation. Many people reacted as if human beings had never felt this way before. Being a historian of the early printed book, I felt a sense of familiarity. On 12 March 1455, Eneo Silvio Piccolomini, secretary to the Holy Roman Emperor (and soon Pope Pius II) wrote that the previous October he had seen five folded sheets from a Bible, 'executed in extremely clean and correct lettering'.[12] Almost as Gutenberg printed his second book, people said print had changed the world. Cardinal Nicholas of Cusa, Papal Legate in Germany from 1446, was an early enthusiast. Martin Luther in his *Table Talk* called it God's last and greatest gift, with a sting in the tail heralding the end of the world.[13] Print, like digital books, offered non-finite freedom, the potential omnipresence of writing. This was not true: early printed books had small print runs. When Luther's 95 Theses appeared, only a few thousand people saw a copy of the original broadsheet. Yet the authorities feared it was impossible to get rid of it. Indeed,

Protestants regretted that the infernal machine had replaced the *viva vox* of preaching.[14] I sensed a synergy between overpowering feelings of five hundred years ago, and those of my generation. I wanted to understand why the book *per se* creates phenomena of fear, or violence.

Captain Henry Bell, agent in Germany for the Stuart kings James I and Charles I, translated Luther's *Table Talk* into English and had it printed in 1652.[15] The frontispiece shows Luther with a small book in his massive hands, a battering ram of a Bible at his feet. In the preface Bell tells a very strange story. Pope Gregory XIII, hearing of the 'last divine discourses' of the heretic, asked Rudolph II to make an Edict throughout the Holy Roman Empire, burning all printed copies of it in existence, and sentencing to death anyone keeping it at home. Years later in 1626, a German acquaintance of Bell, Casparus van Sparr, doing some building works in his grandfather's old house, dug some deep foundations. Lo and behold, a last lost copy of Luther's book happily turned up, in an obscure hole, wrapped in linen cloth, covered with beeswax. Europe now was gripped by a ferocious war of religion, the Thirty Years War, so the book went to Bell in England for safekeeping. Having perfect German, Bell begins to translate; he is slow at the work, but a ghost appears in a dream to hurry him up; he goes to prison for debt, which gives him opportunity for writing. Finally, he gives the text to Archbishop William Laud, who calls it a work of 'eternal memory', and Parliament grants it a licence. Even now, Lady Luck intervenes: the English Civil War erupts, and Laud is imprisoned and beheaded for treason in 1645. No wonder Bell calls his book, after this fabulous farrago of tall talk, a 'miraculous preservation'. If only a tenth of it is true, it is an allegory of the life of books.

I have called my book *Bibliophobia* in reference to the long history, as old as books, of their destruction, literal and metaphorical. It captures a dark side of the book, too easily idealized. Gutenberg's print revolution gets equated with enlightenment and progress. Bibliophiles hopefully outnumber bibliophobes. My subject is not only hostility, but a not unrelated history of bibliomania or what I will call bibliofetishism. We need not be students of Freud to recognise desire *and* anxiety in the same object. In Freud's case of Little Hans in 1909, a five-year-old boy has a phobia for horses and will not leave the house.[16] 'Bibliophobia' is not in any clinical list of phobias or psychoanalytic study of the Oedipus Complex. However, Freud's vocabulary of repression or aversion helps to analyse the medium of letters. Of special interest are ways in which material books invest embodiment and personality—or by obverse, fears of destruction or invasion of identity. The final act of *Hamlet* begins with a prince and some gravediggers; it ends with a litany over his corpse. In the graveyard Hamlet muses on a skull: 'That skull had a tongue in it, and could sing once'. No written record remains, but if it did, writing matter is dead skin: 'Is not parchment made of sheepskins?'[17] *Vitam mortuo reddo* ('I give life to the dead') is the motto in a famous early woodcut of the printing press in action; in French is added below 'I delight the dead'.[18] Laurence Sterne, rewriting *Hamlet* in *Tristram Shandy*, has Tristram cry 'Alas, Poor YORICK!', then leaves two pages printed solid black in mourning.[19] In the life of Yukio Mishima in Tokyo in November 1970, this assumed ritual form. Shortly after finishing *The Decay of the Angel*, the fourth novel in *Sea of Fertility*, he recited death poems before performing seppuku.[20]

Marcel Proust's *À la recherche du temps perdu* begins with the narrator as a child trying to get to sleep while reading a book. 'Je voulais poser le volume': he wants to put away the book, but it has become merged with his consciousness.[21] 'I had not ceased while sleeping to form reflections on what I had just read.'[22] In the course of completing the novel between 1909 and 1922, writing merges in Proust's world with the experience of dying. In *Ulysses*, Joyce begins the chapter 'Calypso' with Leopold Bloom eating and ends with him shitting. In Jeri Johnson's words, Bloom is 'a bodied text, a corpus'.[23] When he enters the jakes, Bloom picks up a book of stories to read; Joyce's brother Stanislaus thought it a joking self-reference to a scrap of fictional juvenilia.[24] Having finished his business, Bloom recycles the pages on his own body: 'He tore away half the prize story sharply and wiped himself with it'.[25] The book incorporates his identity. This is not a modern idea: Aristotle compares literary form with a well-shaped body in the *Poetics*.[26] Horace begins his *Ars Poetica* with a metaphor of an ill-formed book mixing up a human head and foot.[27]

The internet, connoting the social projection of personality on a global scale, with corresponding anxiety of identity theft, is again germane. Desire to eliminate the book feeds off the power it contains. 'Knowledge is power' is a phrase mis-attributed to Michel Foucault: it made him laugh, he said, 'since studying their relation is precisely my problem'.[28] The first systematic bibliocaust took place in the name of Qin Shi Huang, First Emperor of China (Ying Zheng). An edict of 213 BCE, composed by Li Si, himself an author and noted calligrapher, ordered the destruction of historical records, philosophy, and literature, including key Confucian texts.[29] Li Si thought all texts dealing even tangentially with politics should be possessed only by the state. Free-thinking is the enemy of progress. The event came to be known as 'the burning of books and burying of scholars' (焚書坑儒). The story, as told in the *Records of the Grand Historian* a hundred years later, may not be accurate in detail. It is disputed whether the burying alive of 460 Confucian scholars is a mistranslation; medicine and agriculture and prophecy may have escaped the ban. However, many books certainly were destroyed, while (in a nice touch, reminiscent of modern copyright libraries) two copies of each text were simultaneously deposited in the Imperial Library, the one place able to keep them.[30] Li Si's place in the history of censorship is secure. It is my argument that the nexus recorded in the *Records of the Grand Historian* of fire and burial, and of book and body, is also no accident.

To make this case I shall range across a whole history of written artefacts, and a broad global range of books. I therefore begin with an apology, that as a scholar largely of literature and of the printed book, I will describe many things in which I am no expert. However, at the heart of *Bibliophobia* is not so much a scientific history as a pathology of the symptoms of knowledge and oblivion, or past and future, invested in ideas of writing, books, and libraries. Literature runs like a river through it. It works as a palimpsest of similar things, rather than by linear chronology or comprehensive study.

Benjamin and Barthes both saw mortality inscribed in symbolic systems. The French title chosen by Barthes, 'La mort de l'auteur', puns on *Le morte d'Arthur* by Sir Thomas Malory, one of the first books printed by William Caxton. The death of Arthur, like that of Achilles, or Jing of Jin (or for that matter the death of Jesus), is not only a famous narrative but a figure for a principle of narrative. In the modernist novel (in Hermann Melville's *Moby-Dick*, Virginia Woolf's *The Waves*, or Samuel Beckett's *Malone Dies*) a physical book is a trope for how reading processes imitate a life's course. Mrs Ramsay 'turned the page; there were only a few lines more, so that she would finish the story, though it was past bed-time'.[31] While Proust is admired for transcending time, his book accepts mortality.[32] 'Eternal duration is no more promised to books than it is to men', Proust writes in *Le Temps retrouvé*.[33] The book embodies us: in consuming it we die.

In 1935, in exile in Paris, against a background of Nazi tyranny in Germany and imminent collapse in liberal values, Benjamin wrote a first draft of *Das Kunstwerk im Zeitalter seiner technischen Reproduzierbarkeit*. It marked, Eric Hobsbawm says, a transformation in modern experience of the arts.[34] A manifesto for modernism, it critiqued fascist culture by asserting art's revolutionary status 'in an age of mechanical reproduction'. A Latin motto used by Futurists, *Fiat ars, pereat mundus* ('Let art be made, though the world perishes') forms an epigraph: it exposes with equanimity 'the *Führer* cult' of his own nation and the spurious fetishes of Marinetti. While acknowledging the effect of mass media, Benjamin argues for emancipation through challenge rather than decline and fall. Revised in French in 1936, and in German in 1939, his work proposed photography and film as a release from 'genuineness' (*Echtheit*) in art.[35] In the process, art found social function: no longer imprisoned by 'ritual', it entered the domain of the political.

'In principle', Benjamin says, 'the work of art has always been reproducible. What man has made, man has always been able to make again.'[36] However, the concept of the artwork has been characterized up to now by its existence in 'the here and now' (*das Hier und Jetzt des Kunstwerks*): 'its unique existence in the place where it is at this moment' (p. 5). Presence defines art, the inviolability of which is threatened by reproduction. Art has been reproduced throughout history: the ancient Greeks cast or embossed bronzes, terracottas and coins; engraving and lithography (from the seventeenth to the nineteenth century) speeded such processes up. Yet something new is afoot. Photographs and moving images radicalize meaning, by making the eye work without mediation, no longer subject to the hand. Something different results:

> We can encapsulate what stands out here by using the term 'aura'. We can say: what shrinks in an age where the work of art can be reproduced by technological means is its aura.   (p. 7)

Here, Benjamin digresses into a history of Western art before modernity. The patina of a bronze, or provenance of a fifteenth-century manuscript, establishes authenticity. This embeds artworks in tradition, though understanding changes over time. A classical statue of Venus, an object of worship to its original Athenian audience, in the Middle Ages could be seen as a dangerous idol. However, in both cases, what is at stake is 'singularity (*Einzigkeit*) or, to use another word, its aura (*Aura*)'.[37] While the oldest art was magical or religious, 'aura' did not disappear with secularization in the Renaissance. Ritual function transferred to a different form of *Einzigkeit*, such as a theory of beauty or sublimity. Indeed, Benjamin sees art taking on religion's mantle at the Enlightenment. Here he cites G. W. F. Hegel in his *Lectures on Aesthetics*: 'art stands on one and the same ground as religion'.[38] Only as revolutions in reproductive processes arose did art feel a crisis. The sign of this was the vogue of *l'art pour art* (a term Benjamin cites in French, 'art for art's sake'). This can be called a 'theology of art', or even a negative theology, in which the 'pure' art form is felt to be beyond social context or even subjective origin.

What concerns me here is how Benjamin's extraordinary theory of mechanical reproduction relates to the idea of the book. In one sense it seems irrelevant: one of the clichés of cultural history is that mechanization of the book occurred more than 500 years ago, in the invention of a printing press in the German Rhineland.[39] Indeed, even this is a fabrication of Western vanity: paper was invented in China in the year 105 CE; wood block printing appeared there in the sixth century; book binding in about 1000 CE; and moveable type was invented by Bi Sheng in 1041 CE.[40] Of the book, even more than the work of art, it can be said that it has 'always been reproducible'. Indeed, it is of its nature *technological*. Long before print, books were manufactured, on a quasi-industrial scale, producing identical 'copies' of one thing. Francesco di Ser Nardo in the fourteenth century promised to make a hundred copies of Dante's *Divine Comedy* in a single order, a similar magnitude to seventeenth-century print runs.[41] One copy of Dante is (in ideal terms) no different from any other. That is what makes it a book. Michael Suarez and Henry Woudhuysen in *The Book: A Global History* argue that the term 'book' implies 'great diversity of textual forms'.[42] These embrace rolls as well as bound books, using pixels as well as ink; they include newspapers or wax tablets, sheet music or maps.

A book is never bound by material existence as an object: it can be copied a billion times and remain the same. Such is the true sense of Barthes on 'the death of the author', however traduced (by friends and enemies) to mean something more sinister or banal. As we read words on a page, 'the voice loses its origin, the author enters his own death, writing begins'.[43] Writing, to be writing, must be legible to any reader, regardless of origin or creation. Whereas speech escapes a bodily mouth to be heard by the ear, writing is an information system belonging to no one, a medium of its own making. It is abstract to producer and receiver; and equally meaningful to both. I can, of course, know who wrote a writing, or infer from it a 'tone of voice' or style, but I can also (in principle) follow it without such context. Indeed, much writing survives anonymously, with no sign of where or when it arose. Provided a relevant linguistic system has been deciphered, there is no bar to interpreting. The first poet whose name is recorded is Enhedduana of Ur in Sumeria, priestess of the goddess Inanna.[44] Yet we could read her poems, or those of Sappho, without knowing anything about her, beyond a grammar of gender or proper name.

Writing is so ubiquitous in human societies, we often forget to ask what it is. The most extended theoretical model is *De la grammatologie* by Jacques Derrida (1967). The opening chapter is 'The End of the Book and the Beginning of Writing'. What does he mean by 'la fin du livre'?[45] Derrida is not inclined to statements of fact, alluding instead to a mood of Armageddon (long before the digital book) in Marshall McLuhan's *The Gutenberg Galaxy* (1962). McLuhan heralded an end to print, a new age of television and computer. It was cause for celebration: print suffocated the oral and aural. Print's hegemony reduces life to linearity, like a galley of type, so 'All experience is segmented and must be processed sequentially'.[46] McLuhan maker of zeitgeist was pessimistic: 'The world has become a computer'; or 'an electronic brain, exactly as in an infantile piece of science fiction'.[47] He felt triumph at the doom of print. Derrida treats talk of 'cette mort du livre' (p. 18) with heavy irony: 'this death of the civilization of the book, about which so much is said, and which manifests itself particularly through a convulsive proliferation of libraries' (p. 8). What Derrida analyses is not the book's extinction but '*exhaustion*'. Underlying this is not desire for a return to pure speech, unencumbered by print or writing, but the opposite. At the centre of Derrida's argument is a reversal of what he sees as a perennial philosophical bias in favour of speech at the expense of writing.

To summarize this bias he adopts two brief epigraphs: one, a eulogy from Friedrich Nietzsche in the *Birth of Tragedy*, to 'Socrates, he who does not write'; and the other a definition of the nature of writing from Jean-Jacques Rousseau's *Essai sur l'origine des langues*: writing is nothing more than 'le supplément à la parole'.[48] Philosophy, Derrida argues, has made language synonymous with speech, since speech can be taken as an uncomplicated carrier of thought, consciousness, identity, experience, subjectivity and so on. Above all, speech signifies *la présence*, the presence of the speaker who is thereby endorsed and authorized as a human subject. This 'metaphysics of presence' he famously dubbed 'logocentrism'. It has served as a tool of oppression for 'at least some twenty centuries': at the very foundation of patriarchalism, colonialism, and capitalism.

The pronouncements of Derrida on such questions are often received as a form of holy writ, a preposterous result since it repeats the structural bias Derrida means to lay bare. Here I am interested not in what Derrida says about 'logocentrism' but rather 'grammatology'. By this he means neither a history nor a philosophy of writing. He takes the word from I. J. Gelb's classic, *A Study of Writing: The Foundations of Grammatology* (1952). Gelb eschewed traditional approaches written from a 'descriptive-historical point of view'. Instead, he revealed fundamental principles in writing as an idea.

Gelb argues for a science of writing, to be called 'grammatology', independent of other linguistic sciences. Writing is a system of signs in its own right. Derrida turns this into a philosophical principle, making writing an emancipatory value in language. Shorn of identification with the authority of the voice, writing stands for freedom. Within this, features of writing traditionally taken as part of its inferiority to speech—exteriority, embodiment, equivocation—are revealed as a commitment to risk, energy, or creativity. Here, writing's 'iterable' function—a precondition for Derrida of all communication—becomes its latent power. Far from voice being the origin of language's potential, it is only as the link with voice is broken that language comes into play.[49] The term Derrida consistently uses for this is *différance*, a neologism to suggest how 'presence' within language is never perfectly represented, but instead is prone to decay and erasure.[50]

What connection can be made between this and Benjamin's manifesto on works of art? Derrida's 'iterability' shares with Benjamin's *Reproduzierbarkeit* an iconoclastic attitude towards the primacy of identity, presence, authority, intention, meaning, in accounts of literary or artistic valuation. In this context, Benjamin's metaphor of *die Aura* invites investigation. The word *Aura* in German, as in English, is an ineffable residue of a Greek root carelessly left in a Latin equivalent. Greek αὔρα means 'breath', or 'breeze', passing to Italian (such as Francesco Petrarca's *Rime Sparse*).[51] In philosophical fourteenth-century English, 'aura' was used by John Trevisa for a gentle wind. From here it dropped from the language, never used by Shakespeare, and by Milton only in Latin.[52] Revived in the eighteenth century, it expresses a sensory perception almost impossible to verbalize: the aroma of blood, the respiration of flowers, the touch of the wind. From thence it diverges, on the one hand to suggest the spirit of something non-physical (like ether); on the other, the physical character of something illusory or even imaginary (the emanation of living things; or the mystical electricity or 'mesmer' given off by a dead body). The entry in the *Oxford English Dictionary* frankly admits it is somewhere between word and pure metaphor, 'a subtle emanation or exhalation from any substance' (OED, 2.a.).

Benjamin's *Aura* is metaphorical, since plastic art can hardly hold 'breath'. The word connotes metaphysical quintessence, a quality by which a thing is known.

He shares Derrida's antipathy toward the presence of a sovereign author, suggesting a spectral stain of the holy inside artworks even after secularization. A Renaissance madonna, transferred from an altar to the Galleria degli Ufizzi in Florence or Musées du Louvre in Paris, keeps its halo. It is venerated by a crowd in a big exhibition even though deconsecrated from its liturgical or devotional purpose. 'Originally the contextual integration of art in tradition found its expression in cult', Benjamin says. Yet 'the existence of the work of art with reference to its aura is never entirely separated from its ritual function'. It retains the feel of an 'instrument of magic (*Zauberinstrument*)'.[53] Benjamin borrows from the resonant word Max Weber used to explain religion in modernity: *Entzauberung* ('disenchantment').[54] Art in Benjamin retains its spell. In a footnote, Benjamin described its axis of space/time as a paradox. Distance is the opposite of closeness: 'the *essence* of remoteness in an object is that it cannot be approached. Unapproachability is one of the chief qualities of the cultic image'.[55]

A work of art yields to damage over time, or changes in use or context, or transfers ownership, yet retains an essential 'aura'. For this process, Benjamin chooses a second metaphor: *die Spur* ('the trace'). This attaches itself to an object which once had an 'aura'. Chemical or physical analysis reveal such 'traces', which never attach to a reproduction, which lacks patina or residual pigmentation: its physicality is brute fact, denuded of 'aura'. It is significant to recall that 'la trace' is Derrida's term for the least possible residue of presence left in the written mark. In characteristic fashion, Derrida reduces even this irreducible minimum to less than nothing, not a presence but '...rather a simulacrum of a presence that dislocates, displaces, and refers beyond itself'.[56] The 'trace' (or *Spur*, in German translations of Derrida) is the terminus of writing.

Modernity, Benjamin says, is the era of *der Verfall der Aura* ('the decline of aura').[57] In one view, books never possessed 'aura' as art does. However, even a manuscript is not an 'original' like a work of plastic art. We refer to an authorial copy as a 'holograph', but the handwriting of the author is still a 'copy', not the work itself. The written work is inherently 'iterable'. Benjamin creates a rigid break between modern and pre-modern. Idealization of the past consigns to it a presence that has been lost. Yet medieval art, in its time, suffered decay. A madonna did not embody the Virgin Mary in a literal sense. It was a simulacrum, only a transferred relic of the saint. Devotion was made to a person, not the image. Alexander Nagel shows unexpected affinity between medieval art (serial production, the ready-made) and modern.[58] Conversely, post-Renaissance painting partakes of the relic: a piece by 'the circle of Velázquez' or 'workshop of Rembrandt' increases in value ninety-fold if reattributed to the hand of a master. Perhaps this will be taken as proof of Benjamin's thesis. The equivalent to medieval trade in bones is modern art's capacity to treat everyday objects as totems of a cult: Kazimir Malevich's black square; Marcel Duchamp's *pissoir*; Damien Hirst's dismembered shark. Andy Warhol meanwhile pastiches the reliquary in endless 'genuine' fakes for museums.

Artists' stuff always costs money, but never in proportion to 'market price'.[59] There is no commercial reason for raw materials in a Duchamp to affect its valuation more than a Giotto. Still, art's failure to ratify Benjamin's theory is relevant. Photography and cinema have not replaced other art forms, no more than the digital book erased the printed.[60] In conceptual art, video is not treated as cinema, but translated relic. Art is resaturated with 'aura', and fantasies of violence cling to its making. Whether painted, literary, musical or architectural, art works have in common a physical form attuned to metaphysical content, yet the relationship is at some level opaque to explanation or interpretation. Music, more than the visual arts, has undergone modern transformation through reproducibility. From the gramophone (patented in 1887) to the MP3 (in 1993), technologies once things of wonder are now superseded. Music metamorphosed from a medium defined by performance to one defined by dissemination. However, change was not so absolute: musical notation and printed music were revolutionary inventions in their day. Meanwhile, in an age of digital music, live performance has not lost its aura.

Theodor Adorno called form 'sedimented content', in order to express the impossibility of more finite or less metaphorical assimilation.[61] With the visual arts or music, perhaps the *mystery* of relationship is apparent at some level. Writing makes the exchange invisible. Language, as Derrida averred, only *seems* to promise direct access to what it, too, cannot foreclose. Writing is an enigma: blank letters shimmer forth meaning that is only explained by more blank letters. Speech, out of the mouth of one person directly into the ear of another, enacts presence more fully. But speech, too, at some level, is a confidence trick. What gives vocalized sound guarantee of exact communication?

We get by, of course: we converse, read, make sense as we can. However, Benjamin, Derrida, and Adorno, in different ways, suggest the sheer improbability of human inter-communication or intersubjectivity. At the heart of this is a doubt about subjectivity. Speech and writing imperfectly represent us, we fear, but what model do we have for identity? Sigmund Freud in a beautifully speculative essay of 1925 compared memory function to a recently invented device called *Der Wunderblock* ('the magic notepad'). He makes a two-way connection between writing and the mind. When I mistrust memory, he says, I write something on a piece of paper. The surface on which the note is preserved becomes as it were the material part of my memory, the rest of which I carry with me invisibly. I can reproduce this portion when I like, in the certainty it remains unaltered.[62] Yet this does not correspond to how memory works. 'The sheet is filled with writing, there is no room on it for any more notes.'[63] However, in the mind, capacity for new memories is not used up by existing memories: it receives unlimited supply of new, even as it retains the old, permanently (if not reliably or unalterably).

In the century since this remarkable essay was published technologies have in some way replicated Freud's model, suggesting Freud as a wild prophet of the digital. The iPad, it is said, is the *Wunderblock* made flesh. This misunderstands

Freud's project. The technology for a *Wunderblock* is neither here nor there for Freud, whatever his fascination that capitalism followed the tenets of psycho-analysis. The *Wunderblock* is a metaphor, and must be, because human conscious-ness (never mind the unconscious) is non-physical. Derrida in an essay on Freud argued that writing is thus the perfect metaphor for psychic existence.[64] This is as much the case today, even with a far more complete neuroscientific explanation of how physical neurones produce mental affects. Memory is an ideal example since, for Freud, memory is an invisible trace of things once visible. Human memory reveals the 'magical' capacity of mental apparatus for unlimited receptiv-ity and preservation of durable traces. John Locke's *Essay Concerning Human Understanding* makes a similar metaphor for mind: a 'white Paper, void of all characters, without any *Ideas*'.[65] The vast store of ideas comes only with experi-ence. Paper books uncover a mystic connection between the mind's void and the brute fact of experience.

Writing is now around 5,000 years old. Ancient scripts can be divided into seven different types, all of which appear to have independent origins: Sumerian in Mesopotamia (modern Iraq); proto-Elamite in Elam (in modern Iran); proto-Indic in the Indus valley (covering modern Afghanistan and Pakistan as well as north-west India); Chinese in China; Egyptian in Egypt; Cretan in Crete and Greece; and Hittite in Anatolia and Syria. To these can arguably be added an eighth, Mesoamerican, although this writing is much later. At its heart, all writing is a technology for the reproduction of language. The digital revolution currently carries everything before it, but we have been there before, in a series of media revolutions of which only the most obvious is the one called printing. Irnerio in Italo Calvino's *If on a winter's night a traveller* (1979) teaches himself how 'not to read'. It is a difficult task: 'they teach us to read as children, and for the rest of our lives we remain the slaves of all the written stuff they fling in front of us'.[66] What would human history look like without the invention of writing? The secret, Irnerio says, is not to refuse to look at the words on the page, but to stare so intently that they disappear.

The book shows little sign of dying. Yet fear of books is as explicable as love. Between a physical book and its ideal lies essential anxiety. Fantasies of destruc-tion and rebirth revert, as we will see, to the beginnings of the book. Oblivion is fundamental to writing, coming into focus, perhaps, at the advent of new media. Our era is not the end of the book, but rather one in which the *life* of the book is more apparent and therefore fragile and dangerous. It seems that media revolu-tions produce both dreams of knowledge, and paranoia about oblivion. As cor-onavirus threatens social relations, just as climate emergency threatens the planet in which human beings dwell, information technology is at the centre of both, whether in terms of solutions or else potential apocalypse.

Information technology is a new word—the *Oxford English Dictionary* gives 1952 as its first use—but it is not a new concept. The first media revolution was of clay tablets, reed, and stylus, in the thirty-second century BCE. *Cuneiform* is the world's first writing system. More than a dozen languages came to be written using this system. Its name comes from Latin *cuneus* ('wedge'), referring to a characteristic shape made by a stylus when applied to clay by a scribe. Cuneiform is not alphabetic and has no 'letters': it used between 600 and 1,000 characters to write whole words, or parts of them; or syllables (or parts of them).[67] The main two languages in cuneiform were Sumerian and Akkadian. Sumerian has no known relations, while Akkadian (existing in two dialects, Assyrian and Babylonian) is related to Arabic and Hebrew. Hittite, written in a simplified cuneiform, is related to Indian and European languages. Something of cuneiform's versatility and success is shown by its use into the first century CE: it lasted longer than the period separating us from Christ. In a word in Arabic we see a glimmer of the oldest past.[68]

A connection between writing and violence occurs in one of the earliest myths of the origins of writing. Enmerkar, king of Uruk, invents cuneiform to send messages to other kings. The Lord of Aratta, in receipt, knowing that he cannot understand it, submits.[69] Writing spells potency before it is read. In another Sumerian myth, Sargon, cupbearer of Ur-Zababa, king of Kish, tells a dream that frightens the king. He sends Sargon to Lugalzagesi, king of Uruk, bearing a clay tablet, concealed inside the first envelope. The message is his own death sentence but is not conveyed.[70] Sargon survives to become king of Akkad and father of Enheduanna. Similar stories survive in Homer's *Iliad* about Bellerophon, or the Bible about Uriah.[71] In this way writing comes to signify power itself.

Old as these myths are, they were written a thousand or more years after the invention of writing. The earliest examples of writing to survive are more mundane: expense accounts for temples, records of sheep and goats, bills for beer or bread. Yet a connection between information and power is inscribed in many copies of cuneiform. This text (Fig. 1) was written on a cylinder in the reign of Cyrus the Great in the sixth century BCE. Its technology is modernist in feel. The kings of Babylon buried cylinders in the foundations of buildings. These are messages to posterity: in finest script, listing royal achievements. As such they fulfil their objective: sometimes this is the only record we have left of the king in question. But the cylindrical shape was also symbolic: it gave the idea of endless writing, knowledge without limits, power reaching into eternity. The cylinders sometimes contained bleak prophecies of the ends of time and of knowledge.

'The internet is not a tool. It is an alien life form', David Bowie declared in an interview with Jeremy Paxman for the BBC's Newsnight in 1999. In 1996 he was already the first mainstream artist to distribute a song (called *Telling Lies*, perhaps without irony) as an online exclusive, selling over 300,000 downloads; in 1998 he launched his own ISP, called BowieNet. While Paxman scoffed at the internet as little more than a portable vehicle for Reuters news agency, his interviewee looked into the future with awe:

Fig. 1. 'The eternal book'; *The Cyrus Cylinder,* clay, 6th c. BCE. British Museum

> I don't think we've even seen the tip of the iceberg. I think that the potential of
> what the internet is going to do to society, both good and bad, is unimaginable.
> I think we're actually on the cusp of something exhilarating and terrifying.[72]

Ziggy the Prophet uncannily foresaw that the internet is far more than a medium
for information. It is a metaphor for the illimitable ideal of perfect knowledge. As
such it is also a symbol of the possibility of knowledge's imminent destruction, of
the end of culture. Politicians show a manic-depressive attitude to the World
Wide Web: the solution to their problems and yet the key to our fears. The
Millennium Bug was meant to erase every bank and health record from the
planet. Now we are told cyberterrorism holds the greatest threat to mankind.
Meanwhile, in Denis Villeneuve's film *Arrival* (2016), contact with aliens depends
on interpreting a written language completely different in form and system from
anything previously encountered among humans. Linguists and codicologists are
called in to save the world. Do the strange visitors bring a 'weapon', or a 'tool'? It is
an old joke: the Greek word *pharmakon* meant either 'medicine' or 'poison'.
Philosophers from Plato to Erasmus to Derrida have made the *pharmakon* the
emblem of writing.[73] The answer, the future of human existence, lies in deciphering an alien script, one which will either save us or kill us—or possibly both.

In 2017, an object from outer space passed through the solar system: it was
named *ʻoumuamua*, Hawaiian for 'first messenger'.[74] Within the world of the
interstellar probe, it is legitimate to ask if we know any more what a book is, or
what a library is for. For many people, a concept of the book is encapsulated by a
codex, bound by stacking the pages and fixing one edge, using a cover thicker

than the sheets. Early in the second century CE, the Roman poet Martial (*Epigrams*, 1) advertises a work as this new kind of object, with a host of advantages over traditional scrolls. It can be held in one hand, he says; you can carry it with you; it can be your companion on long journeys, if you like. This is because it is made of 'parchment (*membrana*) compressed in small pages'.[75] 'My book (*liber*) is thumbed everywhere', he says.[76] While it took a while to catch on, by the fourth century CE, codices outnumber papyrus rolls. Despite the ubiquity of the roll book in Greek and Jewish traditions, almost all early Christian books survive in papyrus codices.[77] Neither economy nor practicality sufficiently explains the preference. Change coincided with gradual replacement of papyrus by parchment, and adapting binding techniques from other crafts, like weaving and leatherwork.[78] Yet the advantage of the codex shows itself in use: in the development of a particular kind of literature, intended as handbooks for life—one example is a 'gospel' – disseminated in public readings.[79]

In sixth-century CE mosaics in the Basilica of San Vitale in Ravenna, John the Evangelist holds his gospel in his lap, a codex complete with stitching holes and straps; on a table beside him he has a quill pen, a knife to sharpen it, and a pot for his ink (Fig. 2). Gospel writing: the invention of the codex embodies the spread of Christianity. Religions and intellectual revolutions alike negotiate their origins around terms in written media. Hindu *śruti* are defined precisely as words without text, or books 'without beginning and without end'.[80] The Zoroastrian Avesta became canonical in the fifth century BCE via texts such as the liturgy of Yasna.[81] The Jewish Torah consists in a scroll. The earliest copies of the Buddhist Pali Canon are written on palm or bamboo, stacked together with thin sticks, then wrapped in cloth and placed in a box.[82] Islam, like Christianity, and the religion of Mani, founded itself via the power of codices.[83] The Sikh holy book is not a mere book but the last of the gurus, still living.[84] Johann Sleidan wrote in 1542 that by Gutenberg's invention God chose Protestantism to triumph in the Reformation.[85] Three technologies aligned in the stars: ink and paper from China; presses adapted from oil or wine.[86] In turn, Enlightenment liberty declared itself by advances in press manufacture or copyright. The tech gods invoke the digital transformation of democracy and culture.

Whether by cause or myth, in every historic reformation of writing, violence is not far off. Rather than the dying book, perhaps we mean a 'codex in crisis', to borrow Anthony Grafton's phrase.[87] Codices are so universal they do not need naming. (Many people do not know a paperback *is* a codex, as the word is reserved for manuscripts.) Conversely, an e-book, while not a codex, is a book. The word 'book', says Cassiodorus (6th c. CE), comes from Latin *liber* meaning 'free'. It is 'freed' from prior existence as plant (whether tree bark or papyrus leaf). The etymology is false but its ideal of writing as synonymous with freedom is powerful. Writers are always referring to it. François Rabelais inscribes Gargantua's genealogy not on paper, parchment, or wax, but the bark of an elm tree.[88]

Fig. 2. 'Birth of the codex'; Ravenna, Basilica of San Vitale, mosaic, 6th c. CE

Google and Facebook invoke freedom so as to limit the power of democracies to regulate them. The book is not defined by any technology, old or new, it is a continuum of media from cylinder to tablet to scroll to codex to Kindle and so on. In some ways, the digital revolution returned to older techniques of reading, such as 'scrolling down'. Early computerized books imitated papyrus rolls, in which readers visualize the beginning of a text, with only a vague sense where it ends. Indeed, early computerized books were even more like rolls, since file space was finite, and a text was divided into different 'floppy disks'. In the last decade the roll has given way to the 'tablet', where the flick of a finger makes a piece of text visible as it replaces the last. This, too, is an old medium, since tablets existed among ancient Egyptians, Mesopotamians, and Greeks. An erasable one on wax became a universal medium of the Roman Empire for ephemeral text, leading to the phrase *tabula rasa* or a 'clean slate'. Some modern technologies imitate this by providing a portable stylus. Latin used many words interchangeably for a 'book': *volumen* (a 'roll'); *liber* (strictly, part of a larger work divided into rolls, such as Virgil's *Aeneid* or Livy's *History*); *charta* (a papyrus sheet); *libellus* (a portable book, such as the poems of Catullus); *tabula* (a large public document); *tabella* (a temporary notebook).[89]

The conceptual key to the book is not a particular physical form, but the idea of a text with limits, which can be divided into organized contents. In that sense a book is not a physical thing but an *idea* of a thing. Nonetheless, physical constraints, whatever form they take, quantify limits, and what is contained in them. The limits express a boundary between writer, text, and reader; the boundaries are concrete *and* abstract. As I read, my book becomes me, I become my book. Its text—including pages still to be read—is (for the period in which I am reading) constitutive of my mental world. It takes its place alongside other books I have read, interleaves with them, and as I read, collates them together. I recall the words from previous readings, including re-readings (perhaps) of this book, as well as other books. Together, I carry them in my head as a kind of library. If I am lucky, they collect dust in my physical library. But even if not, my head is a history of reading, identical neither with consciousness, memory, nor neural networks.

In the fourteenth century CE, Richard of Bury, Bishop of Durham, wrote a beautiful book in Latin called *Philobiblon*. It is a collection of essays on the acquisition, preservation, and organization of books, mixed with something like an autobiography of reading. Richard collected books and hoped they might survive him in an unbuilt library in Oxford. Instead he died at Bishop Auckland, the palace of the Durham see, his books dispersed at his death. However, at least one, a copy of John of Salisbury, is in the British Library.[90] Richard's work was copied in manuscript and then printed, first in Cologne in 1473, and in Paris in 1500; in England by Thomas James, Bodley's Librarian in Oxford, in 1599.[91] The titles of its chapters would not look out of place in a book about books today:

1. *That the Treasure of Wisdom is chiefly contained in Books.*
2. *The Degree of Affection that is properly due to a Book.*
3. *What we are to think of the Price in the Buying of Books.*

Richard discusses how to control book circulation among students, and the open-stack system in library access. He pays poetic tribute to the book's imaginative place in a full life. 'In books I meet the dead as if they were alive; in books I see what is yet to come.'[92]

In connecting memory with futurity, Richard repeated a common classical trope. Aeneas on landing in Italy inscribes a tribute to the Trojan dead on a shield.[93] Roman tombs are places of writing; indeed, they are among the commonest surviving sources of inscription.[94] They tell us about the dead, and warn us we will die, too. The *Manes*, the spirits of the dead, were believed to reside in and around the tomb; inscriptions, from the time of Augustus on, address them directly: *diis manibus* (D.M.).[95] Mesopotamian, Chinese, Greek, and Mayan tomb inscriptions all contain hopes and warnings at the threshold between life and death. Inside Egyptian tombs, hieroglyphics negotiate the passage of the dead into the afterlife; on the outer door-jambs and lintels, they instruct passers-by to perform proper rituals to ensure afterlife continues.[96] In Munich, we face in rapture an exquisite Attic stele showing a young woman meeting her dead mother, writing faintly visible above them.[97] The epitaph is a favourite literary mode in Virgil and elsewhere because by recording the dead, a book also promises a kind of afterlife. Ovid ends his long poem *Tristia* with the words: 'Forbid the door of my death to be closed!'[98] The book, in providing an epigraph to his life, still offers him the chance of survival.[99]

Books and writing lie between living and dying. It is no surprise bibliophobia is closer to bibliophilia than we care to know. We live in difficult times, candidly aware of threats to freedom. Even in Richard's book, eulogy contains menace. To friends who cannot trust a messenger, he says, we send books. Books keep secrets, and betray them, too. Richard records prisoners using books as 'ambassadors' to plea for their lives with the prince.[100] Boethius, imprisoned by King Theodoric the Great of the Ostrogoths in Pavia in 523 CE, wrote the *Consolation of Philosophy*, cramming it not only with Plato and Aristotle but also Homer, Euripides, and Catullus.[101] Perhaps they came from a mental library since his codices may have been forbidden him.[102] Elizabeth Tudor and Sir Walter Ralegh carved graffiti on prison walls at the Tower of London.[103] Sir Thomas More and Lady Jane Grey are recorded as Tower readers.[104] More's prayer book miraculously survives, an inexpensive Book of Hours printed in Paris, bound with a Latin psalter. In the margin he marked words for attention with his pen, or added comments.[105] Above and below a woodcut miniature of the nativity at the opening of the divine hour 'Prime', More adds his own prayer: 'Gyve me thy grace good lord | to set the world at nought'.[106]

In March 1944, Dietrich Bonhoeffer wrote from Tegel military prison in Brandenburg to his friend Eberhard Bethge. He was reading Wolfram von Eschenbach's twelfth-century epic *Parzifal*, side by side with Goethe's *Faust*.[107] Accused of conspiracy in Claus von Stauffenberg's July plot, he was sent to Buchenwald. Hanged at dawn on 9 April 1945 in Flossenbürg concentration camp, liberation lay just a fortnight away. Prisoners request books for company at the last; yet books can also incriminate. Salman Rushdie in 1990 registered shock in meeting anyone 'for whom books simply do not matter'.[108] He makes a brutal connection of writing and death, reporting the burning of *The Satanic Verses* in 1989. 'These are the contemporary Thought Police', he said.[109] His inevitable reference-point for twentieth-century book-burning is state-sponsored public bonfires of May 1933 in Nazi Germany, in the first months of the Reich.

No more extreme encounter between writing and violence is imaginable than the fate of books described in Primo Levi's *Se questo è un uomo*. He recounts to his readers the impossible suffering of Auschwitz, in which his book itself comes to represent a post-human endurance. 'Non siamo morti', he says of the entrance into the camp, where the sign on the gate (*Arbeit macht frei*) appears to be the last vestige of human writing. 'We are not dead.'[110] For to write is to go on living, and the continuation of his sentence is a primal sign that life has not yet ended. From time to time the narrator intervenes in the present tense in order to express astonishment at past survival: 'Today, at this very moment, as I sit writing at a table, I myself am not convinced that these things really happened.'[111] Levi's astonishment at this particular moment is engendered by a bizarre encounter with a physical book, there in Auschwitz. The book in question is Ludwig Gattermann's *Die Praxis der organischen Chemikers* (1894). From it Doktor Ingenieur Pannwitz (Director of the rubber plant at Buna) conducts an improvisatory chemical examination, the result of which is that Levi is transferred to the factory. In a moment of utterly profound absurdity, he is confronted with the identical maroon-colour hardback volume from which he studied in Turin before the war. 'I stare at the fair skin of his hand writing down my fate on the white page in incomprehensible symbols.'[112] The memory of the copy of 'Gattermann's cookbook' draws forth a parallel account of another book in the next chapter, 'The Canto of Ulysses'. In order to teach some Italian to Jean, the Pikolo of the Chemical Kommando (who is bilingual in French and German), Levi gives an elementary lesson in Dante's *Divine Comedy*. There are no possessions in camp, but Levi holds the book inside his head. Dante, with Baudelaire, Dostoyevky's *House of the Dead*, Manzoni's *I promessi sposi*, and Rabelais's *Gargantua et Pantagruel*, are his unerasable companions in the *malebolge* of Eastern Silesia. Here, he says, *Questo è l'inferno*.[113]

Judaism, Christianity, and Islam have in common that they are 'religions of the book'. The Queen of Sheba, Augustine of Hippo, Martin Luther, and Malcolm X all converted via books. Whether in Asia, Africa, Europe or America, reading processes are spiritual.[114] The assumption goes that holy texts derive sanctity from the divinity that breathes into them. Yet it could be that religions derive power *from* the idea of the book. A book takes an elixir of the human and imparts it to whoever comes in contact. Cassiodorus, fifteen hundred years ago, understood the closeness of 'divine and human readings': each partakes of the institution of writing, the one feeding off the other.[115] Art takes over 'something mysterious' after the Reformation, Hegel says; in this way it prefigures its own dissolution, or *Auflösung*, which some have called the death of art.[116]

Is this what we mean by the death of the book? *Bibliophobia* confronts Benjamin's *Aura* in its ambiguous immanence. An idea of the book is inscribed in human agency. Barack Obama browsed the stacks of his mother's library as a nine-year-old boy, looking for racial origin or political inheritance.[117] Personhood is located in odd rituals accruing to religious books the world over: kissing, blessing, breathing, burying. The Talmud declared Torah scrolls to be impure; rabbis discouraged Jews from storing offerings next to scrolls, in case mice nibbled sacred words.[118] In less explicit holiness, *Liji* was a 'book of rites' in the warring states period (*c.*4th c. BCE), summarizing practice under the Zhou Dynasty. Confucius wrote that 'rites' (*li*) are the most important thing in life: 'I found my balance through the rites.'[119] His books embody more than etiquette: rites and literature restore tradition tangibly in the simplicity of the past.[120] Examples printed on woodblock were still made in nineteenth-century Japan bound in the *fukuro toji* style (stacked sheets of folded double-width thin paper inscribed on one side only).[121]

Books partake of everyday as well as holy rituals: cherished by an owner, left to a friend as the most personal legacy. Natalie Zemon Davis has called early modern French books primary agents in a philanthropic economy of the gift.[122] Wills are the best guides to early private libraries: Elisabeth Leedham-Green's research into Tudor and Stuart probate records at Cambridge University runs to two vast tomes, one a list of the dead, and the other of their books.[123] Yet the personal emotional charge that Richard of Bury found in books—as transitional objects of conscience—also exposes them to danger or state power. Chapter 7 of *Philobiblon* is 'The complaint of books against war'. War, more than plague, is enemy to books. Winged Mercury is strangled, Apollo the python's prey. Aristotle, God's own scholar, is put in chains by Mars.[124] Richard mourns for Zeno of Elea who, failing to bring down a tyrant, bit off his own tongue and spat it in his face.[125] Richard prays to God for peace, and to Jupiter on Olympus as well, just in case.[126]

K. is approached by the Examining Magistrate in Franz Kafka's *Der Proceß* (1925) bearing 'an ancient school exercise-book', with the terms of his indictment. Left in the interrogation chamber, K. asks for some books to help his solitude: an erotic art-book, a novel.[127] In prison, Nelson Mandela's treasured books included his copy of Shakespeare. Mandela signed his name by a passage in *Julius Caesar* to show he was ready to die.[128]

> Seeing that death, a necessary end,
> Will come when it will come.[129]

Yet books have also been used in legal trials for at least 3,000 years in order to prove guilt, via association, or ownership, or even readership. Book burnings in public long predate the Nazis, at least as early as the third century BCE in Qin Dynasty China.

Bibliophobia is not a history. Its motivation is anthropological or philosophical, in meditating what is invested in physical books. It is not about material objects, so much as the interaction between object and subject. In what way is a book held equivalent to a person, or a proxy for a person, in human actions? *Bibliophobia* ranges between the first appearances of writing 5,000 years ago, and the book's recent revenant in digital form. It is a personal study, motivated by chance encounters. When he died, my father, a chemist, left me the first gift he received from my mother, a mathematician, with her inscription inside, from seventy years before.[130] It reminded me of the first Puffin Book she gave me, the curious smell it had, its beautiful Garamond font; or of other books on his shelves, a blue leather *Works of Shakespeare*; or J. R. Partington's *Text-Book of Inorganic Chemistry*, printed the same year, it happens, as Levi's copy of Gattermann.

The book is the ark of imagination. So, writing begins: 'A voice comes to one in the dark. Imagine'.[131] Beckett's voice of imagination is promise and threat. Writing is not mimetic *of* something: it is the how and where of mimesis. A book constitutes the coming into being of writing, so that when revolutions take place in its form (such as new media), a terrible beauty is reborn. Change exposes the sightlines in the theatre of mimesis, making seen the unseen, and making its spectators vulnerable inside the illusion. This is an 'uncanny' beauty, in Freud's sense. Freud contemplates the wooden doll Olympia in E. T. A. Hoffmann.[132] It is familiar, but terrifying. At the heart of the terror is a feeling the doll might be a living thing, even if we know it isn't. Like the ghost in *Hamlet*, desire and fear at the uncanny 'excites a peculiarly violent and obscure emotion'.[133] Is the book an example of a living doll? Erasmus thought so: scripture, he said at the end of *Praise of Folly*, is like the figure of Silenus in Plato's *Symposium*, an idol which contains the mystery within.[134] What follows, is a love-letter for books, even as I recount the violence done to them. The book is not dead or dying, not yet. It has finitude written into it; as scroll, codex, or tablet, writing begins and ends, again. In that sense a book carries our mortality within it: beginning a book for the first time, or finishing it, is a metaphor for life. Closing the book brings mourning. Writing is the trace of morbidity, and reading is a little death. We live inside books, and expire with them, even as they outlive us.

2

The Library as Computer

From high in the roof, the book robot (Fig. 3) swings down in an arc in a vertical plane, 10 m or more in a single movement, between stacks ranking 20 m high. It pauses, chooses a stack, then hovers, humming all the time, hunting for the book that it is programmed to find. The scale of the building is difficult for a human to take in. The void is 24 m high by 24 m wide by 64 m long. In any case, the room is not designed for humans. Oxygen levels are kept at 14–15 per cent, which is similar to trying to breathe at the top of a Himalayan mountain. Visitors watch from a special cage, advised to leave after fifteen minutes for their own safety. This library is not a human environment, for it is designed for habitation by books and robots alone.[1]

This is a library for the twenty-first century. Roly Keating opened the British Library's National Newspaper Building in 2015 at Boston Spa, near Wetherby in Yorkshire. It is a library for an apocalypse designed by Andrei Tarkovsky: bunkers of books or readers, at the edges of the moors, a portent of climate extinction. The building houses 33 km of newspapers, 60 million issues in 280,000 bound volumes, or 450 million individual pages.[2] They are stored in a dark, air-tight, low-oxygen environment, eliminating risk of fire. The temperature is 14 °C; humidity 55 per cent. The concept of a Newspaper Building has now widened to apply to storage of millions of books from British Library collections. Since space at the main site at St Pancras in London is at a premium, it is proposed to house books 262 km away and transport them between the Reading Rooms in both locations. Eventually, it is planned that seven million items will be held at the 'Additional Storage Building' in Boston Spa. All of this makes logical sense: but it is a different matter taking in the logistical exercise of handling books on such a scale of magnitude.

The robotic crane adds a volume to a pile that it is assorting in a plastic bucket. In time, it delivers this to an airlock at the end of the room. There are 140,000 bar-coded containers. It is only at this moment that human intervention takes over, as staff retrieve items from the airlock to send to Reading Rooms, a maximum of 48 hours from ordering to arrival at a London desk. Yet if a human librarian wanted to enter the vault to retrieve a book, using either gigantic ladders or high-wire trapeze artists, it would not be feasible. The books are no longer on fixed shelves ear-marked for their location. Only the crane knows where the books are. It never puts a book back as it found it, absorbing the used item back into the system in the order in which it comes, then remembering where it was.

Fig. 3. 'The mechanical curator', British Library Newspaper Building, Boston Spa, 2015

The books are engaged in an eternal game of musical buckets, finding new neighbours, and slotting in accordingly. Only humans need shelf marks any longer: the
shelves have gone. The retrieval system is fully automated, with the arm moving
between 26,000 locations, capable of holding 89,000 stacks at a time. In principle,
given a large enough vault, the robot could control all of the books ever made, all
by itself.

   Of course, it is not the only futuristic model of the book. Data now are digital:
as indeed is what I write, until it comes out in print. Currently, the world produces 16.3 zettabytes of data per year. This dwarfs the contents of any imaginable

library past or present, even the Library of Congress in Washington, DC, the largest library in existence. Its website declares its collections 'universal', unlimited by subject, format, or national boundary, materials from all parts of the world and in more than 450 languages.[3] Two-thirds of items acquired each year are in languages other than English. It began with the purchase by the US Congress of the library of Thomas Jefferson in 1815 (numbering 6487 books, and costing $23,950), after the British burned the US Capitol, and all its books, in 1814. It now contains more than 38 million books and other printed materials; along with 3.6 million recordings; 14 million photographs; 5.5 million maps; 8.1 million pieces of sheet music; and 70 million manuscripts.[4] There are an estimated 128,731,750 items in the non-classified collections, perhaps more than 168 million in total. Jefferson's library, after a second fire destroyed it on Christmas Eve 1851, is today being reconstructed in a small spiral exhibition bookcase, with blank spaces for catalogue items still unfound.[5]

However, this is nothing in comparison to the World Wide Web. For the internet, now, is a book, too: the book of the world. Unfolding my laptop, the bibliolith opens before me, all-containing. Even a large printed folio takes up just 10 megabytes of data in electronic format. In a rough calculation, we could in theory transfer the whole Library of Congress into around 1.5 million gigabytes. A zettabyte equals a trillion gigabytes. Forbes.com predicts by 2025 that worldwide creation of data will increase ten-fold to 163 zettabytes per year.[6] No wonder, in the internet's hyperbolic world, that litotes is the rhetorical device to make sense of it. A zettabyte truly deserves its modest epithet 'Big Data'.[7]

However, digital euphemism conceals titanic demands. All over the world, megaliths of storage, in monumental bland structures, are built to house data. In place of a metaphor of interconnected network, we now speak of a 'cloud'. The cloud is physical: made of phone lines, fibre optics, satellites in space, cables under the ocean.[8] As well as a staggering consumption of energy in creating or sharing data, there is additional cost in cooling the digital hyperstores, using more water and power. United States data centres consumed 70 billion kilowatt-hours of electricity in 2014, 2 per cent of the country's total energy consumption.[9] Indeed, the figure is so low only because of gains in efficiency. Internet giants, Amazon, Facebook, Google, and Microsoft, invest in hyperscale data centres, reducing need for ever more individual servers. These cloud giants create a new science to maximize data centre efficiency, leading to a slow-down in the industry's overall energy use. However, the metaphor of the cloud, while containing data numbers within human comprehension, is nonetheless finite. Hyperscale savings can only occur once. Meanwhile the demands for data grow and grow. As the cloud gets bigger, it requires more space, and the space creates more and more heat. It is burning the world.

'You books must know your places', says Ahab, who knew better.[10] I first encountered Google on a first visit to the new British Library at St Pancras in

1998. It was an omen. I was trying to find a recalcitrant item in the brand-new Rare Books and Music Reading Room, soon a home from home. I went to Reference Enquiries (in those days a person); she asked me if I had tried Google. It is difficult to convey how strange it sounded on first hearing. Was it a brand name or neologism? It sounded playful: 'to go' plus 'to ogle'. Nobody yet (in my hearing) used it as a verb; that soon followed. Computers had been a daily part of life for a decade, and long ago I had first seen an email as a student in Cambridge, from a physicist friend working at CERN in 1983. But I had only recently finally acquired a laptop powerful enough to use an infant WWW; my first one in 1991 had a clockspeed too slow (although faster than Neil Armstrong's onboard computer on Apollo XI). Moreover, video (even images) was not common, so the net still appeared as a digital library, not as an Anthropocene witch. Dialling in used a phoneline, its echoing feedback dialtone portending nemesis, and it was a relief if a connection wheezed out of the router. The search engines I used were clumsily ineffective: so, when my rescuer at Reference Enquiries typed three words, clicked, *and found exactly the information I was looking for*, I felt myself in the presence of a priest or a magician. Google became my watchword, as for so many others, useful and at the same time clean, transparent, and homely. The fuss-free font was designed to appear non-commercial. Perhaps because I was in a national library, itself free of access, I did not ask why it was free.

In twenty years since my first Google date, people questioned what changed in human memory through the internet's intervention. It is obvious, passing from Gutenberg to Zuckerberg, or Facebook to Fake News, we feel 'a revolution in communication'.[11] Loss meets gain. 'I've almost given up making an effort to remember anything', says *Wired*'s Clive Thompson, 'because I can instantly retrieve the information online'.[12] Thompson refers to the net as an 'out-board brain'. Nicholas Carr in *The Shallows* finds long-term consequences in thinking processes. Relations between short- and long-term memory are not constant in neuroscience. Recalling in different ways, brains change. 'Out-source memory, and culture withers'.[13] Yet as the net began, Umberto Eco felt more sanguine. Anxiety about media is very old, he said in a lecture at Columbia University in 1996: a 'fear that a new technological achievement could abolish or destroy something that we consider precious, fruitful, something that represents for us a value in itself, and a deeply spiritual one'.[14] Eco's paradox is that computers cause more people to read rather than fewer. Aids to memory are as old as writing: indeed, they are one reason why writing was invented. Nonetheless, a question of what humanity would be like, without writing, is *a fortiori* present in the question of what humanity is in the net.

Rewriting Homer's *Odyssey* in *Heroides*, Ovid imagines Penelope writing Ulysses a letter. Don't write back, just come (*ipse veni*), she says.[15] She wants his presence. If only Paris had drowned in the Aegean Sea, before finding Helen of Troy. If so, Penelope would not now lie 'cold in my deserted bed, nor would now be left alone complaining of slowly passing days'. It is anachronistic poetry: real-life Penelope knew no writing.[16] Yet an insistence that writing is no substitute for human presence is belied by Ovid's passage becoming a teaching device in schools for fifteen hundred years, in which pupils were taught how to write letters to make people remember them, far away. Bede the monk, shortly before his death in 735 CE, sends a letter from the River Tyne in Northumbria to his bishop Ecgbert in York because he cannot be with him in person (*corporaliter*). If only they could meet face to face, to share their passion for reading (*legendi*).[17] A later disciple of Ovid is Heloïse in the twelfth century, taught the classics (among some other things) by the academic Peter Abelard, finest thinker of the age. She learns well: and quotes to him the example of the *Heroides* to reproach her (now cloistered) lover Abelard for not writing more letters to her in her misery.[18] Heloïse, Peter Dronke comments, writes 'her own *Heroides*'.[19] In the process, Michael Clanchy argues, Heloïse teaches Abelard to write, not as philosopher, but as poet.[20] Writing preserves the *vox*, the voice, of the author, medieval grammar taught. Petrarch, avid Ovidian, owned a copy of the letters of the French lovers to capture it.[21] He wrote notes in Heloïse's margins, some of them to record his own sexual desires.[22]

After the advent of printing, another Parisian grammar guru called Peter, Pierre de la Ramée (or Ramus), invented new printed means in 1555 to teach presence in writing, recycling Ovid's Penelope topos once more.[23] The *vox* becomes the word. Technology is always trying to stay one step ahead. The codex used quires to create divisions in texts like chapters.[24] Print reinforced encoding of contents via systematic prefatory tables of them, found in any book today, although it took a while to get straight.[25] Ramus's printer André Wéchel in Paris created more tables to dichotomize his logic in columns, making it more accessible.[26] Compiling, archiving, or indexing in print, as Ann M. Blair describes, multiplied new methods to enable readers to search for terms.[27] Novel experiments, reproduced in engravings, engendered accurate diagrams, creating new credibility for science.[28] At some point, hard to know when, the numbered footnote was invented, to help the reader find the original source of knowledge: here goes.[29] The page became 'mathematized' by fresh textual representations of numbers and formulae.[30] Eventually, science invented an idea of 'fact', to help persuade readers of the reliability of truth.[31]

The internet has recreated Penelope's web all over. The problem of *this* web morphed from what humans do with books to what computers do with humans. What Google did next is told in mind-boggling detail by Zuboff. Like the new British Library, 1998 is the date Google incorporated as a company. The founding ideals of Larry Page and Sergey Brin shuffled democratic possibilities by creating an endoscopic search process. Algorithmic searching fed the information society over again. Google's mission, no less, is to 'organize the world's information and make it universally accessible and useful'.[32] The sentence effaces totalitarian assumptions. The web's benefits are so well known as not to need repeating:

knowledge implies unimpeded freedom. The illusion of isolation and privacy in individual internet users creates a sense of limitless choice. The power of Google Search is indeed a wonder to behold. Like a logical missile, if you define a target, you can pinpoint one result out of zettabytes available. You find friends, enemies, and of course your self, at a click, a digital selfie of global self-importance (how many Google searches begin with a proper name). In twenty years from 1998, Google Drive expanded to one billion active users on two billion devices; 500 million users of Google Photos upload 1.2 billion photos per day.[33] In 2017, 1.2 trillion searches were made worldwide.

This conforms to the first of what Zuboff calls 'the two texts' of the digital. The first is a familiar one of authors and readers. Every smartphone owner consumes it. This makes a universe of connection, on a scale never before experienced on earth. Here we are, with our 'friends', composers of our own world: in posts, blogs, photos, videos, tunes, stories, likes, or tweets. For most, it is a world limited only by access to enough storage. Storage is the oldest metaphor of knowledge. All learning depends on memory, Quintilian says, which is like a *thesaurus* (storehouse): the only thing more important than storage is how to find things inside the *thesaurus*, each idea in the right place.[34] Storage and searching are still keywords for Google. Digital storage is the postmodern determiner of desire. Everyone wants more, for more images, music, information. We buy storage in monthly contracts from suppliers, or (if the pinch is more acute), a new smartphone to process it faster, each change of hardware transcending older limits of personal storage. All we wish for now is *everything,* and all at the press of a button.

However, there is 'a second text'. In 1998, it was invisible even to Google. For a while, Google relaxed in performing simultaneous searches in the most efficient way possible, to satisfy its users. However, each search holds an implicit mirror image, of when or by whom a search is made. This, too, is digital data. At the moment Google discovered the existence of this text, it understood how easy, on exponential scale, it is to make money. The discovery came in a banal lucky dip known as 'Carol Brady's maiden name'. Carol was the TV Mom of *The Brady Bunch*, a US sitcom from 1969 to 1974. She began the fiction under a previous married name, Martin, her birth name never used in five series. However, Google's data team discovered in April 2002 that, on five occasions a day, at 48 minutes past the hour, 'Carol Brady's maiden name' attracted the highest nationwide search queries. The solution to the puzzle was *Who Wants To Be A Millionaire?* From Maine to Hawaii, as the time zones rolled past, this was the question on everyone's lips.

There is an innocence about the moment that deserves reflection. For a while, the UK *Who Wants To Be A Millionaire?* (which also began in 1998) became my mantra to demonstrate to students why, as I babbled about James I of England, they should listen. The first million-pound question was: 'Which king was known as the wisest fool in Christendom?' The poor contestant got it wrong, as the students learned. If a million pounds seemed a lot of money, an equation of knowledge times remuneration was changing. As Hal Varian, Google's economist noted, 'Every action a user performs is considered a signal to be analyzed and fed back into the system.'[35] The Brady moment lay in the predictive power invested in search analysis. The key was not information gained by users, but that provided by them, in their searches. This is known as 'behavioural data'. The more data that were gathered, the more behaviour could be predicted. The economics turned out to be stupendous. In 2001 Google's net revenue was $86 million; in 2002, after Brady, this rose to $347 million; $1.5 billion in 2003; $3.5 billion in 2004: a 3,500 per cent increase in four years.[36] In 2014, its market value exceeded Exxon Mobil, making it the second richest company in the world (behind Apple).

The key point is that the 'two texts' are a one-way mirror. All textual relationships imply a mirror: that is what makes them wonderful. In literary theory this is known as mimesis, an idea invented in Aristotle's *Poetics*.[37] The reader sees herself reflected on the other side of the first text, and becomes two selves. While for some, mimesis belongs only to poetry and drama, a theory for how characters create illusory mimics of real people, mimesis can be seen as the principle behind language altogether. Words, we say, represent things. Indeed, in evolutionary anthropology, it has been proposed that mimesis is the fundamental factor leading to the development of human language. In *Origins of the Modern Mind* (1991), Merlin Donald proposed the 'mimetic skill' as the watershed adaptation through which humans gained symbolic control to rehearse the body's movements in a systematic way, to remember those rehearsals, and reproduce them on command.[38] Out of these symbolic traditions came first language and later technology, in the transference of communication to writing and ultimately to computers.

Indeed, it is tempting to find a mimetic relationship in the switch from speech to writing. Aristotle defines this in *De interpretatione*, foundation stone of Western logical tradition: 'Spoken sounds are the symbols of mental experience, and written marks are the symbols of spoken sound.'[39] Such metaphors occur the world over, as in a Chinese fourteenth-century scholar: 'writing is pictured speech, and speech is vocalized breath'.[40] Voltaire's *Dictionnaire philosophique portatif* lends a semblance of algebra: 'L'écriture est la peinture de la voix; plus elle est ressemblante, meilleure elle est'.[41] Writing is better, the more truthfully it represents speech. However, it is important to recognize mimesis as more complex than that. Cognitive neuroscience now regards Donald's theory as over-linear in its picture of evolution in three stages, as well as over-reliant on human exclusivism. So-called 'mirror neurons' exist in monkeys as in humans.[42] Neurons activate whenever an animal performs an intentional action; but they also operate when an animal watches another animal performing the same action. Interestingly, chimpanzees are often better at social cognition than humans.

Similarly, that writing expresses speech does not mean *only* speech. The linguist Edward Sapir is invoked in defence of an idea that written language is point-by-point equivalent to speech, but states: 'this naturalness of speech is but an illusory feeling'.[43] Writing-as-speech ignores variable histories and epistemologies. The alphabet is its *sine qua non*. But does it really match speech? Alphabetic signs can function as single sounds, or as syllables, or as whole words; while syllabic signs (such as in ancient Hittite or Akkadian) can also function as single sounds. Visual morphemes show writing communicates irrespective of speech: 'How much wood would a woodchuck chuck if a woodchuck could chuck wood?' Writing uses signs with no conventionally assigned speech-forms (punctuation is a clear case). Even read aloud (or especially) writing is full of forms that are 'ambiguous and easily misunderstood'.[44] The assumption of correspondence in phonetization of alphabetic systems is as beguilingly misleading as one between writing and pictorialization in ideogrammatic languages such as Egyptian hieroglyphs, Chinese *hanzi*, or emojis. Such symbols are not pictograms, but logographs: words out of words.

Roy Harris demonstrates that Aristotle's original definition of writing presupposes a semiotic interpretation of representation rather than a substitutional one.[45] Nevertheless, mimesis haunts an epistemology of language from cave painting to artificial intelligence. Indeed, mimesis provides the energy for new software systems. We want to represent ourselves better, whatever the medium. Technocrats encourage us to believe each advance in technology advances freedom. Mission statements draw on too simple a mimetic metaphor. For Gelb's exhaustive analysis of the philosophical framework of writing, acknowledging necessary *relationship* of speech to writing, insists it is not the same in different languages. Gelb distinguished three forms of writing: logographic, syllabary, and alphabetic. Chinese characters adopt a different mimetic system from alphabetic European languages: they are logograms, representing a word phrase. Other written systems (like cuneiform) are syllabaries, each glyph a syllable. Egyptian hieroglyphs mixed logographic glyphs (morphemes) with phonetic glyphs.

Ignoring a temptation to create a genealogy of surviving written systems, Gelb desired to find what Assyrian cuneiform, Egyptian hieroglyphics, early Chinese characters, and Phoenician and Greek alphabets, held in common. Gelb constructed an overarching link between idiosyncratic forms: cuneiform of Elamite, Hittite and Sumerian types; Cretan Linear B as opposed to the logo-syllabic forms of Linear A or Cypro-Minoan; or syllabic derivations from Chinese such as Old Korean or Japanese. Writing for Gelb must be an order of 'visible signs', in which a relation of signs within system is arbitrary.[46] It is distinct from pictograms, used (with varying degrees of systematization) among early Indo-Europeans, Semites, and Amerindians. For pictures render their meaning as understandable in their own right, not as part of a system. Gelb is clear that pictograms are not *writing* as such: 'there was a time when man did not know how to write'.[47]

Behind all writing is Penelope's dream of human presence through imaginary speech. Yet only alphabets can be thought of as formally phonetic, and even so, according to the latest consensus, scripts are divided into three types: *consonantary* (in which characters denote consonants alone); *alphabetic* (consonants and vowels); or *abugida* (consonants accompanied by specific vowels).[48] The consonantary systems, including Hebrew and Arabic, are sometimes described as 'abjads' (derived from the first four letters in ancient Arabic); the 'abugida' (from the first letters in the Ethiopic script) is typical of Indic scripts beginning with Brahmi.[49] In an abugida (such as Devanagari, in which Sanskrit is written) each consonant–vowel sequence is a unit, called an *akṣara* in Sanskrit. The Phoenician glyph ʾālep, which carried over into the Aramaic and Old Hebrew scripts, represented the glottal stop; all the other characters in Aramaic and Hebrew at first represented consonants.[50] The Arabic abjad used ʾalif to represent a long *a*, and developed a new sign (*hamza*) to signify the glottal stop. Other characters corresponded to consonants and long vowels, leaving a reader to supply all the short vowels.[51]

The earliest Phoenician script (which unlike cuneiform or hieroglyphs consisted of only a few dozen symbols) was still a syllabary. From its symbols, via complex routes, derived both Aramaic abjad and the radically different Greek phonemic alphabet. Hebrew came to be written in Aramaic square script.[52] A cursive Aramaic script formed Arabic.[53] Perhaps even Brahmi script derived from Aramaic. Early abjads, so seminally important in history, had yet no means to express vowels. Later, maybe under Greek influence, Hebrew and Arabic writing manifested liminal marks for vowels ('diacritics'). They were lovingly called 'mothers of reading' (*matres lectionis*), slashes and dots bespeaking speech.[54] Even so, lacking full representation of vowels, they were not yet phonetic.

The Greek alphabet (dating from 800–750 BCE, made from Phoenician letters) was thus revolutionary. In Gelb's terms, instead of splitting whole words into constituent parts (such as syllables), alphabets build words up from tiniest particles of sound.[55] Much later a variant Aramaic abjad emerged in central Asia, used by Buddhists, Christians, and Manicheans.[56] It is ancestor of the Old Uyghur abjad, and thence the Uyghur alphabet, written vertically, first used in the reign of Genghis Khan. In 1269, Kublai Khan, grandson of Genghis and now emperor of China and Khan of Khans, ordered a new alphabet to be designed from scratch, common to all the Empire's literate languages, Mongolian, Chinese, Turkic, and Persian.[57] It was named Phagspa, after its inventor, a Buddhist monk and Imperial Preceptor, who based it on the Tibetan abugida (derived from Brahmi). For a hundred years, until the fall of the Yuan dynasty, it attempted to regulate the world.

From Greek, the Glagolitic alphabet derived in the ninth century CE with extra letters (perhaps from Hebrew, Coptic, or Armenian scripts) representing sounds in Serbo-Croat, Czech, or Slovak. Further east, the Cyrillic alphabet used Greek uncial and Glagolitic letters to match Russian or other Slavic languages, as well as Turkic, Mongolic, and Iranic, from the Balkans to the Caucasus and into central and east Asia. Indeed, the Roman alphabet itself developed from Greek (via the

Etruscan). Earliest examples are carved in stone, from perhaps the seventh century BCE. Old Italic scripts included Etruscan in central Italy, Nucerian in the south, and the Raetic alphabet of Bolzano in the north. Runic alphabets may derive from Raetic or else from Latin, runes spreading into the Germanic north, followed by the Futhark of Scandinavia and the Vikings.

With the power of the Roman Republic and Empire, aided by sophisticated use of a monumentally legible culture of inscription (still visible from Iberia to Persia or from Northumberland to Sudan) the Roman alphabet conquered the world. The Emperor Claudius, says Tacitus, as well as invading Britain, invented three new Latin letters. Claudius understood from the example of the ancient Egyptians the power conferred by inscriptions in stone.[58] *Rex*: 'this is the king's cup', declares a heavy bowl found near the Temple of Vesta in the Roman forum in 1899: it may have belonged to one of the last kings of Rome.[59] The Romans were not great innovators in the technologies of writing—they borrowed almost everything from the Greeks—but they knew how to colonize and capitalize it. Law they inscribed not on stone, but on bronze, precisely because it was a rarer and more valuable material.[60] When Horace calls his own poems 'more lasting than bronze' (*aere perennius*) he is making a grand claim: because in casting letters in bronze, the Roman Empire aimed to own the world.[61] Augustus placed a complete record of his accomplishments (*res gestae*) onto two bronze pillars on his Mausoleum in Rome.[62] All over the Roman world, people learned to read, not only in the elementary sense, but in constructing the structure of their lives.[63] In the forum, on temples, in cemeteries, using an elaborate code of abbreviations, Roman power was a visible structure. In perfectly formed stone letters, still the standard for computer fonts today, the Romans turned the alphabet into money and property.

Print caught on fast: Erasmus' *Adagia*, an anthology of classical learning, came with an alphabetical index in Johannes Froben's 1515 edition.[64] Dictionaries and encyclopedias quickly used the same device.[65] The West weaponized the alphabet as cultural sirens of speech. Colonial imperialism ensured dominance. As a result, the alphabet comes to some to seem normative, and many non-alphabetic writing systems are transliterated to fit the norm.[66] In the Western mode, normative is regarded as superior. In 2015, Google devolved business to a parent company called Alphabet, to signal domination in futurity. Page and Brin, with minimalist irony, created a website for it with the url 'abc.xyz'. A rival is the Chinese company Baidu (meaning 'a hundred times'). The Chinese Amazon, Alibaba, deploys a name with ambiguous counter-reference to oriental linguistic secrets. Google assumes the alphabet always wins. Alphabets use letters in tens; cuneiform numbered characters in hundreds; Chinese, thousands. Yet despite proliferation, reading speed measured across alphabets, abjads, abugidas, or logograms, is shown to be uniform. The alphabet benefits from false prejudice about its similarity to speech. For while language systems change, writing systems tend to be stable. Even though the Greek alphabet began as phonemic, it devolved to fit different dialects (as did Latin). Modern European alphabets derived from Greek or Latin represent speech imperfectly. When English orthography standardized in the eighteenth century with the ubiquity of printed words, it did so on a basis of written features rather than spoken (to the confusion of non-English speakers today). Indeed, a single sentence in modern English manifests features that are prosodic and others that are syllabic; some alphabetic and some even logographic (numbers, for example). Gelb concludes: 'Writing can never be considered an *exact* counterpart of the spoken language'.[67]

Writing does not directly represent speech, or speech personhood.[68] In turn, artificial intelligence only imperfectly and indirectly responds to human desires and needs. Yet by promising to do so, Google and Facebook draw us in. In the meantime, Zuboff's idea of a secondary mimetic process in the 'second text' has changed everything. At its heart is an asymmetry between personal storage and the capacities of Big Data. In 1986 human knowledge corresponded to the contents of a mega-library, on the model of a Library of Congress, adjusted to the gamut of human languages. At that time, 1 per cent of information was digitized. By 2000 this had risen to 25 per cent. By now the rush to digitize existing books and records was well under way. This accompanied a parallel effort to produce new information in ready-made digital form. The result is that by 2013 it was estimated that 98 per cent of the world's knowledge was digital. Does the robot know everything?

The volume of information on the internet now exceeds pre-digital mass by geometric proportions. Indeed, in Zuboff's words, 'its volume exceeds our ability to discern its meaning'.[69] This is a dizzying statement. It is, of course, of the nature of information to exceed understanding. In the seventeenth century it was a commonplace that the age of the polymath is over. Already before Goethe, there was too much science for one person to know. This was long since true. There are 480,000 items in the English Short Title Catalogue, listing English books between 1473 and 1800 (digitized in Early English Books Online, available for a small fortune from Proquest). Even boastful academics can claim only to read fifty books per week; squaring this twice over a reading life of fifty years makes 125,000 books; allowing no time for processing or thinking. Now God needs a computer (or alternatively, she always was a computer). To sift through vast amounts of information, Martin Hilbert observes, only artificial intelligence will do.[70] Google has hired more computer scientists than anyone else in order to design the computers and algorithms to cope. The book robot in that sense is now redundant. It patiently fishes out book after book for hungry readers, who patiently await in St Pancras for the van to arrive from Yorkshire. But all the human readers in what remains of human history have been left as if light years away. Google alone now employs 2.5 million servers in fifteen locations spread over four continents. Governments and universities lie in its wake.

There is a peculiar freedom, wrote Roland Barthes, arriving in a country not knowing its language. Landing in Tokyo in 1966, he perceived intensely the Japanese language around him, making sense of things (or of him) without his understanding. It is possible to apprehend a language making sense, without it making any sense to me. Barthes felt this especially in relation to Japanese, in which 'the empire of signifiers is so immense'.[71] He also felt instinctively that Japanese constructed reality differently from his own language. Its irreducible difference in that way freed him from the mirage of representation.

Mimesis is the magic spell of language. Writing, as much as images of the dead in the civilization of ancient Egypt, creates what Otto Rank calls 'a double of the body'. In Freud's analysis of Rank, 'the double' creates mirrors and shadows of us, and thus provides 'an insurance against the extinction of the self'.[72] The doctrine of the soul is an intellectual extension of this, as indeed in time 'all the suppressed acts of volition that fostered the illusion of free will'. We have here an outline theory of the origin of religion as well as of writing's magical function. In the third century CE, Serenus Sammonicus, physician to Emperor Caracalla, prescribed a cure for malaria.[73] Sufferers should wear, he said, an amulet in the form of a triangle, bearing the nonceword *abracadabra* (Fig. 4).

A version of the spell is found on Abraxas stones, used by gnostics of the heretic sect of Basilides, who taught in Alexandria in the second century CE. Magical papyri and gemstones bore secret writing as amulets and charms. The first mention of Abraxas is in Hyginus, superintendent of Augustus' Palatine library.[74] Irenaeus, Greek-speaking Bishop of Lyon, refuted Basilides, reporting Abraxas as *archon* ('ruler' of the earthly heaven) via a genealogy in which an unbegotten father begets *nous* ('mind'), who begets *logos* ('word'), and so on in sequence 365 times.[75] Hippolytus, hermetic hunter of magi, supplies a number value to the letters of *ABPAΣAΞ* to add up to 365.[76] A cruciform example survives from sixth- or seventh- century Burgundy in a silver talisman.[77]

In the hillside at Fiesole, high above the Arno, amid the cypresses below the piazza at San Domenico, wonder begins. Giovanni Boccaccio summons a party at a villa as respite from the Black Death in 1348, setting them a task of telling each other 100 stories over ten days. There are no limits to the spells of imagination: *egli sapeva tante cose fare, & dire, che domine pure unquanche* ('he knew how to do and say more stuff than God ever could').[78] Midst the Florentine pandemic they create a little earthly paradise, which Boccaccio with blasphemous scandal calls *Verbum caro* ('the word made flesh'). Daniel Defoe reported an 'Abracadabra' (Fig. 4) still in use in the Great Plague year of 1665 in London, saving occupants of a house during lockdown.[79] Folk etymology derives it from Hebrew, 'I create as I speak', linked to a passage in the Talmud, or Christ's own tongue Aramaic, 'I create like the word' (אברא כדברא).[80] Abracadabra shifts between *abjad* and *alphabet*, from *a* to *aleph*. No document verifies its origin as it descends into the

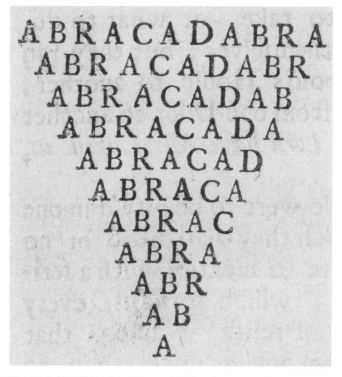

Fig. 4. ABRACADABRA': Defoe, *A Journal of the Plague Year* (London: E. Nutt, J. Roberts, A. Dodd, and J. Graves, 1722), 40. Oxford, Bodleian Library, Vet. A4 e.3659 (1)

vernacular of popular magic. The US Supreme Court in 1948 assured its citizens that charging a jury is no 'matter of abracadabra'.[81] Rushdie voiced in it the magic of railway trains: 'abracadabra abracadabra abracadabra sang the wheels as they bore us back-to-bom'.[82] *Harry Potter* echoes with an 'unforgiveable curse' in Voldemort's death-spell.[83]

> Disappear, O sickness, at the sound of this word.

So writes Sharon Olds in 'Abracadabra Ode'.[84] Will Minerva answer our prayers? Google hardly cares. In the post-corona world, ALPHABET INCORPORATED ('Investors in Humans') imagines new ways to get us to stay indoors, turn on the computer, and give our selves and our data away for free, perfecting, in the process, the dreams of ancient despots.

3

The Message of Ashurbanipal from Antiquity

The Royal Library of Ashurbanipal at Nineveh, dating to the seventh century BCE, is sometimes described as the 'first library' of the world.[1] This is an exaggeration: books were collected a thousand years earlier, in the time of Hammurabi, who compiled lists of kings, and codified the law.[2] Mesopotamia had many libraries before Ashurbanipal, and systems of archiving already extant made his possible.[3] However, Ashurbanipal's stands as an archetype of the first library to have the attributes we expect of a modern library. The collection spread out in multiple rooms organized by subject matter. One group of rooms was dedicated to history and government; another to religion and magic; a third to poetry; and others to geography, science, and so on.[4] The Library of Ashurbanipal even had a kind of catalogue for finding books, arranged by what we would call shelves. The Assyrian king thus matches the ambition of the Chinese emperor fictionalized by Jorge Luis Borges, who maps out his dominion over the world by listing all the things within it, beginning with a taxonomy of all the animals. There are embalmed ones, trained ones, fabled ones, stray ones; all prefaced by 'those belonging to the emperor' and (in a singular case of metastatement) 'those included in this classification'.[5] Foucault borrowed from this parody in his preface to *Les mots et les choses* (1966).[6]

Yet the parody has serious meaning. Borges created it for an essay on John Wilkins's proposal in 1688 for a universal philosophical language which would encode a description of the thing within the name of everything. Human beings create epistemes, Foucault says, by which they organize the world to control it, like Borges's emperor. The Enlightenment created 'catalogues, indexes and inventories' out of the libraries and archives which it built, in order to categorize and lay claim to a totality called truth.[7] In 1690, Gottfried Wilhelm Leibniz was appointed the librarian of the Bibliotheca Augusta in Wolfenbüttel, one of the great early modern libraries of Europe, with 25,000 volumes. He created a new book indexing system and an alphabetical author catalogue.[8] He called for a general empirical database for all sciences. To assist this, he envisaged a *characteristica universalis* (a universal formal language), a *calculus ratiocinator* (a universal logical calculation system), and a community of minds without barriers.

How the king's library at Nineveh looked is deduced from other sites excavated in Mesopotamia, revealing an oblong of spaces set into stone, like multiple ovens, or the funeral boxes in a columbarium. Each niche contained a separate selection of clay tablets. Individual tablets came with accompanying citations, acting as a table of contents. Each group of tablets in Ashurbanipal's library contained a further brief citation to identify it, and each room contained a tablet near the door to classify the general contents of the room. As in a modern library, tablets were organized according to shape and size, as well as contents. Among the finds at Nineveh are inventories detailing the acquisition of clay tablets and of wooden writing boards.[9] For Ashurbanipal's collection was not the result of accretion and heritage: he commanded the library into existence, with the aim of uniting under one roof all the knowledge yet known to mankind. This involved a colossal effort of textual retrieval inside and outside his empire; and another of intensive copying of texts transcribed into his own language in fair copies.[10] The efforts of scribes, combined with the demands of military intelligence, give this ancient archive something of the character of what is now called 'collection development'.[11]

The collection today contains 30,000 pieces of cuneiform, comprising approximately 1,200 distinct texts.[12] Despite the organizational talents of the original librarians, the library had less luck in early excavations. The first discovery, credited to Austen Henry Layard, aspiring diplomat and amateur explorer, was made in 1849 in the south-west palace, the Royal Palace of King Sennacherib.[13] Three years later, Layard's assistant, Hormuzd Rassam, an Iraqi Christian from Mosul, later Iraqi agent for the British Museum, discovered a similar 'library' in the palace of King Ashurbanipal on the opposite side of the mound.[14] A majority of surviving tablets were severely fragmented. Unfortunately, no inventory was made of either find; at the time they got to Europe, the tablets were irreparably mixed up, along with those of other sites. Thus it is impossible today to reconstruct the original contents of either of the two main 'libraries'.

Ashurbanipal (668–c.630 BCE) ruled ancient Assyria at its zenith of military and cultural extension.[15] Greeks named him Sardanapalos; the Bible, Asnapper or Osnapper, 'great and noble' (Ezra 4: 10). Diodorus of Sicily describes his reign in *Bibliotheca historica*.[16] Aristotle mentions him in *Nicomachean Ethics* as someone who could not distinguish the good life from bodily pleasure.[17] Lord Byron wrote a tragedy *Sardanapalus* in blank verse in 1821, set in Nineveh, making its title character the last king of the Assyrian monarchy. Byron dedicated the play to Goethe; its influence spread through Romantic Europe, inspiring a painting by Eugène Delacroix, and an unfinished opera by Hector Berlioz. The historical Ashurbanipal protected Assyrian territory by extraordinary military victories, yet his reign spelt the end of Assyrian empire.[18] Even in ancient times, Ashurbanipal's fame was associated with memory preservation, his conquests dwarfed by his collection of texts at Nineveh. Sources in Persian and Armenian literature recount that Alexander the Great saw the great library of Ashurbanipal and was inspired to create his own at Alexandria.[19] Dying before he could begin work, he left its creation to his successor Ptolemy. Libraries, Mary Beard reminds us, are not mere repositories of information: they are the organization of knowledge, and so control it, and restrict access to it.[20] Not for nothing are library buildings often modelled on fortresses.

Most of the Library of Ashurbanipal is now in the possession of the British Museum and the Iraq Department of Antiquities.[21] Despite Layard's impatience, it can be deduced from the conservation of fragments that the number of tablets existing in the library was once many thousands, and the number of writing boards in the library was 300. The texts are principally in Akkadian, preserved in a Neo-Babylonian cuneiform script. The majority of the tablet corpus (about 6,000) includes legislation; foreign correspondence and engagements; aristocratic diversions; and financial matters. Most precious from a scholarly view is a nearly complete list of ancient Near Eastern rulers. The findings of spies or secret affairs of state were hidden secure in deep recesses of the palace, like a post-modern government data archive. The texts contain divinations, omens, incantations, and hymns to various gods, or concern medicine and astronomy.

Amidst ephemera are works which ever since discovery were hailed as masterpieces of early literature. Rassam found the *Epic of Gilgamesh* (Fig. 5) in 1853. Subsequently, even older fragments have been discovered of the 'Old Babylonian' version (18th c. BCE) known by its incipit, *Shūtur eli sharrī* ('Surpassing all other kings'). Akkadian texts found by Rassam are later, in the so-called 'standard version' (13th–10th c. BCE), with an incipit *Sha naqba īmuru* ('He who saw the deep', or 'He who sees the unknown'):

> He saw what was secret, discovered what was hidden,
> > He brought back a tale of before the Deluge.
> He came a far road, was weary, found peace,
> > And set all his labours on a tablet of stone.[22]

Approximately two-thirds of this longer, twelve-tablet version have been recovered, with the largest copy still being from Ashurbanipal's library. In addition to this wonderful find, the *Enûma Eliš*, a Babylonian creation myth, was discovered by Layard in 1849. It consists of about 1,000 lines divided into seven clay tablets. Like the *Epic of Gilgamesh*, this copy is seventh-century BCE, although the text may be a thousand years older than that. Other literary finds included the myth of Adapa the first man, who was offered immortality, but refused to partake of the food or drink of the gods, as it could be the food of death. Some said that Adapa had the body of a fish, and the bones of carp were found in the oldest Mesopotamian shrines. Even more elusive is the fragmentary tale, *The Poor Man of Nippur*. It consists of three strange economic stories, in which debts (as in Rabelais's *Tiers Livre* or the 2008 bank crash) turn out to be incommensurate with gifts. In the first, Gimil-Ninurta, 'an unhappy man', presents a goat to the mayor. It is interpreted as a bribe, and the poor man receives in

Fig. 5. 'The Flood Tablet'; *Epic of Gilgamesh*, clay tablet, 7th c. BCE. British Museum K.3375

exchange a cup of third-class beer. Debt is as old as writing, for which reason J. M. Keynes studied cuneiform texts.

The Sumerian goddess of writing was Nisaba (sometimes Naga or Nidaba), who also took care of accounts, grain, and harvest, venerated in rituals at Ere.[23] In the Gudea cylinders (c.2125 BCE), she holds a gold stylus and a clay tablet.[24] As writing moved into law and literature, her responsibilities expanded. She is 'wild cow' and 'wild sheep'.[25] In Babylon she declined, and by the Third Dynasty in Ur was replaced by a nerdy male god, Nabu. In Egypt, Seshat, dressed in leopard-skin, was 'Mistress of the House of Books'. She took care of accounting, mathematics, and architecture, under the sway of Thoth, her father or possibly husband, who ruled writing in general, as well as the dead.[26] The oldest civilizations all have complex mythologies of text and writing. In India, Sarasvatī is mentioned in the

Rigveda, one of the four canonical texts of Hinduism. On the fifth day of spring, even today, she helps young children to learn the abugida of the Devanagari script. In the Sarada Tilaka, a collection of Sanskrit mantras of the eighth century CE, she helps us to attain all possible eloquence, and also 'bring radiance on the implements of writing, and books produced in her favour'.[27] Yet long before her, the eagle Garuḍa 'is made not of feathers but metres. You cannot hurt a metre'.[28] Poetry is visualized speech. Garuḍa is the hymn. Buried among the branches of a tree, he reads the Vedas.

The Library of Ashurbanipal is the most capacious metaphor possible both for the survival and the destruction of knowledge. Uniquely among Assyrian kings, Ashurbanipal described himself as a scholar-king, conscious that knowledge was key to his power:

> I have read cunningly written texts in obscure Sumerian and Akkadian that are difficult to interpret. I have carefully examined inscriptions on stone from before the Deluge that are sealed, stopped up, and confused.[29]

Knowledge is a secret for kings alone, all-seeing. The library contains all, from reports of agents (all over the empire) interrogating dissent, to diviners who read the future.[30] Ashurbanipal oversees a comprehensive archive of the world of knowledge:

> I have already written to the temple overseer (?) and to the chief magistrate (that) you are to place (the tablets) in the storage house (and that) no one shall withhold any tablet from you.[31]

Estimates of original contents number 10,000 clay texts; the library may also have contained leather scrolls, wax boards, even papyri. Ashurbanipal's library offers an image of universality in knowledge, and equally one of destruction. Indeed, they are bound together in the story of the Library: without destruction, survival was impossible. A coalition of Babylonians, Scythians, and Medes destroyed Nineveh in 612 BCE.[32] During the burning of the palace, a great fire ravaged the Library. It caused the clay cuneiform tablets to become partially baked, and so, by an irony of chemistry as much as history, preserved the tablets. Other texts inscribed on wax were lost due to their organic nature. The story of Mesopotamia is irretrievably linked to a story of loss.[33]

In 2002, the British Museum launched the Ashurbanipal Library Project, a long-term co-operation with the University of Mosul in Iraq. It aims to bring Ashurbanipal's astonishing library to life. Using modern technology, an ancient place is opened to new readers. In its display (Fig. 6), the Museum in Great Russell Street beautifully reimagines clay tablets in MDF cabinets resembling, yet also subtly different from, the original columbary of the stone library. It is the ancient library seen as if in a modern dream.

Fig. 6. 'Antiquity reconstructed'; Library of Ashurbanipal at the British Museum, 2019

The wonder of books is intrinsic to the experience of them. When Augustine is in Carthage, he longs to meet Faustus, follower of the Persian cult guru Mani. Mani's cult beguilingly mixed books and images, hymns and psalms.[34] The *Gospel* of Mani was divided into 22 parts, named after all the letters of the Aramaic abjad. When he arrives, Augustine is delighted by this eloquence and skill in languages. But has Faustus been seduced by literature?[35] He lacks skill in all arts other than grammar. 'He had read some orations of Cicero, a very few books by Seneca', some poetry, and volumes of the Manichean sect written in a Latin of superior style.[36] Augustine's first love is rhetoric, always, yet Mani's books leave him wanting. 'The books of the Manichees are full of long mythological tales about heaven and the stars and sun and moon': he worries whether wonder is enough.[37] Similarly, when Augustine travels to Rome, his friend Alypius gets into trouble while lost in books, 'walking up and down alone in front of the tribunal with his writing tablets and pen'. Immune to pleasures of money or the flesh, Alypius is tricked and punished for bribery, all while he is *solus cum tabulis ac stilo*. The one way to corrupt him is a passion for books: *hoc solo autem paene iam inlectus erat studio litterario* ('The only thing that nearly succeeded in tempting him was his enthusiasm for literature').[38]

The two global books of modernity are Charles Darwin's *On the Origin of Species* in the nineteenth century and Stephen Hawking's *A Brief History of Time* in the twentieth. Darwin's book cost fifteen shillings on publication in 1859, quickly selling out; an American edition followed in 1860, with a translation into German the same year.[39] By Darwin's death in 1882 it had appeared in six editions in England, fully revised, along with further abridgements and library editions, and been translated into French, Italian, Russian, Swedish, Danish, Polish, Hungarian, Spanish, and Serbian. Hawking's book was published in 1988, for readers with no knowledge of science, and including just one mathematical formula: $E = mc^2$.[40] The book sold more than 25 million copies, plus an app, a film that ignored the book, and an opera that was never completed; it has been translated into forty languages. Like Nicolaus Copernicus on the revolutions of the heavenly spheres, it is sometimes said of each that it is a 'book that nobody read'.[41]

Arthur Koestler was wrong about that, and it is silly to dismiss Darwin or Hawking.[42] However, in one sense it does not matter: their books contain theories of everything, matter or anti-matter, so that we ourselves no longer *need to know*. A metaphysical idea of the book links desire for fulfilment and fear (or desire) of oblivion. Perhaps, as in Freud's *Beyond the Pleasure Principle*, the two drives inextricably meet. If all experience teaches us that every living thing dies, Freud says, 'then we can only say that *the goal of all life is death*'.[43] In its search for knowledge combined with a need to rid itself of knowledge, 'the book' resembles the *Fort-da* game of the child who repeatedly throws the toy out of the cot and then reels it back in on the end of a string. The article on 'le livre' in Denis Diderot and Jean le Rond d'Alembert's *Encyclopaedia* veers between bibliomania and bibliophobia.[44] A book communicates to public and posterity a 'point of knowledge'.[45] Pliny the Younger (prolix himself), said the bigger the book, the better.[46] Yet everyone knew Callimachus the grammarian's view, that 'a big book is equal to a big evil'.[47] A big book is bad news. When is more, less? D'Alembert said every hundred years a list of useful books should be compiled, 'et qu'on brûlât tout le reste'.[48] In a letter of November 1760, Diderot approved book-burnings by China's first emperor.[49] Immanuel Kant, writing in the margin of his own book, *Observations on the Feeling of the Beautiful and Sublime* (1764), lamented the 'flood of books' in which 'the world is annually drowned'.[50] The mathematician Marquis de Condorcet in 1792 commended 'une destruction commune' of aristocratic books.[51] There were plans for a bonfire of leather-bound books owned by Bourbons and clerics, but nothing came of it. Freud agrees there is no antithesis between life drives and death drives.[52]

'My book, stuffed with phrases, has dropped to the floor. It lies under the table, to be swept up', says Bernard at the end of Woolf's *The Waves* (1931). He has been keeping a notebook to archive his whole life, but it turns out to be an unachievable pipedream.[53] Rachel Whiteread's *Untitled (Paperbacks)* is a wonderful evocation of the spatial imaginary of the library, of what books entail (Fig. 7). First shown at the Venice Biennale in 1997, and now owned by the Museum of Modern Art in New York, the work consists of a negative plaster cast of the interior of a library, with the fore-edges of the books turned inward.[54] Whiteread creates, in spectral relief, a roomful of books whose contents and titles appear to be lost. The plaster surfaces are like a haunting of the library, at once there and not there. Examined closely, the size of the books, the texture of their pages, sometimes a

Fig. 7. 'Paperback ghosts'; Rachel Whiteread, *Untitled (Paperbacks)*, plaster and steel, 1997. New York, MOMA

residue of the coloured binding, are still visible. Whiteread's sculpture is a poetic monument at once to the immortality of the book, and its fragility.

Unpacking his library in Paris in 1931, Benjamin perused his books, still not on shelves, 'not yet touched by the mild boredom of order'.[55] Crates wrenched open lay on the floor, 'the air saturated with the dust of wood'. For a book collector, it was a moment of anticipation. After two years in the dark, awaiting a home, the books enjoyed the chaos of the box, arbitrary, confused. Indeed, their natural state is disorder: it is only in a library, above all in a catalogue, that they find order. The dream of Ashurbanipal tells us an intrinsic condition of the book. Tablets are things, yet body forth something abstract, in the form of contents. Every book, however small, organizes itself as a little world. Every library portends a galaxy of worlds, listed in constellations, every book in its place. In shocking foresight, Nineveh librarians created a catalogue of categories to organize tablets. With a little fantasy, these are not so different from Aby Warburg's in his library in Hamburg in the early twentieth century, now in Bloomsbury in London: symbols and images of art (*Image*, first floor); motifs in languages and literatures (*Word*, second floor); transition from magical beliefs to religion, science, and philosophy (*Orientation*, third and fourth floor); and ancient patterns of social customs and political institutions (*Action*, fourth floor). The library of the Sorbonne in Paris in the fourteenth century also began its catalogue with literary humanism, although the Vatican preferred theology first.[56] It took Conrad Gesner's *Bibliotheca universalis* of 1545 to summon the alphabet to organize books.[57]

Contents cannot be reduced to materiality. Taken collectively, indeed, the tablets speak of something more than their individual contents. A library is more than a linear sequence of books: it is a system of knowledge; and the bigger the system, the greater the paradox. The Library of Ashurbanipal was buried by invaders centuries before the famous library at Alexandria was established. Each of these legendary collections was taken as a symbol of the totality of knowledge, in different histories. Alexandria was bigger than Nineveh. The palace library of the Fatimid caliphate in Cairo, before its dispersal by Salah al-Din, was said to contain any book that anyone might want. Ibn Abi Tayy in his twelfth-century *Universal History* claimed it contained two million books.[58] A wild exaggeration, perhaps, but minute compared to the megaliths of the British Library, Bibliothèque nationale de France, or Library of Congress. All these, as the twentieth century ended, moved to new premises or built extensions to accommodate overfill.

These steel and glass temples of post-modernity, embedded in London, Paris, and Washington, DC, proclaim a realm of knowledge beyond the imagination of the past. Yet they emerged to meet a new revolution. Colin St John Wilson made plans for a library at St Pancras in 1962, just as ARPANET (the first packet-switching device) was devised. On 15 December 1996, the BnF moved (just eight years after President Mitterrand's proposal), only to greet a transatlantic datalink between Cornell University and CERN in Geneva. The library abandoned the eery green light of its domed Byzantine hall in rue de Richelieu for an under-ground ziggurat, the size of nine football pitches, stretched between four giant towers. To reach the books, it is necessary to descend into the earth via a vertigin-ous escalator, devised (it is said in W. G. Sebald's *Austerlitz*), 'on purpose to instil a sense of insecurity and humiliation to the poor readers'.[59] The Parisian library, despite high-speed development, ran into huge escalations of cost, due to a mono-lithic high-rise design. The locals jokingly dubbed it the 'TGB' or *très grande bib-liothèque* ('Very Large Library'), a sarcastic allusion to France's high-speed rail system, the TGV or *trains à grande vitesse*.[60] Yet as soon as completed, it was overhauled to assimilate a digital identity in Tim Berners-Lee's web browser known as 'World Wide Web'.[61]

Libraries have built-in obsolescence, side by side with self-contradictory uni-versality. Big is therefore never big enough. In this sense, the epithet Big Data is similar to the hyperbolic oxymoron *très grande bibliothèque*. Knowledge never keeps up with itself.[62] This paradox relates to another: knowledge disappears as inevitably as it arrives. The motivation for the book robot in Boston Spa was that newspapers, printed on thin and poor-quality paper, are damaged irreparably through storage. A 1959 report to the Virginia State Library concluded that most library books printed in the first half of the twentieth century would be unusable by the end of the twenty-first.[63] One aspiration of the digital age has been to transfer knowledge to a medium immune to decay, one not material in the first place. However, archiving is an inextricable problem of the digital age.[64] Systems, platforms, software programs, go out of date in a decade. The rush for retrieval takes place in another office at Boston Spa, a little museum of computers from the 1970s or 1980s. Amstrads, BBCs, and early Apples already look quainter than a penny-farthing bicycle or even an Assyrian chariot. Yet there is method: the British Library runs every program it can find while it can, to preserve knowledge otherwise lost.[65]

In this respect, the Library of Ashurbanipal has advantages. It is still here, thirty centuries on. Yet its fragments tell their own story of data loss. The Ashurbanipal Library Project has counted 30,943 pieces. These are pieces of pieces, barely yield-ing a whole. Books, even digital ones, are physical, and the first law of physical things is decay. The project partner is the University of Mosul, a city far older than London. Not be to be confused with Nineveh across the Tigris (now known as Nebi Yunus, after the prophet Jonah buried there), it is populated largely by Kurds. Mosul is first mentioned in Xenophon but is much older.[66] After Alexander's con-quests in 332 BCE it fell under the Seleucid Empire, changing hands again with the rise of the Sasanian Empire in 225 CE, becoming part of the Sasanian prov-ince of Asōristān. Christianity arrived as early as the first century. Mosul was an episcopal seat in the sixth century, then annexed to the Rashidun Caliphate. The first mosque in the city was built in 640 CE by Utba bin Farqad Al-Salami.[67]

In its Arabic form and spelling, Mosul, or 'Mawsil', stands for 'linking point', we might say 'Junction City'. Its markets attested to this role: a meeting place of Arabs (in a Sunni majority), Assyrians, Jews (both Iraqi and Kurdish), Iraqi Turkmens, Armenians, Yazidi, Mandeans, Romani, and Shabaks. All this has changed. The Jews began leaving in the 1950s. Of perhaps 70,000 Assyrian Christians once in Mosul there may be no one left. The American invasion of Iraq began a year after the Ashurbanipal Library Project was inaugurated. Two of Saddam Hussein's sons were killed in Mosul in July 2003. Subsequently, the city became synonymous with violence. Car bombs and suicide attacks began in 2004. In 2008, 12,000 Assyrian Christians fled after a wave of murders. On 10 June 2014, the Islamic State of Iraq and the Levant took control. Archaeological catastrophe conceals a murderous list of human victims.[68] The tomb of Jonah is gone, alongside the oldest monastery; also, the fourteenth-century mosque of Nabi Jerjis, 'prophet George'. Amid wreckage in Mosul Museum is further record of loss, reminiscent of the library of Assyrian kings: wholesale burning of thousands of books or manuscripts.[69]

The library of the University of Mosul once had a million books, maps, and manuscripts. Mohammed Jasim, Director of the Library at its destruction, described it as among the finest in the Middle East, with some books a thousand years old. Among its treasures was a Qur'an from the ninth century, but it was principally a working library for modern students of science, philosophy, law, history, literature, and the humanities. Six hundred thousand books were in Arabic; many of the rest were in English. During nearly three years of Islamic State rule, the university closed down. In December 2016, as the Iraqi Army pushed into Mosul, ISIS fighters set the library alight. Visitors reported they could smell the charred books a block away. Irina Bokova, the director-general of UNESCO, called the burning of the books 'an attack on culture, knowledge and memory'.[70] At Mosul they now call it 'a library without books'. The difference between the libraries of Nineveh and of Mosul, then, is the difference between entropy and iconoclasm—or, as I will go on to call it, the less well-known but equally venerable art of biblioclasm.

4

Living in the Tower of Babel

In Auschwitz, Primo Levi says, the confusion of languages was a fundamental component of living: 'a perpetual Babel, in which everyone shouts orders and threats in languages never heard before, and woe betide whoever fails to grasp the meaning'.[1] Fifteen or twenty languages were spoken, yet polyglossia was not a means of communication. *Innumerevoli sono le proibizioni.*[2] Language is a negative entity, expressed in arbitrary prohibitions without number. The linguistic rule of the camp is 'to reply 'Jawohl' to every command: 'never to ask questions, always to pretend to understand'.[3] When the Buna factory is built by the labourers of the Lager, they call it *Babelturm, Bobelturm*, the Tower of Babel. It is cemented by hate and discord, in 'the insane dream of grandeur of our masters, their contempt for God and men'.[4]

Morbid fantasies about the ends of knowledge are in this way never new:

And the whole earth was of one language, and of one speech.

[4] And they said, Go to, let us build us a city and a tower, whose top may reach unto heaven; and let us make us a name, lest we be scattered abroad upon the face of the whole earth.

[5] And the LORD came down to see the city and the tower, which the children of men builded.

[6] And the LORD said, Behold, the people is one, and they have all one language; and this they begin to do: and now nothing will be restrained from them, which they have imagined to do.

[7] Go to, let us go down, and there confound their language, that they may not understand one another's speech.

[8] So the LORD scattered them abroad from thence upon the face of all the earth: and they left off to build the city.

[9] Therefore is the name of it called Babel; because the LORD did there confound the language of all the earth: and from thence did the LORD scatter them abroad upon the face of all the earth.

The first part of Genesis 11 marks the end of the primeval Yahwistic story, before the birth of Abraham and the beginnings of Jewish history. It is an aetiological saga, explaining why there are so many nations and languages on the earth.

Fittingly, in view of its subject, it relies on a Hebrew pun (indeed these verses are full of puns): Babel is the Hebrew word for Babylon, one of the foremost city names of the ancient world, synonymous with human civilization; but it also means 'confusion' or 'medley', from the verb *bālal*, to 'stir up' or 'mix up'. The associations reverberate further: for Babel was often understood popularly to mean 'the gate of God'.[5] In this way, Genesis 11: 1–9 speaks of human imagination as an instrument of inevitable hubris. Its themes of ultimate knowledge and its inevitable failure, of a global language and the confusion of tongues, of a universal culture which leads only to division and dispersal, could not be more modern. Have knowledge and paranoia always gone together?

Yet while the story of Babel is thirty centuries old, the *image* of Babel is more recent.[6] Its oldest known representation is in an eleventh-century CE sculpture in the cathedral of Salerno; more famous is the thirteenth-century mosaic in the Basilica di San Marco in Venice.[7] All this changes in humanist northern Europe. Babel became ubiquitous, especially via the work of Peter Bruegel the Elder. Bruegel painted the subject at least three times, two versions of which survive. The first of these, signed in 1563 (now in Vienna), is radically different in emotion from the later one, now in Rotterdam. They have acquired mythographic status, influencing every representation of the Tower thereafter.

The Vienna Tower dominates the landscape as if it were the rock of Gibraltar, high above the sea (see Plate 1). The top of the tower (Pl. 1) is above the cloud level, and its bulk even casts a shadow on the land below. It is an image of doom as well as hubris, in line with an Old Testament theology of the curse put on a blasphemous and covenant-breaking nation.[8] To the Genesis story, Bruegel adds elements taken from the *Jewish Antiquities* of Josephus, written in the first century CE.[9] This is his source for identifying Nimrod as the architect and engineer of the tower project. According to Josephus, the Jews built the tower thinking it slavery to submit to God. Visually, Bruegel's sources are probably the work of earlier Flemish artists, such as the Grimani Breviary and a panel by Joachim Patinir.[10] Yet unlike those works, Bruegel makes his tower, while stark and impenetrable, teeming with human bodies. They are at work on the building, which therefore seems contemporary with the viewer, rather than a venerable antiquity. The painting indeed is meticulous in its presentation of a vast array of building technologies. On the viewer's left, the building appears to be approaching completion; the stonework appears as if polished, and architectural ornaments such as architraves and balconies are in place. Towards the centre, scaffolding can be seen behind the finished walls, as if they are Hollywood props; the core of the building is only gradually coming to fruition, and roofs are unmade. On the right, much of the site is still rubble, awaiting form. The city is, still and always, under construction, perhaps unfinishable; but it also seems already to be undergoing a process of inner decay. Like the Forth Bridge, once finished at one end, it will no doubt need rebuilding at the other. The tower is a symbol of permanent modernity and fragility. It fills the eye's view, reaching to the roof of the sky; but as it does so, it crumbles before our eyes, as if for every brick or stone supplied, another may fall. Human labour works in vain, but it is indefatigable and inexhaustible.

Like most of Bruegel's images, *The Tower of Babel* (1563) is resistant to easy interpretation, while thick with hermeneutic signposting. It is an essay in human folly, more specifically the sin of pride. It contains a number of precise historical and biblical allusions, while being clearly fantastical in conception. Architecturally, the tower is reminiscent of the Colosseum. Yet it also leans perceptibly to the left, in a spiral, like the campanile in Pisa. It may be that the lean is an optical illusion created by the spiral, which is already a feature of Babel images, including the Bedford Hours and the Grimani Breviary; in the case of the Malwiya minaret at the Great Mosque of Samarra in Iraq, the spiral was realized as architectural fact, not fantasy. This ninth-century CE modernist masterpiece, a geometry more perfect and starker even than Frank Lloyd Wright's New York Guggenheim (1959), was badly damaged by a bomb in the Iraq War in 2005.[11]

While Bruegel could only have imagined that exquisite building, the city spread out on either side of the lower part of the *The Tower of Babel* (1563) is historical: this is sixteenth-century Antwerp. Antwerp at the time was the fastest growing port in the world, taking advantage of the decline of Bruges before the rise of Amsterdam. Its population doubled between 1440 and 1500, then doubled again by the year of Bruegel's painting.[12] The fortress walls of the river Scheldt and the nearby church towers can be recognized from contemporary landscape views of the city such as by Lucas van Valckenborch. Meanwhile, a procession wanders up towards the stone mountain, more or less at the viewer's point of perspective. They are led by a cardinal and a courtier, stumbling over the masonry, and indeed the masons. It is argued the Vienna painting contains an attack on Philip II of Spain and the power and wealth of the Catholic Church.[13] This is a painting hot with political and social meanings.

Babel is the most plastic image of the book in the Western world. On the one hand, it is a synonym for literary confusion. Yet the tower itself is also a metaphor for the potential for language to mean in the first place. 'Language stands halfway between the visible forms of nature and the secret conveniences of esoteric discourse', writes Foucault.[14] The names of things were originally lodged in the things they designated, the myth of Babel suggests; the destruction of the tower marks the end of this realm of transparency. Renaissance images of Babel suggest that transparency might yet be restored. In Bruegel's Rotterdam version (Fig. 8) a more optimistic, Utopian interpretation is offered. The building is now closer to completion: five full spirals are in place, lending the edifice a monumental architectural sense of classical (or at least Renaissance) order. The top part of the building is still in progress and, given some necessary support from a Department of Media, Culture, and Sport, this *grand projet* looks as if it may yet come to fruition,

Fig. 8. 'Babel I'; Peter Bruegel, *The Tower of Babel*, oil on panel, *c.*1565. Rotterdam, Museum Boijmans Van Beuningen

as a usable national library. Bruegel's new panel speaks lyrically of order, and a logic of grace, as well as of insane, hubristic insatiability. If discord is the ultimate result, the aspiration embodied in its construction is idealistic.

Bruegel turned Babel into an ambiguous icon, mixing light and dark. Yet it also fills the frame: the book as Babel forms an ultimate human aspiration as well as a codename for human failure. The dark side is more apparent in an engraving of 1547 by Cornelis Anthonisz (or Teunissen), *Fall of the Tower of Babel*. Teunissen's image (Fig. 9), unlike Bruegel's, is inescapably one of violence. In the top right corner of the engraving there is an inscription which explicates this: 'BABELON' followed by 'GENESIS 14'. Babel appears in Genesis 11; Teunissen has conflated this passage with a verse from Revelation 14:

[8] And there followed another angel, saying, Babylon is fallen, is fallen, that great city

Babel is not destroyed in Genesis, but early in the Hebraic commentary tradition, in the Midrash, the top is burnt and the bottom swallowed up by God, with the middle section left to erode over eternity. In the Babylonian Talmud it is explained

Fig. 9. 'Babel II'; Cornelis Anthonisz. (Teunissen), *Fall of the Tower of Babel*, etching, 1547

that God fears that there will be no end to man's ambition; or that God foreknows that man will turn knowledge into an idol.[15] The destruction of the Tower is an image of the origin of forgetting: anyone who enters Babel forgets what he has learned. The angels of the Lord can be seen in Teunissen's image riding on the clouds, wielding trumpets as they throw down lightning rods onto the Tower, which collapses in on itself in gigantic fragments. At the foot of the scene, like a cameo from Book 2 of the *Aeneid*, the inhabitants flee from a Troy that is in flames, while capitals, pedestals, and tympana rain down on them.

Lightning is also in evidence in Maarten van Heemskerk's version (Fig. 10), reproduced in Philippe de Galle's engraving of 1569. Van Heemskerk is definitely in Babylon. The architectural language is as if he had seen a ziggurat, although he can't have done; he seems to have derived it from the account of the temple of Zeus Belus in Herodotus. Herodotus describes 'a square of two furlongs each way, with gates of bronze. In the centre of this enclosure a solid tower has been built, of one furlong's length and breadth.'[16] This is thought to derive from an account of the Etemenanki Ziggurat at Babylon, which is mentioned in the *Enûma Eliš*, the creation myth discovered in Ashurbanipal's library.[17] Here we come full circle: for

Fig. 10. 'Babel III'; Philippe de Galle, *Tower of Babel*, engraving, 1569. Rotterdam, Museum Boijmans Van Beuningen

some scholars think that Sumerian writing is the source of the Babel story in the Bible.[18] Van Heemskerk certainly knew Herodotus, and takes the trouble to present the Babylonian citizens in Persian-style dress. Obelisks (including one with a spiral ramp) and statues of lions adorn the sophisticated cityscape. Doom is overtaking the people, as massive cylinders of brick explode, and fire spreads through the upper levels. The fall of Babel is the fall of the world: the confusion of tongues is the final catastrophe of culture.

Van Heemskerk the antiquarian is acutely aware that his reading of ancient sources reflects on current conditions. Literacy interweaves at several levels, from ancient Sumer to biblical Israel, to Renaissance commentary on them. Why is the myth of Babel so powerful in the second half of the sixteenth century? A number of explanations seem possible. Bruegel's images in particular show an interplay with the concerns of northern European humanism.[19] Architecture as a historical concept consciously plays with philosophical meaning. Erasmus is strongly present in all Bruegel's work, especially *Netherlandish Proverbs* (1559), which consciously plays on the humanist masterpiece *Adagia*, the most popular scholarly book of the century.[20] Here Erasmus is felt in a classicizing idealism but also in a conflict between present and past (Babylon and Antwerp) and in the complex ethical interpretation this embodies. Babel asks us how we view the past, and how antiquity as it were reads modernity. Bruegel's relationship with the past is always paradoxical: he is the artist of belatedness, reworking late medieval genres in a nostalgic present, yet forever new. W. H. Auden's Brussels meditation on Bruegel, 'Musée des Beaux Arts', was written in December 1938, a month after Kristallnacht, when the synagogues were smashed up and civilization set on fire:

> About suffering they were never wrong,
> The Old Masters: how well they understood
> Its human position.[21]

Bruegel's Babels contain within themselves a miniature of the sixteenth-century wars of religion. In the Vienna panel we see the corruption of the church and the descent into chaos and destruction. In the Rotterdam panel, by contrast, we see an optimistic vision, even a new order of reform. The Low Countries were the perfect vantage-point to encounter the war between old and new in the 1560s. Antwerp was at the crossroads of the old Duchy of Burgundy and the Spain of the Habsburgs; a centre of the early Reformation, then a bastion of the oncoming counter-Reformation.[22] It was also the third largest printing centre in Europe, after Venice and Paris.[23] In May 1572, Bruegel's humanist friend and collaborator, the printer Christopher Plantijn, produced his magnificent eight-volume Polyglot Bible. Combining texts in Hebrew, Aramaic, Greek, and Latin, Plantijn's *Biblia Sacra* printed in Antwerp promised a unification of the dispersed languages of antiquity.[24] The Polyglot Bible was an antidote to Babel, a linguistic cure for confusion. For Babel is like a book, a container of all the writing that can be written, a library that contains all other libraries. The spiral shape of Bruegel's Rotterdam version of Babel recalls an idealized library under construction: like the Biblioteca Nazionale Marciana in Venice, designed by Cardinal Bessarion after the Fall of Constantinople to be a second Byzantium, a home for learning as a universalized theory of knowledge.[25] One of its early purchases was the Grimani Breviary, with its image of Babel. The tower's architecture symbolizes a Platonic form: Babel as a mathematical formula for language.

Violence is not only metaphorical here. In 1510, Raphael completed his *Disputation of the Holy Sacrament*, in the Stanza della Segnatura in the Pope's apartments in the Vatican.[26] It is a sacred equivalent to the better-known *School of Athens*, which he painted the year after. The experience of viewing it is overwhelming: the figure of Christ enthroned, in the centre of the fresco, is lifesize. Below, the Holy Spirit flies down, against a disc of gold, to meet the sacrament at the imagined altar. The host is set in a monstrance, inscribed with the name of the Pope, Julius II. Among a pantheon of theologians, both church fathers (Jerome and Augustine) and scholastics (Thomas Aquinas and Bonaventure), Julius's uncle, Pope Sixtus IV, grasps a giant book, perhaps his treatise on the Blood of Christ. Dante and Savonarola lurk in the background. The saints 'write the Mass',

Giorgio Vasari wrote in a brilliant analysis, while others debate (*disputano*) the Host.[27] It is Vasari's account that has given the fresco its modern title. Some argue that the painting figures forth an array of heretics who vie (unsuccessfully) in theological argument. Notwithstanding, the room bears the mark of heresy in a literal sense. In May 1527, the unruly army of the Emperor Charles V, made up of German, Spanish and Italian mercenaries, sacked Rome. The assault was brutal and swift: by the time the violence ended, nearly half the city's population lay dead in the streets. In the papal stanze, a pike of one of the German soldiers left its mark on Raphael. The word 'LVTHER' appears in one place directly below an image of a bound book; and elsewhere 'vKIMP', standing for *vivat Karolus Imperator*: 'long live Emperor Charles'. The graffiti are authenticated by Benvenuto Cellini in his *Vita*.[28] The violence of the graffiti is a reaction to papal power.[29] But it attests to the power of the book itself.

The yearning for perfection and the will to oblivion are connected in modernity's idea of the book. However, twenty-first-century anxiety about the death of the book is bound up with ideas that go back to the sixteenth century. This is not accidental. The sixteenth century, like the twenty-first, was a period of intense change in media. McLuhan's *Gutenberg Galaxy* popularized this idea in the 1960s, describing the way that the printed book changed 'the *forms* of experience and of mental outlook and expression'.[30] He compared this with two other epochal moments in history: the phonetic alphabet in pre-classical Greece in the eighth century BCE, and what he calls (already in 1962), the 'electronic age'.[31] The modern state, and a sense of the 'public' were, he felt, unimaginable without the typographic reorganization of print culture. In a more scholarly vein, Elizabeth Eisenstein's *The Printing Press as an Agent of Change* (1979) proposed that print culture provided the conditions in which changes in religion, science, and historical understanding emerged. She identified a number of ways in which print reoriented European mentalities. The dissemination of knowledge, its standardization, its organization, its preservation, and reinforcement, were all dependent on technological features of print. In the shift from hearing to reading, and from writing by hand to reproduction by machine, she sees the origin of 'data'.[32]

Academic fashions change quickly. For a time, McLuhan was the darling of the airwaves, with his buzzwords such as 'the medium is the message', implying that the nature of a medium (the channel through which a message is transmitted) is more important than the meaning or content of the message.[33] Reportedly via a typographical error, this transferred into the title of his 1967 multi-media compilation, *The Medium is the Massage*.[34] The book was composed in collage style with text superimposed on visual elements and vice versa. McLuhan spawned a thousand talkshows and university modules called 'the birth of the book'. That term is reductive (like all intellectual shorthands) and demonstrably false. Gutenberg did not invent print (which the Chinese had been using for a thousand years) and print did not invent the book. As a result, McLuhan (and also Eisenstein) came to be pilloried for technological determinism.

McLuhan denied that his approach was deterministic, and instead desired to understand the part played by technologies of information in intellectual revolutions. While his guru status has passed, his attention to the power and allure of media has come back into focus recently because his idea of the 'electronic age' has become all the more powerful. The history of the book is more cyclical than made up of terminal points. The scroll is making a comeback on e-books, iPads, and Androids. Revisionist historians of textual bibliography have made a case for the printing revolution as being slower and more paradoxical than the stereotypes of 'revolution'.[35] Print did not disseminate as widely as often assumed, it was slower in achieving standardization, and it coexisted with manuscript for centuries. Yet no amount of revision can alter the fact that print was felt at the time to be a profound intervention in human culture, just like the internet now, even as we also misinterpret the World Wide Web.

McLuhan distinguished between media such as print, photography, radio, and cinema (which he called 'hot media'), and media such as speech, cartoons, the telephone, and television ('cool media'). Hot media are rich in sensory data; cool media provide fewer sensory data, and consequently demand more 'participation or completion by the audience'.[36] He was not only talking about media in the modern sense: hieroglyphics he called 'cool', while the alphabet was 'hot'. Fabulous as the terminology appears, McLuhan is sensitive to the way that the physical media of knowledge are embodied processes. This reaches back to a seminal statement on the status of the physical book from the age of print. 'The images of mens wits and knowledges remain in Bookes', wrote Sir Francis Bacon in *The Advancement of Learning*.[37] Bacon attests to a mediation between cognitive and material worlds, later commented on by Milton in *Areopagitica: for the Liberty of Unlicenc'd Printing* (1644), 'For Books are not absolutely dead things':

> I know they are as lively, and as vigorously productive, as those fabulous Dragons teeth; and being sown up and down, may chance to spring up armed men. And yet on the other hand unlesse warinesse be us'd, as good almost kill a Man as kill a good Book; who kills a Man kills a reasonable creature, Gods Image; but hee who destroyes a good Booke, kills reason it selfe, kills the Image of God, as it were in the eye.[38]

The occasion of this eulogy of the book was a temporary end to censorship due to the collapse of Star Chamber in the English Civil War.[39] On 14 June 1643, an Act of Parliament was passed 'to prevent and suppress the licence of printing'.[40] Despite the focus on print, Milton's mode of address is consciously oratorical, in the manner of Demosthenes in the Athenian court of the Areopagus. Advocating freedom for books, Milton suggests a book is both a thing and not a thing, commensurate with yet distinct from its contents.[41] It is like 'Dragons teeth', from the story of Cadmus, the founder of literacy, who killed the sacred dragon of Ares, and sowed the teeth to make ferocious warriors, the legendary *spartoi*, ancestors of the Theban nobility.[42] A book is an object, yet stands for the meanings seeding within. It is less and more than contents alone, a metonym for words we read or thoughts we have as we read. The book as a form of life transposes from military to domestic spheres. A book is cared for or discarded, loved or abused, just as an article of clothing or furniture takes character from its owner. Old books have additional value in carrying a presence of other readers from the past.

'Et si je suis homme de quelque leçon, je suis homme de nulle retention', says Michel de Montaigne in his essay 'Des livres'.[43] His reading surpasses his capacity for retention. As well as sensory record, books embody memory and past thoughts, better than a mind. Indeed, doubly: for a book contains both reader and author. In Milton's poetic terms, books 'contain a potency of life in them', since they 'preserve as in a vial the purest efficacy and extraction of that living intellect that bred them'. The book thus achieves a mystery of transforming something immaterial into concrete form. It is not extravagant for Milton to claim for a book 'a life beyond life', or the 'Image of God'. Destroying a book, he says, is homicide or worse—for a book encloses more than one life. A book binds writer and reader, reader and reader, across space and time. Paradoxically, regardless of material survival of physical copies, a book is immortal and imperishable. While some see the intimate link between body and book as diminished by passage from handwritten to printed form, Milton shows metaphor is as important as material. The physical object does not so much reify experience as draw attention to the process of mediation. Something similar happens with the digital book, which in contrast to the printed object appears as the unburnt, perhaps the incombustible. It consumes within.

The battle of the books rages eternally in human history. Milton raises, as he always does, ghosts of Christian controversy and the classical past. Yet why did Christianity succeed paganism, and not, say, Manicheanism its rival?[44] Originating in Persia, the texts of Mani spread to the western Roman Empire and east to China. Followers claimed Mani was a reincarnation of the Buddha, of Zoroaster and Krishna, as well as Jesus.[45] Most texts were written in Syriac, a variety of Aramaic; some in an abjad script peculiar to Mani, and attributed to his personal invention.[46] While it is tempting to see esoteric writing and language as barriers to Manicheanism's spread, the opposite is true.[47] Gnostic ideas found perfect marriage with secret writing.[48] It is persecution that brought nemesis, beginning with the Sasanian Empire in Iran.[49] In Rome, Diocletian burned Manichean leaders alive, along with their scriptures. Theodosius I dealt death to Manichee monks east and west.[50] The Abbasid Caliphate in Baghdad branded Manicheans 'dualist heretics'. An inquisition began in 780 CE, headed by a *ṣāhib al-zanādiqa* ('master of heretics').[51] In China, the Emperor Xuanzong declared

Manichees heretics in 732 CE, for confusing the Chinese populace's idea of Buddhism.[52] When the Emperor Wuzong attacked Buddhism in turn, he had the Manichean priests dress like Buddhist monks and then killed.[53] While Manichees lasted longer in China than anywhere, they were called 'vegetarian demon-worshippers', and in 1370 the Ming abolished them forever.

Religions like to think of themselves as separate, but they are meeting all the time, as Buddhists met Zoroastrians in Shapur I's Persia, Jews and Christians in Muhammad's Arabia, or paganism, Mithraism, and Manicheanism in Roman north Africa.[54] Augustine converted to Manicheanism then Christianity in between Theodosius I's imperial decree *Cunctos populos* of 380 CE, declaring the Nicene Creed the only legitimate religion in the Roman Empire; and his three laws of 391 and 392, outlawing pagan ritual sacrifice, and condemning to death Manichean monks.[55] Augustine's subsequent literary campaign against Manichean writing succeeded so well that in Western Europe the original writings of Mani could only be gleaned from refutation within Augustinian texts.[56]

Mani occupies a counter-text in the margins of official doctrine by the great doctor of the church. Once an acolyte of the Manichean bishop Faustus of Mileve, Augustine later wrote *Contra Faustum*, thirty-three books attacking the heresy point by point.[57] Six hundred years after the last followers of Mani disappeared, the Bogomils in Bulgaria were accused, nonsensically, of being his followers.[58] In the west, phantom medieval 'Manichees' were hunted down.[59] Augustine was recopied in manuscripts like this one from Fécamp in Normandy (Fig. 11). Faustus reaches despairingly from the ground on his back, pointing to his book; Augustine towering over, his head reaching into the vault of the cathedral and his crozier so powerful it escapes the limits of the margins altogether, slams down his own book in turn. This is a cultural war of books, not just of ideas.

Christian conversion follows as night follows day. In a garden in Milan in 386, under a fig tree (in case Eve is listening), Augustine heard a voice telling him to 'pick up and read'. The book to hand is a Bible, and the verse he chooses at random tells him to convert. So he does. 'Then I inserted my finger or some other mark in the book and closed it'.[60] The rest is history: Augustine's conversion narrative was exemplary for centuries. It is taken as automatic, though Augustine presents it as gradual if momentary. William James disputed the instantaneous interpretations by evangelical Christians of the experience of Jan Hus, Martin Luther, or John Wesley.[61] What is similar in Luther is the presence of a book. He meditates 'day and night' not just on the Bible but one verse in Paul, Romans 1: 17.[62] He hates the one Latin word *iustitia*, but then suddenly understands its meaning differently. This word is now 'the sweetest', and opens the gates to paradise.

John Bunyan's conversion is presented as more spontaneous, during a game of 'cat', in which a player swings a cudgel at a piece of wood so that it leaps in the air like an animal. A voice comes to Bunyan from heaven: 'leaving my Cat upon the ground', he sees Jesus, looking at him rather displeased.[63] Yet the voice does not

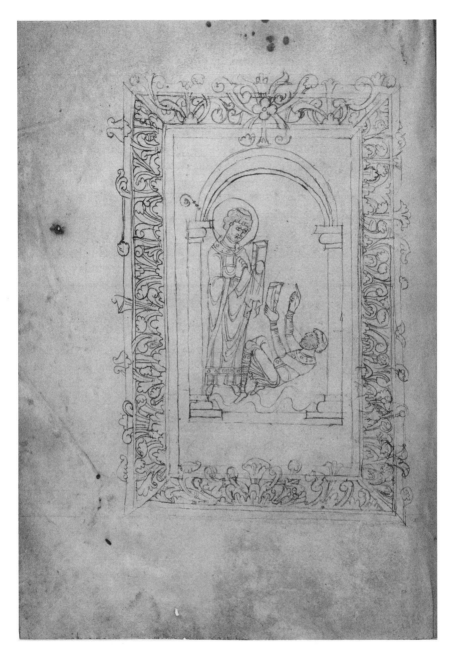

Fig. 11. 'Augustine against heresy'; *Contra Faustum Manichaeum*, ink on vellum, 11th c. Paris, Bibliothèque nationale de France, MS fonds latins, 2079

arise from nowhere. Like the spiritualist Anna Trapnel in Southwark, or other converts of the 1640s and 1650s, he had just been listening to a sermon.[64] His head in any case is full of Paul's letter to the Romans, which is always the book in question. Religious autobiography is thus intimately connected with the act of reading books.[65] Paintings of Augustine's conversion, such as by Benozzo Gozzoli in San Gimignano, typically show him reading. Caravaggio depicts Jerome (Fig. 12) one better, reading and writing at the same time.

Jerome lays his book on top of another book, reading so intently he appears to have forgotten that he is writing. Jerome is the classic saint of the study, painted by Caravaggio not only in this example from Rome around 1605, but in another version from Malta a year or two later. The subject inspired many artists, such as Antonello da Messina and Dürer. No saint is more bookish than Caravaggio's, his left hand gripping the fore-edge, while his right arm extends across a third of the canvas, from his nose to his pen, which lies on a third book, atop another still. This is the book incarnate. Books are always converting. Evangelicals plied Paul's letter to the Romans from the Mayflower to nineteenth-century midwest America.[66] Russian Orthodox missionary priests did the same in the 1840s among the Inuit in Alaska.[67] Meanwhile, the dangerous words of Mani appeared lost forever. But in the nineteenth century, manuscripts of Mani were found on the Silk Road near Bulayiq, now held in Berlin.[68]

Fig. 12. 'Writer as reader'; Michelangelo Merisi da Caravaggio, *Saint Jerome Writing*, oil on canvas, 1605–6. Rome, Galleria Borghese

While the iconic status of Babel always concentrates on the archaic, it is an image that quickly metamorphoses into the futuristic. By 1679, when Athanasius Kircher created his widely known engraving *Turris Babel*, he was able to take advantage of recent archaeological tourism in Babylon itself, by the Italian Pietro della Valle.[69] Kircher's Babel would not look out of place in Fritz Lang's *Metropolis* (1927). The Jesuit Kircher (1602–80) was a polymath, who wrote on geology and medicine as well as adventures in the emerging field of comparative religion.[70] At his university in Rome he created a *Wunderkammer* of objects from around the world. Central to all his other interests is language itself. His interest in Babel went deeper than the surface, since he desired to uncover the universal language that preceded it, and in the interim he made it his business to decipher as many of the ancient tongues as he could master. He claimed to have uncovered the riddle of hieroglyphics, although his confidence later proved unfounded. He did, however, show a link between ancient Egyptian and Coptic. Years of study of Sinology led to his *Encyclopaedia of China*. He insisted that Chinese ideograms were inferior to hiereoglyhics, because they referred to specific things rather than complexes of ideas. Although Eurocentric, his speculations theorized writing as an art.

Kircher's mythographic analysis of Babel, which includes conclusive proof that, while the building was huge, it did not reach to the moon, is complemented in the modern era by Borges's story, 'La biblioteca de Babel' ('The Library of Babel'). The idealized library that he describes is in fact a tessellated projection of a real library—the National Library on Calle Méjico in Buenos Aires—of which Borges was the blind director:[71]

> The universe (which others call the Library) is composed of an indefinite and perhaps infinite number of hexagonal galleries, with vast air shafts between, surrounded by very low railings. From any of the hexagons one can see, interminably, the upper and lower floors. The distribution of the galleries is invariable. Twenty shelves, five long shelves per side, cover all the sides except two; their height, which is the distance from floor to ceiling, scarcely exceeds that of a normal librarian.[72]

The Library is a symbol of infinity or eternity. In this way it figures within itself both truth and certainty. As such it is a mystery, a mystery sacred in significance. Indeed, the Library *in toto* is an emblem of divinity. Rather than the letters giving access to the divine, the very idea of the divine is prefigured in the existence of the Library. For the Library is everything that is or can be: 'in other words, all that it can be given to express, in all languages' [*todo lo que es dable expresar: en todos los idiomas*] (pp. 81–2).

Like a theory of everything, the universal book at first brings happiness: 'All men felt themselves to be the masters of an intact and secret treasure' [*un tesoro intacto y secreto*]. Humanity's basic mysteries are unfolded; official 'inquisitors' [*buscadores oficiales, inquisidores*] appointed for the task, Now comes the catch. The search is bottomless, impossible, or blasphemous. A heretical sect abandons the search for certainty and instead leaves it to chance: in an odd premonition of the computer, Borges imagines random selections of letters and symbols to be searched, which will eventually lead to the improbable revelation of the quintessentially canonical book.

Borges's story perfectly captures the crossfire in the battle of books. He understands the counterweight of inevitable censorship: 'the hygienic, ascetic furor caused the senseless perdition of millions of books'. Yet the holocaust of forbidden secrets is a mirage. Total censorship is impossible: some believe every copy in the Library is unique, others posit the Library contains several hundred thousand imperfect facsimiles. Still others search, as a result, for the idea of the one book that will be the perfect compendium of all the rest; or else the one librarian who has discovered this book, and read it through, and who must now be God himself. Even seemingly random collections of letters, it is surmised, in some book in the Library have acquired some 'terrible meaning' in one of its many 'secret tongues'.

Tú, que me lees, ¿estás seguro de entender mi lenguaje?[73]

'You who read me, are you sure of understanding my language?', the narrator asks, plaintively.[74] If one myth is the Library as universe, of language reaching for ever and into all places, the opposing myth is annihilation, a world where no book any longer exists. It is difficult not to see in Borges's story the riddle of the internet made flesh.

This is the dystopian fiction of Ray Bradbury's *Fahrenheit 451* of 1953, and François Truffaut's film of the same name a decade later. In Bradbury's imaginary society, all books are forbidden: any that remain are hunted down and torched by state 'firemen' who wear on their helmets the symbolic number 451, 'the temperature at which book paper catches fire and burns'. While a bookless culture descends into torpor and conformity, the act of destruction itself is ritualistic and redemptive: 'It was a pleasure to burn', the book begins.[75] Guy Montag is a 'fireman', employed by the state to incinerate any books that are found. Despite his job, he comes into contact with remaining book-lovers and secretly keeps a book himself. '"There must be something in books, things we can't imagine, to make a woman stay in a burning house; there must be something there"', Montag says.[76] The bookhunt turns inwards, and he is ordered to set fire to his own house. Instead, he turns the flamethrower on the chief fireman.

The message derived from *Fahrenheit 451*, repeated at Bradbury's death in 2012, is that the fiction is a warning against state censorship. Specifically, the book is ubiquitously conflated with the book burnings in Nazi Germany in 1933. Yet it must be said that Bradbury himself rejected this interpretation. For him, the book concerned a different media revolution: the cultural dynamic of television, turning the young into zombies, incapable of independent thought. In the interests of science, it needs also to be said that Bradbury got his chemistry wrong. The classic paper of 2001 by Jens Borch and Richard E. Mark fixes the auto-ignition of paper at 450 °C, or 842 °F; the full equation involves the thermal conductivity, density, and specific heat capacity of the material, in ratio with heat flux.[77] To understand a relation of fire and writing requires deeper analysis.

II

BOOKS AND VIOLENCE

Dort wo man Bücher verbrennt, verbrennt man auch am Ende Menschen

Heinrich Heine, *Almansor* (1821)

5

The Book-Fires of 1933

In May 1933, in the square in front of the Opera in Berlin (Fig. 13), Nazi students joined together in a theatrical bonfire of *undeutsche* ('un-German') books.[1] Similar bonfires were planned in thirty-six university cities, and took place in thirty, many on the single night of 10 May, although continuing sporadically up to 21 June.[2] During the days leading up to the burnings, book-covers and title-pages were torn from their bindings and nailed onto posts in stark public display. Placards were printed to advertise the intended events. The idea was to co-ordinate the events between eleven o'clock and midnight for maximum impact.[3] Large crowds (reportedly 40,000 in Berlin) attended the conflagrations in manifest-ations of solidarity and popular will; in some cases, the presence of troops salut-ing the fires provided a more insidious message of collective endorsement. The Deutschlandsender, a semi-official radio station, broadcast the event live, which was also shown later on newsreels.[4] Before the Staatsoper in Berlin, or the cath-edral in Münster, or the town hall in Munich, books were stacked in piles twice the height of a man and burned through the night. Among the authors burned were Karl Marx, Sigmund Freud, and also Heinrich Heine, Thomas Mann, Bertolt Brecht, Upton Sinclair, and Jack London. 20,000 volumes in Berlin alone were burned.

Hostility to intellectual culture erupts here, Hobsbawm says, in all-out war with modernism.[5] Scarcely hidden is outright racism, foretelling the Holocaust. The Nazi book-burnings, preserved in hundreds of photographs, present a cul-minating image to the history of human censorship. In all, over twelve years, up to the end of the Third Reich in 1945, it is estimated a hundred million books were destroyed.[6] To this literary holocaust, the 1933 burnings are understood as a haunting prelude, an unprecedented display of ideological violence leading directly to systematic suppression of prohibited printed matter.[7] In the post-war imagination, the burnings symbolized the idea of a totalitarian state of the mind, expressed in popular culture by *Fahrenheit 451*.

In present-day Bebelplatz, on the site of the events of 10 May, dedicated to memory of the night, lies a small monument, easy to miss (Fig. 14). Designed by the Israeli sculptor Micha Ullmann in 1995, it consists of a glass plate set into the square. Underneath, for the most part blocked off from the viewer, only the top part visible, is an array of empty bookcases. It is said that Ullmann made it large enough to hold 20,000 books, the total originally burnt. Nearby, a plaque set into the cobbled stones bears lines from Heinrich Heine's play *Almansor* (1821): *Das*

Fig. 13. 'Berlin in 1933'; bonfire in Opernplatz, photo 1933. United States Holocaust Memorial Museum

war ein Vorspiel nur, dort wo man Bücher verbrennt, verbrennt man am Ende auch Menschen ('That was only a prelude; where they burn books, they will in the end also burn people').[8] Students from Humboldt Universität across the road hold a book sale in Bebelplatz every year to mark the anniversary.

Like the burnings, Ullmann's *Denkmal* (German for 'memorial') is best viewed at night, the eery effect of neon lamps revealing the ghosts of the missing volumes in their shelves. In 1933, the student committees drew up meticulous plans for how the books were to be assembled on the pyres, in order to provide the optimum stage and visual effect for their display. Faculty, dressed in academic robes, students in SA uniform, the Hitlerjugend carrying flags, processed behind marching bands playing German folk songs and marches.[9] Nine students were given the task of throwing books on the pyre, each given his personal category of books.[10] Instructions were given for the incantation of *Feuersprüche*, ritualistic chants of denunciation; texts were provided for the students to use as they tossed books into the flames. These texts created a bizarre formal antiphony between the obscene characteristics of the books and the ideals of true German culture. The declamations concluded with a litany of the names of offending authors:

Fig. 14. 'Berlin today'; Micha Ullmann, *The Empty Library*, wood, plaster, paint, glass, electric lighting, air, silence, 1995. Berlin, Bebelplatz. Photo Angela Serena Gilmour

Gegen Klassenkampf und Materialismus
Für Volksgemeinschaft und idealistische Lebenshaltung
Marx, Kautsky.[11]

In this example of a *Feuerspruch* distributed from Berlin on 9 May, the text consists of nine triads, each with a one-line strophe (*Gegen*) paired with a one-line antistrophe (*Für*) and a one-line chorus, a miniature roll call of literary pariahs. This is repeated as a kind of liturgy: 'Against the soul-destroying overestimation of the sex life; for the nobility of the human soul; Sigmund Freud'. The Freudian school is ostracized for inciting the sex drive; Erich Maria Remarque for his betrayal of the soldiers of the world war. Using such a text as a template, students were encouraged to improvise further lists, following the lines of the black trinity of Jewish, Marxist, and Freudian writers.

The presence of specific names in these stylized maledictions has been taken to suggest that the 1933 burnings were part of a systematic campaign of censorship, with its own index of prohibited books. The American Civil Liberties Union was founded in 1920 just after the First World War. It arrived in the wake of the Communist Revolution in Russia, as civil liberties came under attack from the US Attorney General, Mitchell Palmer, who rounded up thousands of so-called 'radicals', searching them without warrant, and deporting many. Since 1983, the ACLU has marked Banned Book Week annually, in which the Nazi book burnings, and Bradbury's *Fahrenheit 451*, always play a prominent part.[12] The definition of civil liberties depends, often, on whom you are talking to. The ACLU has taken a different view: censorship is always wrong. It played a prominent part against Senator Joe McCarthy's purges in the 1950s; in the Supreme Court victory in *Roe* v. *Wade*, and in favour of LGBT rights; in defence of *Ulysses* or later, *Harry Potter*. In June 2020, it filed a suit for journalists in the District of Columbia US Court in *Black Lives Matter* v. *Donald J. Trump*. Yet in 1978, it also defended a neo-Nazi group who wanted to demonstrate in a district of Chicago where many Holocaust victims resided.

Meanwhile on 5 June 1956, the United States Food and Drug Agency invaded the offices of Wilhelm Reich, Freud's Jewish former student, who escaped from Nazi Germany in March 1933, the day after the *Völkischer Beobachter* published its attack on *Der sexuelle Kampf der Jugend*. Reich in America got up to peculiar things, but his deeper American crime was a scientific and political interest in the female orgasm. Looking for drugs and machinery, the FDA seized instead six tons of Reich's books and papers. On 23 August they all went into the New York Gansevoort Public Incinerator on 25th Street: including the pre-war *Sexual Revolution* (1936) and *Mass Psychology of Fascism* (1933). Psychiatrist Victor Sobey reported Reich had to pay for the burning, while he himself was made to load up the truck, as if he was digging his own grave before being shot.[13]

Both British and US leaders routinely profess themselves defenders of free speech. The UK government in 2020 meanwhile defends the rights of old statues of slave-owners but rejects the concept of Islamophobia, just as the British Labour Party for a while tried to amend the International Holocaust Remembrance Alliance's definition of antisemitism. Free speech is a bespoke form of absolute value which can be adapted for the occasion. Censorship is one of those things for which hardly anyone talks in favour but happens all the while. Much of what we think about it leads from the European and American Enlightenment. In Britain, the lapse of the Licensing Act in 1695 ended the monopoly of the Stationers' Company over the book trade, and also its comprehensive system for the examination of books.[14] Already, in the British civil wars, censorship proved prone to ambiguity.[15] The temporary stay in royal censorship in the 1640s produced more printed books and a larger lay readership.[16] The new disorder in 1695 led directly to the world's first copyright statute under Queen Anne in 1710. The Act transferred the rights to a book from the printer to the author, and at one swoop gave such rights a time stop.[17] If Defoe's joy at moral rights was spiked by limits on making money, Jürgen Habermas nonetheless views the change in the eighteenth-century order of books as crucial in the emergence of the idea of public opinion and the public sphere.[18] Freedom to print anything, however, was quickly forestalled by the Blasphemy Act of 1698. In the 1720s, an idea of obscenity emerged in the prosecution of Edmund Curll for publishing the French pornographic classic *Venus in the Cloister*; and shortly afterwards, in the furore caused by John Cleland's *Fanny Hill, or Memoirs of a Woman of Pleasure*.[19]

Sex has been involved in a trade-off with profanity, atheism, and politics ever since. *Pace* Habermas, it is not so much a public sphere as the boundaries of erotic privacy that is at issue.[20] How far is it necessary to control what goes on in people's bedrooms, or else their heads? This ambivalence readily crossed the Atlantic from Europe to America, with consequences still visible in the USA today. Jefferson wrote to Abigail Adams from Paris in June 1785 about a treasonable incident at the French court, involving (to add to the spice) an ambassador and a princess.[21] The scandal was the subject of a popular song known to pretty well everyone, Jefferson reports insinuatingly (without letting Abigail in on the sordid details); it was even printed (with licence) in a book called *Les quatre saisons littéraires*. But once it passed inside *Le Journal de Paris*, the reviewer was seized in his bed overnight, and the journal suppressed. Jefferson pokes fun at the *ancien régime* but cannot resist a libertine squib at a brand-new American republic, which will probably go to war (he surmises) rather than allow the publication of a naughty song.

The Continental Congress of 1774 proposed that a free press would enable 'the ready communication of thoughts between subjects'.[22] The American dream founded itself on unity in the state, corrupt behaviour by officials to be abolished through shame in the newspapers. (*Plus ça change, plus c'est la même chose*, the editor of *Le Figaro* said later.[23]) Virginia's Bill of Rights in 1776 stated: 'freedom of the press is one of the great bulwarks of liberty, and can never be restrained but by despotic governments'; yet the same state in 1792 passed an Act 'Against Divulgers of False News'. Only Pennsylvania of all thirteen commonwealths and states permitted 'truth' as a legitimate legal defence in its Constitution of 1790.[24] The First Amendment of the US Constitution in 1792 conferred only conditional liberty: it constrained the US Congress from attacking free speech. Who will guard the guardians? Liberty is a transgressive term, shifting shape as to who is granting it. Such arguments reach back and forth to despots long gone, still to come, and very much present. They also attach to every new idea in any new book.

In 1663, a papal ban was imposed on the works of René Descartes.[25] As a Catholic who died in 1650 in Protestant Sweden, he was buried in a graveyard for orphans; when his remains returned to Saint-Étienne-du-Mont in Paris, a funeral oration was refused on suspicion of atheism.[26] Meanwhile church and state argued over the fate of his writing. Finally in August 1671, Louis XIV forbade the teaching of Cartesian philosophy in French universities by royal decree. However, he did not prohibit the publication, sale and distribution of Cartesian books.[27] Similar ambiguity prevailed in Italy. In 1633, the Roman Inquisition condemned the Copernican astronomy of Galileo Galilei, an event which persuaded Descartes to withhold publication of *Du monde*.[28] For a while, in Florence, Galileo continued to enjoy the protection of the Medici Grand Dukes.[29] Family ties allowed them to take pride as inheritors of the neo-Platonist intellectualism of Lorenzo the Magnificent.[30] The whims of princes are fickle, however, and under Cosimo III, Cartesian philosophy and Galilean science were suppressed in favour of the Florentine Inquisition. Baruch Spinoza requested an interview in Holland in 1667 with Grand Duke Cosimo, but he would not see 'such a man'.[31] Prague was safer territory: Johannes Kepler successfully defended Galileo and Copernicus under Rudolph II.[32]

It might be thought that the Netherlands was the one safe place for free speech. Indeed, often by sea via Rouen, or by road south through Liège, Holland was so much the regular source for illicit books that they became known in the trade as 'livres d'Hollande'. Descartes's *Principia philosophiae* in 1644, and Thomas Hobbes's *Opera omnia* (1668), appeared in Amsterdam for want of any licence elsewhere. For decades Amsterdam, freedom's beloved, was the only place to print Pierre Bayle's *Dictionnaire*, or even Locke's *Essay* (in a French translation).[33] It wasn't just philosophical genius Holland was happy to allow: scatology and heresy found a ready ear.[34] However, the prince of Dutch rationalism, Spinoza, proved a step too enlightened for the Calvinists in the United Provinces. The Leiden pensionary Pieter Burgersdijk advised that the *Opera posthuma* of 1674 contained 'very many profane, blasphemous, and atheistic propositions'.[35] The States of Holland banned not only this work, which included the sublime *Ethics*, but the whole of Spinoza's philosophy, including reprints, summaries, and extracts. Despite being educated in the Torah as a Portuguese Sephardi, he was issued with a ḥērem (חרם), the strongest form of Jewish censure, by the Amsterdam synagogue, on account of his ideas about the authenticity of the Hebrew Bible.[36]

In such circumstances, it went by the board that Spinoza should be added to the papal Index of Prohibited Books. Bayle led the polemical riposte to the Inquisition as enemy incarnate of philosophy and science.[37] However, a binary of enlightenment and inquisition will not do. Jonathan Israel argues that it is a myth that Spinoza's *Tractatus Theologico-Politicus* 'ever circulated freely'.[38] Johann de Witt, Holland's Pensionary, preferred not to make a formal provincial ban, but the anti-Socinian legislation of 1653, set up to defend the Holy Trinity from defamation, had many powers to inspect bookshops and sequestrate copies. Moreover, even the Cartesians felt ill inclined to defend Spinoza. An Utrecht professor wrote in April 1671 to Leibniz (still studying law in Nuremberg, and not yet turned to mathematics), calling the Tractatus a *liber pestilentissimus*.[39] More gracefully, young Leibniz replied that Pascal's *Pensées* was a *libellus aureolus*.[40]

Censorship is a much more ambiguous topic than it appears in diatribes about free speech. 'One must not ban any books now', writes Kant, but only because banning them encourages the vanity of bad authors to write more rubbish.[41] Spinoza, subtly, argues that the only way to maintain peace and freedom is to grant sole power over religion to the sovereign.[42] Yet this power is supported in turn by then granting people freedom to philosophize.[43] Meanwhile the government of the United Provinces attempted to steer a path between forcing conscience and allowing unlimited freedom to believe. The latter was indeed regarded as an impossible legal fantasy or the province of fools and poets. Nonetheless, it is notable that the Dutch, even when they disliked books, did not burn them. Dirck Volckertsz Coornhert in his 1589 *Trial of the Killing of Heretics and the Constraints of Conscience* vilified Calvin for carrying over Catholic practice of burning heretics into Protestantism.[44] The Netherlands associated fire with foreign tyrants. Hugo Grotius in his *Remonstratie* of 1615 extends the feeling to books, noting with disapproval the burning of the Talmud by the popes.[45] Nonetheless, Johan van Oldenbarnevelt was executed for circumscribing belief in the wrong Protestant God in 1619.[46] His protégé Grotius escaped imprisonment in 1621, smuggled out by his wife in a bookchest. In voluntary exile in Richelieu's France for much of the rest of his life, he dedicated *De iure belli ac pacis* ('On the Law of War and Peace') to Louis XIII in 1625.[47]

Burning books answers to a different need than the delicate indelicacies of censorship. The Nazi burning rites of 1933 did not even try to define illicit literature. A formal index was not compiled until cultural policy tightened in 1938.[48] By the end of the war, 5,485 book titles had been banned in Leipzig, a number that is at once sinister and oddly modest in comparison to the totalitarian objectives of the Nazi state.[49] Local figures may be a gross under-estimate. As early as 1934, the Bavarian police had a list of 2,293 authors of 6,843 seized and forbidden books.[50] The problem is not only that books are sometimes hard to count, but also that book-haters are vague in their sentiments. Censorship as a subject is larded with a mythology of specificity, as if censors always read what they object to, and comprehend their own instinct for prohibition. In a bull of November 1487, Innocent VIII demanded all printed books be examined for approval.[51] The Fifth Lateran Council's decree on printed books in 1515, *Super impressione librorum*, backed up by Leo X's bull, baulked at the sheer scale of reading required, calling for burning of books simply because they had not been presented for approval.[52] From Paul IV's Indexes of 1557 and 1559, to Pius IV's of 1564, lists of banned books veered onwards toward a mania for list-making and deep unclarity of purpose. The Pauline Index of 1559 banned outright the complete works of Pietro Aretino, Erasmus, Niccolò Machiavelli, and Rabelais. Thousands of books were destroyed, but printers complied only grudgingly and sporadically. The Tridentine Index repeated the same authors but silently dropped the blanket application: only six of Erasmus' works were now listed.[53] The ironies escalate. Alfred Rosenberg organized some of the book-hunting and burning in 1933, then himself was placed on the Papal Index by Pius XI in February 1934.[54]

It is in the nature of imaginative writing to elude and satirise the censors even as they proceed. Andrei Platonov's *The Foundation Pit* (Котлован) was finished in 1930 but only published in the Soviet Union in 1987. Voschev is fired from the machine factory and joins a group digging an enormous foundation pit to support a housing complex for the country's proletariat. The pit is never finished, and the workers begin to be liquidated. Instead, the remaining workers are set to dig graves and make empty coffins. 'The dead are all special', they are told. This evident satire of collectivization was too much for Soviet officials. Yet Platonov was a lifelong Communist, editing the Moscow magazine, *The Literary Critic*, and working as a war correspondent in the Great Patriotic War. Stalin called him both an idiot and a genius. Although *Happy Moscow* was not published until 2012, Platonov published many books and stories; Vassily Grossmann spoke at his funeral in 1951 after his death from tuberculosis. Writing escapes even as the body succumbs. Ismail Kadare's 1981 novel *Palace of Dreams* (Albanian: *Pallati i ëndrrave*) similarly presents the totalitarian state by creating a ministry of dreams set in the Ottoman Empire. The state dedicates itself to the interpretation of the dreams of all its citizens. The innocent Mark-Alem, who narrates the story, unaware of his own complicity, ends up as head of the infamous Tabir Sarai. The Albanian Writers Union condemned Kadare, accusing him of attacking the socialist government of Enver Hoxha. The Party has raised you to Olympus, and can cast you into the abyss, he was told. Yet the Politburo also fretted that purging an international author would backfire.

From Ovid to Fyodor Dostoyevsky and Bertolt Brecht, or the poet Khet Mar from Myanmar today, writing is synonymous with exile, both actual and mental. It is this sense of the book as transgressive totem to which the book-burners respond. Censorship in the literal sense proves harder. Although blacklists of books existed before the Nazis came to power, censorship remained in the power of the regional States and was inconsistently applied. In some areas, lists of around a thousand volumes were proscribed in 1934. Yet by 1935, the Prussian police specifically banned not one of the authors declaimed in burnings.[55] The May 1933 burnings created confusion over how to choose books, random printed matter piled on as fuel for a general incineration. Stormtroopers later burned many books not illegal, being ill-equipped with proper lists of unacceptable books. For 'unacceptable', read Jewish. The Hitler Youth burned Heine's poems in Düsseldorf, his birthplace.[56] The reason is summed up in the journal *Der deutsche Schriftsteller* in 1937: 'Heine is not a poet, he is a Jew.'[57] Yet after the Nuremberg Laws of 1935, the question of what is a Jewish book turned to niceties of whether it was three-quarters- or only half-Jewish. With odd bibliographical self-pity, the persecutors described the task of listing Jewish books in full as a 'Herculean labour'.[58] Hercules had not yet concluded by the end of the War. Jewish could mean by a Jewish author; or even featuring a Jewish character (Dickens's *Oliver Twist*). In practice, a mishmash conflation of Bolshevik, Marxist, and Jewish became a rule of thumb, as it did for the visual arts, such as in the Mannheim exhibition which coincided with the book-burnings, from 4 April to 5 June 1933. Entitled *Kulturbolschewistische Bilder* ('Images of Cultural Bolshevism'), it put together paintings, sculptures and graphic works by fifty-five artists, including

Max Beckmann, Marc Chagall, Robert Delaunay, André Derain, Franz Marc, Edvard Munch, Emil Nolde, and Oskar Schlemmer.[59] Art, like theatre, was easier to control than books.[60]

The Latin verb *censeo* was derived from proto-Italic **kensējō*, 'to give an opinion', related to Sanskrit शंसति (*śáṃsati*, 'to declare'). It is an odd etymology for modern 'censorship': an act of declaring turning into a decree condemning an act of declaring. Two censors were elected in republican Rome under the presidency of a consul, although following different auspices (omens from the behaviour of birds).[61] Birds, we should remember, mean different things at different times. The censors' authority maintained the census, supervised public morality, and regulated government finance. Cicero in June 50 BCE congratulates Appius Pulcher on his election as censor, telling him to be mindful of one of his ancestors.[62] Ecclesiastical Latin took over these meanings in confused form, mixing theological judgements with campaigns against heretics. Erasmus tried to clear the meanings up in his New Testament scholarship, but as ever complexity was the sacrificial victim.[63] Erasmus, as we know, joined the Index.

It is in the nature of censorship, Freud declared in *The Interpretation of Dreams* (1900), that it allows something untrue to be said in place of something true.[64] The names of demonized authors (such as Freud) in 1933 are uttered as shibboleths, chthonic symbols of vilification. Their enunciation is part of a parodic sacrament, just as the pyrolatry is a spectacle of representational immolation. The book burnings of May 1933 were both more and less than acts of suppression. Contrary to general myth, they did not enact an official policy of the newly formed Nazi state. They were organized by a Nazi student organization, the Deutsche Studentenschaft, initially (at least) as a propaganda effort to upstage a rival group, the Nationalsozialistische Deutsche Studentenbund. In Berlin the ceremonies were endorsed by the professor of political pedagogy; in Bonn, by professors of philology and the history of art.[65] Joseph Goebbels, appointed to the Reichsministerium für Volksaufklärung und Propaganda in March 1933, spoke in Berlin, but he was not the instigator. While permission of local gauleiters in various cities was sought in advance for public demonstrations, the police and SA carrying out searches of private houses, it was members of student associations who raided lending libraries and booksellers. Students wrote and distributed *Feuersprüche*, just as students disseminated twelve theses of ideological justification. These theses, bearing the ominous title, *Wider den undeutschen Geist*, 'against the un-German spirit', were drawn up by committee in April and promulgated (with maximum publicity) for the main events in May.[66]

While burnings clearly relate to censorship, something else is needed to comprehend them as cultural events. The students had no plan as yet for total obliteration of unwholesome literature. They were indulging in fantasy. Their language is a sinister distortion, typical of bibliophobic rhetorical style. With deep irony, they declare themselves bastions of *Aufklärung*, the German word for 'enlightenment', used by Hegel of his hero Spinoza. Alongside comes *Werbung*—'promotion' of true values. In one way, it is not specific books of vilified authors that is the target of violence, but the book as idea and object. The twelve theses of April 1933 (Fig. 15), following classic Nazi doctrine, align an archaic model of German culture with an idealized vision of the people, *das Volk*.[67] Both oral and written,

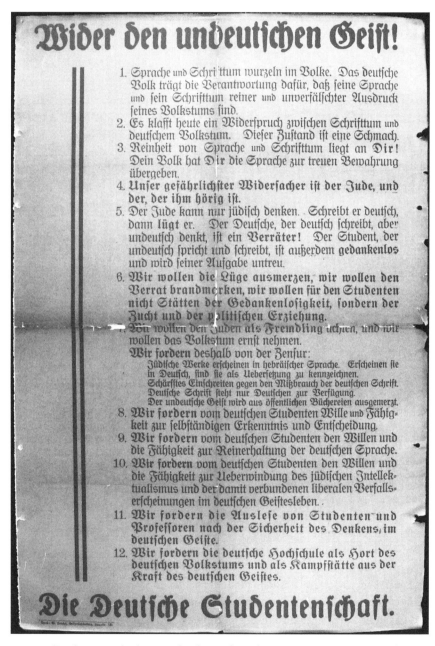

Fig. 15. 'Student prose'; *Theses wider den undeutschen Geist,* poster 1933. Würzburg, Staatsarchiv, Akten der Deutschen Studentenschaft, I 21 C 14/I

'speech and literature' (*Sprache und Schrifttum*) are rooted in the German people (Thesis 1). Yet this is (according to the Theses) no longer verifiable; 'today, a chasm of contradiction between literature and folkdom has opened up' (Thesis 2): 'Es klafft heute ein Widerspruch zwischen Schrifttum und deutschem Volkstum'. Underlying the menace ('this state of affairs is a disgrace', *eine Schmach*) is not only distaste for contemporary literature, born of bourgeois sophistication and moral decadence. The denunciation of *Schrifttum* embraces fear and loathing of the written, *Schrift* itself. The written is conceptualized as an embodiment of the gaping wound in the culture of the people. The populace is split from its own speech, from identity, or its own presence. The letter is the enemy of German 'spirit' (*der deutsche Geist*). To reach the roots of German culture is to search for unmediated original orality.

In writing, the symbolic function of language is transferred from the mouth to the eye. It is this which brings fire into play, in that it provides punishment for the sense of sight. In Freud's analysis of Hoffmann's 'Sand-Man', the most terrifyingly uncanny aspect of the story lies not so much in the doll coming to life as in the imminent fear of blinding. The Sand-Man—embodied within the sinister form of Coppelius the lawyer—shouts 'Eyes here! eyes here!', seizes the boy, and threatens to put red-hot coals in his eyes.[68] At this moment, the memory of the father's death is compounded into a strange delirium, a ring of fire. It is a primal fear, as old as Oedipus, Freud remarks. Burning marks out the removal of sight, so that the very agency of knowledge is purged and expunged.

Allied to a catastrophic dialectic of speech and writing is a parallel anxiety about the vernacular. German meaning, it was said, had been travestied. Just as speech is divorced from writing, meaning is divorced from expression. 'A Jew can only think in Jewish' (Thesis 5); if he writes in German, he is a liar. Translation implied treason of the mind. The theses yearn for pristine, unspoilt speech acts, and for immaculate purity (*Reinheit*) of meaning. Once more, this involves logical violation in the theses, what we might call unhealthy predilection for paradox: *Der Deutsche, der deutsch schreibt aber undeutsch denkt, ist ein Verräter* ('the German, who writes German but thinks un-German, is a traitor').[69] Contradictoriness is no bar to pathological violence. Indeed, irretrievable, archiviolithic purity of speech and language is part of its manic glamour. Cut loose from embarrassing contingencies in German writing, literature, or culture, a German spirit is restored as indivisible spoken word, single in meaning, and transparently vernacular.

6
The Making and Unmaking of Libraries

To seek to understand the sources of extreme forms of public violence is neither easy nor comfortable for a historian. The students in 1933 coined a term with self-conscious zeal, *ein Verbrennungsakt*, carrying connotations of a religious rite and ceremonial performance. The bonfires evoked an act of sacrifice, or purification and fumigation, alongside those of destruction, cremation, and annihilation. The students knew well, too, that book burnings bring a strong of historical memory. Primary among the historical parallels vauntingly invoked by the students was the German reforming hero Martin Luther. More than once, Hitler was referred to as 'ein zweiter Luther'. The picture of Hitler, pursuing a second German Reformation, was identified with the fearless knight in the celebrated engraving by Albrecht Dürer, *Knight, Death and the Devil* (1513). The Twelve Theses printed in bullet-point style broadsheet consciously recalled Luther's monumental 95 Theses of October 1517, using a Lutheran dialect, *Wider den undeutschen Geist*, where modern German would use *Gegen*. Luther's destruction of the papal bulls in a bonfire at Wittenberg in 1520, in the presence of Luther's own students, was used by the Nazi Studentenbund to inscribe its actions as a form of legacy. This was conflated with other exemplary cases such as students burning symbols of Napoleon at the Wartburg in 1817; a 1922 burning of *Schundliteratur* at Berlin's Tempelhof Field; and the burning of the Versailles Treaty with the Dawes and Young Plans by Nazi students in 1929.[1] To reinforce the association with Luther, one of the chosen sites of the 1933 book burnings was Luther's own university, or rather (since the original no longer existed) its descendant in Halle, Universität Halle-Wittenberg, where a bonfire occurred on 12 May.

If the Nazi students chose a specific set of iconoclastic moments in German history to lend their own rites of destruction a distinctive aura and cultural meaning, the burnings aroused further powerful memories in the minds of witnesses, whether in sympathy or in horror at what was taking place. In Switzerland, where the liberal press, as elsewhere in Europe, looked on in baffled shock, the *Neue Zürcher Zeitung* of 11 May 1933 compared the Berlin burning with an auto-da-fé from the Spanish Inquisition. The phrase was repeated in Joseph Roth's essay 'Das Autodafé des Geistes' ('The Auto-da-fé of the mind') in the autumn of the same year.[2] 'The European mind is capitulating', Roth declared. He was still optimistic: 'God is with the vanquished, not the victors!'[3] Stefan Zweig, the Austrian-Jewish novelist, covertly examined the Nazi threat to civilization in a biography of *Erasmus* (1934), in which he pointedly described Erasmus fleeing Louvain because it was too Catholic, and Basel because it was too Protestant.[4] These early modern parallels are used to give voice to Jewish identity under threat.[5]

On the opposite side, the Dominican Inquisitor Tomás de Torquemada, ironically from a Spanish Jewish *converso* family, was invoked as avenging angel. Others, with similar ambiguity, recalled the burning of the library at Alexandria by order of Caliph Umar I in 640 CE. In this way, the burnings connected to central images in European imagination. The library of Alexandria, one of the wonders of the ancient world, has haunted Western culture for two thousand years. The Ptolemaic kings of Egypt, successors to Alexander the Great—the story goes—founded the *Mouseion* (origin by etymology of 'museum'), a research centre cum scholarly academy, or (in E. R. Curtius's phrase) 'a cult organization under a priest of the Muses'.[6] The academy's purpose was to organize all knowledge, and so the *Mouseion* aspired to an incredible ambition: to house 'all of the books of the world' under one roof.[7] This first extended discussion of the library is in the *Letter of Aristeas*, a Jewish scholar of the second century BCE.[8] The library, of course, has long since vanished. Both the story of the creation of this universal library—and the story of its destruction—have inspired legends, and legends of legends.

Who made the library, where it was, whether it existed at all, are matters that still create controversy, and forlorn archaeological dives into the Mediterranean. The tyrants of the sixth century BCE, Pisistratus of Athens and Polycrates of Samos, were said to have had libraries; no doubt Plato had one.[9] After the death of Alexander the Great in 323 BCE, Ptolemy I Soter became king of Egypt, and according to Diogenes Laertius, attracted several Greek intellectuals to his court, including Demetrius of Phaleron.[10] As reported in the *Letter of Aristeas*, Demetrius started purchasing books for him at Alexandria.[11] What is at issue is not the ruined remains of the temple, or the library which is said to have annexed it—although millions of UNESCO dollars were recently spent on excavating the site under the sea, and rebuilding a simulacrum of the library above ground.[12] The Alexandrian library is equally significant for the apocrypha of mythology that surrounds it. The library has inspired endless retelling of stories, some true, and some perhaps not, both of the creation of the collection and of its loss. These myths are themselves two thousand years old. A papyrus fragment of the second century CE, discovered in 1914, records Zenodotus of Ephesus, who specialized in classifying poetry, as the first librarian, followed by Apollonius of Rhodes.[13] Callimachus, the poet, is claimed as the first author of a catalogue.[14] The names of other great librarians of the third and second centuries BCE, notable editors and grammarians, are reverently recorded.[15] The number of books was also a matter of mythic proportions. Demetrius Phaleron is said in the *Letter of Aristeas* to have reported the number of papyrus rolls as 200,000, but that he hoped to increase it soon to 500,000. In the twelfth century CE, the Byzantine scholar John Tzetzes recorded that Callimachus mentioned 490,000 rolls.[16]

The numbers spoke less of precise calculation than of giving a mathematical name to infinitude. From ancient times, the Alexandrian Library stood for completeness, a synecdoche for the universe of knowable knowledge. If the Library did not contain something, it could not be known. Equally, the stories immediately became myths of knowledge that no longer existed. The storehouse of the past was now depleted, rolls had perished, the sum of knowledge was no longer complete. The largest figures for the contents of the library were given after the library was known to be lost. Aulus Gellius speaks of 700,000 rolls; Ammianus Marcellinus simply called it 'priceless'.[17] Even a writer who claims to have been inside says it is no longer the library it once was (as modern users do of the new BL and Bodleian). Yet such writers are few: for most, the Library is a memory, a story at best second- or third-hand. The Library is a figure both of completeness and of decline. There was a time when all knowledge was known, but it is irremediably in the past. These are what James Raven calls 'the resonances of loss'.[18]

Alongside the legends of the creation of the Library, therefore, there grew up another counter-memory of its disappearance. The early stories were of natural wastage. All libraries, of course, are prone to the passage of time, decomposition, or disintegration, as well as to the more cataclysmic ravages of fire, flood, or insects.[19] Later, however, the Alexandrian Library attracted to itself legends of deliberate destruction by human intervention.[20] There are at least three different legends, in fact. In Plutarch's *Life of Caesar*, perhaps now the most widespread version, Julius Caesar set fire to his fleet in the harbour of Alexandria to avoid its capture by the Egyptian navy, only for the fire to spread, taking the 'great library' (τὴν μεγάλην βιβλιοθήκην) with it:

> when the enemy tried to cut off his fleet, he was forced to repel the danger by using fire, and this spread from the dockyards and destroyed the great library.[21]

Readers (like myself) who learned this story at school may be surprised to know that little evidence exists for its historical occurrence. Dio Cassius (3rd century CE) mentions the destruction of books during a battle, but may not be referring to a particular collection.[22] It is only in Aulus Gellius' *Attic Nights* (2nd c.) that a whole library, hundreds of thousands of scrolls, is reported as given to the flames, 'not intentionally or by anybody's order, but accidentally by the auxiliary soldiers'.[23] In a later version of events from imperial Rome, the Library is said to have been destroyed when Alexandria was razed in 272 CE by the Emperor Lucius Domitius Aurelianus.[24]

If the story of Caesar, true or not, is a narrative of insouciant negligence comparable to Nero fiddling in the fire of Rome, later accounts are more malign. In these histories it is the Library itself that is ordered to be destroyed, and its status as a sanctuary of knowledge which is the contention at issue. Here, religion enters the legends with a vengeance. The library mentioned in the new post-Christian account is characterized as a centre of pagan learning—standing adjacent to a great pagan temple, the Serapeum. Once again, in archaeological terms, this creates confusion, since it is probable that this is a different library from that of classical legend, which was adjacent instead to the temple of Rameses. It is as a repository of paganism—containing, among other things, Aristotle's own collection of books—that in 391 CE Theophilus, Archbishop of Alexandria (backed by the Emperor Theodosius I), closed the temples and their libraries.[25]

Knowledge was evil; had not Adam been evicted from Paradise for wanting to know? In about 416 CE, Orosius makes clear that there is by now no large library left in Alexandria.[26] Yet there was something contradictory about this story of a clash of religion with classicism. Alexandria was a thriving centre of Christian learning in the third century CE, with intellectualism of various kinds mixing freely with pagan mythology and heresy.[27] Origen was appointed teacher at the school at the age of eighteen, working there for two decades.[28] Christianity was controversial: in 202, Emperor Septimus Severus ordered Roman citizens openly practising the religion to be executed. After moving to Caesarea, Origen defended Christianity against the arguments of the pagans in *Contra Celsum*, using Plato at length to show philosophy and theology compatible.

The *Letter of Aristeas*, earliest source of the existence of the Alexandrian Library, reports it was precisely the presence of so much learning that made it possible for the Hebrew scriptures to be translated into Greek. For 'in the country of the Jews they use their own characters, just as the Egyptians use their own arrangement of letters and have their own language'.[29] There follows the mystical story of how seventy scholars simultaneously translated the text, each coming up with an identical version, known by the time of Augustine as the Septuagint.[30] However, doubts about the story were expressed as early as Jerome, and then repeated by Renaissance humanists such as Juan Luis Vives.[31] In modern times, Bruce Metzger argues that the whole tale of the library is invented by Aristeas as part of his propaganda for the authenticity and canonicity of the Septuagint version.[32] This ambiguity about literary evidence and concepts of the holy disturbs early Christianity up to Isidore of Seville in the sixth century CE, who devoted a chapter of his *Etymologies* to the concept of the library (*de bibliothecis*). Isidore conflated the words *biblion* ('a book'; also *the* book, the Bible) and *theke* ('a depository') to suggest the archive is the place where the sacred is kept hidden and preserved.[33]

In a parallel story to the culture war between pagan and Christian in the iconoclastic purges of Theophilus, Caliph Umar is substituted as an Islamic anti-type.[34] Umar ruled Alexandria from 634 to 644 CE, and was said to have consented to the burning of the Library in the twentieth year of the هِجْرَة (*hijra*)—by Christian reckoning December 642.[35] As with the Archbishop, the Caliph created an epigram for the occasion: 'If these writings of the Greeks agree with the Qur'an, they are useless and need not be preserved; if they disagree, they are pernicious and ought to be destroyed'.[36] According to Ali ibn Yusuf al-Qifti in his *Ta'rikh al-Hukama* ('Chronicle of Wise Men') there was such a mass of material in the library that it took six months to burn.[37] Nevertheless, in this account, there is a strange mixture of contempt and love for learning. The Caliph wishes to have a report on books that he owns, and is told they come from Sind, from India and Persia; from Jurjan (ancient Hyrcania) and Armenia; from Babylon, Mosul, and Byzantium.

Edward Gibbon in *The Decline and Fall of the Roman Empire* (1788) was belligerently sceptical about the story concerning the Caliph, finding its source only in the thirteenth-century *Specimen historiae Arabum* of Gregory Abulpharagius, a Jewish Christian writer known also as Bar Hebraeus, or Abu 'l-Faraj in Arabic. In characteristic polemical style, Gibbon used his exoneration of Arabic blame to add fuel to his philippic against the Christian inheritors of the Roman world, and especially Archbishop Theophilus, 'the perpetual enemy of peace and virtue; a bold, bad man, whose hands were alternately polluted with gold, and with blood'.[38] In so doing, Gibbon repeated the confusion of the palace library with the library of the Serapeum, which Theophilus did destroy. Gibbon triumphantly declares the Christians as the greatest barbarians of them all. Yet Gibbon's scepticism has not prevented the story of Umar from encouraging Islamophobia down to modern times. The idea of the destruction of the Alexandrian library has entered legend as powerfully as the legend of its creation. In the UNESCO project to restore the great library of Alexandria in modern times, it has been suggested that the dream is still colonial, perhaps demoting Islamic material in favour of the Western classical tradition.[39]

The fantasy of the destruction of knowledge on such a voluminous—it is tempting to say encyclopaedic—scale, also has complex roots. It is strongly embedded in notions of sacred knowledge—whether this be pagan, Jewish, Christian, or Muslim—and its embodiment in written texts of scripture. It is also connected with conflict between these systems of sacred knowledge. Gibbon runs down Christianity in favour of Islam, just as earlier and later Christian traditions used the story of the Caliph against their Muslim enemies. In turn, this external threat to religious truth intercalates with questions of orthodoxy and heresy within a particular religion. Sometimes both processes coincide.

Qifti presented his narrative of Umar as arising out of a dialogue between 'Amr ibn al-As or Amrou, the Emir who occupied Alexandria, and a survivor of the Greek Christian community after the Muslim occupation, John Philoponus (or John the Grammarian).[40] Amrou was a subtle scholar much interested in disputing the divinity of Christ via the Qur'an in comparison with the Gospels. He was persistent enough to check the accuracy of the Patriarch's citations of Greek translations, against the original Hebrew text of Genesis. Philoponus, in turn, while a Christian, was so thorough an Aristotelian that he was suspected of heresy against orthodox Christian doctrine, especially the controversy over Christ's divinity, which was of great concern to Islamic scholars.[41] Sometimes it was unclear whether the grammarian was a heretic or a pagan.[42] It is in the midst of these learned debates about the nature of Christ, or the doctrine of the Trinity, or the coherence of the gospels and of Christian law, that Philoponus makes the fatal error of admitting the continued existence of the great Alexandrian library. The learned Amrou wishes to consult it, but in seeking permission from the Caliph he is ordered instead to burn it.[43] Yet here, too, there are deviations and digressions in the narrative: one of the texts they need turns out to have been lost already, in a previous fire.

Knowledge and destruction always go together, as in the myth of Babel (see Pl. 1). This is characteristically presented as a battle between learned and unlearned. Tacitus (without knowing German) said the Germans were visionary savages prone to human sacrifice and worshipping trees.[44] Being Tacitus, he also said the Romans were worse. The Goths then sacked Rome, so other Romans called them barbarians. This led, so we're often told, to the 'dark ages', but the epithet covers later lack of understanding. This is history as written by victors; to which we might add, literate and Latinate victors. Augustine wrote that when Alaric the Goth invaded the city, the pagans blamed the Christians, so that he was inspired to write *The City of God against the Pagans*.[45] The Goths were less barbaric than the Romans, Augustine felt, knowing his Tacitus.[46] Nor were they always un-Christian: Walafrid Strabo in a history of liturgy reports Goths translating scripture (*divinos libros*) into a Germanic language.[47] By the time of Charlemagne, the boot sat on the other foot, Germany claiming the imperial crown of Rome. Charlemagne's *patrius sermo* or 'paternal language' was a form of 'rustic Roman', a Romance ancestor of French. By the 790s, however, his court at Aachen spoke a version of Old High German. The Emperor himself also spoke Latin and a little Greek.[48]

The new Christians now needed new pagans to find unlearned. In York, the poet and monk Alcuin, who later served at the court of Charlemagne, reports that Bishop Ælberht kept a wonderful library 'all under one roof' (*uno sub culmine*).[49] According to legend, this remarkable collection of books was dispersed by the Vikings, during the ravages of the Great Heathen Army in 866–7 CE, led (it was said) by the sons of Ragnarr Loðbrók.[50] Alcuin described with even greater horror the earlier raid of the Northmen on the monastery of Lindisfarne off the Northumbrian coast on 8 June 793: 'They desecrated God's sanctuary, shed the blood of holy men around the altar...and trampled the bodies of the saints like dung in the streets.'[51] Holy Island mattered so much, as the site of the relics of St Cuthbert, but it was also the centre of English Christian writing and bookmaking.[52] Paganism and illiteracy are regarded as more or less synonymous in such accounts. Bede hoped that by reading his book, the *Life of Cuthbert*, readers would feel 'a burning desire' for the kingdom of heaven.[53] Alfred the Great, in a preface to his translation of Pope Gregory the Great's *Pastoral Care*, presented the Danish invasions as a devastating loss for English learning.[54] Meanwhile he made his own translations of Boethius'

Consolation of Philosophy and Augustine's *Soliloquies* into a symbol of scholarly reform and a learned vernacular.[55] Yet the Icelandic sagas, too, are among the wonders of literature; and Snorri Sturluson's *Prose Edda* begins with Adam and Eve and Noah's Flood.[56] Although this dates from later than Bjorn Ironside and Ivar the Boneless, syncretism took place before conversion to Christianity.[57] By the eleventh century Danish followers of Odin and English Christians alike read pagan Virgil for fun.[58] Long before this, Bede referred to the history of the English people as partaking *ea quae fama vulgante collegimus* ('vernacular fame'), an echo from Virgil.[59] Anglo-Saxon Christian schools taught Virgil all the time, and Bede's *Life of Cuthbert* is full of Virgilian presence.[60]

Yet if the monks believed themselves to be the repository of all useful knowledge, in other circumstances they could appear as the enemy of learning. The fifteenth-century humanist Poggio Bracciolini graduated from legal copying as a notary to work under seven different popes, rising to become *apostolicus secretarius* under Pope Martin V. Just before Poggio took this post, the papal office lay vacant for two years after the antipope John XXIII escaped from the Council of Constance disguised as a postman, and the cardinals and bishops debated how to end the western schism. Poggio used the interval to hunt for manuscripts in the monasteries towards and beyond the Alps. In this, he followed in the footsteps of Petrarch, who in 1345 rediscovered Cicero's *Letters to Atticus* in the chapter library of the cathedral in Verona.[61] From here, Petrarch reached back to elements of early Roman civilization considered lost irretrievably. Historical consciousness worked in odd ways. Petrarch wrote anachronistic letters to Cicero and to Livy, to whom he introduced the idea of Christ's incarnation.[62] Poggio copied Cicero's letters in 1408.[63] Petrarch's personal library, often obtained through monastic channels, included rarities, such as the *De re rustica* of Varro, who fought with Pompey against Julius Caesar. Varro's *De lingua Latina*, one of the most important sources for knowledge of early Latin, was probably given to him by Boccaccio.[64] The political edge to Italian humanism is shown by Poggio's mentor, Leonardo Bruni, who reinvented the foundation of Florence to make it part of the ancient Roman republic.[65]

In February 1416, Poggio set out on the snowbound roads west and north of Constance. He recounted his discoveries in letters to the book-collector Niccolò Niccoli, whose handwriting later formed the model for the italic style in the printed books of Aldus Manutius.[66] Poggio exoticizes the wildness of Switzerland in a bid to outdo Petrarch: the journey into the wild is presented as a synecdoche of the journey into ignorance. Petrarch's sense of the wild is always somewhat domesticated and comfortable, an Arcadian sojourn in the south of France at worst. Poggio instead describes a mental itinerary into the world of the profane, centred on Baden, a thermal spa in the middle of nowhere in Aargau, after admiring the Rheinfall (which he calls 'Caesarstoul', *Caesaris sedes* or Caesar's throne) in Schaffhausen. He compares the Baden baths to the ancient Romans taking the waters at Puteoli, splashing in a reference to Leonardo Bruni's recent *Oratio Eliogabali* of 1408, a spoof of ancient free love and literary oneupmanship.[67] This is mixed in with Poggio's religious syncretism. He recounts to Niccolò his Hebrew lessons at the hands of a convert from Judaism to Christianity.[68] He calls himself an imitator of Jerome. From here he enters (he proclaims in rapture) the service of the goddess Venus.

There are thirty baths in Baden, Poggio reports with leisurely sprezzatura. In the public baths, women, men, boys, and maidens, mingle promiscuously, he half-quotes from Virgil.[69] But he turns prim *Aeneid* into porn: the bathers are 'displaying their private parts and their buttocks'.[70] In the private baths, a prophylactic fence divides the sexes, but with no guards, plenty of touching takes place, on both sides and in between. Now Poggio interpolates his tale of ancient luxury with his tale of ancient and modern learning. He presents himself as an Italian with no inkling of German, but he may be making mutual deafness between the Roman and the Gothic a literary trope: he knows the German word, *Mädchen*.[71] Linguistic, scholarly, and sexual traffic is his point. He refers to Jupiter appearing to Danäe in a shower of golden rain, from Ovid's *Metamorphoses*.[72] The image of holding property in common he takes from Plato's *Republic*.[73] These references are mere commonplaces, staging posts to his crowning point, which comes in a reference to the wholly profane and illegitimate name of Epicurus:

> What a great centre of the Epicurean way of thinking this is. And I believe that this is the place where the first man was created, which the Hebrews call Ganeden or the garden of delight. For if pleasure can make life happy, I do not see what is lacking in this place for complete and perfect happiness.[74]

As well as in Eden, we are in the earthly paradise at the climax of Dante's *Purgatorio*. There, Dante leaves behind the terrace of lust, and the temptations of Sodom, and—encouraged by the fictional presence of Virgil—passes through fire to find Beatrice. Here he finds innocence but also a ravishing *locus amoenus* of human pleasure, in which dreams of fair to middling women are well to the fore, Matelda as well as Beatrice:

> Non credo che splendesse tanto lume
> sotto le ciglia a Venere, trafitta
> dal figlio fuor di tutto suo costume.[75]

Somehow in the allegory, Dante mixes in a critique of the Avignon papacy and a farewell to Virgil. He swims over the river of Lethe, possibly to forget the classics and find God.

Poggio's letter is a *commedia buffa* of risqué fantasy and learned allure. Yet it is also a commentary on the Latin language and on Greek hermetic philosophy.

Eros is ever in conversation with Athene, as they were perhaps in his scandalously prosperous marriage to Selvaggia, a noble Florentine girl not yet eighteen years old. Perhaps his favourite discovery was a complete copy of Quintilian's *Institutio oratoria* in the monastery at St Gallen, long known only in fragments.[76] Bruni in a letter to Poggio rhapsodized over the return of Quintilian 'whole and entire'. Europe gave thanks: in Rome, Lorenzo Valla borrowed Quintilian for his critique of scholastic logical method.[77] Erasmus encountered Quintilian in the monastery of the Augustinian canons in Steyn near Gouda in South Holland; in *De copia* he described Quintilian as the key to the abundance of language and literature.[78] In the backwoods of Saxony, Luther claimed he liked Quintilian above almost any writer.[79] Rhetorical eulogies aside, Poggio placed a polemical edge on his repristinations. Valla wanted to use a new philology to reopen the Bible and theology. Erasmus found Valla's *Adnotationes in Novam Testamentum* in a monastery in Louvain in 1504, laying the foundations for his Greek New Testament of 1516, replete with humanist annotations.[80] Poggio's own opinion was that theology and humanism are different realms of thought. While never demeaning his literary style with anything like an argument, Poggio leads Valla in a satirical charade, loosely modelled on Dante, from the streets of imperial Rome, to the inferno of Satan, to the Elysian fields of the immortal heroes at Troy, back to Lorenzo's miserable scholarly hut.[81]

By far Poggio's most sensational rediscovery, of course, was *De rerum natura*. Poggio spotted Lucretius' name on the spine of a book in a monastic library, which he never revealed, perhaps Fulda in Germany. Recognizing the author from Cicero, he opened the cover in 1417 of a complete manuscript of a poem in six books or seven thousand lines, thought lost forever. He lent it to Niccoli, who did not give it back for fourteen years, but fortunately made other copies, since the original does not survive. Lucretius Regained was more problematic than Lucretius Lost, however. In Poggio's discovery, Stephen Greenblatt declares, 'the world became modern'.[82] Lucretius described nature through the eyes of Epicurus. Epicureanism was a byword in post-classical thought for attacking Stoicism, the predominant ancient theory of ethics. Poggio means 'Epicurean' in this way in a letter from Baden in 1416: a guide to the pleasurable life. Yet Epicurus meant something more monstrous. This is a world not only without a Christian God, but with no need for pagan gods either. The universe is made of 'atoms', each human being an arbitrary string of matter. As we die, atoms recombine into some other matter. For unorthodox writers of classical bent this was fabulous news. Printed in 1473, the book spread, as if in brown bag covers. Erasmus wrote a colloquy 'The Epicurean', in which Hedonius ('the hedonist', the star character), says paradoxically, and with a wink to his author, 'there are no people more Epicurean than godly Christians'.[83] Montaigne loved his copy, scribbling in it endlessly; it, too, was lost for centuries until found in Cambridge University Library in the 1990s.[84] But to other humanists, the book smelt of a canker that would not go away.

Thomas More's *Utopia*, avant-garde in many ways, makes the ideal islanders Epicurean in the old sense as followers of pleasure and opponents of Stoicism. However, Lucretian mortality of the soul is a heresy too far even for utopians.[85]

Humanists heralded monasteries as sacred keepers of a knowledge monks no longer understood. Cincius Romanus in the summer of 1416, hearing Poggio's successes even before he found Lucretius, replied German monasteries were full of Latin books. Vitruvius on architecture or Priscian on grammar were back in plain sight, and hope rose for all the lost works of Cicero and Livy to return soon.[86] In Cluny in Burgundy, Poggio found the complete forensic orations of Cicero, previously known only in parts. Yet Poggio complained in 1421 that he hated a book-hunter's life, longing for the Curia in Rome.[87] The 'Sirens', as he called lost books, had now drawn him to England, perhaps why this Italian snob was so miserable. What drives him on? By now, rumour of lost Latins was spurred further by the greater treasure of lost Greeks. Yet what spurs Poggio is the sense of loss itself, compounded by the chimera of the northern dolts who keep losing things. To Niccoli he writes that it is hardly worth bothering looking in Germany any more, as the country is full of thieves. As for English libraries, they are too new to have anything worth looking for. The cathedral library at Salisbury is so useless it does not even have a copy of Origen. He can't be bothered to go to moribund Oxford at all.[88]

In truth, monkish Oxford was not quite so barbarian as Poggio made it sound. Indeed, Humfrey of Lancaster, duke of Gloucester, who gave 281 books to the university at his death in 1447, was reading Poggio himself, at least in his aristocratic imagination.[89] In the same decade, the Paduan scribe, Milo da Carrara, was copying books in England.[90] In the opposite direction, British barbarians by now toured around Italy.[91] Joshing talk of filthy books found in filthier countries is part of a literary game, but it is also part of a deadly serious denomination of the book as artefact. Poggio employs complex strategies to mark out Christianity from paganism, libertinism from divine letters. He does not want to soil profanity with latent puritanism. His attack on Valla's *Elegantiae linguae latinae* sets out a ground all the more familiar in modern times, of secular against sacred. In this, inadvertently, he repeats the strategy in reverse of Alfred the Great, who used the spoliation of the monasteries to prove the superiority of the English to the Danes. It is not so far, either, from the stories of Alexandria, which prick out hard divisions between Islam and Christianity.

In truth, even after the dispersal of the Fatimid library by Salah al-Din, the Ayyūbid dynasty which he founded, and which spread from Egypt across the Levant and into the Maghreb, nurtured the collection of books. Collecting is always intimately related to destruction. In Cairo, the library of the vizier needed fifty-nine camels on three trips to instal the tens of thousands of books in the citadel.[92] Syria, too, saw an efflorescence of Sunni book culture. The Mamlūks, who originated as a military class in the Abbasid Caliphate of Baghdad, gradually took power in Egypt and in 1250 claimed the sultanate.[93] The Mamlūk Sultans were not native speakers of Arabic, yet they sought to legitimate their rule by claiming Cairo as the successor to Baghdad as guardian of Sunni Islamic culture. Their name, meaning 'slave', implied non-Muslim; they defied outsider status by adopting Sufism, promoting Arabic poetry and appropriating the Ayyūbid practice of attaching a madrasa (Islamic school) to the sultan's mausoleum.[94] Libraries flourished under the Mamlūks in other religious institutions such as mosques. These were on a scale comparable to the largest monasteries in Christian Europe. The Mahmudiyya madrasa held 4,000 volumes. Private libraries among the Mamlūks dwarfed their Christian analogues: a fourteenth-century judge in Damascus and later Cairo owned 5,000 books. A century later, the historian Ibn Hajar was said to have a library twice that size.[95] The catalogue of the library of the Ottoman Sultan Bayazid II (1447–1512) numbered over 7,000 titles. By comparison, the legendary library of the Hungarian King Mátyás was a third of that. The library of the Sorbonne in Paris held 1,722 books in 1338. Cambridge colleges in the fifteenth century possessed about 200.[96] Bibliophile Petrarch, whose library was so fine that the Republic of Venice bought a house for him and his books to live in, perhaps owned only around the same number.[97]

A century after Poggio, John Leland trawled English monasteries, seeking lost books in Glastonbury.[98] By now Thomas Cromwell had closed them in the name of Henry VIII's Reformation.[99] Leland, a sentimental Catholic, went book-mad, lamenting voguish barbarism. *De viris illustribus* mixed noble worthies with rural travelogue, noting where the best books were still to be found, in spite of Cromwell's agents.[100] Leland in 1534 can find just two books of note after Tudor Vikings left York Minster.[101] John Bale, Carmelite friar cum Protestant zealot, followed Leland by editing a printed bibliography of English literature in 1548.[102] He died a colonial bishop in Ireland. As Christianity split, so did the battle of books. Yet still the library acts as emblem of divisions of knowledge. Books are agents for transgression as well as authority. This is how the Council of Constance reverberates in Poggio's story: after 1415, western Christianity reunified, by cutting out heresy's unwanted heart, and dragging Jan Hus from Prague as scapegoat.

Learning and unlearning are imagined in popular mythology of global history as polar opposites. Nowhere is this truer than the 'classical heritage', presented so often as a justification of Western racial superiority or imperial right. Classicism is never innocent or unself-consciousness. A century after Poggio, Machiavelli described his exile from Florence in 1513 in a letter to Francesco Vettori, ambassador at Rome. He is living on a farm, like rusticated Cicero, and like Cicero, wherever he is, his head is always in his books. In the afternoon, he goes to his aviary, a book ever in his pocket (Dante or Petrarch; or else Tibullus or Ovid). He is like a character in a play by Plautus, a bird cage on his back. As evening comes, he returns home to his study. He takes off his day-clothes, full of mud and dust, and puts on formal courtly dress. Here, he enters into the presence of *antiqui homines*, imbibing his humanist birthright, and asking classical great men the reasons for their actions, who in their kindness do not fail to answer him.[103] He is, J. G. A. Pocock says, 'conversing with the ancients by reading their books'.[104]

Machiavelli behaves as if there is one classical tradition, which informed his little book, *The Prince*, and taught him how politics is to be done properly, in perpetuity. Classical civilization, however, exists in many forms: Chinese, Indian, Japanese, Arabic, Persian, and others. Destruction of knowledge is an act of colonial power, as one classicism seeks to conquer another. The British burned down the Royal Library of the kings of Burma in the third Anglo-Burmese War in 1887, not before taking treasures back to the Victoria and Albert Museum in Kensington. In the early twentieth century, the Gyeongbokgung palace in Seoul, a miracle of Korean Confucian scholarship, was wrecked by the invading Japanese imperial army. In August 1914, the German army set fire to the library of the Catholic University in Louvain in an act of terror to control the population. In the Second World War, Japanese forces deliberately destroyed Chinese national libraries in Beijing, Shanghai, Hunan, Baodong, and elsewhere. Auden's 'Spain, 1937' uncovers classicism's claim to follow unchanging tradition, while adapting to impose new tyranny:

> Yesterday the belief in the absolute value of Greek;
> The fall of the curtain upon the death of the hero.[105]

Library websites emanate auras of organic accumulation, as if books collect themselves. Assembling a library, Peter Brown comments, is 'a crushing investment'.[106] More often, libraries are a result of cash, war, theft, and colonialism. Ceolfrith, Bede's guardian, grew stellar libraries at Wearmouth and the abbey of St Peter at Jarrow on Tyneside, maybe by means of a lucky purchase of Cassiodorus' second-hand books.[107] The Medici stole monastic books to fill the Laurentian library in Florence. Oxford and Cambridge colleges acquired their medieval manuscripts in the dissolution of English monasteries. Cardinal Bessarion, born in Constantinople, laundered books under the eyes of the Ottomans in Turkey after 1453, later donating them to the republic of Venice as the Biblioteca Marciana, the 'first public library'. Two Archbishops of Canterbury fleeced books after the Reformation to create Lambeth Palace Library, which yet only escaped the clutches of Cambridge University by a fluke in the British Civil Wars.[108] William Laud did the same after the pillages of the Thirty Years War, for the Bodleian.[109] The Bibliotheca Palatina, jewel of Renaissance Protestant Heidelberg, ended up as booty in the Vatican Library. Great European and American libraries assembled 'Oriental Departments' in a free lunch for centuries, before the Calcutta Public Library opened in 1836, the Kyoto Prefectural Library in 1898, or the Imperial Library of Beijing in 1909. The Jagiellonian Library in Kraków lost thousands of books in the Second World War, then made up for it with a stash of prize books, including holographs of Mozart and Beethoven from the Berlin Staatsbibliothek, found in another monastery, in Silesia.

Learning is a moving target. St Gallen in Switzerland, for Poggio a parvenu rubbish tip, was a miracle of scholarship at the time of the Magyar raids in the tenth century CE. From there, Notker hailed Bede as a 'new sun in the west, ordained to illuminate the whole globe'.[110] Scholarship forever moves between birth in a desert and burial in an abandoned archive. In the 1980s, Abdel Kader Haidara, curator of the library in Timbuktu in Mali, journeyed across the Sahara and along the River Niger, tracking ancient Islamic and secular manuscripts supposedly hidden in the trunks of desert shepherds. Then, after 9/11, Al-Qaeda turned up in the Maghreb.[111] In Timbuktu, Haidara saw them arrive in 2011, led by a radical triumvirate of a Tuareg and two Algerians. Over two years, this 'badass' librarian transported 377,000 manuscripts by river and road past jihadi guards and Malian soldiers to Bamoko in the south of Mali.[112] Books left behind in other libraries in Timbuktu meanwhile were blown up along with works of Islamic art. Yet the saved books, too, faced new dangers of mould and humidity.

Book are always at risk. William Dalrymple cites *The Book of Protection*, a volume of Nestorian charms and spells: 'By the power of the voice of our Lord which cutteth the flame of the fire, I bind, expel, anathematise the bullets of the engines of war.'[113] Al-Qaeda is not the only brutal army in history. UNESCO envies magical formulae handed from the angels of Adam to King Solomon. Sitting in Hotel Metropole in Alexandria in 1994, Dalrymple recalls how the oil wars of the twentieth century destroyed Mediterranean and Middle Eastern civilizations, where Jews, Christians, and Muslims had lived together for centuries. He wrote this when Beirut in Lebanon was a city in flames, but Syrian Aleppo and Homs safe havens. The ironies of history never abate. In about 1509, Leo Africanus visited Timbuktu, dazzled by intellectual riches.[114] The city boasted private libraries with 700 or 1,600 books; a dictionary of Arabic in twenty-eight volumes by an Andalusian grammarian; a treatise on poetics by Al-Khalil ibn Ahmad, a ninth-century linguist of Iraq.[115] Leo encountered in Mediterranean Africa and Europe Arabic translations of Plato, Aristotle, Hippocrates' medical texts, and Ptolemy's geographies; Latin translations of the jewels of the Persian scholar Avicenna, ethical and scientific works.[116] Yet in 1591 Ahmed Baba, confronting the Moroccan Sultan's army, asked why Muslim brothers ransacked and burned his 'small library'.[117] Recalling him in prison in Marrakesh, or scholars dispersed to Ghana or the Ivory Coast, it is hard not to think of ravages of British imperialism in northern Africa, or recent American wars in Iraq and Afghanistan.

Elias Canetti finished writing his first novel, *Die Blendung*, in 1931, two years before Hitler's rise to power. Published in England at the end of the war with the title *Auto-da-fé*, it tells the story of Herr Doktor Peter Kien in Vienna, a forty-year old philologist and scholar of China. Eschewing sex or any human contact, he lines his apartment throughout with books, leaving room only for a small divan to sleep on. He believes himself to be in the possession of the largest private library in the city, and carries a part of it with him whenever he goes out. 'Books, even bad ones, tempted him easily into making a purchase.'[118] He descends into further psychosis. He marries his housekeeper Therese, because she takes such care of the library; but on their wedding day, she throws out some books to make room for herself to sleep. Kien contemplates killing her. 'Books have no life; they lack feeling, and perhaps cannot feel pain'; but books are still better than humans.[119] No wonder Canetti's book is called 'the end of modernism'.[120] At the novel's climax—how else is it supposed to finish?—the library burns.

Alexandria's ancient library symbolizes to Western minds pristine knowledge. Ultimately, however, it becomes as much a figure for the unity or coherence of one sacred system against another, or sacred in relation to profane. Its destruction equally omens failure and annihilation in intellectual systems of any kind. The fantasy of a burning library thus relates to concepts of truth and final meaning. In a letter to the Emperor Manuel I, John Tzetzes—like many scholars since, obsessed with the lost library—tells of a dream which lasted all night. Towards the end of the dream, he catches sight of a book he's coveted for many years, which will provide a key to all his mysteries: only for the book to curl up in flames before his eyes.[121] Even while the binding burns, the letters, as if of a divine quality of their own, continue to be visible. He wakes up; the book disappears: but its script, perhaps its meaning, exists still in indelible form in half-remembered nightmare.

7

Incombustible Heresy in the Age of Luther

Why do people burn books? Burning satisfies a fantasy of oblivion, appealing to authors and scholars as well as dictators and philistines. Virgil desired the *Aeneid* to be burned at his death, only for Augustus to save it, although the puritanical emperor would gladly have destroyed all of Ovid.[1] The second Earl of Rochester gave proof of how obscene his poems were by asking for them to be burned at his death; but copies of the poems were so widespread as to make the order moot.[2] The will of Emily Dickinson was more wilfully ignored by her sister Lavinia in 1886.[3] Max Brod reported that in Kafka's desk after his death he found an instruction for all his writings to be 'burned unread'.[4] Brod preferred not to burn them, following other self-contradictory desires of his friend, expressed in a letter of 1921: 'The impossibility of not writing, the impossibility of writing German, the impossibility of writing differently.' To these, Kafka added a fourth: 'the impossibility of writing'.[5] Books and violence resonate in Kafka's imagination. If we want books to make us happy, he wrote in a letter in 1904, we would be better off with no books. The only books worth reading are the ones that wound us: 'like the death of someone we loved more than ourselves'; or 'like a suicide'.[6]

At one level burning answers to a functional purpose. Burning is a means of destroying books quickly. Yet fire is not the most efficient enemy of books.[7] Water is the element used in the book industry for elimination of unwanted surplus, turning paper back to the pulpy mess from which it came.[8] Destruction, of course, can be purposive: and nowadays book-burning is seen as a subset in the techniques of censorship. Yet 'censorship' is a nineteenth-century Western appropriation.[9] It was reinvented as the inversion of the liberal idea of a free press. John Stuart Mill made the classic statement in 1867:

> If all mankind minus one, were of one opinion, and one, and only one person were of the contrary opinion, mankind would be no more justified in silencing that one person, than he, if he had the power, would be justified in silencing mankind.[10]

Biblioclasm is much older, and more powerful, than an instrumental means of state censorship. It answers to a deeper fear. Just as the Chinese invented printing centuries before Gutenberg, so records of book-burning in China precede the apocryphal stories of Alexandria, going back to the third century BCE, and the Qin First Emperor.

The order to burn books is quoted in *Shiji* (the *Historical Records*) by Sima Qian, the Grand Historiographer:

> Your servant requests that the records of the historians apart from those of Qin should all be burned. Apart from those copies which the scholars of broad learning are responsible for in their official capacity, anyone in all under Heaven who dares to possess and hide away the *Songs*, the *Documents*, and the sayings of the hundred schools, should hand them all over to a governor or commandant and they should be indiscriminately burned. If there is anyone who dares to mention the *Songs* or *Documents* in private conversation, he should be executed. Those who, using the old, reject the new will be wiped out together with their clans.[11]

The books no doubt burned quickly, made as they were at this time of strips of bamboo, sewn together with silk 'like Venetian blinds'.[12] Far from glorifying the First Emperor, Sima Qian writes a century later from the point of view of the Han court which replaced him. By this time the period of the Warring States was over. The burning of the books, like the burning of the Library at Alexandria, is a piece of propagandist counter-theatre, making sense of an earlier case of propaganda. Sima Qian is in the business of rewriting the past in the form of a new 'universal history'.[13] Central to this is the canonical status of Confucius as historian and philosopher. In the process, he rejected the Qin emperor as an aberration, and the Qin's totalitarian attitude to books is part of this denunciation.

Borges was fascinated by this mythology of the book in more than one direction. In his 1961 story cum essay *La muralla y los libros* ('The Wall and the Books') he drew attention to the coincidence of the order to burn the books with the first building by the Qin of the Great Wall of China. Burning books and constructing walls may be considered the common tasks of rulers, he muses, and yet: 'Walling in an orchard or a garden is ordinary, but not walling in an empire'.[14] Borges conjectures that the emperor walls in his empire because he knows instinctively that it is perishable, while he destroys the books because he senses in some way that they are sacred:

> Perhaps the burning of the libraries and the erection of the wall are operations which in some secret way cancel each other.   (p. 223).

The two actions, Borges suggests, are caught in apposition because each crosses a boundary between the material and immaterial, and between the universal and the individual. The burning of a book draws attention to the fact that it is a material object in its own right. Once again, the concept of censorship is inadequate to this, as it reduces the book to the sum of the ideas contained within it. It sees the suppression of books as conterminous with the suppression of ideas. Yet books are physical objects with their own physical laws and their own form of life. Neither do they come into being only by being read. Books signify by being bought, owned, borrowed, given, or received.

Whether on view in a church or temple, or in a court of law, or of a prince, or someone's bookshelves in an office or the home, books carry a meaning and a value. The Qin approach to books was far more ambiguous than the burning myth allows. In a 1975 excavation of a Qin burial, 1,100 bamboo strips of writing were found mixed up with the bones.[15] On the emperor's tours, he made pilgrimages to the mountains and left *stelae* rich in texts.[16] Stranger things can happen to a book than being read, although no human activity is odder, perhaps, than reading. Books can be worn on the body like jewels, kissed, buried in shrines, held up in veneration, torn up in shreds, defaced, individual words erased or cut out, or covered over with paper patches. The apocryphal Acts of Paul and Thecla in the fourth century CE are bound up with a host of erotic and ascetic practices.[17] Books, like other objects of human manufacture, are invested with desires, fears, anxieties, and longings, well beyond their material dimensions, but which attest also to a material existence in time and space which goes beyond their physical owners or makers. A book may outlive its reader by a thousand years or more, but like its human reader it is transient and perishable, so that it can be destroyed in a moment.

Book-burning is an iconic part of tyranny in many countries and periods. The Roman Emperor Domitian publicly burned writing.[18] The books of Arius were burned after the First Council of Nicaea in 325 CE. The books of the Nestorians were burned when they were defined as heretical in 475 CE. Al-Hakam II, the Umayyad Caliph of Andalusia, collected books from Damascus, Baghdad, Constantinople, Cairo, Mecca, Medina, and Basra. He had books translated from Latin and Greek into Arabic, especially on science and philosophy, but also Orosius' Christian history and the *History of the Franks*. But under the reign of his successor, his vizier Al-Mansur submitted to religious pressures and had much of the library burned, especially the 'ancient sources', Greek books of astronomy and logic.[19] In the early thirteenth century, during Pope Innocent III's campaign against the Albigensian heretics, it was said that the books on both sides were exposed to a trial by fire. While the Cathar books burned freely (Fig. 16), a book by Domingo Guzmán (later St Dominic) miraculously floated above the fire grate.

The incident was a primal scene in the foundation of the Inquisition, taken for centuries as proof of its authority. A painting of the event by Pedro Berruguete was commissioned in the 1490s by the General Inquisitor Tomás de Torquemada for the Dominican convent of Santo Tomás in Ávila, along with another panel of an auto-da-fé.[20] The book is immaculately preserved, in sumptuous binding, above St Dominic's head. The image asks a question of us: what role do books, and writing itself, play in heresy trials? Here, John Arnold argues that we pay

Fig. 16. 'The Cathar heresy'; Berruguete, *St Dominic and the Albigenses*, tempura and oil on wood, *c*.1495. Madrid, Museo del Prado

attention to 'depositions as texts', in order to register the power relation that is built into 'the written-ness of the records'.[21]

Reading is 'always a practice embodied in acts, spaces, and habits', says Roger Chartier.[22] Many Cathars in Languedoc were illiterate and it is suggested their books were few. However, the Dominican Bernard Gui referred in his manual of inquisition to two kinds of book essential in identifying heretics: the New Testament in the vernacular, and works of Cathar theology.[23] Each pair of *perfecti* needed a copy of the Occitan New Testament to perform the ritual of *consolamentum*. There were hundreds of *perfecti*, and hundreds of depositions mention the ritual; there must have been many copies.[24] In Bernard's second category, Pierre (priest and double agent) admits possessing a calendar with a 'book of the faith of the heretics'.[25] The Inquisitor needs to find a book to locate heresy physically. The Cathars obliged by making books talismans for their most secret beliefs. Carlo Ginzburg in *The Cheese and the Worms*, about sixteenth-century Friuli, argues it is not books alone, but an encounter between written page and oral culture, that produces the 'explosive mixture' in Menocchio's head.[26] Menocchio owns an eclectic range of books, hermetic and prosaic: a Bible, saints' lives (Jacopo da Voragine's *Legenda Aurea*), Boccaccio's *Decameron*, and perhaps an Italian translation of the Qur'an.[27] In Montaillou, Ladurie suggests books formed an informal circulating library, like 'little blue books' in the eighteenth century. Pierre had no difficulty returning an illicit book to its owner. Books carried ambivalent status rather than extant arcane ideas. The pseudo-priest Arnaud de Verniolles handled Bibles, Gospels, a calendar, and Ovid on the art of love.[28] Jacques Fournier, later the Avignon Pope Benedict XII, examined Arnaud in 1318 during the persecution of the Cathar heretics. He had no difficulty detecting a second clandestine identity behind illegal performance of the Mass: a narrative of homosexuality. The book is the labile form of latent heresy.

The earliest Buddhist texts were transmitted orally, only later committed to scripts in a variety of languages, such as Pali, Gāndhārī, and Sanskrit. Diverging texts led to arguments about which were canonical, and which were considered *buddhavacana* (the word of the Buddha). The earliest Buddhist schools, developing in India, accepted the Pāli Canon, also known as the *Tipiṭaka* ('three baskets').[29] From here later developed Theravāda Buddhism, dominant now in Sri Lanka and south Asia, including Myanmar and Thailand. However, this branch rejected the Mahāyāna *sūtra*s, which were accepted in China and Japan, leading to Mahāyāna Buddhism. Mahāyāna *sūtra*s warn against the charge that they are not word of the Buddha, vigorously defending their authenticity.

Violence also occurs across religions. Pope Gregory IX warned the European clergy in 1239 of the dangers of Jewish rivals to the Bible. Not content with the old law given to Moses and transliterated into Christian tradition, the Jews have another, oral, scripture, the Talmud or 'teaching'. The volume of this, Gregory states ominously, 'exceeds the text of the Bible'.[30] In June 1240, the Disputation of Paris, sometimes known as פריז משפט or the *Procès du Talmud,* took place at the court of King Louis IX of France. The Franciscan Nicholas Donin, a Jewish convert to Christianity, assembled passages from the Talmud, allegedly containing blasphemies against Christian doctrine, attacks on historical Christians, and obscene folklore. A man called Jesus was boiled in shit in hell for eternity; Adam copulated with all the animals in Eden before choosing Eve. The Talmud was defended by four Jewish rabbis. The Disputation originated in ignorance among the Catholic clergy that any Jewish writing existed apart from the contents of the Old Testament. Donin was previously associated with the Karaite Jews, and used the occasion to attack rabbinic tradition.[31] The outcome was that a huge number of Jewish texts were burned on 17 June 1242, numbering 24 wagon loads. The burning, which took place in the Place de Grève, was described by Meir ben Baruch, the Maharam of Rothenburg. His *kina*, or lamentation, *Shaali serufah baesh* ('Ask, you who were burned') is sung today by Ashkenazi Jews: 'My tears formed a river that reached to the Sinai desert and to the graves of Moses and Aaron. Is there another Torah to replace the Torah which you have taken from us?'[32] The book again is an incubus of humanity.

In 1034, the library of Avicenna in Isfahan was destroyed by Sultan Mas'ud I. Genoese mercenaries during the crusade of 1109 burned the library of Dar al-'ilm in Tripoli after the city's surrender to Baudouin, Count of Boulogne, first Christian king of Jerusalem. In 1193, the Nalanda university complex, the most renowned collection of Buddhist texts in the world at the time, was sacked by Turkic Muslims. In 1204, the Imperial Library of Constantinople was destroyed by knights of the Fourth Crusade, and its books burned. When Christian Constantinople fell for the last time in 1453, the Ottomans removed, sold, or destroyed, thousands of manuscripts. In 1499, the troops of Cardinal Cisneros ransacked the library of the Andalusian Moors at the madrasa in Granada, took the books to the Plaza Bib-Rambla, and burned them. When the Swiss scholar Gesner began searching the libraries of Italy and Germany for lost manuscripts, his motivation was the destruction of the library of Buda in Hungary by the Turks in 1526.[33]

So the litany goes on, Christian on Jew and Muslim, Muslim on Buddhist and Christian. This begins to explain the pathological reaction burnt books arouse. Umberto Eco's *Il nome della rosa* (1980) creates a fantasy library, designed like an impenetrable labyrinth, at the centre of which lies an unmentionable book, the lost second volume of Aristotle's *Poetics*, on comedy. Rather than let the book be found, the librarian sets fire to his own library, before the judgment of the inquisitor, none other than Bernard Gui himself. The abbey burned *per tre giorni e per tre notti* ('for three days and nights').[34] Books invoke mourning, as they provoke savagery. Daily news stories confirm it. In September 2004, in a fire at the Anna Amalia library in Weimar, 30,000 books were lost, another 40,000 damaged by smoke and water used by firefighters. Christina Weiss, Minister of Culture, made an elegiac press release: 'The literary memory of Germany has suffered terrible damage. A piece of the world's heritage has been lost for ever.'[35]

At the same time, the fire inspired acts of heroic retrieval. Firefighters and residents formed a human chain to save 120,000 books, including a 1534 Bible owned by Luther, and in another nice literary trope, the world's largest collection of copies of Goethe's *Faust* (a character well used to fire). Later, a copy of the first edition of Copernicus's *De revolutionibus orbium coelestium* (1543) was recovered from among the charred items. Human reverence is not the only factor in survival. Using a conservation technique which itself possesses powerful symbolic meaning, the damaged books were frozen in an effort to preserve them. In some circumstances fire itself can even keep a book alive. In a wonderful inversion of the processes of nature, the library of Herculanaeum, destroyed in the eruption of Vesuvius in 79 CE, is being newly investigated to see if the carbonized scrolls can be read by radiographic methods beyond the power of human eyesight.[36] Works by Epicurus, which without fire would have been dumped or disintegrated, have been kept intact by the extreme pyroclastic heat of the volcano. Their reappearance has the feeling of a miracle, as if the Alexandrian library could be resurrected and the known works of Aeschylus or Sophocles multiplied twentyfold.

Yet it is not only the book as a material object that is mourned. Other venerable artefacts of human culture, such as votive statues, wall paintings, or funeral urns, possess a similar aura of irreplaceable value and of the immanence of the human subject. Christina Weiss's word 'memory' provides a clue to the peculiar status of the book as text. The book is a vessel as well as an object. What gives the book a peculiar status as a human artefact is not either its material substance or its abstract contents alone, but the way in which it subtends a boundary between object and meaning, surface and depth, matter and spirit. A book is a liminal object. It extends both inwards and outwards at the same moment. The aura surrounding a physical book is conjured up by the way in which it offers the ultimate charisma of a meaning made flesh. A book promises physical access to something which is not physically there. It offers a bridge from the world to words, and hence also the mind that reads those words, even to consciousness itself. This is also what provokes the fantasy of power involved in its destruction, and the violent triumphalism that accompanies this. For the liminality of the book is also a source of ambiguity. Even though, in the book, a transaction between physical and mental universes appears to take place, the exact location of that transaction cannot be found. A book is a way through from one side to the other, but the sense that the route through can be apprehended or measured is entirely an illusion, at least in the current state of neural science. The book represents a conundrum, in the way that the brain of a human person represents a conundrum.

Ovid was exiled by the Emperor Augustus for *carmen et error* ('poetry and error'; it is Ovid's joke not the charge sheet) to Tomis, a remote village in what is now Romania, on the very edge of the civilized world. He knew that Augustus wanted the ban to apply to his books as well as his person, but instead he turned the idea of censorship upside-down. At the end of *Metamorphoses*, he declared his book was now his indelible afterlife, an out of body remnant of him.[37] In *Tristia*, he wrote to his wife in Rome that his writings were his *maiora monimenta*, the better part of him.[38] They gave him a 'second body' at home.[39] This conundrum is a source of fascination, but it is also disturbing. This is one reason why in earliest human societies, writing itself as a medium was considered to confer a mysterious power, and also to contain a mortal danger.

> He who my inscriptions and my foundation-stones shall conceal, shall hide, to the water shall lay, with fire shall burn, in dust shall cover, in a house underground (?), a place not seen for interpretation shall set, the name written shall erase, and his own name shall write.[40]

In Assyrian and Egyptian culture (as in others later), writing has been held to contain the spirit of the human person who is represented within it. Dealing with such magic required a special affinity with the sacred, sometimes left to priests. In modern societies, a residual power in the book, even when not apprehended in religious terms, remains. Almost all US presidents have sworn the oath of office while holding a book, although there is no requirement, and the book has not always been a Bible. This is enhanced by the way in which a book is more than the sum of the writing which it contains. A book is not just a collection of written signs. It is a physical object with a perceptible volume, density, and mass. In this way it resembles a human body, and like a human body it is organic, permeable, perishable—and combustible.

By occupying an interface between matter and mind yet failing to deliver in either sense what is promised, a book is capable of creating both desire and longing, fear and loathing, in equal measure. The actions of the Nazi students in 1933 are the most blatant realization imaginable of a hatred for the book as representative of ideas that are held to be so different as to be anathema. Yet they also witness to bibliophobia, in its root sense of a fear of the book, something uncomprehended or unavailable for full analysis. By burning books in gigantic pyres they make books a fetish. The fetish consists in the incomplete, perhaps unfinishable relation between the form of a book and its contents. The Nazi students fear books not only because they hate what they think they contain, but also because they do not know what they contain, or how they do it. The book is mysterious to them, and burning it one form of compensation for that mystery.

If at one level book-burnings are easy enough to read—tawdry, hysterical, and brutal as they are—at others they certainly are not. This applies with the more force when we consider the longer history of violence towards books in which the Nazi students incorporated themselves. The histories of loss and multiple heresy involved in the legends of the Alexandrian library suggest this in one way; Luther's burning of the Papal bulls in another. The Nazi students were not the first to recognize the iconic significance of Luther's actions. In 1817, on the three-hundredth anniversary of the posting of the 95 Theses, German students demonstrated at the Wartburg in Thuringia against the reactionary ideas in force in the German small states, in favour of a liberal, modern, and national state. As a marker for revolutionary sentiments, at a key moment in the rise of post-Napoleonic national consciousness, a printed pile was picked for a symbolic pyre.[41] Anti-nationalist and Jewish works joined a copy of the *Code Napoléon* in the flames. Luther offered straightforward precedent: a German patriot, folk hero, and radical ahead of his time, railing against forces of foreign, imperial, reactionary power.

What was the significance of Luther's action in 1520, however? Luther stood at a watershed. In the aftermath of the 95 Theses of October 1517 his fate was uncertain. For two years, a series of theological disputations and examinations determined his position. Up until then, the Luther affair was 'a German event'.[42] However, on 15 June 1520 a papal bull *Exsurge Domine* ('Arise, O Lord') set out his provisional excommunication.[43] If he did not recant within sixty days, Luther was a heretic. Luther determined to accept his destiny in the most dramatic manner, planning his incendiary gesture in advance.[44] He first wrote about it in a letter in July, five months before the event.[45] It was no secret: Elector Frederick the Wise was informed. A close confidant of Luther, Frederick's secretary, Georg Spalatin, told his master, as the execution of the plan approached, that it would take place in the pulpit of the castle church in Wittenberg.[46] Luther and Spalatin discussed shrouding the event in classical garb by imitating the ancient Roman practice of extinguishing torches in a formal condemnation.

As it happens, Luther abandoned the humanist touches and changed venue (Fig. 17). The new surroundings carried their own meaning. The humanist professor of Greek, Philipp Melanchthon, in a public notice in the city church, invited professors and students to the chapel of the Holy Cross, just outside the city's Elster Gate.[47] This was the location of the town's carrion pit. On 10 December 1520, at nine o'clock in the morning, the spectacle took place under the aegis of Johann Agricola. During the morning, Luther was still trying to obtain from the faculty of theology copies of the *Summa theologiae* of Thomas Aquinas, and Duns Scotus's commentary on the Sentences, to add to the fire. The theologians refused, so Agricola made do with copies of the canon law, a confessional manual by Angelo di Chivasso, and a few books by Luther's literary opponents, Jerome Emser and Johann Eck.[48] Bystanders added other volumes to the pyre. In a letter written a month later, to his monastic superior, Johannes von Staupitz, Luther reported his own appearance at the bonfire, 'trembling and praying'.[49] In a last dramatic flourish, as if on impulse, Luther lifted up a copy of the papal bull against him, *Exsurge Domine*, and threw it on the burning pile. Few there will have known what this last document on the fire was. If it is the burning of the papal bull that is now remembered, for Luther's audience the canon law was the true sensation.

Typically, Luther liked to present his action as improvisatory, but it was a staged improvisation. He gave a lecture justifying his action to his students the next day. Unusually, the lecture was delivered in the German vernacular, a gesture of defiant national opposition in itself.[50] The lecture survives only in reported form; its

Fig. 17. 'Luther burning books in 1520'; woodcut, Ludwig Rabus, *Historien des Heiligen Auserwählten Gottes Zeugen* (Straßburg, 1557)

effect, according to one very partial witness, was electric. Luther wished to be seen acting on the spur of the moment but also in the interests of justice. The burning was a circus show, but the moment of decision facing his audience was a point of no return. Luther told his students they faced a choice: this was no longer child's play. Pope Leo X had declared him an agent of error. Luther was prepared to risk his own earthly life in the interests of the only truth as he recognized it. His students faced the same stark alternative. The reporter of the lecture had no doubt: Luther was the angel of the living God foretold in Revelation 14: 6, tending the sheep of Christ while shepherds sleep.

By the end of the month, with that combination of theatre and media of which he had become a master, Luther brought out a pamphlet, *Why the Books of the Pope and his Disciples were Burn*ed *by Dr Martin Luther*, published in German and Latin.[51] It was a bravura performance, even by Luther's standards in this *annus mirabilis*, in which his three major Reformation tracts were published in less than six months. In the first sentence he brazenly declares that the books of the pope of Rome have been burned 'by my will, advice, and help'.[52] He lists five sensational reasons for his scandalous action. First, he claims apostolic authority: in the Acts of the Apostles, 19: 19, in a gathering of believers before St Paul at Ephesus, the early Christians themselves had brought their old books of pagan magic and burned them in public:

This piece of scripture was commonplace among early modern book-burners, since it suggested God is a book-burner himself. Editions of the Papal Index used it as a frontispiece into the eighteenth century. God encourages iconoclasm against idolaters or demons, it just depends who is on God's side. Denis Crouzet suggests a mental connection between image-burning and book-burning in sixteenth- and seventeenth-century France.[53] Eustache le Sueur painted the subject for Notre-Dame in Paris in 1649 (Fig. 18), vindicating Paul as true preacher just as false preaching is condemned. Luther, by calling the Pope a demon, endorses his own efforts as apostolic: [*sie*] *brachten die Bücher zusammen und verbrannten sie öffentlich*. In a more political turn, Luther distances himself from defiance of the present holder of the papal office, Leo X, or the Emperor Charles V, by stating that the current orders against his own writings result from bribery and corruption. Fifth, he finishes by asserting that he has not indulged in book-burning for its own sake, in a wilful display, but in response to actions of others. They have burned his books, now he is burning back.

The Lutheran book-burning has the opposite meaning from the one extracted four hundred years later by the students in 1933. While Luther appears to be a pre-emptive cleanser of literary sinfulness, he poses himself rather as a counter-insurgent, protecting truth against its violent official enemies. Luther places himself on the side of the persecuted rather than the persecutor. Like Paul and the early Christians, he burns books in defiance, as a dissident against the grain of a powerful enemy. It is not for nothing that he concludes with a motto from the greatest of all biblical saviours of lost causes and makers of spectacular revolutionary gestures, Samson: 'As they did to me, so have I done to them' (Judges 15: 11). To uphold God, he brings the temple down.

In turning the tables, Luther created a series of mirror images to reflect back on his oppressors. In a flagrant parody of the literary style of the bull, Luther extracted thirty errors from papal documents, mostly direct citations from canon law, to demonstrate the heresy of the pope. The tone of this combines righteous anger with savage irony. Burning the pope's books, and then announcing the action as sheer reasonableness, is the ultimate figurative statement of Luther's *gran rifiuto*. On a literal level, his act of burning re-enacts and reverses the process to which his own books have been submitted. Burning Luther's books had been a specific stipulation in the papal bull, confirmed in a papal circular in August 1520. All Luther's books and writings containing the errors were also condemned: they

Fig. 18. 'Holy fire'; Eustache Le Sueur, *St Paul Preaching at Ephesus*, oil on wood panel, 1649. Paris, Musées du Louvre

were not to be read, circulated, or preserved, but burned. In a twist, the papal command requires that the burning take place 'with ceremony'.[54] Two nuncios distributed the bull within Germany. Johann Eck took responsibility for Electoral Saxony and south Germany, Girolamo Aleandro for the north and west.[55] He delivered the bull to the emperor in the Netherlands, and negotiated with the secular arm to carry out its mandates. Not least of his undertakings was to initiate the authorities in the art of book-burning. He ordered the burning of any pamphlet supporting Luther and contrary to the Faith, of which a spate was expected; Ulrich von Hutten's *Vadiscus* was one of the texts which duly received his opprobrium.

Aleandro was a cultivated choice for destroyer. A future cardinal and Archbishop of Brindisi, he was a learned humanist, who had lodged at the house of Aldus Manutius with Erasmus. Former lecturer in Greek at the Sorbonne, he became Leo X's librarian at the Vatican. The image of librarian turned book-burner is an edifying irony. On 26 September, Aleandro arrived in Antwerp to meet Charles V. An edict from Antwerp signed two days later proclaimed that on finding any books by Luther or his followers, *hi omnes publico cremarentur igni* ('these should all be burned by public fire').[56] By the time Aleandro reported his proceedings with the emperor in a letter in October to Leo X after Charles's coronation in Aachen, the first burning had taken place. On 8 October, around 80 Lutheran books were burned in Louvain marketplace, in the presence of the theologians, who had been among the first to condemn Luther in 1519.[57] Oecolampadius wrote a report, taking his information from an eyewitness. Erasmus, resident in Louvain at the time, referred to the burnings in Louvain, Antwerp, and Ghent: 'soon all the books of Luther will be cooked'.[58] The lines of the battle of the books were now drawn. Erasmus' epigram was quoted by Louvain scholastics; it was easier to burn Luther's books than remove his ideas from people's hearts: *Facile est Lutherum eximere e bibliothecis; at non facile est illum eximere e pectoribus hominum.*[59]

Another burning soon took place in Liège, after a decree of condemnation was placed in public view on 17 October. In the meantime, Aleandro made the case to Frederick the Wise to turn Luther over to the emperor for trial, and burn all his books. Forcing the issue, Aleandro arranged further burnings in Cologne on 12 November and Mainz at the end of the month.[60] By now it was clear that burnings formed a propaganda campaign to endorse papal authority through public violence. At the same time, by encouraging crowds to attend the burnings as mass spectacle, Aleandro hoped to make them rituals of incorporation, by which the public would become complicit in the condemnation of the heretic. A public executioner performed the incinerations, suggesting a formal juridical sentence applied to books. The scale of the shows magnified, implying literary annihilation. Pageantry increased, with speeches of denunciation and sermons of malediction. Locations were selected for maximum visual power and mass enthusiasm.

Yet in Cologne, the fire was boycotted by the Archbishop and Chapter, and students took to attempting to rescue Luther's volumes from the flames. In Mainz, Aleandro was personally threatened, and the public executioner at first refused to carry out his task, since public opinion did not consider that Luther's books had been condemned. The burning had to be postponed to the next day.[61] An action devised by Aleandro to foster or coerce a spirit of public uniformity served instead to create an image of division. This was followed by a literature of complaint against the burnings, not only by religious sympathizers of Luther but also by humanists. Ulrich von Hutten wrote a poem, full of questions and quips, a 'Lament over the Lutheran Conflagration at Mainz'.[62] The humanist Wolfgang Capito reacted to events in Mainz with gloom; he warned Luther to calm things down.

If Luther responded in one direction by calling the burnings childish and stupid (*puerilis stultitiae*), in another he was planning a retaliation, a publicity stunt all of his own.[63] Luther's bonfire of 10 December, in turn, quickly became embroidered in the telling, by opponents and supporters. On one hand, the Bishop of Brandenburg fantasized that Elector Frederick had packed a ceremonial guard with horsemen and footsoldiers to accompany the pyromaniac monk into the city. On the other, the exuberant *German Requiem for the Burnt Bull and the Papal Books* declared that the action liberated the soul of the German people, even of the souls in purgatory.[64] By burning canon law, Luther released the shackles of the dead for ever. The new requiem was a song for joy.

The atmosphere of cultural revolution increased after Luther's appearance before the emperor at the Diet of Worms in April the following year.[65] In two days of examination, Luther articulated his defiance in more precise terms than ever, Charles V concluding that the monk was beyond the pale. The Diet also marked a turning point in the campaign against books. On 8 May an imperial edict was issued from Worms in German, Dutch, French, and Latin. This multilingual ban imposed a *Vernichtung* of Luther's writings: literally this means 'annihilation'. The terms of the ban were comprehensive: anyone is condemned who buys, sells, reads, keeps, transcribes, prints, or causes to be written or printed any book by Luther (*kauf, verkauf, lese, behalt, abschrieb, druck oder abschrieben oder drucken lasse*).[66] All offenders are put under *verdambnus*. The edict strains for a metaphor to put Luther's written remains out of sight, beyond existence, obliterating even a memory or intuition of them. A formal order is made for all his books, not only writings condemned in his examination but anything bearing any trace of his authorship, to be put to the flames: *mit dem feur zu verbrennen*. Yet fire is not enough. As if the ashes of the books might cause offence, the edict looks to liquidate them further, to waste them away entirely (*genzlichen abzethun*), or turn them into nothing (*zu vernichten*), to erase them or wipe them from the earth (*zu verdilgen*). However, the terms of the abuse draw attention to its failure. The authorities could not burn Luther, he kept getting away; even his books seemed incombustible.

The firestorms began in earnest. On 13 July the edict of Worms was proclaimed in Antwerp in the Grote Markt in front of magistrates. A vast crowd gathered, buyers and sellers, farmers from the country up for Saturday market. Aleandro, in a triumphant letter to the emperor, reported every window crammed with people, *con grande et tacita attentione* ('rapt in huge and silent attention').[67] The elements of a mass religious rite in place, the bonfire begins, four hundred books by Luther (three hundred from booksellers, the rest from private individuals). Antwerp's mounting book trade, at the crossroads of Europe, made it the centre of the Lutheran market outside Germany.[68] Aleandro calls the burning timely as thousands of Luther's books have been printed locally. In another letter the next day to Joannes Vigilius, he calls the burning 'beautiful'. The same month, on St James's day, 25 July, another grand burning took place in Ghent. The feast day of a saint is significant: it suggests a festival aspect to the spectacle, and protection of the cult.

In view of the size of the crowd—tens of thousands of people—it is likely that the location was the Vrijdagmarkt, directly adjacent to Bij St Jacobs. The Vrijdagmarkt was the main political focus of the city and the place of public execution. To emphasise the theatricality of the event, and its religious seriousness, there was a long procession, a public promulgation of the bull, and a solemn sermon. For the burning, a giant platform was constructed; here, according to Aleandro, 'più di ccc^to [i.e. 300] libri di Luther' were combusted, some printed locally, some in Germany.[69]

Aleandro is at pains to describe the burning in festive terms. Even the emperor is said to have joined in the jollification: 'et Caesar passovi appresso et fece un bel riso et festa di tal cosa' ('the emperor passed close by and smiled broadly at the festive proceedings'). As with any bonfire and procession, the occasion was a communal endorsement and recuperation. By initiating the crowd in violence, the bonfire was designed to bind people to a collective will. The works of heresy are desecrated, brought down from their pedestal, and shattered in public view. Yet the act of incorporation was not entirely successful. In several cases, Lutheran students indulged in impromptu rescues of forbidden books. Sometimes they substituted scrap paper for precious Lutheran volumes; sometimes, in eagerly repeated stories, they swapped anti-Lutheran books for the originals. There is an element of counter-ritual here: a carnival overturning of the measures of suppression, and an element of magical reversal in the burning of the books of the oppressor.[70] In the process, the books of Luther are turned into relics.

Further burnings took place in Bruges in August, and also in 's-Hertogenbosch, Utrecht, Deventer, Trier, and elsewhere; there were at least three more bonfires in Antwerp in 1522. From the Empire, the practice spread: formal burnings of Luther's books took place in 1521 in Paris and in London, in the churchyard of St Paul's Cathedral. The event was reported by the Venetian ambassador. King Henry VIII was sick with ague, but John Fisher, Bishop of Rochester, gave a two-hour sermon denouncing Luther.[71] Cardinal Wolsey's participation emphasizes the element of pageantry and display:

> The Cardinal was under a canopy, an unusual thing, and after the oration gave the blessing, whereupon all went out of the church processionally, into the churchyard, where there was a lofty platform, which we ascended in great confusion.[72]

On 27 September 1521, the Inquisition at Valencia was congratulated on having detected and burnt 'Lutheran' books. In Italy it might have been the same story, except Lutheran books were hard to find. A reprint of a Lutheran work was printed in Venice in 1518, the only book published in Italy with Luther's name on the title-page before the twentieth century. Other early copies condemned in

Fig. 19. 'Triumph of Humanism'; Hans Holbein the Younger, *Hercules Germanicus*, woodcut, c. 1522. Zürich, Zentralbibliothek

Venice, Bologna, Naples, Turin, and Milan were imports. The main conduit for heretical material was Venice, but while a Lutheran book was found in 1520, the Venetian Inquisition only began burning books after 1547, in Piazza San Marco and the Rialto.[73] Padre Marin, father inquisitor, claimed to have burned 'an infinite number' of books, but was presumably exaggerating.

Felipe Fernández-Armesto has argued that censorship is equal on both sides in the Reformation, citing Luther's escapade outside the Wittenberg town gate as evidence.[74] This is even-handed history at its most insidious. Luther's bonfire party, scandalous and politically explosive as it was, hardly counts as censorship at all: he did not have the power, never mind the will, to suppress the dissemination of all the copies of his own bull of excommunication, never mind all the books of canon law in Europe. Yet it speaks volumes about the volatile status of the book within the culture of the time. In around 1522, Hans Holbein the Younger produced a broadsheet woodcut (Fig. 19) depicting Luther as *Hercules Germanicus*, a German demi-god. He bears Hercules's club and his lion-skin, and a rope through his nose holds the pope by the throat. Beneath his feet he tramples the intellectual élite of the scholastic Middle Ages: Aristotle, Peter Lombard, Aquinas, Duns Scotus, Ockham, Richard Holcot, and Nicholas of Lyra.[75]

The image presents Luther as a demoniac force, eagerly destroying the great bookmen of the past. Ironically, it survives only in one copy, almost by accident within a manuscript book in Zürich, itself perhaps the victim of censorship. Yet it is just as easy to see Luther as a bibliophile as a bibliophobe. He was an avid reader, not least of the authors he here treads on. He was also the most prolific producer of books of his time. Bibliophobia is not always readily distinguishable from bibliophilia. Aleandro, after all, was a literary humanist and man of culture. The people who energetically propagate literature will also often be the same people who are at pains to curtail it when produced from the wrong hands. Yet it is not enough to attribute the violence shown towards books by the avidly bookish simply to an antipathy to a contrary viewpoint. The battle of the books represented within Holbein's woodcut not only demonstrates the controversial status of ideas on the eve of the Reformation, it declares the status of the book as the most powerful and public engine of cultural controversy. The book is perceived as a weapon and is thus an object of fear as well as awe.

8

The Bondage of the Book

C'est une étrange chose que l'écriture: 'Writing is a strange invention', says Claude Lévi-Strauss in *Tristes tropiques* (1955):[1]

> The only phenomenon with which writing has always been concomitant is the creation of cities and empires, that is, the integration of large numbers of individuals into a political system, and their grading into castes or classes. Such at any rate, is the typical pattern of development to be observed from Egypt to China, at the time when writing first emerged; it seems to have favoured the exploitation of human beings rather than their enlightenment. This exploitation...made it possible to assemble thousands of workers and force them to carry out exhausting tasks [...]. My hypothesis, if correct, would oblige us to recognise that the primary function of written communication is to facilitate slavery.[2]

It is a bleak statement that the origin of writing lies in enslavement ('l'asservissement'). Lévi-Strauss formulates writing as an oppressive equation of subject and object. In Leviticus, 'letters are things in themselves', Mary Douglas states.[3] Law and writing are commensurate: 'As it is written in the law of Moses'. So says scripture, citing itself.[4] Writing encodes inclusion and exclusion: what lies within the law, and without. 'Before the Law stands a doorkeeper', Kafka writes in his impenetrable parable of the same name, 'Before the Law'.[5] In *Der Proceß*, the priest tells K that his story forms part of the writings (*die Schriften*) that precede the law: but there is no law outside the law, and thus no writing to preface writing.[6] Writing becomes the law. Written law embodies the system of exchange from archaic times, Marcel Mauss says, and 'no gift is free'.[7] 'L'homme est né libre, et partout il est dans les fers.'[8] Man is born free, Rousseau writes in *The Social Contract*, and everywhere is in chains. Perhaps in its simplest sense, writing is an estrangement of original nature. In his chapter on slavery ('De l'esclavage'), Rousseau makes writing one of the conventions by which natural freedom is 'alienated'. Rejecting the arguments of Grotius and Hobbes, Rousseau asserts that slavery in natural terms is absurd: 'il ne signifie rien'; it exists only by means of being written in law.[9]

Lévi-Strauss, grandson of a Brussels rabbi, sailed to Brazil in 1935 an ex-schoolteacher: for four years, until the outbreak of war, he undertook the only ethnographic fieldwork of his career. For this period, between bouts of university work, he travelled in what he described later as 'un monde perdu'—a lost world, about the size of France, three-quarters unexplored, frequented by small groups of native nomads. For several months he settled among the Nambikwara, a people wiped out over the previous two decades since the building of the telegraph line in 1915: from ten or twenty thousand down to only a thousand or two. Their material culture was sparse, leading to Lévi-Strauss calling them 'survivors from the Stone Age'.[10] They used weapons, but no canoes; the women carried possessions in baskets, making objects to measure, by hand, as need arose.

For Lévi-Strauss, the Nambikwara constitute a society before culture. They sleep on the ground, hunt, and bathe; most of their time is spent preparing food. The Nambikwara language, which Lévi-Strauss endeavours to learn, has several dialects. However, they have no writing. One day, the apprentice anthropologist conducts an experiment, what he calls a *leçon d'écriture*. By this, the Nambikwara encounter writing for the first time; yet it is also a 'writing lesson' in a general sense, by teaching a truth *about* writing. Lévi-Strauss hands out sheets of paper and pencils. At first, the Nambikwara are mystified; but after a while, Lévi-Strauss discovers they 'are all busy drawing wavy, horizontal lines' (p. 296). He wonders what the lines signify: for they are not drawing a particular image or sign. Rather, they imitate the *action* of writing: they do what they think he is doing. The chief, however, does something additional, leading Lévi-Strauss to assume he has 'grasped the purpose of writing'. He asks for a writing pad, and if Lévi-Strauss asks him for something, he does not speak, but writes in the pad. This *writing* consists of yet more wavy lines. Even so, the chief, on completing a line, will inspect it carefully and exchange pieces of paper with Lévi-Strauss, as if they are sharing information, ticking one script off from another. In this counterfeit of textual exchange, is the chief deluded? No, Lévi-Strauss concludes: for in the transaction, while no meaning is shared, it appears to the other Nambikwara *as if it has*. The chief has persuaded them that 'he was in alliance with the white man and shared his secrets' (p. 296).

From this moment on, something appears to have gone wrong in the relation between the anthropologist and his subjects. There is an uncomfortable atmosphere between them. Lévi-Strauss interpolates a comic interlude made up of embarrassing and sometimes frightening episodes. As a result, he ends up lost in the middle of nowhere; his mule runs off; he loses his pistol and his camera. Alarmed, he abandons himself to the situation and to a feeling of savage anxiety. He is rescued unexpectedly by two of the Nambikwara who go out looking for him, finding him and his equipment without any trouble. Yet Lévi-Strauss is 'perturbed by this stupid incident'. He cannot sleep. In his attempt to make sense of things, he concludes that writing has interfered in their relationship, and not in a good way. The Nambikwara have come to an understanding of the function of writing, not as an intellectual system, but as a symbolic order of power.

This, Lévi-Strauss concludes, is the originary purpose of writing. It is not a question of acquiring knowledge, or of remembering or understanding, but of increasing the power of one person or group at the expense of others. He goes on to speculate how this has happened in every civilization over time. For writing exists as an institution even in societies where a large majority of inhabitants have never learned to handle it. Lévi-Strauss recalls travelling in the Chittagong hills in eastern Pakistan, where the inhabitants are almost all illiterate, but where there will always be one scribe who acts on behalf of the whole community. The villagers cannot read, but they all 'know about writing' (p. 298): they know its power, and that the scribe is the agent of power, who often combines this function with being the moneylender. He has a hold over them.

What is the relationship between writing, violence, and slavery? Slavery is as old as civilization. The Code of Hammurabi (1760 BCE) and the Hebrew Bible describe it as long-established practice. Early Egyptian and Chinese slavery are based on public labour. Slavery is associated with conquest and ethnicity: the word derives from a term for the Slavic peoples. This relates to a question of language: *barbaroi* is the Greek term for those who know no Greek, which makes them babble like 'bar-bar-ians', to some extent beyond the law. Citizenship in Athens connected at some level to literacy.[11] A small number of slaves was literate, employed as scribes by lawyers and teachers. Plato mentions a slave reading and copying an important text.[12] This continued in republican Rome; Cicero constantly promises to free Tiro his scribe, but there is too much work for him to do. Cicero loves him, clearly, and writes to him often: *Cura, cura te, mi Tiro.*[13] He asks after his health and orders him not to sail before recovering. This relationship is unusual.[14] The demand for education of aristocratic boys led to importation of large numbers of specialist Greek slaves. Cato the Elder owned Chilon, a *grammatistes* who 'taught many boys'.[15] Cato taught his own son himself, but Plutarch says it was uncommon.[16] By the late republic slavery was structural to the Roman economy. A quarter of the inhabitants of Rome itself was enslaved. Yet this is dwarfed by the figures for the empire outside Italy, in which permanent war made slavery ubiquitous.

When Cristoforo Colombo saw birds (perhaps northern curlews) off the Bahamas in October 1492, he understood the 'writing lesson' of Lévi-Strauss instinctively. For Columbus, taking possession is principally 'the performance of a set of linguistic acts', says Greenblatt.[17] Columbus notarized everything: he declared ownership of places and things, witnessed them, archived them. In 1452, *Dum diversas* ('Until different'), a papal bull of Nicholas V, legitimized a trade in slaves as result of war. This consigned Saracens, pagans, and unbelievers to hereditary bondage. In 1513, the *Requerimiento*, drafted by the jurist Juan López de Palacios Rubios, ordained in law the divine right of Castile to subjugate and exploit the territories of the New World. This outlined a short history of creation for the benefit of indigenous peoples, catechizing the nature of Adam and Eve, and how God made St Peter ruler of all the people on earth. Dominion is owed to him by native Americans as much as by anyone. By virtue of this document being announced on arrival, the new lands (whether Tierra Firme or any islands) are declared perpetually Spanish, and their inhabitants Christians and vassals, by their own consent. The only glitch is that natives do not speak Spanish, nor can they read the *Requerimiento*. Hence a subclause: obey, or you, your wives and children are slaves to be sold.[18]

Illiteracy performs enslavement, literally. This is reinforced by the curious coincidence that 1492 was also the final year of *Reconquista*, in which the last part of the Nasrid kingdom of Islamic Iberia fell at Granada. The first archbishop in the city, Hernando de Talavera, gave the Muslim population a 'choice': convert to Christianity or leave. Meanwhile he commissioned a Spanish–Arabic dictionary to help dismantle 'cursed Mahoma'.[19] The Reyes Católicos, Ferdinand and Isabella, conflated crusade and colonization, in which all pagans are the same. Talmudic and Qur'anic books burned in autos-da-fé in Spain, and when conquistadores moved into Mexico, the same happened to Mayan texts, and in Peru to the Inca. In historic triangulation, censorship adapted new rules for books. Ferdinand and Isabella established prior censorship in July 1502.[20] Booksellers and printers needed licences, provided by a variety of officials in Granada, Valladolid, Toledo, Burgos, and Salamanca. When Charles V retired in 1556, processes against heretical books redoubled, in Spain, and throughout its American Empire.[21]

The fantasy of empowerment through literacy also works in opposing ways, to justify conquest. Marching into Mexico City in 1520, soldiers of Hernán Cortés turned to each other, reports Bernal Díaz, saying they felt like characters out of a romance like *Amadís de Gaula*.[22] Colonizers project a fantasy of the willing enslavement of their victims.[23] Lévi-Strauss's meditation on the power of writing could not be more pertinent to early colonization, on both sides of the negotiation of literacy. Jean de Léry's *Histoire d'un voyage faict en la terre du Brésil*, published in 1578 after he spent two months among the Tupinamba in Brazil, describes their language to record a specific *lack* of writing: they know nothing of letters, holy or profane, and use no characters by which to signify.[24] Father Bernabé Cobo (1582–1657), the Jesuit missionary, arrived in South America in 1596, returning to Europe only sporadically, for instance in 1632 with a sample of quinine. He lived successively in the Antilles, in Venezuela, and in Peru, writing two ethnographic studies, *Historia general de las Indias* (1653), an encyclopaedic account of flora and fauna with descriptions of pre-Columbian peoples and their buildings; and *Historia de la fundación de Lima* (left in manuscript in 1639). Accounting for Inca religion and customs, he comments on writing as a system of knowledge: 'Since the Indians did not have any form of writing, there are many things about them that cannot be determined', he says.[25] That is a classic statement of the problem of history without written records, making study of preliterate societies inherently obscure. But Cobo also insinuates that the Peruvians did not understand things about themselves.

A dozen years after *Tristes tropiques*, Derrida turned his story into an archetype of a theory of writing in *De la grammatologie*. 'L'histoire est très belle', he acknowledges; indeed, a 'parable' of writing in the Western world.[26] Lévi-Strauss extracts from his 'incident' with the Nambikwara a series of principles for the institution of writing. It is hierarchical, mediating power relations; it functions in an economics of capitalization (the chief employs it in exchange of gifts); it performs rites akin to a quasi-religious cult. The incident lays bare, too, a dynamic in anthropology. Derrida notices that travelogue takes the form of 'les confessions'. Lévi-Strauss confides terrible witness to a reader of primal violation ('la pénétration'). The anthropologist enters an Amazon paradise, infecting innocent humanity by way of the serpent of writing. Innocence lost is never regained. Not only is writing the original carrier of violence in society, it repeats it in a scientific discourse of analysis. Modernity transgresses the primitive world twice over.

Derrida calls Lévi-Strauss's trope 'rousseauiste', and ostentatiously demonstrates its origins in Rousseau's *Essai sur les origines des langues* (1781). Here Derrida finds his famous phrase, 'this dangerous supplement': Rousseau makes writing supplementary to speech, while the social contract is traduced by violence. Rousseau's chapter on writing ('De l'écriture') describes written language as degradation: 'It becomes more regular and less passionate. It substitutes ideas for feelings. It no longer speaks to the heart but to reason.'[27] A generation before the discovery of the Rosetta Stone, Rousseau constructs a typology of writing. The Mexicans, in pictograms, and the Egyptians, use 'figures allégoriques', representing not sounds, but 'objects themselves'. In this, they used 'passionate language'. Chinese writing then 'truly represents sounds and speaks to the eyes' (p. 17). A third system, the alphabet, 'our' way of writing, breaks the speaking voice into constituent parts. It does this not so as to 'represent speech, but to analyse it'. He concludes, against all prevailing wisdom about writing's origins: 'The art of writing does not at all depend upon that of speaking'. Writing fixes language, and thus alters it:

> It changes not the words but the spirit, substituting exactitude for expressiveness. Feelings are expressed in speaking, ideas in writing.

The verb he uses is *suppléer*: to 'stand in' for, or 'make up for', something lacking.

Derrida's sensational reading of Lévi-Strauss via Rousseau relies not on *Tristes tropiques* and the *Essai* alone: he minutely analyses the major anthropological corpus of Lévi-Strauss, and in Rousseau traverses not only classic political treatises (*Discours sur l'inégalité* (1754) and *Du contrat social* (1762)); but also literary works such as *La Nouvelle Héloïse* (1761) and *Émile: ou de l'éducation* (1762). Above all, he quotes that extraordinary experiment in autobiography known, after Augustine, as *Les Confessions de Jean-Jacques Rousseau*, published posthumously in 1782. In *Confessions*, Rousseau describes how his mother died nine days after he was born: 'I cost my mother her life, and my birth was the first of my misfortunes.'[28] More startling still is his first memory of consciousness: 'I had feelings before I had thoughts', he says; he has no idea what he did to the age of five or six; he cannot remember when he first learned to read.

However, he can remember the first book that he read through, *un roman* ('story') left him by his mother: from this first moment of reading he dates his 'first uninterrupted consciousness of himself'. Rousseau associates reading with consciousness and experience, calling it a 'dangerous method'. Reading in the *Confessions* is a primal sexual scene, just before the narrative where he is spanked by his nanny and first feels sexual arousal. Flogging, of course, has been associated with education since the Bible.[29] Quintilian attacked its use in the schoolroom.[30] Erasmus reasoned that reading and writing work better without it.[31] Locke's *Some Thoughts Concerning Education* argued that flogging arouses passion rather than reason, and teaches mental enslavement.[32] Nonetheless, the association of violence with teaching the elements, including to black slaves and white naval cadets, reaches deep inside the fiction of the nineteenth century, such as Harriet Beecher Stowe's *Uncle Tom's Cabin* (1852) and Melville's *White-Jacket* (1850).[33] Melville sees an erotic connection; Thomas Hughes completes the metaphorical picture by having Arthur in *Tom Brown's Schooldays* (1857) thrashed with one book for losing another. So powerful is the work of memory in *Confessions* that spanking and arousal are synonymous. Rousseau needs an idea of corporal punishment to feel desire, and imagines pain if he meets a young woman reminding him of his nanny. He finds in this an abject shame and diminution of subjectivity. But it also defines his self for the rest of his life. Agency, desire, and violence go together, and reading is at the heart of this.

What do we make of this complex of ideas? Derrida uses Lévi-Strauss and Rousseau to construct an antitype. The 'writing lesson', he says, sets up a necessary connection of writing and violence. Writing degrades purity of feeling via economic corruption. It creates authority and colonization, by which the identity of the native innocent is subsumed within that of the civilized master. Lévi-Strauss explicitly notes: 'the primary function of written communication is to facilitate slavery.' What justifies, Derrida asks, the assumption that writing is 'l'asservissement'? He might as easily have said 'la libération'. The problem, Derrida concludes, lies in a model of priority, writing coming after spoken language in time. What Rousseau appeals to, is an original presence, away from which writing falls: and this is the reason he associates it with violence and his own sexuality.

Derrida's theory of the 'metaphysics of presence' gave rise to a deconstructive literary and philosophical practice beyond my scope. But it leaves open a question whether he is right not to associate writing with violence. Perhaps we could change emphasis to understand the structures in writing which lead Rousseau to his observation. A connection between literacy and slavery is very old. Not content with using illiteracy as a prerogative for bondage, the Spanish censored and revised the pictographic literature of the overseas world to enforce state security.[34] Literacy is used over again in baptism of conquered natives as Christians. The practice was borrowed by the Protestant Dutch when Admiral Jacob van Neck navigated the Indonesian archipelago in the 1590s. On the way, an inhabitant of Madagascar is converted and given a new name of Laurens. An accompanying text states that conversion takes place by 'listening to a sermon'.[35]

The violence of writing is more originary than Derrida cares to confess. Between 1740 and 1834, Alabama, Georgia, Louisiana, Mississippi, North and South Carolina, and Virginia all passed anti-literacy laws for slaves.[36] The 1739 amendment to the Negro Act in South Carolina forbade slaves from being taught to read and write, punishable by a fine of £100 and a six-month jail term. In Virginia, assembly 'of negroes for the purpose of instruction in reading or writing, or in the night time for any purpose, shall be unlawful'.[37] What does this show if not a 'primary function of written communication is to facilitate slavery'? The violent slave-catcher Ridgeway in Colson Whitehead's novel *The Underground Railroad* nails it: 'Get them off the plantation and they learned to read, it was a disease.'[38] We reach for analysis in recoil to the shock at such symptoms. Does writing enslave because it is an *enclosure*, chaining knowledge in a container (script, book, archive)? Is its embodiment of forms of *technology* (clay tablet, codex, manuscript, printed book, e-book), a means of mechanizing the techniques of power? Does the fact that the exchange is a hermetic act conceal the structures of bondage, so that text becomes fetish, or keeping of secrets an archival ritual? The book, we realise, is a form of *symbolic order* as well as cultural capital.[39] The promise that it contains of freedom, imagination, and mystery, are its poisoned chalice in return. The book's capacity for liberation is the verso to the rectilinear logic of servitude. 'That worst sort, an abolitionist with a printing press', snaps Ridgeway.[40]

It is not just a matter of the violence of prohibition on literate slaves, but the reluctance of a master race to give up sentimental attachment to the privileges of imaginative freedom. John Adams described the passages on slavery in Jefferson's *Notes on the State of Virginia* (1783) as 'worth Diamonds'.[41] For a slave-owner, they are indeed relatively enlightened: Jefferson envisaged emancipation for slaves, and education at the public expense, 'according to their geniuses'.[42] Refined, rational, *rousseauiste* that he is to his core, however, there is something missing in his account of black culture in Virginia. They have 'no poetry'. He says this even having read Phillis Wheatley's *Poems on Various Subjects, Religious and Moral* (1773); but for him, the first published African-American book of poetry is mere 'religion'. Washington admired them more, but then he was no critic. Washington's largesse had even deeper foundations; at his death there were 317 slaves at Mount Vernon, compared to a mere 130 at Monticello on Jefferson's, not including the children of Sally Hemings. Jefferson's deafness here contrasts with his lament at the loss of 'the records of literature' among native American peoples.[43] He deeply mourns the passing of the language of the Mattapony, and the Powhatan, so that we can never now know the character of those people in the way we do northern Europeans. It is a gaping blank in Jefferson not to see a discrepancy. The size of the hole in his mind is revealed by how he broaches it in a letter to Adams thirty-five years later: while still waiting for emancipation, he bluffly demurs: 'What a bedlamite is man!'[44]

The book's symbolic order is shadowed in the fantastic chapter 'Cetology' in *Moby-Dick*. Cetology is a branch of zoology designed to classify whales. Yet the whole idea of the whale, above all in Melville's master-narrative of whales, defies classification. Leviathan is a figure for what cannot be explained (as in Milton's *Paradise Lost*).[45] The narrator embarks on an impossible task, hitting on an idea of comparing a whale to (guess what) a book. Indeed, he classifies the books by size: the FOLIO whale (the *Sperm Whale*); the OCTAVO whale (the *Grampus*); and the DUODECIMO (the *Porpoise*).[46] Yet the whale, even as a metaphor for the book, cannot contain the whale. 'Leviathanism', after several pages of Linnaean patience, exhausts the writer. Like Cologne Cathedral, it remains unfinished. 'God keep me from ever completing anything', Melville laments, before resuming his book's relentless passage towards Ahab's terrifying destiny.[47]

Writing and violence is not a constant equation. Book-burnings, or other forms of mutilation, come and go with time. They emerge at moments of pressure and attention. The Library of Alexandria became an object of dispute as the codex took over the world of the Middle East, aiding new forms of religious zeal and conquest, Muslim and Christian. Luther's immolation of the books of canon law took place, and the burning of his own books in turn, in the second generation after Gutenberg's machine. Rousseau's essay on writing and language emerged at a time when mass publication of books using automatic technologies led to renewed efforts of control. Adam Smith regarded copyright as an extention of property. Yet copyright only emerged in the eighteenth century out of a system of royal and ecclesiastical privileges, undergoing fraught negotiation.[48] *La Nouvelle Héloïse* joined the Index Librorum Prohibitorum; *Émile* was banned on publication in Paris and Geneva, then publicly burned in 1762.

'The education of Rousseau is the only means to help civil society flourish', Kant wrote in the 1760s; for Rousseau's doctrine alone allowed for equality.[49] By 1785, Kant's categorical imperative appeared to confirm that slavery denies the status of persons as ends in themselves.[50] Yet his own writing on black Africans barely recognizes their human nature.[51] Hegel's 1807 chapter on the 'master–slave dialectic' is not optimistic. If slavery is a political aberration, Hegel found it difficult to eliminate in theoretical terms. His famous chapter on the 'master–slave dialectic' describes a 'trial by death' between 'being for itself' and 'being for another'.[52] The terminology of *Herrschaft und Knechtschaft* needs a little exegesis.[53] Hegel trained at the Protestant seminary in Tübingen, where Luther was at his fingertips. Luther's *Von der Freiheit eines Christenmenschen* ('On the Freedom of a Christian') is one of his three golden pamphlets of 1520, as well as perhaps his most famous work written in German. It begins with two apparently contradictory statements juxtaposed as inalienable truths: *Eyn Christen mensch ist eyn freyer herr* and *Eyn Christen mensch ist eyn dienstpar knecht*.[54] 'A Christian is a free lord over all things and subject to no one | A Christian is a bound servant of all things and subject to everyone.'[55] To explain how both are true, Luther cites scripture (1 Corinthians 9: 19) and then medieval theological commonplace. Mankind is twofold in nature, spiritual and bodily (*geystlicher und leyplicher*); and both inner (*ynnerlich*) and outward (*eußerlich*). In the diversity of nature, human beings are thus caught in an inevitable and violent contradiction (*stracks widdernander seyn*).

While Hegel's master-slave dialectic is usually taken to mean a struggle between two different persons caught in a social and political bind, in which only one can overcome, Susanne Hermann-Sinai uses the Lutheran context to support an alternative reading. Here, freedom and unfreedom are caught in 'internal struggle of self-consciousness'.[56] Perhaps, indeed, the two are not incompatible. Hegel read about Toussaint's slave revolt in Haiti in the German periodical *Minerva*.[57] He could see, if only ambiguously, like the Marquis de Condorcet or Georges Danton at the National Convention in 1793, how inner freedom requires universalization in abolition of slavery.[58] Certainly, Hegel sees it as inevitable corollary that self-consciousness is independent *and* dependent: it exists 'only as something recognized'.[59] In the first edition of Kant's *Critique of Pure Reason* (1781), the object of inner sense is the soul, while the object of outer sense is the body. The 'influence of external things', whether a priori or as 'appearances', is subject to 'inner sense'.[60] In Hegel, the making of self into 'other' must be subject to sublation or *Aufhebung*. Such an action is ambiguous, Hegel says, because it involves a return to itself, or a receiving back of itself, even as it declares its otherness. *Aufhebung*, indeed, always has apparently contradictory implications of preserving *and* changing. Consciousness exists 'within itself', and 'for itself', and yet also 'outside itself' (§184).

Is this the terrifying secret of writing? It enslaves as it liberates, in that it makes the inside an outside, occluding a relationship between inner and outer. A slave conscious of slavery is victim to a violent conflict of ambiguity.[61] No wonder Derrida exclaims Hegel to be *dernier philosophe du livre et premier penseur de l'écriture*.[62] Hegel's work may be 'reread as a meditation on writing', he says.[63] Writing, Hegel declares in *The Phenomenology of Spirit*, is 'expression of the inner' as 'externality'.[64] Later, he ascribes to this the alienation of culture. In the estrangement of self-consciousness is inflicted 'external violence of the unchained elements'.[65] Fifty years before Darwin, Jacques Lacan notes, Hegel provided the 'ultimate theory of the proper function of aggressivity' in human beings.[66] A conflict of master and bondman creates a crisis of subjective and objective to be traced all the way from Stoicism to Christianity to modern universal state. Could we even say that freedom and bondage are *sublated* in writing? This is the logic of *aggressivité* inherent in writing from Sargon to Facebook, in a promise of communication that at one and the same time (indeed, in the same action) threatens publication with cancellation or suppression. In writing, narcissism meets the fear of nothingness; or to borrow from Lacan's reading of Freud, Eros merges with death instinct, like Dante's kiss.[67] Indeed, the mirror-like process of mimesis enacts ambiguity. In *Glas*, Derrida's hypertextual homage to Hegel, the sheets of the *Phenomenology* are as it were torn into strips, alongside Jean Genet's dismembered Rembrandt. The dialectic of 'maîtrise et esclavage' makes the death penalty a manifestation of liberty, putting natural life into play as 'la condition d'une subjectivité libre'.[68]

Books are inherently ambivalent. Augustine the bibliophobe, and refuter of heresy, is Augustine the bibliolater, reading and writing on gargantuan scale. Augustine writes against Donatists, Manicheans, Pelagians, academics, pagans, Jerome, even against himself in his *Retractions*.[69] But he never stops writing. In 1529, Erasmus placed the *Retractions* first in his edition of Augustine, in front of *Confessions*. It is an emblematic motif of the contradictions of writing. Luther, too, writes against Johannes Eck and Jacobus Latomus, then Erasmus and even Huldrych Zwingli. He writes *with* Augustine on justification by faith, against him on the unity of the church. Luther contradicts Luther on the same page. Yet he, too, keeps writing. Both Augustine and Luther wrote at tumultuous times not only for the church, but for the book. Augustine discusses in a letter the advantages of a codex. The twenty-two *quaterniones* of *The City of God* may readily be bound in two codices, he says, one of ten 'books' and one of twelve; alternatively in five smaller volumes.[70] Luther collaborated with the printing house of Melchior Lotter to transform the appearance of his printed works and their capacity to distribute his ideas. He first came across the firm in Leipzig, where they printed his Leipzig Debate in 1519.[71] In 1521, he persuaded Melchior the Younger to move to Wittenberg with capital and type founts for a new press; Lucas Cranach provided the paper from his mill. In September 1522 this resulted in Luther's New Testament.[72] Freedom and bondage are never far apart here, most of all in Luther's 1525 homage to Augustine in opposition to Erasmus on the free spirit of writing, *De servo arbitrio*. Heresy indeed is derived from the Greek word αἵρεσις meaning 'choice': the Latin word *arbitrium* is both a virtual synonym and the philosophical shorthand for a free will.

The jumble of books in the head of Menocchio the Italian miller creates a one-man heresy. This makes him feel 'my opinions came out of my head'.[73] Ginzburg retraces this operation of heretical networks. The Italian Qur'an conjures up a god of nature separate from Christ. The *Fioretto della Bibbia* allows him to imagine an original chaos before the world began. Mandeville's travels, in the form of *Il cavalier*

Zuanne de Mandevila, opens up alternative belief-systems, like Montaigne's contemporary essay 'Des cannibales'. Reading Léry on Brazil led Montaigne to declare that values are relative: 'qu'il n'y a rien de barbare et de sauvage en cette nation'.[74] Westerners call the Brazilian nation 'barbarous' by comparing Christianity; there is nothing inherently savage about it. Lévi Strauss's concept of *La pensée sauvage* refers similarly not to barbarous peoples but to an untamed state of the human mind.[75] It is something like this that Menocchio finds in Mandeville. In the margins of fantastic tales of India and China, or Pigmies and two-headed men, he discovers comparative religion. Heaven and hell exist only on earth; the soul is mortal. Idols and images on the island of Chana are worshipped not because God is made man, but because valiant people are loved by a god of nature.[76] Boccaccio's tale of the three rings from the first day of the *Decameron* turns in Menocchio's head into an allegory of toleration for different points of view.[77] In Ginzburg's account, these are fragments from a whole. It is the Inquisitor who puts them together with inexorable Christian logic. The Inquisitor finds heresy *ad libitum*, giving each a name: faith in idols denies the incarnation; three rings reject the Trinity.

Books lie at the heart of all anxieties in Lévi-Strauss's 'writing lesson', raising questions about identity. A person without books is without name or rights. Simultaneously, a book opens a window into a person's head. Such access is at some level baffling, and always dangerous. Writing is thus an index of rebellion and freedom as well as heresy or enslavement. No image of writing signifies more strongly than the author at the stake.

Jan Hus was burned at the Council of Constance (Fig. 20) in 1415. A huge paper hat was put on his head bearing the word *Haeresiarcha* (the leader of heresy). Asked to recant, he refused, saying, 'In the truth of the gospel which I have written, taught, and preached, I am ready to die'.[78] His books, as is shown graphically in this early chronicle, were burned with his body. In this way Hus prefigured Heine's famous epigram. As history turned to farce by way of tragedy, Heine's books were burned in ironic travesty in 1933. Luther said it was progress for men to burn books in preference to flesh. It is a cliché, repeated for example by Freud in 1933. Yet Luther and Freud both knew such a judgement was optimistic. Rather than emerging into a more liberal world, the sixteenth century turned out to be as violent as any in history before the twentieth. If wars of religion concerned what was in people's heads, they were also about how ideas got there, or could be prised out. Religious interiority became subject to political scrutiny, without knowing where it was. How do I know what is going on in your head? Writing acted as a faultline, as it was the best physical evidence for the identification of the *ynnerlich*. Just as significant as writings produced by the accused was the presence of suspicious books in their homes. Readers, as much as writers, needed surveillance.

Crouzet describes 'une mélancolie violente' evident in the French Wars of Religion.[79] Many early trials of Lutherans in France turned on ownership of

Fig. 20. 'Burning of Jan Hus'; Diebold Lauber, MS of the Emperor Sigismund, *c*.1450

books.[80] The Paris Index expanded lists of prohibited items.[81] Indictments in the archives of the Parlement de Paris show ruthless search for heretical books (or legal or rhetorical just in case).[82] In 1542, anyone with a copy of Calvin's *Institutes* had to hand it over in twenty-four hours.[83] Political trials, for sedition or treason, followed. Yet this raised more ambiguity: does ownership of a book entail readership? Does reading entail assent? Is it enough for an accused to show intention to read? The standard defence was that reading took place to uncover heresy or sedition. Censors appointed by church or government fell under suspicion: nobody was purer than pure. First, it had to be decided what books were foul. Here, honour is due to the Index, printed in Rome in 1559 and 1564, imitated over all Catholic Europe.[84] Once again, print is not incidental. The 'index' in a benign sense was the industry's favoured device.[85] With new technology, a malign version was inevitable. The Index advanced until the century's end, every book examined in detail. It was an impossible project, expurgating paragraph by paragraph, line by line. Research in the archives of the Office of Propaganda in the Vatican has shown it less systematic than unimaginably tedious.[86] In 1597, the inquisitor in Padua burned 29 sacks of books.[87] Display created symbolic meaning beyond practical effects. The body of writing *in toto* was subject to the single master-reader of the Church. In any case, printed books were not accurately reproduced: prone to error, each edition, or single copy, was *unicum* to a degree. Nobody could be secure of the precise contents of every copy in practice.

An example is the fate of some of Petrarch's sonnets. *Rime* 136-8 came to be known as 'Babylon Sonnets' because of their attack on the Avignon papacy, such as in RVF 138:

> Fontana di dolore, albergo d'ira,
> scola d'errori et templo d'eresia,
> gia Roma or Babilonia falsa et ria,
> per cui tanto si piange et si sospira.[88]

The reference to Avignon as Babylon changed meaning after Luther's other 1520 tract *The Babylonian Captivity of the Church*, where the pope is a 'whore of Babylon'. Now a 'school of errors' or 'temple of heresy' (in Petrarch's words)— written in defence of Rome against its rival—was interpreted instead as potential attack on Rome. Pope Paul IV's Index of 1559 prohibited three offending sonnets in Petrarch, permitting the rest to be read. Existing manuscripts show interference.[89] Printed copies are treated more roughly. In a book now in the Beinecke Library (Fig. 21), printed in Venice in 1552, the text of the sonnets is inked out so that they cannot be read, in retrospective compliance with the Index; the commentary is left untouched. In another example printed in Venice in 1549, in the University of Pennsylvania Library, a sonnet is expurgated using a brush with thick ink, the commentary in lighter ink. Paper was then pasted over the sonnet text to hide it;

Fig. 21. 'A censored Petrarch'; *Il Petrarca* (Venice: Domenico Giglio, 1552), fos. 214ᵛ–215ʳ, Yale University, Beinecke Library

in a final act of suppression, paper was glued over the fore-edge, so the book could not be opened at these pages.[90] A later reader has freed the imprisoned sonnets from their covering paper, as happened to many censored copies. Meanwhile, in printed editions post-Index, Babylon sonnets were omitted pre-publication. In a 1595 Venice edition in the Beinecke, a printer has inserted *Qui mancano tre sonetti*, then left two blank pages. A reader has taken the opportunity to add them back, handwritten, dated 1596.[91]

The machinery of expurgation was low-tech and old-fashioned, relying on pen and glue. In an edition of the minor works of Jerome from Basel in 1525, the text of the doctor of the church is left intact, but the name of the editor, Erasmus, appeared in the Index and so has been blotted out later in whitewash paint. This includes eliminating him from the running heads at the top of the page.[92] The preface is obliterated entirely, four leaves cut out with a razor and the remainder whitewashed out. The technique is meticulous but at another level meaningless: whole sentences are left with the single name *Erasmi* removed. A nightmare of total censorship was thus exactly that: a bad dream. There is instead an element of public display, its only purpose to show that violence has been done. Four hundred years later, in response to the Russian army's similar practice of blacking out words, sentences, or paragraphs in newspapers, Freud first developed the concept of censorship within psychoanalysis. In a letter to Wilhelm Fliess in 1897, he calls this *Russian censorship*: 'Words, whole clauses, and sentences, are blacked out so that the rest becomes unintelligible.'[93] This *Zensur*, Freud says in *Die Traumdeutung*, 'ruthlessly deletes whatever it disapproves of, so that what remains becomes quite disconnected'.[94] It is easier, perhaps more salutary, to forget than it is to remember.

Lacan called this censor 'the other of language', a superego synonymous with the name-of-the-father, or 'the symbolic function which, from the dawn of history, has identified his person with the figure of the law'.[95] Father: author: lawgiver: the gender of *logos* is hardly accidental. It is 'the symbol of an authority at once legislative and punitive'.[96] Perhaps writing could be identified as a socio-linguistic 'symbolic order' that binds the unconscious to public or communal property. Indeed, Lacan acknowledged the reference to Hegel in his use of the term 'symbolic'. 'The unconscious is structured like a language' (*comme un langage*), he said famously.[97] He names this in a 1957 essay 'the agency of the letter': the 'material support that concrete discourse borrows from language'.[98] While it is clear that Lacan refers to the semiotic function in language rather than its material form, he recognizes the symbolic as a form of physical fetishism, to the extent of making an ironic aside to his love of fragmentary letters in a Garamond typeface.[99] Indeed, this is one of the reasons Lacan rejects a model of communicative expression as explanation of the system of writing (p. 161). Writing's representative function goes beyond mime or 'dumb-show'. It is the realm of fantasy itself.

Writing in this sense is a figure for what Hegel calls *Anerkennung*, or 'recognition': to become conscious of an external object, as something distinct from the self, requires the reflexivity of *self*-consciousness. One consciousness exists as 'Being for itself', which is mediated through another consciousness ('Being for another').[100] One is lord and the other is slave. Recognition (or 'acknowledgement'—*Anerkennung*) comes about only through a process of mediation. The existence of writing is one physical form taken by this mediatory reflexivity. The master-slave dialectic is a double reflexivity (Being-for-itself *and* Being-for-another) and constitutes, Hegel says, 'a trial unto death'. Writing, we could say, causes the self to see the other not as essence; rather, 'in the *other* it sees *its own self*'.[101] In that sense, writing is political precisely because it is mimetic. It is a dialectic of enslavement combined with empowerment. In the hinge between one face of the page and the other, identity and property, as well as law, become inscribed. Writing exposes self-consciousness to an external violence. Books and violence thus come together in the most primal of fears and longings.

Law is enacted by the reading process, in a coercive transaction between the lines, or under wraps. A relationship of reader to text is contingent and imaginatively oblique. The material form of language creates similes for readers to fantasize meaning. A book is in parts, it wears a jacket: a language of meaning is a tangled web ('text', after all is a metaphor).[102] On the verso of the unnumbered inserted flyleaf of *Glas*, Derrida remarks: 'Il rejoue la mimesis et l'arbitraire de la signature dans un accouplement déchaîné'. His uncoupling of mimesis and signifier is passionate and unbound. 'Our chains rattle, even as we are complaining of them', Coleridge wrote in 1817 of his own writing.[103] Since the invention of the codex it became common to figure meaning, or mind, in terms of a binary or bond between contents and covers. Who has used a laptop without wondering about the peculiar way in which it folds in two, enclosing patterns of reflection between keyboard and screen, fingers and eyes, mouse and hand, in referential equilibrium?

René Girard in *La violence et le sacré* (1972) argued religious violence is always founded on mimetic desire.[104] We borrow desires from others. Far from autonomous, desire for an object is provoked by that of another for the same object. This means the exchange of subject and object is not direct: there is an indirect triangle of subject, mimesis, and object. Girard's theory is criticized for its monolithic view of the sacred, not least by Emmanuel Lévinas.[105] Girard, he felt, gave an incomplete view not only of holiness, but also of the history of violence, not least in the Holocaust (in which, although he is silent on the subject, most of his family died). Yet if applied not to a fundamental theory of the place of sacrifice in world religions, but to writing as the subject of suffering, Girard's concentration on the *mimetic* may not be misplaced. Derrida remarked that imitation is central to the idea of language in Rousseau, and equally to his sense of the origin of art:

> the essence of art is mimesis. Imitation redoubles presence, adds itself to it by supplementing it.[106]

The book provides not only a place where mimesis is observed, but a principle of mimesis in its very form. The book is the metaphor in which metaphor is revealed; it is the originary site of proscription. Derrida makes play with Rousseau's fascination with the idea of holy scripture and his concentration on taboo.[107] But writing is a place of death: indeed, writing in Rousseau's *Confessions* is a figure for death itself. At the end of book 8, Rousseau declares how a terminus of writing anticipates dying: 'My confessions are not intended to appear during my lifetime, nor that of those they may disagreeably affect. Were I master of my own destiny, and that of the book I am now writing, it should never be made public until after my death, and theirs'.[108] Proust worries constantly at the end of *Time Regained* that he will die before he finishes writing.[109] In *Malone Dies*, Malone writes: 'I shall soon be quite dead at last, etc. Wrong again. That is not what I said, I could swear to it. That is what I wrote'.[110] Which does Beckett mean?

As books burn, the spectacle offered, perhaps, is an opportunity to absolve the mind of ambiguous imaginings. The ashes of a book promise finitude, both an end to hated ideas and meanings, and closure for the problem of meaning they open up. To the censor, they offer the hope that offending ideas might disappear; to the secular state, watching in attendance, they offer the equally welcome promise that society might unify. Aleandro and Charles V smiled in the smoking air of Antwerp with some agreement of emotion. Yet the smell of burnt paper and vellum left another residue. The book, in the moment of destruction, left behind unsettling reminder that it is a material object.

Yet it was not, we have seen, only organic. The mystery or meaning within could not be eradicated. Mimesis brings a logic of freedom in the verso page of bondage. It confers on books seemingly sacral status, and it is no coincidence that sacred books invoke the most violent antipathies. 'Violence is by nature instrumental', writes Hannah Arendt: it is aimed at something.[111] The Nazis derived perverted joy in destroying Jewish books, in the knowledge that Judaism is a religion of the book. Yet books evaded them, as well as suffered violence. In the ghettos of Europe heroic efforts preserved written memory despite all efforts to suffocate it.[112] Dina Abramowicz acted as librarian in Vilnius as Jews awaited deportation to Poland or stoning and shooting in Lithuania. 'Who will come to read books here?' she asked: yet the library lent 100,000 volumes in a year. The status of books within Semitic beliefs, Judaism, Christianity, and Islam, as also in religions such as Hinduism, Buddhism, and Sikhism, always involves a burden. Investment in written words celebrates a mystery of meaning, as marks on the page encrypt a secret. The stormtroopers incinerated books to erase a culture, like the Romans burning the Temple in Jerusalem. But the holy of holies remained intact. The holy is precisely not material.

III

SACRED TEXT

Mais même dans ce sens-là, le seul que je puisse comprendre, je ne serais pas tenté d'être bibliophile. Je sais trop pour cela combien les choses sont poreuses à l'esprit et s'en imbibent

Marcel Proust, *Le Temps retrouvé* (1927)

9
The Mystery of Arabic Script

The *mihrab* at the Mezquita or Great Mosque of Córdoba is approached from the north, and stands on the far side of the building, perpendicular to the entrance. Following the style established in the Umayyad Caliphate, the Mezquita has an enclosed courtyard (now the Patio de los Naranjos) and a covered arcaded hypostyle hall for prayer, supported by 856 columns made of jasper, onyx, marble, granite, and porphyry. The site of course has been disfigured by Christians—the Emperor Charles V declared that in building the Capilla Real, 'You have destroyed something unique to make something commonplace'.[1] Gothic verticalism traduced the horizontal architectonics, although aesthetic vandalism protected the Mosque from outright destruction. It is thus possible to traverse one side to the other keeping the Christian aberrations to the east. The vestibule built by Sultan Abd-al-Rahman III (945 CE), leads to the constructions of Abd-al-Rahman I (785 CE) and Abd-al-Rahman II (833 CE).[2] A first impression is dazzled by complex forces (Fig. 22). A canopy of arches, many of them doubled, often in distinctive horseshoe shape, surmounts the forest of short columns that ties the building together. Together, the arches create a sense both of infinity, and yet also of a precise mathematical universe. It is a perception which cannot be conveyed by a photograph: for as the body moves, so the geometry moves with it, a straight line transforming into a diagonal, or vice versa, so that the columns dance as the mind adjusts to space in time.

The *mihrab* itself was built by Al-Hakam II (961 CE). Fourteen new cross-aisles were built, almost doubling the building in size, and moving the *qibla* wall further south. Even so, not until a further rebuilding to the east did the intricate tesseration of pilasters become complete.[3] Seen from a distance the *mihrab* is a miracle of light (Fig. 23). While the foreground of the building (amidst the columns and arches) is a magnificent penumbra, entirely roofed in—today with low-level electric lighting but originally illuminated only by 356 oil lamps—the *mihrab* was designed to allow in the full effect of distant sunlight suffused from behind by windows in the ceiling, a dazzling shimmer of gold.

The architecture of this part of the mosque was the work of a craftsman specially brought in from Constantinople, along with a vast supply of raw materials needed for his work.[4] The overall design, and the effects of lighting, were borrowed from the Great Umayyad Mosque of Damascus, the model for building throughout the Arab world for two hundred years after its construction.[5] There

Fig. 22. 'Praying arches'; the Mezquita in Córdoba, photograph by the author

Fig. 23. 'The sense of the holy'; the *mihrab* at Córdoba, photograph by the author

were four *mihrab*s in the mosque at Damascus, one of the most celebrated being that 'of the Companions': it became known as the 'pearl' (*al-durra*). The symbolism of the pearl was enhanced by a distinctive use of the architectural ornament of the conch or scallop shell. This, too, is a feature repeated at Córdoba. A verbal motif of light is thus mixed with its physical manifestation. At Damascus, great golden chains were used for hanging lamps in the Great Mosque: creating 'an association between actual illumination of the building and the iconographic allusions to radiance in its decoration'.[6] At Córdoba, this blaze of light was further reflected from the elaborate and expensive use of gold mosaic to surround the *mihrab*.[7] Light was more than a metaphor for spiritual illumination: on Fridays, the caliph led the prayers as directed by Islamic law, his body framed in the show of light.

The *mihrab* expresses something of the paradoxical status of the mosque. 'Wherever you pray, that place is a mosque (*masjid*)', the Prophet Muhammad stated.[8] While for practical reasons this has come to mean a communal building designed for prayer, it is prayer (or literally in Arabic *sajda* 'prostration') that makes a mosque, not the other way round.[9] The prophet defined not a building, only a direction for prayer, at one point Jerusalem. Now, the faithful, wherever they may be, should now turn their faces toward 'the sacred place of worship' (*al-masjid al-ḥarām*).[10] This sacred place is the Ka'ba in Mecca. In Medina, Muhammad built a house, now one of the most venerated places in Islam.[11] It has been repeatedly enlarged and restored, so that it is hard to know its original appearance: it may have had a central open courtyard with a colonnaded roofed structure around it made of mud (adobe).[12] Strictly, however, a mosque does not need a roof, or even enclosing walls. It is defined instead by an orientation, the *qibla*, which is usually signified by a wall to give it physical formation, although the *qibla* is not a physical thing but a concept. The function of the *mihrab*, then, is to be a physical mark for the *qibla*. Whereas the *qibla* is a concept, the *mihrab* is a place, if a minimal one.

According to the early Islamic historian al-Waqidi (*c.*740–823 CE), the first mosque to make an architectural feature of the *mihrab* was at Medina.[13] Here, it was said, the Prophet planted his lance to indicate where people should pray.[14] The characteristic form of the niche—perhaps derived from Coptic building practice—spread from Medina throughout the Arab world. The word *mihrab* originally had a non-religious meaning and simply denoted a special room in a house; a throne room in a palace, for example. Niches were used in the ancient world for statues of the gods in pagan temples; for the Torah in synagogues; later, for images of the saints in Christian churches. However, a niche is by its nature only a metaphorical room; and the key point about this 'room' in Islam is that it is always empty. As Robert Hillenbrand comments, the 'willed austerity' of Muhammad's example and practice was never entirely left behind, however multiform mosque buildings became, and however elaborate the patterns of architecture.[15] The *mihrab* at Córdoba is a case in point. It is not so much a niche as the seeming entrance to a palace. The great horseshoe arch suggests a space behind it which is much smaller in fact than it appears. It is surrounded by mosaics, and above that, by a giant inscription, on two levels, one of blue letters on gold, and a larger one above, in reverse, gold letters on blue. Within the niche there is an architectural space of sudden height, leading to a roof made in elaborate design with tiny portholes of light.

Nevertheless, the essential feature of this *mihrab*, as of others, is its emptiness. At the core of this is a beautiful form of abstractness or resistance to a physical idea of presence. The *mihrab* suggests the mystery within without foreclosing it, or even representing it. Something similar has been identified in what has been called the first work of Islamic architecture—the Dome of the Rock in Jerusalem (late 7th c. CE). Modelled on Byzantine buildings in Syria and Palestine, it shares with them the use of coloured marble columns and piers, and wall decorations also made of marble plaques, often incorporating mosaics in which thousands of tesserae of glass and stone are set closely together.[16] A building of eight sides is surmounted by a high wooden dome, the lead roof of which is plated with gold. This dome spans the internal central space above the rock supported by twelve stone circles in groups of three, each group separated by a heavy pier made of masonry. Doors open at the four points of the compass. Inside there is a lavish system of decoration, including a display of mosaics even more magnificent than on the exterior. These consist of zoomorphic patterns of trees, plants, fruits, and jewels. There is no narrative; indeed, no human forms at all. Right at the top of the decoration, just below the ceiling, at the top of the arcade, is a narrow line of inscription in Arabic from the Qur'an in gold on a blue ground. It totals 240 m in length.[17]

An outright ban on human figuration is often said to be one of the oldest features of Sunni Islam, but this is a Western misconception. Idolatry in the form of physical figures of false gods—*awthān* (Q 22: 30; 29: 17, 25) and *aṣnām* (Q 6: 74; 7: 138; 14: 35; 21: 57; 26: 71)—is rejected in the Qur'an.[18] However, the Qur'an contains many narratives of people. *Tamāthīl* ('likenesses') in one context (Q 21: 52) seems to be a synonym of 'idols', but in another (Q 34: 13), it appears in a list of desirable objects made for Solomon by the jinn. The Qur'an does not ban figuration, rather it does without it. There is nothing *like* God, so God cannot be represented.[19] He is worshipped directly without human mediation. Over time an absence of figuration hardened into law, but what is just as interesting is what happens instead, in place of figuration. Byzantine art long used stylized versions of vegetal and floral motifs as a way of setting off or framing larger themes; such artists when employed in early Muslim buildings made what was subsidiary in Christian art into the central object.[20] In the Umayyad Mosque at Damascus this decoration included some landscapes—including one large panel showing a great river with fabulous colonnaded pavilions running along the bank, with smaller landing sites for boats, the whole scene shaded by giant trees. This may suggest the paradise promised in the Qur'an for true believers. Still, there are no human figures. In other parts of the mosaic, the vegetal patterns take over entirely, transformed into an art of sheer geometry and abstraction. At the heart of these are placed, as at the Dome of the Rock, inscriptions from the Qur'an. This foreshadows what Sheila Blair describes as the dominant theme in Islamic culture as it developed over the next fourteen hundred years: writing itself.[21]

The opening of Sūra 96 of the Qur'an (Iqra' ('Read/ Recite') or al-'Alaq: 'The Blood-Clot') is generally reckoned to contain the first words revealed by God to the Prophet Muhammad:

In the Name of God, the Merciful, the Compassionate,
Recite: In the name of the Lord who created,
created man of a blood-clot.
Recite: And thy Lord is the Most Generous,
who taught by the Pen,
taught man that which he did not know.[22]

Sometimes these words are interpreted as meaning that writing was new to Arabia in the time of the Prophet; sometimes that mankind is able to learn from writing what otherwise would be unknowable. Whichever interpretation prevails, the importance of writing is confirmed throughout the Qur'an: Sūra 68 (al-Qalam), declares 'By the Pen, and what they inscribe.' The word for 'pen', *qalam*, meant either a reed pen (from Greek, *kalamos*) or a shaft of light: in either case, later commentators agreed, the pen was the first thing created by God, so that he could write down the things to come. In Sūra 50 (al-Qaf), it is said: 'two noble angels sit on man's shoulders recording his every action and thought. The one on the right notes down good deeds, the one on the left evil ones' (Q 50: 17–18). On judgement day, according to Sūra 69 (al-Haqqa), every man's deed will be accounted in the Book of Reckoning (Q 69: 18–19).

Arabic was the language of revelation. From early times, its script was held in the highest regard, as the shape which gave form to its contents. Old Arabic poetry before the Qur'an was already regarded as the highest expression of art. In general poems were composed to be recited in public, with the *qaṣīda* or 'ode' as the verse-form most esteemed of all. Such poems were memorized for oral performance. Nevertheless, however Sūra 96 is to be interpreted, writing in Arabia went back several centuries before Muhammad, with examples in classical Arabic as early as the fourth century CE in Syria, and other dialects several centuries before that. While classical Arabic has twenty-eight distinctive sounds or phonemes, the *abjad* used for its writing has only eighteen letter-forms or graphemes. The same grapheme is used for as many as five different sounds. So: *bā'*, *tā'*, *ṯā'*, *nūn,* and *yāʾ* are all represented originally by the same shape. Whereas many other languages use two forms of writing (a *monumental* form in which each letter is separate, and a *cursive* ('handwritten') in which they are connected together in a more or less continuous flow), Arabic only has a cursive form. Within this, though, individual letters change their shape according to the position within a word. The same letter can have four different forms: one where it stands alone; one where it begins a word (initial); another when it ends one (final); and another again when it is in the middle of a word (medial). There are no majuscule and minuscule case forms.

Like all Semitic languages, Arabic is based on a system of roots, in which usually three (sometimes four) consonants ('radicals') connote general concepts. Around the radical a series of related concepts groups, in ever-widening pattern. Thus, the combination *k-t-b* is a root conveying 'writing'; from here derive cognates, such as *kātib* ('writer' or 'scribe'), *kitāb* ('book'), *kutubī* ('bookseller'), *kuttāb* ('school'), and *maktab* ('place of writing', 'office').[23] The verb 'to write' is *kataba*; *mukātaba* is 'a letter', such as I might write to you or you to me; but also equally other forms of writing, such as a 'contract', or 'manumission of slavery'). *Mukātab* denotes the person written to. Thus the root and the grammatical form of the Arabic language define virtually every word in the lexicon. Sometimes only context will determine what is the meaning between identical forms of the root *k-t-b*: for example, *kataba* ('he wrote') versus *kutiba* ('it was written').

Perhaps as a result, Arabic has a natural tendency to abstract profusion and also to an alignment of form and content (or at least, the metaphorical illusion of such). In Arabic, the first letter of the *abjad*, written as a tall vertical stroke, is *alif* ('aleph'). It is also the most common letter in Arabic, often compared metaphorically, especially by mystics, to a standing person refusing to prostrate. Blair comments how an individual scribe will make play with these endless repetitions of the same stroke, like soldiers on a string.[24] While in Greek, philosophers have tended to define language according to its spoken form, so that language in essence is one person speaking to another, in Arabic it is just as idiomatic to think of thought as instinctively written in form. The world is the mind of God written out in front of us, not the creation of a God who speaks.

It is hardly surprising, then, that calligraphy is also the basic art form of Islam. Arabic script showed some early developments to accommodate holy writing. On the Dome of the Rock, the earliest dated evidence for the writing down of the Qur'an, diacritics are already used to distinguish different sounds with the same grapheme: *bāʾ* has a short stroke under the letter; *tāʾ* two strokes above; *t̲āʾ* three strokes above; *nūn* one stroke above; and *yāʾ* two strokes below. In this way the *bismillah* (the invocation to God) and the *shahada* (the profession of faith), along with several quotations from the Qur'an, are run on from each other in a continuous visual sequence beginning counterclockwise.

Another early development was a new format of manuscript. Most manuscripts of the period, such as Christian Bibles, were written in a 'vertical' format (that is, when a page is taller than it is wide). This was also the format used in other Islamic books, but rarely (for two centuries or so) for the Qur'an. Instead, a horizontal format was chosen. This made the Qur'an instantly distinguishable from other holy books, which either used 'vertical' pages, or (like the Jewish Torah) were written as a scroll.[25] Thousands of such manuscripts and fragments survive, from very large examples for public reading in a mosque, to tiny devotional copies. Some were on parchment using reed pens. The horizontal lines are highly regular, and a careful and stately script was developed. The writing resembles in that way a public inscription rather than the quick everyday style in evidence in secular circumstances. In the Qur'an letter shapes are repeated in patterns which acquire a distinctive aesthetic; even spaces are carefully regulated. An especially lavish example (Fig. 24) is the Amajur Qur'an originally given in 876 CE to the city of Tyre and long kept in a storehouse in the courtyard of the Great Mosque of Damascus. It is now scattered around the world, with a majority of surviving leaves in the Museum of Turkish and Islamic Art in Istanbul. Like this double folio from the Ashmolean Museum in Oxford, each page of the manuscript contained just three lines of script. No gold is used, so that its decoration lies rather in its meticulous geometry: the space between letters is the same as that between words. The vertical line along which the text begins is so regular as to be almost tangible.[26] Yet there are no diacritical marks and vocalization is minimal: so that the text is almost useless to someone who does not know it by heart.

The result is that the 77,000 words of the Qur'an are spread out across thirty volumes, each one comprising 200 folios. It has been estimated this required the skins of more than 300 sheep.[27] While this makes the Amajur MS an object of exceptional size and expense, ornamentation of other kinds is common. A tenth-century CE Qur'an in Harvard University Art Museums is written in gold and silver on a parchment dyed in blue, in imitation of the mosaic lettering found in buildings.

Decoration also marked the divisions between parts of the text. While the earliest manuscripts of the Qur'an may not always mark out verses from each other, or provide any headings for the individual suras, such practices quickly developed. In time, circles or teardrops used for this purpose might be replaced by medallions of increasing size. In the ninth century CE horizontal decorative bands were used to introduce each *sūra*. A different colour of ink and size of font could be used to show that this part of the text is not sacred. Such textual divisions could also incorporate vegetal and leaf-like forms, similar to the decorations found on buildings. A frontispiece to a ninth- or tenth-century Qur'an now in the Chester Beatty Library, Dublin, has a highly geometric pattern in gold. While parchment leaves were often kept loose in boxes, tooled leather bindings, such as

Fig. 24. 'Geometrical script'; fragment of Amajur MS, Kufic script, ink and colour on parchment, 9th c. CE. Oxford, Ashmolean Museum, EA 1996.53

those in the library of the Great Mosque of Kairouan in Tunisia, survive from the ninth-century.

Two developments, one technological and the other artistic, mark the beginnings of the golden age of the arts of the Islamic book. Chinese papermaking first travelled into Islamic lands in the eighth century CE.[28] Although the Qur'an often continued to be copied on parchment, because of its precious and conservative associations, paper was a more flexible medium for calligraphic arts and also cheaper, so encouraging more widespread experimentation.[29] Secondly, around 900 CE, Ibn Muqla, secretary and vizier at the Abbasid court in Baghdad, invented proportional handwriting.[30] He calculated a length for *alif*, the first letter of the abjad, based on a precise number of dots formed by the nib of a pen on paper. From this he elaborated a formula for the size of all the other letters. The result was a script known as *muḥaqqaq* (made in conformity with the *ḥaqq* or 'truth'): a script that is accurate, but also thereby just so, or ideal. Handwriting was now rounded rather than the angular scripts of early times.[31]

The most famous example of the result of this writing revolution (*c.*1000 CE) is the Qur'an of Ibn al-Bawwab ('the son of the doorman'). A 'doorman' was a salaried position in a library, paid about the same as the librarian.[32] It was said a manuscript by Ibn Muqla was copied by Ibn al-Bawwab in such a way as to be indistinguishable from his model's. His style was adopted in Fatimid Egypt, and Salah al-Din later sent one of his volumes as a gift to Damascus.[33] Only one complete Qur'an by him (Fig. 25) survives: a small volume (just 17.5 cm × 13.5 cm), each page with fifteen lines of round script.[34] The letters, exceptionally even in thickness, are in brown ink, sometimes with blue and gold. Headings for suras and other textual divisions use further colours (white, gold, and red) although always with an austere sense of harmony and lucidity. It is both simple and ornamented. Yet every aspect of artistic style in this masterpiece flows as if in sympathy with the formation of the letters itself. This is not so much an art of writing,

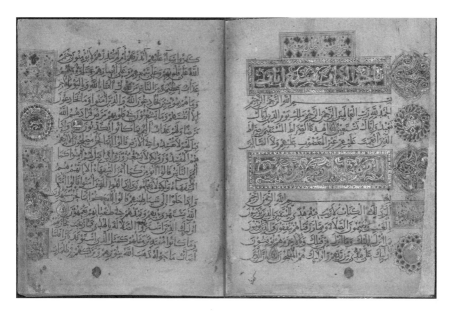

Fig. 25. 'Calligraphy as art'; Ibn al-Bawwab Qur'an, *naskh* and *rayḥān* script, ink and gold on paper, 1000 CE (391 AH). Chester Beatty Library, MS 1431

as writing transformed into a new art form. The letters of the abjad connote geometric wonder.

Baghdad, seat of the Abbasid caliphate, became the centre of the finest calligraphy, in a proliferation of round scripts codified by Yaqut al-Mustasimi as the Six Pens. Hülagü, grandson of Genghis Khan, sieged Baghdad in 1258, sacking its great library, assuming the title 'Il Khan' (or 'lesser khan').[35] Yet calligraphic art bloomed in the Ilkhanate, a southwestern corner of the Mongol Empire. The sultan Ghāzān converted to Sunni Islam in 1295, and the Ilkhanids eventually ruled over Iraq, the Caucasus, part of what is now Turkey, and all of Iran. Examples of Baghdadi work from this period show the limits of the possible. Paper is made from cellulose pulp of a variety of plants, suspended in water, captured on a wire screen, and then dried into flexible sheets. A Qur'an produced in Baghdad in c.1301–7 (701–7 AH), perhaps begun for Ghāzān, has very large bifolios (50 cm × 35 cm).[36] Each page is rubbed to the smoothest possible surface, offering almost no resistance to the nib. It was copied by Aḥmad al-Suhrawardī using five lines of black *muḥaqqaq* script. The text is then framed by a magnificent polychrome illumination painted by another artist, employing a vivid range of floral and vegetal motifs.[37] Another Baghdad Qur'an, perhaps by the same scribe, is twice the size; to lift the paper when wet, Blair writes, represented a Herculean task: there are a thousand bifolios.[38]

This was commissioned in 1306 by Ghāzān's successor, Sultan Öljaytü, raised as a Buddhist, baptized as a Christian in 1291 (his name taken from Pope Nicholas IV), then a convert to Sunni Islam with his brother in 1295. A mega-scale thirty-volume (*juz'*) manuscript was copied for Öljaytü at Hamadān in 1313 after he turned Shī'ite, and includes a Shī'ite prayer; it was designed for public reading in a mosque.[39] The calligrapher, 'Abdallāh ibn Muhammad ibn Mahmūd al-Hamadāni, wrote in gold, outlined in black, marked with blue diacritics.[40] He was also the illuminator, creating *sūra* titles in white on a blue ground with a gold decoration; in the opening pages, there are star-polygons, along with rectangular panels in an 'infinite' pattern. His artwork is sparing in its use of gold strapwork, with a vivid use of blue; the silhouette style is called by James 'almost ethereal'.[41] A third Qur'an commissioned by Öljaytü for his mausoleum, was finished in Mosul in 1311 (710 A H). The calligrapher is not known from any other work. Each volume has an illuminated frontispiece, showing dazzling arrays of polygons like stars on the page, using red and blue.[42] The script (Fig. 26) is in gold *muḥaqqaq*, with black diacritics, inside a rectangular frame, with repeated geometric patterns in an artistic style of extraordinary mathematical complexity and beauty.

Öljaytü's Hamadān imperial Qur'an was bequeathed in 1326 to an emir in Cairo, and so survived intact, escaping the invasion of Iraq by Timūr (Marlowe's Tamburlaine).[43] It then provided a model for copyists and illuminators under the Mamlūk sultanate.[44] Between 1250 and 1517 the Mamlūks came to rule over Egypt, Syria, and the Hijaz, ending the westward advance of the Mongols, re-establishing the Abbasid caliphate in Cairo, and acquiring sovereignty over the holy places of Mecca and Medina.[45] The Mamlūk sultans set about a programme of construction of vast building projects, often combining a madrasa and a mausoleum, with a *khānqāh* (a teaching institution for ṣūfīs) and *zāwiyya* (a school of ṣūfīs), as centres for popular Sufism.[46] A *waqf*, or religious endowment, maintained the complex, also providing for the recitation of the Qur'an, using specially commissioned copies, increasingly in multi-volume form (*rab'a*), contained in elaborate boxes made of bronze inlaid with gold and silver. Each *juz'* was read by a different person.[47] Calligraphy was taught in special schools, *maktab aytam*, in huge buildings.[48]

The earliest surviving example, created in 1304, in seven volumes, was commissioned by Rukn al-Dīn Baybars, later Sultan Baybars II, perhaps for a new *khānqāh*.[49] Mamlūk calligraphy did not yet use *muḥaqqaq*, and the scribe uses a large gold form of *thuluth*, outlined in black, a script usually reserved for ornamental *sūra* headings. The calligrapher, Ibn al-Wahid, a Syrian, made a fortune from his trade.[50] This Qur'an is notable for elaborate frontispieces and other artworks, produced by a team of illuminators led by Abū Bakr, known as 'Sandal'.[51] The frontispieces to volume 2, by Muhammad ibn Mubādir, involve hybrid interlocking octagons and tile-patterns. This may show that the artist was earlier trained in Ilkhanid Baghdad. The same artist illuminated another Qur'an in Cairo

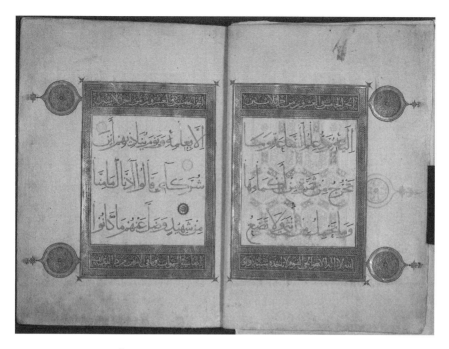

Fig. 26. 'Big books'; Öljaytü Qur'an (Mosul), *muḥaqqaq* script, ink and gold pigment on paper, 1310-11 CE (710 AH). London, British Library MS Or 4595, fos. 2ᵛ-3ʳ

with two finispieces and a beautiful frontispiece (Pl. 2) with a central panel surrounded by four rectangular panels and medallions (see Plate 2).[52] In two white Kufic inscriptions at the top and bottom are two Qur'anic quotations, referring to the holy book itself: 'Indeed We have sent [the Qur'an] down in a Night of Blessings' (Q 44: 3, top), and 'Indeed We have sent down [the Qur'an] in the Night of Destiny (Laylat al-Qadr)' (Q 97: 1, bottom). Side panels contain trees of gold palmettes. The centrepiece, in simple blue and gold, composes a perfect infinite pattern: repeating twelve-armed star polygons, the outer limbs interlocking to form squares. At the centre of each is the artist's signature motif, an octagon.

Star polygons, twelve-armed, or sometimes even sixteen-armed, are a feature of Qur'ans created later in the century for the Umm al-Sultan madrasa, some presented by Sultan Sha'bān and others by his mother, Khwānd Barakah. The frontispieces consist of a square geometric trellis with a surrounding *chinoiserie* border.[53] Another Qur'an also now in the National Museum of Cairo, completed in 1372, is extremely large (74 cm × 51 cm).[54] Most pages have 13 lines of text, but for the opening pages a new style of writing was used, known as *jalīl al-muḥaqqaq* (large *muḥaqqaq*), twice the standard size. The calligrapher's nickname was al-Muktib ('teacher of writing'); the illuminator, Ibrāhīm al-Amidī, was from Anatolia. As well as dark blue, gold, black, and white, his colours include brown, light blue, green, orange, red, and pink. The text of Q 1 is spread out over a double-page. There are just three lines of text, in black outlined in gold, of a gigantic size, a single *alif* measuring more than 5 cm.[55]

The question of scale in Islamic art of the book is developed at the other extreme in a technique known as *ghubār*: the script of 'dust'. These minuscule letters are less than 3 mm tall, and can be as small as 1.3 mm. It was said to have been invented to write messages for carrier pigeons, but Iranian calligraphers applied the method to amulets, talismans, and, when asked, whole copies of the Qur'an. A boxed set made in Tehran (perhaps 13th or 14th c.) includes the entire text divided into thirty *ajzā'* (plural of juz').[56] Each page is just 4 cm × 4 cm, with just 3 cm of text nonetheless presented in seven lines.

Writing is not itself sacred, but it *contains* the sacred, and in the attunement of one with the other, a kind of miracle occurs. Talismans occur in Judaism, Christianity, and Islam; the word is Arabic, derived from Greek τέλεσμα, meaning 'completion'. The Zalfiqar talisman, enclosing a five-line prayer, was used by the Mughal emperor and by the Janissary cavalry as protection in war. Islam requires writing, and writing acquires a patina of the holy. As if in recognition, writing draws attention to its materiality within Islamic culture. One feature of this is bookmaking, another is public inscription. Classical Greece used inscriptions widely, whether on the walls of buildings or on *stelae*. In the Republic and Empire of Rome, the art of monumental writing became a tool both of official propaganda and private identity. The Forum of Augustus assembled an elaborate epigraphy of inscriptions alongside statues.[57] A marble tablet found near the Via Pinciana in Rome bears a poem of fifty lines memorializing Allia Potestas. It is a eulogy to her ability to keep two young lovers at once, who are as inseparable as Orestes and Pylades while she was alive, but who fight now she is dead.[58]

From around 2300 BCE, long predating anything in classical epigraphy, is the Anubanini petroglyph located in what is now Kermanshah province in Iran.[59] Anubanini, king of the Lullubi, is depicted driving his foot into the chest of a captive. This is joined by an inscription in the Akkadian script, beginning: *Anubanini, the mighty king, king of Lullubum, erected an image of himself and an image of Goddess Ninni on the mount of Batir*. There follows a curse invoking eight Mesopotamian gods by name, bringing doom on anyone who damages the monument. Around a third of the petroglyph was destroyed during the Iran–Iraq war. Nearby, close enough to make it possible that there is a direct influence, Darius I the Great (550–486 BCE) ordered the construction of a complex rock relief carved into the cliff of Mount Behistun in western Iran. The multilingual inscription measures 15 m high by 25 m wide, occupying a place 100 m above the road between the ancient capitals of Babylonia and Media. It is written in three languages: Old Persian, Elamite, and Babylonian (a variety of Akkadian).[60] The Old Persian text contains 414 lines in five columns; the Elamite text includes 593 lines in eight columns, and the Babylonian text is in 112 lines. Sir Robert Shirley saw the monument in 1598 and thought it was Christian in origin. In the eighteenth century it was transcribed by the German surveyor Carsten Niebuhr, and then the Old Persian text was partly deciphered by Georg Friedrich Grotefend. Gradually, in a manner similar to the decipherment of the Rosetta Stone, the inscriptions of the other languages were worked out one by one. The inscription begins with the ancestry and lineage of Darius, and continues with a list of his territories, and a long series of rebellions he had to put down. Despite its importance to Assyriology, it suffered target practice by Allied soldiers in the Second World War.

Near Persepolis, the Ka'ba-ye Zartosht ('Cube of Zoroaster'), a mysterious quadrangular building, originating from the Achaemenid Empire, perhaps also in the reign of Darius I, bears a later trilingual inscription. Writing in the third century CE, the Sasanian king Shapur I described in Middle Persian, Greek, and Parthian his campaigns against the Roman Empire, and the Zoroastrian fire temple he built.[61] While public inscription in the Middle East had already been known for over two thousand years, the place of inscription in Islam is nonetheless distinctive, both in its continuity and its cultural coverage. The earliest Islamic building, the Dome of the Rock, bears an inscription; the dome of the mosque in the terminal of the King Khalid International Airport at Riyadh, Saudi Arabia, built in 1984, has an inscription almost identical in design.[62] A band of gold with geometric patterns in black, is surmounted by white letters on a blue ground, written in the *thuluth* script. As at the Dome of the Rock, this begins with the *bismillah* (the invocation to God); it is followed by the first seven verses of Sūra 57 from the Qur'an (al-Hadid; 'Iron'). The quotation combines a declaration of the majesty of God with an assurance that charitable gifts on holy projects will be rewarded.

Inscription from the Qur'an is found on the earliest Islamic coins as well as buildings. It is found on all the decorative arts: in metalware, woodwork, ceramics, and textiles. Yet as well as occupying space on decorative objects, writing could rightly be said to constitute the art of decoration. While this is found all over the Islamic world, it reaches an apex in the Alhambra in Granada in southern Spain. Here the aesthetic and the religious become one, incorporated into the visual design of the palace, so that in the words of José Miguel Puerta Vílchez, 'the buildings themselves if deprived of their solid fabric could remain standing in the imagination, constructed only of words'.[63] An immediate feature of the surviving buildings (only a third of the original structure is intact) is the contrast between the plainness of the exterior and the lavish ornamentation of the interiors, so much so that a visitor is astonished on first entrance inside the palaces. One way of explaining this is in the Islamic concentration on the life within. Inwardness applies equally to the religious life and to domestic life. However, the contrast between outward form and inward content also applies to Islam as a religion of the book. Islam is a constant equilibrium built around the idea of contents: the container (script or book) and the meaning within. The inner can be found only through expression of the outer.

The Muslim conquest of al-Ándalus (the Iberian peninsula) in the eighth century CE was lightning-fast. Christian and Jewish communities in the early period were tolerated in exchange for taxes (*jizya*), as *dhimmī*s. During this time, both under the Emirate which reported directly to Damascus, and then under the Caliphate of Córdoba, Granada was a relatively unimportant outpost. It was after the Caliphate of Córdoba collapsed, and especially after the fall of Córdoba to Christian rule, that Granada reached its apogee as the Andalusian capital. It was at this point, under the first Nasrid King Muhammad I (1238–73), that the Alcazaba (a fortified citadel) began to be built on the Alhambra.[64] In the fourteenth century CE under Yusuf I (1333–54) and Muhammad V (1354–91), this fortified castle was transformed into the most luxurious palace in Europe. One feature of the decoration of the Comares Palace (the king's residence) is how omnipresent it is. In some rooms, such as the Hall of the Ambassadors, decoration occupies all available space. It is the largest room in the whole palace, forming a perfect cube, yet every part of every wall, and even the ceiling, is adorned.

Many arts are combined. The lowest order of the wall uses ceramic tiles in the style known as *azulejos*: glazed tiles cut and formed into patterns. The design is extraordinarily intricate. The overall pattern is made up of a multitude of different small pieces, each individually cut. The *azulejos* had to be assembled piece by piece, like a mosaic. The central design in this room is a star with eight points, out of which a series of other stars form a concentric circle. Colour as well as shape is used to define the geometry of the whole. Each large star is made up of fragments of other stars, alternated with polygons of a dazzling variety. The principle is a form of tessellation: a square is rotated at an angle of 45°, and then superimposed, forming a first star of eight points. Each star of eight points is then divided via irregular quadrilaterals and hexagons. The small pieces are very often incomplete in terms of their own geometry, an array of stars as fragments, but the overall design is a dazzling mathematical perfection.

Above this level is a large section in stucco, gypsum plaster mixed with marble or alabaster dust. It has an architectural advantage of being strong and consistent, and the decorative advantage of being cheap, and (unlike tiles) easy to carve or mould. Within a wall it is adapted to form columns and vaults, yet does so in a manner seeming part of a whole, though sumptuous and detailed. In the Hall of the Ambassadors, stucco reaches 10 m, right to the ceiling. Each wall is divided into four piers with three alcoves behind; just below the ceiling is a row of six windows. This creates a profusion of levels of decoration: some floral, some vegetal, some geometric, repeating the star pattern from the *azulejos*, but with twelve points instead of eight. The overall effect is multiplicity and fullness. Indeed, the building has the character described by Johan Huizinga in *Herfsttij der Middeleeuwen* (1919) as *horror vacui*: 'a fear of emptiness', although here it is perhaps better called love of copiousness.[65] This is topped by the use of a third artistic material in the ceiling: a vault, 18 m high, made of cedar wood. This uses a technique known as *muqarnaṣ*: prisms or polyhedra cut concavely at the bottom, combined with polychrome patterns of inlay in different colours of wood. Once again, the design comprises concentric stars in seven crowns, leading to a small central cupola. The stars are made to appear as of different sizes, like a canopy of constellations, row upon row and yet without any sense of exact regularity. The four diagonals of the ceiling are said to represent the four rivers of paradise, and the cupola paradise itself.

At the heart of the design of this architectural masterpiece is something easy to miss even when standing within the great hall itself. From the top to the bottom of each wall, often occupying the function of a frieze, is a vast array of Arabic writing. While some of the inscriptions in the Alhambra are informative—recording the date of construction of a monument or the personage for whom it was built—others are properly speaking iconographic: they embody, enact, or interpret, architectural purpose of composition.[66] There are two types of calligraphic script in use, Kufic and cursive. Kufic, derived from script used in early Qur'ans in Iraq, is rectilinear, angular, and with no vowels and few diacritical marks. It was a script in favour for inscriptions on stonework throughout the Islamic world.[67] The cursive script in use in the Alhambra differs from the rigorously proportioned *muḥaqqaq* script of the Baghdadi masters. It often has exaggeratedly rounded forms, with elongated final letters, enabling an interweaving and enjambment of letters and even words. In the Hall of the Ambassadors, inscription reaches as high as the eye can see, to a wooden frame beneath the roof, onto which is painted in white (now faded) the entirety of Sūra 67 (al-Mulk, 'Divine Sovereignty'), consisting of 30 verses.[68] This begins on the north wall, describing the orderliness of the cosmos and proportions of the stars of the heavens, referring directly to the design in the ceiling. Below is a cascade of writing (Fig. 27), included in a mesmerizing pattern of banderoles, cartouches and medallions. Writing dazzles the viewer: it is hard at first to make out which parts are script and which ornament. Since in the standard ordering of the sūras, Q 67 is followed by Q 68 (al-Qalam; 'the pen'), it is clear that writing is seen as divine.

On the walls, there are a series of epigraphic friezes, beginning in a large strip below the ceiling and above the windows, a continuous repetition of the phrase 'There is no victor but God'.[69] The script here is Kufic, and is the largest in the room, a proportion which is diminished in every order below so that each frieze can comfortably be read at whatever height. Eight different texts are dispersed at different levels: the *fātiḥ* ('the victor'); a praise of the Sultan Al-Hajjaj; and praises

Fig. 27. 'Writing as architecture'; Comares Palace ('Hall of the Ambassadors'), Granada, Alhambra, 1333–54. Photo: author

and blessings.[70] Some of these are single-word calligrams: not strictly speaking writing, but letter designs in a geometric pattern signifying words such as *baraka*, 'blessing'.

However, not all the writing is derived from the Qur'an: in the central alcove there is a mystic poem in six verses, composed especially for this room, used as a throne room, describing the throne and its meaning. The poem imagines the inhabitants of the room:

> From me, both by day and night, mouths salute you
> with wishes of good fortune, happiness and friendship

and salutes its maker, Yusuf I:

> My lord Yusuf, sustained by God, clothed me
> in dignity with robes of undeniable distinction

In the Hall of the Ambassadors, it can truly be said that the walls speak.[71] Poetry is written into the fabric of the building, and at the same time the building takes on the character of poetry. Mural poetry is a genre synonymous with the Alhambra, which contains the largest collection of classical Arabic wall poems in the world. This began under the leadership of the politician and scholar Ibn al-Hakim from Ronda. The walls of the buildings become a site for a peculiar form of *qaṣīda*, a genre which merges petitions to patrons with an aesthetic panegyric. In the chancellery, a close relationship arose between the court poets and the calligraphers and scribes. Indeed, often they were the same people: the virtues of writing clearly and beautifully were interpreted both as a mental and a physical gift. An early exponent was Ibn al Jayyab (1274–1349), a court poet who reached his peak under Yusuf I, not only in the Alhambra but in the madrasa, condensing the traditionally long eulogistic style into short poems which could be transferred to a wall. His successor was Ibn al-Khatib (1313–*c*.1374), who composed the poems in the niches and alcoves of the Hall of the Ambassadors, the only work of his to survive. After him comes Ibn Zamrak (1333–93), who became the muse for the enormous building programme of Muhammad V. His work can be seen in the Courtyard of the Myrtles, the Hall of the Boat, and the Palace of the Lions. Praise of his monarch merges seamlessly with descriptions of religious and courtly pageants.

The longest poem on the walls of the Alhambra is in the Hall of the Two Sisters. Here 24 distichs run anti-clockwise around the inside of the hall, sixteen carved into circular cartouches and the remaining eight into rectangular ones, alternating all the way, white script on a blue ground. The verses are taken from a 146-verse *qaṣīda* originally recited at the circumcision of the Emir 'Abd Allah, the son of Muhammad V. The poem begins in the first person as if the voice of the garden itself, in long lines divided into two parts:

> I am the garden that with beauty has been adorned |
> Behold my loveliness and my high standing wall will become
> clear to you

This turns into an evocation of the cosmic blessings supplied by the stars in the heavens above, especially the Pleiades and Orion:

> They seem to be arches of turning celestial spheres |
> that even cast a shadow upon the pillar of the dawn when
> it breaks

Each verse is given its own calligraphic identity, joined to the one preceding and to the one following at the same height, so that the room can be read by the viewer in continuous ease. The skill of the calligrapher in fitting each verse to the size of a cartouche, whether circular or rectangular, is exquisite. The script in the rectangular cartouches is distinct from that in the circular. The wall is made to talk, assuming the voice of the first person feminine. Architecture is translated into poetic form so that it is hard to say where one ends and the other begins. Praise of place and word intermingle.

One final example of the miracle of writing materialized in architectural form is the Mexuar Oratory, in the part of the palace complex which just precedes the

Fig. 28. 'Writing in the *mihrab*'; Mexuar Oratory, Alhambra, 1363-7. Photo: author

Comares. It dates from the time of Yusuf I, but was substantially redesigned and refurbished under Muhammad V. It is highly unusual in relation to the traditional mosque or *masjid*, which whether in Medina or Damascus or in Córdoba was an enclosed building inside a courtyard, with no view outside. Here, by contrast, there is a magnificent view of the Albiacín on the opposite side of the city of Granada. The oratory surrenders to this vista (Fig. 28) in elegant arched windows on one side, at right angles to the *mihrab*, aligned precisely with the direction towards Mecca. The view thus forms a visual counterpoint to the *qibla*. Natural beauty is then enhanced and embellished by a full display of calligraphic art. The north wall above the windows has six orders of writing, devout and eulogistic by turns. On the top is a frieze in Kufic script with the repeated phrase, 'Praise be to God for the bounty of Islam.' Nasrid shields and the motto of the Sultan are placed in cartouches below. Two friezes of 'There is no victor but God' in cursive script next frame a series of large medallions containing an exclamation praising Muhammad V. The arches of the windows are then decorated with further short blessings in piers.

This fabulously intricate design is surpassed again as we view the *mihrab* itself. Here there are eight orders of script, covering the entire upper wall, and surrounding the upper portion of the niche. The base of the arch of the niche is given over to two kinds of invocation to prayer. Around the arch are circled eight calligrams, each incorporating the name of Allah, written in Kufic script, with a different attribute of God inscribed in diminutive cursive script above. The arch is then framed by a three-sided rectangular frieze repeating the same praise of God three times on each side and four times in the upper band, all in Kufic calligraphy. Above and around, framed into every axis and corner, are cartouches and friezes of different sizes. In these the dominant refrain is repeated over and over again, 'There is no victor but God.' It is the prevailing motto of the whole Alhambra palace, from the outside gates through the Mexuar and the Courtyard of the Myrtles, into the Comares and the Palace of the Lions. It is only appropriate that the mihrab, the religious centre of the complex as well as the private chamber of the ruler, has this motto inscribed all over, both in frame and in detail.

Writing and building have become one. Below the last line of calligraphic architecture, the lower half of the *mihrab* is a rare example of empty architectural space. Here the embodied is placed on an absolute dividing line with abstract white space. Bare plaster wall expresses the mystery of meaning surrounded by the exorbitant flourish of script.

10
The Unnameable Hebrew God

For a thousand years, the Jewish community of Fustat in Egypt deposited old books and other written detritus in a storeroom (known as a *genizah*) in the Ben Ezra Synagogue in Old Cairo. The word *gĕnīzāh* (גניזה) is derived from the triconsonantal Hebrew root *g-n-z*, which suggests a concept of 'hiding'; the Talmud had a notion of 'concealment' or 'storing away'.[1] Originally, perhaps the meaning was 'to hide' or 'to put away'; but later, as many words do, its meaning transferred from an action to a noun for a place where one puts things. In that way *genizah* is perhaps best translated as 'archive' or 'repository'. In ancient Persia, *ginzei malkā* was an Aramaic term for 'the royal archives'.[2] What we put away we intend neither to forget, nor exactly to remember. It remains *there*, for safe keeping, ready to be found; but in the meantime, it might as well never have existed.[3] Fustat for centuries was also home to the book market, the *sūq al-kutubiyyīn*, and also the paper mill.[4] The *genizah* at Fustat, like other examples in the ancient and medieval world, was a storage area within the synagogue. It was located high up in the air and could be reached only by a ladder. Its function may be associated with a very old practice of burying a holy man with a *sefer*, a holy book, either from the Tanakh (the Hebrew Bible), or else the Mishnah or the Talmud or any work of rabbinic literature.

Such practices are widespread in the world's religions, for instance in Buddhism and Christianity. Their purpose in time transferred from person to book.[5] In early Islam, old copies of the Qur'an were not thrown away but instead ritually interred, in the ground or in the walls of a building such as a mosque. Indeed, that is how many of the oldest manuscripts of the Qur'an survive at all, and in such good condition.[6] The best way to destroy a book is to use it and then throw away the pieces. Put it in a cupboard for long enough and the fact that you have forgotten it, preserves it. If the *miḥrāb* provides a leading metaphor for the contents of a book, for the mystery within, the *genizah* is a deep metaphor for what happens to books over time. They collect and leave traces, secrets packed away, half-forgotten. They become absorbed into each other, merging and interpenetrating within the archive, whether a library or a human mind.

Perhaps all libraries are a kind of *genizah*. In the Muslim world, Qur'ans and oceans of poems and letters gathered in the great libraries of the Umayyad Caliph in Damascus and in Córdoba, or the Abbasid ('House of Wisdom') in Baghdad, and the Fatimid in Cairo.[7] Meanwhile, from mystical origins the contents of a Jewish *genizah* broadened. It became taboo to bury any words from scripture;

then by curious mental transference, any word written in Hebrew whatsoever. In time, cemeteries often became sites for *genizot*. Paper-interment is known to have been practised throughout the Middle East, in Morocco, Algiers, Turkey, Yemen, and Egypt. In the strictest sense the taboo forbade the throwing away of any writings containing the name of God. This became a very wide category, from the Torah to any piece of writing including an invocation to God, which might mean all kinds of secular document such as a wedding betrothal or a contract. This was not limited to Hebrew writing, because many languages used by Jews used the Hebrew script: Aramaic, Judeo-Arabic, Judeo-Persian, Judeo-Spanish, or Yiddish.

Indeed, the Cairo Genizah, the most famous of all, contains the most comprehensive assemblage of medieval Jewish records of any kind. In curious fashion, its rediscovery has followed the trajectory from sacred to secular that is implied by its own contents. At a certain point the *genizah* simply became too full to be used any more. It was then left alone and ignored until the eighteenth century, when rumours arose of paper treasures. In the mid-nineteenth century fragments began to appear on the literary market, attributed vaguely to the Cairo Genizah, until in 1896 two Scottish scholars and twin sisters, Agnes S. Lewis and Margaret D. Gibson, travelled to Egypt and returned in some excitement to their home in the Madingley Road in Cambridge.[8] Lewis and Gibson had earlier worked on the Codex Sinaiticus Syriacus, the oldest manuscript of the gospels in Syriac. Like that manuscript, their new find from Cairo was a palimpsest, involving the over-writing of one text by another, often done for practical reasons to save valuable parchment, although sometimes involving an esoteric purpose. The linguistic demands of this new *genizah* text required a different kind of expert, so they enlisted the help of the legendary Moldavian scholar Solomon Schechter. Schechter took one look at the document and swore the sisters to secrecy. He was certain that they had chanced upon the first-ever known Hebrew text of Ben Sira, the Wisdom of Sirach (or Book of Ecclesiasticus). A work of ethical teachings from the second century BCE, it had survived only in a Greek translation, outside the Hebrew Bible but part of the canonical Christian Bible of both the Orthodox and the Catholic churches. The find was therefore sensational, and Schechter was determined to verify it and travel to Cairo: to purchase the rest of the collection found by Lewis and Gibson, in case the *genizah* contained the rest of Ben Sira.

Altogether perhaps 400,000 items, many tiny, survive from Cairo's *genizah*.[9] Westminster College, Cambridge, built out of the home of Lewis and Gibson, still owns 1,700 fragments from the Fustat hoard. The remainder is distributed between the Jewish Theological Seminary in New York (where Schechter moved after Cambridge); the John Rylands Library, Manchester; the Bodleian Library, Oxford; and, by far the largest repository, the Taylor-Schechter Genizah Collection at Cambridge University Library. Here, stored on the sixth floor of Giles Gilbert Scott's monolithic tower, which stands as a modernist Gothic temple to learning, lie 193,000 manuscript fragments. It is a modern *genizah* of the ancient *genizah*. The state of the hoard when Schechter found it was atrocious: it took the labour of years to disassemble texts from the assorted dust and pigeon shit of centuries.[10] Schechter, wearing a special mask, suffered physically and mentally from painstaking attempt to decipher secret sacred texts. After he left Cambridge for New York, attention turned to other kinds of document. These include a mass of previously unknown Jewish poetry. They also include everyday letters, business deals, law contracts, leading to the fullest appraisal ever likely to be made of Jewish religious, communal, and personal life, Hebrew and Arabic literary traditions, or relations between Muslims, Jews and Christians, from the ninth to the thirteenth centuries CE.

Some of the texts in the collection are older than the *genizah* itself. This example found by Schechter (Fig. 29) is a palimpsest, where a Greek text of Psalm 22 (Masoretic numbering) has been overwritten with a liturgical hymn (*piyyut*) based on texts from Leviticus by the Galilee poet Yannai. The writing in Greek, which can be seen faintly in columns that have faded to a red-brown colour, is in a biblical majuscule hand dated to the seventh century CE, with no accents and little punctuation. The writing in Hebrew stands out prominently in black, in a square Oriental hand of the tenth century CE. Even though the under-text is scriptural, it is the poem by Yannai which ensured its presence in the *genizah*, because the Hebrew letters are themselves considered holy. The Greek meanwhile is in several columns because it is a fragment from the *Hexapla*, composed by Origen in Caesarea in the third century CE. This was a parallel-text Bible (possibly the first ever) which contained the Hebrew text in conversation with five texts in Greek: a transliteration; the translation by Aquila; that by Symmachus; then the Septuagint; and the translation by Theodotion.[11] It was copied in a bifolio, with three columns on each page. This copy is not only the oldest example to survive, it even preserves the format of the text, including the gutter at the fold of the codex: on one side are Columns III, IV and part of V; on the other, the far right of Column II, then Columns III and IV.[12]

Vellum, the material from which the manuscript was made, was expensive. Text from an unwanted book was therefore frequently scraped off to make way for text in another. Some of the oldest texts of the Greek New Testament survive under later Latin texts; a fragment of the Qur'an (the Sana'a palimpsest) survives this way from perhaps fifteen years after the death of Muhammad. In the opposite direction, holy texts cover pagan texts such as a sixth-century CE fragment in Greek from the *Iliad*.[13] The Romans used a Greek word *palimpsestus* for this effect on wax tablets or vellum. Cicero in 53 BCE received a batch of several letters from his friend Trebatius.[14] They include one that is a palimpsest; Cicero admires his thrift but is left wondering what was on the previous scrap? He hopes Trebatius has not been rubbing out Cicero's letter in order to substitute his own.[15] Cicero's joke plays on how palimpsests figure the vulnerability both of friendship (cohabitation on the page) and memory (one letter overwritten by another). This

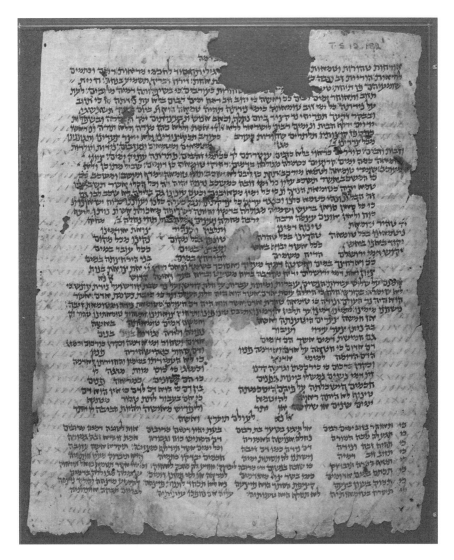

Fig. 29. 'Palimpsest in vellum'; Upper text: *piyyuṭim* by Yannai, c.10th c. CE, Under text: Origen's Hexapla on Psalms 22, majuscule, 7th c. CE. Taylor-Schechter Genizah Collection T-S 12.182. University of Cambridge, University Library

reinforces how writing acts as a metaphor for memory in Cicero generally. Memory stores things, like letters on a page.[16] Palimpsests suggest how one memory becomes overlaid. In the act of remembering one thing, another is forgotten: and yet a trace of the older memory remains in the fabric of the new one. In the case of the Genizah palimpsest of Origen and Yannai, this happens at the level of communal memory. One language overwrites another, one community merges with another, in textual form.

Gérard Genette, in *Palimpsestes: la littérature au second degré* (1982), suggests that all texts prompt their readers to remember or reread a previous text. Paraphrasing Borges, he says 'literature is not exhaustible, in the way that no single book is'.[17] The book thus acts cognately to the musical and sacred term 'parody': reworking something old into something new. In this way books act as forms of cultural exchange. Early Muslims referred to Jews and Christians as ʾAhl al-Kitāb (الكتاب), the 'people of the book'. The Qur'an suggests a community of faith between different scriptures, among which it mentions the Torah (*tawrāt*), the Gospel (*al' injīl*) and Psalms (*zabūr*) by name, and in general more ambiguously scrolls or leaves (*ṣuḥuf*).[18] Sometimes the Qur'an pays tribute to the religious and moral virtues of communities receiving earlier revelations, and refers to Muhammad asking these 'people of the book' for contextual information. The Qur'an also uses this term three times in order to refer to a gnostic group called the Sabians. Later Muslims have also at different times, sometimes controversially, bestowed the term on Zoroastrians, Samaritans, Hindus, and Buddhists.

The term refers at some level to co-existence and a degree of toleration. The Jews of al-Andalus, for example, were culturally Arabized; many literati were polyglots who wrote in Arabic, imitating the idiom of Arab literature.[19] Moses Maimonides was born in Córdoba at the end of its golden age, a denizen until the Berber Almohads conquered the city in 1148 and abolished dhimmitude.[20] New conditions newly constrained liberties, and it was rumoured Maimonides had converted, although he alludes to his conversion as false.[21] He escaped to Fez in Morocco, composing a commentary on the Mishnah, then travelled to Palestine before settling in Fustat. Thus, some of his writing, including in his own hand, survives in the Cairo Genizah.[22] In the other direction, Averroës (Ibn Rushd), chief jurist of the Almohad caliph in Córdoba, was disgraced in 1195 and forced to live in the Jewish city of Lucena. He may have escaped to Fez; while there is no record of him meeting Moses, Moses loved his books on Aristotle.[23]

Cultural interpenetration also applies to bookmaking. The script in Andalusian Qur'ans developed uniquely, based on Maghrebi script. The earliest dated illuminated Qur'an from Spain is 1090 CE: it is decorated at the beginning of each sura.[24] A Córdoba MS of 1143 has carpet pages designed in a centred interlace pattern.[25] Interlace patterns in carpet pages are sometimes continuous, in an illusion of extending infinitely beyond the frame; this reflects the architecture of the Nasrids in the Alhambra. Jewish illuminated Bibles borrowed decoration from Islamic repertoire until late in the Middle Ages, even when produced under Christian rule. The earliest decorated Hebrew Bibles are close in date to the first Qur'an carpet pages.[26] The Ben Asher Codex was found in the Karaite Synagogue in Cairo by Abraham Firkovich, around the same time as the discovery of the Fustat Genizah. Spanish Hebrew illuminated Bibles have close parallels in Islamic design: carpet pages, decorated chapter headings, the marking of *parashot*, and verse counts.

The first surviving Sephardic illuminated Bible is from Toledo in 1232, at a time when the city had been in Christian hands for nearly 150 years.[27] It has modest ornamentation, including a few spared-ground frames and medallions against a background of brown ink. Its formal language is entirely indebted to Islamic art. Another Bible, now in Marseille, features the first coloured carpet pages in the Toledo School.[28] Remarkable in these Bibles is the near absence of representational imagery. Narrative is rare and then only in the margins.[29] Representation is limited to picturing the Temple in abstract form. The first depiction of the Temple occurs in the Parma Bible, with an abundance of decoration, including a micrographic carpet page in a large centred star pattern. Here is depicted a seven-branched menorah (Fig. 30), together with wick tongs and ash scoops on each side, and a three-stepped stone with other details.[30] A simple frame makes one unit out of all, together forming the Ark of the Covenant. In a moment of wild uncanniness, the most unrepresentable object in Judaic culture becomes represented.

A third of the population of Muslim al-Andalus was Christian, known as Mozarab, a term (like 'queer') at first derogatory, later self-identifying. The

Fig. 30. 'Revealing the Ark'; Parma Bible, ink and gold pigment on vellum, Toledo, 1277 CE. Parma, Biblioteca Palatina, MS Parm 2668, fo. 7ᵛ

Mozarabs spoke a Romance language; Arabic was known only to the political elite. Only a few works can justifiably be called 'Mozarabic' in the full sense of the term—that is, created by the Mozarabic population of al-Andalus. The design of the Biblia Hispalensis (produced in Seville, 988 CE) is full of allusions to Islamic design, horseshoe arches intermingling with round.[31] The use of arches—usually polylobed and superimposed—is readily recognisable from its use in Andalusian Islamic architecture, as at Córdoba.[32] In the opposite direction, as Muslims settled in Christian reconquered lands, they were called *mudéjares*. A *mudéjar* design became prevalent in architecture and architectural sculpture.[33] Synagogues were designed using motifs from Islamic art.[34] There is absence of figurative motifs and a trend for abstraction, in geometric formal patterns. *Mudéjar* art is hard to define, since it uses Islamic formal elements often created by Christians and Jews. This dynamic phenomenon metamorphosed under influence from Nasrid Granada and the Maghreb.

What is striking is Iberian diversity: Christians in al-Andalus; Muslims in Christian Castile, until the savagery of *Reconquista*; Jews in all regions. Al-Hassan Al-Wazzan was born in Granada to a Muslim family; in 1492 his family escaped to Morocco; in 1518 he was captured by Christian pirates and presented to Pope Leo X. He converted Christian as Yuhanna Al-Asad; in Italy he was called Giovanni Leone; as Leo Africanus he published the first geography of Africa.[35] Here we uncover broader meaning in 'people of the book'. Conversion in religion is equivocal, Maimonides said in 'Epistle on False Conversion'.[36] Multiculturalism meets obsessive religious identification. There were words for a Christian living under Arab rule (*mozárabe*), a Muslim under Christian (*mudéjar*), a Christian converted to Islam (*muladi*), a Jew to Christianity (*converso*), a converted Jew who stayed a Jew secretly (*marrano*), or a Muslim forced to be Christian (*morisco*).[37] Pluralism in shared culture, defined by arts of the book, is countered by horrific violence. In 1391, pogroms in Christian Spain killed an estimated 100,000 Jews, with 100,000 'converts' and 100,000 refugees; prelude to 1492's expulsion of all Jews, and later, in Aragon (1609) and Castile (1614), all Muslims. Alternative views manifested only in specular form, such as shortly after Constantinople's Fall in 1453, when Nicholas of Cusa wrote *De pace fidei* ('on the peace of faith'), a dialogue in heaven of different religions, including Islam and the Hussite Christian heresy. He posits a theory of *una religio in varietate rituum* ('one religion in diverse rites'); in another work he discusses the Qur'an in a Latin translation and credits Judaism with partial access to the truth.[38] Faiths can meet and trade in Constantinople; the cardinal makes no call for reconquest.

Mystic Nicholas dwelt on infinity, or scholastic ignorance, and played a board game with Italian aristocrats ('Game of the World'). In reality, Christianity provoked a peculiarly violent culture of religion. At some level this related to book culture. While aniconic features of Jewish and Islamic religion negotiated scripture's transcendental status, Christianity cherished confusion. Islam struggled to keep body out of bounds. In the incarnation, Christianity doubled up embodiment with the equally abstract doctrine of the Word. Scriptural study embraced figuration equivocally, from Origen on.[39] Eusebius wrote that Origen interpreted Matthew 19: 12 so literally he had a physician castrate him.[40] In fact, Origen's *Commentary on Matthew* says only an idiot reads books that way.[41] Scholars argue the cut one way and another.[42] Yet violence is there for all to see, 1,000 years later, in manuscripts showing Origen put a knife to his own testicles.[43] A later Christian theologian followed Origen's example in reading, and perhaps in genital fate. 'Where is that learned lady Heloïse, for whose sake Peter Abelard was castrated, then became a monk at Saint-Denis?', sang François Villon in *Ballade des dames du temps jadis* (1461).[44] Abelard wrote *Historia Calamitatum*, an autobiography of literary trauma.[45] As always, *Omnia in figura*: Origen is the past master of letter and allegory.[46]

The so-called 'lead books' of Sacromonte symbolize such problems. Discovered between 1595 and 1604, in caves on a hillside outside Granada, they comprised 22 volumes of circular leaves of lead, sown with wire and bound in metal folds. Along with books were found burnt human remains, identified on more lead plaques as belonging to Caecilius of Elvira, patron saint of Granada, martyred under the Emperor Nero.[47] Into the books are inscribed a mixture of Latin and Arabic, the latter using a script which *morisco* scholars from Albiacín, who 'discovered' the books, identified as 'Solomonic', that is pre-Islamic. This sensational event crossed lines between sectarian Christianity in Granada and its largely Muslim past.[48] The lead books donated an invented memory of a much older Arabic world before and outside Islam, yet not quite yet Christian. Some letters are unidentified; the text is obscure; one part, 'the mute book', was never deciphered.

The 'lead books' contain teachings and prophecies of the Virgin Mary. Addressed to St Peter, they excise St Paul from Christian memory. Allusion is made to the Immaculate Conception of the Virgin, but in other respects the text is tailored to Islamic sensibility, suppressing the cult of images, the divinity of Christ, and the doctrine of the Trinity. The lead speaks Islamic language of 'God is one'. No wonder the books perplexed early readers. It is suggested they were written by, and for, *moriscos* keeping their original faith.[49] Yet they were authenticated by the Archbishop of Granada and received the patronage of King Philip II of Spain. Soon, Protestant scholars in the Netherlands dismissed them as fakes. In 1682, the Holy Office in Rome, where they were taken for safekeeping, condemned them as heresy and forgery. Not until 2000 did they return to Sacromonte, home of flamenco and the Romani of Granada, who fled there after 1492. Only now scholarly access opens up; meanwhile relics of Caecilius are still venerated.[50]

Texts divide, texts remain. Diego López de Zúñiga led a team of editors in 1502 to create a parallel text of Hebrew, Vulgate Latin, and Septuagint Greek, with an Aramaic Targum underneath. Just after publication he embroiled Erasmus in controversy. In a wider sense, a 'people of the book' reverberates more broadly than its meaning in the Qur'an or of *dhimmī* in early Muslim societies. In Judaism, *Am HaSefer* (עם הספר) is self-referential, affirming how a people adheres to sacred text. Nonconformist Christians (Baptists, Methodists, Puritans, and Shakers) took 'people of the book' to refer to them. In such contexts, self-identity forms in the name of religion. Yet the foundation of religions on scriptural texts is no accident. The text contains the Faith to such an extent as to become equivalent: religion in the word, as it were. While one faith differs from another, each regarding itself as true in exclusion to all others, they have in common a reliance on the mystery at the heart of writing. The mark on the page confers meaning. The inner is realised through construction of an outer. The divine is a word-god.

In Judaism, as later in Christianity and in Islam, the idea of sacred writing finds a natural home. Curtius, in the classic study, makes a connection between the book as material object and the *idea* of the book within a culture.[51] The symptom of this exchange is a capacity to conceive of a book symbolically, as metaphor for something other to itself. More unexpectedly, we find that material form has something to do with the symbolic value ascribed to it. The Greek word Pentateuch (the word in the Christian church for the most sacred part of the ancient scriptures, known to the Jews as the Torah), means literally the 'five containers' in which the scrolls of the text were kept.[52] The scroll early became a metaphor for what the scroll contained—and perhaps in an extended sense also for the mysterious relation between the text of God's words, and the spiritual sense of what those words are taken to mean. 'Writing' as an idea comes to the fore only in Deuteronomy; what we call 'book' is first called 'tablet' or 'ark' in Exodus or 2 Samuel, and only in 2 Kings becomes a 'scroll'.[53] This metaphor, like all good metaphors, slid easily in both directions. The laws given to Moses were written on stone tables, in turn taken as the embodiment of divine ordinance. It becomes a natural figure of speech to speak of law as 'written with the finger of God' (Exodus 31: 18). Metaphors mediate easily between different formats in which God's book is inscribed. Those who are of God are written into his 'book' (Exodus 32: 32); those who have sinned are blotted out.

As new media arise, so God's work changes its medium. Sometimes God writes in wax. Still, God discloses himself best in a scroll, the superior written technology of the ancient world. God witnesses his purposes in a scroll (Isaiah 8: 1); at the end of time, 'the heavens shall be rolled together as a scroll' (Isaiah 34: 4). Hebraic metaphors carried over into the Greek of the Christian New Testament. In a vision of the world's end, 'the heaven departed as a scroll when it is rolled together' (Revelation 6: 14). However, early manuscripts of the New Testament are usually codices, often divided as separate sections: gospels; the 'Apostolos' (Acts); the Pauline corpus; and Revelation.[54] The passage of time in the world is reconceived as a book which opens and finally is closed. Here, what Curtius calls 'the magnificent religious metaphorics of the book', reaches symbolic apotheosis. God's entire intervention in creation is imagined as a book. As Ezekiel begins prophet's life by eating the divine book (Ezekiel 3: 1), so it is as a book that St John the Divine imagines the enunciation of the apocalypse (Revelation 5: 1). When the dead come before God at the end of things, the books open, 'and whosoever was not found in the book of life was cast into the lake of fire' (Revelation 20: 15). It is not difficult to see how a sense of the symbolic meaning of the book translates into a mystical value in the artefact. The second commandment forbidding image or likeness of what is in heaven or earth (Exodus 20: 4–5) rested more burden on the written word.

The 'holy' writings come to be not only the law but also part of worship.[55] Josephus describes how the Torah was read in the Temple court.[56] The Mishnah tells that the scroll is handed by the hazzan to the head of the synagogue, who gave it to the segan, then on to the High Priest.[57] In the *Sefer Torah* used in synagogues in later times, the pristine state of the text was preserved by the masoretes: the law is to be inscribed only on parchment, in rolls, with no markings of any kind, undertaken by a trained scribe (*sofer*). Skins of 'clean' animals are scraped of hair and treated with salt, flour, and gallnut.[58] A good example is a Sephardi manuscript of the fifteenth century CE (British Library Add. MS 4707), written in square Hebrew script on parchment in 42 uniform lines, 268 columns in total. One from the nineteenth century, now in the Jewish Museum in Berlin, survives (as many do) with its rolls intact, as it would have been used in the synagogue (Fig. 31).

When not in use, the scrolls of the Torah are stored in the Holy Ark (*Aron Kodesh*).[59] This was a cabinet or niche in the synagogue, dressed with a mantle, a breastplate, silver bells, and sometimes a crown.[60] This injunction is observed to the present day. The architecture of the synagogue was designed to contain it and to suggest its presence. In the fourteenth-century El Tránsito synagogue in Toledo, later a Christian chapel, two windows were set high in the east wall in order to represent symbolically the twin tablets of the law. Excavation indicates that the Ark was placed beneath the windows.[61]

Outside of sacramental use, codices of the Hebrew scriptures could be decorated. The marginal instructions of the masoretes in medieval Hebrew Bibles were reduced to a micrographic form of script and then bent into vegetal or animal shapes to decorate the page.[62] Framing a word, line, or page with drawing and colouring was commonplace, usually in dots or lines or geometric shapes but sometimes encompassing living and even human forms. This does not diminish embodiment of the sacred within writing. The idea in the Kabbalah of the secret significance of the letters in which the Torah is transcribed is traced to the first century BCE. The idea of a magical charge inscribed into letters found graphic form in the tradition of illumination, and also in the commonplace use of amulets (*kame'ot*), potent objects worn close to the body, offering protection against illness or disaster. The tefillin are a phylactery or leather box of parchment scrolls inscribed with the Torah; Maimonides approves the use.[63] Jewish amulets (Fig. 32) contain Kabbalistic inscriptions, angelic names, or variants on the divine

Fig. 31. 'Purifying the book'; Torah scroll on wooden rollers, 19th c. Berlin, Jewish Museum

name. Mystical designs combine in geometric forms, such as the star of David, triangles, squares, or pentangles. In a silver Syrian bracelet, hinges are covered in Hebrew characters forming Kabbalisitic prayer, encircling a wearer's wrist.[64] In a seventeenth-century plaque (3 cm square), the names of the four rivers of the Garden of Eden (Pishon, Gihon, Chidekel, and Perat) snake around each line, reversing each time, left to right, right to left, and so on.

Fig. 32. 'Hiding the word'; Amulet, silver, 17th c. (?); British Museum 1867,0709.5

The divine name is the ultimate talisman of sacred text in Judaism. In Talmudic tradition, the name of God could neither be uttered nor written. The one used in the Torah is four consonants יהוה (YHWH). This was the 'proper name of God', the name God used of himself. As such, it is not of human invention. At the same time, it is known only via rendition in human forms of language. No better instance of the tension fundamental to writing could be invented. The four letters of God's name contain divine revelation. From early times revelation transformed into taboo.[65] By the third century CE utterance of the sacred *tetragrammaton* (Greek for 'four letters') became a capital offence. Here the metaphysics of naming collided with the problem of transmission of the Hebrew Bible. Early sources (oral and written) of the Hebrew Bible disappeared over time: in acts of censorship, in the politics of war (the destruction of the First and Second Temples), and because of fragility in textual media. Despite a written tradition of 3,000 years, the oldest complete Hebrew Bible is no older than 1008 CE.[66] It uses the Masoretic text with vowels (known as the Tiberian vocalization). Hebrew Bibles are thus predated by Greek manuscripts even though those are translated from it, in versions such as the Septuagint. This indeed is the origin of *tetragrammaton*, referring to the problem of rendering God's name in Greek. By now, a taboo existed over using the letters, so that the Septuagint instead says κύριος, or 'Lord'.[67] However, it may be this word imitated Christian practice. No early New Testament uses a *tetragrammaton*.

Obscurity mixes with euphemism in order to produce a prodigious philological problem, which scholarship struggles to control.[68] Instead of being called

Yahweh, God is known by substituted terms, such as *hakadosh baruch hu* ('The Holy One, Blessed Be He'), or *Hashem* (השם, 'the name') as well as the more familiar *Adonai* (אֲדֹנָי, 'Lord', equivalent to the Greek *kurios*). As well as the *tetragrammaton*, God is known by other names, *El, Elohim, Eloah, Elohai, El Shaddai*, and *Tzevaot*, together forming 'the seven names' of God.[69] In Greek, over sixty different renderings of the unutterable are identified.[70] The secret names are subject to powerful forms of mysticism and kabbalistic interpretation. This is compounded by a discovery, in the Cairo Genizah and the Qumran Caves (known popularly as 'Dead Sea Scrolls') of forms of Hebrew script older than Masoretic.[71] Indeed, manuscripts in palaeo-Hebrew script themselves acquire hermetic connotation.

The Aleppo Codex, purchased by the Karaite Jewish community in Jerusalem and then transferred to Cairo, where it was seen by Maimonides, ended up in Syria (hence its name).[72] Kept out of view in a *genizah* and then an iron safe for five hundred years, it re-emerged in the riots of 1947 when the Aleppo synagogue was burned down, only to disappear again. In 1960 it was smuggled into the state of Israel at the behest of Izhak Ben-Zvi, biblical scholar cum Israeli President, where it is now in the 'Shrine of the Book' in the Jerusalem Israel Museum, a modernist white dome also containing the Qumran scrolls. Much is missing: only 294 of (an estimated) 487 pages survive. Only the last section of the Torah is extant. While it was once thought that the damage was caused by fire in the Aleppo synagogue, scientists reveal that dark marks in the book are caused by fungus not fire. Some scholars instead accuse members of the Jewish community of tearing off missing leaves and keeping them privately hidden.

Memory of historical *genizot* merges with a broader sense of a *genizah* as container of forbidden material. An early account draws attention to how it combines sacred and taboo: 'A genizah serves ... two-fold purpose of preserving good things from harm, and bad things from harming'.[73] Writing deemed heretical (sometimes including books now canonical, such as Proverbs and Ecclesiastes) are *ganuz*, because their words contradict each other. They are censored by being buried out of sight. Religious texts 'that time or human error' render unfit for use cannot be thrown out, but instead require *genizah*: removal to a clay jar or other safe place, that 'they may decay of their own accord'.[74]

The *genizah* may sound like an ancient or recondite practice but it still exists today: in Jerusalem you will find a *genizah*, shaped just like a large recycling box, alongside other bins on the street. Tins, glass, cardboard, holy writ, all have their proper place in the modern world of waste. Waste is virtually a condition of modernity. Until the twentieth century everything was recycled: clothes handed down, scraps of them reused to make patches for other clothes, or manufactured to form pieces of string, or indeed pulped in order to form the raw material used in making paper. Paper, in turn, was hardly ever truly 'waste'. Aristocrats paid the price for highest-grade paper in letter-writing; this was remixed to make 'pot', the grade for printing. As a book disintegrated, its pages would be recycled: as wrapping for meat, or butter; or, at the bottom end of the cycle, to wipe shit from the arse.[75] Ben Jonson referred to his dramatic rival Thomas Middleton using sheets from a play to 'cleanse his posterior'.[76] Anthony Burgess made the same joke for his fictional poet in the novel *Inside Mr Enderby* (1963). Enderby composed lyrics seated on a toilet, whereby throwing away the worst was all the more practical and to hand.

Keeping paper is a different matter. This has happened, as we might say, 'since records began': it is virtually a mathematical law of the archive that the longer ago, the less survival. The great age of the paper archive was from the mid-nineteenth century to the mid-twentieth, as increasingly more and more paper was condemned to retention. Historians of this period are cursed by an overload of information. Then the telephone intervened, and in our own time email and SMS. Caught up in this is a constant law of tension between preservation and loss. How much are we prepared to keep of ourselves, and how much are we ready to lose? History is full of stories of people burning their letters, or else requesting their descendants to do the same in their name. The past is prone to taboo, even when not strictly sacred: indeed, it is profanity which frequently motivates the desire to destroy. Hallam Tennyson left the poetic manuscripts of his father Alfred to Trinity College, Cambridge, on the basis that they be kept on display but forbidden from publication. For years, delicately balancing respect and memory, they were kept in a glass case in a public room yet under lock and key. The poet's editor, Christopher Ricks, was allowed to consult them, but not to transcribe them even in the annotations to his first scholarly edition of 1969. Wishing to emend the word 'love' in 'Semele', Ricks used a scholarly joke, referring to an 'evil setback', that is (via the rules of acrostic crosswords) the word should be 'EVIL' backwards, that is 'LIVE'.[77] A few months after the edition came out, Trinity College lifted the embargo, to the chagrin of Ricks, who set about the task of a second edition, three times as long.

Tennyson junior was alarmed at the prospect that manuscripts would reveal his father was homosexual. Biography has emerged as a major genre of modern writing, identity politics meeting tittle-tattle. Lives are published of stupendous size, digging inside the enormous paper record in the archive, welcomed in proportion to how many secrets they betray. At the heart of this is a mislaid concept of privacy. Article 8 of the European Convention of Human Rights guarantees a 'right to respect for privacy and family life' from the state and its institutions, with restrictions prescribed by law. Yet intervention of the state in the realm of privacy began in the interest of invading, not protecting it. In 1534, Henry VIII's Treason Act expanded to include not only those who had actively planned the death of the king, but those who might even be thinking of it, or who:

do maliciously wish, will or desire by words or writing, or by craft imagine, invent, practise, or attempt any bodily harm to be done or committed to the king's most royal person, the queen's or the heirs apparent, or to deprive them of any of their dignity, title or name of their royal estates, or slanderously and maliciously publish and pronounce, by express writing or words, that the king should be heretic, schismatic, tyrant, infidel or usurper of the crown.[78]

Treason was extended from exterior acts to interior thoughts. Moreover, in order to identify the malicious interior thoughts of its subjects, the state had to find evidence that would stand up in court, and its first recourse was to 'words or writing'.[79] The mental world of citizens was to be examined by accessing their own archives.

In this definition of treason there emerged a new opposition between 'private' and 'public'.[80] Whereas in earlier times much of life was conducted in an uninterrupted public sphere, historical change sees new interest in what has come to be seen as private life. Among them is the condition of writing. Until the 1450s, manuscript was the only medium available, in a multiplicity of forms and styles. Heterodox groups like Lollards in England developed their own style of book production.[81] In the passing of books from person to person the Lollards were called 'known men', that is, known by their books.[82] By the 1530s handwritten books were swamped by printed versions of old Lollard texts.[83] With print, new prohibitions came in, inferring different modes of being. In the digital world, the private world is changing again. Data capture by Google or Facebook exposes privacy daily. These data are unerasable—preserved in files in an indefinite manner. One of the first cases in law against Google was under the Spanish Data Protection Agency, in which ninety individuals claimed 'the right to be forgotten'. The Agency concluded citizens have a right to request the removal of information that Google possessed.[84]

Zuboff argues that surveillance capitalism invades privacy on an unprecedented scale. This is no doubt true, a fundamental ethical and political issue facing human society today. However, in arguing previous media advances were more favourable to human freedoms, Zuboff is guilty of sentimental nostalgia. For her, the Gutenberg revolution was a moment of democratization and liberation.[85] The execution of Thomas More under the Treason Act in 1535 gives pause for a different reflection. More at his own trial stated that the new law made a subject prone to surveillance that only God should be capable of. More was condemned on hearsay, via a phrase he was said to have said hypothetically, to Sir Richard Rich.[86] More was more circumspect: 'Non sum Oedipus, sum Morus', he writes in reported dialogue to his daughter, Margaret Roper.[87] Oedipus is a riddler, but More claims 'by mouth and by wrytyng' to be a simple soul, 'the Kyngis trew faythfull subiect'.[88] The Archbishop of Canterbury, the Lord Chancellor, and Mr Secretary Thomas Cromwell demanded a last interview in the Tower of London. Would More confess it was lawful for his King's Highness to be Supreme Head of the Church? More will say no more. Come the time, to God alone I 'declare my trouthe towarde his Grace before him and all the worlde.'[89] Cromwell digs up a story of More examining heretics, forcing them to own the Pope is the church's head: surely it is as well to be burned for one as beheaded for another? In patient exactness, fate foretold, More replied his end lay not 'betwene heading or burninge', but 'headinge and hell'.[90]

'C'est la faute des pronoms, il n'y a pas de nom pour moi.'[91] Beckett's unnameable narrator has no pronoun by which to call himself, and therefore no name. Has he forgotten his name, or did he never have one? If only More had had less of a name. Writing lies at the heart of the problem of privacy and information in society. We think it is a transparent medium, but it is nothing of the sort. The state has collected information about citizens since writing began: indeed, more or less, that is the first recorded purpose of writing. At the heart of the conundrum is the issue of storage. Solomon Schechter's meditation on the origins of the *genizah* is evocative:

> The word is derived from the old Hebrew verb *ganaz*, and signifies treasure-house or hiding-place. When applied to books it means much the same thing as burial means in the case of men. When the spirit is gone, we put the corpse out of sight to protect it from abuse. In like manner, when the writing is worn out, we hide the book to preserve it from profanation. The contents of the book go up to heaven like the soul.[92]

The book contains us. It is our archive, constituting at once a site for personal identity, a treasure house of human memory, and an opportunity for surveillance and oppression. The *genizah* in this way is a kind of moral fable, taking us from the storehouse of history right up to the digital age of the impossibility of forgetting.

11

How the Alphabet Came to Greece from Africa

Socrates is telling a story, as is his custom, at the end of a long day. He sits with his friend Phaedrus under a plane tree by a stream on the outskirts of Athens. The cicadas are singing loudly. The two men have been walking all day in the country-side, and while they walk, Socrates gets Phaedrus to read out loud a speech by Lysias that is written out on a scroll under his cloak. This speech by Lysias, the foremost orator of the day, argues in favour of indifference: if you're in love with someone, your reasoning will be biased and prone to jealousy. Socrates affects to think that the speech is brilliant, yet also claims he can make up a better one on the spot. Phaedrus, he says, has given him a *pharmakon*, a drug to get him out of his home city and into the country.[1] The drug in question consists in speeches 'bound in books' (*en bibliois*): by this means Phaedrus can persuade him to go anywhere in the world.

Books are the most powerful drugs in the world, Socrates says. They make you do anything without you knowing why. At this point he gives his own speech on love, which at all points in the dialogue is imagined as between men, one older and one younger. Desire can be a good thing: indeed, nothing good happens without desire. But pleasure gets in the way and leads us astray. The lover should be thinking only of what is best for his beloved, yet looks for pleasure instead. The only solution is not to bind ourselves to love, but always to be ruled by judgment rather than desire for pleasure.

Nothing is simple in Plato's *Phaedrus*, however. Suddenly, Socrates is inter-rupted by the *daimonion*, a supernatural voice from inside him—somewhere between conscience and unconscious—telling him that he has offended the gods. He confesses that he thought both speeches, Lysias' and his own, were terrible. Love, he now admits, cannot be bad: it is a gift of the gods. Socrates commits himself to give a second speech or *palinode*, a recantation, in which he will say the opposite from before. Now he praises love, even though it is a form of madness. For madness is the ultimate gift of the gods, and comes in four kinds: prophecy, from Apollo; sacred ritual, from Dionysus; poetry, from the muses; and love, from Aphrodite. He goes on to give a rapturous defence of love, an essay on the immortality of the soul and on the nature of the human, expressed by an allegory in which the soul is compared to an exquisitely formed chariot, made up of a pair of winged horses and a charioteer. The horses represent the dual nature of humanity, which is lifted heavenwards by its wings, but weighed down by the body and the emotions; reason, in the person of the charioteer, guides the horses but cannot control them completely. In this, the soul is also like love itself. The charioteer is filled with warmth and desire as he gazes into the eyes of the one he loves. One horse has higher desires but the other is overcome by a desire for sex. Perfect love is the combination of human self-control and divine madness.

Even now, Socrates (or is it Plato?) changes tack again. As if the nature of the soul and of love was not enough, Phaedrus and Socrates now discuss the speeches as speeches. It is at this point that Socrates tells his tale:

> I heard, then, that at Naucratis, in Egypt, there was an ancient god of that country, one whose sacred bird is called the ibis, and the name of the god was Theuth. He it was who invented numbers and arithmetic and geometry and astronomy, also draughts and dice, and, most important of all, letters.[2]

Theuth, or Thoth, was an ancient Egyptian deity usually represented as a human body with the head of an ibis. Originally a moon god, he was thought of as the reckoner of times and seasons and hence possessed many kinds of specialized numerical and linguistic skills. Most especially he served as the scribe of the gods, and was credited with the invention of writing (γράμματα or *grammata* as Plato puts it) and Egyptian hieroglyphics. Plato calls Thoth the inventor of the art of writing also in the *Philebus*, but it is not a compliment.[3] When King Thamus asks Thoth what are the qualities of the various arts, the god replies that writing 'will make the Egyptians wiser and will improve their memories'.[4] Thamus disputes this, saying that Thoth has been misled by paternal affection as 'the father of letters'. Writing does not help us to remember things, indeed it makes us forget them. For, by putting trust in the marks on the page as an aid to memory, we forget to remember ourselves. Writing offers the appearance of wisdom but not wisdom itself. In reading, we only *seem* to know things, but remain ignorant inside.

In his repudiation of writing as a science of knowledge, Socrates repeats the word *pharmakon*. It is a word with many related meanings: 'medicine', 'remedy', 'recipe', but also 'elixir', 'potion', 'poison', 'drug'. Drugs promise to do us good but can also do us harm. They also make us dependent on them. The problem with writing, according to Socrates, is twofold. Its effects can be profitable and malign, equally. Yet also its use rids us of responsibility and agency. The two problems are of course connected. Here we come to the metaphilosophical heart of the dialogue. Ostensibly about love and sex, it is also about how to make arguments and fictions and speeches. Rhetoric is the medium of the dialogue, and also its object of discussion. Rhetoric is a false friend, persuading us of things that we should know are not true. Intrinsic to bad rhetoric is its status as writing. Philosophy should not be bound to the written, but to the spoken word. This is because speech keeps us closer to the presence of the person making it, and retains our agency.

The account of writing in the *Phaedrus* is full of irony. Anyone who considers himself to have created a work of art (*techne*) out of the written form is a simpleton; as is anyone who thinks that anything that is written down can ever be 'clear and certain'.[5] Yet what is Plato himself doing if not creating a work of art by writing down the spoken words of Socrates? And are his readers fools for taking from this something clear or true? Here we need to realise that Plato, like us, was living at a period of profound change in the medium of writing.[6] Lysias along with the other sophists was placing new emphasis on written texts, not only by rhetoricians, but also by lawyers, politicians, and physicians. In this way, even though Lysias was himself a notable orator renowned for his performances in the Athenian Areopagus, he placed himself in the vanguard of a literary movement that threatened the hegemony of the spoken arts, as exemplified by Socrates and his school. In carrying a papyrus roll on his person, Phaedrus is an example of the new trend.[7]

Plato is part of both worlds. On the one hand, he places himself at the feet of the master who most represented the old world of face-to-face teaching. On the other hand, he is a dedicated producer of the new form of *techne*: a medium of artistic prose aimed at a sophisticated reading public. While in the earlier *Gorgias*, Plato clung to the ideal of politics as an essentially oral sphere, after the *Republic* and by the time of the *Laws* he is more open to a literary form of doing philosophy.[8] Whatever the true relation of Socrates the philosopher-oracle to Plato his scribal amanuensis, it is a relation of paradox. A medieval manuscript image of a treatise on fortune-telling by Matthew Paris, now in the Bodleian, shows uncannily a myth of role-reversal: it is Socrates who sits at a writing desk, pen in hand, while Plato stands behind him, prodding him into action, and directing his thoughts with a wagging finger. Derrida made half of a book ('Envois' in *La carte postale*) out of the idea, when he came across a postcard version of the image (Fig. 33) by chance in 1977, while on a lecture tour in front of baffled Oxford philosophers. Had the medieval illuminator simply made a mistake, Derrida wondered, in figuring Socrates writing? If so, it is a Freudian slip: Socrates turns his back on Plato, 'who has made him write whatever he wanted while pretending to receive it from him'.[9] Who is author, the scribe or prophet?

Perhaps this is one reason why the *Phaedrus* as a whole is so jokey, and why in the section on the origins of writing the jokes are full of nervous tension. We may compare the way that in the great age of television, in the 1950s and 1960s, theatre directors of the classical school both promoted Shakespeare's plays as intrinsically superior to the moving image, and then also said that Shakespeare, if alive today, would be writing for TV. Or, to bring the comparison up to date, we could note how contemporary commentators at the same time ostentatiously declare the necessity of going digital while also joshing that Google is turning us into idiots.[10] 'My mind is going', laments HAL the supercomputer towards the end of Stanley Kubrick's *2001: A Space Odyssey* (1969); 'I can feel it. I can feel it.' We

Fig. 33. 'Hunt the writer;' Matthew Paris, *Socrates and Plato*, ink and pigment on parchment, 13th c. Oxford, Bodleian Library, MS Ashmole 304, fol. 31ᵛ

cannot now turn back the clock, says Nicholas Carr in *The Shallows*; but the Internet is changing the way we live and communicate, remember and socialize. The web is the instrument of universal distraction: we surf, and surf, until we cannot remember what we were searching for.[11] The result, Carr says, is a kind of inevitably superficial form of thinking. At worst the net even fosters ignorance, especially since in the end only the web knows. As soon as we have found the answer to one search, we look for another. And because we have found something on the internet, we believe it to be true.

While Carr is careful not to make his book a lament for a paradise lost of proper knowledge, others readily predict the internet is at once the doom of learning, and the origin of fake news, dumbing down, and 'alternative facts'. It is interesting then, to notice that twenty-first-century CE fears about fundamental changes in the way that we think and that we remember, due to changes in the technology of writing, have their correspondence in the Athens of the fourth century BCE. For this new invention, Socrates says, 'will produce forgetfulness in the minds of those who learn to use it, because they will not practise their memory'.[12] Phaedrus shows that he knows that Socrates is partly joking: 'Socrates, you easily make up stories of Egypt or any country you please' (275b3). Plato in turn makes it clear that his own text is partly playful. According to Diogenes Laertius, Plato himself was a tourist in Egypt in his twenties, hoping there 'to see those who interpreted the will of the gods'.[13] While there he fell sick and had to be cured by the priests. Plato no doubt expected his readers to know all the slurs against him. Everyone in Athens now wants to have a *logographos*, someone who can write speeches for you, to save you the trouble: a ghost writer, a hack, a spin doctor. We are all logographers, now, Plato appears to say (himself included). The reader is only too aware that Plato nonetheless never speaks in his own texts in his proper voice, so that his role as author is always ironic. Yet irony is also in its way deadly serious.

Derrida in the twentieth century returned to this passage as an iconic moment in his revelations about the origins of Western philosophy. Philosophy, he says, is founded on a rejection of writing. It claims instead, like Socrates, to utter truth in the speaking voice. King Thamus of Thebes is the political representative on earth of Ammon Ra, the king of the gods. Ammon has no need of writing: for he is the god who speaks (*dieu-le-roi-qui-parle*).[14] Inevitably, this god is a father figure, and like all fathers, he is 'suspicious and watchful' of the talents of his sons—in this case, of Thoth and the gift of writing.[15] Philosophy in turn, Derrida states, is all too ready to play the father, the voice of truth, omnipresent and at the same time all too obviously present, ordering, making us obey. Is Derrida playing the father in telling us to ignore the father?

If Plato has his tongue partly in his cheek, we can be sure that Derrida always does, too. Yet he is noticing powerful metaphors at play in Plato on the relationship between language and *logos*, speech and writing—and not merely as metaphors either.[16] Writing is the illegitimate child of speech, Socrates says, the bastard word that traduces the true one. Philosophy should speak instead with the voice of 'the living and breathing word of him who knows'.[17] Only speech has the full presence of knowledge. By contrast, Socrates says, writing is 'very like painting' (275d2). The people in paintings look like living beings, but they cannot talk. Writing, like painting, is merely an image (*eidolon*). This is of course a profoundly Platonic concept. In books 2, 3, and 10 of the *Republic*, Plato expounded at length on the theory of *mimesis* (or 'representation'). The poets promise a world as real as ours, he says, but it is a false promise. It is but a shadow of a shadow, a world of fakes. In a similar way, writing is a form of substitute world, an image or an idol. It takes the place of the real world of speech, but it can only do so in attenuated and derivative forms.

Derrida pays detailed attention, playful and serious, to the many faces of the Egyptian god Thoth. Ammon is identical with Ra, the sun god, and also with Min, the god of fertility and creation. He is therefore often symbolized by an egg; Thoth his bastard son is a bird—the ibis—born from an egg. Thoth as the moon corresponds to Ra as sun. If Ammon simply is, and says, Thoth is hence his messenger. Although Plato makes no mention of this, Thoth was indeed often identified with the Greek god Hermes. Thoth, like Hermes the messenger, is a trickster, a fraudster, who can take on different identities, a jack-of-all-trades, a joker, a wild card.[18] Here the very substitutive quality that makes Socrates shudder becomes the source of Thoth's power. He is the shapeshifter, or metamorphosis itself. In his power over numbers as well as written letters, he readily extends such powers over games of chance or dice. He is actor, dancer, gambler, fool, all at once. It is not surprising then, that he is also the master of *pharmakon*: doctor, pusher, dealer, quack.

These are the qualities ascribed to writing in ancient mythology. Derrida revels in the transgressive possibilities of writing as an alternative guise to the logocentric metaphysics of presence. Writing celebrates difference, subversion, risk. This is what makes it often the enemy of power, the place where rebellion can begin. Yet just as Plato's *Phaedrus* sometimes deliberately overplays the hand of Socrates, Derrida, too, artfully exaggerates the counter-insurgent energy of Thoth. Thoth's magic is alluring as well as dangerous. Thoth was the divine scribe who recorded the lives of the kings.[19] Seshat, his female counterpart ('she who writes'), was the mistress of the royal libraries. Thoth counted the years of the reign by adding a notch to represent the rib of a palm leaf. Adopting the form of a baboon, he surrounded the head of the human scribe, reading or perhaps creating his thoughts. The power of Thoth extends into death, as he weighs the heart on the scales as the person ceases to exist. We see this in exquisite detail in a Book of the Dead (Fig. 34). In the Papyrus of Hunefer (*c*.1275 BCE), the scribe Hunefer's heart is weighed on the scale against the feather of truth, by the jackal-headed god of death, Anubis. The ibis-headed scribe of the gods, Thoth, writes the result with a stylus on the right-hand side of the image. If the heart is identical in weight to the feather, Hunefer passes into the afterlife. If not, he is devoured by the chimera Ammit, who is lowering underneath, equal parts crocodile, lion, and hippopotamus. Recording life in writing doubles up, so that one becomes understood in the terms of the other, life as hieroglyph. 'For it goes without saying', Derrida the philosopher says, 'that the god of writing must also be the god of death.'[20]

What part is played in this by the hieroglyph itself? 'Hieroglyphics' is a Greek word first coined by Clement of Alexandria in the second century CE, although

Fig. 34. 'Thoth, god of writing': Book of the Dead of Hunefer, painted papyrus, 19th Dynasty, 1292–1189 BCE. British Museum, EA9901.3

he was following Egyptian practice, in which the script was called *mdw-ntr* (*medunetjer*, 'god's words').[21] In the fifth century BCE, Herodotus used the term *hiera grammata* ('sacred letters') to distinguish it from a second Egyptian script which he called *demotika* ('common').[22] In fact there were four different kinds of script in use in Egypt over the four thousand years of its ancient empire.[23] Herodotus uses the strange script of the Egyptians as part of his description of their lifestyle as truly alien to his own mind and culture. They are religious to excess he says, beyond any other people; their men are circumcised; they make their bread from spelt. The oddity of the Egyptians is summed up, however, by their writing, which goes from right to left, although he recognises that the Egyptians find this natural, and the Greek way awkward. At some level, Herodotus and other Greek writers such as Strabo and Diodorus of Sicily regard the hiero-glyphic script as unintelligible.[24] In this they make a double take: they recognize that it signifies, but they do not understand how.

It is the pictographic nature of Egyptian writing which paradoxically makes it so mysterious. Rock pictures of animals in hunting scenes, or in the breeding of cattle, date back perhaps as far as 5000 BCE. Later there are boat pictures, not surprising in a culture dominated by the Nile and the Mediterranean: but in some cases, the drawings begin to feel as if they are saying something more, if only we could see it. In one example, known as Tomb 100 at Nekhen, the will to commu-nicate is almost palpable: but is it an origin myth, or an autobiography, or some-thing else entirely?[25] The earliest evidence beyond such speculation comes from Abydos around 3200 BCE. In the tomb of a very wealthy man around 190 labels in wood and ivory have been found, which are carved with pictorial signs listing the contents of the tomb. The labels have holes in them to tie them to the goods they describe, although the goods are (of course) lost. Some signs represent num-bers; others perhaps the goods themselves; others, place-names; others perhaps administrative terms.[26] In a slightly later development, writing comes to represent a box, or perhaps a box within a box: the container of a substance, such as a piece of pottery, itself bears the mark of a box, with a pictogram within it. Here we have the earliest traces of the proper name: the word for a thing, or the name of a person, or the person with the thing. It is a moment both profoundly philosophical and literally incomprehensible.

It is in the next millennium, from 3000 to 2000 BCE, that Egyptian comes into its own, in the early dynastic period and the Old Kingdom. Menes 'the founder' established the kingdom with Memphis its capital at the apex of the Nile delta. The patron god of Memphis was the craftsman Ptah, who was said to have created the world by giving names to things. The culture of Memphis was scribal and bureaucratic, and scribes were often priests. The scribal caste encouraged the idea that their function was quasi-mystical. Yet while outsiders like Herodotus imagined that hieroglyphics are entirely pictorial, they are not. Thus while many hieroglyphs are literally logograms—a picture corresponding to a single whole word (such as 'sun', ear')—many others are phonetic: that is, they represent sounds. This is a consonantal system, with no vowel characters. Modern classification lists 26 uniconsonantal hieroglyphs. That is very close to the statement in Plutarch that Egyptian uses an alphabet with 25 letters.[27] An owl represents an *m*; a quail chick a *w*.

However, to call this an alphabet is a misnomer, since there were two additional groups of Egyptian phonograms: about eighty bilaterals (combinations of two consonants, such as *mw*, *nw*); and seventy trilaterals (three consonants, such as *nhb* or *hfn*).[28] This is not the end of the story, since many bilaterals and trilaterals have more than one sound value. The system as a whole is prone to many ambiguities, and there are many homonyms. To distinguish between homonyms, or to provide a shorthand for the reader, or perhaps just to enrich the aesthetic of writing, there is another whole subset of hieroglyphs known today as 'determinatives'. Thus, the words for 'writing' and 'scribe' share exactly the same bilateral sign. To differentiate, there is an additional glyph of a papyrus roll to represent 'writing'; and a seated man to represent 'scribe'.[29] Perhaps the most charming example for modern tastes is the Egyptian solution to the word for 'cat', an animal considered sacred. The word is composed of three phonogram signs (a bilateral and two uniconsonantals) followed by a determinative. The phonetic result is *m-y-w*, making up a wonderfully onomatopoeic sound rather like 'meeow'; the fourth glyph is a seated cat, with its tail curling up on its back, in a perfect picture of self-containment.[30]

Hieroglyphics are perhaps the hardest of all writing systems to systematize or to symbolize. The story of how they came to be 'deciphered' through the trilingual cryptic crossword of the Rosetta Stone, has come to be a central icon for the mystery of writing itself (Fig. 35). This grey and pink granodiorite stela was carved in 196 BCE with a priestly decree in three blocks of text, hieroglyphic (14 lines),

Fig. 35. 'Romancing the stone'; hieroglyphics, Rosetta Stone, stela in grey and pink granodiorite, Ptolemaic, 196 BCE. British Museum EA 24

Egyptian demotic (32 lines), and Greek (54 lines). The name of Ptolemy V appears in a cartouche in hieroglyphics. The last text in hieroglyphics was composed at the end of the fifth century CE. At around this time a Hellenized Egyptian called Horapollo produced a list of nearly 200 signs, but his *Hieroglyphica* was lost to posterity, and the quest began again only in the Renaissance when Cristoforo Bundelmonti found a manuscript copy of this work. However, Horapollo had no understanding of the phonetic content of the signs, and created an often fanciful symbology instead. The glyph of a vulture was interpreted as 'mother' using an elaborate allegorical interpretation on the basis that vultures reproduce entirely on the female side, whereas the solution is simpler: the vulture is the trilateral sound *mwt*, which is also the word for 'mother'.

The Jesuit Athanasius Kircher in the seventeenth century CE, who collected Coptic manuscripts, and realised that this language was descended from ancient Egyptian, reproduced hieroglyphics in *Oedipus Aegyptiacus*. However, he, too, was mesmerized by the symbolic possibilities of pictographs. Only after Napoleon's soldiers found the temple stela at Rosetta was progress fully possible. Even so it took several scholars to piece it together. Joseph de Guignes, a French orientalist, identified the existence of the determinatives; the Danish scholar Georg Zoëga said that some hieroglyphs were alphabetic; leading eventually after many byways to Jean-François Champollion and his *Précis du système hiéroglyphique* (1824).[31] Here, Champollion declared that hieroglyphics were a combination of phonetic and ideographic signs, and began to give them accurate values.[32] However, he still suffered from a shortage of texts; it was only in 1828, after a period studying examples in Italy, then working as curator of the Egyptian Collections at the Musée du Louvre, that he journeyed to Egypt itself. In a letter to the Grand Duke of Tuscany in June, he announces his impending departure.[33] On 18 August he records in his diary seeing the Arab Tower and the Column of Pompey in the harbour at Alexandria.[34] While examining the necropolis at Saqqara in October, Champollion realized that the idea of 'hour' was expressed in a group of hieroglyphs including a representation of a star, serving no phonetic function in the word. He recorded in his journal his stunning act of enlightenment, calling the star glyph 'le déterminatif de toutes les divisions du temps'.[35] Seeing stars everywhere, he found that the Egyptians had names for different dates or times, all using this one glyph. Writing to his brother, Champollion describes with wonder his new knowledge of the hours of the ancient days and nights, amidst the devastated remains of the cemetery of the citizens of Memphis, a 'désert affreux', virtually lost to the possibility of study.[36]

Part of the problem of hieroglyphic is its flexibility: while it is usually written and read from right to left, it can also occur left to right. The text can be written horizontally, but it can also be written on a vertical axis. The combination together of logographic, phonetic, and hybrid determinative glyphs, and the division into three types of phonetic sign, make for an interpretative puzzle which is not altogether resolvable. Indeed, Gelb in his ground-breaking *Study of Writing* proposed that a syllabic solution was possible as an alternative to a consonantal. This has not found support among Egyptologists.[37] However, Gelb's theory was not based on a different reading of the signs themselves. He agreed about the absence of vowels, something found only in Semitic writing systems; and that the non-semantic signs are all of one kind. But he argued that they could not be consonantal because no other writing system has ever developed in a direction from the logographic to the consonantal, and indeed such a trajectory is 'unthinkable'.[38] The ancient Oriental systems, such as Sumerian, Hittite, and Chinese, and indeed the modern writing of native Americans and different cases in Africa, all derived from a logographic original to create syllables. This followed a natural psychological impulse, to divide the world into words, and then words into component syllables. The consonant, by contrast, is only imaginable in Gelb's terms on the principle of stitching together different parts of an alphabet, as indeed happened with the first ever alphabetic system, in ancient Greek.

Gelb's hypothesis has been consigned to the footnotes, but it is worth reconsidering on philosophical grounds, not as a criticism of Egyptology, but as a contribution to the enigma of writing. It is conventional, as we saw in Part I, to describe written marks as Aristotle does, as symbols of spoken sounds. Hence, we describe as homonyms two words that are spelled the same and sound the same but have different meanings. A 'book' is both the thing you have in your hand, and a collection of bets made on a horse; 'air' is both what we breathe, and a tune we sing. However, the definition is a classic case of a chicken and an egg. We say 'homonym' when it is not clear whether we mean 'homophone'—a coincidence of sound—or 'homograph'—a rhyme of orthography. By way of example, in English, at least by some speakers, the word 'once' is pronounced identically to 'wants'. It is nonsense to say that either of these written words in modern English is a 'representation of a sound'. One derives from an Anglo-Saxon adverb *ænes*, the other perhaps from an Old Icelandic verb *vanta*. Variations in sound of many kinds have come into being ten or more centuries since, across languages and also regional dialects. Even now, some readers of this paragraph will dispute harshly that no educated English person could confuse the two. One thing all will agree is that the distinction is only clarified by reference to words in dictionary spellings. If anything, the sounds follow the user's sense of the written word, rather than the other way around. The priority of spoken over written is presumed ultimately because everyone concurs that spoken languages existed before written ones. Yet the presumption is somewhat jejune when we consider that written languages are five thousand years old, and that the evidence for how a language sounded in earlier times is always only to be judged on written evidence. No one living has ever heard ancient Egyptian spoken, or ever will. The lack of written vowels makes its sound system especially opaque. A recent announcement that a mummified priest had been made to speak again via a CT scanner in Leeds missed the point: it merely reproduced the sound the vocal tract makes in a mummified state.[39]

Hieroglyphics were especially preserved for monumental purposes. For practical purposes, scribes used a shorthand version which came to be known (via Clement of Alexandria) as *hieratic*. For the scribes, though, they were the same thing: the one was a simplified version of the other. Hieratic was never used on stone, but only on pots or papyrus: it was used for accounts and for writing letters. Demotic was a third script, an everyday form used for business purposes and more widely understood. Hieroglyphs were thus an increasingly specialized form of writing, eventually becoming archaic and perhaps artificial.[40] But for certain purposes only the monumental script would do, most of all in communicating with the gods. In temples, or other buildings associated with the gods, hieroglyphics were mandatory. This also applied to the words of the pharaoh, especially when he is an intermediary between the gods and the people. This also applied to places where the divine and the earthly coincided, most of all in tombs and cemeteries. A special form of literature arose known as the Books of the Dead.

Books of the Dead (Fig. 34) consisted of a number of magic spells intended to assist a dead person's journey through the Duat, or underworld, into the afterlife. The tradition of writing these lasted well over a thousand years and were the preserve of priests. They were always written in hieroglyphics, often in archaic forms, sometimes on a vertical plane. They could be inscribed on tomb walls or places in the coffin or a burial chamber. Most texts within a Book began with the word *ro*, which can mean 'mouth', 'speech', 'spell', 'utterance', 'incantation', or 'chapter of a book'. This ambiguity reflects the similarity in Egyptian thought between ritual speech and magical power.

As in ancient Assyria, therefore, scribes became a special class of people, with quasi-sacred powers. Indeed, writing in this context itself comes to be seen as sacred. Curtius's survey of the idea discovered its origin in the ancient Near East and Egypt.[41] Here we find holy and cult books, the possession of which is restricted to a priestly caste. Writing is a mystical act and scribes are accorded a corresponding status as its masters and interpreters. The earliest inscriptions in the tombs of kings acted not only as a literary record but also as physical totems for the pharaoh to avert danger in the afterlife and to communicate with the gods.

By contrast, Curtius asserted, in classical Greece there was 'hardly any idea of the sacredness of the book' (p. 304). The *Phaedrus* was a prime case. Is this a case of secularization, whereby the ancient sacred traditions wither and transform themselves into a kind of modernity? Ascribing a proleptic modernity to ancient Greece is a popular trick within the Western tradition that claims an innate global superiority. Against this, we could set Curtius's evidence that in the Hellenistic period the Greeks did acquire a 'culture of books'. In later grammarians, indeed, things came full circle, and Homer, in whose writing no figure of the book appears, began to be regarded as sacred writing. Roman literature shows a similar pattern, in the main eschewing an imagery of the book, although the last book of Martial's *Epigrams* is an exception. He offers his dinner guests a gift to take home, to each of which he attaches a dedicatory poem. They are all writing objects: books, writing tablets, styluses, and so on. A three-leaved tablet will seem like an excellent gift if it bears a message from your girlfriend; but a wax one might be even better if you need to erase the details of an assignation.[42] When Martial was rediscovered in the twelfth century, this love of the book, albeit profane, found a ready Christian home.

For a modern reader, what lends further power to this idea of secularization is the development of the alphabet. The alphabet appears to rid writing of its chthonic power. If the pictogram is like a shibboleth, and drawing it is a magical act, the alphabet is a clinical tool of science. The first pure alphabet in human history is the Greek one: from it derive all the European types, whether Coptic, Latin, Gothic or Slavonic. Yet the origins of the Greek alphabet are one of the great mysteries of writing. It did not arrive suddenly, or even from Greek soil. The Greeks traditionally called Kadmos (Cadmus) the Phoenician the founder of writing. Herodotus indeed called the Greek letters *phoinikeia grammata*, 'Phoenician characters'.[43] The historian claimed to have seen examples of an archaic alphabet in Thebes, the home of Kadmos. They were forgeries, but Herodotus had his geography right. Phoenician writing consisted of twenty-two syllabic signs, each designating a consonant plus an unspecified vowel. Ultimately derived from Egyptian, it spread to Palestine, Syria and northern Mesopotamia. The earliest Greek inscriptions (8th c. BCE) show similar shapes, and converted four consonantal signs into *alpha*, *epsilon*, *iota*, and *omicron*. From other Phoenician signs it created two letters: a consonantal *digamma* and a vocalic *upsilon*.[44] In so doing, the Greeks made a profound innovation: the articulated vowel. One of the two earliest examples yet found is the 'Cup of Nestor' on the island of Ischia (*c.*750—700 BCE). It is a jokey text about drinking and sex, possibly alluding to Homer, written from right to left: the first word contains three vowels, as clear as Neapolitan sunlight.[45] The earliest example of the Greek alphabet in Italy, perhaps even older, is almost all vowels: *EUOIN*, a drinking exclamation to the god Dionysus.[46] Within 200 years, in Miletus, two more glyphs emerged for long *e* and *o* vowels. All the sounds of words could now be rendered in full, and a text could be read continuously, without supposition.[47]

Barry Powell has added a beautiful speculation to this theory. Noticing the coincidence in time between development of the Greek alphabet and the writing down of the final form of Homer's *Iliad* and *Odyssey*, he wonders if the desire to vocalize writing fully is connected to the needs of dactylic hexametric poetry—the alternation of long and short syllables in flexible but predictable patterns. Unlike other Indo-European metres, which are based on syllable counts, the hexameter allows for the substitution of two short syllables for one long. It creates an aesthetic response out of a sense perception of the ear. The *aiodos*—the singer of songs—is characterized in the *Odyssey* as the hero of language-making. The *Odyssey* presents within itself the formal performance of a host of songs, often performed at banquets. Some are as short as 141 lines ('The Adultery of Ares and Aphrodite'; *Odyssey* 8. 226–366) but at its longest—the apologue of Books 9–10 – Odysseus sings 1,960 lines in one shot, and then, when Alkinöos begs for more, sings another 709 lines.[48] Such performances may have been typical of the kind of oral poet of whom Homer was an example. The hexametric line was here an aid to memory. Yet this is nothing in comparison with the feat of reciting the *Iliad* or the *Odyssey* as a whole. Memorizing it is a staggering feat, and all modern attempts have failed.

Homer himself had no need for writing, and it is commonly assumed never saw his poems written down. Although there are references to 'baneful signs' in the text of *Iliad*, book 6, it is assumed among commentators that these are not written signs: the Homeric heroes are all illiterate. And yet, at some point, with enormous consequences for Homeric verse itself as well as world literature, 'writing, with all its mystery', came to Homer, and his work was written down.[49] This, not the oral poems, is what we have. Within a generation, Greek myth and legend begin to be found on Greek pottery, with feasts, dances, contests, and battles on land and at sea. While it is not possible to prove direct influence from Homer, an eighth-century BCE representation of a man riding on a keel while others drown, appears to be Odysseus leaving the island of Helios (*Odyssey*, 12: 403–25).[50] Powell's conclusion is fanciful but sensitively told: the Greeks needed writing to keep Homer alive, and once they invented it, transformed their own world.

Writing never looked back, so to speak. The Greek alphabet, according to Gelb, is 'the last important step in the history of writing'.[51] 'Nothing new', he says, has happened since. The alphabet appears to be the quintessential sign of modernity. While the origins according to Powell are poetic, the alphabet is the engine of clarity and transparency. Homer himself, while as full of metaphor as the wine-dark sea, can be recited by anyone, simply by learning the letters, and parsing them out, one by one. With this act, it appears, the myth of Thoth disappears. He can no longer lord it over us with his Eleusian mysteries, his rituals of chance and death. The scribe as spell-master and priest is gone.

Kadmos lived in the middle Bronze Age, five hundred years too old to make up Greek writing. Another story gives another hero credit for the alphabet: Palamedes, son of Nauplios.[52] He, too, is Phoenician: Virgil traces his descent from Belus (the Bible's Baal), prime among Phoenician gods.[53] If Palamedes gets no lines in Homer, he belongs in his world. Odysseus feigned madness so as not to go to Troy. Palamedes placed Odysseus's baby son Telemachus in front of his plough; by picking his child up, the father confessed he was not mad, so went to war.[54] Odysseus' hatred is the common theme of these ephemeral stories. Another post-Homeric myth has Palamedes carry a letter from Clytemnestra to Helen, through which Odysseus and Menelaus fail in their embassy to get Helen back.[55]

In other places, like the lost play *Palamedes* by Euripides, he teaches the Greeks to write, to put their letters in order, adding consonants to the seven existing vowels.[56] Writing, Palamedes declares, provides (as in Plato), 'remedies for forget-fulness'. But *pharmaka*, we know, harm as well as heal, so *Lethe* is not appeased.

Palamedes is a cousin to Thoth (like Hermes): and like both, he is inveterately inventive. He records the laws and devises the numbers; he measures time; he invents coinage and dice.[57] Above all, he puts things in order, like the letters in this sentence: he makes things 'march in a row', which was the root of the word for alphabet in Greek.[58] 'Palamedes replied: "I did not discover writing—I was discovered *by* writing",' Philostratus wittily says.[59] Writing was always waiting for the right guy to find it: invention is really discovery. Powell speculates the Greek alphabet was invented simultaneously to Homer because someone needed to write it down to remember it. It can never be proven, but it is a beautiful idea for no other reason than that the *Odyssey* is the poem of memory, looking backwards to return among heroes, or grieving for their passing.

> But come my friend,
> Tell us your story now, and tell it truly.
> Where have your rovings forced you?
> What lands of men have you seen, what sturdy towns,
> What men themselves?[60]

Odysseus struggles to recall and longs to forget, putting off death by telling his tale, or speaking to the dead in the effort to bring his comrades back to life. The *Odyssey* is the primeval tale of literature coming into being, so perhaps also of writing as becoming.

In the late 1480s Aldus Manutius arrived in Venice on a mission to print texts in Greek.[61] In Rome he befriended the humanist Giovanni Pico della Mirandola; he started printing late, forty years old. Before his work, only ten Greek books (such as Homer) had been printed in all Europe. To find scholars, he searched the sizeable Greek community in Venice.[62] Between 1495 and 1498, he produced a landmark five-volume edition of Aristotle.[63] Old Byzantium reconvened on the Adriatic lagoon in Aldus's *Neakademia*, talking Greek in imitation of Plato's famous school.[64] In 1507 Erasmus lodged there, editing *Iphigenia in Aulis* and *Hecuba* by Euripides. A year later Erasmus bought a copy of *Rhetores Graeci*, including the long-lost Aristotle's *Poetics*. When he edited a Greek New Testament in Basel in 1516, the printer Froben used a Venetian model for his Greek type.[65] In all, the Aldine press made 75 texts of classical and Byzantine authors.[66] A per-fect Greek fount became a holy grail for Renaissance printers. Claude Garamond, whose Roman type was so wondrous that the Aldine company adopted it after the master's death, next tried to cast in metal a more venerable alphabet, making legendary *grecs du roi* for use in Robert Estienne's 1550 edition of the New

Testament. In 1578, Estienne's son Henri published all Plato, source of the Stephanus pagination still in use.

Imagining a 'future for writing' in 1952, Gelb envisaged utopian rationalization. He foresaw a reformed script, a descendant of the International Phonetic Alphabet, to eradicate the shortcomings of the Latin.[67] Ironically, he wrote this just as the computer age came into being. Now the letter morphed again, from the stroke of the pen in ink, or stamp of printed fount on paper, to a purely electronic realm. To achieve this, letters of writing are translated into code, then generated back from the bowels of the machine. The new process only goes to show that mystery lies dormant in writing after all.

Indeed, Zuboff's term to describe Google's armies of computer scientists interpreting the omni-mass of modern data is 'the new priesthood'.[68] It is a metaphor she uses often, with a conscious nod to hieroglyphics. Yet is it so inappropriate? Plato tried to demystify writing by demonstrating its innate ambiguity. The coding of supercomputers is immune to ambiguity, but it is not short of mystique. It is worth remembering that Erasmus, great master of the revolution of the printed word, invented a figure for the process of writing which itself uncannily recalled the *Symposium*. Socrates, he says, was called 'more ugly than the Sileni'.[69] A Silenus was a small figure of carved wood. On the outside it appeared as the caricature of a drunken old man, the tutor of Bacchus, ugly and priapic. But on the inside, by the cunning of the artist, was represented the figure of a deity. What better icon or metaphor, Erasmus asked, was there for the miracle of writing. Is not the text of Plato—above all the *Symposium*, where Alcibiades extols the Silenus—an example of this mystery: how dark, physical letters contain miracles of light within?[70] Daring himself to go further, Erasmus asks, is not Holy Scripture itself a Silenus? The language of the Hebrew and the Greek Old and New Testaments is often crude and vulgar by the highest classical standards, but Christ himself is found within.

Erasmus was familiar with the attempts of Horapollo to interpret the Egyptian hieroglyphics, but he doubted his capacity to succeed. The 'priest-prophets and theologians of Egypt', he said in another of his Adages, *festina lente*, thought it wrong to express the mysteries of wisdom in 'ordinary writing'.[71] To hide the truth from the uninitiated *hoi polloi*, they drew the shapes of animals and inanimate things. In order to interpret this secret language, Erasmus speculates, it would first be necessary to learn the properties of every object in the universe, and the nature of each separate creature. Such knowledge, of its essence, was either impossible, or given only to the very few.

Christians in Erasmus' time gave a name to this figure of secret knowledge, whom they called (following old Roman tradition) Hermes Trismegistus. Hermes, the messenger of the gods, mediates between life and death. Marsilio Ficino, Pico della Mirandola, and Giordano Bruno all speculated whether this figure was a pagan prophet who foresaw the coming of Christianity, or who could convey a *prisca theologia*, a single unified theology which lay at the heart of all religions.[72] Exegetes of the Qur'an identified the prophet Idrīs with Hermes Trismegistus, and some Arabic genealogists claimed Muhammad was his descendant.[73] In the medieval Arabic tradition, there were three figures called Hermes. The first (who is identified with Enoch), built the pyramids and wrote the whole knowledge of mankind on the walls to preserve it from the flood. After the flood, the second Hermes studied science in Babylon; the third wrote scientific works in Egypt.[74] Cicero recorded the existence of five Mercuries in *De natura deorum*.[75] Cicero thought that the Egyptian name for Trismegistus was Them; Ficino was also familiar with Lactantius, where he is called Thoyt.[76] In his commentary on Plato's *Philebus* in 1469, Ficino put two and three together in concluding that Hermes is the western name given by ancient Greeks living in Egypt to the eastern god Thoth; and that Mercury is simply the Latin equivalent.[77] In *Pimander*, Ficino proclaimed Hermes 'three-times-greater' because he is philosopher, priest, *and* king. A source of wisdom older than Plato, and ruler of all philosophers, he is honoured for his responsibility for the invention of writing.[78] Mercurial Thoth is thus a permanent symbol of the obscure power of writing, from hieroglyphics to Google. We may no longer think of writing as sacred, but we have not ceased to worship it.

12

The Characters of Chinese

Hangul, the script of Korea, is perhaps the most scientifically proficient writing system in the world. Unlike other scripts (Fig. 36), it arrived out of nowhere, with no previous grammatological genealogy, in January 1444 CE. It was also the invention of a single person: King Sejong the Great (1397–1450), the fourth king of the Joseon Dynasty.[1] It was promulgated in the *Hunminjeongeum* ('The Correct Sounds for the Instruction of the People'), which was originally also the official name of the script.[2] This document was written in classical Chinese, which until then was the written script for the Korean language (known as *hanja*). It contained a preface by Sejong explaining the origin and purpose of Hangul, and outlining the alphabet letters *(jamo),* with brief descriptions of their corresponding sounds, and examples. The document then instructs the head of the Hall of Worthies, the Confucian scholar Jeong In-ji, to provide detailed explanations, in what became known as the *Hunminjeongeum Haerye*.[3] This was 65 pages in its original publication, and demonstrated (again in *hanja*) how the letters were to be formed (as initials, medials, or finals); how they were to be combined; and how to use them.

The astonishing feature of the Hangul system, still remarkable if introduced now, is that it is based on a completely original theory of the representation of sound. There are five basic consonants (*k, n, s, m,* and *ng*) each of which is given a graphic shape corresponding to the shape of the mouth and throat in uttering it. Each of these signs could be doubled or added to, in order to create all of the other consonant sounds. The vowel signs are entirely different in structure, and given a metaphysical explanation, evoking the three elements of Heaven (dot), Earth (horizontal line) and Mankind (vertical line).[4] These signs could be combined in different ways to produce eleven vowels and diphthongs. The whole system was based on a sophisticated phonological analysis of fifteenth-century Korean, distinguishing each syllable into its onset, peak, and coda. It made a conceptual and graphic distinction between vowels and consonants. In addition, instead of being arranged in a row side by side, Hangul letters were written in syllable blocks. It is a comprehensive linguistic design, alphabet and syllabary at once.

Hangul has lasted five hundred years but changed over time. Revisions resulted from disputes between phonemic purists and those who favoured the regularity of whole morphemes, making verb and noun shapes correspond to each other. Sejong belonged to the latter school; Jeong In-ji to the former. The Hangul

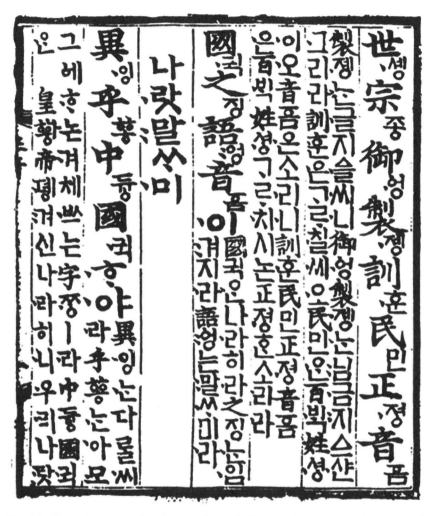

Fig. 36. 'Inventing new writing'; a page from the *Hunmin Jeongeum Eonhae*, a partial translation of *Hunmin Jeongeum*, the original promulgation of Hangul, 1443. Gansong Art Museum, Seoul, National Treasure No. 70

alphabet originally consisted of 28 letters, with 17 consonant letters and 11 vowels. In South Korea today, modern Hangul consists of 24 letters (14 consonants and 10 vowels). In North Korea the total is 40, which includes 5 additional tense consonants and 11 compound vowels. For anyone arriving in Seoul for the first time, and seeing the letters in operation, as I did on the Satnav of my friend's car, it is like language turned to logic. As Hyosik typed in, the letters moved into blocks of up to four in mathematical dance. There is a current fashion for writing instead in a line. Personally, I hope it is resisted; my mother loved geometry.

The introduction of Hangul was part of a philosophical theory of the rational basis of the state and of monarchy. The Joseon king was defined, according to Confucian ideals, as 'a transcendental being with the mandate of heaven'.[5] Symbolic objects and rituals expressed the sovereign status of royalty, and exerted power and authority over the country: legislative, judicial, and executive control. Sejong's reputation rested on political reforms: he established a Hall of Worthies (*Jiphyeonjeon*) at the Gyeongbokgung Palace, an elite group of scholars; he vastly increased the size (and professionalism) of the civil service (no longer limited to the noble class); he promoted scientific technology, in agriculture and the military; and he reinforced Confucianism as a socially normative teaching, suppressing Islam and at first also Buddhism.[6] The new script was intricately related to what can be described as a textual culture of politics.

The Korean elite reverted to the Chinese Hanja system after Sejong's death; to his profuse writings were added *Annals of the Joseon Dynasty*, a minute description of the official business of the monarch, and also a detailed inventory of his daily life. Over thirty volumes were meticulously compiled over 400 years.[7] There were *Daily Records of the Royal Secretariat*; and over time an anthology of *Exemplary Accomplishments of the Monarch*.[8] These recorded edited highlights of the deeds of former kings, turned into a manual of emulation for the current Joseon king. The *Genealogy of the Royal Family* (Seonwon-Rok) recorded information on the family tree, duly amended reign by reign. Begun under King Taejong (reigned 1400–18) it was supplemented by two other family trees of less direct members of the royal clan.[9] The Records of the Royal Palaces (*Gunggweolji*), begun in the reign of Sukjong (1674–1720) located all buildings in the royal palace complex, every wall and piece of furniture in its place.[10]

Already in the Goryeo Dynasty a Chinese envoy in Korea reported that 'the Royal Library by the riverside stores tens of thousands of books'.[11] The Chamber of Scholarly Advisers was founded in the 1250s, merging military and civilian values.[12] It is not much of an exaggeration to say that, between the downfall of Goryeo in 1392 and the annexation of Korea by Japan in 1910, the state was realized as a book of record. This combined a codification of tradition with a textualization of political and ethical life. Literary production controlled the life of every Korean citizen, even the large majority who were denied access to power by virtue of being unable to read. Government officials were ranked in eighteen levels, which were semi-hereditary but reinforced by state examinations (*gwageo*). Although some tests were military, the most prestigious was literary, in four parts, rigorously scored and ranked.[13] Candidates were examined on the Four Books and Five Classics of Chinese Confucianism, followed by the *chinsa-kwa*, which tested writing skills in poetry and documentary prose. Excellence here was the fast track to the levers of bureaucracy, the secretariat, ministries, offices high and low, the judiciary, academies, and archives of state. There were special Offices for

Paper Production, for Woodblock Printing, and Moveable Type.[14] Nonetheless, the number of books in circulation was small and strictly controlled for use by scholar-officials.

If writing and the book often owe their origins to sacred purposes, the Korean model is a demonstration of a cardinal link between technologies of writing and the mechanism of power and control. The Korean monarchy participated in state rites at every stage, so that the seals of office and documentary record of the life of the king were buried in a shrine after death. The Royal Ancestral Rites were codified over again in the late nineteenth century.[15] At the same time scholarly culture modernized, revising and reforming the Korean bureaucracy's literary methods.[16] In 1894, it adopted for the first time Hangul, used in popular and literary contexts for centuries, in official documents.

Despite a modern bias towards decoupling secular from religious, the two are not separate. While the Babylonian scribes dedicated their work to Nabu, the god of writing, knowledge was a key to power, and information was preserved about every level of society.[17] Whatever the demands of Thoth, the original hieroglyphic writing under King Den in 2800 BCE was ready-made to keep accounts. Egyptian rule embraced planning, made possible by keeping the most rigorous possible records of the annual flooding of the Nile. Yields of land were matched to the height of the flood, and taxes calculated accordingly.[18] Religion and politics merge in the technology of writing. The first ever book produced in the world using moveable type is not Gutenberg's 42-line Bible, but the *Jikji*, published in Hanja in Heungdeok Temple in Cheongju in July 1377, some 75 years before a press was set up in Mainz.[19] The text of the *Jikji* (Fig. 37) was written by Baegun (1298–1374; Buddhist name Gyeonghan), chief priest of Anguk and Shingwang temples. It comprises a collection of analects by monks, designed by Gyeonghan as a guide to Buddhism, Korea's national religion under the Goryeo Dynasty (918–1392).[20]

The technical accomplishment of the *Jikji* is the more remarkable since Chinese writing contains so many characters. Modern Chinese has over 60,000 characters in total, although most texts in practice require no more than 2,000. The earliest dictionary of characters by Xu Shen in the first century CE already contained nearly 10,000.[21] Nevertheless, printing began in China nearly a thousand years before the West. It was certainly well established by the eighth century CE.[22] The printing was done with woodblocks, employing ready-made skilled trades in wood carving.[23] The Diamond Sūtra, another Buddhist text, is the world's oldest printed book, dating from 868 CE, printed from seven blocks stuck together to create a single scroll.[24] The polymath Shen Gua described in the eleventh century a form of earthenware moveable type, using pieces of clay hardened in a kiln. Although nothing of this date survives, it is comparable to practical experiments using metal in Korea in the thirteenth century, before the *Jikji*.[25] Moveable type

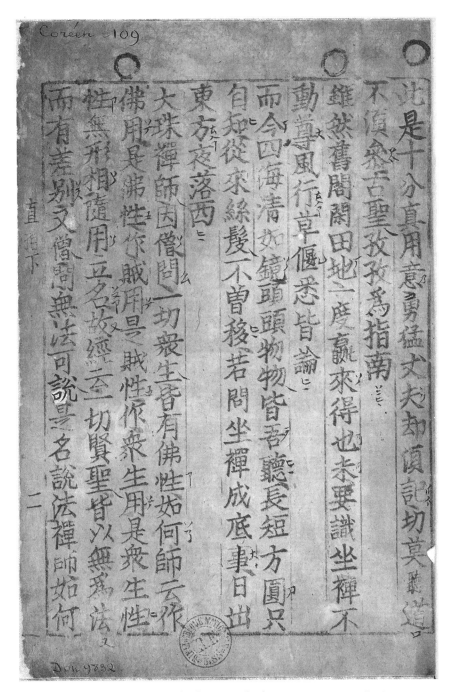

Fig. 37. 'The first moveable type'; *Jikji*, printed ink on paper, 1377 CE. Paris, Bibliothèque nationale de France, MS coréen 109

was necessary in Korea (said an early Joseon king) because importing books from China was difficult due to the distance, and because wood was easily burned or defaced.[26] It was also more feasible, since Korean print runs tended to be in tens or twenties, as reading was restricted to a governing scholar class.

Papermaking was first developed in China during the Han Dynasty in the second century CE.[27] The Chinese took paper to Persia, from where the Muslims took it to India and Europe. Early Chinese books were calligraphed paper rolls. In the Tang Dynasty, Buddhist texts came to be folded as in an accordion, and less liable to tear.[28] In addition to Buddhist sūtras, maps and calendars were made this way, a style of bookmaking that spread to Japan, where it was called *orihon*, used continuously for a thousand years, to the nineteenth century. A little later in the Tang period, a fashion arose for 'butterfly binding', single leaves folded into two pages, then laid on top of each other, in as many sheets as necessary.[29] This was called *detchō* or *kochōsō* in Japan.[30] Opened, the pages stand up resembling a butterfly's wings. This binding was mainly used for printed books; as convenient as a codex, it led to a profusion of books that were easy to use and read. For religious reasons, rolls were still preferred for Buddhist texts until modern times.

In the Heian period, the last classical age in Japan before the rise of the *shōgun*s in 1185 CE, Buddhism, Taoism, and other Chinese influences were at their height in the capital Kyoto. The Japanese imperial court now saw its golden period in literature and art. In a new type of binding, *yamato-toji*, folded pages were placed one inside the other in fascicles, sewn together with thread along the fold.[31] Another, older form of binding spread again from China, as old as the Tang and popular in the Ming, where a page was handwritten or printed on one side only, folded with the text showing upwards, then placed on top of the last sheet. Assembled pages were sewn together, the stitches in the blank margins next to the loose edges. In this way, the spine constitutes the sewn end, and the open edges are in folds. In Japan, this 'pouch binding' was known as *fukuro toji*.[32] By the late sixteenth century, it was the standard format for printed books, continuing right through to the Meiji in the late nineteenth century.

The Japanese writing system combines logographic *kanji*, adopted from Chinese characters, with syllabic *kana*, which consists of two types: *hiragana* for native words and *katakana* for foreign loan words. In early times only Chinese was written; then *man'yōgana* developed, appropriating *kanji* from Chinese, but interpreted phonetically rather than semantically. Originally it may have come from Korea; it was not reformed until the Meiji, when it was simplified into *hiragana* and *katakana*. In the Tokugawa period, between 1603 and 1868, books were printed using *man'yōgana* in Edo and Osaka as well as Kyoto. Artists and craftsmen combined in producing books, and women were often responsible for the binding, with some active as publishers and booksellers.[33] Machine printing did not begin in earnest until the 1880s.

With its influence reaching for so long into Japan and Korea, Chinese can properly be called the most important literate culture in history. Four times in antiquity, writing arose *de novo* in separate cultures: in Mesopotamia, in Egypt, in China, and in Mesoamerica. Of these, only Chinese has not needed modern decipherment, since it has been in continuous use from generation to generation to the present day.[34] While there are incised marks on pottery nearly 7,000 years old, the earliest unambiguous attestations of Chinese writing are inscriptions from Anyang, dating from about 1200–1050 BCE from the last stage of the Shang period. These consist of divinatory inscriptions on ox scapulas or turtle plastrons, supplemented by some bronze inscriptions.[35]

The Chinese characters in use today are the direct descendants of the Shang script. The Shang system is logographic: each character stands for a single word. There are two different kinds: unit characters, which consist of one graphic element alone; and compound characters, which are made up of two or more component parts.[36] Every character thus stood for a single syllable; but due to the flexibility of the compound system, a single character could correspond to different words, according to context. The idea of the purely ideographic nature of early Chinese writing has had a long hold in the West, and in the Renaissance, this seemingly hermetic function of language was highly attractive, making Chinese a parallel case to the interpretation of hieroglyphics. The twentieth-century imagist movement in poetry similarly found in Chinese characters an ideal of what Ezra Pound called in his manifesto: 'Direct treatment of the "thing", whether subjective or objective'.[37] Without knowing a word of Chinese, Pound produced a miniature poem of his own in 1913, 'Fan-Piece, for her Imperial Lord':

> O fan of white silk,
>> Clear as the frost on the grass-blade,
> You also are laid aside.[38]

Pound continued to project his 'ideogrammic method' in *Cathay* (1915), a full collection of Chinese 'translations' and imitations.[39] The ideographic character of Chinese continues to be controversial. William Boltz has argued for a 'crypto-phonogram' theory of the development of Chinese script, partly on the basis that a purely semantic writing is a fantasy.[40] Yet for Chad Hansen, to call this 'fantasy' is a purely Western canard.[41]

No modern reader could read the Shang script, since it uses many character forms long out of use. Early scripts differ from each other considerably despite following the same principles. This changed in the third century BCE, when the state of Qin united all China for the first time. One of the Qin emperor's goals was to standardize Chinese writing.[42] His Grand Councillor Li Si established what are known as the 'Small Seal' script (as opposed to the older 'Large Seal' forms).[43]

Here we encounter again the mystique of the First Emperor, and the problems of interpretation this entails. The megalith of the First Emperor dominates the modern myth of early China: he is the builder of the Great Wall as well as an empire that lasted two thousand years; while his army of terracotta warriors, discovered by accident by farmers digging for a well in 1974, have occasioned magnificent global exhibitions—and stereotype images of a new Chinese imperialism.

We should beware of taking too literally the creator myth of Ying Zheng, the man who became Qin Shi Huang. While everybody knows the fictitious cliché that the Great Wall can be seen from space, it is the reconstructed wall of the Ming Dynasty (1368–1644 CE) that is now in the mind's eye, and the original structure of the Qin is hard to quantify.[44] Similarly, while Li Si certainly intended to unify the Chinese writing script, silk manuscripts dating from after the end of the Qin Dynasty show that variation existed in practice. The idea of unity is instead the retrospective interpretation of Xu Shen a hundred years later, when he created his lexicon of the Small Seal script, explaining all the characters within his own structural interpretation, and as a by-product creating a whole category of non-standard characters, which through the success of his formula then themselves ceased to be.[45] A third omnipresent mythology has built up around the Book Burnings, discussed above. For while they are remembered now as an image of the intolerance of free speech, this image is a creation of the Han Dynasty that followed, part of a decision by Sima Qian to present Qin Shi Huang as a monster of destruction.

Nonetheless the idea of Qin Shi Huang as a creator god is hardly an accident, as it is the very idea he wished to promote.[46] Writing is a central tenet of the mythography. It is also the channel of authority in early China altogether, from the Warring States to Qin and then on to Han and beyond. Writing instrumentalizes assent and obedience in early China, in the establishment of what Mark Edward Lewis calls 'a textual canon' as the fount of imperial authority.[47] This canon is like a textual double of the state, in which texts become the double of the ruler. Such texts take many forms: divinatory records, communications with ancestors, government documents, collective writings of philosophical traditions, speeches attributed to historical figures, chronicles, poetry, commentaries, and compendia. Lewis calls this the 'encyclopaedic epoch': the 'ideal of the recently created empire as the image of the all-inclusive state'.[48] An equation is made between intellectual and political authority, in which the state (after the death of Confucius and the burning of the books) embodies its yearning for textual unity in a single corpus of official literature: legal documents, histories of the past, and verse.

The irony is that it was in the interests of a single textual corpus built into the fabric of the imperial library that Li Si carried out the burning of the books in the first place. Rather than an act of arbitrary censorship, Li Si's motive was intellectual control via the dissemination of writing. Perhaps, after all, the terracotta army has its relevance. The forced labour of 700,000 convicts and labourers was employed in the construction of the imperial tomb, of which the 7,000 individually cast figurines of warriors so far discovered is but a fraction of the original mausoleum.⁴⁹ What the emperor sought was not immortality in Western terms but what the Chinese called *bu si* ('non-death').⁵⁰ The totalitarian conception of the tomb is shown not so much by the famous mimetic faces as by the extraordinary planning and logistics needed to produce them. Beyond soldiers and weaponry lay further representational mania: a map of the known world, its rivers carved out and filled with mercury, a living simulacrum of the universe.⁵¹ 'The king of Qin waved his whip and drove the contents of the cosmos before him', wrote Sima Qian, for once hardly exaggerating, at least in terms of the Emperor's imagination.⁵²

The emperor desires to simulate the universe in its entirety, and it is a literary model that he has in mind as well as an artistic one. In symbolic terms, the empire and the book are one. 'Writing was neither routine nor commonplace', states Michael Nylan of the Han Dynasty that followed the Qin.⁵³ If the Western cliché of literary culture is to see it as casual in style and ornamental in purpose, China is an antidote. Higher literacy required long training; it was associated with hereditary privilege; and its motive was the assertion of political authority. Nonetheless, it was not the slightest degree functional in form. This was a consummately artistic concept of writing, which prized elegance and eloquence from the tiniest detail of presentation to the largest considerations of philosophy.⁵⁴ The *Yantie lun* ('Debates on Salt and Iron'), a first-century BCE treatise on monetary policy and price stabilization, is written in dialogue form, with fictional representations of reformists and modernizers, expressing cultural ritual and wisdom, using the model of Confucius' *Analects*.⁵⁵ A century later, Yang Xiong's *Fayan* ('Exemplary Talk') takes rhetoric itself as the key to Chinese civilization. Classical learning is the highest form, because it teaches the art of imitation (*ru*).⁵⁶

Such writing manifests itself as a physical entity as well as a structure of ideas. Calligraphy is a principal form of Chinese art, with its rituals of brush and ink. The model can be intricately small-scale or equally gargantuan. On Mount Tai, the most sacred of China's mountains, there is a wall of granite known as the Great Vista (*Daguan feng*). Here the first emperor ascended to the summit to declare the unity of China.⁵⁷ For a thousand years after, the emperor carried out the Feng and Shan sacrifices to pay homage to heaven (at the summit) and earth (at the foot of the mountain). *Daguan feng* is covered in huge Chinese characters. The largest (and oldest) inscription was composed in 726 CE by the Tang emperor Xuanzong. Much of it is in tetrasyllabic verse. Xuanzong addresses the spirits of his ancestors, and also the gods of heaven and earth. His intended readership is also inscribed on the side of the mountain: every person who will ever make the ascent, from now until the end of time, and who looks upon the words.⁵⁸

Fig. 38. 'Buddha on the mountain'; Diamond Sūtra inscription on Mount Tai, Shandong

The inscription bespeaks a kind of totality, expressed not only in the grandeur of its statements about meaning over time and scale of readership, but in the gigantic size of the lettering, the lavish gold pigment ornamenting in each of the 1,008 characters, and the dazzling landscape context of the peak itself. The declaration inspires awe at every level. It is *yuzhi yushu*—'composed by the emperor and transcribed by the emperor'. His power is unchallengeable and embodied in writing.

Elsewhere, on the north-east side of the mountain, is Sūtra Rock Valley, in which in the sixth century the Buddhist Diamond Sūtra was cut in characters 50 cm across. Unlike a polished marble stele, which in China (as in classical Rome) could be inscribed using a transfer from written sheets that could then be traced, the granite of Tai meant that the artist worked directly onto the stone (Fig. 38). Kneeling, the monks scraped out the adamant surface of the slope into 900 characters, and then brushed in the red pigment by hand afterwards. Understandably, mistakes were made, especially perhaps when a monk returned to work after a night's sleep, or else was in need of one. Yet whether for religious or for political purposes, the result was, in Robert Harrist's words, 'monumental and immeasurable'.[59] In total, there are 22 temples, 97 ruins, 819 stone tablets, and 1,018 cliff-side and stone inscriptions located on Mount Tai. The mountain continued to be carved during the Ming Dynasty (1368–1644) and the Qing Dynasty (1644–1912).

The Kangxi emperor (reigned 1662–1722), who was a tireless calligrapher in general, ever making gifts to Chinese literati (earning sycophantic gratitude), arrived on Mount Tai in 1684. By now Great Vista peak was something of a graffiti park. The emperor could hardly erase the existing characters, so instead he inscribed just two letters onto 'Cloudy Peak' (*Yunfeng*), making up for number in sheer size: they are each 100 cm tall. A special plinth was carved to frame them, and in the next generation two poems by the Qianlong emperor were added. He was the last emperor to inscribe on the side of the mountain, but there is a modern postscript. In 1962, a stone inscription was added to the slopes of Mount Tai, based on a hand scroll of the *Poem on the Long March* by Mao Zedong (1893–1976).[60] Chairman Mao never visited the mountain himself, but the work of his hand is there for all to see. Zhou Enlai and Guo Moruo were other enthusiastic calligraphers in the Communist Party.[61] Mao, whatever his doubts about invoking the methods of the old aristocratic class, was a past master at employing the politics of writing (and of letters) on a scale even his imperial forebears would have marvelled at.

Public inscription is one of the many ways in which the Communist Party under Mao exerted literary culture as an instrument of power and control. The marks of literacy made Party ideology omnipresent in everyday life. The ultimate example is perhaps the quickest-selling book of all time, and one of the most widely published: Mao's so-called 'Little Red Book'. *Mao Zhu Xi Yu Lu* ('Quotations of Chairman Mao') dubbed 'the Mao Bible', sold 720 million copies between its first publication in May 1964 and the first bilingual Chinese–English edition of August 1967.[62] Volumes of Mao's *Selected Writings* circulated in the 1940s before the founding of the People's Republic of China; in 1951, an authoritative edition appeared, in chronological sections, printed in Beijing in 200,000 copies. Three supplementary volumes produced between 1952 and 1960 covered new writings and speeches, the last issued in one million copies (a posthumous fifth volume appeared in 1977).[63] By 1964, the four volumes of Mao were the foremost sources of knowledge in China as well as by far the most common reading matter.

For the selected version, two trial bindings, in light and dark blue, were made before two different formats were approved, both containing the same text, with 250 pages divided between thirty chapters. At this point the book was intended only for the political department of the People's Liberation Army. A version in white printed paper wrappers, with the title in black characters inside a red box, was made for high-ranking officers; but for brigade teams, the binding was provided by an innovative technology, a red vinyl textured plastic, incised with the title and a red star. To create a buffer between vinyl and the thin paper inside, stiff white cardboard was inserted adjacent to the linen-backed spine, with sewn head and tail bands.[64] It is not known how many copies were produced of the first edition, since it was created from stereotyped plates simultaneously in different cities. Yet almost immediately the idea of the book was expanded from an ideological army manual to an unlimited mass market for the largest population in the world.

Modernist plastic and cheap paper combined to give the new book an iconic status, a commodity fetish specially designed for Marxists, we could say. Either in perfect timing with the Cultural Revolution (which broke out in 1966), or else as an intrinsic part of Mao's new political direction, the book-object became synonymous with the total politics of the new state within a state.[65] Members of the Red Guard (Fig. 39), in real life as well as ubiquitous posters, brandished their copies aloft, as if they were breviaries or Bibles.

Revolutionary violence in the meantime caught up with the printing process. Lin Biao, head of National Defence, wrote an endorsement, a Maoist *nihil obstat*, in his own calligraphic handwriting: 'Study Chairman Mao's writings, follow his teachings, and act according to his instructions.' But he made a mistake with his brush, an error only discovered after the first edition was printed, and only corrected in the third. The aura of Lin, an ally of Mao since 1928, and Commander in Chief of the volunteer forces in the Korean War, grew with the new book containing his signature, so that in 1969 at the Ninth Congress he was designated Mao's heir and successor. A classic victim of the volatile politics of the Cultural Revolution, he was then accused of plotting to assassinate Mao, denounced, and the aeroplane carrying him to exile was shot down over Mongolia on 12 September 1971. An order followed that his calligraphic endorsement should be torn out or otherwise defaced from every copy of the book, on pain of arrest.

By now there was a standard sequence of preliminaries: a half title printed in red, *Workers of the World, Unite!*; a title-page, with title and central star in red; a photographic image of Mao in a sensitive portrait in brown ink, often with a protective tissue guard; and the facsimile autograph of Lin Biao in brown or black ink. The second edition of March 1965 added two new chapters, and the third another, for a total of 33 chapters and 270 pages. In August 1967, the publication was further transformed in the bilingual Chinese–English edition produced by the East is Red Publishing House in Beijing. Now the book became a global proselytizing device, as nations and languages received the word of Mao in the hope of a socialist conversion worldwide: in order of publication, English, French, Japanese, Spanish, Russian, Vietnamese, German, Italian, Portuguese, Mongolian, Arabic, Hindi, Albanian, Indonesian, Urdu, Nepali, Hausa, Norwegian, Pashto, Thai, Burmese, Swahili, Persian, Esperanto, Korean, Lao, Tamil, Bengali, Rumanian, Hungarian, Polish, Greek, Serbian, and Braille.[66] Among many gullible or devout readers, my teenage self counts as one. The number of copies in circulation by Mao's death was in the billions; one estimate is 6.5 billion.[67] By the end of the 1970s circulation had stopped, and a counter-order came for millions and millions to be pulped as obsolete paper. Total royalties earned are a matter of speculation.[68]

On 8 August 2008, ideographic hauntings entered the digital age. At the Opening Ceremony of the 29th Olympic Games in Beijing, massed ranks of scribes in kitsch red costumes danced, holding bamboo-slip scrolls, reciting extracts from Confucius' *Analects* (论语). 'Harmony is what is most prized in the

Fig. 39. 'Little Red Book'; Mao Zedong above Red Guards with Little Red Books

practice of the rites.'[69] After a visual tribute to brush, ink, stone, and paper (the four elements of Chinese calligraphy), the display metamorphosed into a gigantic machine, first printing press then digital press, pixels self-reproducing in a binary vortex of alternate pressed and depressed electrical charges.[70] In one move, the choreography of film director Zhang Yimou mirrored the Chinese government's desire to combine the cultural power of ancient calligraphy with the digital revolution that the new China wields on a global scale.

This constituted a radical reframing of the Chinese script in relation to modernity. The classic western view was stated by Hegel, who contrasted the ideographic opacity of the Chinese writing system, with the rational simplicity of the Western alphabet. In what might be considered an example of Orientalism, Hegel called Chinese writing 'at the outset a great hindrance to the development of the sciences'.[71] In time, during the colonial years of the late nineteenth and early twentieth centuries, the Hegelian view was adopted by Chinese intellectuals themselves. There were simply too many signs, which took too long to learn, and in any case did not correspond to speech and thus inhibited memorization. One fruit of this self-denigration was the reform proposed by several members of the May Fourth Movement of 1919 to create a new vernacular writing system, *baihua*, to reflect the spoken Chinese of the modern world.[72] A parallel script reform was *Zhuyin* or *Bopomofo* (after the first four syllables in the conventional ordering of Mandarin syllabaries), which reduced the number of characters to 37, with four tone marks, as a newfound phonetic writing system.[73] Officially recognized by the government of the People's Republic of China, it is still in use in Taiwan today.

Meanwhile the Communist government in mainland China commissioned a different reform under the leadership of the economist and linguist Zhou Youguang. This is the system called Hanyu Pinyin, using romanization as a way of reinforcing a phonetic script.[74] Initially, traditional Chinese writing posed a problem in the world of computers, since ASCII code could only deal with a finite number of characters (the 26 Latin letters, 10 digits, and punctuation marks).[75] This was an additional argument in favour of Pinyin. However, in time coding caught up not only with Chinese but also with many other non-western writing systems, using an input method editor. Tablet computers allow users to interface with a stylus, simplifying the computer usage of Chinese further. As with other arguments about the triumph of the Roman alphabet, the idea that Chinese is fundamentally unsuited to the age of the iPad has been revealed as neo-colonial twaddle. It is possible, by way of a linguistic coda, to see the bold confidence of the representation of Chinese writing in the Beijing Olympics, as indicating new life in an old script. Chinese writing has been the most successful writing system in history. It has its own independent way of representing language and reality. As well as the voice of speech, it manifests the body of things, and thereby also the body of the human. Andrea Bachner winningly calls this a 'corpography', a written form of embodiment.[76] The only caveat is the totalitarian model the script continues to evoke at so many moments in Chinese politics. Watching the Opening Ceremony in 2008, too, beauty carried a shadow of menace. Not only the dancers, but the written characters they figured forth, appeared as the chosen instruments of an unseen power.

IV

THE CULT OF THE BOOK

A good Booke is the pretious life-blood of a master spirit, imbalm'd and treasur'd up on purpose to a life beyond life

John Milton, *Areopagitica* (1644)

13
Words and Images

In December 1929, in the last issue of *La révolution surréaliste*, René Magritte produced a series of images with captions under the title, 'Les mots et les images'.[1] The words appear in Magritte's characteristic cursive handwriting, while the images are engraved directly from his drawings; an original draft survives entirely in Magritte's hand in the Musées royaux des Beaux-Arts in Brussels.[2] The evident implication of the twinning of the two products of Magritte's hand is a theory of correspondence between verbal and visual; and yet the initial proposition of the manifesto is the opposite: 'un objet ne tient pas tellement à son nom'. No object attaches itself so readily to its name that one could not find for it another which corresponded just as well. As Magritte descends down the page, he loses no opportunity for the playful rearrangement of word and thing by association, substitution, superimposition, or fusion of one with the other.

He laid out the principle in a letter to Paul Nougé in October 1927, explaining the work *Découverte*, which he had painted earlier that year: there he had merged two concepts with no logical connection, *femme et bois*, painting a 'woman' as if made of 'wood' (or vice versa).[3] The result was not a combination of the two but a new thing entirely. Surrealism, he said, was not the equation of word and thing, but a refusal to take either as paramount. In *La révolution surréaliste*, the most perfect example is his statement: 'Tout tend à faire penser qu'il y a peu de relation entre un objet et ce qui le représente'. Proof how little relation exists between word and referent lies in a pair of images placed beneath, using Magritte's idiosyncratic childlike literalist graphic style, of a French country house surrounded by tress (Fig. 40). The images appear absolutely identical, except for the words accompanying them, 'l'objet réel' and 'l'objet représenté'. The joke is that a thing after all is indistinguishable from its representation; except for a further joke that, rather than Magritte engraving the same image twice, he has instead drawn it a second time free hand, with minute cases of 'spot the difference' in execution.

We are living through a new age of the visual, what has been called a 'pictorial turn'.[4] In an era of data deluge, visualization is the key to new technologies. Visual representation structures the processing of information on a scale scarcely imaginable a generation ago. Indeed, technology, it is said, is changing the way that the brain thinks. Just as training primates to use tools leads to

LES MOTS ET LES IMAGES

Un objet ne tient pas tellement à son nom qu'on ne puisse lui en trouver un autre qui lui convienne mieux :

Il y a des objets qui se passent de nom :

Un mot ne sert parfois qu'à se désigner soi-même :

Un objet rencontre son image, un objet rencontre son nom. Il arrive que l'image et le nom de cet objet se rencontrent :

Parfois le nom d'un objet tient lieu d'une image :

Un mot peut prendre la place d'un objet dans la réalité :

Une image peut prendre la place d'un mot dans une proposition :

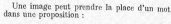

Un objet fait supposer qu'il y en a d'autres derrière lui :

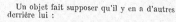

Tout tend à faire penser qu'il y a peu de relation entre un objet et ce qui le représente :

Les mots qui servent à désigner deux objets différents ne montrent pas ce qui peut séparer ces objets l'un de l'autre :

Dans un tableau, les mots sont de la même substance que les images :

On voit autrement les images et les mots dans un tableau :

Fig. 40. 'Verbal icon'; René Magritte, 'Les mots et les images', printed book, 1929. Brussels, Musée royaux des Beaux-Arts de Belgique

observable growth in visual and motor skills, so the human mind adapts to new media just as it learns to master them.[5] Within this dominion, we are routinely told that the age of writing is giving way to the age of the image. Neuroscience is invoked to provide an explanation: the left brain tending towards the word, favouring the rational, the linguistic, and the logical; and the right brain towards the image, favouring the visual, the emotional, and the intuitive. At around the time of the invention of the internet, it became fashionable to see this in large-scale cultural terms, in which left-brain linear thinking was contrasted with the new possibilities that the digital age opened up of a move to right-brain holistic thinking.[6] In its cruder forms, the argument also suggested a division on gender lines.

Although posed as the newest of the new, these divisions run deep in human cultures. In the Sanskrit text *Viṣṇudharmottara Purāṇa* (6th–11th c. CE), a distinction is made between Viṣṇu (the Supreme Being) as image, and Viṣṇu as text. Vajra the king asks the sage Mārkaṇḍeya why, if god exists everywhere, do people make images of him, and why do they believe that he resides in this image?[7] Mārkaṇḍeya replies that in himself, Viṣṇu exists without boundaries, having neither beginning, nor middle, nor end. However, out of love (*anugraha*) for Hindu people, and to make himself approachable, Viṣṇu presents himself as an image. The image is a 'condensed' (*piṇḍita*) form of him, and thus has proportions and occupies space (with a beginning, a middle, and an end). All of this, of course, is also presented here in textual form, in one of the Purāṇas ('Books of received wisdom'), collections of myth, folklore, and other teaching.

Julius Lipner has described the bewildering hierarchy of Hindu texts.[8] Hinduism of all religions is the most equivocal about writing, the most attached to speech as having superior value, and the most sceptical about how holy scripture is. The Purāṇas (3rd c. CE) are held to be less holy than the original Hindu texts. The most sacred and beloved of these is the Veda ('knowledge'; 1200 BCE onwards). It represents an infallible 'hearing' (*śruti*), by ancient sages of the sacred words left in the world by Viṣṇu. The Veda nonetheless combines a sense of the upholding or protection of oral tradition with its potential destruction or violation.[9] A second order of textual revelation exists in the *Brāhmaṇas*, representing the rituals of sacrifice; then the Āraṇyakas, 'forest-texts', and fourthly the Upaniṣads. This is followed by a radiating circle of mythological narrative texts in the form of the *Mahābhārata* ('The Great Tale of the Bhāratas'; 4th c. BCE–4th c. CE) and the *Rāmāyaṇa* ('The Coming of Rāma'). Nonethless, the *Mahābhārata* claims to be 'on a par with the Vedas' because it is 'supremely purifying'.[10] All these textual forms coexist with rampant imagistic representations.

The story (Fig. 41) of the exiled hero Rāma (the seventh incarnation of Viṣṇu) and his devoted wife Sītā was first told 2500 years ago. Lakṣmaṇa and Sītā resolve to go into exile with Rāma. Seated in the pavilion on the left, Sītā distributes her

Fig. 41. 'Viṣṇu in pictures'; *Rāmāyaṇa*, watercolour on paper, 1649–53 CE. British Library Add. MS 15296

jewels; in the pavilion on the right, Rāma and Lakṣmaṇa give away their jewels, horses, elephants and camels. Text sits side by side with this watercolour. Originally containing 450 images, the manuscript was prepared by a single scribe in collaboration with many painters. It was prepared for Maharana Jagat Singh, ruler of the Rajput kingdom of Mewar in Rajasthan.

Viṣṇu in *Moby-Dick* picks up the Vedas lying at the bottom of the ocean. He becomes incarnate in the whale, which 'sounding down in him to the uttermost depths, rescued the sacred volumes'.[11] Self-mockingly, Melville merges the Indian god with all the mythologies in his head: Perseus, St George, Hercules, and Jonah. Cultic books and cultic images are not infrequently put in combination, often presented as if in semiotic conflict. A battle between image and text in religious terms is strongly present especially in the three Semitic religions, Judaism, Christianity, and Islam. This conflict then plays off in a different direction in the historical division that has been constructed between modernity and pre-modernity. Here, the pre-modern has been reconstructed to present a precise historical narrative, after which humankind rejected imagism at the same time as rejecting religion. This is the cultural work ascribed to the revolution of print culture.

McLuhan's concept of the *Gutenberg Galaxy* poses print as an epochal precondition of modernity. Culture is simultaneously technologized and secularized, through which print enables a triumph of individualism. This is of course a Western view of world history. Print was not invented by Gutenberg at all, and by the fifteenth century was nearly a thousand years old. It is also not a secular invention (although perhaps that could also have been extrapolated from the most famous of Gutenberg's works being a Bible). The oldest surviving printed book in the world is the Diamond Sūtra, produced on 11 May 868 CE according to the Western calendar: 'On the 15th day of the 4th month of the 9th year of the Xiantong reign period, Wang Jie had this made for universal distribution on behalf of his two parents.'[12] The Diamond Sūtra is one of the most important Mahāyāna scriptures in East Asia. It begins with an image, of the historical Buddha addressing his elderly disciple Subhūti, surrounded by an assembly gathered under a grove of trees.[13] As image and text, and as a cultic object, the Diamond Sūtra suggests an alternative mythology of the meaning society gives to the material existence of books.

This ambiguity is also present in McLuhan, who far from glorifying print, celebrated its imminent implosion at the hands of movies, television, and the incipient age of the computer, which he foresaw with uncanny zeal. The printed revolution was giving way to what he called 'the global village' of the future.[14] Mankind in the electronic age is freed from the slavery of print. Such a conception conflicts with the pervading cliché (popular in the digital revolution) that the visual (in the use of the internet) has either invaded or appropriated the techniques of writing and reading. While the popular press is full of fears that reading and writing are on the wane, superseded by the cheap thrills of instant visuality, whether Youtube surfing or game consoles, it is obvious enough that the internet, far from bringing about the end of reading, has reinforced it to the extent of twenty-four hour saturation. Technology not only *allows* reading, but also might be thought to mandate it. We used to go home from work and at some point feel free of a gaze of text; now, email follows us to bed, where international timezones (reinforced by COVID-19) mean that even in rest from one task, another arrives from 3,000 miles away, so the reading day begins again at midnight. Text, like money, never sleeps.

At the heart of this problem is a question whether visual thinking is in some sense the antithesis of verbal thinking, even that it is a different world or order of ideas. Such an insight has existed since the Enlightenment, in the theory of the distinction between art and literature developed by G. E. Lessing in *Laokoön, oder, Über die Grenzen der Malerei und Poesie* (1767). This was allied to Lessing's long-standing rejection of Horace's theory of imitation in favour of Aristotle's theory of mimesis. In particular, he denied Horace's truism *ut pictura poesis*—that poetry and painting are fundamentally alike.[15]

Painting and poetry, in their imitations, make use of entirely different media of expression, or signs—the first, namely, of form and colour in space, the second of articulated sounds in time.[16]

This is the reason why literature lends itself so naturally to narrative, since it unfolds in time. Painting, by contrast, exists in space not time. Taken to its logical conclusion, verbal language has no place in the appreciation of visual art, since it belongs to a different cognitive domain. In relation to visual art, the senses take over, in the direct response of feeling. In the opposite direction, Friedrich Schleiermacher, founder of modern hermeneutics, objected to the idea of pictures in poetry. No poem should 'look like an axe or bottle'.[17] Text is the means by which an author communicates thoughts that are prior to the creation of the text. The text is the place where these 'inner thoughts' become 'outer expression' in language.[18] The pictorial in this sense is an aberration of the hermeneutic method, acting as a barrier to higher understanding.

Lessing's father was a Lutheran minister, and he himself took his master's degree at Wittenberg. Schleiermacher took the chair in theology at the new Lutheran University of Berlin in 1810. There may be a trace, then, of Protestant influence in the Enlightenment epistemological division between the verbal and the visual. The historian Carlos Eire has called the Reformation 'the triumph of the word over the picture'.[19] The word of God, spoken by a 'jealous God', expressly forbade the making of any image of God:

> Thou shalt not make unto thee any graven image, or any likeness of any thing that is in heaven above, or that is in the earth beneath, or that is in the water under the earth.[20]

Condemnation of the image went hand in hand with zeal for the letter of the law, or as might be said, the law of the letter. There is indeed a phenomenological edge to this. The visual incorporates the world of the material and is limited to it. The world of the spirit is by definition immaterial and invisible, beyond the reach of images, which can, by seeking to imitate it, only become idolatry. By contrast, the biblicists often turned away from material and physical manifestations of the spiritual (in the world of things) with revulsion. For Eire, the Reformation was most successful, as in Calvin's Geneva, when it succeeded in harnessing popular revolutionary iconoclasm.[21]

Aber das wortt gottis ist geistlich | und allein den glaubigen nutze, wrote Andreas Karlstadt in his 1522 treatise on the abolition of images.[22] The word consists of spirit alone. Karlstadt had been appointed city preacher in Wittenberg while Luther went into hiding under the imperial ban. Meanwhile, in January 1522, the council, without the consent either of the bishop or of Elector Friedrich the Wise, declared a church ordinance that 'the images and altars in the church should be removed, in order to prevent idolatry, for three altars without images are enough'.[23] Action proved as loud as words, and the City Church was raided, with altars stripped and images broken. In rural Saxony, an image of St Francis was hung from the gallows in 1524.

This was not idle vandalism but organised purgation. The element of orchestration is shown not only by the church order but also the words of the preacher in exhorting the congregation to zealous action. Luther's hymn *Ein feste Burg* provided a martial call to arms. This pattern was followed in turn in Germany, in Switzerland, in the Low Countries, and in England and Scotland, as the Protestant Reformation spread.[24] John Knox describes with relish how stones were thrown at the tabernacle in St John's church in Perth in May 1559.[25] In May 1562, a riot of image-breaking followed a sermon in Rouen.[26] Margaret Aston has compared the radicalization of the iconoclastic congregation through collective actions such as orations and hymn-singing to French revolutionary songs of 1789–93 such as 'Ça ira' and the Marseillaise.[27] An engraving (Fig. 42) of the 1566 *Beeldenstorm* in Antwerp by Frans Hogenberg shows articulate, clinical violence. The altarpiece is attacked with an axe, while men mount ladders to smash stained-glass windows above. There is an element of military efficiency about this vandalism, reinforced by the caption at the bottom of the image, which declares that once the Calvinist religion has finished its business not an image will remain standing.

Calvinism had scripture to warrant its position on images in churches. The second commandment prohibits the use of 'graven images' to represent God. Laws

Fig. 42. 'Art under attack'; Frans Hogenberg, *Beeldenstorm*, engraving, 1566. Rijksmuseum

against false gods increased in specificity and in violence in Exodus 34: 13 and Deuteronomy 12: 3:

> And ye shall overthrow their altars, and break their pillars, and burn their groves with fire; and ye shall hew down the graven images of their gods, and destroy the names of them out of that place.

Clément Marot's metrical version of the Ten Commandments was sometimes used in France as a musical accompaniment to the burning of images.[28] Image destruction took on a religious and even a ritual air. This was no indiscriminate rage, but what Natalie Zemon Davis calls 'rites of violence': religious acts of reform and cleansing.[29]

However, as Joseph Leo Koerner has shown, Lutheranism had ambiguous feelings towards images.[30] Luther disapproved of the iconoclastic arguments of Karlstadt. After the destruction of the early 1520s, Wittenberg allowed images to return to churches. A striking example is the Stadtkirche, subject of the violence of 1522, which contains no pictures surviving from before 1521, yet is today crammed with religious art. Primary in this iconographic display is the Wittenberg Altarpiece of 1547 by Lucas Cranach the Elder. It takes the form of a traditional triptych, a Lord's Supper as centrepiece, flanked by Baptism to the left, Confession to the right. The images contain subtle inflections of Protestant feeling. They are denuded of sacramental symbolism. The Lord's Supper is an everyday meal, in which apostles dress in contemporary sixteenth-century costume, for all the world like Lutheran pastors. Baptism emphasizes the community (*Gemeinde*) at work; Confession is represented by a scene of adult colloquy and piety. These are signifiers of word and faith in action, without the sanctified mediation of holy church.

Most puzzling of all, and the subject of a lengthy analysis by Koerner, is the predella at the foot of the triptych. This shows 'Luther Preaching to the Wittenberg

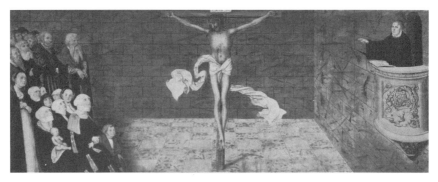

Fig. 43. 'Luther and the Cross'; Lucas Cranach the Elder, Predella, oil on wood panel, 1547. Wittenberg, Stadtkirche

Congregation'. On the one hand, this is a traditional Christian subject, found in any number of Catholic churches in northern Europe. Christ on the cross takes centre stage, adorned with his wounds (Fig. 43), and presenting his suffering to and for us. Yet there is something odd about the scene. Christ is not alone. On the left is a congregation, obviously meant to represent the full diversity of the Wittenberg citizenry, men of differing ages, all standing; (seated), a mother with a baby, a young child, older and younger women; and at their back, the only woman standing, visibly pregnant. All, young and old, male and female, are rapt in concentration, staring at the scene on the right. Here Luther himself stands, in his pulpit, open door behind, his hand outstretched towards Christ. This is the subject of the predella: not crucifixion as such, but Christ crucified, as preached by a minister of God. Above all, seemingly without impiety, the painting is unafraid to represent Luther himself in action: painted indeed in the year of his death.

The uncanniness lies elsewhere than overt presentation of the triumph of Lutheran doctrine. It is in the relation of image and representationalism. The crucifix is not only an image, it *is represented as* an image. The centre of the visual plane exists in a different dimension from its surroundings. Although, when the viewer looks intently, the cross is situated in a pictorial pavement beneath Luther's pulpit, it is an effect of *trompe l'œil*, since the cross also exists as a crucifix in line with the viewer. Christ is not a body in the same world as other bodies in the picture, but an icon, such as might be seen in sculptured form in a thousand churches. It is, if you like, a double form of mimesis: the cross as representation, or symbol, rendered again in the space of the preaching assembly. Luther stares into the void, not at Christ in person, but the 'cross' as idea.

The theology of Luther is synonymous with two things. On the one hand he is known for *sola scriptura* ('words alone'), 'the word of God', scripture revealed as it were in itself, with no need for the accretions of Christianity collected over the centuries.[31] On the other hand, he is known for the 'theology of the Cross', a faith connected entirely to the central moment in the Christian narrative, when Christ takes on the sins of all human beings to make them his own.[32] This duality in Luther also involves formal dualism, between Christ as word, the *logos* that makes God visible (as in the gospel of John, 'In the beginning was the word'); and Christ as Cross, the embodiment of suffering at the heart of the Christian condition. Cranach's painting expresses the dualism brilliantly, we might say unnervingly well. The viewer is transfixed by the cross; but also, the cross is a word, a linguistic symbol representing the whole of Luther's theology. Christ is in the middle of the viewer's perspective, and yet not there in the narrative framework of the image.

The paradox of the painting is, in Koerner's words, 'to represent a hidden God'.[33] In the 1520s Luther developed a theory known as *Deus absconditus*: God is hidden from us, but through this absence is made present to us.[34] The roots of this lay in medieval mysticism, in the negative theology by which God is both there and not there. In artistic terms, this is equivalent to the sense that a pictorial image is a physical thing, an object in our world, but simultaneously something conceptual. Indeed, without that conceptual framework it is not art at all. 'A picture serves as reading' (*pro lectione*), Pope Gregory the Great wrote in 600 CE.[35] Dispute between verbal and visual depends not on difference but on the 'interrelationship of word and image'.[36]

Enlightenment theory of the nexus of verbal and visual repeats the ambiguity. Indeed, for Schleiermacher in his 1799 essay on religion, 'everything mysterious and marvellous is proscribed and the imagination is not to be filled with empty images'.[37] Twentieth-century art theory often accepted this Enlightenment paradox with open arms. Clement Greenberg asserted in the 1950s that painting should express itself in purely optical terms. Verbal explanation contaminated art, Greenberg said, which is an autonomous world, free from the reading of texts, perceived as 'self-evident' to the eye.[38] Greenberg responded to movements in art. In *Der Blaue Reiter* almanac (1912), Wassily Kandinsky distinguished the letter as part of a linguistic code from writing as a 'thing'. On first sight, a reader looks at marks on the page as 'a physical form that quite autonomously creates a certain outer and inner impression'.[39] Kandinsky aimed ultimately for direct equivalence between sign and referent, in which painting could achieve its goal of a universal, non-discursive language. This idea became fundamental to Expressionism.

Simon Morley has called the opposition of verbal and visual theories a 'policing of media boundaries'.[40] Morley contrasts this with the evident fascination with written language found in modern art. An example is Pablo Picasso's Cubist still life *Au Bon Marché* of 1913 (now in the Ludwig Collection in Aachen).[41] Morley illustrates (with a facsimile from the Bibliothèque nationale in Paris) how Picasso used a sheet from the newspaper *Le Journal* (dated 25 January 1913), cut up into fragments and juxtaposed with his own distorted drawings of bottles and other ephemera.[42] The incorporation of fragments of newspaper titles, advertisements, billboards, brand names, and logos is a prime feature of Cubism, whether in Picasso or in work by Henri Matisse, Georges Braque, or Juan Gris. Greenberg explained the presence of letters and words in Braque and Picasso by saying that they are denuded of their literal meaning and turned instead into flat visual surfaces. Braque, late in life, recorded in conversation with Dora Vallier a more nuanced view. The letters, being in two dimensions, combined with three-dimensional representation in such a way as to disturb or deform visual expectations: they 'permitted one to distinguish the objects that were situated in space from those that were outside space'.[43] What Braque means can be illustrated by the ground-breaking work *Fruit Dish and Glass* (1912), now in the Metropolitan Museum in New York.[44]

This is the first ever-example (Fig. 44) of a technique known as *papier collé* ('glued paper' or 'paper cut-outs'), distinguished from other forms of collage because formed entirely from cuts of paper, and contemporary with poetic experiments in cut-ups. In a shop in Avignon, Braque bought a roll of wallpaper

Fig. 44. 'Paper-cut'; Braque, *Fruit Dish and Glass*, charcoal and cut-and-pasted printed wallpaper with gouache on white laid paper, 1912. New York, Metropolitan Museum

known as *faux bois*, that is, a simulation of oak panelling. The viewer of the image is immediately confused by a visual pun about the nature of representation. The paper is designed to be seen in three dimensions as panelling. Transferred to the painting, the eye has to recompose rounded space as flat. To this, Braque adds free-hand drawings in charcoal, of a glass bowl, pears, and grapes; and what looks like a dish and a wine glass (or is it a candlestick?) The 'wood' wallpaper at the top of the image invites the viewer to see it as the panelled walls of a café; that at the bottom of the image, at right angles, represents perhaps a table. His drawn objects both occupy this space and evidently also conflict with it. Perceptual distortion is increased by the writing in the image, which consists not (as elsewhere in Braque or Matisse) of cut-outs, but oddly drawn letters in imitation of cut-outs. To add to the effect of disorientation, Braque adds textures, in the form of sand and *gesso*.

Braque's own description of his multi-media techniques as distinguishing 'objects that were situated in space from those that were outside space' alludes to his own training in *trompe-l'œil*. The picture both is, and is not, a representation, confusing the viewer's attempt to understand it as either. The most famous example of the technique is the surrealist manifesto piece by Magritte, *The Treachery of Images* (1929).[45] Below an image of a smoking pipe is a statement in italics: *Ceci n'est pas une pipe*. The image is transparently a pipe: but it is also *not a pipe*, since it is only a representation. Magritte's landmark image is so synonymous with movements in modern art that it is often forgotten this is one of the oldest ideas in art, going back to Zeuxis in the fifth century BCE. Pliny the Elder recounts a legendary story that Zeuxis' painting of grapes felt so real that birds flew down to eat them; not to be outdone, Parrhasius invited Zeuxis to unveil his painting from behind a curtain, only for Zeuxis to discover the curtain itself was painted. Zeuxis declared his fellow artist the winner, because 'I have deceived the birds, but Parrhasius has deceived Zeuxis.'[46] If eighteenth-century art theory often quoted the story simply to promote spatial illusion in painting, Pliny and his Renaissance followers (such as Erasmus) took the story as an exemplary case of the limits of mimesis.[47]

As well as explaining his work, Braque's words are a marvellous commentary on Cranach's cross in the Wittenberg predella. We know the image is a form of mimesis; but we no longer know what mimesis is, or what its boundaries might be. Intriguingly, the brilliant modernist collector Hélène Kröller-Müller, champion of abstract art (one of the earliest buyers of Vincent van Gogh and Piet Mondriaan), first bought outstanding examples of Cubism (such as by Braque and Gris), then later acquired early modern art to hang alongside, to show their abstract affinities. *Playing Cards and Siphon*, a 1916 piece by Gris featuring the Cubist favourite *Le Journal*, is made to mimic, retrospectively, a still life of a wall by Heyman Dullaert from the seventeenth century.[48] Dullaert pins books and journals to a panelled wall beside a quill pen and pair of wax seals, misplacing objects in space so as to confuse the viewer's sense of the world of material things.[49]

W. J. T. Mitchell repositions visual theory to break a barrier between verbal and visual. He argues for close and often combative relations in 'the sisterhood of the arts'.[50] Rather than the categorical divide of Lessing's temporal and spatial fields, he sees Lessing as an example of 'protracted struggle for dominance between pictorial and linguistic signs, each claiming for itself certain proprietary rights on a "nature" to which only it has access'.[51] Renaissance, Enlightenment, and Modernism are three momentous periods of semantic struggle, in which the construction of nature is at stake. This is not to deny the philosophical importance of a view of 'nature' in either verbal or visual art, Mitchell says; but to deny to either art pre-eminence in solving the borderlines of the dispute. The mimetic possibility of art to represent nature is a permanent dialectic within both fields. Indeed, one explanation collapses into the other: painting finds relief in linguistic equivalents; the philosophy of language reduces words to 'images' that they signify. Magritte's distinction of 'l'objet réel' from 'l'objet représenté' mimics the distinction between *signifié* and *signifiant* developed for the contemporary science of linguistics, first used in *Cours de linguistique générale* by Ferdinand de Saussure in 1916 (which featured an image of a tree juxtaposed with the word 'arbre').[52]

Mitchell's framework can be applied outside the world of theory to understand moments of cultural violence within both artistic fields. My book has focused on moments of bibliophobia or biblioclasm. Perhaps it is time to consider how bibliophobia relates to what is often seen as a different phenomenon. Iconoclasm is in the news, because of recent events such as the blowing up of the Buddhas of Bamiyan in Afghanistan in 2001.[53] This is associated with Islam in particular as peculiarly aniconic, that is, categorically opposed to artistic representation. However, Islam, even in a religious sense, manifests artistic aspirations in proper worship of God. This art is concentrated on writing, an art *of* writing not mutual opposition. Iconoclasm, rather than innate in Islam, is (in Mitchell's suggestive historicization of art theory) a form of periodic enthusiasm and distress. The same is true of Judaism, prone to iconoclasm and stark religious forms of written art. While in twenty-first-century culture wars, aniconic Islam fights art-loving Christianity, this is falsification. The word 'iconoclasm', and its philosophical roots, appear first in Christian context, in eighth-century Byzantium.

The Emperor Leo III, saving Constantinople from the Arabs in 717–18 CE, convinced himself that Muslim success in conquering Christendom was due to Christian failure in upholding the Second Commandment in Exodus 20: 4 ('Thou shalt not make unto thee any graven image, or any likeness of any thing that is in heaven above').[54] Military victories of Leo III and his son Constantine V vindicated ideological opposition to idolatry; reversals under Empress Irene signified refutation of her opposition to iconoclasm between 797 and 802 CE.[55] At the heart of the struggle was a theological argument about signs: how words imagine things, how visual objects represent meanings.[56] Yet for many reasons, iconoclastic struggle became a wider cultural war. On one hand, it entailed increasing division between East and West after the Second Council of Nicaea. At stake was the relation of church and state: whether an emperor had a right to determine public doctrine. While some held the emperor Leo III correct, others took a liberal view on images. This meant making Constantine V a heretic for proscribing images. Constantine's arguments led to acts of violence not only against images but persecutions of people using them. In the counter-reaction, he was compared to the pagan tyrant Diocletian. Meanwhile Charlemagne in the West summoned the Frankfurt theologians to debate a similar issue. Pope Hadrian I refuted their arguments, but soon died. His successor Pope Leo III, in defence of image-making, sought allies in the Frankish kingdom, leading to the imperial coronation of Charlemagne at Aachen in 800, so that for the first time there were two Christian Empires.

Lurking in this arena came a shift in written culture. In both East and West, Christianity reappraised Christian and pagan literature. When Byzantine debate about images reached Charlemagne by letter, he determined that the Latin church would stay neutral.[57] Dispute over images transferred to debate about a 'renewal' in texts, so that the inheritance of Christian antiquity required new policing of the boundaries of correct feeling and interpretation. The Carolingian court adopted a new handwriting style, known as Carolingian minuscule, sometimes attributed to Alcuin of York. In reality the development was more complex, with a new script arising out of Irish and English models in the Carolingian monasteries of Luxeuil, Corbie, Tours, and elsewhere.[58] Charlemagne ordered Alcuin to model a new standard of legible text for Jerome's Bible.[59] The script reflected a taste for philosophical, scientific, and literary study, as well as a standard for copying biblical and sacred texts. As we will see in Chapter 14, the script takes on a character of the sacred, as if letters are sacred things.

In the East came a parallel 'Macedonian Renaissance'. Once again, this accompanied a textual revolution. From the tenth century, Byzantine manuscripts of classical and early Christian Greek works were gradually rewritten in a minuscule style, and few of the older uncial manuscripts were preserved.[60] By the eighth century, Byzantine learning declined, cut off from Latin Christianity.[61] The ancient corpus of texts in Greek, pagan and Christian, was recopied in Byzantium after the ninth century. A corollary of this was that texts not copied were lost for ever. What we now think of as a canon of ancient Greek literature is the product of this culture of Christian textual reform. As by-product, the modern Greek vernacular of the time was lost in translation to a fabricated Attic form.

The iconoclastic emperors banned images of Christ, the Virgin Mary, and the other saints. Ultimately the ban failed, and later in the Middle Ages, Byzantine churches developed the use of the iconostasis, in which a screen covered in icons totally conceals the altar from the laity except when the central doors are opened.[62] In the meantime a variety of complex and subtle defences of images emerged. One example, the ninth-century Khludov Psalter, contains a series of miniatures directed against the iconoclasts, which require intense efforts of interpretation.[63] In one illumination on fo. 67ʳ (Fig. 45), the miniaturist illustrates a verse from Psalm 69: 21, 'They gave me gall to eat; and when I was thirsty, they gave me vinegar to drink'. He shows a picture of the soldier offering Christ vinegar on a sponge attached to a pole.

Below he interpolates a contemporary image, showing John the Grammarian, last iconoclast patriarch of Constantinople, rubbing out a painting of Christ with a sponge attached to a pole. Like other images, its polemic is witty, with a cartoon caricature of John the Grammarian's wild hair, but it also shows the mixed energies of iconoclastic debate. The defence of images works not by images alone but in a highly literary way. The reference to Christ on the cross is a classic case of typology, cross-referencing Old Testament verses with New.[64] The image is dominated not by self-explanatory veneration, but complex and articulate meaning. This is reinforced by the rhetorical device of the analogy with the destruction of the icon using the pole. Another image shows directly the iconoclast council of 815, which reinstated the ban on images. As the heretical council, called by the Emperor Leo V, discusses the ban, another group of clergy attacks an icon of Christ using whitewash. Yet instead of whitewash, four streams of blood emerge, washing round the feet of the iconoclasts. This, too, uses typology, the four streams of blood acting as an inversion of the four rivers of Paradise, which were often depicted by Byzantine artists as emerging from the foot of the cross. The images thus play on a literary tradition which was the bastion of the opponents of images who insisted on the primacy of the lettered version of scripture. Many images in the Khludov Psalter indeed contain explanations of drawings next to them, little arrows pointing from text to illustration, to show which line a picture refers to, or how to understand them.

Byzantine art crossed to Russia after the conversion of Kievan Rus' in 988 CE. The pre-eminent Russian iconist is Andrey Rublev in the fifteenth century. Undaunted by any anxiety of figuration, his most famous works are the *Old Testament Trinity* (1408–25, where three figures appear to Abraham at the Oak of Mamre); and the *New Testament Trinity*, more familiar to western eyes but all the more troubling in visual iconography. Scruples put to one side, in 1654 the Russian archbishops placed a curse on the two-fingered gestural sign of the cross and imposed a three-finger sign symbolizing the Holy Trinity.[65] Imperial Russia encouraged a profusion of icons, Mary and Christ, popular and official, into the early twentieth century. It was supported by propagandist theory such as Dimitri Sosnin's *On the Wonder-Making Icons and the Christian Church* (1833). Evolving from the early Byzantine *templon*, in Byzantine and Russian churches the nave is separated from the sanctuary by an iconostasis or icon-screen.[66] Reinforcing ideology, the Russian word писать (*pisat'*) means (as in Greek) both 'to paint' and 'to write'. The prayer-image, says Oleg Tarasov, represents the drama of incarnation as both 'struggle' and 'mirror'.[67] Icons are not made, but 'appear'. The 'appearance' (Russian: *yavlenie*, явление) of an icon is a synonym for miraculous discovery.[68] The idea is like a premonition of a surrealist or Dadaist manifesto. In 1915, Malevich placed his *Black Square* in the corner of the exhibition hall, the position reserved for an icon in Russian homes. He called it 'the zero of forms', a black square in a white frame.[69] After the October Revolution of 1917, he defined

Fig. 45. 'Against iconoclasm'; Khludov Psalter, ink and paint on parchment, 9th c. CE, Historical Museum, Moscow, MS 129

Suprematist art in three stages attached to three square icons: black for the economy, red for revolution, white for pure action.

A century after Rublev, arguments in art replayed at the Reformation, the presence of icons in Byzantine churches drawing Protestant criticism.[70] To reform, or to radicalize? Tridentine Catholicism reacted with new images, and agitation around the sacred monogram of Christ.[71] Protestant iconoclasm revived anxieties of centuries.[72] Idolatry, it said, discovered fetishism in things, such as crucifixes. A Kent preacher in 1542 admitted he would tear down the cross on which Christ died if he could.[73] Aston calls the initial phase of iconoclasm 'iconomachy' (the Greek word used for example in the Byzantine controversy): war not against images but against idolatry.[74] Idolatry also attached to ritual. In the eucharist, the sanctification of bread and wine into the body and blood of Christ took place with a host of physical gestures: kneeling, raising the hands, moving the elements on the altar, breathing on the ritual book, kissing it. Martin Bucer followed Luther in identifying such practices as ritual idolatry, which he called *artolatreia* or 'bread worship'.[75] Arguments about proper worship lie deep in Christianity. *Latria* is worship due to God alone, argued Aquinas, citing Augustine.[76] Wyclif used the same word to infer a transgression between consecrated host and worship of images.[77] Scruples over objects in worship (and bodily relics) was but a short step from outright iconoclasm. In the Calvinist Reformation, it turned (in Patrick Collinson's word) to 'iconophobia'.[78] Nonetheless, Collinson argued iconophobia to be short-lived, lasting perhaps a generation.

Iconoclasm is often pictured as essential to Protestantism, an aversion to the visual. That is exaggeration: Protestant iconoclasts distinguished art from a manifestation of the holy. They destroyed not art in general, out of aesthetic horror, but art objects used as devotional repositories for divine presence. Contrary to stereotype, they liked art in Old Testament or other contexts, and happily recycled religious art forms into new kinds of domestic, familial, or patriotic image.[79] Oliver Cromwell gave an inlaid ivory cabinet with illustrations from Ovid's *Metamorphoses* to his daughter as a wedding gift.[80] Melville, not entirely in jest, found the illustration of whales in books a kind of idolatry.[81]

Juxtaposing iconoclasm with bibliophobia is salutary. The two often appear opposites: one, a perverted religious fervour; the other, religion secularized. Once art loses sacred power, it gives way to art alone. Such views ignore a complicity of verbal with visual realms. Reformation attitudes to art betray a dualism, but of complex kind: fractured between word and body, representation and word. As Koerner argues, modernity has not abandoned this dispute but accentuated it. Post-Romantic art, he says, contains 'vestiges of the sacred'.[82] Visual theory, following Mitchell, places painting close to the semiotics of writing. Meanwhile, Jay David Bolter argues, writing in the digital age rediscovers (in hypertext) its own visuality, what he calls 'writing space'. The stability of printed pages has given way to 'fluidity' in the electronic page, where it is difficult to see where mind ends, and writing begins.[83] Writing is not reducible to linguistic sign or to physical object: it is an ephemeral marking. Perhaps in the electronic age it is not 'any longer a text' at all.[84] Artists such as Cy Twombly rediscover writing as a visual affect. Twombly creates surfaces teeming with writing, or at least with the mimicry of writing. Making something to look like a sequence of words in his own hand, but often isn't, Twombly reimagines writing's surface as physical.[85] This is not new: epigraphy throughout republican and imperial Rome gave voice not only to the commands of power or needs of business, but to intimate memories. A widower in late republican Rome tells of his pain and loss: why did he not precede her?[86] In Gallo-Roman Lyon, lettering was an artistic device.[87] 'Where you are, I was, where I am, you will be', a tomb says to us.[88] Writing as art is an installation of personhood and mortality.

14
Kissing the Book

'I grew up kissing books and bread', Rushdie writes in *Is Nothing Sacred?*[1] In Bombay when he was a child, the devout would kiss holy books. 'But we kissed everything', he says: dictionaries, atlases, Superman comics. Kissing was a mark of redemption for an 'act of clumsy disrespect' in dropping a slice of chapati or a book, 'food for the body and food for the soul'. 'Hold the Holy Book before me that I may touch it', says Don Sebastian to the priest in *Moby-Dick*.[2] In similar vein, Henry David Thoreau in *Walden* calls the written word 'the choicest of relics'.[3] Writing for Thoreau is at once 'intimate' and 'universal': 'the work of art nearest to life itself'. An 'Antique Book', in Emily Dickinson, is not just a 'mouldering pleasure' but an 'Enchantment': it brings Sappho back to life.[4] These are modern remainders of an ancient supposition that books are a form of sacred treasure. Thoreau recalls a story from Plutarch told in Pliny the Elder. Alexander the Great, finding a gold casket inlaid with pearls and precious stones among the booty of King Darius, chose to place in it the works of Homer: 'the most precious achievement of the mind of man'.[5] Is Rushdie's book (or Melville's) secular memory? Thomas à Kempis, the medieval mystic theologian, said that a reader on picking up a book should hold it in the arms like holy Simeon taking up the baby Jesus.[6] When you finish reading, Thomas said, you should close the book, give thanks, and kiss it (*osculandum*).[7] Rushdie responds by feeling that the touch of the sacred has not left the book. His own novel has been exposed to 'bewildering ferocity'. Faced with the ambiguity between sacred and secular politics, he feels a shudder, just as Thomas More when asked to prove his loyalty to the king in 1535, by kissing the book: 'I aunswered that verily I neuer purposed to swere any booke othe more while I lived'.[8]

Until just over a hundred years ago it was still the law in England that an oath in court had to be sworn by kissing a copy of the Bible.[9] However, in 1888, the Oaths Act made provision instead for a secular gesture: 'If any person to whom an oath is administered desires to swear with uplifted hand, in the form and manner in which an oath is usually administered in Scotland, he shall be permitted so to do'.[10] The Hon. Secretary of the Northern Counties Branch of Medical Protection in Newcastle-on-Tyne called kissing the book as 'a most uncleanly and offensive procedure'. A few years later, a judge at the Bloomsbury County Court sneered at a witness, 'if you have got a fad about microbes, you should say so, and I will swear you Scotch fashion'. The *British Medical Journal* demanded that judges take microbiology more seriously. It estimated 30,000 persons annually kissed the

New Testament in the City of London Court, while a police-court usher reported the covers of his New Testament worn smooth and polished from the pressure 'of numberless lips, bearded and beardless, blooming and faded, honest and lying, foul and sweet', as some 49,760 witnesses were sworn in that court annually.[11] The courts require quarantine, from superstition as much as from a deadly virus.

What does the paradoxical and contradictory phenomenon of kissing the book mean? It is of course a ritual gesture, which the *British Medical Journal* dismisses as a routinized action, redundant to the instrumental function of certifying the sincerity of a contract. This concurs with Mary Douglas's analysis of modern ritual as 'a despised form of communication'.[12] Evidence of the equation of ritual and hypocrisy is shown in James Gillray's 1798 cartoon etching of British politicians. Jacobins queue up to kiss the book in proof of honesty, swearing turning to perjury: 'I SWEAR, that he is perfectly well affected to his country!—a Man totally without dissimulation'.[13] A Bible in George Eliot's *The Mill on the Floss* is so worn by kissing and swearing it looks like a 'well-cured ham'.[14]

However, another suspicion lurks in 'the Scottish fashion', of inhering in the physical object some magical power. Kissing is akin to idolatry, an image of God in a material container. It also reifies the interior thoughts, opinions and beliefs of a book's reader. The faith of the individual somehow resides in this object rather than in the scripture contained within it. The context for the Oaths Act in 1888 is a discussion in Richard Baxter's *Christian Directory* of 1673, where a question is asked on Christian Ethics:

> *Quest.* IS it lawful to lay hands on the book and kiss it in swearing as is done in England?[15]

The opinion of 'some scrupulous Brethren in *Scotland*' is adduced as evidence in the negative, although Baxter himself adjoins a different reply:

> *Resp.* To take an Oath as imposed in England with laying the hand on the *Bible* and kissing it, is not unlawful.

This raises the issue of the material culture of the book in exquisitely literal form. It also puts into the sharpest relief the relation of the idea of the book as object to the idea of the book as a sum of cognitive contents. Why do I feel so strongly the power of an oath in a Birmingham coroner's court, as I hold the book in my hand? The extrapolation of a book as a physical fetish in place of its contents is a mirror image for the fundamental paradox lying within language itself: physical signifiers standing for immaterial signifieds.

These are exactly the questions, of course, that arise also in relation to iconoclasm. Images abounded in churches as substitutes for the bodily presence of a saint. The cult of the saints originated with the collection and veneration of bodily relics of saints, skulls or bones or clothes, which conveyed what Peter Brown has called *praesentia*, 'the physical presence of the holy'.[16] This conveys what Brown beautifully describes as 'a yearning for proximity'. Relics were transported, bought, sold, and often stolen, so that sites of holiness sprang up all over Europe and not just in the middle East where the original acts of the apostles had taken place. Paulinus of Nola, who himself took a fragment of the true cross home to southern Italy, compared relics in a poem to 'life-giving seeds' scattered around the world.[17] Reliquaries, made of precious materials, were designed to carry them.[18] Holiness became as portable—we might say sociable—as the relics themselves. In turn these new sites became places of pilgrimage. Miracles became associated not only with the original lives of the saints but also with their earthly remains. Their presence warded off the presence of evil, or the touch of them healed the bodies of the dying or the incurable. The blind, the crippled, and the possessed, congregated at these shrines, as if in the presence of Christ himself.[19]

Jerusalem was the ultimate goal of pilgrimage for obvious reasons; Rome was more frequented because easier to get to; it was rivalled to some extent by the shrine of St James the Great at Compostella in Galicia. There was some difference in practice: in Byzantium, it was desirable to touch and kiss relics; while Pope Gregory the Great commented that in Rome this would be considered sacrilegious.[20] By the later Middle Ages, kissing was commonplace.[21] In England, Canterbury and Durham had the most devotees, as the shrines of the remains of St Thomas Becket and St Cuthbert. However, the supply of such objects was limited, and over time an image might be used instead, with the same veneration applied to them.[22] At Walsingham in Norfolk pilgrims flocked to the site of where an apparition of the Virgin Mary appeared in 1061, and where an image was placed and a replica house built of the place where the Archangel Gabriel appeared in the annunciation. In that sense, images come to have the function of 'transitional objects', as described in the psychoanalytic theory of D.W. Winnicott.[23]

Hans Belting suggested the term 'cult images' to reflect the use of relics as a kind of image devotion.[24] In a western adaptation of Byzantine religion, 'likeness' came to function as 'presence'. Some early reliquaries imitated the venerated object in the design of the receptacle made to hold it. Prime among these are 'head reliquaries', such as that of Pope Alexander I at the Abbey of Stavelot near Liège in Belgium. A silver 'antique' head encases the skull so as to impersonate the saint alive.[25] Representation thus takes over from embodiment. Transitional objects signify to people as symbols, Winnicott says, even without them 'fully understanding the nature of symbolism'.[26] He gives as an example the Eucharist in Christian practice, which raises the added question whether the elements of the Mass are a substitute for something, or else the thing itself. Images, indeed, as described by Eamon Duffy in relation to the later Middle Ages, could function not only in the cult of the saints, but in mediating the holy sacrament. Images acted as more than illustrations or explanations of the sacred: they were sacred themselves.[27] Douglas makes the point that before the Reformation, ritual is understood to be 'efficacious', whereas afterwards (in Catholicism as well as Protestantism) it came to be judged according to standards of spontaneity and social usefulness.[28]

Books have a curious transitional status in the symbolic field of holiness. On the one hand, denigrators of images held up books as a kind of antidote to idolatry. The books of the Bible, as containers of doctrine, upheld the world of faith against 'superstition'. The foolish believe that if they 'gaze on a picture of St Christopher they will not die that day'; that praying to an image of St Barbara will save them in battle; that supplicating to St Erasmus will make them rich, says Erasmus the humanist.[29] In the colloquy, 'A Pilgrimage for Religion's Sake', a man is shown the finger of the apostle Paul; he kisses it, in wonder, but then expresses a misgiving: the joint of the finger is surely too large to be human. His companion bursts into laughter.[30] Then the story of William of Paris is told, a great collector of relics, who acquires some of the milk of the Virgin Mary, and becomes one of the richest men in Europe.[31] In his edition of the works of Jerome, Erasmus rejects the miracles of the saintly life of his master and instead proclaims the miracle of his writings: 'to me the greatest miracle is the miracle of Jerome as he expresses himself to us in his many works of lasting quality'.[32] He is only half kidding in reimagining the book as a kind of reliquary, for mental remains. Above all, Erasmus pins his faith on the miracles of the writings of Christ collected in the New Testament. In his preface to his edition of the Greek text in 1516, he called this the true body of Christ.

In Zürich in 1523, Huldrych Zwingli declared that the Bible was the sole guide to doctrine and worship. He declared the images in the city's churches to be idols, and urged their removal. In May 1524, the council gave the order, and in the iconoclastic riots that followed, relics were thrown away and images smashed.[33] Yet although Zwingli claimed his inspiration to be Erasmus, Erasmus himself deplored the violence, and distanced himself from Zwingli's insistence that in the Mass, we only witness a commemoration of Christ's sacrifice. Erasmus was caught between the idea of the image as symbolic or efficacious. He was also equivocal, at least in jest, about the power of books. In another of the colloquies, 'The Holy Feast', revelling in his love for the wisdom of the ancients, he adds in a marginal afterthought, 'St Socrates pray for us'.[34] In reply, one of the interlocutors hopes that Virgil and Horace will be canonized as well.

In the opposite direction, then, the book can become an object of veneration as much as a protection against idolatry. The ancient practice of using books of the Bible as objects for divination, rather like the use of copies of Homer or Virgil in *sortes Virgilianae*, is shrouded in a certain amount of mystery, and some doubt its authenticity.[35] Yet Augustine allows the narrative of his own conversion to follow the same pattern, where words chance upon the first line he beholds, this time in a copy of Paul's Epistles: chance makes up his mind to follow a holy life as a result.[36] A book as an artefact of the holy is as much a 'transitional object' as an image, in that sense. The devil could be warded off by pen and ink as much as by relics and images, Cassiodorus, 'book-producer of the Lord', said.[37] Gospel books and psalters were revered as objects from early times. The gospels originated not so much as a new genre as an adaptation of Greco-Roman biographical literature.[38] For a long time they circulated separately, both the canonical and the 'apocryphal' ones, as precious 'lives' of Jesus, literary sanctuaries.

In the Carolingian Renaissance, Alcuin argued that all books might take on an aura of the sacred.[39] 'Letters are immortal', Rabanus Maurus wrote in a poem:

> For the fingers rejoice in writing, the eyes in seeing,
> And the mind at examining the meaning of God's mystical words.[40]

The design of biblical books from the seventh century to the ninth CE shows attention to physical form, crossing a boundary between textual and visual in ways that parallel Islam and Judaism. The Book of Durrow, probably produced in Ireland in about 700 CE, contains decorative pages to initiate each gospel, using carpet pages and elaborate renditions of opening letters or words.[41] Incorporation of symbols of the evangelists, and of the Chi Rho symbol (a visual anagram of Christ's name in Greek, even though the text is in Latin), breaks down a distinction between word and image. This book culture seems to have been shared across Europe from Northumbria to the Mediterranean, making attribution and dating complex and controversial. The Echternach Gospels, named after a monastery in Luxembourg (now believed to have produced them), were once thought to be from Lindisfarne.[42] It was a natural assumption since manuscripts of the period transgress national boundaries: Echternach was founded by Willibrord, a Northumbrian monk. The book is decorated throughout, beginning with the prefatory letter by Jerome to Pope Damasus. The lion symbolising St Mark's Gospel leaps over an abstract geometric pattern of purple squares and a maze-like architectural border of red lines. Evangelist portraits originated in late antique Roman manuscript illumination; here it is made exceptionally vivid in colour and ebullience of stylization.[43]

The Lindisfarne Gospels, produced around the same time, is an example of a work of art in book form, the masterpiece of a single illuminator and scribe, named in a later colophon as Eadfrith, bishop of Lindisfarne.[44] The colophon associates the book with the cult of St Cuthbert, and it was perhaps used to celebrate the translation of the saint's relics in 698 CE. We see here the connection between body and book as the indication of the presence of the holy. The holiness of the book is partly manifested in the costliness of its production. The skins of 150 calves were used to make its vellum pages.[45] In the ninth century, a binding was added by Billfrith, embossed with precious jewels, alas later pillaged.[46] While the text used lamp black to create a lasting legible impression, the variety of pigments used in the illumination has long drawn astonishment.[47] A pioneering assessment of the chemistry of the book surmised that lapis lazuli was imported from the foothills of the Himalayas. In fact, the minerals found are more local, but the ingenuity involved in their production is all the more remarkable: green from verdigris, a copper byproduct; blue from woad; red from red lead; purple from *crozaphoria tinctoria*, a plant extract. This latter colour could be made more blue by adding stale urine to increase the level of alkaline.[48] Eadfrith took such care that he made technological innovations, such as developing a predecessor of a lead pencil in order to pre-rule the pages before the addition of script or illustration.[49] If he had used the furrowed lines previously employed by illuminators, the complex variety of pigments would have been mixed and the visual definition would have been lost.

This carpet page (Fig. 46) shows a cross extended to the size of a full page, embedded in a complex field made up of a dozen different colours, abstract in overall design but composed (once the eye looks closely) of birds' beaks, peacock feathers, vegetal curls, and what are perhaps loose-limbed human legs.[50] The ornamentation shows motifs familiar from metalwork and jewellery, comparable to Islamic prayer rugs, perhaps familiar in Northumbria at the time.[51] An alternative influence is Coptic manuscripts which also show Islamic influence. Michelle Brown comments on the combination of iconic and aniconic features in the cross-carpet pages.[52] Rather than the crucifix serving as a type of narrative art, with emotive features of suffering or grief, Christ appears to be embedded mystically in the cross as sign, concealed yet revealed.

Slightly later in production, maybe late in the eighth century, in Iona, perhaps in Ireland, the Book of Kells is even more extravagant in its textual representation.[53] Figures of humans, animals and mythical beasts combine with Celtic knots and other interlacing patterns in vibrant colours. Its mythical attribution to the hand of St Columba himself (d. 597) attests to the way that the book has become a sacred object in its own right. Many of the images are based on human figures, such as Christ enthroned, or the Virgin Mary and Child (the oldest known example in a western manuscript).[54] The design becomes the more elaborate in the text of the Gospels, all four of which was given an introductory decorative programme.[55] Each Gospel was originally prefaced by a full-page miniature containing the evangelist symbols, followed by a blank page. Then came a portrait of the evangelist, facing the opening text of the Gospel. The ornamentation of the opening few words of each Gospel is lavish to the point that the text becomes

Fig. 46. 'The zoomorphic page'; Lindisfarne Gospels, ink and pigment on parchment, 8th c. London, British Library Cotton MS Nero D. IV, fo. 26v

almost illegible. At the opening of Matthew, the first page consists of just two words: *Liber generationis* ('The book of the generation'). The *lib* of *Liber* is turned into a giant monogram that dominates the entire page. The *er* of *Liber* is presented as an interlaced ornament within the *b* of the *lib* monogram. *Generationis* is broken into three lines and contained within an elaborate frame in the right lower quadrant of the page. The border and the letters themselves are further decorated with spirals in a zoomorphic pattern.

After this treatment of the generations of Christ, the decoration of the book of Matthew begins all over again. The second opening is even grander. A miniature of Christ is followed by the only carpet page in the whole of the Book of Kells, then a blank page is a prelude to a Chi Rho monogram, the single most lavish miniature of the early medieval period, which serves as an incipit to the narrative of the life of Christ (see Plate 3).

The Chi Rho consumes the entire page (Pl. 3). The letter chi dominates, one arm of the letter swooping downwards and across. The letter rho crouches as if into the embrace of the arms of the chi. Each letter is divided into compartments that are lavishly decorated with knot work and other patterns. The background is likewise a mass of swirling and knotted decoration, circles within circles, polygons, crosses, and diamonds. Within this mass of decoration are hidden animals and insects mixed with foliage and vegetation. Within the crossed arms of the chi, three winged angels arise in an ecstatic vision.

Brown comments on how in the Book of Kells book merges with icon, and speculates on how its overpowering symbols of the holy could have interacted with a society seemingly 'unprepared for their appearance'.[56] Carol Farr is more practical in her analysis, indicating the liturgical nature of some features of the design. Yet she, too, comments that the Book of Kells is more for show than for function.[57] The book as it were oversteps its own bounds. It is self-consciously excessive in its lavish decoration. It draws attention to its own status as a book, and yet also to something more than a book, a sacred object in its own right. The image of the book *as* book is indeed characteristic of Northumbrian and Irish books. The traditional symbol for St Matthew of the winged angel or man is rendered in the Echternach Gospels as an *Imago hominis*, or 'image of a man' (Fig. 47).

The character of man is exemplified by the holding of a book. The face of the man is highly stylized. The shape of his body is turned into abstract forms, which match the knotted patterns of the margins. This contrasts with the figurative delicacy of the representation of the evangelist's hands, in which four fingers hold each of the two leaves of the book, the thumb curled under and behind. He shows the book to the reader, while mirroring the stance of the reader himself, his book in hand, homo legens.

This is paralleled in the Codex Amiatinus, the manuscript which Abbot Ceolfrith took with him on his last journey to Rome, intending it as a gift for the

Fig. 47. 'Image of man'; Echternach Gospels, ink and pigment on parchment, 8th c. Paris, Bibliothèque nationale de France, MS. lat 9389, fo. 18v

Fig. 48. 'Unpacking the library'; Codex Amiatinus, ink and pigment on parchment, 8th c. Biblioteca Medicea Laurenziana, MS Amiatino 1, fo. V[r]

shrine of St Peter the Apostle. He died en route in Langres in Burgundy. This enormous book contains both Old and New Testaments, on 1030 leaves made from the skins of 515 animals. Its decoration is so Mediterranean in style that it was long thought to be Italian in origin, but it was probably produced in Wearmouth-Jarrow in the early 8th century CE.[58] It contains a wonderful image of a scribe at work (Fig. 48), posed as the prophet Ezra. The iconography of the prophet's body appears to be the same as the evangelist Matthew in the Lindisfarne Gospels, suggesting a shared decorative scheme.[59] The scribe is at work on three different illuminations. The tools of his trade lie at his feet. Behind him, in a manner liable to touch the heart of any scholar or bibliophile, is a cupboard full of bookshelves, with no fewer than nine books on display.

Book culture saturates these great books. The Codex Amiatinus was revered as the most accurate copy of Jerome's new Vulgate translation. The Echternach Gospels has an odd inscription, claiming that it was corrected against a codex, which had belonged to Jerome himself.[60] The statement is surely spurious, but it suggests an attention to *praesentia* parallel with the codex sharing in the holy status ascribed to the bodily relics of saints or to the holy image. Reliquaries carried the body of the saint, man-made objects enfolding the divine. A striking feature is the way that the materials used in making a reliquary seem often to be themselves organic.[61] In a similar way, books are made to draw attention to the way that they are made 'from the skin of animals'.[62] In images and books, animal remains merge into representation, just as presence merges into likeness.

We can refer in this way with something more than metaphorical resonance to a cult of the book. Stephen of Ripon in his *Life of St Wilfrid* refers to the saint's gold and purple gospel book being kept in a jewelled box, and Michelle Brown believes the Lindisfarne Gospels were stored in a 'book-shrine' when not in use.[63] Just as a skull or fibula of a saint might later be encased in a sculptural metal object imitating a head or a leg, so the *cumdach* was invented to enshrine a book as a transitional relic of a saint.[64] Five early examples survive. In some, the book survives while the case was later pillaged for its precious materials, such as that of the Book of Kells, stolen in 1006 CE. One for the Book of Durrow, venerated as a relic of St Columba, disappeared in the seventeenth century. In the opposite direction, the Soiscél Molaise survives from the eleventh century CE, while the Molaise Gospels have gone. It has a wooden core with silver-gilt facing representing the symbols of the four evangelists, along with an inscription calling it a 'shrine'. Some examples of *cumdach* show signs of being carried on the body, perhaps around the neck, sometimes as a battle standard. The Domhnach Airgid or 'silver church' (Fig. 49), associated with the relics of St Patrick, was originally made in the eighth century and substantially remodelled in around 1350. Christ crucified is in three-dimensional relief, with another panel showing St Patrick presenting a gospel book.

Fig. 49. 'Book-shrine'; Domhnach Airgid, silver, 8th c. remodelled in 14th. Dublin, National Museum of Ireland, NMI R.2834

As carriers of the holy, books became holy in turn. It is here that kissing comes into focus. In 1628, Bartolomeo Gavanto traced the origin and mystical significance of the Roman rites, and their rubrics (manual acts of the priest in ritual). He found the formula *Haec sunt verba Sancta* ('these are holy words') to be very ancient, associated from early times with a gesture (by priest or deacon) *osculans librum* ('kissing the book').[65] An *osculum* in Latin means 'little mouth'; it can be chaste, but the *osculum infame* (devil's kiss, on the anus) shows it is not always. The term remains throughout Europe into the sixteenth century, such as the 1519 printed Trondheim Mass.[66] In the Sarum Use, widespread throughout England from the thirteenth century onwards, a number of rubrics during Mass connote the sacred presence of the book during ritual: not only kissing the missal but also raising it above the head or level with the heart, or breathing on it, censing it with incense, moving it to one side or other of the holy elements of bread and wine.[67]

In this way the book becomes, like the image, another kind of transitional object. Icons, like relics, frequently bear signs of having been kissed. Kissing is the most transitional of human gestures, in which a body secretes part of itself, or (to put it frankly) shares mucus, to mark exchange of feelings. Kisses are mentioned in the Vedas and in early Sumerian and Egyptian poetry. A papyrus fragment feathers a fleeting 'success to the mouth': is that Sappho's kiss?[68] 'Give me a thousand kisses', Catullus tells Lesbia, more ebulliently, in Sirmione by Lake Garda.[69]

How many are enough, he asks her: as many as in the sands of Libya.[70] Johannes Secundus of The Hague wrote a book of kisses in 1541 (*Liber basiorum*), explored empirically in relation to his Spanish lover, Neaera.[71] He discusses kissing as food; kissing as wound or bringer of death; kissing to merge souls: it was one of Montaigne's favourites.[72] Everyone knew the spurious poem by Plato in the *Greek Anthology*: 'My soul was on my lips as I was kissing Agathon'.[73] John Donne concealed this homo-erotic reference in a verse letter to Sir Henry Wotton:

> SIR, more than kisses, letters mingle Soules
>   or, thus friends absent speake.[74]

'Chaste lovers covet a kisse'; Donne was quoting Castiglione.[75] Thomas à Kempis tells penitent souls to greet one another with a kiss.[76] Although associated primarily with sex, Baldassare and Thomas remind us that much kissing is quite innocent. A mother's first action towards an infant, after feeding, may well be to kiss; later, we kiss our children to greet them; in some parts of the world (less so in queasy England) we kiss in social ritual (twice in France or Poland, thrice in the Netherlands), greeting a member of the family, or a friend, young or old, male or female. Indeed, the kiss is so innocent that Freud expresses himself disappointed. It is 'held in high sexual esteem among many nations', he says snootily, despite the organ involved leading to the digestive tract.[77]

What Freud recognises is a substitutive value that kissing acquires. We kiss, transferring value from one area to another, knowing that this will endow additional imaginative power. A child moves from sucking a mother's breast to 'the lips of another person'.[78] Children, Freud notices, endow kissing with magical (and secret) significance, like a taboo. Disabused of such fantasy (for instance, that babies are conceived by kissing) they retain a frisson of excitement about the kiss, which perhaps never quite disappears in adult life. In an insight full of suggestion for religious kissing, Freud states in *Analysis Terminable and Interminable*: children are 'like primitive tribes who have had Christianity thrust upon them but continue in secret to worship the old idols'.[79]

The idea that kissing might be idolatrous became a fetish in the early Reformation. This tore with palpable violence through ambiguities of centuries. The kiss of peace is of course scriptural. In Romans 16: 16 and elsewhere it is called the 'holy kiss' (ἐν φιλήματι ἁγίῳ). The kiss marks (in physical form) a sense of belonging to the church. The writings of early Christian fathers show that it was incorporated immediately into the liturgy of the Eucharist. That it retained a sense of shock in transition (kissing between men; between women; worse still, men and women) is reflected in later practice of substituting for the kiss a transitional object (known as the Pax, or 'peace'). In the thirteenth century, apparently because of concerns over the sexual, social and medical implications of actual kissing, an object with a flat surface, later with a handle, would be passed from person to person, along with a cloth.[80] Each person would kiss the object (not each other), and wipe it clean. The social stakes appear in breaches in etiquette. In 1494, Joanna Dyaca was accused of breaking the *paxbrede* by throwing it on the ground, 'because another woman of the parish had kissed it before her'.[81] In sharing the *portepaix* ('the peace-carrier') the parish sublimates charity and flirtation.[82]

Perhaps to get around these problems, the Tridentine Mass in 1570 ordered that the sign of the peace be exchanged only between members of the clergy, unless royalty were present. In the modern Church of England, as in many other cases of Anglo-Saxon embarrassment, the problem is displaced onto the shaking of hands. However, in the sixteenth century, kissing, and kissing the book in particular, is routinely used as an example of how to demarcate the boundary between proper worship and idolatry. In the English translation of Erasmus's *Explicatio in symbolum apostolorum*, commissioned by Thomas Boleyn in 1533, Erasmus states that in church when we 'kysse the gospel boke' we do not 'worshyp the parchemente | or yᵉ gold | or the yuory | but we do worshyp the doctrine of Christ'.[83] In a similar way, 'A christen man | if he dothe bowe his hede to the ymage of Christe crucified | he knoweth that none honoure is due to the wodde or tree'. It is not the image that is worshipped, but 'that thynge | which the ymage doth represent'. No wonder Adam Phillips calls the kiss 'a symbol of betrayal'.[84]

Using a book in legal trials as a proof-test in presentation of evidence (or guarantee of mental assent) was well established before the Reformation.[85] John Fitzherbert's *Boke of Surveying* in 1526 establishes the practice that a tenant in order to confirm terms in agreement with a landlord, should 'kysse the boke', and pay a penny, 'as the custome is'.[86] This practice is confirmed in the 1538 *Institutions in the lawes of Englande,* where it is explained: 'Fealtie is as moche to saye as a fidelitie or faythfulnes'.[87] Laying hands on a book, or kissing it, gives corporeal validation to 'faythfulnes' within. This could have many meanings. Touching the holy book in some sense acts as a taboo on the witness, attesting to his seriousness in making his fingers and lips liable. Or it could be the holiness of the book somehow transfers to the act and strengthens it. Or it could be the bodily gesture is a signal of the public nature of the contract, a sign of completion.

There is a spectrum of values posited in the book. At one extreme is concordance between the book as object and the presence of a person: a human body transmitting itself into the form of the book. In this sense a book is felt to have bodily presence of its own: the book itself, *qua* object, is 'holy'.[88] At the other extreme is a sense that physical action is more like a token for something else— interior assent or contract. This is an alternative view of the book as merely signifying, metaphorically, its contents. None of this is explicitly stated. Yet a need for some explanation is shown by the gloss of 'as moche as to saye as a fidelitie', and also by a caveat at the end: 'but he shall not knele as he that dothe homage'. The encoding and decoding, positive or negative, of manual and bodily actions is a feature of sixteenth-century forms of attention.

Kissing the book also featured in heresy trials. *The Testimony of William Thorpe* is an autobiographical account of his trial before Archbishop Thomas Arundel in 1407.[89] The Lollard Thorpe is required without feigning to kneel and lay his hand 'vpon a booke and kisse it'.[90] Once more, kissing acts as exteriorization of interior oath. This use of an oath to manifest the state of a person's faith was sensitive among Lollards, not only since it was dangerous. It broke the rule that conscience is a pact with God. Thorpe's trial was printed in 1530 in Antwerp with Reformation works by William Tyndale.[91] By now, it was argued *ex officio* oaths in trials should be illegal, as the pact was sacrosanct, and an oath an invitation to blasphemy, barred by the third commandment.[92]

In question is the boundary between outward sign and inward sense. This forms a nexus of anxiety with idolatry, prime location of controversy to Lollards and later evangelicals. Wyclif warned of idolatry in images, but attributed divine power to the Bible.[93] Thorpe declared that no one should kneel or pray in front of images, 'ne kissen hem', or make offerings to them.[94] A little later in in the trial, Thorpe is asked whether it is lawful 'to knele doun and touche þe holy gospel boke, and kisse it, seiynge "So helpe me God"'.[95] Thorpe equivocates, seeing his danger, but argues that since a book is nothing other than the material it is made of, it is unlawful 'to kisse it', because it is forbidden to make an oath on a material object. Here, he cites Jerome and John Chrysostom. For the gospel does not consist in letters on a page, but in its meaning for a believer: 'þe gospel hidde in þe lettre'. He derives this from Jerome's prologue to the Vulgate Bible.[96]

What is interesting is how kissing, rather than clarify a boundary between material and meaning, blurs it. John Frith, a controversialist in the early sixteenth century, finds the task hard. Honour is due to God's word. A believer owes reverence to scripture, not only abstractly, but also physically, whenever he must 'take the boke in his hande'.[97] A slippage occurs between cognitive and bodily, confirmed by apparent confidence that 'yf he kisse the boke for the doctrines sake that he lerneth there oute' the believer is to be commended. Frith hesitates, then applies a distinction: clouding the book in incense is childish, he says; 'But yf he shuld knele downe & praie to his boke then he did committe playne idolatrie'.

Why is kneeling idolatry but kissing a mark of respect? What is it in physical gesture that makes it interpretable in these ways, or in an object that enables us to make distinctions about its objective status, and its subjective reception? In the reign of Mary, the Catholic bishop Edward Bonner repeats the argument word for word from the Protestant Frith:

> when we do kysse the booke of the Gospels, we haue not suche affection, and loue, to the parchement, paper or letters made with ynke, as for theyr sakes to

kysse the boke, but hauynge onelye respect to those holsome comfortable and
holy sayinges whych are in the boke conteyned.[98]

He reiterates with confidence the same distinction between container and contents.

The familiarity of the gesture of kissing in legal oaths probably lent naturalness
in referring to it as equivalent to assent, yet there is some Freudian form of denial
going on. Imagine if every time we agreed with a sentence, we kissed the page.
What tipped the argument in these decades was a spatial context of kissing the
book, as Erasmus puts it, *in ecclesia* ('in the chyrche'). The issue came into focus
in manual actions by the priest using the gospel during Mass, especially once the
rite was translated into the Reformed context of the Book of Common Prayer in
1549. Each nuance of gesture in relation to doctrine and scripture now came into
acute bodily focus.[99] We see this in the text of rubrics, which act as stage directions to the words in ritual. The rubrics maybe look to us like glosses, yet they
attest to a problem of embodiment. The 1549 edition takes extravagant care in
what to allow or to exclude: in baptism, the unction of oil on the child's head
remained, but *ephphatha* (meaning 'be opened', signalled by anointing the ears
and lips with spittle) dropped; in 1552 unction was abolished, but signing the
cross approved, a cause of anxiety for a hundred years.[100]

Other gestures, not mentioned in rubrics, continued to be performed by priests
familiar with the Roman rite. Bucer commented on these to Thomas Cranmer
in 1550:

> there are people who endeavour to represent that Mass of theirs...with all the
> outward show they can, with vestments and lights, with bowings and crossings,
> with washing the chalice and other gestures...with breathing over the bread and
> chalice...with moving the book on the table from the right side of it to the
> left...with displaying the bread and chalice.[101]

Where does word end and gesture begin? The boundary Bonner maintained
between ink that is physical and the 'sayinges whych are in the boke conteyned'
becomes hopelessly blurred when we recall that reading, and speaking, are also
physical actions.

We are wrong to assume that anxieties about images and idolatry are different
from ones about words and meanings. The problems increase in the confessional
conflict of the Reformation, and also in the culture of the printed book. At first,
Protestants insisted they knew the boundaries. Thomas Becon in *The displaying of
the Popish masse* articulates a distinction between Lord's supper and bread-
worship through contempt for gesture: 'Onely when yee rehearse the Name of
Iesus, they learne to make solemne courtesie, and so a peece of the Gospell being
once read, they stroke themselves on the head, and kisse the naile of their right
thumbe'.[102] During *Sanctus*, he notes with glee, 'W[th] lifting up your hands, ye

speake with a loud voice, & that ended, ye kisse the Masse-booke', lips joining the page at the point where the red rubric of the Canon begins. This is quoted in a 1637 reprint of Becon, responding to Laudian revivals of ritual in the 1620s and 30s. One such was bowing at the name of Jesus, a practice never mentioned in any rubric of the Book of Common Prayer. Others, like signing with the cross in baptism, existed all along. In Civil War Essex, records survive of extreme measures to prevent ritual taking place: the child snatched from the priest's hands, or the face covered with a cloth, or the curate's hand being twisted behind his back.[103]

Yet even if signing the cross was excluded, laying on of hands was allowed. And even when the wedding ring was banned in marriage service, the 1645 Puritan *Directory of Public Worship* (which replaced the Book of Common Prayer), made the couple take one another by the right hand at the saying of vows.[104] Behind the scruples lay a complex, perhaps unresolvable tension between sign and signified. Cranmer, in one of the prefatory elements in the 1549 Book of Common Prayer, allowed external ceremonies as endorsement of faith and doctrine, 'not in bondage of the figure or shadow, but in the freedom of the Spirit'.[105] This is a highly metaphorical form of phrasing. Baxter in the *Christian Directory* defended kissing the book (as opposed to signing the cross, which he resisted), on the grounds that 'Significant words, gestures, or actions are not therefore evil, because they are significant'.[106] On the other hand, Laurence Chaderton, Master of Emmanuel College, Cambridge, teacher of John Harvard, in 1605 defended the sign of the cross in a memorandum, but he continued to worry that 'to make signes or representations of spirituall thinges pertains only to god'.[107] However, what was baptism if not an action involving physical manifestation of spiritual things? Calvin, with verbal care, called baptism a 'covenantal seal'.[108] However, he still used water.

Puritanism is accused of blind literalism by James Simpson in *Permanent Revolution*.[109] Iconoclasm to us is a catastrophic anti-aesthetic violence, even while relics and icons attract modernist derision. Is this a faultline in modernism rather than medievalism? The theory of affordances in phenomenology suggests how objects cue changes in human behaviour. Iconoclasm is best understood, perhaps, as a conflict over affordances. Puritans displayed in this conflict not only outbreaks of cultural violence but sometimes a deft awareness of the vexed semantics of metaphor and holy objects. We are all 'sons of Adam, borne free', they said.[110] Throwing off the shackles of idolatry enabled religious freedom, they thought. Sir Thomas Aston here makes the same claim as the peasant rebels of 1381; Christopher Hill traced this trajectory from the Levellers and Diggers of the 1640s to Thomas Paine in *The Rights of Man* (1791).[111]

Exponents of alternative cognitive worlds in the sixteenth century struggled over distinctions that have come to be maintained more absolutely in modernity. In the Reformation, representation is still raw. More shows how Tyndale's invocation of the name of Christ depended on the image-creating capacity of the word he is trying to deny:

> And yet all these names spoken | and all these wordes wrytten | be no naturall sygnes or ymages but onely made by consent and agrement of men | to betoken and sygnyfye suche thynge.[112]

In return, in the *Answere vnto More*, Tyndale plays with different image-meanings of the cross, as object, metaphor or metonym, as he describes the idolater going about his life with no sense of the difference, crossing himself with 'a legyon of crosses':

> And where he shuld crosse him selfe | to be armed and to make him silfe stronge to beare the crosse with Christe | he crosseth him selfe to driue the crosse from him | and blesseth him selfe with a crosse from the crosse.[113]

An idolater cannot tell what a word is, so no longer knows what a thing is, either. The cross outside the world of words is not a cross. Every word, every image, is brought back to its signification. It is More's genius to turn the argument back on Tyndale's world of words: these, too are 'representations'.[114] If Tyndale makes the image an empty vessel, More threatens to make Tyndale's word an empty signifier.

Here comes the crux (pardon the metonym). This is not a world in which a realm of images is threatened by rampant bookmen. It is one in which images and books face the same threat and the same promise. Transcendence is threatened with annihilation. The battle against images is not about objects but how they signify, what they are held to contain. This folds back onto the book the epistemic uncertainty of images: in what way is a book a thing? Alexandra Walsham has drawn attention to the way new forms of relic culture grew up after the English Reformation. She cites examples not only of Bibles, but also catechisms and other devotional books, being used for their healing powers.[115] David Cressy has called such cases, books as 'totems': a Bible being used as a talisman during childbirth, or another as a cure for sleeplessness.[116] In the Civil War, Parliament marched with Geneva Bibles on poles, facing Royalists with a King James Version. A favourite anecdote is from more modern times, when a woman in New Hampshire in the nineteenth century 'ate a New Testament, day by day and leaf by leaf, between two sides of bread and butter, as a remedy for fits'.[117] Equally notorious is the medieval story of St Hugh of Lincoln shocking the monks of Fécamp in Normandy by kissing the bone of Mary Magdalene so enthusiastically that he bit part of it off.[118]

Eating the book is a comic setpiece for historians. Yet eating books is an old idea:

> Moreover he said unto me, Son of man, eat that thou findest; eat this roll, and go speak unto the house of Israel. So I opened my mouth, and he caused me to eat that roll. And he said unto me, Son of man, cause thy belly to eat, and fill thy bowels with this roll that I give thee. Then did I eat it; and it was in my mouth as honey of sweetness.[119]

Ezekiel's words are some of the grandest (and weirdest) in Hebrew scripture. Yet they attest to a profound (and common) metaphor of reading as digestion. Augustine compares the reading process to a cow chewing the cud.[120] Nourishing the mind with reading, he says, is like nourishing the body with food. Bede referred to Caedmon hearing words by day and 'ruminating' them in the night to write poems.[121] The idea attests to a quizzical, even baffling consciousness, that literary acts are acts of the body as well as the mind, and enact violent transaction between the two. In the sixteenth century this idea of violence found frequent literary expression, although nothing so graphic as its iconic form (Fig. 50), in Dürer's brilliant, savage, dionysiac representation of the urgent mystery of reading in the woodcut sequence of his *Apocalypse*.

> And I took the little book out of the angel's hand, and ate it up; and it was in my mouth sweet as honey: and as soon as I had eaten it, my belly was bitter.[122]

John the Divine's astonishing quotation from Ezekiel is rendered in Dürer as an image of the visionary prophet sucking the text with elemental force of spirit into his throat, choking or gagging on the letters of the book. Dürer uncovers a manic, imaginative panic at the sixteenth-century apotheosis of literature: the moment of humanism.

In the Preface to his edition of Jerome in 1516, Erasmus hailed the written word as the most lasting of human treasures, more saintly than saints, calling books 'relics of the mind'. How can we (he asked) pay respect to slippers, tunics and napkins of martyrs, yet neglect the books they wrote? Books are the precious remains of a person, living and breathing, yet we leave them to be 'gnawed at will by bug, worm, and cockroach'.[123] We find a legacy of this conflict of sanctity and disgust throughout medieval Christianity. The codex became a holy object, to be carried aloft, elevated, kissed, bowed down before. Text, in a similar process, was transformed into a kind of image. Gospel books, either in the lettering of the Lindisfarne gospels, or in the coverings of books such as the Echternach jewel book now in Nuremberg, make the word palpably holy.[124] The cover, made in the eleventh century in Trier, consists of an ivory plaque of the resurrection, with traces of paint. Surrounding it are panels in repoussé gold relief, depicting signs of the evangelists. At the outer boundaries are filigree gold work and enamel.

In waves of iconoclasm this came under attack. Kissing images was redescribed as idolatry. Modernity regards such practices in turn with a little disdain. Yet William Dalrymple found images being kissed, and even eaten, in Syria in the 1980s.[125] The reification of the book was not lost at the Reformation. Images in churches were torn down, but what replaces them? Elizabethan Injunctions ordered giant inscriptions of the Ten Commandments where parishioners formerly saw an image of Christ and the Last Judgment (the 'doom'). In Thornham in Norfolk a fragment survives of scripture written on the nave. The letters are so

Fig. 50. 'Devouring the Book'; Albrecht Dürer, *Apocalypse with St John the Divine*, woodcut, 1498

huge as to cover the whole west wall in its undamaged state, saturating church in text. Histories of the church date them as mid-sixteenth century, but the text used is the King James Version of 1611. A few miles south, among the marsh churches near King's Lynn, there are versions of the Ten Commandments from the mid-seventeenth century. It is a visual echo of the profusion of medieval graffiti in churches, many in Norfolk: names, symbols, crosses, pentangles, Solomon's knots, faces, text, even music.[126]

Is a sense of the book as sacred entirely lost? 'When two or three study the Torah together', the rabbis explained, 'the *Shekhinah* [divine presence] is in their midst'.[127] Is this a facet of a text's holiness, or else of freestyle interpretation? The Jewish word Midrash derives from *darash*—to go in search of something. When Rushdie writes of a book falling to the floor as a sacrilege, for which a kiss is absolution, it is easy to see in it a secular survival. Yet Augustine referring to himself as chewing a book is not literal, neither is Thomas à Kempis when he embraces a book like a baby.[128] It helps to recall that Thomas was a professional scribe, who commended his art as an aid to devotion.[129] In the five pages that Proust takes to describe the first kiss with Albertine, it is clear that it is not body parts (lips, cheeks, neck, nose, or nostrils) that have become a fetish, so much as the kiss engendered as writing: 'le moment qui précède le plaisir, pareil en cela à celui qui suit la mort'.[130] The pleasure of writing exists in parallel to the mystery of language: somehow the letters in ink on a page take shape in our heads as feelings. Yet words do not escape embodiment, whether as sounds or written marks. The same is true of a book, or any object which holds writing. The book contains within it the desire for the object and itself becomes the object of desire. My books take on the imprint of my body, they share its quirks and foibles. Between contents and cover, between letter and figure, sense and reference, as also between the eye that reads and the lips that speak or kiss, lies a range of implicature that folds in both directions.

15

Books Under the Razor

In York Minster Library, there survives a pre-Reformation missal, a small folio. It was printed in France for use in York.[1] In five hundred years of its life, to this day, it has not moved outside a small triangle in north Yorkshire, between York itself and the edges of the Dales and the Moors. The Calendar contains an 'obit' (record of the death) of John Best, rector of 'faysbe', dated 14 August 1530.[2] This places the book in Faceby, a small village in the Moors near the Cleveland Hills. The current church there is a nineteenth-century building, but the original dated from the twelfth century; it was and is a tiny church with minimal decoration. A signature ('Rich: Lumley') also appears on the title-page. Richard Lumley was vicar of Stainton near Middlesbrough from 1667 to 1687, and then of Guisborough (also in North Yorkshire) until his death in 1694. Lumley bequeathed around 250 books to Stainton Vicarage. From there, like all Stainton's precious books, it was deposited in York Minster Library for safekeeping in 1911.

However, the sensational aspect of the book is concealed by these details. The opening of the *Te igitur* at the beginning of the Canon, as in many missals, is illuminated by a figure of the crucifixion, in this case a woodcut (Fig. 51) which has been coloured in with contemporary paint. But this is not what a modern handler of the book sees. Instead, the eye is confronted, we might say assaulted, by a vigorous slash, diagonally across the image of the Cross. Below, through the last half dozen leaves, is another, deeper gouge, in the opposite direction to the slashed crucifix, we might even say forming a reverse cross or saltire. These cuts are made with a very sharp instrument indeed, either a dagger or some kind of razor. On the facing recto, the mutilation begins again on a woodcut of God the Father Enthroned (also found in many missals at this point), who wears (following traditional iconography) a papal tiara. Here the damage is deeper still, cutting through seventeen leaves. Another cut focuses very precisely on the image of God the Father (who may or may not be confused with the Pope), from the top of his throne down to his lap, slicing between the eyes and through the nose of God.[3] There is also a smaller cut, diagonally, right across God's face and cheeks.

The book is an astonishing example of iconoclasm. This may have been done in the 1530s, when many books were defaced by the order of Henry VIII; but it is more likely that it happened under Edward VI in the late 1540s. It is unusual in several respects: unlike Henrician defacements, it attacks not the cult of the saints, but the image of the Saviour. Unlike Edwardian iconoclasm, it is aimed not at images or icons, but a book. However, the book is also uncanny. The sheer

Fig. 51. 'The wounded missal': *Missale*, hand-painted printed book, 1516. York Minster Library, Stainton 12, sig. N2v

savagery of the mutilation is over-determined, or a form of supplementary violence. It is disturbing, like a physical wound.

The Stainton Missal bears marks also of other textual attacks. A circular in June 1535 from Thomas Cromwell to the bishops, ordered the word *papa* ('pope') to be erased in the following books:

> all manner prayers, orisons, rubrics, canons in mass books and in all other books used in churches, wherein the said bishop of Rome is named or his presumptuous and proud pomp and authority preferred, utterly to be abolished, eradicated, and erased out.[4]

In 1538 the erasure of the Pope was extended to the cult of St Thomas Becket:

> from henceforth, the days used to be festival in his name shall not be observed, nor the service, office, antiphoners, collects, and prayers, in his name read, but erased and put out of all the bokes.[5]

In September 1538, Thomas's shrine at Canterbury was dismantled, its treasure removed and carted away, and his bones disinterred and possibly burned.[6]

Something, odd, though, happens in the proclamation. The cult of Thomas Becket is felt to reside not only in relics, or images that form a transitional substitute for the body of the saint, but in his very name. Zeal against idolatry is transferred into the realm of the onomastic or semiotic. To declare that 'the said Thomas Becket shall not be esteemed, named, reputed, nor called a saint' is to bring down not only a visual order but a world of words. It is not enough for the name not to be: it must be seen not to be. In that way, names are treated as things, the very mode of representation subject to destruction.

The book was under suspicion in the 1530s. Henry VIII took personal interest in acts of erasure, emending documents to insist on visible enforcement. Bureaucracy joined zeal in this process. The censor's gaze fastened on publication but also a book's appearance, annotations, and prologues.[7] Marginalia were forbidden, scripture restricted to 'plain sentence and text'. One surviving copy of Matthew's Bible of 1537, produced under royal copyright, has its annotations overpainted in brown.[8] A proclamation in April 1539 excoriated the heterodox possibilities implicit in interpretation of scripture. Remedy lies in only allowing graduates of Oxford and Cambridge and licensed preachers to expound the Bible. In an extravagant injunction, Henry extended his ban to cover all forms of reading: no person is allowed to read the Bible in church 'with any loud or high voices'; divine service is to be spent in silent prayer or silent reading. Even at home, reading is to take place silently and preferably in solitude. If doubt of meaning is experienced by the reader, he is to resort to an expert in private.[9] A draft, revised in Henry VIII's own hand, bristles with textual ironies. Henry railed against the insidious process of annotation, but riddled the document with his own annotations, scribbling into the margins (and between the lines) further intimidations against the text and its readers. The draft asks that the Bible be read quietly and reverently, the king adds 'quietly and with silence', and 'secretly'.[10] Whereas the king's statutes previously promoted biblical reading, he now sought to privatize the reading process almost beyond a reader's knowledge. A Gloucestershire shepherd in 1543 complained that Christ's sheep were forbidden the gospel.[11]

As a theory of publication, reading, and meaning, Henry's words carried an ominous premonition. Surviving missals and other service books manifest how decrees are carried out to the letter, or rather the anti-letter, of the law. The quarrel between word and image is nowhere more obvious than in the rigorous attention to detail by censors carrying out instructions. In Ranworth in Norwich the service for St Thomas Becket was defaced with faint diagonal lines, and easily reused in the reign of Mary.[12] Perhaps the oddest case of failure to comply is in King Henry's own Book of Hours, where neither the name nor the image of the saint is removed.[13] Royal privilege extends far indeed.

Under Edward VI in 1548 and 1549, iconoclasts turned biblioclasts, no longer content with names alone. After the Act of Uniformity all mass books were to be turned in and torn up. Only twelve manuscripts survive of the York Missal, itself a sign of the rigour of the iconoclasts. How do we explain this? Margaret Aston's wonderful last book, *Broken Idols of the English Reformation*, proves how close verbal and visual are in a culture war of 'Word against Image'.[14] The worst idols, Aston points out, pretended to speak, 'whose heads nodded and lips moved', as if conveying the word to believers. 'Haue not your idols giuen aunswer? haue they not wagged their heades and lips, &c. O shamelesse dogges & blasphemous idolaters', denounced William Fulke.[15] Iconoclasts reserved a virulent bile for such apparent delusions. In brilliant shows of pastiche, Hugh Latimer delighted in demonstrating how famous relics (like the Rood of Boxley) might be fakes, revealing the automaton that lay beneath the moveable eyes of the dumb idol.[16] Sometimes relics were burned.[17] Calvin set out a formal case in his *Traité des reliques* of 1543: relics connote a pagan superstition 'to make idols of them'.[18]

Reformers endorsed such principles at extreme lengths, pulling heads from torsos of stone, whitewashing walls to render images invisible, even recommending silent prayer to purge liturgy of the taint of ritual. However, violence was not invisible. Iconoclasm was left in plain sight, visual remainder enacting a doctrinal reminder.[19] Sculptures were left with heads torn from the socket of the neck; faces of saints in roodscreens scratched and their eyes gouged. Latimer's desecration of fake display of relics was itself a public display. The living blood of Jesus, for which a new apse had been built in Hailes in Gloucestershire in 1270, was deconstructed literally and philosophically by Latimer in 1538.[20] Transferred to London, the blood was paraded and then tasted at Paul's Cross, said to be honey coloured with saffron.[21] In that way, violence was mimetic as well as anti-mimetic. Indeed, without any apparent recognition of the contradiction, the new doctrine ordered destruction of books as well as images.

What, then, is the significance of pages mutilated so brutally in the Stainton Missal? Here the savage violence of intervention falls on the Canon of the Mass. At this point, the priest raises his hands a little, joining them, looking briefly up to heaven, then bows deeply before the altar and rests his hands on the book. After the gospel is read, the priest says, privately to himself, *Benedictus qui venit in nomine domini*, and kisses the book. At the singing of the *Veni creator* the celebrant washes his hands. Thirdly, before the consecration, at the words *Sit signatum, ordinatum, et santificatum hoc sacrificium nostrum*, there is a threefold signing of the cross over the bread and wine.[22]

The initial *T* was signalled hierarchically in manuscripts throughout northern Europe by elaborate decoration, and sometimes a miniature. The canon was styled in larger script for ease of reading, often copied (later printed) on parchment even if the rest of the book was on paper. Directly preceding the Canon, in late medieval manuscripts and printed copies throughout the sixteenth century, there was often a full-page illumination of the Crucifixion, as in British Library

MS Stowe 10.[23] On beginning the Canon, the priest would kiss the image of the Crucifixion. In a Pierpont Morgan example produced around 1400 in France, probably in Troyes, for use in the cathedral of Châlons-sur-Marne, the miniature has a small gold cross in the lower margin, so that the priest might not damage the miniature in kissing the cross.[24]

The Stainton Missal has the traditional Crucifixion image, overpainted in red, blue and green. At the foot of the cross is a border, and in the middle of this there is a decorated abstract cross, rather like the Châlons example, painted in black. Here, the black colouring is smudged. It is thus likely that, as in many missals, it bears the residue of the lips of the priest as he kissed the book before raising it, anticipating the elevation of the host. Don Skemer in *Binding Words: Textual Amulets in the Middle Ages* quotes Michael Camille as saying that copies of missals are often damaged irreparably by kissing. This must be romantic exaggeration. But copies such as a Flemish Hours exported to England, now in the British Library, show visible traces of ritual use, which verge on damage.[25] John Lowden has speculated that another devotional book, produced around 1490, may show extensive signs of kissing. Three pages are painted black, on which large drops of blood trickle down. The third page has been thoroughly worn.[26] This is testimony to the physical presence in surviving books of the embodied memory contained in their use. The sensitivity of the York use to manual performance—to washing the hands, to signing over the bread, to elevating the host, above all to kissing the book—has its mirror image in the physical horror felt by Protestants.

Nothing in Henrician censorship prepares us for the Stainton Missal. Damage to the Canon is of a different order of magnitude. The knife makes seven cuts in all. A likely reconstruction is that the book was attacked three times over: first the woodcut on the verso (Christ crucified); then the page is turned to the right, and cut in a crossways action back through the previous leaves. The cutting takes place in different directions, in diagonal pattern. The action is repeated on the recto, across a second woodcut of the enthroned God the Father, dressed like the pope. Delving deep into the book, seventeen leaves are cut. Then a few pages are turned together, with another crossways slash, through fewer leaves. Finally, violence turns back to the woodcut of the 'pope': his head is bisected vertically, and sideways. These wounds are smaller but more precise. It is hard to resist the analogy of a bodily assault. Three crossed wounds: on God the Son, God the Father, and the Canon of the Mass. The book is ritually slaughtered.

Comparisons with other cases of similar damage are few and far between. Damaged books are likely to have been thrown away or their pages reused for binding or other purposes. At Lambeth Palace Library, there is a Primer of 1537 where the damage is considerable, but unlike the Stainton Missal, it appears to be less a targeted assault on liturgical function, and more like an attempt to make the whole book unusable.[27] A different comparison can be made with a copy of the same Primer of 1537 in Canterbury Cathedral Library.[28] The first two folios of 'The Letany' are slashed, although the names of the Saints remain intact except for 'Thomas', which has been torn out leaving a triangular shaped hole where part of his name should be. In some ways it is difficult to make any generalization from the Stainton Missal, beyond the brute fact of its witness to physical violence. We are left with the anger still present in the book, like a bodily memory of the emotional past; and with other witnesses of preservation, in the way that the book has come down to us. How do we explain historical anger?

At the same time the Stainton example shows a surplus of violence, something uncontainable. Physical remnants of iconoclasm often show an extraordinary ambiguity. Visiting the church in Faceby, and seeing an engraving there of the old church, it is hard not to be struck by the extreme poverty of the building, little more than a sheepcote. A layperson from the village might, like other iconoclasts in England and the Netherlands, be reacting to the divergence between his own circumstances and the richness of an illuminated book. In a fifteenth-century Flemish manuscript of a Book of Hours at Lambeth Palace Library, the text for the feast of Thomas Becket has been erased (Fig. 52), following the public orders, and in addition, the saint's face is defaced. A single cross appears through Thomas's visage, and many other saints' images are scratched through, with a kind of randomness. In one case, the baby Jesus has been damaged. Arendt's controversial concept of the 'banality' of violence comes to mind.[29]

In the case of the Stainton Missal, the violence is less arbitrary, in seven separate acts of the knife, some more deeply gouged than others. Anger can even be interpreted a little. It is noteworthy that while the cross is cut through, the body of Christ is untouched. Is this a conscious act of mercy, even a recoil from sacrilege? On the other hand, God the Father is given no grace whatsoever. However, the memory of the book does not end with its mutilation. The book survives its dismemberment: it is kept, after the Reformation and after iconoclasm. Is it itself a form of relic, the sacred body of a wounded church? And yet its survival is not, as we might expect, recusant or Catholic. At the end of the sixteenth century someone used it to record the escape from assassination of James VI, a Scottish king (and by upbringing a Presbyterian). In the seventeenth century it lingers on, passing at some point into the hands of a Yorkshire vicar, and thence into a Church of England parish library. It is then, a transitional object for us, too, in the passage of human memory. 500 years old, it bears marks of use from just before the Reformation and just after, in turn ritual and iconoclastic; and then passes out of recorded usage and into the archive. And there, in the archive, it lies, dormant and yet viscerally embodied still.

A missal is a holy object and makes us think it is a special case of religious violence. 'As good almost kill a Man as kill a good book', says Milton in *Areopagitica*.[30] Yet good Puritan that he is, Milton extends the sense of the sacred to any book whatever:

Fig. 52. 'The face defaced': *Hours*, ink and paint on vellum, Flemish for English use, 15th c. London, Lambeth Palace Library, MS 496, fo. 54v

> Many a man lives a burden to the Earth; but a good Booke is the pretious life-blood of a master spirit, imbalm'd and treasur'd up on purpose to a life beyond life.

The image of embalming, or impregnating a dead body with spices, to prevent it from decay, is a striking one for a book, especially in *Areopagitica*, which rejects the Index of the inquisition, or of Church of England prelates, in order to translate the book from its cultic origins onto the political state.[31] At some level Milton exorcizes the book of ritual. Yet in demystifying the book, or defumigating it from incense, Milton resacralizes it. He attests to a mystery in the book as object, something preserved in it like a human presence. Perhaps this explains a parallel case of early modern biblioclasm in the same decade. It is a very different book, one of the oddest surviving copies of Shakespeare, a Second Folio of 1632 which once belonged to the library of the Real Colegio Seminario de los Ingleses (or English Seminary) at Valladolid. The copy was first described by Sir Sidney Lee in *The Times* in April 1922, and soon acquired by the Shakespeare Folio collector, Henry Folger.[32] The questions Lee asked were glaring enough. Why were young Jesuits, training for the mission in Spain, reading an English dramatist? Also, why does the book bear inside its front end-papers the certificate of Guillermo Sánchez (see Ch. 14, Fig. 57), a censor for the Holy Office, or in other words, the Spanish Inquisition?

> Opus auctoritate Sancti officii permissum et expurgatum eadem auctoritate per Guilielmum Sanchaeum e Soc[te] Jesu.[33]

A third question, obviously related closely to the second, is why the entirety of just one play, *Measure for Measure*, has been neatly cut out using a sharp instrument.

The most arresting commentary on the book is made by Greenblatt, in an interview on the enduring mystery of Shakespeare in the *Washington Post*. As Greenblatt speaks to the Head of Reference at the Folger Shakespeare Library, Georgianna Ziegler dramatically (or ritually) holds up the Valladolid Shakespeare as a testament to the power of books. By way of formal explanation, it is suggested that the missing text of *Measure for Measure* could be due to the play making light of Catholic doctrine. But there is something still unexplained, the interview continues: 'People do things to sacred texts', Greenblatt says.[34] Greenblatt's sly conflation of Shakespearean Folio and holy writ is not meant to be bibliographically accurate. He knows perfectly well that religious censorship is more subtle and venal in its motivations than this.

Copies of Shakespeare in Spain, even rumours of them, are rare in the seventeenth century. A First Folio is said to have been owned in Valladolid itself by the Count of Gondomar, Spanish ambassador to England from 1613 to 1622 and afterwards Spain's leading expert on English affairs. A noted bibliophile, he is reported to have bought a Shakespeare in London for his library in the Casa del Sol. In one version of the story it was burned by mistake by a servant during decluttering; in another it is reused as wrapping paper.[35] The presence of a copy of Shakespeare in a Spanish Jesuit seminary is doubly curious. Lee, perhaps romantically, thought he was encountering Guillén Sánchez, one of a select group of Spanish clerics reading English in the period. However, was Sánchez Spanish? Patrick Ryan, SJ, in a letter to *The Times* the day after Lee's article, made the brilliant suggestion that Guillén Sànchez is the Spanish pen name of Father William Sankey.[36] He was born in Lancashire in 1609 and entered the novitiate at Watten (near St Omer) in the Spanish Netherlands in 1628. In 1639 he was in Ghent.[37] The records of the College in Valladolid say he arrived in Spain from Flanders in January 1641, professing the four vows in 1643.[38] For two months in 1649 he was in charge of the College. In 1651 he moved to Madrid, to become Rector of St George's English College until 1662.[39] He visited England briefly, but died in Flanders in 1682, aged 73.

The first reader of this Spanish Shakespeare was English, not Spanish, albeit a distinctive kind of English reader. The Sankeys were Lancastrian. Like much of the neighbouring gentry, they adhered to the Roman Church despite Elizabethan persecution. However, William himself lived almost all his adult life, from his teens to his seventies, in exile communities. He was never a missionary, but a career priest, bureaucrat, and long-term domiciled expatriate. All his surviving words, spoken or written, are in Spanish. To all intents and purposes, he is a naturalized reader. As for expurgation, Sankey's methods are tireless yet not exhaustive. Many plays are untouched—more than half of the 36 plays in the Folio. He makes marks in 7 out of 14 comedies, 5 out of 10 histories, and 3 out of 12 tragedies. Sankey gives mixed messages. Some censorship is moralistic, in sexual bowdlerizing of comedies. His largest interventions relate to the life of a priest: *King John*, and *King Henry VIII*.[40] Both plays refer to monks and priests; in the latter case (Fig. 53), to the English Reformation, which cut Sankey off from faith and homeland. In *Henry VIII*, the censor's zeal puts Shakespeare 'under erasure' (to use Derrida's phrase) to the point that text can barely be seen under censorious black ink.[41]

But what happens when *Measure for Measure* is removed altogether, the final act of violence?[42] This is not writing under erasure but writing in oblivion. The excision appears to have been made using an instrument like a razor; the cuts are sharp, although with occasional reverse movements as the instrument catches the paper. What brings this into being? There is hardly a proper answer to this question. Censorship always contains a tension between what is there and what is not there, between the text seen and unseen. Here, however, censorship opens up different ways of reading, requiring imagination, to see what happens when we look between the lines.

There is a parallel history of Spanish censorship of plays. Bartolomé de Torres Naharro, of Jewish *converso* descent and himself in holy orders, wrote plays that were published in 1517 in a volume entitled *Propalladia*. It was only after his death and after the Reformation that they ran into trouble. A ban was placed by the Inquisition in 1559, and in 1573 a full expurgation was undertaken. In one copy of Torres Naharro in the Biblioteca Nacional at Madrid, the examiner

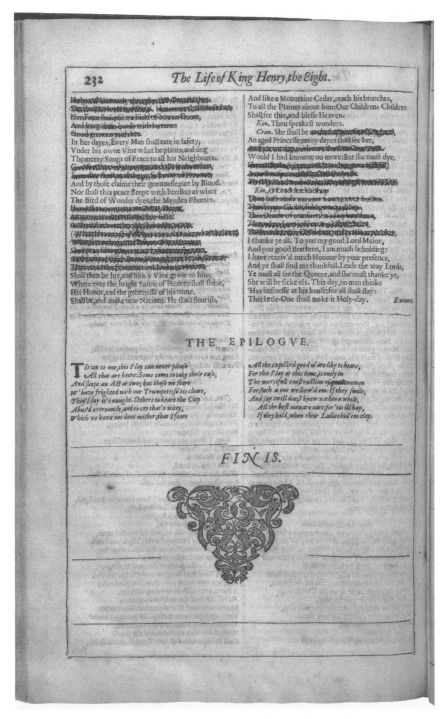

Fig. 53. 'A censored Shakespeare'; *Mr. William Shakespeare's Comedies, Histories, & Tragedies, Published according to the true Originall Copies* (London: Thomas Cotes, 1632), Washington DC, Folger Shakespeare Library, shelf mark: Fo.2 no.07, sig. y6v

(a friar in the monastery of St Jerome at Seville) went further. He dated his act 2 June 1585: 'The comedy called *Jacinta* was taken out and torn up because it was prohibited in the catalogue printed in 1583'. The excision was incorrect as the play had not been banned. A later reader redeems the excessive zeal of the friar by adding the play back, copied out by hand.[43]

Is the excision of *Measure for Measure* an example of an excess of zeal or paranoia? Perhaps both are present. However, here lies an unexpected kink in the history of censorship. The usual model is functional. Censorship aims to remove something offensive from a text. By definition it knows what it is looking for. A settled version of orthodoxy pre-exists for censorship to act on. Yet the expurgators often used censorship to work out what orthodoxy was. Gigliola Fragnito comments on the Roman Index that 'the censorial apparatus was not the well-oiled machinery that has often been depicted; rather, it frequently jammed, and changes of mind, reversals and dithering gave it a markedly erratic course'.[44] Indeed, Fragnito argues, the Herculean ambition of the Index, responded to a sense of failure, or a sense of the inevitability of this failure.

In the twenty-five years following Clement VIII's third Index of 1596, a bureaucratic mania ensued—with all the farce and incompetence that energetic bureaucracy brings with it. After a while, specialization was introduced to assist the process. Works on medicine and philosophy were sent to Padua; those on astrology to Venice; historical texts to Milan; books on duelling to Parma, Piacenza, and Cremona; texts on canon law to Bologna; those on civil law to Perugia; and literary works to Florence.[45] There was a complaint in Padua that after they had finished with an author from one point of view, it had to go on to other cities for further expurgation, perhaps even undoing previous work. Yet the Congregation of the Index itself aspired to a comprehensive collation of expurgations. Naturally, these processes are full of irony and contradiction. One cardinal worried that when more than half of a sentence is removed, the rest might become hard to understand.[46] Are the censors permitted to add to a text to restore the sense?

In Fragnito's words, 'The central apparatus had been crushed by the weight of a project for the disinfestation of an unmanageable quantity of books'.[47] A number of factors brought it down: the slowness of the expurgators; habitual meanness in paying them; inefficiencies of transporting material. Beyond the impossible magnitude of the task in hand there were further questions: what if, in the effort of voluminous, inexhaustible expurgation, the censors had omitted, or worse misinterpreted or transgressed, matters of orthodoxy? This suggests something more mysterious and less practical about the operation of censorship. It does not always know what it is looking for, and it does not always know what it has found when it has finished looking. What the act of crossing out means, what the word that is crossed out means *when it is crossed out*, what the difference is between the word scored and unscored, what the words to one side or the other of the purged word mean, is open to interpretation. In this context, interpretation is anything but free: the mind making sense of the text is backed into a corner, fearing error, perhaps reeling from it, and trying to work out how to manoeuvre around it.

In a letter to Ernst Jünger in 1956, published as *The Question of Being*, Martin Heidegger speculated about the problematic nature of defining anything, let alone words. To make his point, Heidegger crosses out the word 'Being' but lets both the deletion and the word remain. He had been experimenting with placing words under erasure since his 1929–30 lectures, *The Fundamental Concepts of Metaphysics*.[48] In *The Question of Being*, he says: 'Since the word is inaccurate, it is crossed out. Since it is necessary, it remains legible'.[49] The sign of crossing through (*Durchkreuzung*) is not the same as the merely negative act of crossing out (*Durchstreichung*). Iconoclasm, we could say, most strikingly the Stainton Missal, is an example of *Durchkreuzung*. The cross remains, even as Christ is slashed. Yet the missing play in the Valladolid Folio gives us *Durchstreichung*, properly defined. It is a case of the totally obliterated, the absolutely expurgated, absent text. What can be said between the lines of a text where all the lines have been removed? Where there is no proclamation outlawing the text, or reason for removal? What was William Sankey looking for, and what did he find when he had finished, when he had blotted whole scenes into incomprehensibility, or cut an entire play with a razor?

Of course, there are instrumental reasons for expurgation. *Measure for Measure*, with its friars and confessors, its nuns and whores, is more than minimally anti-Catholic. However, the censor also does not know in advance exactly what is problematic. It is not because the censor knows what he is doing that he cuts out an entire play. If he could so readily understand the play, then as with *Henry VIII*, he would just cross out words and speeches. It is because he cannot make complete sense of the play that he finds it troubling enough to remove it altogether. In this respect, it is interesting to consider how the play itself mirrors the action of religious censorship, and in the process ambiguates the boundaries of religious orthodoxy. *Measure for Measure* is about the discovery of orthodoxy, the enforcement of it, and the triumphant display of it. Yet it is also a play about the dismantling of orthodoxy, not by outward rebellion but by a kind of decay from within. The play gets into the heart and mind of the censor himself, and it appears that the censor does not enjoy this. The play is concerned throughout with systems of religious control, with the desire to enforce conformity by violent means. It articulates social control down to the interior thoughts of citizens. In the process, it examines the means orthodoxy uses to carry out its scrutiny, including torture.

What Sankey agonizes about most in Shakespeare is the Protestant calumny, well known to the Jesuit order, that Catholic priests were conjurors and charlatans, forever prone to acting in disguise or fabricating extravagantly theatrical miracles. Priests are portrayed as moral enforcers, agents of the Inquisition in extracting secret information under the ecclesiastical power of pardon. In

Measure for Measure, the Duke's caricature of a fake priest is displayed in excruciating detail, supervising the conscience of Isabella, and then in turn almost everyone in the play. No intervention by the Duke as friar is more extreme than when he takes on the role of her brother Claudio's confessor, the night before his execution. This is an extraordinary scene, one of the most remarkable in all Shakespeare. It is a scene of quietus, of deathly silence and extreme unction. One fact troubling Father Sankey the confessor is that the friar abuses his position to play games with the minds of the penitent. The friar breaks the seal of confession in order to manipulate events. The Duke plays God, pretending to hear the last confession of Claudio before his death, in order to encourage him into following the Duke's plans. Or perhaps Sankey is most troubled, like many spectators of the play, by the agony of confrontation between brother and sister, which the friar forces them into conducting.

Claudio is offered the temptation of release from prison. Isabella is there to tell his brother he must die. But she will also tell him that he has a chance to escape death, only it is a choice he must not take, since it is a choice that will imperil both his soul and hers.

> ISABELLA   Dost thou think, Claudio,
> If I would yield him my virginity
> Thou mightst be freed?[50]

It is one of those scholastic bargains with theology the play is full of. Claudio is steadfast: 'Thou shalt not do't.' With the solace that imagination gives, Isabella retorts that if it were only her own life at stake, she would willingly give it up. 'Thanks, dear Isabel', Claudio replies, perhaps a little curtly.[51] Is there a more intimate scene in Shakespeare? It is the more charged with emotion in that it is shared between brother and sister and not between lovers, and that it faces up to death and not to love. And yet, just at the point where we have learned to empathize with Claudio in his desperation, the play makes him turn again. He hates himself for having put his sister in this position. Death is his ultimate reconciliation with God. Like the condemned heretic, he has no choice but to recant his life of sin and embrace his own execution as the ultimate kindness of the Church and of God. Is there a more disturbing scene in Shakespeare, in its moral ambiguity, its astonishing privacy and exposure, its closeness to the promise of mortality? If it was this that drove the censor to his ultimate act of amputation, and reach for his razor, for a moment we can perhaps feel some sympathy.

16

Shakespeare and Bibliofetishism

At the end of *The Tempest*, Prospero makes his famous farewell. As well as leave-taking, it records a punctilious performance of quasi-religious ritual involving drowning a book:

> PROSPERO   But this rough magic
> I here abjure; and when I have required
> Some heavenly music—which even now I do—
> To work mine end upon their senses that
> This airy charm is for, I'll break my staff,
> Bury it certain fathoms in the earth,
> And deeper than did ever plummet sound
> I'll drown my book.   *Solemn music.*[1]

The scene invokes an ambiguity central to the play. The mood is of religious ceremony. At the point of Prospero's farewell, this is a ritual not of mourning but public penitence: *They all enter the circle which Prospero had made, and there stand charmed.* The 'Solemn music' assists at a ceremony of purgation that is nevertheless not staged.[2]

On 1 December 1987, the Chinese artist Huang Yong Ping, dumped a load of art school textbooks, including a translation of Herbert Read, inside a washing machine (Fig. 54). Mixing Dada and Chan Buddhism, it was a reaction to the state of art theory in post-Maoist China, as well as to the cultural capital of books. It was a symbolic act, carrying connotations of purifying as well as destroying, or washing away; and also of jumbling up tradition and modernity, or East and West, in an anticolonial gesture.[3] Two years earlier, in *A 'Book Washing' Project*, he had taken all the books from his bookshelf and put them in the wash to create a pulp. At some level these installations are also a commentary on the millennium-old tradition of burning books, going back to Qin Shi Huang and reaching up to the Cultural Revolution. Drowning books is a form of anti-burning, cathartic, even baptismal. Water opposes fire, by putting it out.

Prospero's book gives us the opportunity to reconsider what Greenblatt calls 'the mimetic economy'.[4] While offering at first sight a model of the stage's relation to state institutions, Greenblatt concludes that the principal beneficiary of Shakespeare's legacy was not the theatre but 'the institution of literature'. He recounts a story told by H. M. Stanley, how in Mowa in central Africa in 1877 the

《中国绘画史》
和《现代绘画简
史》在洗衣机里搅
拌了两分钟 1987.12.1

Fig. 54. 'Drowning books'; Huang Yongping, *A Concise History of Modern Art after Two Minutes in the Washing Machine*, Chinese teabox, paper pulp, glass, 1987. Walker Art Center, Minneapolis

chief Safeni demanded that he destroy his travel notebook, or otherwise the whole country, its crops and its women, will become infertile, and his people will die. Stanley does not wish to destroy the book, which contains 'a vast number of valuable notes', plans and sketches of ethnological and philological interest.[5] By a clever trick he substitutes a copy of the works of Shakespeare and sets fire to that. Safeni is satisfied; Stanley gets to keep his notebook. The colonization of Africa is saved by the Burning of Shakespeare. For Greenblatt, the episode is iconic. Only the Bible rivals Shakespeare in metanarrative purpose. For modernity, though, the Bible comes second, and 'Shakespeare *is* the discourse of power'.[6] Shakespeare's book becomes Prospero's Island.

In Peter Greenaway's film *Prospero's Books* (1991), the old magician has a large library, including *An Atlas Belonging to Orpheus* and *An Alphabetical Inventory of the Dead*. For British worshippers of Shakespeare, there is further irony: since just before D-Day, the BBC has run a highly idiosyncratic weekly radio programme called *Desert Island Discs*. An autobiographical interview allows a celebrity of the day to imagine herself a sovereign subject surrounded by an ocean. The allusion to *The Tempest* is maybe not unconscious. To while away solitary confinement, the guest is provided with eight pieces of music, along with three books. One book is chosen personally, the other two are compulsory: an English Bible, and (what else) a copy of the *Complete Works of Shakespeare*.

'Desert Island Shakespeare' raises significant questions about the book as material object, and how its status has changed over time. How does Prospero's drowning of his text relate to Stanley's burning of Shakespeare's book? For Greenblatt, the book is triumphant, in what we can see are Marxist terms, because of its exchange value. Unlike the Globe Theatre, fixed in time and place, Greenblatt says, the book is 'supremely portable', and detached from its physical and geographical origins. It is 'endlessly reproduced, circulated, exchanged', thus conforming to a ruthlessly capitalist model of cultural poetics. If the Globe appeals to a pre-modern ideal of community or gift culture, the Shakespeare Folio is like the invention of paper money or of capital itself.[7]

In Volume I of *Das Kapital*, Marx states that while a commodity, in the first place, is 'an object', it becomes commodified only in so far as it has a 'value-form'.[8] However, this is a paradox, something we cannot resolve easily. Rather proving Greenblatt's point about the triumph of Shakespeare, Marx quotes from Falstaff to say what he means:

FALSTAFF Why? She's neither fish nor flesh; a man knows not where to have her.[9]

'The value of commodities is the very opposite of the coarse materiality of their substance, not an atom of matter enters into its composition'.[10] The value of commodities has a social reality: indeed, value only realizes itself in a social relation of commodity to commodity. This is what Marx calls 'the riddle presented by money'.

While a commodity appears at first sight as something 'trivial', we might say *a mere thing*, it is anything of the sort: 'Its analysis shows that it is, in reality, a very queer thing, abounding in metaphysical subtleties and theological niceties'.[11] This has nothing to do with usefulness or functionality. Wood can be transformed into a table, but remains wood. Yet in becoming a commodity 'it is changed into something transcendent'. Indeed, worse still, the existence of things *qua* commodities, even the value-relation that makes them products of labour, 'have absolutely no connexion with their physical properties'. Thus, linen becomes commodified first as paper and then as book. To find a corresponding analogy to this mysterious process Marx has recourse to the religious world. In religion, he recalls, the products of the brain appear as beings endowed with life, in a process called by philosophers of religion a 'fetish'. Fetishism, Marx declares, 'attaches itself to the products of labour, so soon as they are produced as commodities, and which is therefore inseparable from the production of commodities'.

As David Harvey comments, this section in *Capital* is written in a distinctive, even literary style: 'evocative and metaphoric, imaginative, playful and emotive'.[12] For some economists and political scientists, indeed, the 'fetish' concept is treated as extraneous to Marx's argument, not to be taken too seriously. But for those with a philosophical or literary interest, so Harvey continues, it is 'the golden nugget', even 'the foundational moment to Marx's understanding of the world'. Marx's concern is to show how market systems and the forms of money 'disguise real social relations through the exchange of things'. The freedom of the market is no freedom at all: it is a 'fetishistic illusion' (p. 42).

In *Lire le Capital*, Louis Althusser transfers the idea of the fetish to the sphere of reading and writing. He does so historically, by juxtaposing 'a theory of history and a philosophy of the opacity of the immediate'.[13] This is what he calls the *fetishism* of reading: 'the illusion of an immediate reading of them [is made] the ultimate apex of their effects: fetishism'. The 'fetish' is thus a signifier for hermeneutic surplus, or the unquantifiable. Althusser's argument here originates in a seminar at the École Normale Supérieure early in 1965. It bears the marks of its time in assuming a radical epistemological break in the early modern period between the transparency of pre-modernity and the 'opacity' of modernity. Lacan dated the break to Erasmus; Althusser prefers Spinoza.[14] Behind either choice lies secularization. The aspiration, Althusser declares, is bound up with 'the religious fantasies of epiphany and parousia, and the fascinating myth of the Scriptures, in which the body of truth, dressed in its words, is the Book'.[15]

Lisa Jardine read the Renaissance as the period in which books turned into economic commodities.[16] This imitated the economic historian Richard A. Goldthwaite's theory of the rise of 'consumer culture' in the demand for art in Renaissance Florence.[17] Modern history of the book, as in the work of Don McKenzie, founds itself on a principle of the preponderance of economic over ideological factors in the minds of printers. McKenzie comments on how Māori identity in the 1850s found expression in print culture for economic not religious reasons.[18] It must be admitted these are Western and capitalist conceptual distinctions, which do not appear so inevitable elsewhere in the world.

'Read thousands of books, travel thousands of miles', is a thousand-year-old proverb by the neo-Confucian scholar Liu Yi (1017–86). In the late twentieth century it was reapplied in the work of new-wave artists in Communist China. Over a three-year period, Xu Bing carved over 4,000 fake Chinese characters in order to print 400 books of nonsense text, called *Book from Heaven*.[19] In his October 1988 exhibition at the National Art Gallery, Beijing, multiple copies of the books lay on the floor, while overhead, as if in a giant sail or cloud, huge paper sheets with the same characters curved across the room, the walls hung with the same script. It was called 'a sea of books'.[20] Xu Bing recalled how he grew up surrounded by books, as his parents worked in Beijing in the University Library; however, by the time he reached manhood, 'the entire country read only one book', Mao's Little Red Book.[21] He became, he said, saturated with the exterior appearance of books—book bindings, styles of calligraphy, varieties of brush and ink, or techniques of typesetting—without knowing any of the contents. At the end of the Cultural Revolution, he caught up with lack of reading as if in a feverous booksickness, suffering afterwards the results of over-consumption in such a short period in time. These cultural forces produced, he says, a peculiar 'awkwardness'.

This ambivalence is seen in Song Dong's *A Room of Calligraphy Model Books* (1995), in which calligraphic style-books are cut into strips, and then reassembled on the floor like a carpet, an electric fan running over them, creating a rippling pattern like the wind in a field. Hong Hao has been called a 'book artist' by Wu Hung, such as in *Selected Scripture* (2000), a collection of large prints created over more than a decade.[22] Each represents as if one page from a limitless encyclopaedia, which is nonetheless forever unrealized as it only exists in these single disaggregated sheets. By this means Hong Hao rids the book of its 'functionality and contextual continuity'.[23] Although all of the pages come from a book, the viewer never knows what the book is about. The contents of the book are deconstructed so that its logic (or epistemology) entirely disappears. The interesting thing here is the close attention paid to the traditional media of Chinese writing—the *guohua* that is so central to Chinese culture—in the form of ink or paper, or the thread-bound scroll, or butterfly binding, or painting album. The book is reformed as both concept and pure form, disassociated from meaning or intelligibility. A powerful example is Qin Chong's *Birthday* (2002). Four separate installations are each made from hundreds of sheets of pure white paper assembled into a tight pile (Fig. 55), that is then set on fire.[24] The ream of paper is distorted in shape into something like a rhomboid or ziggurat, in which the trace of charcoal is the dominant visual impression. It is an image in which emotion and politics are strongly linked. In a brilliant commentary on his own work, he remarks how history and memory are reversed: the visible part of the book is blank, while 'the part that no longer exists is that which has been recorded'.[25]

Greenblatt deflects this political energy in a comic primitivism of bookburning. Stanley, Greenblatt muses, maybe made it all up. But Stanley only did so, knowing Shakespeare's power. In that sense a book's commodification mimics reality—commodity fetish is also object fetish, even when imaginary.[26] In such a way Hamlet began to colonize China.[27] Francis Hitchman, author of *The Penny Press*, accused social reformers a few years after Stanley of making books 'a species of Fetish', with a twist of Islamophobia in calling Nonconformists 'Mahometans'.[28] Early in *Moby-Dick*, Queequeg turns the pages of a 'marvellous book', something he has never seen. Ishmael tells him 'the purpose of the printing', which Queequeg compares to his wooden idol. Ishmael cannot make out if he is George Washington or a cannibal.[29] The Dutch took the fetish to Indonesia, an archipelago of 700

Fig. 55. 'Charred paper as art'; Qin Chong, *Birthday II*, paper, ink, ash, 2002. Venice Biennale

languages. Multatuli penned the anti-colonial novel *Max Havelaar* in 1860, show-ing how commodities like sugar and coffee were starving the country of rice.[30] Just before independence in 1949, the Dutch interred the Marxist novelist Pramoedya Ananta Toer; he wrote the anticolonial novel *The Fugitive* in prison.[31] As an intermediary in social and political relations the modern book still pos-sesses its charge. The Shakespearean Folio is an object of such cultural value in our time that it is rarely possible for anyone other than scholars or royalty to be allowed to touch it. One sign of fetishism is kleptomania. The Shakespearean bib-liophile James Orchard Halliwell was accused in 1845 of stealing that rarest of books, a first quarto of *Hamlet*. To make the story more Oedipal or Ophelian, the owner in question was the father of his fiancé, Henrietta Phillipps.[32] In a digital age, desire to touch old things, especially with an aura like a First Folio, is newly enhanced. Touching the Folio is the nearest we come to the sacred body of the author.

Peter Stallybrass in an essay on 'Marx's Coat' takes the fetish outside its theoretical home in order to uncover its ideological origins: 'the fetish as a concept was elaborated to demonize the supposedly arbitrary attachment of West Africans to material objects. The European subject was constituted in opposition to a demonized fetishism, through the disavowal of the object.'[33] This perception distinguishes between objects that may be called 'fetishes' and the 'fetish' as an idea. *Calling* something a fetish, then, is a kind of fetishization: a religious or other practice is objectified, reified, we might say often trivialized, as a surrender to a supposedly pre-historic form of subjectivity. William Pietz's brilliant anthropological analysis ('The Problem of the Fetish'), argues that an 'untranscended materiality' attaches to otherwise disparate fields in which fetishism has become central: ethnography and the history of religion; Marxism and sociology; psychoanalysis and the psychiatry of sexual deviance; or aesthetics and philosophy.[34]

The idea of the fetish, Pietz argues, came into being at a very peculiar point in colonial history, a triangulation of Christian feudalism, West African lineage ties, and emerging capitalist merchant systems. Indeed, we can see this in the history of the word, from the late medieval Portuguese *feitiço*, to the sixteenth-century pidgin *Fetisso* on the African coast, to various northern European versions of the word *fetisch* via a 1602 text by the Dutchman Pieter de Marees.[35] The fetish, Pietz insists:

> could originate only in conjunction with the emergent articulation of the ideol-
> ogy of the commodity form that defined itself within and against the social val-
> ues and religious ideologies of two radically different types of noncapitalist
> society, as they encountered each other in an ongoing cross-cultural situation.[36]

The 'fetish' is an inherently relational term, meaningful only in the axis by which a society comes to imagine itself in contradistinction to a pre-capitalist society. And yet, in post-Enlightenment theories of subjectivity, it occupies a much stranger territory, able to transcend almost any disciplinary boundary as a key to the mysteries of object relations or the social organization of subjectivity. This is so despite the fact that the term is almost always cited within double- or even triple-bluff scare-quotes, above all via its most famous rendition in Freud as universal substitute for the castrated penis.[37]

Within this, Shakespeare's book proffers a re-engagement with the material 'fetish' of knowledge as it enters the dangerous epoch of apparent dematerialization. A sense of the book as an object with an aura lies at some distance from that other contemporary concept, the ebook as devoid of any physical value whatsoever, a mere container of knowledge. The internet as a metaphor for information itself has fostered an idea of knowledge as a vast, indeed illimitable, abstract entity. Yet this has generated in turn a profound cultural anxiety about those moments when a boundary between knowledge as infinite system, and knowledge as physical entity, comes into question. Take the Ed Snowden affair, felt as a wound by governments and civil liberties groups alike. This involved a palpable fear of a breach of the infinite web of knowledge as a totality. Somewhere out there I am only an algebraic signifier in a hypothetical algorithmic chain.

The lives of books on shelves, as objects within lives, gain ever closer attention. A new discipline of the material culture of the book has arisen in the last generation to study it.[38] Here, the material textuality of Shakespeare's books meets halfway a philosophical and anthropological question about how to read Shakespeare. 'Look,| Not on his Picture, but his Book', Ben Jonson's poem 'To the Reader' in the prefatory material of the First Folio, commends.[39] What does it mean to look on his book, rather than the words in his book? Shakespeare himself recognises the book as 'fetish':

> CALIBAN   Why, as I told thee, 'tis a custom with him
> I' th' afternoon to sleep. There thou mayst brain him,
> Having first seized his books; or with a log
> Batter his skull, or paunch him with a stake,
> Or cut his weasand with thy knife. Remember
> First to possess his books; for without them
> He's but a sot, as I am, nor hath not
> One spirit to command—they all do hate him
> As rootedly as I. Burn but his books.[40]

If 'discourse *is* power', as Greenblatt avers, then Caliban feels that power *is* discourse. The anxiety of cultural capital is attested by the extreme violence Caliban invokes in countering the fetish. He will smash his oppressor's skull, and so 'brain him'. Power is invested in the physical object of the book, and can only be answered by physical rebellion. To disempower Prospero, it is necessary to take away his book.

Religious travesty is common on the early modern stage. The witches in *Macbeth* do things in threes, like the sacrament of baptism. 'All hail' (three times) is an anti-masque, John Kerrigan says, to the 'theology of the Jacobean threefold monarchy'.[41] The most notorious necromancer of all, Doctor Faustus, faces damnation as an end without limits. As the clock strikes twelve, in a last bargain with his soul, he offers to burn his books:

> FAUSTUS.
> No Faustus, curse thyself. Curse Lucifer,
> That hath deprived thee of the joys of heaven.
> *The clock striketh twelve.*
> O, it strikes, it strikes! Now, body, turn to air,
> Or Lucifer will bear thee quick to hell.
> *Thunder and lightning.*

Oh soul, be changed into little waterdrops,
And fall into the ocean, ne'er be found!
My God, my God, look not so fierce on me!
Enter Devils.
Adders and serpents, let me breathe a while!
Ugly hell, gape not. Come not, Lucifer!
I'll burn my books. Ah, Mephistopheles!
Devils exeunt with him.[42]

The offer, it appears, comes to nothing, and Faustus falls into the pit with the dev-ils. Marlovians used to assume that this magical power is subsumed onto the book as mere instrument or container. An alternative view is that the book holds a power of its own, which it subsequently confers onto the magician.[43] To Caliban, indeed, a magician without a book is nothing, 'He's but a sot, as I am' (3. 2. 93). Prospero's renunciation of the 'fetish' at the end of *The Tempest* thus makes fetish-ism into metaphysical enquiry, or mimetic self-reflection, rather than a mere site of materialist text.

In 'Marx's Coat', Stallybrass argues that the invocation of 'fetishism' *repeats* rather than illuminates the problem it purports to explain. European colonizers did not fetishize objects: 'on the contrary, they were interested in objects only to the extent that they could be transformed into commodities and exchanged for profit on the market'.[44] In the process, Stallybrass creates a turn on Marx's celebrated appropriation of the 'fetish'. For Marx, Stallybrass notices, uses the 'fetish' satirically to counter the triumph of capital. If European capital ridiculed the fetishism of objects, Marx in turn ridiculed the society that thought it had surpassed such worship, but instead displaced it onto money.

The history of the book in modernity asserts a move to the secular that is also a move to economic value. In late capitalism, more than ever, we recognize also a remorseless drive to treat Shakespeare and literature (the humanities in general) as having value only as they can be turned into capital. Nagel shows how cult objects of Renaissance Italy today demand of us a nuanced understanding of secularization and modernity.[45] It is possible to put it more strongly: that the tra-jectory of modernity and secularization needs reversing. The art object as fetish has never been stronger. As Matthew Bown declares: 'The art market today is a market in crypto-relics, no more, no less'.[46] Rather than assuming holy books or icons are holy because of religious origin, perhaps we should consider the reverse: religions acquire their sense of the sacred partly from an aura of personhood sur-rounding the books, objects and artworks that embody them.

No contemporary object has become as much a fetish as the plastic and alu-minium dreamworld of Steve Jobs (Fig. 56), as realized in the iPod, the iPad, and the iPhone. Any user of Apple products (including this author, typing away on a Macbook Pro) will recognise the habits of a cult. The mystique surrounding a

Fig. 56. 'Post-modern icon'; Steve Jobs launching the original iPhone, 9 January 2007

new iPhone has nothing to do with the labour that went into making it, or the functionality of its microcomputer, or even its exorbitant price in comparison to all the other products that do the same thing in a saturated marketplace. The religious exemplar of the unforbidden Apple is linked to a brand that endows a magical quality once acquired. By possessing it, my body becomes an extension of the smartphone, partakes of its cool, its sleekness. It turns into an example of what artificial intelligence theory has called 'the extended mind'.[47] The minimal lines, the metalized curves, make me a futuristic cyborg within a sect.

The smartphone, to use Althusser's language, is 'overdetermined'. It stands in line with commodity fetishes back to Shakespeare's First Folio. Jobs is a modern Prospero. Dropping out of college in 1972, he audited a course in calligraphy, inadvertent source of the multiple typefaces and proportional fonts of the Mac.[48] With the iPhone, Apple turned the smartphone into a book, and simultaneously turned Shakespeare into a species of smartphone. Meanwhile, the Folio as commodity gets examined from all angles.[49] Every copy is catalogued; its price is indexed, from first purchase for £1 bound in 1623, to the latest sale at American auction for $6.16 million.[50] Folger founded his Shakespeare Library, one of the world's nicest libraries, to contain 82 precious relics; the Meisei Library in Tokyo has another 12. Here (Fig. 57) is the Second Folio, owned by the Jesuits in Valladolid, Martin Droeshout's luminously weird engraving of 'gentle Shakespeare' shimmering above the censor's signature.

Such is the external face of the idol, concealing the kernel within. Ink, founts, letter-heads, have been examined to a degree that reveals the identity not only of individual printers but of compositors.[51] A new technology has been invented to take measure of this knowledge.[52] Yet in the process, like the builders of Babel, we know too much. So much is known about the Folio, it is impossible to make reasonable comparison with any other book. In that sense, no statement about the First Folio has proper scientific validity: it is unfalsifiable. The First Folio is a fetish of book history all on its own.

We can learn here from Althusser's latterday scepticism about historical contingency and the power of explanation: 'overdetermination' is not a theory of the social sciences but a metaphysical aporia. This might be one last lesson to emerge from the way that Shakespeare's text attests to the presence of the book as a cultural form. Rather than conforming either to the unmediated neo-materialism offered by 'thing theory', or alternatively to the transvaluative chicanery of 'cultural capital' in the art world, we can recognise the function of the modern book as a form of boundary object.[53] It is not only Protestants who are newly certain that books have merely symbolic function, and so are containers rather than objects in their own right. The whole status of what it is for a book to contain something comes into question. This is one reason Shakespeare's plays—*Hamlet* or *Macbeth*—are shot through with complex representations of the book as symbol. In *Hamlet*, the book becomes a symbol of memory; *Macbeth* abounds with metaphors of the book as a repository of time and a figure for death.

In the opposite symbolic direction, the book becomes a metonym. In Act 2 of *The Tempest*, when Caliban is made to swear his loyalty to his new masters on the island, the drunken Trinculo and Stephano swap the book for a bottle:

CAL.   I'll swear upon that bottle to be thy true subiect, for the liquor is not earthly.

'Here, kiss the book', cries Stephano, at which Trinculo, good as his word, and loyal as ever to liquor alone, kisses the bottle. 'Hast thou not dropped from heaven?', Caliban avows. 'The fetish mimes the forms of authority at the point at which it deauthorizes them', Homi Bhabha observes.[54] Even so, in his signal deauthorization, Caliban is made to prove his religious conversion by a ceremony using a new ritual form:

CALIBAN   I have seen thee in her, and I do adore thee. My mistress showed me thee, and thy dog and thy bush.

Fig. 57. 'Face of the idol'; *Mr. William Shakespeare's Comedies, Histories, & Tragedies, Published according to the true Originall Copies* (London: Thomas Cotes, 1632), Washington, DC, Folger Shakespeare Library, shelf mark: Fo.2 no.07, title-page sig. πA2ʳ

STEPHANO   Come, swear to that: kiss the book. I will furnish it anon with new contents. Swear.[55] [*Caliban drinks.*]

The transference is not an indication of lost ritual, but of the power and mystery involved in the book as thing. Marx would have liked this moment in the play: it is the aesthetic self-acknowledgement of the fetishistic encounter. To come to terms with the book as thing, yet without turning it into capital, we need a renewed attention to a theory of the idol, or a philosophy of the object as work of art.

V
THE BODY AND THE BOOK

En resolución, él se enfrascó tanto en su lectura, que se le pasaban las noches leyendo de claro en claro, y los días de turbio en turbio; y así, del poco dormir y del mucho leer se le secó el celebro de manera, que vino a perder el juicio.

Miguel de Cervantes, *Don Quijote de la Mancha* (1605)

List of Plates

Plate 1 'The Library of Babel', Bruegel the Elder, *Tower of Babel*, oil on wood panel, 1563. Vienna, Kunsthistorisches Museum

Plate 2 'Islamic carpet page'; Opening page of illumination facing Q 2, by Muhammad ibn Mubādir, Cairo, *c*.1306–10; Dublin, Chester Beatty Library, MS Is 1457.1, fo. 1r

Plate 3 'Christian carpet page'; Trinity College Library, MS A. I. [58], fo. 34ʳ

Plate 4 'Writer as martyr'; Jacques-Louis David, *Marat at his Last Breath*, 1793. Brussels, Musées Royaux

17

The Book Incarnate

In the days of Charlemagne, and Louis the Pious, books routinely were called bodies.[1] Catholics still understand *corpus* in two senses: Christ's bread as Christ's body, or an author's works. Claudius of Turin, bishop from 817 CE to his death in 827, quoted an anonymous fifth-century commentator on St Mark. The word, like mankind, has a body and a soul. To explain what it means—'literally'—is to explain it *carnaliter*, as living flesh.[2] Later Holy Roman Emperors were less learned and less sentimental. On 20 May 1631, Johann Tserclaes ('the monk in armour'), Count of Tilly and leader of the forces of the Habsburg Emperor Ferdinand II, mounted a final assault on the Lutheran city Magdeburg.[3] The offensive took six months; the army reached the city's outworks at the beginning of May. Tilly offered terms for surrender, but they were turned down, some citizens hoping for relief from Gustavus Adolphus of Sweden, 90 km away in Potsdam. A final assault began at seven in the morning, from five different directions. Imperial troops together with the Catholic Liga numbered 18,000. The city's total population was just a few thousand more; there were 2,500 regular troops defending the city. Although sacking a resisting town was standard practice in this murderous war, the massacre of Magdeburg was exceptional. It was reported in no fewer than twenty newspapers, 205 pamphlets, and 41 illustrated broadsheets, disseminated not only in the princely courts of Germany but as far afield as Paris, Amsterdam, London, Rome, Madrid, and Stockholm.[4]

Magdeburg is a flagrant symbol of the violence of war in European history. A census of February 1632 could find only 449 inhabitants left. Much of the city was in rubble still in 1720.[5] After two companies of Croats crossed the Elbe and entered a side gate, a fire broke out, spreading fast after an apothecary's house (used to store gunpowder) blew up: 'Then there was nothing but murder, burning, plundering, torment, and beatings.'[6] Looting broke out everywhere. Finally, though, 'when there was nothing left to give', Otto von Guericke's eyewitness account tells, 'the misery really began'. All-out violence took over, as 'the soldiers began to beat, frighten, and threaten to shoot, skewer, hang, the people'. Charred bodies were still being thrown in the river without burial a fortnight later to prevent spread of disease. 'I believe that over twenty thousand souls were lost. It is certain that no more terrible work and divine punishment has been seen since the Destruction of Jerusalem', wrote Gottfried Heinrich Graf zu Pappenheim in a letter.[7]

The bare figures of carnage are swamped by a mythological sensationalism of violence. Reports of the massacre of children, and mass rape of women, surrounded Magdeburg from early in the multitude of pamphlets.[8] The city became a byword for atrocity to go along with Drogheda and Wexford in 1649. *Magdeburgisieren* was a verb to describe utter destruction of a city. Schiller, Goethe, and Brecht turned Magdeburg into poems and plays. Protestant propagandists created a myth of the Magdeburg maiden (*Magde* is a synonym of *Mädchen*) who immolated herself rather than surrender. In the opposite cause, 'Magdeburg justice' was a euphemism justifying a similarly vicious response to Catholic pleas for mercy in the Thirty Years War. Individual tales of slaughter and heroism abound. In the midst of the city, in the cathedral, Reinhard Bake, the Lutheran pastor, struggled to save the congregation gathered to thwart the terror, up to 4,000 desperate people, mostly women and children. As the Croatian soldiers overran the nave, Bake held up his Bible. He was slashed several times by a sword, but the Bible he was holding in his arms lasted long enough that his assailant abandoned the idea and let him live.

Magdeburg preserves the famous Bible on public display. Bake eulogized Magdeburg's miraculous survival in Latin, comparing the city to Troy in Virgil's *Aeneid*:

> Venit summa dies et ineluctabile fatum
> Magd'burgo! Fuimus Troes, fuit Ilium et ingens
> Gloria Parthenopes![9]

Luther went to school in Magdeburg for a year and in 1524 he proclaimed the Reformation there in a sermon.[10] An earlier siege of the city, after it refused Charles V's Augsburg declaration in 1548, made Magdeburg a standard-bearer for Protestantism. The printed book was at the heart of this. In five years, led by the Lotter family (who had worked with Luther as early as 1519), the Magdeburg presses printed 460 works, mostly polemical pamphlets of religious resistance to the emperor.[11] With Luther now dead, Matthias Flacius Illyricus took up the literary challenge. The Croatian theologian and Hebraist moved from Wittenberg to Magdeburg and early in 1556 assembled a group with the task of creating the first Protestant history, from the birth of Christ to modern times.[12] The result, the so-called Magdeburg Centuries, produced thirteen volumes of apparently universal history (with a heavy confessional slant); it was followed by twelve volumes of *Annales Ecclesiastici* to present the Catholic version of history by Cesare Baronio (1588–1607).[13] This was, it seemed, the world in a book.

The printed versions of the Magdeburg Centuries and of Baronio appear to transform human life into a powerful new medium. This is accorded a confessional axis, which adds considerably to the burden of violence attaching to the book, so evident in Magdeburg in 1632. The elephant in the room in the history of the book is always the coming of print in the West, which coincided more or less exactly with the Reformation. Yet printing changed very little between 1500 and 1850.[14] When Michel de Montaigne visited the Vatican Library on 6 March 1581, he made no distinction, indeed, between print and manuscripts. Popes kept libraries from at least the time of Agapetus and Gregory the Great.[15] A new library was proposed by the humanist bibliophile Nicholas V in 1448, who later added finds from Constantinople; it was officially opened by Sixtus IV in 1475.[16] Montaigne was shown a myriad of books, including 'livres escris à la mein', hand-written copies of Seneca and Plutarch.[17] Among classical treasures he admires an *Aeneid* of Virgil, in large lettering, with long, narrow characters he describes as 'quelque façon gothique' and attributes to the time of Constantine. This was the Codex Romanus, a fifth-century illustrated manuscript once described by Agnolo Poliziano.[18] An Acts of the Apostles is in gold Greek letters, as fresh as the day it was made, the characters so thick you can feel them. 'Je crois que nous avons perdu l'usage de ceste escriture.'[19]

As well as a sense of the lost past, the books indue another feeling of strange-ness. He sees a 'book from China, in strange characters'; they are painted with a brush onto a material which, he says, is much thinner than paper, so that writing is made on one side only.[20] The sheets, he says, in a remarkable early Western description of butterfly binding, 'are all double and folded at the outside edges'. He sees the bark of a tree with writing, and a piece of ancient papyrus with inde-cipherable characters.[21] Books have a power beyond words, and a life as things. The Breviary of St Gregory the Great feels to him as if it has descended 'de mein en mein', suspending disbelief for a moment, into his own hand from that of the pope.[22] This was the Sacramentarium Fuldense, copied by a monk from Regensburg at Fulda around 1000 CE.[23] At the time of Montaigne's visit, it was believed to be the oldest Roman liturgical manuscript in existence. Another book, he says, is annotated by Thomas Aquinas, in a handwriting worse than his own.[24]

Books confer a mysterious power: an Arabic patriarch of Antioch whom he meets a week later, who knows no European languages, prepares a remedy for the stone for him, which he puts in a pot, along with the patriarch's strange writing. One day he dines with the French ambassador and with the scholar Marc-Antoine Muret, and argues with them about Solon's Law, and how land was described in Greek. Only 'du sens propre de la langue' can we learn the limits of freedom.[25] Muret, meanwhile, was attempting to make sense of hieroglyphics, which replaced Greek characters in a manuscript of Seneca.[26] At some level, the books appear to Montaigne as obscure as the monuments in which the half-ruined city of ancient Rome abounded. In the Vatican Library he sees a statue of Aristides and tries to read his character from his face. At Easter he sees a display of the sacred Veronica, the cloth with which the face of Christ was wiped, and retained his image via his blood. At St John Lateran the heads of St Paul and St Peter are revealed, with 'their flesh, colour and beard, as if they were alive'.[27]

It is in this meeting-place of body and book that Montaigne locates the true miracle of writing. It has a life beyond life. I am myself the material of my book, he says in his preface to the *Essais*, a phrase which finds its echo in Roland Barthes: 'Le livre du Moi'.[28] Barthes imagined a book that might become a facsimile of himself: *Roland Barthes par Roland Barthes*. Yet the book also resists his ideas, Barthes says; paradoxically, it consists of 'what I do not know'. In the discrepancy, he discerns a certain violence, what he calls a theft of language, or '*meaning-for-myself*'.[29] When Henri-Jean Martin undertook to explain *The History and Power of Writing*, he found violence and writing connected throughout history, tracing the equivalence between swearing on a book or holy relics. Charlemagne used a Bible as he would other objects of symbolic value: a branch, a piece of turf, 'a rod to grant power, or a knife or a sword'.[30] Charlemagne's literary projects are not discrete: they are a consolidation of power.[31] Martin, collaborating with Lucien Febvre, noted that around the same time in China, Feng Tao attempted to print the whole of Chinese literature on wood blocks.[32]

Martin comments curiously on the figure of Etienne Dolet, an Orléans scholar and later printer in Lyon, who campaigned against intolerance but was himself 'always a violent man', who killed a painter in a fight.[33] Dolet's career began with a defence of a monk converted to Lutheranism who was burned at the stake by the Parlement de Toulouse; and it ended with his own burning in the Place Maubert in Paris. Dolet is seen today often as emblematic of the stormy origins of print. Yet in his dying, Reformation anxiety recalled medieval heresies. Motivation was not only religious: Edward I, defeating William Wallace in 1298, ordered the burning of a library of Scottish books, supposedly including revered volumes King Fergus II brought from Rome in 400 CE.[34] According to Boccaccio, Dante's *Monarchia* was burned in Lombardy.[35] Closer to Luther are condemnations of John Wyclif and Hus. Wyclif's books were burned in the presence of the Oxford university chancellor in 1411 at Carfax.[36] They burned again in Prague for Archbishop Zbyněk Zajíc as prelude to Hus's condemnation in Bohemia, the books in a ritual on their own before Hus himself was put to the flames in 1415.[37] Reginald Pecock, outspoken critic of Lollard heresy, was also convicted of heresy.[38] Examined, he requested his books be burned at Paul's Cross in London in December 1457, as part of his recantation. Oxford repeated the incineration later that month, and again in 1476.[39]

The Reformation arrived at precisely the right moment in northern Europe to enforce the shape of censorship established in Iberian Islam, Judaism, and the Americas. Change is volatile, not linear. A key identification of heresy in Catholic doctrine is that it is never original, so all heretics are doomed to repeat the errors of the past. The word means 'choice', Aquinas says; choice can lead only away from

God.[40] Ownership of books played a central role in heresy trials.[41] With Hus in 1415, there is an element of concremation with the body of the heretic. Images of Hus burning at Constance exist in many forms, distributed in woodcuts or manuscripts.[42] In some he wears a hat with heresy inscribed as if on his body; in others, books are used as tinder for the fire. The books are burned (see Ch. 8, Fig. 20) as part of a ceremony of expulsion from the body of the Church. The books stand in for the body of the heretic, in some way interchangeable.

Executioners searched the charred remains, breaking up Hus's smouldering head and placing it back in the fire; they found his heart among the intestines, so skewered it with a stick and roasted it. Hus's books are subject to the same rule of absolute annihilation. The writings are purged and erased from the face of the world, thrust into oblivion. Print culture facilitated syncretism and heresy, but also enforcement of new orthodoxy. This is John Foxe's answer in *Actes and Monuments* in 1563 to the rhetorical question, why did Luther's reformation succeed while Hus's failed?[43] The theology is the same, Foxe deduced, so the difference is in volume of copies. He gave a materialist account to Luther's revolution, success ascribed to the number of readers. In this he over-estimated print runs, and underestimated dissemination of manuscripts. By the later Middle Ages, manuscript production in cities was an industry using professional scriptoria.[44] Foxe (like some modern historians) overstated practical effects in early print. In counter-action to Eisenstein, a consensus now finds print culture at its zenith only centuries later.[45] Stability in printed texts has been misunderstood.[46] Uniformity of orthography, authorship, or copyright has often been exaggerated.

Nevertheless, print brought a change in writing's social meaning. To gauge economics of dissemination, historians sometimes ignore this. Foxe's epigram that print brought down the papacy is dismissed as providential fantasy. Yet why did Foxe think it, and why did his readers believe him? The important issue, Alex Gillespie writes, is how a book is imagined, not just what it is.[47] A printed book was felt as a different thing from a handwritten book. A manuscript is a unique document, the work of a single scribe whose hand can be identified, for example in a manuscript of Chaucer.[48] While only for expensive books did purchaser meet scribe, a manuscript book is a personal artefact.[49]

We need to search, McKenzie said, for 'human presence in any recorded text'.[50] Incunabula mimicked handwritten copies by simulating manuscript decoration.[51] Such methods were fake. It is human labour that casts type in composing sticks or transfers it to a galley to be set in a forme.[52] Ink was applied by hand, and paper placed by hand onto the press, at which point another hand pulled a bar to apply pressure in capturing ink into text.[53] Gutenberg's printing press in Mainz adapted old technology rather than created *ab ovo*. By the beginning of the fifteenth century, images of saints (with accompanying text) and playing cards were printed in woodcut.[54] Mass-production in a modern sense became possible only in the nineteenth century.[55] Indeed, the formal name for the mechanism in use between 1450 and 1830 is the 'hand press'.[56]

Yet printed books are different, by carrying the mark of a machine.[57] Its production appeared anonymous, as ink no longer bore an impression of human agency. At the same time, whatever its circulation, text became inherently reproducible. Nobody knows how many copies circulated in Germany of Luther's Ninety-Five Theses. No estimate will ever account in any case for the sensational reports given at the time of its dissemination, or general cultural reputation.[58] No doubt the number of readers was smaller than usually thought. Yet supporters and detractors projected onto the Theses a fantasy of dissemination, a fantasy with material effect. Although scepticism is proper, revisionism can be misplaced. Part of print's power lies in mythology. It is easy to see, in the present century, sitting (as I do) at a laptop accessing a World Wide Web, that technology is more and less than means to an end. The internet endows powers beyond conceptual reach, yet while information is said to be 'everywhere', it is not.

The materialist evidence for Foxe's belief in print is wrong, but he was right to be a materialist. Luther was a new kind of theologian and heretic, as printed author.[59] Although a university doctor, who never tired of proclaiming such authority, he derived his reputation from a sense (misplaced in fact) that printed books were everywhere. Erasmus, not a doctor except by honorary degree, edited a bilingual Greek and Latin text of the New Testament, endowed with authority unimaginable from such a source two generations earlier.[60] Erasmus benefited, while complaining about the abundance of books.[61] Medieval theology drew on institutional practice, of universities, religious orders, and the Church. Print transcended boundaries, its mode of production unfixed.

At the same time, a link between book and origin loosened. It is not a radical break with old perceptions that brings revolution so much as ambiguity in writing's status, rather as in the emergence of digital books. A medieval inquisitor hoped to remove all memory of heresy by extirpating every copy of a heretical writing.[62] In 1410, heresy was still personal. John Badby went way beyond the bounds of ordinary Lollard unorthodoxy by not only denying the 'real presence' of Christ in the sacrament of the altar, but also stating anyone partaking of it in the mass would be damned.[63] If the host in every parish is the body of Christ, he said, there must be 20,000 gods in England. How could a loaf be divided in so many parts and remain whole? Sentenced to be burned at Smithfield, as soon as the flames began to rise, he cried out from the stake. Was it a plea for mercy, as one chronicle suggests?[64] Prince Henry (Hal in Shakespeare's *Henry IV*) ordered the burning to be halted halfway. Badby was scooped out, subjected to an improvisatory examination on theology. Henry promised him his life and pardon if he recanted, along with a pension of threepence a day for the rest of his life.[65] Badby refused. Back he went into the fire, the confessor cheerfully anticipating the flames to continue in Hell.

Heresy in print was less readily eradicated. Foxe printed the story of Badby with a woodcut of his burning, but the link between heretic and book was now less direct.[66] Heretical ideas were accessible more remotely: a printed book was harder to destroy: not literally, of course, but figuratively.[67] There were always more editions. A first attempt to censor a printed press was in 1475 in Germany, with books submitted to the Bishop of Regensburg. A printer was arrested in Cologne; decrees in Mainz demanded pre-sale inspection of books at the Frankfurt fair. In a bull of 1487, Innocent VIII warned of printed books.[68] This bull set penalties for transgression: excommunication, fines, and book-burnings. Further bulls followed from Alexander VI in 1501 and Leo X in 1515. These measures feared loss of control in the flow of ideas. In 1514, orders came to burn works by the German Hebraic scholar Johannes Reuchlin in Cologne, Louvain, and Paris. The most sensational instance was not in Germany, but Florence. In a 'bonfire of the vanities' on 7 February 1497, the Dominican friar Girolamo Savonarola consigned to the flames blasphemous paintings, with piles of print: works by Boccaccio and Petrarch, Pulci's *Morgante* and other chivalry, books of magic, or with obscene pictures.[69] Something similar happens in book-burnings, such as Aleandro's in the Low Countries. Register Books in the city archives of Antwerp show in detail books marked up for signs of Lutheran heresy or sedition against the Emperor or English king.[70] Cuthbert Tunstall and Thomas More in London searched high and low for heretical books after copies of Tyndale's New Testament began to arrive in 1525, but they were a little disappointed at the results; rain and the 'meagre supply of books' spoiled the fun of the bonfire.[71]

At the same time Montaigne was visiting the Vatican in Rome, Edmund Campion made the journey in the opposite direction to return to England as part of the Jesuit Mission to reconvert Protestant England. He arrived in London disguised as a jewel merchant in June 1580, moving from house to house in Berkshire, Oxfordshire, Northamptonshire, Lancashire, and the North Riding of Yorkshire.[72] Campion's mission partly worked through the printed book. His *Rationes decem* ('Ten reasons') were printed clandestinely at a secret press at Stonor Park in Oxfordshire, called the 'Greenstreet House press'.[73] Sensationally, 400 copies were placed on the benches of St Mary's Church in Oxford at the university Act on 27 June 1581. However, as Woudhuysen remarks, manuscript circulation rivalled print dissemination, and in some quarters was favoured, because of freedom from government control, but also because of its 'personal appeal'.[74] In July, Campion was apprehended at Lyford Grange and taken to London, his arms pinioned and wearing a paper hat, inscribed 'THE SEDITIOUS JESUIT'.[75] Interrogated over three months, often under torture, he produced a defence of his faith in a 'Letter to the Lords of Council', circulated in manuscript.[76] It was printed by Campion's enemies, bearing the title *The Great bragge and challenge of M. Champion a Iesuite*, after the event.

Indeed, as one of the poems on the martyrdom of Campion declared, probably by Henry Walpole, sainthood is partially carried by 'paper inke, and penne'.[77] Walpole reputedly stood so close to the scaffold that he was spattered with Campion's blood. When the poem was later published, the printer was sentenced to lose his ears. These marks of the body, Gerard Kilroy suggests, are transferred onto paper. Unable to gather around a physical shrine, the recusant community created a 'literary *memoria*' to act as a bodily substitute.[78] In this form they circulated as relics for decades after the death of the saint. Gertrude Thimelby, who left England to become a nun at Louvain in 1658, transcribed many poems by hand.[79] In another manuscript circulating in the English Civil War, thirty-two poems are copied from the work of one of Campion's successors in the Jesuit mission, Robert Southwell, who was executed at Tyburn in 1595.[80]

'Language is a skin', says Barthes: 'It is as if I had words instead of fingers, or fingers at the tip of my words.'[81] Not for nothing did Nancy Pollard Brown call the search for Southwell's work a 'paperchase'.[82] Sometimes the manuscript bore the hand of the author and saint himself: such as Stonyhurst MS A.v.4, which contains Latin as well as English poems, in Southwell's handwriting, which takes two different forms, formal and informal, italic and secretary.[83] Another (Stonyhurst MS A.v.27, now in the Jesuit Archives), not in Southwell's hand, which contains his letter to his father as well as fifty-two poems, bears the childhood inscription of Hieronima Waldegrave, who died in the Benedictine Abbey in Ghent in 1635.[84] The paper is much older, and it is possible the poems were copied at any point between 1592 and 1609.[85] However, Southwell circulated early in print as well as manuscript. Some works, like the beautiful prose poem *Marie Magdalens Funerall Teares*, passed the censors of the Archbishop of Canterbury and Bishop of London. The Harmsworth MS at the Folger Shakespeare Library combines manuscript texts bound up with a copy of the first edition of *Saint Peters Complaint*. This was printed in 1595, the year of Southwell's martyrdom; but later editions also carry the same date on the title page, as if a calendar year for the saint.

This mixed register of print and manuscript in heterodoxy is seen on the opposite confessional side in the same decades. The pamphlets of the eponymous Martin Marprelate caused a print sensation, excoriating John Aylmer, Bishop of London, and John Whitgift, Archbishop of Canterbury. Like Campion's work, they had to be printed in secret: the first was printed in East Molesey in Surrey, at the house of Elizabeth Crane, by Robert Waldegrave. On the run from the agents of Whitgift and of William Cecil, Lord Burghley, the Queen's Treasurer, the operation moved to Fawsley Hall, Sir Richard Knightley's mansion in Northamptonshire. By January 1589 the press was in the house of John Hales in Coventry, and then wheeled to Job Throkmorton's residence in Haseley nearby.[86] Of course, these addresses do not appear on the title pages, which prefer the jazzier locations of 'Oversea | in Europe', or 'Printed on the other hand of some of the Priests', or 'not farre from some of the Bounsing Priestes'. Much of the controversy that surrounds the tracts regards the doubtful question of authorship, whether by Throkmorton or John Penry; as also the scurrilous replies by Thomas Nashe (written at Whitgift's behest as part of a literary campaign). This bears some similarity with the way that Campion's pamphlets were 'answered' by Meredith Hanmer. Copies of Campion were marked up for censorship (surviving in York Minster Library); in a similar way, Penry's treatise proving that the Reformation of the Puritans was being slandered to the Queen, is marked with crosses and underlinings in the Huntington Library copy.[87] By 1593, Penry was also in prison, under torture. On 23 May he wrote a confession in his own hand: 'I John Penry doe heare as I shall aunswere before the Lorde my god in that dreadfull day of iudgmente set downe summarye'.[88] In another, apparently written the night before his execution, he begs Cecil for mercy. The handwriting bears visible evidence of distress and perhaps of torture, as his hand struggles for control of the pen. At the same time, he makes a declaration of identity somewhere between avowal and disavowal: 'I aunswer y[t] my name is John Penri & not Marten Marprelat'.[89] In death as in life, he appeals to the heart and 'lyfe blood' of religion.[90]

While much of Reformation book history is dedicated to one side of the religious conflict or the other, they have more in common than sets them apart. Earle Havens has recently discussed the extraordinary prison graffiti that survive on the walls of the Tower of London, written by Catholics as they awaited trial. In a similar way, at Lambeth Palace can be found wall graffiti of Lollards and other heretics. Text and body merge with each other in the work of the hand. Meanwhile, over and again, both are destroyed together, brought to equal oblivion. In Tudor and Stuart England, David Cressy shows, fire elicited 'spectacle and spectators'.[91] Henry VIII's Act of Parliament in 1543 specified heretical works by name for burning.[92] Books were burned at Oxford University in 1550.[93] Latin liturgical books were burned by order on 1 February the same year.[94] Under Mary, the torch was passed to English prayer-books. In 1556 John Hullier, of Eton and King's College, Cambridge, was burned to death on Jesus Green. Books in the fire included a Book of Common Prayer; Hullier opened it to read, until the smoke got into his eyes.[95] More practically, the articles of the newly incorporated Stationers' Company in 1557 provided for systematic burning of prohibited books, but also for recycling for other purposes if this was more convenient.[96]

Sedition and heresy come together in the statutes under Elizabeth I, as they had under her father.[97] The antiquarian John Caius's treasured stash of medieval liturgical books and vestments in his rooms at Cambridge took three hours for iconoclasts to burn in December 1572.[98] The right hand of John Stubbs was cut off in public in 1579 for defying the queen's intended French marriage. Merry sonnets as well as heretical or seditious works were burned at Stationers' Hall.[99] Under James I, the bonfire moved open air at Paul's Cross in London in the cathedral's shadow, conveniently close to the Hall, where the books were examined.[100] Under Charles I, William Prynne's *Histrio-Mastix* was judged in 1637 to have libelled Queen Henrietta Maria. Prynne's body was mutilated and his book humiliated; yet this didn't end the searches.[101] The Chancellor of the Exchequer ordered Prynne to be placed in a pillory, first at Westminster, then Cheapside, a paper over his head declaring his crimes. At each place, one of his ears was removed. The public hangman punished the books, placing them in a fire in front of the pillory, 'as unfit to be seen by any hereafter'.[102] What is described here is not efficient censorship but a condition of paranoia. Burning is the manipulation of shock and awe.

A relationship, natural or imagined, between books and human bodies is a familiar trope of early modern writing.[103] A goodly book, says Rabelais in the prologue to *Gargantua*, is full of high conceptions; to get at them, the reader must 'break the bone, and suck out the marrow'.[104] Rabelais claimed the best conditions for composing were eating and drinking. In Swift's *Battle of the Books*, the ancient and modern books in St James's Library fight each other to the death. Just as the human body is corrupted and decomposes in the ground, so 'a restless Spirit haunts over every *Book*, till *Dust* or *Worms* have seized upon it'.[105] Bookworms and earthworms cohabit body and book. A book is a *corpus*, it wears a jacket. Not for nothing was the name for the plank which held the paper in the printing press a 'coffin'.[106] Sterne's *Tristram Shandy* constantly reminds the reader that the book she is reading is organic matter prone to material decay: 'so taking hold of the two covers of the book, one in each hand, and letting the leaves fall down as he bent the covers back, he gave the book a good sound shake'.[107]

Miraculous preservation by means of a holy book is a stereotype into modern times. When the mafia tries to assassinate Homer Simpson, he ensures Ned Flanders stands next to him. The first bullet hits Ned's Bible; the second is taken by a large piece of the holy cross, which he happens to be carrying on him. Flanders checks his chest pocket but he has no spiritual ammunition left: 'I think I'll go inside', he shrewdly reflects.[108] Irony shadows violence. In 1856, the *New York Tribune* called attention to Henry Ward Beecher, of the New England Emigrant Society, who 'believed that the Sharps Rifle was a truly moral agency, and that there was more moral power in one of those instruments, so far as the slaveholders of Kansas were concerned, than in a hundred Bibles'.[109] The rifles became known as 'Beecher's Bibles' as a result. The arms were shipped to rebel slaves on one occasion in a crate marked 'books', although there is no evidence to support an apocryphal story they were marked 'Bibles'. It is a mirror image of when Tyndale's New Testament was shipped with Lutheran books into the German Steelyard in London in the 1520s, in the guise of cloth, to escape Henry VIII's agents.[110]

A three-way metonymy between Bibles, bodies, and bullets mixes metaphors of deliverance and enslavement. Nat Turner, who led the slave rebellion in

Southampton County in Virginia in 1831, was known as 'The Prophet'. His uprising preached the Bible. God's kingdom confronted the Anti-Christ of the realm of the slaveowners: the Serpent was now loosed, and Christ had laid down his yoke for the sins of men.[111] Sethe in Toni Morrison's *Beloved* (1987) escapes from her plantation Sweet Home with similar ideas:

> And she said she always wished she could read the Bible like real preachers. So it was good for me to learn now, and I did until it got quiet and all I could hear was my own breathing.[112]

Morrison based the character on Margaret Garner, who escaped from Kentucky over the frozen Ohio river in 1856 but was apprehended under the Fugitive Slave Act of 1850.[113] The abolitionist, Harriet Tubman, nicknamed 'Moses', rescued slaves from the Act on the Underground Railroad. She countered white interpretations of the doctrine of obedience in the New Testament with a narrative of deliverance from the Old.[114] Meanwhile, slave Bibles were edited to enforce obedience.[115] In the redacted version, they omitted to state that in Christ there was neither Jew nor Greek, 'bond nor free'.[116] 'Talk of salvation could give an African ideas', thinks grandmother Ajarry.[117]

In 1859 Tubman helped Captain John Brown plan the raid on Harper's Ferry in West Virginia. Thoreau's address to the citizens of Concord, Massachusetts, in defence of Brown, stated: 'I think for once the Sharps Rifles and the revolvers were employed in a righteous cause'.[118] Thoreau called Brown a Spartan and Puritan, primed for 'a perfect Cromwellian troop'.[119] Bullet-proof Bibles, or Bible-assisted bullets, reach back from the American to the British Civil Wars. When Bunyan enlisted at Bedford as a soldier for the parliamentary cause, he took up position as a sniper, but was replaced by another at the last moment: 'as he stood Sentinel, he was shot into the head with a Musket bullet and died.'[120] Bunyan is saved by providence for God. Richard Baxter reported many 'strange Preservations'. A bullet shot through the fur of a man's hat but stopped at the lining.

> Another had a small Bible in his Pocket, and a Musket-Bullet shot into his Bible, which saved his Life.[121]

Baxter referred to *The Souldiers Pocket Bible* first issued by Cromwell in 1643 and in general use among the New Model Army. It was a condensed pamphlet version of the Bible text, a small octavo about the thickness of a modern passport. Carried on the person, it was buttoned on the inside near the heart, under the soldier's outer coat. It divided into headings providing useful admonitory warnings: *A Souldier must consider that sometimes Gods people have the worst in battel as well as Gods enemies.*[122] A similar edition was produced for soldiers on both sides in the American Civil War.[123]

Fig. 58. 'Soldier's Prayer-Book'; London, Imperial War Museum, K 85/1847

The Imperial War Museum contains a small collection of First World War Bibles and prayer-books, such as Fig. 58, preserved with such tales attached to them. One of them, a pocket soldier's edition of the *Book of Common Prayer*, has a bullet hole tearing all the way through the book, and other shrapnel damage. Another has the bottom right-hand corner blown away, while the rest is covered in blood. It is not clear whether the soldier survived the shrapnel. However, the paper wound shows how the soldier carried the book on his person in battle, whether as a source of consolation in quiet moments of reading in the trenches in the long hours out of battle, or as a gift from home. It could equally be a badge of faith, a phylactery, or a lucky charm. German soldiers on the front in Flanders sometimes carried Nietzsche's *Also sprach Zarathustra*.

The connection between book and body is thus longlasting and deep-rooted. In Dublin in 1916, Marsh's Library lay between the British Army barracks in Kevin Street and the barricades of the insurgents at Jacob's Biscuits factory. 'Khaki Hamlets don't hesitate to shoot', reports Joyce in *Ulysses*.[124] According to the annual minutes of the Library Trustees, British machine-guns shattered the windows of the reading room, 'injuring' five books. The entry wounds were small at the spine, the exit wounds five or six times larger at the fore-edge. Some pages are ripped to shreds, others compressed by the pressure of the impact of the projectiles. The books, which come from the collection of a seventeenth-century Huguenot, have never been repaired, and are left as relics.[125]

Beyond issues of faith and superstition—hardly uninteresting—lies a deeper question about the commensurability of the history of the book with the history of human embodiment and identity. By a strange irony of history, when Graf Pappenheim, the general who accompanied Tilly in the command of the imperial forces which sacked Magdeburg, himself died in battle not long after, his left breast pocket contained a sheaf of papers covered in his blood.[126] They, too, have been preserved as a souvenir of war, on display in a modern museum.

'In the hands of the Dadaists', Benjamin says, 'the work of art became a bullet.'[127] More prosaically, 'The pen is mightier than the sword' is an expression first coined in relation to another anti-hero of the Thirty Years War, Cardinal Richelieu. In Edward Bulwer Lytton's play of 1839, *Cardinal Richelieu: Or the Conspiracy*, the Machiavellian bureaucrat surmises the age of direct political violence is over, so that written communication now does the work of the powerful. By the 1840s, this became a commonplace in the opposite sense, a consolatory sentiment for liberals everywhere. In the age of Charlie Hebdo, the sentiment acquired more sinister meaning, the odds becoming that much worse. Transferring the metonym from pen as sword, to book as victim, a different synergy occurs between human and symbolic worlds.

Nearly a millennium before Magdeburg, St Boniface, sometimes known as the 'Apostle of the Germans', was born as Wynfrith, deep in Wessex, some time late in the seventh century, possibly at Crediton in Devon. In England he wrote a Latin *Ars Grammatica*; a treatise on verse; and some Old English riddles. In 716, he left for the Low Countries to become a missionary among the Franks, and later the first Archbishop of Mainz.[128] He was killed at Dokkum in Frisia in 754 in a massacre along with 52 others.[129] His remains were transferred first to Utrecht and then to Fulda in the mid-point of modern Germany, where he had earlier founded a Benedictine monastery in anticipation that it would be his resting place.[130] From here his cult arose, Fulda a prime site of Christian Europe, reaching throughout the Germanic worlds and lasting to the present.

The cult of Boniface symbolizes the foundation of Germany and even of Europe. His creative zeal is central to the idea of Catholic Germany, while his alliance with the inheritors of the legacy of Charlemagne—with the early Pippinid and Carolingian lords, and especially with Charles Martel—aligned the imperial family with the papacy.[131] The historic Boniface thus exchanges places with the historiographical Boniface, who has been reappropriated over and over again in the creation of successive myths both of Germany and of *magna Europa*. In the anniversary years of 1805 and 1855, Catholic nationalism was aroused in contradistinction to the Lutheran jubilee of 1817. In 1954, by which time Boniface's death had been redated by a year, Konrad Adenauer, himself a Catholic German, addressed a crowd of 60,000 for the 1200th anniversary in Fulda with a hymn to European unionism: *Das, was wir in Europa gemeinsam haben, [ist] gemeinsamen Ursprungs* ('What we in Europe have in common is of common origin').[132]

Fulda is fundamental to the cult of Boniface. Yet while his sarcophagus still lies under the altar of the cathedral, formerly the abbey church, this is not a cult of bones alone but one of books. Books lie at the heart of the story of Boniface. He was a writer himself; his works were copied in libraries and schools of the Carolingian Renaissance; one survives from the eighth century.[133] He was active in the circulation of classical authors, including Virgil, and Servius' commentary on Virgil.[134] It is appropriate for such a bookish man that in the eleventh-century Fulda Sacramentary, he is seen holding a liturgical book as he makes the sign of the cross over the head of a novitiate.[135]

This creates a balancing image of book with the martyrdom scene below, narrating an episode recounted in the early *vitae Bonifatii* (a rich literature of hagiography dating from the eighth and ninth centuries), which culminates in the murder of the aged saint in Dukkum, between Franeker and Groningen in the northern Netherlands. In the first *vita*, by Wilibald, an Anglo-Saxon priest, Boniface tells his companions to abandon arms since scripture tells us 'not to render evil for good but to overcome evil by good'.[136] The saint is killed and the ransackers, drunk on wine from the monastery, start killing each other in arguments over booty. A remnant, clearly not of bibliophiles, is angry, expecting different treasure: 'they broke open the chests containing the books and found, to their dismay, that they held manuscripts instead of gold vessels, pages of sacred texts instead of silver plates'. The killing spree feeds on books instead. An orgy of book destruction ensues, the fields littered with scattered pages, others drowned in the marsh.

Perhaps this episode gives rise to the most vivid martyrdom story of Boniface, occurring only in the *vita altera*, probably by Radboud, Bishop of Utrecht from 900 to 917. This repeats Wilibald except for one additional anecdote, a report said by Radboud to be added by an eyewitness, where at the point of death Boniface holds up a copy of the gospels, swords and axes raining on him. The book protects him, but the saint is overcome by his assailants, and attains his crown in heaven.[137] By the time of the fourth life of Boniface, the eleventh-century *vita* by Otloh of St Emmeram, this martyrdom account had become associated with the so-called Ragyndrudis Codex.[138] The cover of the codex bears signs of violence—beyond wear and tear—and the book's insides are marked by incisions.[139] The Ragyndrudis Codex has come to be revered as one of Fulda's prize relics, almost as precious as the sarcophagus and its contents, and attached to the history of the saint as supposedly one of three books found on the battlefield by the surviving monks.

There is no evidence, in fact, that the Ragyndrudis Codex was ever in Friesland, never mind that Boniface owned it.[140] The first life of the saint mentions no damaged book, and when it first appears in Radboud it is a gospel. The Ragyndrudis

Codex is not a gospel. It dates from the early eighth century, its contents mainly anti-heretical, specifically anti-Arian (the anti-Trinitarian heresy). Its true owner is another figure entirely, the enigmatic 'lady Ragyndrudis' mentioned in the first person in an inscription on fo. 2v. She was a 'laywoman of some wealth and education', perhaps from St Omer in northern France.[141] The book bears no literary signs of Boniface's campaigns of conversion in northern Germany. There is every possibility the book was translated to the Fulda cultic site much later, and the story of its violent association with the saint may also be a later retrospective accommodation, as Patrick Geary has argued was common practice.[142] Just as relics are bought and sold, so stories attaching to their possession are transferred. Yet this hardly makes the book of any less interest. For Peter Brown, it is the transferability of a cult from place to place, generated by the practice of translation, that makes the Christian sense of the holy distinctive, different for instance from Sunni Islam, where the singularity of place is much stronger.[143] Like the relics of the disciples of the Buddha, or the cult of the saints in Sufism and Shi'ism, Christian cults in late antiquity acquired an astonishing form of mobility, in which all kinds of appropriation take place.

Further to this, however, is the meaning and significance of *praesentia* in relation to books. *Praesentia* is defined by Brown as 'physical presence of the holy, whether in the midst of a particular community or in the possession of particular individuals' (p. 88). A book may seem to us at first sight lacking *praesentia*: mediated, semiotic, hermeneutic. Yet Michael Aaij suggests that in the case of Boniface, the Ragyndrudis Codex became a substitute for, or alternative version of, a literary *vita*.[144] Borrowing from Barthes and his celebrated invention of the 'booklife'— 'Le livre | la vie'—Aaij argues that the 'tortured book' is a 'booklife', a metonymy for Boniface's whole life and mission.[145]

Mis libros (que no saben que yo existo) | son tan parte de mí. 'My books (which do not know that I exist) | are so much part of me', writes Borges in a late poem.[146] Indeed, they express me better than the words I write, he says. Like the lines of his face, as he runs his hands over them, or his grey hair, as he stares blindly in the mirror, the books on his shelves reflect his life. It is better that way: the voices of the dead speak forever. The Ragyndrudis Codex is a *vita*—the book has a life, not only in that its physical condition tells Boniface's story, but also as an object with its own story (Fig. 59). For, as Barthes declares, 'I cannot *write myself*'.[147] Writing and self are both subject to irony and to mimesis. What the book offers is thus a simulacrum of substitution. In a recent examination of the vellum of the Ragyndrudis Codex, it has been suggested that one of the many marks and scratches left inside it is the residue of a nail. The book may have been nailed to a tree, as is reported in a number of tales of counter-crucifixion narratives.

This is an object that has acted and suffered, the marks of suffering borne on the body. This endows it with cultic status among a saint's relics. Marco Mostert considers it likely that Radboud's recension of the *vita* made its way to Fulda,

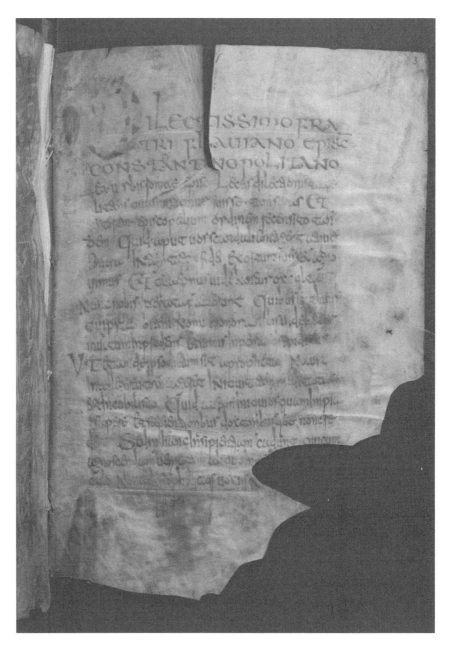

Fig. 59. 'Martyred book'; Ragyndrudis Codex, ink on vellum, 8th c. Fulda, Landesbibliothek, Codex Bonifatius 2.

where legend attached itself to damaged books.[148] By the tenth century books had been elevated to contact relics, connected by more than imagination or metonymy to Boniface. The Ragyndrudis Codex is tortured in the way Boniface's remains are a tortured remainder of martyrdom. This might seem peculiar to Boniface, or early Christianity in general. However, the relation of book to personhood is deeper, bound up with the physical object as container of ideas or thoughts. A book is special, of the most intimate relation to owner or reader.

18

The Hand in the History of the Book

What are books for? A twenty-first-century reader readily imagines an answer to this question in terms not so different from Petrarch in the fourteenth century:

> A book I keep for the sake of both its author and its giver and have always in my hands: a handy little volume, of tiny bulk but infinite sweetness. I open it, to read whatever meets my eyes—for what could meet them there except pious and devout thoughts?[1]

Petrarch is taking a day trip from Fontaine de Vaucluse near Avignon in southern France to Malaucène, at the foot of Mont Ventoux. From here he makes a hazardous ascent to the top, which he described years later in a letter to Brother Dionigi of the Order of St Augustine in Borgo San Sepolcro near Arezzo in Tuscany. It has become one of the seminal accounts in the history of mountain-climbing. 'At first, overwhelmed by the unfamiliar breeze of the air and the wide open panorama, I stood like one dazed.'[2] At the summit he can see the Mediterranean Sea at Aigues Mortes to his left, and the river Rhône directly before him, like a fat, lazy serpent; behind him, at least in his mind's eye, he can see right into Italy. He is transfixed by memories of his student days in Bologna, and at the same time made dizzy by imagining the sight of the great mountains of classical antiquity, Athos and Olympus. His reverie renders him vulnerable, caught between heaven and earth; in consolation he reaches inside his pocket for a book.

The book in question is a copy of Augustine's *Confessions*, a gift, it happens, from the recipient of the letter he is writing—Fra Dionigi. The book is a substitute for his friend—a transitional object—and also for its author. For the book carries *the thoughts* of the author into *the mind* of the reader. This link between body and mind then takes physical form in a kind of game played by Petrarch on Gherardo his brother, who has shared the journey upwards from the comforts of home to this perilous ravine. Petrarch opens the book at random: 'By chance the tenth book of the work came to hand'. Petrarch reads out aloud, and what comes from his mouth astonishes himself as much as his listener. 'And men go forth to marvel at the heights of mountains and the vast waves of the sea and the broad flow of rivers and the compass of the ocean and the cycles of the stars, and they leave themselves behind.'[3] The tally with his experience that day strikes him dumb, and from this moment, all through his return right down to the foothills, he is silent. 'I turned my inward eyes upon myself': *in me ipsum interiores oculos reflexi.*

External and internal, the book as object and as contents, interior sensation or exterior, all merge in the encounter on the mountain. This is the miracle of the book. It crosses boundaries: not only between thing and thing, but even between thing and nothing. Reading a book is truly metaphysical. The word 'book' in Germanic languages has been derived from writing runes on the bark of a tree, because of its relation to the word 'beech'.[4] *Liber* in Latin or *livre* in French refers to fibrous plant matter; *codex* comes from *caudex*, the stem of a plant, or the axis between stem and root. While a *liber* is in two dimensions, the *codex* is two axes folded in three dimensions. In Sanskrit *bhūrjá-* in its masculine form means 'birch tree', or in its feminine, the birch bark used for writing. The Tibet Museum in Lhasa exhibits examples of books made from the bark of birch trees. In Roman traditions, it was thought that the earliest books had been written on bark; the Christian writer Cassiodorus speculated further, using the pun in Latin on *liber* meaning free: a book as it were 'is the bark of a tree, removed and freed'.[5] The idea may be fanciful philology but is an interesting starting-point for a philosophy of the book. Just as Michelangelo's *Awakening Slave* presents a captive body breaking free from inside the marble, 'as though surfacing from a pool of water', so thought is trapped in the tree and then opens forth in the leaves of a book.[6]

The key feature of the book in Petrarch's words is that it is *semper in manibus*, 'always in my hands'.[7] His expression is so redolent of our own lives that we can easily picture him now, as if with an Oxford World's Classics paperback of the *Confessions*. However, the book in question was a humanist manuscript codex. It is a curious if obvious feature of books, little commented on, that the form of the codex imitates in size, appearance—and number—the human hands. The oldest surviving manuscript of the Greek Bible, containing the Septuagint text of the Old Testament as well as the New, is the Codex Vaticanus in Rome.[8] It is a quarto, measuring 27 cm × 27 cm. It has around thirty lines of text per page. Codex Sinaiticus, now in the British Library (also 4th c. CE), has four narrow columns of text per page, averaging 15 words per line.[9] These figures are little different from texts long predating the codex. Two cuneiform examples in the British Museum, from the reign of King Ammiditana (c.1683–1647 BCE), are divided into twelve to fifteen ruled lines of text.[10] They were copied by Bel-ushallim, son of the exorcist Abibi; one is an educational text, the other a magic spell.[11] It is wrong to call them 'books' exactly, since they are single tablets. Yet in size (one is 7 cm × 11.3 cm) they resemble a paperback page. Most e-books generate around ten words per line, in common with manuscripts in Carolingian minuscule from the tenth century CE, just like many texts from the print shop of Aldus Manutius in Venice in 1500. The first Kindle reader, launched on 19 November 2007 by amazon.com, was 12.5 cm. × 20 cm. in size.[12]

In this way, Chartier emphasizes the importance of situating the digital revolution within a *longue durée* of the book in history.[13] Books of all kinds are objects created for the convenience of the hand in connection with the eye. Augustine in

The City of God draws attention to his readers turning the pages of his book as an act of making mental sense of it.[14] Gillian Clark suggests he was referring to Horace, who tells his readers to 'turn over' the Greek poets, day and night.[15] The word 'manuscript', Christopher de Hamel reminds us, means 'written by hand'.[16] Books of Hours survive in greater quantities, he says, than any other object from the Middle Ages.[17] In that sense they could be said to be *for* the hands as well as by them. Liturgical books were always emphasizing their handiness: the main medieval everyday book for priests was called either a breviary or a *Portiforium*: for carrying.[18] Covering hundreds of feasts and ferial days of the church year, they might be portable only for plump hands. Books of Hours, by contrast, are often dainty, designed for private use at home.

Early examples were richly decorated and very expensive; but by the early Tudor period an unbound printed copy could be purchased for 3*d*. or 4*d*.[19] Pious women especially desired them. They provided a digest of the liturgy, with all the most important rites, including the mass and offices for the dead; also bidding prayers and prayers to the Virgin. But they were often small enough often to be carried in a sleeve or on a belt. Walsham calls them 'jewels for gentlewomen', although they didn't have to be that gentle.[20] The point is that they are books not only for reading but for touching and handling, praying with as well as from. Duffy exquisitely ascribes to them 'a history of intimacy'.[21] In the paintings of Hans Memling everyone has got one: in the *St John Altarpiece* from Bruges, it is Barbara and St John the Evangelist who are reading; in the *Virgin and Child between St James and St Dominic*, Mary manages to keep reading while holding her baby and entertaining the saints, although Jesus crumples the page to try to stop her; in the *Donne Triptych* Jesus is at it again, as the Virgin reads and an angel eats a plum; the donor, Elizabeth Donne, is luckier in having an older daughter and so keeps concentrating on her Hours.[22]

Some of these books are large, such as the *Très Riches Heures du duc de Berry*, with its dazzling blue illuminations of the calendar months and seasons by the Limbourg brothers and Jean Colombe.[23] In others, handiness is by no means incompatible with exquisite decoration. The Breviary of Charles the Bold is smaller than a Kindle, made in Valenciennes with miniatures by Simon Marmion.[24] A Marmion *Hours* might be bigger, but its illumination of St Luke painting the Virgin is minuscule, taking a quarter of the leaf.[25] Gerard David made a tiny panel (9 cm × 7 cm) in Bruges in about 1490. It was small enough to fit like a mouse in the palm of a hand during devotion.[26] He repeated his feat in a Book of Hours for Margaretha van Bergen.[27] The rubric granted an indulgence of 11,000 years' exemption from purgatory, if a person were to recite the prayer written beside the image. In the 1530s, Simon Bening painted tiny landscapes for the calendar of an Hours for the Use of Rome.[28] For the Hours of Isabella of Portugal, he made some of the smallest paintings of the period, showing the life of the Virgin, which were sent to Spain to be stuck as insets in the upper half of larger leaves, themselves illuminated further. The entire leaf is

16.7 cm × 11 cm; yet Bening's image of 'The Mocking of Christ', a third of half of that, shows every detail in every face.[29]

A minute Qur'an dated 1352–3 uses diminutive *naskh* script.[30] In 1800, the London publisher John Marshall created the *Infant's Library* in seventeen volumes, with coloured pictures on one page and text facing, including a history of England the size of 'a mouse's tail'.[31] Buddhist books of Dharma are still made today, 5 cm square. A student recently gave me a copy of Shakespeare's poems the size of my thumb. Yet a book need not be handy to show evidence of use of the hands. One of the books Shakespeare used most in writing plays was Raphael Holinshed's *Chronicles* of the English kings, a vast folio in two columns. A Shakespearean scholar noticed he had a tendency to cite passages from outer columns, towards the top of the page, a sign of skim reading at speed.[32] The eye's needs ensured the triumph in the West of codex over scroll, then folio, quarto, and octavo in printed formats.[33] The number of words per line co-ordinates with what the eye takes in within a single glance.

Meanwhile pages act like a mirror of a person's hands. In the medieval iconography of the Annunciation, the Madonna is typically caught by the Archangel Gabriel in the midst of reading a book. It is as if one form of conception transfers over into another. Giovanni Bellini's diptych for the organ of the church of Santa Maria dei Miracoli in Venice shows exquisite arrangement of hands: the angel carries a lily in his left, as an offering, while simultaneously holding up his right hand in greeting. Mary's right hand is pressed against her chest in humility, while her left holds down the page while reading. Antonello da Messina twice painted the Virgin caught in the act of reading. In the Palermo version, her hands part before her chest, over a book, lying on a rest in front; her mind is visibly caught in mid-sentence as Gabriel arrives. In the 1476 Munich version (Fig. 60), her hands cross her body, while the open pages of the prayer book are flat in front of her, one page caught in the moment of turning, just as her thoughts are.

The hands are constantly employed in reading. Tristram Shandy's father 'shut the book slowly; his thumb resting, when he had done it, upon the upper-side of the cover, as his three fingers supported the lower side of it, without the least compressive violence'.[34] Sterne himself sat for a portrait in 1765 in Florence in via Santo Spirito, opposite Palazzo Manetti. The artist Thomas Patch, who emigrated after a homosexual indiscretion, shows Sterne in the final state of tuberculosis, communicating with a figure of Death.[35] After Sterne died, Patch turned it into an etching (Fig. 61), 'And When Death Himself Knocked at my Door'. Sterne the author stands in mid-view, his hands across his chest for all the world like an annunciate Virgin. Death the archangel meets him crossing the half-open door, hourglass in one hand and walking-stick in the other. To Sterne's side on a desk is a book and quill pen with inkpot; behind it, a statue of a goddess or a saint in a case.

Darian Leader draws attention to the hand's implication in ideas of identity and autonomy, calling it 'manual agency'.[36] The hand is used in making out the

Fig. 60. 'Reading hands'; Antonello da Messina, *Virgin Annunciate*, oil on wood panel, 1476. Munich, Alte Pinakothek.

world, and the individual's relation to it, from babyhood on. In later life, we are always looking to do things with our hands; purposefully, but also in unconscious denial of activity. From medieval times onwards, a panoply of hand technologies emerged to keep idle hands at bay: fans, gloves, pipes, umbrellas, pens, pocket-watches, cigarette boxes. In Italy, a joke goes around now that the mobile phone was invented to give young people something to do with their hands, once cigarettes were banned. 'Everywhere we look', Leader comments, 'people are busy with their mobiles.'[37] Books, too, keep hands busy. It is hard not to be reminded of Rousseau's obscene euphemism in the *Confessions*, when he refers to the first time he heard about the kind of book 'which one reads with one hand'.[38] Less scandalously, in manuscripts or early printed books, an image of the hand (a 'manicule') is used to point to interesting details and structure the text.[39] At the heart of this, William Sherman suggests, is the cognitive stimulation provided by hand-eye co-ordination.

Typically, I begin reading a book in the grip of both hands, the pages on either side held between thumb and forefinger. As I relax, I transfer a book to hold in one hand only, or swap as it grows tired. Many types of artificial book-holder are

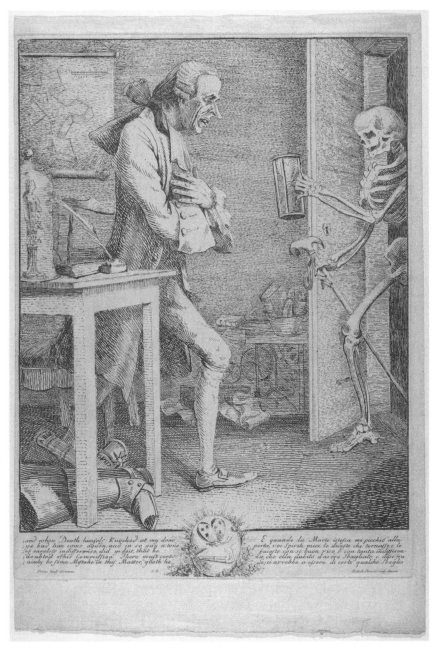

Fig. 61. 'Death of the author'; Thomas Patch, Sterne as Shandy: 'And When Death Himself Knocked at my Door', etching, 1769. New York, Metropolitan Museum, 2013.939

devised to assist the process, the preferred mode for handling rare books in libraries. These, too, act in imitation of the body, a reader's helpmeet. Most readers prefer contact through fingers, keeping intimacy with the book in the process of reading. It may be this is one reason, despite advantages of economy or functionality, the e-book stalled in its relentless conquest over a traditional paperback. As I drop one book, 'I take up another', says Montaigne, if only to put off boredom.[40] The book acts as an extension of the hands, even a form of prosthetic. The book is an alien hand, or a third hand for the mind's use.

The importance of Petrarch's phrase *semper in manibus* goes way beyond convenience or portability. A book, we might say following Heidegger, is *zuhanden* rather than *vorhanden*, 'ready-to-hand' rather than merely 'present-at-hand': it is ready for use, like Petrarch's *Confessions*.[41] It is not a mere lifeless object, to which we then subsequently confer meaning; it is 'manipulable in the broadest sense and at our disposal'.[42] Indeed, Heidegger gives as an example of his fundamental concept of *Zuhandenheit* ('handiness') the way that, even in relation to a book that we can never read (such as one in an unknown language) we see it as a *book* and not as paper with black marks.[43]

This is a means of understanding the way in which a book is a form of hand technology. *Technik* ('technology') for Heidegger is not simply a way of making things, but a way of knowing them. It is a form of *revealing* things that precedes the making. Technology is not defined according to its instrumentality, Heidegger insists, but through its capacity to 'bring things forth' (*hervorbringen*). A book is an exemplary case in point: it discloses itself, that is, opens the world out to human intelligibility, through *Unverborgenheit* or 'unconcealment'.[44] A book is a thing and yet more than a thing: it conveys being. While literary history has given the prior claim to authorship in the relation between books and identity, it is worth remembering that reading as well as writing confers autonomy.

In the *Confessions*, Augustine recalls how Ambrose his mentor would escape from the crowds of pious admirers who constantly surrounded him by taking time out either for food or for reading. By reading, he could be somewhere else, even without moving. Leader suggests a similar function in the smartphone: being attached to the handheld device allows someone to abstract herself from the situation she is in, 'to be absent while being nonetheless physically present'.[45] My mind is elsewhere. With beautiful sensitivity Augustine suggests that this motivation was also present for Ambrose:

> often when we were there, we saw him silently reading and never otherwise. After sitting for a long time in silence (for who would dare to burden him in such intent concentration?) we used to go away. We supposed that in the brief time he could find for his mind's refreshment, free from the hubbub of other people's troubles, he would not want to be invited to consider another problem.[46]

Famously, Augustine distinguishes between two kinds of reading here, 'silent' (*tacite*) and 'otherwise' (*aliter*). The 'other' kind of reading is reading aloud, a kind of reading which in the modern world has become unfamiliar (except for children or on audiobooks while we travel) but which in Ambrose's time was normative. *Lectio* was a public activity: something that was done for and among others, such as by monks for the whole community at dinner; or teachers (like Ambrose) for the benefit of their students, interrupting themselves to supply commentary on difficult words. In this way *lectio* has become the root of the modern word 'lecture', whereas in earlier times reading and talking were in closer proximity. For Augustine, it is a surprise perhaps not so much to see Ambrose reading silently at all, as that he *never* reads out loud.[47]

We encounter here a very old scholarly controversy, which might appear arcane and boring if it did not intrude on such important territory in the history of books or the human body. It begins, as many controversies do, with an odd prejudice of Nietzsche. The German people have forgotten how to read aloud, he says in *Beyond Good and Evil*; they read with their eyes only, they have put their 'ears away in a drawer'.[48] The ancients, he says by contrast, if they read at all (which they did seldom), read out loud. Nietzsche's prejudice is not only in favour of the sound of language (and therefore with a sentiment for poetry), but also in a sense *against* reading in general. In *Ecce Homo* he boasted that for years he read nothing— the greatest favour he ever did himself.[49] Modernity has become 'depraved' by reading books and forgetting how to feel directly.

Over time, the motivation for this view got lost but the assumption grew in strength. A classic article in 1927 by the Hungarian classicist Josef Balogh argued that silent reading was almost completely unknown in the ancient world, citing (of course) Augustine on Ambrose along the way.[50] Forty years later came a lonely counter-voice from the Homeric scholar Bernard Knox, that while reading aloud was standard, silent reading was by no means extraordinary.[51] Meanwhile medieval textual scholarship offered a technological explanation, first suggested by Balogh, that ancient readers relied almost entirely on texts written in *scripta continua*—with no spaces between words. Malcolm Parkes argued that as Latin culture shifted towards a class of readers for whom Latin was an unfamiliar foreign language, a series of textual innovations were introduced, such as word-breaks and also punctuation.[52] For these readers, for the first time, Latin became a 'visible language'. Later, Paul Saenger provided comparison with neuroscience to suggest a fundamental distinction in textual cultures. Reciting texts orally was necessary in antiquity for 'the reader to hold in short-term memory the fraction of a word or phrase that already has been decoded phonetically'.[53] Spaces between words enabled silent reading, which in turn freed up the reading of more complex texts.

Contrary to Nietzsche's bias towards voice over literary text, Saenger argues for the superiority of eye over mouth. Over time an idea of cognitive shift has been repeated in accounts of the triumph of the book—and of literacy—in modernity, by cultural theorists as varied as McLuhan, Eric Havelock, Jack Goody, Walter Ong, or Lucien Febvre.[54] Among influential (and elegant) proponents of this is Alberto Manguel, who argued silent reading encouraged the simultaneous comparison of several books left open together.[55] Chartier states it 'radically transformed intellectual work, which in essence became an intimate activity, a personal confrontation with an ever-growing number of texts'.[56] Yet for others this version of the history of books has become that worst kind of heresy, an urban commonplace. Especially strong here has been the outcry of classicists, following Knox's lead, such as A. K. Gavrilov and Myles Burnyeat.[57] They pointed out that while the Greeks always used *scripta continua*, Latin from the second century BCE onwards was often written *interpuncta*, with dots between words. Fashions on this score in fact went backwards and forwards, rather than following a teleological line. In any case, it is evident that readers learned sophisticated methods in deciphering *scripta continua*, which casts doubt on the idea they were inhibited from complexity.[58]

Reading aloud, beyond a basic level, always involves being able to read silently ahead. Quintilian comments that 'we have to keep our eyes on what follows while reading out what precedes'. This, he infers, is an intrinsically complex mental task, since the voice 'is doing one thing and the eyes another'.[59] Lucian in similar vein in *Adversus indoctum* says that the reader's lips are 'still busy with one sentence while your eyes are on the next'.[60] This comes in a work addressed 'against an ignorant book-collector', so it is hardly surprising that it has a sophisticated sense of the reading process. The preface to Quintilian's *Institutio* describes how long his bookseller has been waiting for this text: time spent, he says, 'to go over them again more carefully, with a reader's eyes'.[61]

The funny thing is that the same citations used to prove silent reading in the ancient world, are used by others to show it was nonetheless very rare. Classical literature abounds with stories of secret reading. In Euripides' *Hippolytus*, Theseus the King discovers the dead body of his wife, Phaedra, with a letter tablet hanging from her hand. Chorus and audience are forced to wait while he reads to himself, until the sickening revelation in the letter that she was raped by his son Hippolytus.[62] Cydippe in Ovid's *Heroides* says she read the long letter of Acontius silently (*scriptumque tuum sine murmure legi*) because afraid the gods might be listening.[63] In a grimly contrasting case, Julius Caesar in Plutarch is presented as silently reading over a letter during the proceedings of the senate against the conspirator Catiline. Cato challenges Caesar to read it out, believing the letter is from Catiline and proves Caesar's guilt; Caesar makes a show of handing it over reluctantly, only for it to be exposed as a love letter to him from Cato's sister. Cato's determination to unseat his enemy is turned to his own embarrassment.[64]

What these examples demonstrate is complex interplay between reading and speaking. Cicero, discussing the question of whether the deaf enjoy poetry, commented sensitively that 'far greater pleasure can be derived from reading than hearing verse'.[65] This is a direct rejection of Nietzsche's philippic against the cloth ears of fellow Germans. Silent reading is partly a debate about modernity. Reading aloud is felt to be a primitive staging post on the road to a textual future. Yet is the anthropology dividing oral from literate cultures a false one? The only evidence for oral traditions in the past is by definition literary. The hyper-literate society of the internet, by contrast, is hardly silent. It revels in metaphors which cross the boundary between hand and mouth. Facebook mashes text with a person's mug-shot as if as a mouthpiece; Twitter gives song to the miniaturist lyric of its pre-cisely limited character sets. The internet, via Youtube or countless imitators, is able freely to cross the boundary between sounded and unsounded text.

There are ancient precedents for mixing metaphors between speech and writ-ing. The Jain religion is not based on any divine revelation of truth. Instead it is expressed through the Jinas, royal beings who renounce the world and attain all-knowing wisdom. The twenty-four Jinas give voice to the 'divine sound' (*divyadh-vani*), the source of all knowledge, which is understood by all human beings in their own language. Wisdom passes from one Jina to another, until it is resolved into the voice of the last, Mahāvīra (6th–5th c. BCE). Over time, and with the passing down of this oral tradition through a body of texts, knowledge gradually becomes lost. The writing is like a sound we cannot (any more) quite hear. Yet the texts are all we have, and all the more precious for that.[66]

At times of transition, such as in Anglo-Saxon England between *Beowulf* and Alcuin of York, the literary and oral intermix. A. B. Lord thought *Beowulf* was written down by its poet, who nonetheless composed as he sang; Alcuin joked about a fellow-monk tripping up in reading his poem.[67] Medievalists locate the formation of 'textual communities' from the tenth century onwards.[68] This becomes, if they are not careful, a premonition of modernity. However, ancient as well as modern culture was a mixture of textual and oral. Augustine, we remem-ber, was a pre-eminent giver of sermons; Cicero, before him, is even more famously the author of spoken orations. The pulpit and the law court are their arenas. Yet the line from Cicero to Augustine to Petrarch is equally a literary one. Petrarch uses the form of the written letter to communicate with his lost masters. Through their letters his masters speak to him. Socrates and Jesus are the great sages who gave wisdom without writing things down; yet their wisdom is known via the dialogues of Plato or Xenophon, or the scriptures of the New Testament (or the apocryphal gospels).

Cicero was caught by Augustus' assassins at his villa near the sea. 'Herennius cut off his head (by Antony's command), and his hands'.[69] In the *Life of Antony*, Plutarch furnishes a gruesome detail: Antony ordered 300 heads to be placed upon the rostra of the Roman forum, plus 'that right hand with which Cicero had written the speeches against him'.[70] Why did Antony insist on the hand of Cicero, when his tongue was already silenced? Plutarch confers agency on the hand that writes against Antony (κατ' αὐτοῦ λόγους ἔγραψε). Shane Butler has used this episode to cast doubt on the emphasis laid on oral culture in describing the ancient Roman world.[71] The significance of the oral within a wide variety of cultures, including Roman, has been a commonplace since Walter Ong.[72] However, Cicero belongs as well to a complex written culture, Butler shows. To take one example, Cicero launched his career as an orator in the law courts against Verres, corrupt Roman governor of Sicily. For his speech he had to collate a miasma of written texts: the public records of Sicilian cities, depositions, accounts, letters, public inscriptions on stone and bronze, wills, treaties, pamphlets, contracts; alongside literary pasquinades, or even books of prophecies of the Cumaean Sibyl.[73] Cicero was highly familiar with writing materials; his secretary Tiro, a freedman from slavery at last, who took his name, is said to have invented a form of shorthand.[74]

The stock image of Cicero rising up in court to assail the hapless Verres is therefore too simple. In addition, while the collected 'speeches' of Cicero *In Verrem* constitute a quarter of the Ciceronian oratorical repertory, many of them were never 'spoken' at all. Following the setback of Cicero's opening speech, the hapless Verres fled the scene and declined to appear in court; the rest were issued as writings.[75] Thus, as with the Philippics, Cicero's hand in his own publication has been downplayed. Butler recounts how during one day during the Catiline conspiracy Cicero brought the city of Rome to a standstill, one piece of writing following another. Cicero refers to himself as writing his speeches. In the interflux of writing and speech, history has favoured instead the idea of a conflict of meaning between the two. In one image, writing gradually triumphs over speech; in another, the spoken word is always superior.

A parallel may be drawn with conflict over the status of scripture at the Reformation.[76] By 1520, Luther was declaring any conflict over doctrine should follow the written word of scripture.[77] He claimed the authority of Augustine, who in a letter to Jerome stated that he would accept no judgements unless 'they prove it to me by Holy Scripture'.[78] More dangerously, Luther found support for inalienable proof by scripture in Wyclif's *De veritate sacrae scripturae*.[79] This put him in heretical company. In reply to Luther, Catholic controversy put together a mass of arguments in favour of what came to be known as 'unwritten verities'.[80] Whereas the word of God in Luther is entirely a written object, More counter-argues that it is *aliud scriptum...aliud non scriptum*. The sacraments, for instance, are revealed *partim scripto, partim non scripto*.[81] This takes More into a dispute at the heart of modernity. For lurking behind a question of scripture is not only a question of authority, but also about the status of texts, or language as language. How does text relate to meaning? How do we know what we mean?

Spoken testimony is superior to written, More insists. Indeed, writers of the New Testament, like St Paul, would have preferred to give us spoken doctrine. Writing is unreliable. Indeed, pushing into uncharted water, More finds problems in Paul's Epistles:

Very many of his epistles, as of the other apostles also, are lost, and of those which are extant, some are translated incorrectly, some are translated ambiguously, the copies in the two languages do not agree at all points, and there is incessant controversy about their meaning.[82]

Tyndale in *The Obedience of a Christen Man* of 1528 took up cudgels in reply:

I answere that Paul taught by mouth soch thinges as he wrote in his pistles. And his tradicions ware the Gospell of Christe.[83]

In Tyndale, speech is given back as writing, in profound metaphysical disturbance. For More, writing is essentially material and thus perishable. However, God is imperishable. He therefore only exists as spirit and as spoken word. More plays (with humanist learning) on the Greek $\pi\nu\epsilon\hat{\upsilon}\mu\alpha$, meaning both 'holy spirit' and 'breath'. In the *Dialogue Concerning Heresies* (1529), More fixes on the corruptible composition of parchment:

And so was it conuenyent for the lawe of lyfe | rather to be wrytten in the lyuely myndes of men | than in y^e dede skynnes of bestes.[84]

Had not St Paul himself said scripture was written not with ink but the living spirit of God? Indeed, he continued, 'the letter killeth, but the spirit giveth life'.[85]

Something curious is going on. In More's deconstructive turn on writing, writing returns even as he repudiates it. For proof of the authenticity of oral tradition comes in the form of a proof-*text*. All the spoken promises of Christ that More quotes are written texts. More cannot evade writing. In ultimate vindication of the spirit against the letter, More translates Paul's famous phrase: 'For the letter kylleth, but the sprete geveth lyfe'. Here the English 'letter' translates the Greek $\gamma\rho\acute{\alpha}\mu\mu\alpha$, meaning literally 'the written mark'. Yet Paul's *dictum*, too, is a $\gamma\rho\acute{\alpha}\mu\mu\alpha$, dead letter inscribed on dead flesh of an animal, promising the life of the spirit. More only receives the spirit of the verse by following the letter, in an act of reading, tracing the obscure mark of its sign in an interpretation of its meaning. And this interpretation he, too, delivers in writing, in the text of the *Dialogue*.

In such arguments we see a false opposition of oral and written, or mouth and hand. In More's repudiation of the pre-eminence of written scripture he dismisses writing as a creature of the body, written on dead flesh (sheepskin or the calf of vellum manuscripts). Writing, Michael Clanchy reminds us, was considered less trustworthy than speech in medieval legal practice.[86] He warns against prejudice in favour of literacy. By contrast, modern recuperation of text celebrates its disembodied status, neural networks in a purely mental realm, what Leah Price has called 'the progressive disappearance of the reader's body'.[87] It is worth returning to Augustine here. For Ambrose's reading, even silent, is still bodily. 'When he was reading, his eyes ran over the page and his heart perceived the sense, even though his voice and tongue were silent.'[88] The old battle over noisy reading in the ancient world is misplaced. As Chartier has observed, both kinds of reading co-existed long after the supposed defeat of one by the other. Early modern readers often read aloud, in the household, at school, for sociability.[89]

Mary Carruthers argues that what is at stake in Augustine's account is not sound or silence but two different experiences of reading. One reading is part of public business of the day, sharing ideas and interpretations, whether in the class-room or the marketplace. The other, the kind practised by Ambrose, is internal-ized and in Carruthers's word, 'meditative'.[90] Augustine's metaphor for this type of reading is bodily. In his Sermons, he refers to reading not as a formal activity but something he calls 'rumination', like the cow chewing the cud.[91] This was a dom-inant metaphor in medieval theories of reading. It was traced back by Jerome to Ezekiel's vision of eating the book, seen in Dürer (Ch. 14, Fig. 50), not to empha-size prophetic weirdness, but rather to normalize it. We eat the book and store it in our bellies, as we wait for its fruit to restore and feed us. In the same passage, Jerome likens this to Samson finding honey in the carcass of the lion (Judges 14: 8).[92] Later, Hugh of St Victor compared reading scripture to walking in the forest. While reading we pick flowers and fruit from among the trees, taste them as we go, and by and by chew them (*ruminamus*), absorbing them into the mind.[93] Rabelais turns metaphor into joke: 'I have the word of the gospel in my mouth', Gargantua says, a good glass of wine to wash it down, before shitting and pissing it all away.[94]

While these ideas are the staple of the medieval art of memory so brilliantly recovered by Carruthers, they fed off ancient metaphors of the reading process. Seneca described reading as like the flight of a bee, gathering flowers in order to make honey.[95] The bee then places each piece of nectar into a separate cell in the honeycomb, every nugget in its own place. Then later, rediscovering our reading, we can blend the nectar from different sources into one sumptuous jar. Seneca, too, uses the metaphor of the stomach, processing the mass of substances within itself; only through digestion does knowledge become ready for use. As if to prove his own point, Seneca derives the image of the bees from his own reading of Virgil's *Aeneid*.[96] In an extended imagination of the metaphorical process, he declares that it is uncertain whether it is the action of the bees which creates the nectar, or something inherent in the properties of the flowers.

Whether it is the property of the book we linger upon, or the imprint on the mind as it is affected, it is clear that reading is both bodily and yet also intersub-jective and intercommunicative. It also changes as we live. Petrarch in a letter to Boccaccio in 1359 CE commented on his reading of Virgil, Horace, Livy, and Cicero, over the course of a lifetime (he was now in his fifties). I eat in the morn-ing and digest in the evening he says; and likewise, a book that I swallowed as a boy, I ruminate as an old man.[97] Sometimes I have read something so long ago that I forget where I first came across it, and forget the author. Suddenly, in the business of the day, preoccupied with something else, a reading comes back to me from the deep past, thoroughly absorbed and yet striking me as totally new. Petrarch, too, borrows the analogy of the bee.

Elsewhere, in his *Secretum* (or 'secret book'), Petrarch creates a dialogue between himself and Augustine. Augustine remarks on how Francesco is 'running through in your mind all your reading and a whole lifetime's experiences'.[98] But in all this, he says, Petrarch does not 'go deep enough'. Later in the book Augustine provides a remedy. Whenever you come across something in your reading that excites you, 'make sure it is deeply impressed on your memory'.[99] For the strongest passions—like anger or lust—are aroused in reading, yet also processed by reading, which helps us to understand them, to ameliorate them, or indeed to live with them. As an example of this deep reading, Petrarch enters into a commentary on another passage from Virgil, the cave of the winds in *Aeneid*, book 1.[100] Augustine listens to Petrarch's *lectio* of Virgil, and expresses admiration for 'the hidden meanings' Francesco finds in poetry. In his cave, Aeolus rules over 'the struggling winds and roaring tempests', but only just, so that the mountain shakes around them. Just so, in the mind, our passions, deep inside us, are hard to bear. We try to chain them down, but they shake us to the core. In reading, we make sense of life, even as we encounter, there, the likenesses of our own passions.

Delightfully, Augustine expresses doubt whether Francesco's insights are present in Virgil's intention or are what he himself wanted to find. Every reading is a dialogue, that is, as Petrarch represents in a fictional dialogue between himself and his mentor. It is a form Petrarch says that he learned from Cicero, just as Cicero learned it from Plato. It is easy enough now to feel distance from ancient and humanist accounts of reading. Carruthers comments that modern readers like to think they are 'objective', whereas the medieval reader is frank in recognising reading as physiological *and* psychological: 'it changes both food and its consumer'.[101] Carruthers wrote this just before the intervention of the internet. Perhaps we are readier now to recognize a physical component in reading. The metaphor of a book as like food, and reading as digestion, has never gone away. We can also still acknowledge difference in kinds of reading. One is everyday, summed up by interaction with the smartphone from morn to night, in bed waking up, or failing to sleep. Preoccupied with business, we glance at the screen, checking a fact or a figure. Digressing, the internet takes us from place to place, one article to another, in the stream of consciousness incited by the great demon Google. We bookmark one place and forget it next moment. Every so often, we are distracted into forgetting ourselves.

Yet there is that other kind of reading, the 'deep reading' beloved by Petrarch. On top of a bedside table, ready at hand as we put the phone down, likely sits a pile of books: a long novel, maybe from this year's prizelist, or a classic we meant to read when younger, or want to read again; or a revelatory piece of non-fiction.

Fig. 62. 'Child's book'; Vincenzo Foppa, *Young Cicero Reading*, fresco from the Palazzo Banco Mediceo, Milan, 15th c., mounted on canvas. London, Wallace Collection.

At my side today, waiting for me to turn away from news of impeachments, fake elections, or viruses, I have Alexis Wright's *Carpentaria*, an Australian *Ulysses*. Petrarch reads Cicero awaiting uncertain afterlife; my book keeps me company as I prepare for climate apocalypse.

In the Wallace Collection in London there is a fresco (Fig. 62) commissioned for a palace in Milan which was given in 1455 by Francesco Sforza to Cosimo de' Medici. The artist, Vincenzo Foppa, reveals a young child sitting on a bench. The bench is at right angles to a window seat, looking out on an arcade of cypress trees behind. The child is rosy-cheeked and wears a pupil's smock in a similar pink shade; one hand grips the thigh above the knee, the thumb bent to the side; the other hand holds a book, or better caresses it, the open pages firmly balanced against the chest in order to keep the place safe and to aid a steady eye in reading. The head is quite still; the neck is bent towards the book; the lips are tight shut; the eyes are relaxed but completely concentrated. One foot is planted on the floor; the other, casually yet also in active poise, balances the body against the stone wall. Another book lies open on an unused lectern and a third is on a shelf below; if the reader needs more, a further pile lies on a bookshelf behind. To complete the scene, at the child's back, an inscription reads M. T. C I|CERO.

For a long time, this appeared to refer to the reading matter in Foppa's fresco, until in 1950 Ellis Waterhouse conceived 'a suggestion so obvious that it has never been made', that the young reader—not his book—is Cicero.[102] Waterhouse drew attention to a passage at the beginning of Plutarch's *Life of Cicero*, where Cicero's talent as a budding scholar and reader is so precociously obvious to fellow students 'that their fathers used to visit the schools in order to see Cicero with their own eyes and observe the quickness and intelligence in his studies'.[103] The two references in the image are not after all unconnected. Plutarch in the same chapter himself creates the arc between early skill as a reader and writer of poetry, and later fame as an orator. Reading Cicero was the centre of educational practice from antiquity to the Christian fathers to the Carolingian age, or from Petrarch to Erasmus to the Elizabethan schoolroom of Shakespeare.[104] Chartier calls these 'communities of readers'; to uncover the literary and autobiographical currents, he calls for 'an archaeology of reading practices'.[105] To read Cicero is always to be put into contact with Cicero the reader. Good readers make good writers, and vice versa. Jerome, who dreamt anxiously that he was becoming more Ciceronian than Christian, wrote in another letter to Pope Damasus that 'to read without also writing is to sleep'.[106]

The child reader in the fresco is connected to the child reader in us all. At the same time, as if through the window behind the child, the image of reading in action points to its power. It has a capacity to transport a reader wherever she wishes. This is caught most of all in an implied movement of the child's eyes, guided as it is by his hand, which holds the book so carefully between forefinger and thumb. It is a moment of mimesis: an imitation in painting of the act of reading, which tells the story of the book's gift of imitating nature, or even feeling itself. At times since the Enlightenment a connection between reading with the body and the eye has been lost, in an idea of reading as automatic mechanical process in the brain. In Cicero, however, in life and death, the business of hand, eye, and mouth were always unified. When the head and hand of the dead orator went on display in the rostra, it was said that Roman citizens saw in them not the vestiges of Cicero but the doom of Antony his assailant. Plutarch tells how Augustus later paid a visit to the son of Cicero's daughter Tullia; the boy has a copy of Cicero's works in his hands, and terrified, hides the book. But Augustus sees it, takes it from him and reads a good while from it, silently, in front of the boy. As he finishes reading, he declares Cicero 'a learned man and a lover of his country'.[107] Cicero, λόγιος ἀνήρ, and his book, live on, surviving death itself.

For Darian Leader, the opposition between hand and mouth, or between eye and mouth, is a false one. Newborn babies spend most of their waking life touching their bodies. For a fifth of their time, focus is concentrated on 'contact between hand and mouth'.[108] As the mouth sucks on the mother's breast, the hand grips itself into a fist. In substitution for the nipple, the baby will suck its own hand, a thumb or finger transferred only at the last instant before feeding. Thumbsucking, Freud reminds us, has 'nothing to do with the purpose of ingesting food'.[109] At other times, as the hand reaches out to an object to inspect it, it will be tested first in the mouth. Later, the hand learns to reach for things independently, always guided by the eye. Child psychologists call the gradual liberation of the hand from the mouth the quest for 'autonomy'.[110] Selma Fraiberg has referred to the hand's 'morbid alliance with the mouth', demonstrating that a triadic relationship between hand, eye, and mouth is never lost, even among the visually impaired.[111]

The different senses are not in competition with each other, indeed can be substituted for one another. In Milton's *Paradise Lost*, touch and taste are virtually synonymous, through the strange Latin homonym by which taste (*sapere*) is knowledge (*sapere*). Eve, addressing the forbidden tree of knowledge as she prepares to eat from its fruit, says:

> O Sovran, vertuous, precious of all Trees.[112]

As if pleased with herself for noticing the pun, she hails the tree's 'Sapience, hitherto obscur'd'. Jean Piaget noticed with wonder a similar synaesthesia in young infants. He observed how when he opened and closed his eyes in front of his children, his daughter would open and close her mouth, while his son would open and close his hands.[113] Freud noticed the *Greiftrieb*, the infant's mirror-drive between manual and oral grip.[114]

The hand is the site of agency, something transferred to the book as we hold it in our hands, something that we attribute to the book as an extension of ourselves. Biological and cognitive life come together in its pages. Is the source of a book's power precisely its capacity for transference, an in-between space transcending relationship? In Dante's *Inferno*, Paolo and Francesca recall a forbidden moment of sexual intimacy, which has condemned them for eternity, as a primal scene of shared reading. Francesca recounts to Dante in Hell how she and Paolo got together one day to read about Lancelot:

> Noi leggiavamo un giorno per diletto

'We read one day for delight'.[115] As they read, their eyes are suspended between them in the same activity, and then as their eyes meet, when they turn from the book, they blush. Yet it is one moment in particular which overmasters them. As the book reveals Lancelot kissing the mouth of his lover Guinevere, their own lips move in imitation:

> la bocca mi basciò tutto tremante.
> Galeotto fu 'l libro e chi lo scrisse:
> quel giorno più non vi leggemmo avante.[116]

As they finger the book in front of them, Paolo's mouth meets tremblingly with Francesca's in a kiss. The book was a go-between (a 'Galeotto'), as was the author who wrote it. In a beautiful example of saying more by saying less, Dante makes Francesca confess that, on that day, they did no more reading together. It is easy enough to see an alliance of mouth and hand in the actions of fictional readers, how their senses become confused in the mimesis represented in the Arthurian legend of sex and betrayal. It is less easy to see Dante's subtle invocation of his own art of imitation, as the reader senses the power of Dante's book, its passion a conveyance between hand and mouth. The book's tacit secret is to be the place where experience is exchanged with the other.

19

Written on the Flesh

In 1990, the artist Shirin Neshat returned to Iran, a year after the death of Ayatollah Khomeini. She commented on enormous differences in Iranian culture, having lived in voluntary exile for over a decade in the United States: 'The change was both frightening and exciting.'[1] At the heart of this was public physical appearance. *Unveiling* (1993) explores the politics of the female body, expressed in a dialectic between Islam and the West, femininity and masculinity, public and private, antiquity and modernity.

This photograph is a self-portrait (Fig. 63). On the subject of the veil, it manages to be both neutral and ambiguous. Neshat is hardly concealed by the veil: rather, her eyes are the prime subject of the image, emphasized both by make-up

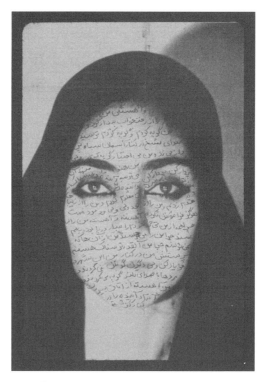

Fig. 63. 'Writing the self'; Shirin Neshat, *Unveiling*, black and white photograph, 1993. New York, Hemispheric Institute

and by the black and white medium. Her mouth, by contrast, is muted and scarcely visible. In place of her voice, the entire oval of her face is inscribed by text. This consists of a poem by Farough Farrokhzad (1935–67). Poet, iconoclast, and film-maker, Farrokhzad spoke for and to female identity and sensuality, before her death in a car accident at the age of 32:

Was not the woman who turned to dust
In the shroud of her waiting and chastity
My youth?[2]

Inscription, too, then is here ambiguous. The text is written in Farsi in the Persian abjad. Does it signify her words, or is it imposed on her, perhaps like the veil? The title 'unveiling' implies a potential for liberation, but also could be meant in the sense of revealing towards the gaze of the viewer. The words of the poem only succeed in signifying, meanwhile, to someone who can read them. The script is based on modern Persian printing rather than manuscripts. To a Western eye it may appear as if in undifferentiated (and ornamental) Arabized or Islamic calligraphy, a subject by which Neshat is fascinated. The photograph challenges female stereotypes within Islam and at the same time also challenges Western exoticism and Orientalism.

In *Women of Allah* (1994), Neshat continued this visual language of writing on the body. A series of photographs show pairs of hands, as if disembodied, palms open, covered in Persian writing, painted in Farsi calligraphy comprising texts by the thirteenth-century CE Persian poet and mystic Rumi. They are like pages of a book opened in front of the viewer. In the background, photographed in black against a black background, an image of a rifle is discretely embedded into the image, sometimes pointed towards us. Neshat gave this sub-section of her work the blankly ironic title 'Stories of Martyrdom'. Are these the hands of martyrs, or their victims? The writing appears to mimic the conventional appearance of a tattoo. Yet examined closely, the ink is not on the hands, but superimposed onto the photograph. It belongs to the body but is not *of* the body.

The Book of Kings (2012) revisits Neshat's earlier and most famous work. The title refers in English to the eleventh-century CE *Shahnameh* by Abul-Qasim Ferdowsi, one of the longest epic poems in the world (three times the length of the *Iliad*). Of central importance to Iranian culture, its 50,000 distichs tell the mythology and history of the region, from the creation of the world to the origins of civilization (fire, cooking, metallurgy, law), ending with the Islamic conquest of Persia. Ferdowsi provides a commentary on the rise and fall of nations, the transience of the world, and the moral virtues: justice, truth, reason, and love. The mythical sections of the poem stress the need for wisdom. In the historical parts (which omit the Achaemenid monarchs, such as Cyrus, Darius, and Xerxes, and take Persian history up to Alexander, here called Sekander) there is a greater emphasis on courtly culture, on luxury and erotic pleasure.[3] The poem is framed by the exaltation of God and praise of Muhammad, but also shows a preference for Persian over Arab culture. Demons teach an early king to write, so that 'his heart glowed like the sun with this knowledge'.[4] They teach him thirty writing scripts, including Greek and Chinese. While the poem was written at a point when the Middle Persian language (*Pahlavi*) was mixing with Arabic, Ferdowsi is understood to have emphasized classical Persian at the expense of Arabic words.[5] The epic also inspired a long and rich artistic tradition in manuscripts, producing some of the most sumptuous examples of Persian miniature painting, including narrative and chivalric scenes, battles and love-making.[6]

Neshat's work refers directly to the exquisite manuscript tradition of the *Shahnameh*, and to its status as a national icon independent of religion. Her *Book of Kings* consists of a series of photographs of both men and women, once again often inscribed with texts and images in imitation of tattoos. In 'My house on fire', a man vigorously strikes with his fist his own heart, which is itself stamped with an icon. Some of the images are named 'Patriots', each with the personal name of the male subject of the photograph attached. The arm is raised against the heart once more, but with a relaxed grip, suggesting steadfastness. In 'Patriots', every part of exposed skin is covered in writing. It is clearly superimposed, however, as if imprinted onto the body. The margins of the original manuscript are visible; the text becomes smaller from top to bottom, with the letters diminishing in size from the forehead (where they are largest) to the fingertips. In 'Villains', text is replaced by image: the legs, or in another case the torso, of a man is covered by a martial illustration from an engraved copy of *Shahnameh*, showing a company of cavalry on horses and elephants. An archer fires arrows at a fallen enemy, or a soldier on horseback beheads his opponent; blood is picked out in virulent red against the completely black background of the photograph.

Most moving of all the images of the *Book of Kings* is a series called 'Mourners'. Ahmed and Ghada, an old man and a woman, gaze directly to camera. They are both dressed in black; Ghada wears a black headscarf. The skin of their faces, the only part of the body that is visible, is pixellated as if to suggest script, which is nonetheless so minuscule that it barely registers as writing. Rendered in a sepia colour, it merges with the contours of the visage. The wrinkles of the face appear like lines of writing, as if the face has written out its suffering in physical form, or else writing has subjected identity to a textual patina. Over and again, a question is raised in the mind of the viewer of the part taken by writing on the body. Does it speak on behalf of the subject, or against or across it? Neshat constructs a complex visual language drawing on two thousand years of calligraphic art in Iran. Art and writing intertwine in medieval Persian culture, in ceramics and architecture as well as manuscript illuminations.[7] In the twentieth century, the Saghakhane Movement transferred the visual graphic of Farsi calligraphy into modern art.[8] Neshat draws on diverse ways Persian and Arabic art understands writing in decorative terms. The subtle politics of her images evokes writing as semantic but also poetic or abstract. She is aware of a long history of imposing meaning on texts, and the ambivalence of the human person when subjected to those meanings.

Implicit in Neshat's work is the controversial sense of tattoo in Islam, and its contrasting reputation in Sunni or Shia contexts. Forbidden by Sunni clerics, tattoos are common in Shi'ite societies, although not using text from the Qur'an. The word 'tattoo' is Polynesian, adopted in the West by Captain James Cook in his *Journal on Tahiti* in July 1769. Melville in a 'peep' at life in Polynesia in 1842 recounts a visit to the tattoo artist: 'The idea of engrafting his tattooing upon my white skin filled him with all a painter's enthusiasm'.[9] Men and women employ the 'method of Tattowing', Cook says. They use lamp black, pricking it under the skin with 'very thin flatt pieces of bone or Shell'.[10] These tattoos were not of writing but figures of men or animals, mixed with elaborate symbols such as circles and crescents. Cook's surgeon compared the facial incisions of the Māori in New Zealand with engravings.[11] Sydney Parkinson and Herman Spöring, employed as artists to makes drawings of zoological specimens, digressed into 'living pictures' of the islanders, as in a 'Portrait of a New Zealand Man' (Fig. 64), in pen and ink wash.

Tattooing indeed is older than human writing. The 'iceman' discovered in the Alto Adige on the Alpine borders between Italy and Austria in 1991, carbon dated to 5,300 years old, has 61 tattoos of dots and crosses on his lower spine and legs.[12] Figurines in Egypt showing women with tattoos may be even older. Mummified remains of Egyptian women with tattoos have been dated to 2000 BCE.[13] In Leviticus 19: 28, there is a ban on tattoos, which implies that they were known among the early Israelites:

Ye shall not make any cuttings in your flesh for the dead, nor print any marks upon you: I am the Lord.

In Isaiah 44: 5, it is said that after redemption the Jews will declare 'I am the Lord's man'; according to some interpretations of the Hebrew, this will be confirmed by tattoo.

Here we uncover the mixed message of the tattoo. The Greek word *stigma* is derived from the verb στίζω meaning to prick or embroider. The Greeks were aware that their northern neighbours in Thrace, especially women, wore marks on their bodies of shapes and sometimes animals. In vase-painting they are sometimes portrayed as Maenads or madwomen who have murdered the poet Orpheus. In literary evidence, Herodotus expresses surprise that the marking is a sign of nobility among Thracian women; women who are *astikton* ('unmarked') are thereby accounted low-born.[14] Herodotus is also aware of tattooing in Egypt. Here he comments on a slave who escapes from his owner to the temple, where

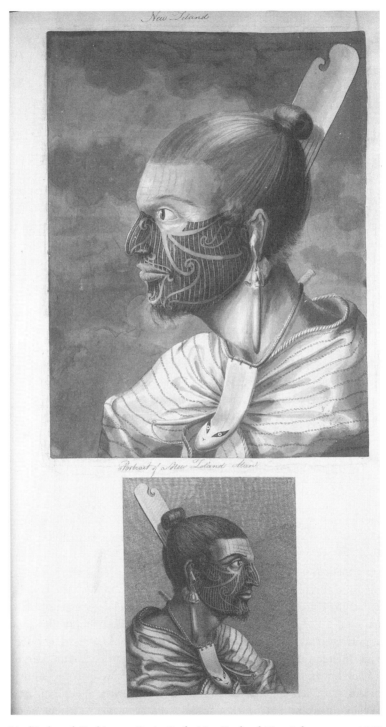

Fig. 64. 'Body art'; Parkinson, *Portrait of a New Zealand Man*, ink on paper, 1768–70. London, British Library Add. MS 23920

he takes on religious *stigmata*, which mean that he is the gift of the god, and no one can touch him.[15] The tattoo thus hovers between the outlaw and the sacred.

The Greeks associated tattooing with slavery, and most of all with the great enemy, the Persian Empire. Indeed, in the past the word *stigma* was often taken by scholars to refer to branding rather than tattooing, such as in the passage where Herodotus describes Xerxes crossing the Hellespont into Europe and marking prisoners of war with the *stigmata basileia*, the royal stamp.[16] Branding has long been at question in histories of slavery under the Persian Empire.[17] This theory is overturned by C. P. Jones in favour of tattooing.[18] He cites several passages to show that over time the practice transferred across into Greek practice, acquiring a kind of taboo, as a foreign practice infiltrating home culture, always in a degrading way. In a sadistic passage in comic writing from the second century BCE, a woman has a lover's betrayal satirized onto his own forehead with the vengeful proverb 'know thyself'.[19] Other references collected by Jones refer to runaway slaves inscribed with words that display their crimes.[20] He explains, in this way, Paul's famous metaphor in Galatians 6: 17, where Paul refers to himself carrying on his body the *stigmata* of the Lord Jesus. The allusion appears to confuse bruising with tattoo ink, as in Aristophanes' *Wasps*, where Xanthias says that he is στιζόμενος by a stick.[21] In a reverse case in Revelation 17: 5, the whore of Babylon has her trade written on her forehead. Travesty in classical tattooing is most evident in the *Satyricon* of Petronius. The male lovers Encolpius and Giton attempt to evade one of their many sexual farragoes by painting their faces as if punished with a *stigma*.[22] Pretending to be slaves on the run, they hope to go unpunished. As ever it is a cock-up.

Early Christianity shows the sensitivity of *stigma*. Cyprian in the third century CE expresses concern about condemned clerics receiving a *secunda inscriptio* on the forehead.[23] The 'first inscription' in this context implies the invisible mark made by baptism, now contradicted by punitive action under the persecution of the emperor Valerian.[24] During the Arian controversy a century later, Hilary complains that orthodox Trinitarian bishops have been tattooed on their foreheads.[25] An earlier edict by the emperor Constantine in 316 commanded that markings on the face should be banned, because 'fashioned in the likeness of the divine beauty'.[26] Inscription should take place on hands, or calves, only. However, in a direction of counter-travesty, *stigmata* could be redescribed as a badge of honour. Mark Gustafson calls the contrary process 'voluntary tattooing'.[27] A Manichean has the words 'Mani the disciple of Jesus Christ' written on his thigh. Procopius of Gaza reports many Christians marking their wrists or arms with the name of Christ or the sign of the cross.[28] This appears in a commentary on Isaiah, where the idea of reclaiming identity on the body with the sign of the Lord is a recuperation from the outright condemnation in Leviticus. Perhaps the most interesting example is from the Byzantine era. The iconoclastic emperor Theophilus punished two brothers Theodore and Theophanes for the crime of worshipping images by first beating them and then tattooing them with twelve lines of cod poetry on their faces. They later became saints, under the reverently uncanny name of the *graptoi*, 'the Inscribed'.[29]

Baptism and iconoclasm show a deeper ambivalence in identity suggested by a tattoo. This reaches beyond the comfortable model of graphic art and self-expression proposed as motivations for modern tattoos. As late as *Walden* in 1854, Thoreau defends tattooing against stereotype of 'hideous custom'.[30] Melville thought 'tattoo' related to a similar-sounding Polynesian word 'taboo'.[31] This word, too, was first encountered by Cook; he thought it 'of very comprehensive meaning', suggesting a sensitive semantic range such as 'consecrated, inviolable, forbidden, unclean, or cursed'.[32] It is clear to Melville that 'tattoo' was also 'a religious observance', but like 'taboo', he found it at some level 'inexplicable'.[33] From the anthropology of Polynesian languages, Freud derived 'the oldest unwritten code of law of humanity'.[34] It is akin to the Roman concept *sacer*, or the Hebrew word קֹדֶשׁ (*kodesh*), that which is separate or set apart. This is what Marcel Mauss and Émile Durkheim called 'the ambiguous character of sacred things'.[35] The Talmud describes the holy of holies as a cube containing the tablets of the covenant.[36] Somewhere, somehow, writing is always hidden. One of Freud's taboo patients avoided writing her name for fear it would get into the wrong hands, to threaten her personality. Eventually she gave up writing altogether.[37] Taboo is 'older than the gods', says Freud.

In *Moby-Dick*, Queequeg reproduces the 'queer round figure' of the tattoo on his arm as his signature on paper: Captain Peleg over-interprets it as a cross to classify him as a Christian.[38] Compare the curious fate of pagan Aphrodite or Venus in the Roman Empire, in this first-century CE head (Fig. 65), made in Athens in the Praxitelean style. At a later date, the eyes of the statue have been gouged and the mouth damaged. The act of blinding and muting the goddess is then completed by marking her forehead with the sign of the cross. She has been mutilated but also Christianized, perhaps an example of repurposing pagan figuration in Christian terms. Or is it perhaps a branding, an enslavement of the old religion to the new, in a reversal of Christian persecution? Inscription is essential to the objectification of the body which takes place in the punishment of a crime, says Foucault. The submission of the body is simultaneous with the representational subjection of the mind, which is made 'a surface of inscription for power, with semiology as its tool'.[39] The blank stare of the marble goddess makes this only the more clear in its abstraction: the body is marked by power, pure and simple.

The extreme example is tattooing at Auschwitz, by which prisoners were marked for ever with a number on the left arm: 'baptized', as Levi calls it with lethal irony.[40] Foucault draws attention to the literalness of the law in this respect. In eighteenth-century France, the traitor wears a red coat, on which is inscribed, back and front, the word 'traitor'. A parricide has his head veiled and the image of

Fig. 65. 'Converting pagan gods': damaged head of Aphrodite, marble, 1st c. CE.
Athens, National Archaeological Museum

a dagger on his shirt. In Bavaria, a poisoner is dressed in a red shirt embroidered
with snakes.[41] Lévi-Strauss found a similar dynamic in tattooing in the practice of
the Māori people. Its cultural purpose was, he said, 'to stamp onto the mind all the
traditions and philosophy of the group'.[42] However, in an anthropological analysis
of Polynesian tattooing, Alfred Gell distinguished between the 'outside-facing'
skin and the 'inside-facing' skin. Rather than the marking of the body being one-
directional, he described a 'traffic, mediated by the skin': 'the skin continually
communicates the external world to the internal one, and the internal world to
the external one'.[43] The skin conveys subjectivity as well as depriving it. In appearance, the goddess looks like a forced convert who has taken on the sign of the
cross in reversal of paganism. If Aphrodite could speak, what would she
feel inside?

Judith Butler objects to Foucault that in some circumstances the body acts as
'surface and resistance' which can disrupt the 'regulatory practices' of a regulating
régime.[44] Butler argues that bodily inscription is a paradox, caught between exter-
nalization and internalization, in a similar way to Gell's argument about
Polynesian culture. In Japan, likewise, punitive acts of tattooing become replaced
by the voluntary art of *irezumi*. The punitive form was non-representational;

irezumi as a figurative art was used at first to hide the mark of stigma, then flourished as representational body art in its own right.[45] In medieval Jerusalem, pilgrims would acquire tattoos as souvenirs of the journey and as marks of faith, inscribing the names of Jesus or Mary or else the sign of the cross.[46] In 1612, William Lithgow put away Scottish Presbyterian taboo so as to combine a tattoo of the Jerusalem Cross with one of the crown of his king, James VI and I of Scotland and England.[47] Convicts transported to Australia between 1817 and 1853 were identified by name and physical description by the authorities. A piece of tattooed skin surviving in the collections of Guy's Hospital in London shows an illiterate convict turning the tables: remaking his own life in his own image, he has represented Adam and Eve, alongside the symbol of the Hope and Anchor, a common trope of convict autonomy.[48] In the Soviet Gulag, prisoners in concentration camps tattooed their heads with the words 'prisoner of Brezhnev'.[49] The ironic act of self-branding at once parades a travesty of the action of the powerful, and at the same time subverts it by enabling an act of subjective autonomy. Yet the irony, too, is prone to further degradation. In the *Genealogy of Morals*, Nietzsche describes internalization as a form of enslavement.[50]

Freud in *Totem and Taboo* extended his general discussion to cover the 'giving of names'. Naming is 'the essence of totemism' and a part of the 'technique of primitive writing'.[51] For Foucault it is one more step to the argument in *Surveiller et punir* that crime and punishment are discursive as well as physical. Punishment works in encoding semiological control, manifested in legislation, confession, or denunciation.[52] Within the system, literal inscription is inherent to punishing crime, which is made evident to all, to the perpetrator as much as to the public that bears witness. The law 'explains, justifies itself, convicts: placards, different-coloured caps bearing inscriptions, posters, symbols, texts read or printed, tirelessly repeat the code'.[53] Foucault's evidence is based on *ancien régime* France, but can be found in Tudor England. Thomas More campaigned rigorously against Lutheran heresy in 1529.[54] A proclamation listed proscribed opinions but did not proscribe specific books.[55] Another followed in June 1530, naming books for the first time, specifically by Tyndale, Frith, and Simon Fish, along with English translations of the Bible, in pursuit of More's earlier arguments. 'Having respect to the malignity of the present time', the proclamation declares, the vernacular Bible will only add to 'the inclination of people to erroneous opinion'.[56]

In 1530, More used prerogative powers of Star Chamber to extend prosecution of heresy into censorship. It was the first foray of the English state into such areas. On 25 October, arrests were made of John Porseck, a man named 'Seymour', and some associates. The charge was 'having books against the king's proclamation'.[57] The men were sent to the Tower of London, and then subjected to a peculiar form of 'public penance'.[58] They were led through the streets of London on horseback, facing back-to-front. The deposition stipulated that they were to wear papers declaring the details of their humiliation on their bodies. After this, Protestant books would be burned at Cheapside. Another case in London repeated More's practice from the first. Bishop Stokesley sent to More further prisoners accused of distributing Tyndale's New Testament. They included Tyndale's brother John, and the merchant Thomas Patmer. Examined in Star Chamber by More himself, the same penance on horseback was repeated.[59] Their coats were 'pinned thick' with the proscribed books found in their possession; they were humiliated using rotten fruit as in the stocks; books burned.

The punishment carries a clear structure of travesty and formal degradation, in which the accused bears inscription of crimes upon the body. Yet in Foxe a generation later (of a merchant, Thomas Sommers), the event is reclaimed with a kind of carnivalesque fury:

> he should ryde from the Tower into Cheapside carying a new booke in his hande, and behanged with bookes rounde about him, with three or iiij. other Marchauntes after the same order.[60]

Sommers, however, turns the tables. The biblioclast meets a match in the heroic bibliolater. Sommers, Foxe narrates, interrupted the gaolers in scriptural haberdashery:

> I haue alwayes loued to goe hansomly in my apparell, & takyng the bookes and openyng them, he bound them together by the stringes and cast them about his necke (the leaues beyng all open) like a coller

In a curiously ritualized action, he turns books into artful bibliophile neckwear. In one direction, Sommers secularizes the gesture, calling it 'apparell' in a conscious visual joke. Yet he also appears to reclaim the sacred status of the book to derive his own identity as a martyr to the cause as a bastion of the holy in the Babylonian captivity of the Church.

This mark of transgressive reappropriation is continued in the climax to Foxe's narrative, the burning of Tyndale's New Testament in a public display of bibliophobia:

> But when M. sommers saw that his new Testament should be burned, he threwe it ouer the fire: which was seene by some of Gods enemyes, and brought to him agayn, commaundyng hym to cast it into the fire: which hee would not do, but cast it thorow the fire. Which thyng was done .iij. times. But at last a stander by tooke it vp, and saued it from burning.

What exactly is the status of the book as object here? For a writer of Foxe's stamp, the consistent view would to deny books, or other objects, having sacred value. Yet the lines between image and book, or object and subject, have become blurred. Sommers and his fellows find the word crossing a physical boundary and inhering within a book's covers. Yet still it is not quite plain what it is imagined is happening here. This is not a miracle story, but of value being placed in a book as object by its human readers. They wish to protect it, rather than pray to be protected by it, and so save the book from burning.

Punishment in Foxe is marked via the body, as in the confession of Robert Barnes:

> kneling vpon his knees, he consented to abiure, and the abiuration put in hys hand, he abiured as it was there wrytten, and then he subscribed with his owne hand.[61]

Subscription takes place on the knees and in and with the hand. Indeed, Foxe widens the field of inscription on the body to make the structure of the body mirror the form of a book. In the case of John Porter, punished for the crime of reading the Bible, he describes first how the new English Bibles are chained inside the church. The book is anthropomorphized by its suffering position, or process of enforcement. When Edmund Bonner, the Bishop of London, who has allowed the printing of the vernacular Bible only on sufferance, catches sight of Porter, he 'rebuked hym very sharpely for hys readyng', and places him in a punishment which strangely mirrors the posture of the book: 'Boner sent him to Newgate, where he was miserably fettred in yrons both legges and armes, with a coller of yron about hys necke fastened to the wall in the dungeon'.[62]

In Porter's punishment the body undergoes transference, taking on the character of a book. His body imitates the suffering book, deriving sanctity from conformity. The book is martyr and heretic, similar to the Ragyndrudis Codex. Yet Foxe interprets the image in different fashion. First, he describes the treatment of books as a reverse iconoclasm, so that biblioclasm becomes a true mark of the sacred. As with early Christian narratives of *stigmata*, he links this to travesty. The sacred book is subjected to insult and injury, yet humiliation becomes a triumph of the oppressed. An indivisible connection between body and book survives but is transformed in the process. It is not the body of the saint conferring holiness on the book, but the book conveying holiness to a reader.

Foxe redraws sacred boundaries in two of the most perverse narrations in his whole work, combining disinterment and desecration of human remains. Wyclif, distinguished Oxford philosopher, escaped formal condemnation to die of natural causes in 1384.[63] But the Council of Constance on 4 May 1415, proclaimed him heretic in death. In Foxe's pithy summary, the Council concluded 'in condemning hys bookes, then of his articles, and afterward burning of his bones'. Orders are made for 'all such bookes, treatises, volumes, & workes' to be found, and then 'to burne & consume them with fire'.[64] Books were burned at Carfax in Oxford in 1411.[65] Yet elimination is not sufficient; the body must be consumed. While Wyclif was already dead and buried – better late than never – his remains were burned in 1428.[66] With gruesome relish, Foxe relates how the skeleton was dug up from the ground at Lutterworth church, the ashes thrown into the River Swift. His publisher, John Day, commissioned a woodcut image, in which an archdeacon gleefully tosses a bone into fire; in iconic tribute, far left a skull is in flames.

Such events reinterpret the religious past into Foxe's lifetime. In Book 12 of *Actes and Monuments*, he recounts how in the reign of Mary (when Foxe was in exile in Basel with the printer Oporinus), Cardinal Reginald Pole made a visitation of Cambridge University: 'which place', Foxe says archly, 'especially seemed to have nede of reformation'. His account is based on an eyewitness version by Conrad Hubert, published in Latin and German.[67] An indictment was made at Great St Mary's, where Bucer, the German Protestant theologian, lay buried, having spent the last years of his life as Regius Professor in Cambridge; and at the grave of Paul Fagius (a continental Hebrew scholar) at St Michael's Church.[68] Bucer is exposed to posthumous examination. It is a weird exhumation: 'that his dead carkas might forthwith be digged vp (for so it was nedefull to be done) to the intent that inquisition might be made as touchyng hys doctrine'.[69] In legal charade, Bucer and Fagius are cited for heresy; when (oddly enough), they fail to show up on demand, a scaffold is erected to denounce their crimes in public.

The travesty of ritual now enters its manic pomp. A full procession takes place, with the Mayor of Cambridge as secular power, priests in robes carrying banners and censers:

> This place was prepared before, and a great post was set fast in the ground to bynd the carcasses to, and a great heape of woode was layd ready to burne them withall. When they came thether, the chestes were set vp on end, with the dead bodyes in them, and fastened on both sides with stakes, and bound to the post with a long yron chayne, as if they had ben alyue. Fire beyng forthwith put to, as soone as it began to flame round about, a great sort of bookes that were condemned with them, were cast into the same.

Foxe adds a powerful layer of irony. A 'great multitude of countryfolke' arrives for market from villages outside Cambridge. Observing the condemned men are already dead, 'partly detested and abhorred the extreme cruelty of the Commissioners toward the rotten carcasses, and partly laughed at theyr folly in makyng such preparature'. Why were dead men so elaborately tied up? They could hardly 'runne away'.

In Day's woodcut (Fig. 66), the coffins are chained upright at the stake, in the posture of condemned bodies.[70] The crucial phrase in the indictment is 'as if they had ben alyue': it is a bodily mimesis. Bucer's books, acting as tinder, also form substitutes for Bucer's body. Two men take books from a basket (far right) at the foot of the pyre, throwing them into the flames. Above and to the side, single leaves of dismembered books fly up in the force of the updraught. A grand

Fig. 66. 'Burning bones and books'; *The burning of Mayster Bucers and Paulus Phagius bones and burning of theyr bookes with a solemn procession*, John Foxe, *Actes and Monuments* (London: John Day, 1570)

procession encircles the bonfire, a banner of the pope and crucified Christ aloft. Some hold lighted torches, others carry books and rosaries. There is a canopy with a bishop or other dignitary underneath. A caption reads *Salue festa dies*. This is a ritual incorporation of heretical books and bodily remains.

The whole is carefully reminiscent of contemporary prints of an auto-da-fé, grand public displays such as that of Valladolid in May 1559 which Foxe's printer Day produced in 1569 in a translation of a description of the Spanish Inquisition by Reginaldus Gonsalvius Montanus.[71] The woodcut shows a composite archetypal scene with the stake at the epicentre.[72] There are two scaffolds, one to the left for the prisoner, the other to the right for the Inquisitors. Two processions encircle, the first formal, led by priests and choirboys singing from open books, followed by candle-bearers; then the penitent in costumes bearing inscriptions; then the condemned in chains; then secular and ecclesiastical dignitaries on horseback. The Valladolid woodcut helped create the *leyenda negra* by which English Protestantism characterised the bloodthirsty habits of the Spanish.[73] It was a characteristic of the Inquisition in Spain, as in heresy trials in general, that books were equivalent to human bodies. This was part of a shared language of punishment: as the body is burned, so is the book, in a procedure of immolation. In Spanish trials, if a heretic was not present, the body was burned in effigy.

In this sense the book is an effigy of an effigy. As late as the nineteenth century, the mark of the heretic is written on the body. Between 1808 and 1814, Francisco de Goya y Lucientes sketched nearly forty brush and ink drawings collected in his Album C. Goya earlier produced parodies of the Spanish Inquisition in his engravings known as *Los Caprichos*, and in the paintings, *The Holy Office* and *Tribunal of the Inquisition*.[74] After autos-da-fé were abolished in 1689, burnings were rare and concealed. In 1814, after the Napoleonic wars, despite a campaign for abolition, the Inquisition was confirmed by the absolutist government of Ferdinand VII.[75] Around half of Album C is devoted to drawings in which penitents wear badges of shame: the *sanbenito*, a garment similar to a scapular in yellow with red saltires; and the *coroza*, a conical hat made of paper, of different colours according to the condemnation. Goya's images cite in ironic detail what Foucault calls the discursive regime of punishment, the semantic detailing of indictment and confession, contrasted with the miserable bodily humiliation of the accused.[76] Each image is titled with a mock indictment beginning P^r ('for') and then replicating the judicial formulae used by inquisitors in trial records. The sardonic edge is most evident in 'For discovering the movement of the earth', in which Galileo is presented between blocks of immoveable stone. The abyss between judgement and rational justice is all the more painful in P^r *hober nacido en otra parte* ('For having been born somewhere else') and P^r *linage de ebreos* ('For being of Jewish ancestry').[77]

Goya used the finest French paper for these drawings, giving them a luminosity in contrast to his use elsewhere of irongall ink, a mixture of brown and grey tones.[78] In P^r *mober lo lengua de otro modo* (C89: 'For wagging his tongue in a different way'), Goya presents a prisoner in the foreground, prosecutor and tribunal in shady background.[79] The charges are written on the *sanbenito*, rendered by the artist as illegible scribbling. The saltire of the tunic appears in ironic double meaning as a cross in a mark of erasure. The *coroza*, too, appears as gibberish. P^r *que sabia hacer Ratones* (C87: 'Because she knew how to make mice') deals with a case of supposed witchcraft (Fig. 67).

Here the savage ironies of inscription and identity are at their most obscene. A woman is seated on a raised platform for full display; her mouth is gagged, her hands and feet are bound together. Inscription appears as an act of violence: in place of the saltire on the *sanbenito*, her charges are handwritten on her body in cross formation against her heart: 'They put a gag on her because she talked. And struck her in the face'.[80] Goya interpolates his own person in her defence, adding to the charges *Yo la bi*, as if to say, 'I saw her.' The woman's *coroza* is daubed with images of mice, in place of the devils that appeared in the sixteenth century,

Fig. 67. 'Graffiti on the body'; Francisco de Goya, *P^r que sabia hacer Ratones*, brush, bougainvillea and brown ink wash, bougainvillea pen ink on paper, 1810–11. Madrid, Museo Nacional del Prado, D04055

signifying death by burning. The woman herself, while speechless, expresses with her eyes her outrage. As in the *stigma* of the tattoo, inscription here forms an act of ironic retrieval, as the indictment is adopted as a kind of badge of pride by the condemned. Writing and the body are tied together by hidden bonds. The book crosses over the realm of the sacred and of the forbidden.

20
Book Burial

The Buddha at the end of his natural life left directions for the disposal of his body. Having already attained nirvāṇa in life, after death he underwent *parinirvāṇa*, a nirvāṇa-in-death. Meanwhile the Buddha's earthly remains are to be cremated by his disciples and his ashes buried within a large mound named a *stūpa*. This is the account given in the *Mahāparinibbāṇa Sutta* originally written in the Pali language perhaps in the fourth century BCE. The last words of the Buddha appear here as *vayadhammā saṅkhārā appamādena sampādethā*: 'All composite things are perishable. Strive with diligence for your own liberation.'[1] A historical site for the mound was identified in the third century BCE by the Emperor Ashoka at Kuśinārā, now Kushinagar in Uttar Pradesh in northern India.[2] Ashoka constructed an elaborate *stūpa* there, later enlarged into a temple with a great reclining statue of the Buddha.[3] After the Muslim invasion in the twelfth century CE the monks abandoned the site, which was only rediscovered in the nineteenth century by British archaeologists, who unearthed the 1,500-year-old Buddha image.[4]

Buddhism is a religion of reliquaries, containers for the remainder of the human body after death. The cremation relics of the Buddha were divided between eight royal families for veneration; Ashoka was said to have created 84,000 *stūpa*s for them.[5] After the dispersal of the original pilgrimage sites, body parts of the Buddha came to light all over Asia. In Kandy in Sri Lanka there is the Temple of the Tooth; in Colombo, the Gangaramaya Temple houses some of the Buddha's hair. Over time, reliquaries became increasingly elaborate, taking the form of the pagoda in East Asia and the *chedi* in Thailand. So much for the literal sense of the *stūpa*. However, the *stūpa* also has a vibrant figurative life in Mahāyāna Buddhist texts. In ch. 11 of the Lotus Sūtra, an enormous *stūpa* emerges out of the earth, measuring thousands of metres high and wide.[6] It floats in the sky above the disciples, who hear the voice of the Buddha from inside. The door of the *stūpa* opens: it contains not relics but a second living buddha, named Prabhūtaratna. He declares that, wherever he is taught, his *stūpa* will appear. In this version (Fig. 68) of the Lotus Sūtra, dated 1257 CE, from the Kamakura period in Japan, the text is inscribed by Sugawara Mitsushige. The coloured illustration shows the two buddhas revealed behind the open door of the *stūpa*, deep among the clouds.

What we have in this tradition, then, is a principle of duplication or even proliferation. The image of two buddhas seated side by side inside a *stūpa* is a widespread motif in Mahāyāna Buddhist art. Relics meanwhile are found everywhere in Buddhist religious practice. *Śarīraḥ* means 'body' in Sanskrit; in the plural,

Fig. 68. 'Text as relic'; Mitsushige Lotus Sūtra, handscroll, ink, colour, and gold on paper, 1257 CE. New York, Metropolitan Museum, 53.7.3

śarīrāḥ means relics, which include pieces of bone as well as the cremated remains of the Buddha or other spiritual masters; in addition, the pearl- or crystal-like bead-shaped detritus that are believed to emanate from cremation. Stories have been told of pearls of *śarīra* raining down during funerals of eminent monks. Relics are said to have apotropaic qualities, warding off evil or bringing good luck, or else conveying blessings to those in contact with them.[7] Yet in an extended sense the Dharma of the Buddha, his teachings or wisdom or doctrine, can be considered *śarīra* as it appears in textual form within *sūtras*.[8] As the essence of the Buddha himself, a *sūtra* came to be equivalent to a relic: a 'dharma body *śarīra*'.

The Lotus Sūtra since early times comprised a comprehensive teaching of Mahāyāna Buddhism. Originally in Sanskrit, it was translated several times into Chinese, including by the monk Kumārajīva, who reached the court of the Buddhist Emperor Yaoxing in 401 CE.[9] His translation was associated with a miracle which mystifies its physical formation: 'it is said that at the time of his cremation, his tongue remained unburnt'.[10] Ritual actions accompanied reading: bathing, wearing special clothes, burning incense. The Lotus Sūtra held special powers over the human body. A nun memorized the whole of the *sūtra* and recited it daily for twenty years; a voyeuristic official, who watched her, received a magical punishment in which his penis dropped off.[11] In compensation for this miraculous connection between text and body, bodily actions were prescribed: for each Chinese character (there are 69,384 in the text), monks and nuns conducted a separate prostration, in which they knelt and touched the ground with their heads.

In the culture of the *sūtra*, the copying and recitation of the text was more than a practical or instrumental act. Precious materials were used, as well as the most expensive paper and binding materials. Dharma or the Buddha's teaching was in a process of degeneration, consisting of three epochs: zheng fa ('True Dharma'), when the Buddha's revelation of enlightenment was directly available; xiang fa ('Semblance Dharma'), during which teachings continued in an enfeebled replica of truth; and mofa ('Final Dharma'), where Buddhist practice disappears and even sacred texts are destined to vanish. Five practices were considered essential for the promulgation of dharma: copying, preserving, reading, reciting, and explaining. Elaborate rituals for copying the Lotus Sūtra developed in China and then made their way to Japan. The monks of the Chinese Tiantai, followed by the Tendai sect in Japan, created rules in which each part of the process had to be performed by a monk: growing the hemp in order to make the paper; making brushes from grass which he also grew; making the ink from graphite. No animal products could be used in this process.

It was in Japan that this tradition around the Lotus Sūtra became strongest. Every character of the Lotus Sūtra came to be considered a living buddha. The monk Ennin turned the text of the *sūtra* into literal instructions to be performed over and again: 'Wherever this *sūtra* is taught, read, recited, copied, or wherever it is found, one should build a seven-jeweled stūpa of great height and width and richly ornamented.' [12] There is no need for a relic inside, as the *sūtra* itself is a relic, indeed it is the body of the Buddha. Japanese copies of the Lotus Sūtra included illustrations in which each character is drawn inside in a *stūpa*, each enshrined as a buddha would be.[13] Some copies foreword each of the ten scrolls with a frontis-piece on indigo paper, focusing on a gold pagoda nine storeys high, with two bud-dhas sitting together inside. Text interweaves with image: the drawing of the pagoda is formed out of characters taken from the *sūtra*. In this way, the copying of the *sūtra* is turned into the building of a *stūpa*.

In the eleventh century CE, the practice began in Japan of burying the *sūtra*. The sacred text, even though copied at great expense, was never intended to be read: instead it was consecrated, enshrined, and then placed within a temple or inside a sacred mountain.[14] The interment of the books accompanied the same ritual actions as for the burial of the dead. However, the object of the ceremony was not mourning but survival. Inscriptions sometimes declare the *sūtra* is a kind of 'time capsule', buried during *Mappō* (Japanese for 'Final Dharma'), and ready to be unearthed in the far distant future when Maitreya achieves buddhahood, cal-culated to the little sum of 5.67 billion years.[15] The *sūtra* was buried in a cylinder, often bronze, and this cylinder was contained once again inside a second casing of stone or ceramic. This would be placed into an underground chamber lined with stone and even packed in a preservative layer of charcoal. The chamber was marked with a gravestone inside a mound surmounted by a *stūpa*.[16] One such twelfth-century CE Japanese bronze cylinder (Fig. 69) in the Kaikodo collection has a lid in the style of a pagoda and elaborate seals.[17] Most often the interred text was a Lotus Sūtra.

Fig. 69. '*Sūtra* mound'; *Sūtra* container, bronze, 11th–12th c. Kaikodo
Collection, Hawaii

The *Sensoji kyo* manuscript from Sensoji temple in Tokyo has a text in ten volumes, copied by a single calligrapher on decorated paper, dyed brown with clove
extract. Max Moerman identifies such examples of 'bibliolatry' as entirely in keeping with the sacramental logic of Mahāyāna Buddhism.[18] After they were buried,
less secure containers became damaged and the text sometimes decayed. Seashell
texts have survived in such cases from the sixteenth century, inscribed with *sūtra*
text; or even stones with a single character on them. Such practices reflect the
increasingly esoteric practices of Nichiren Buddhism. One monk in veneration
for the Lotus Sūtra declares that he who 'discards even a single character or dot
commits an offense greater than killing his father and mother a thousand or ten

thousand times'.[19] *Namu Myōhō Renge Kyō* (南無妙法蓮華經), referring to the Japanese title of the *sūtra*, became a mantra; the Buddha was said to have 'wrapped up a jewel within the five characters and hung it from the necks of the immature beings of the last age'.[20] On Sado Island, more than 100 *honzon* survive, calligraphic objects of devotion representing the scene at Vulture Peak when the assembly rises in mid-air to venerate the two buddhas.[21] Yet the character of text is suffused by belatedness: meaning is immanent within burial, ready to come into being when the Buddha returns. Japanese Buddhism buried the text to preserve it, a virtually infinite deferral until a time so far off it can barely be imagined.

It is not only in a belief in the power of relics that early Christianity bears similarity with Buddhism. Sacred text in both cases is not only a repository of doctrinal meanings but a holding place for the divine being: not only the site where God is found, but where he is. Sacred books from very early times have a ritual purpose as well as an evangelical one. Constantine ordered fifty volumes of the divine scriptures, with ornamental binding, legible and portable, to be copied 'for reading in church'.[22] Paul the Silentiary's poem describing the inauguration of Hagia Sophia in Constantinople in 562 CE records that the book of gospels was raised in procession through the church.[23] The design of early bindings also suggests that books were carried above the head by bishops or priests, and were meant to be seen, touched, or kissed, as objects of reverence.[24]

In sixth-century CE mosaics at the Basilica of San Vitale in Ravenna, the four gospels are placed on four different altars (Ch. 1, Fig. 2). Relics increasingly were buried in the foundations. The ceremonial entrance of the gospel, marking the beginning of the liturgy, was understood as a procession in which the altar, as Christ's resting place, represented the last post.[25] Holy books thus have a natural affinity with tombs and altars. At the very period at which Christian liturgy became formalized in early sacramentaries, gospel books provided the focal point of ritual.[26] Liturgy in general can be said to incorporate the book, or else make the body part of the book. In Jewish ritual, the Torah is read four times a week; when the scroll is taken out of the Ark, congregants may touch it with their hands or a prayer shawl. When the reading begins, the scroll is lifted above the head of the speaker.[27] At the Seder table, the Haggadah is chanted.[28] Central to Muslim liturgy is *rak'a*. Verbal formulae combine with intricate series of physical movements: standing, bowing, kneeling, and prostrating. In dawn prayer, hands are raised level with the earlobes, as the *fātiḥa* and a *sūra* from the Qur'an are recited. Attention of the ear and heart are one.[29] Early Christian books are often understood not so much as texts as a 'visual argument' in which a sense of the holy is enshrined.[30]

The book thus becomes a kind of shrine. It is not surprising to find receptacles designed for carrying holy books at this period resembling reliquaries in appearance. One such is the so-called Throne of St Mark, long associated with a relic of the true cross supposedly given to the patriarch at Grado in northern Italy by the Emperor Heraclius, who rescued it from the Persian emperor Chosroes II. The strange design of this 'throne' allowed the true cross to be displayed as it was stored inside while a gospel could be placed on top. This is similar in type to one in the Syriac–Coptic monastery of St Jerome in Saqqara. A throne in Aachen also has space for a relic inside. The object at Grado is, in Cynthia Hahn's well-chosen words, 'both buried and displayed treasure'.[31]

A more literal connection between literary and corporeal remains is a book known as the Cuthbert Gospel (purchased in 2012 after a fundraising campaign by the British Library). A twelfth-century inscription in the book states it 'was found lying at the head of our blessed father Cuthbert in his tomb (*in sepulcro*) in the year of his translation'.[32] This records the last stage of Cuthbert's long journey after death, arriving in 1104 in the still newish Benedictine priory and cathedral of Durham. The book was now several hundred years old. It is no longer thought to be from Cuthbert's lifetime; Richard Gameson dates its script to just after the Codex Amiatinus, in the early eighth century.[33] Gameson is doubtful the book was designed for interment, certainly not the construction of the shrine at Lindisfarne in 698. However, this does not diminish a retrospective association of the book with the body of the saint. The twelfth-century *Historia translationum* records the temerity of the first monk to open Cuthbert's coffin in Durham, or astonishment at finding a little gospel of St John on a shelf next to the saint's head.[34] Somebody, after all, at some point buried the book inside a coffin.

One theory is that the book (Fig. 70) is similar in kind to Irish so-called 'pocket gospels', a term invented by Patrick McGurk (in a riff on the popular series *Livre de poche* begun in Paris in 1953). In that way the book is a last remainder of the origin of the gospels as literary documents, similar to other biographies of late antiquity.[35] Whether the purpose of the Irish books was personal or 'pocketbook' in nature is unlikely; however, several came to be associated with relics and were buried in coffins. While it is often said that the Cuthbert Gospel survives so perfectly because of protection within a tomb, contact with nails and metal nameplates damaged some of them. One of the most interesting, the Stowe Missal, has extracts from John's gospel along with a Missal and a treatise on the Mass. At the end it contains spells against loss of eyesight and diseases of urine. It was placed in a shrine in Tipperary in the eleventh century, opened by chance in 1733.[36] Closer in appearance to the Cuthbert Gospel is a tiny copy of John, probably Italian from the fifth/sixth century, now in Paris. It contains an image of the cross, recalling John's presence at the crucifixion; and marks out the verse *Ego sum uitis vera* ('I am the true vine'), a line which appears to have inspired the floral design of the binding of the Cuthbert book. It also contains a paper note declaring that the book was found inside 'la chemise de la Vierge', confirming its discovery inside a medieval reliquary containing the undergarment of the Virgin Mary, the most precious relic of Chartres Cathedral.[37]

In any event, the lections marked in the Cuthbert Gospel show its association on first use with masses for the dead. By the time it was found in 1104, it had

Fig. 70. 'A saint's pocket-book'; Cuthbert Gospel, binding, birch boards covered with decorated red goatskin, 8th c. London, British Library Add. MS 89000

come to share space inside Cuthbert's coffin with a number of secondary relics of the saint. Among these are textiles, a pectoral cross, a comb and scissors, a small portable altar, and a chalice and paten. At later times, other books were added to the saintly hoard. It is hardly surprising, then, to find that stories collected quickly about the miraculous powers of the book. Bishop Ranulf Flambard, during a sermon at the reburial in Durham, displayed the gospel in mysteriously perfect condition. It was placed in a red leather satchel tied with frayed silken threads.[38] The condition of the book appears to this day as something of a miracle. When the book was examined in 1806 at the Society of Antiquaries of London, the script was compared with the Lindisfarne Gospels, and the binding (it was said) 'seems to be of the time of Queen Elizabeth'.[39] That was 900 years out; by the 1860s the binding was redated to be contemporary with the creation of the manuscript. This makes it the oldest surviving intact example of Western bookbinding. In tooled red goatskin, with uniquely raised motif, its geometrical decoration recalls insular manuscript design, and the interlace border relates to Anglo-Saxon metalwork. As Arnold Hunt commented charitably, the Antiquaries' mistake is not surprising; even now, the binding is in better state than books of fifty years old (Fig. 70).

There is little doubt that its uncannily pristine condition was felt from early time to have something in common with the incorruptible body of the saint. Bede reports the discovery of the immaculate body in his *Life of Cuthbert*, the bishop kissing the clothes the saint had worn.[40] Cuthbert died on Lindisfarne on 20 March 687. Disinterred and reburied in 698, his remains, it was said, had not decayed after eleven years in the ground. As with the contemporary case of Æthelthryth, abbess of Ely, the uncorrupted body at the moment of translation was taken as proof that the saint had found favour with God. The book acquired a similar status and shared the holy qualities of Cuthbert's earthly remains. When one of Bishop Flambard's assistants in Durham stole a thread from the frayed sling containing the gospel, and used it to tie his shoe, his leg swelled up in physical consequence of his crime. He was only cured after the Prior told him to propitiate the saint by putting the thread back with the book in the tomb.

Identifying the saint's book with his body acquired validity from proximity within the tomb. Does sanctity transfer itself through physical contact, or through metonymic association? We can hardly say. The *Historia translationum* records an anecdote that Cuthbert wore the gospel round his neck, just as the Paris jewel-book was found wrapped in a cloth which had touched the Virgin's skin. By the time of John of Salisbury, it was said that Cuthbert had cured the sick by a laying-on of the gospel, a tale not recorded in any Life of Cuthbert, such as Bede's. Reginald of Durham, also in the twelfth century, seems to have been conflating more than one tradition when he reported a monk wearing a *vita* round his neck. Reginald also says that when William Fitzherbert, Archbishop of York, visited Cuthbert's tomb in about 1153, the sacristan, dressed in an alb, carried the gospel ceremonially to the high altar and hung it round the archbishop's neck, tied by its sling. William opened it and showed it to those around him. At a quiet moment after the feast, a lay-brother and scribe called John could not help himself. Taking the book from what now seems to have been a triple covering of red satchels, he sneaked away to examine the book at his leisure, with unwashed hands, Reginald adds. He too, was taken ill with a fever and had to seek the intercession of the saint.[41]

Durham Priory was dissolved in December 1539. At this point, the book, preserved among the holiest relics of northern England's most important saint, disappeared from view. Archbishop James Ussher mentions it in the possession of the antiquarian Thomas Allen of Gloucester Hall in Oxford in the seventeenth century.[42] However, it was not in Allen's book catalogue, made in 1622; and did not join the rest of Allen's manuscripts when Sir Kenelm Digby donated them to the Bodleian Library in 1634.[43] There is little trace of it until it was presented to the Society of Jesus at their house in Liège in 1769 by the Revd Thomas Philips, who received it from the 3rd Earl of Lichfield. When the English Jesuits moved to Stonyhurst College it went with them. Despite Philips's recusant credentials, the Jesuit community does not seem to have been aware of the book's odour of sanctity until the nineteenth century, when it came to serious scholarly notice.

The book, we might say, is firmly secularized, turned from relic to antiquarian curiosity. Is it only age and evident beauty which make the hairs stand on the back of my neck in the Ritblat Gallery at the British Library? Like everything in the shrine of Cuthbert, the gospel was formally desacralized, dissolved, deconsecrated, in the savage ripping apart of the tomb in 1540. The 'visitation' of Dr Ley, Dr Henley, and Mr Blythman is described in a manuscript account of the priory's last years, now known as *The Rites of Durham*, written in 1593. King Henry VIII's commissioners brought a goldsmith who removed the gold and silver and precious stones, enough in value (it was said) to redeem a prince. Climbing on top of the chest containing the coffin, strongly bound in iron, the goldsmith took a hammer and smashed it open. The sight of the saint within was nonetheless a profound shock: 'thinking to haue found nothing but duste & bones', the goldsmith looked instead on an intact human body: 'and when they had openede yᵉ chiste they found him lyinge hole vncorrupt wᵗʰ his faice baire, and his beard as yt had bene a forth netts growthe, & all his vestmᵗ vpon him as he was accustomed to say mess wᵗʰ all'.[44]

Despite their best efforts, and the repeated cry of Dr Henley to 'cast downe his bones', the saint's body survived. The 1593 text attempts to reconstitute, or make whole again, rituals broken apart by the Reformation. It contains a liminal structure at the heart of its memorial function as a 'description or brief declaration of all the ancient Monuments Rites and Customes' of Durham.[45] We could characterize this as a dialectic of the full and empty. What was full has been emptied out; what was decorated is stripped; what was present is now absent. Where once was life, there is now only monument and memory. Deeply embedded here is a host of metaphors concerning containers, which no longer contain what they were built for, like Duffy's phrase, *The Stripping of the Altars*, or Shakespeare's line, as if straight out of a postcard of Rievaulx Abbey:

Bare ruin'd choirs, where late the sweet birds sang.[46]

The prime example in the *Rites of Durham* is the description of the choir of the now refounded cathedral. This first part of the work only survives in a manuscript which once belonged, appropriately enough, to Bishop Cosin, who used it to reimagine the Book of Common Prayer after 1660. For the writer of 1593, however, the choir is a place of irredeemable loss. It is extant, but redundant, obsolescent, extinct: defined by its closeness to a former shrine of the saint, a place no longer there. Over the high altar, he says there was 'placed in uery fine Alabaster the picture of our lady standinge in the midst, and the picture of Sᵗ Cuthb: on the one side and the picture of St Oswald on the other beinge all richly gilded'.[47] The image stands *in place of* the saint, a substitute in physical form. Here the text records an image now absent from us, the altar stripped. In imitation of this loss, it describes the elaborate sequence of containers that collectively encode the function of the altar as a secret lodging of the dead Christ. Within the choir there was suspended a rich and most sumptuous canopy for the sacrament. This container holds another, 'a marvellous fair pyx', underneath the canopy with the host inside it, and the pyx itself covered with a white cloth. This (as it were) Russian doll (host within pyx under cloth under canopy) of sacred containers prompts a sudden memory of event as well as space: the High Mass in the abbey church, the epistoler followed by two monks singing *Gloria Patri*, the revelation of the blessed sacrament of the altar, and in the midst of this, the gospel book: 'a maruelous faire booke which had the Epistles and Gospells in it, & did lay it on the altar the which booke had on the outside of the coueringe the picture of our sauiour Christ all of siluer of goldsmiths worke'.[48]

The book has a metonymic function in the presentation of the lost sacrament, just like the incorrupt body of the saint in the narrative of the shrine's defacement. The absent presence (or present absence) of the shrine is the centre of the manuscript's holy memory. Cuthbert's shrine brings forth an exalted and yearningly fulsome prose, yet the shrine is only an outward face to what lies within, carefully revealed in staged showings:

> at this feast and certaine other festiuall dayes in the time of deuine seruice they were accustomed to drawe vpp the couer of St Cuthberts shrine beinge of Wainescott where vnto was fastned vnto euy corner of ye s^d Cover to a loope of Iron a stronge Cord wc^h Cord was all fest together over ye Midst over ye Cover. And a strong rope was fest vnto ye loopes or bindinges of ye s^d Cordes wc^h runn vpp and downe in a pully vnder ye Vault wc^h was aboue over St Cuthb^{tes} feretorie for ye drawinge vpp of ye Cover of the s^d shrine and the s^d rope was fastned to a loope of Iron in ye North piller of ye ferretory: haueinge six silver bells fastned to ye s^d rope, soe as when ye cover of ye same was drawinge vpp ye belles did make such a good sound y^t itt did stirr all ye peoples harts that was wth in ye Church to repaire vnto itt.[49]

What lies within? The 'ferretory', a word derived from Latin *feretrum* and φέρετρον in Greek (from φέρω 'I carry'), is a carrier for housing the relics of a saint. We have already seen how for Cuthbert it was custom-made, a coffin with an inserted shelf containing further artefacts including the saint's gospel. The writer of the *Rites of Durham* has never seen the gospel within the shrine, evidently, or at least makes no mention of it. But he does remember a book, in the form of a wonderfully oblique reference to a legend from the saint's life. The 1593 text describes how, during the ninth-century translation of the body of Cuthbert by sea from

Chester-le-Street south to Crayke in Yorkshire on its way to Ripon, during 'boysterous windes and raginge waues', the book fell out of the ship into the bottom of the sea. Cuthbert appears to a monk in a vision, and concerned for the safety of his gospel, commands that he search for it up and down the seashore. It is found, three miles inland, driven there by some wave or wind or else some holy power. Like the uncorrupted body of the saint, the book is intact and untouched: 'wcʰ holy booke was far more beautifull and glorious to looke uppon both within and without then it was before, beinge nothinge blemished with the salt water, but polished rather by some heauenly hand, wcʰ did not a little increase theire ioy'.[50]

The description of the book (said to have a jewelled binding) does not match the Cuthbert gospel we know, and the author may have confused the copy given to Stonyhurst with another British Library treasure, the Lindisfarne Gospels. Yet its unblemished state is in line with the Cuthbert gospel, resonating with the 1593 witness's similar rendering of the saint's uncorrupted body. The book, like a shrine, acts as a *feretrum*, a carrier of the sacred. Yet it does so in a way more oblique than a reliquary containing a saint's body. As Brown remarks acutely, *praesentia* always held in it a paradox (or contradiction) between proximity and distance, identification with a specific site and a sense of the impossibility of ever finally reaching into that site, to the space within. The holy as a 'mere thing', Hegel says, has a 'character of externality'.[51] It exists, palpably. However, it therefore has to be sought in a specific location. Pilgrimage offered an (ultimately) unsatisfiable desire: promise of proximity and yet realisation of distance. Indeed, Alphonse Dupront suggests, this is the point of pilgrimage, 'une thérapie par l'espace', therapy provided by distance despite the difficulty of obtaining its object.[52] Brown argues that the physical lay-out of the grave as shrine articulated a sense of ultimate distance or denial, a final withholding of the sacred object:

> the shrine in late antiquity is an art of closed surfaces. Behind these surfaces, the holy lay, either totally hidden or glimpsed through narrow apertures. The opacity of the surfaces heightened an awareness of the ultimate unattainability in this life of the person they had travelled over such wide spaces to touch.[53]

The shrine is a disclosure and a closed surface. The holy is touchable and untouchable. Gabriel Josipovici calls it 'a journey into the experience of distance itself'.[54]

Book burial has served different purposes in different cultures. In the Jewish *genizah* it is associated with safe disposal. Such practices are not only ancient. The Copenhagen synagogue recently created a makeshift *genizah* in the graveyard as a resting place for texts. 'As the Torah lives, so a Torah scroll can die', says Rabbi Kathy Cohen of the Reformed Temple Emanuel. A New Jersey synagogue has created a ritual.[55] In the communication between sacred and everyday, connection is made between text and body. A text is a living thing, deserving respect in its passing. Something of the same is found early in Islam. Fragments of the Qur'an have been discovered in a small building inside the courtyard at the Umayyad Mosque in Damascus, among the earliest known texts.[56] They are from scrolls (like the Jewish Torah) as opposed to the dominant Islamic form of the codex. They survive at all only because buried behind the wall, as they wore out and became unusable. In 1972 at the Great Mosque at Sana'a in Yemen, when plaster was being removed, a stash of early manuscripts was found. Not realizing their significance, the workers packed them into potato sacks. They include the Sana'a Palimpsest.[57] Written in the Hijazi script, one Qur'anic text has been overwritten with another (Fig. 71).[58] The find drew attention to the materiality of the Qur'an, and at the same time the sensitivity attaching to its material state as a container of the sacred.

Somatic rules applying to handling the Qur'an are often noted. Busbecq, ambassador at the Ottoman Empire in the sixteenth century, observed it was a

Fig. 71. 'Burying the Qur'an'; palimpsest, ink on parchment, upper level 8th c. (?), lower level 7th c. (?). Yemen, Dār al-Makhṭūṭāt, Ṣan 'ā' 1 / DAM 01-27.1

fearful offence to sit on a copy, even by mistake. In the nineteenth century, Edward Lane, in a study of Egyptian social customs, remarks it was improper to hold the book below the girdle. Jacques Jomier in interviews in Egypt in the twentieth century heard that a Qur'an should be at the top of any pile of books. 'I believe in God, in his angels, in his books', said the man.[59] Today, it is commonplace for readers to sit on the floor, the book on a chair in front, an image found in Persian manuscripts showing a *maktab* in the fifteenth century.

In Q 56: 77, the Qur'an refers to itself as a 'preserved book' (*maknūn*), to be touched only by the purified. The essence of the book is the secret inside. At the same time, it provides boundaries for what is pure. Much discussion is given to whether non-Muslims may touch the Qur'an. Alternatively, boundaries exist in the dimensions of the book itself: its characters are holy, but the margins or binding maybe not. In Hinduism, the Vedas were considered an oral tradition: writing was unclean, like seeing a dead body or having sex, and purification needed before reciting Vedas. The *Mahābhārata* condemns anyone who sells the Vedas, or sets them in writing, declaring they will go to hell.[60] Yet in time, of course, Hindu sacred writing became central to its tradition. At this point, new negotiations took place over what Mary Douglas calls 'matter out of place'.[61] While funerals for Hindus customarily consist in cremation followed by scattering ashes over water, a version of burial was practised for special saints. This was known as *samādhi* ('coming together'), a word usually associated with deep meditation. Perhaps under the influence of Buddhist *stūpa*s, monuments came to be constructed for the interment of either full corpses or cremated ashes.[62] In Vrindavan on the banks of the river Yamuna in Uttar Pradesh, there is a sixteenth-century temple which contains the grave of *Chaitanya Mahaprabhu*. Nearby is an extraordinary *granthasamādhi*, or 'book tomb'.[63] While this case seems like a lonely example of Hindu veneration of the book, there are many other cases of the water immersion of books on the Yamuna or other places along the Ganges. It is not uncommon for a tourist to see a cremated book sailing past, alongside more familiar tales of the macabre involving burning bodies on water.

It is tempting for Western eyes to see in such practice signs of superstition or exoticism. Yet they are not so far away. A boundary between life and death is observed through writing. Books are used to contain secret messages for the living by the dead; or vice versa. Dante Gabriel Rossetti, when his wife Lizzie Siddal died of laudanum overdose in 1862, placed in her coffin two books, hidden in her hair: a Bible, and a manuscript of his own poems written while she lay ill. Regretting loss of the manuscript a few years later, he had a friend dig up the coffin to retrieve the book: it was wet, decayed, and worm-eaten, so only fragments remained legible.[64] Sir Thomas Browne wrote in *Urn-Buriall*:

> But who knows the fate of his bones, or how often he is to be buried? who hath the Oracle of his ashes, or whither they are to be scattered?[65]

From the seventeenth to the nineteenth century, the commonest term for the writing authors had left behind them was 'remains'. Books and bones at some level are part of the same signifying system. They are relics, remnants, revenants. The cemeteries of the nineteenth century, Samantha Matthews observes, are full of writing, just as Romantics from Byron to Tennyson thought of their writings as forms of sacred remembering.[66]

Perhaps the most striking example of book disposal in world religion is in Sikhism. After the age of human gurus—lasting over 200 years until the turn of the eighteenth century CE—the sacred Sikh scripture embodies divine presence, as a *textual* guru, known indeed as Guru Granth Sahib. In common speech a distinction is made between scripture as *jot* or *sarop*: the spirit of the meaning of the holy text, discussed in public readings or private meditation, versus the physical 'form' of the text.[67] It is not unlike the distinction in Latin Christianity between *spiritus* and *littera*, holy 'spirit' within outer shells of letters. Much Sikh worship surrounds the veneration of the *sarop* of the Guru Granth Sahib. In the Sikh place of worship (the *gurdwara* or 'guru's door') the sacred text is placed on a throne, draped in cloth, and decorated with ornaments. Before entering, women and men remove shoes and socks, wash hands and feet, and cover their heads. They are entering the presence of the holy. Devotion takes place in prostration. Whenever a reading stops, the book is covered, until at the end of the day, the book guru is closed ceremonially and carried in procession on the head of a barefoot attendant, to rest the night alone. It is a mistake to maintain a rigid distinction between presence and absence, or subject and object. For *praesentia* is not something bodily or inhabited: it is always a form of metonymy. It is a process of transference: from living person to body in grave; from body to site; or site to cult. In the presence of the book we live and die.

VI

GHOST IN THE BOOK

Ainsi, lecteur, je suis moy-mesmes la matiere de mon livre
Michel de Montaigne, 'Au Lecteur' (1580)

21
The Book After the French Revolution

The body of the writer lies slumped in front of us (Pl. 4), his pen still caught between the thumb and forefinger of his right hand, his left gripping a freshly inscribed letter in his own handwriting. Writing is his final mortal act. His head, following the direction of his right hand, has jerked backwards, and his face is caught directly in our viewpoint, the mouth slightly open, and the eyes in the midst of closing. A thin trickle of blood falls from a wound in his neck; a bedsheet, which unbeknown to him, has transformed into his winding sheet, is also bloodstained. Meanwhile his body is an object of mystery to us. It has, as it were, disappeared from view. Knowing the story of the death of the author, Jean-Paul Marat, we know he is lying, dying, in a bath. Yet we could be forgiven for thinking he is crawling into his sarcophagus, or perhaps simply falling into death. (See Plate 4).

'Do Books Make Revolutions?' is a famous question asked by the great historian of the book, Roger Chartier, on the occasion of the bicentenary of 1789.[1] Chartier cited authorities as legendary as Alexis de Tocqueville and Hippolyte Taine to manifest a stereotype of the French Revolution as created by books, especially ones by Voltaire and Rousseau. Yet it is a conundrum, Chartier asserts, that the idea of reading's power often accompanies indifference to a history of physical books. Historical materialism fights at some level with a form of anti-materialism. His question is therefore reversible: did the Revolution change the ideological function of the book? Hobsbawm favours a different materialist reading in which demand for books follows education, and 1848 figures as a more revolutionary year than 1789.[2] The modernist view of the book seems to be based on a deconsecration of the book as material object. Karl Popper epitomizes this prejudice. His autobiography begins in his father's library: 'the physical shape of the book is insignificant', he says. What matters is 'contents, in the logical sense'.[3] Carlo Ginzburg, in an essay on those quintessential modern masters of scientific method, Freud and Sherlock Holmes, argues that this has a historical origin: the more books have become mechanized, the more they have effaced their materiality and commodity.[4] In the dialectical terms of bibliophobia, we have reached, it seems, a threshold, in which writing is denuded of association with either holiness or embodiment. A book is a mere book, equivalent to a mundane sense of contents. Letter appears to give way to spirit alone, never more so than in a pile of forgotten paperbacks or a Kindle on a holiday.

Book historians have responded to Chartier's challenge in contrary ways. Robert Darnton charted the records of the Société Typographique de Neuchâtel to show how a Swiss printer supplied forbidden books and pamphlets to booksellers throughout the *ancien régime*. Pornographic novels, utopian fictions, and scandalous libels enriched and undermined French literary and political life.[5] Later, Darnton mapped how the Enlightenment trinity of Voltaire, Diderot's *Encyclopédie*, and Rousseau, often produced from Switzerland, flooded markets from Blois to Lyon, or Besançon to Montpellier.[6] In another direction, bibliography has followed the suggestion of McKenzie to investigate not authors but 'printers of the mind', in the practices of printing-houses and the economics of publishing.[7] Darnton fulfils this aim in relation to the *Enyclopédie*.[8] In England, James Raven analyses the effects of credit and risk on the business of books in the Revolutionary era, and the changing legal context in relation to sedition and censorship.[9] Within this scholarship, a conflict exists between the idea of the book either as an instrument of the Enlightenment, or as an economic commodity. Analysis by William St Clair shows how both can be true: London publishers advertised a large number of titles, but squeezed the supply to keep prices high.[10] All too briefly, the monopoly relaxed in 1774 to allow a reading nation to develop.

The repeal of the Licensing Act in 1695 and emergence of copyright law in 1710 are no longer seen as the watersheds in freedom they used to be.[11] Nevertheless, the idea of intellectual property built into interpretation of the US Constitution appears to mark the historical terminus for the idea of the book as a holy thing. In recognizing 'the Progress of Science and useful arts', Congress establishes limits to its own powers by transferring them to a free press.[12] Yet with freedom comes nostalgia for the age of enchantment. Leonard Woolf sighs with regret: 'The making of books was a handicraft a hundred years ago'; now it is an industry, 'set up on Monotype machines'. Virginia Woolf chooses to be optimistic in an age of democracy, wanting books for everyone, 'tramps and duchesses', but laments a price too high for many to afford.[13] 'How Should One Read a Book?', she asks: with imagination and insight; yet the greater part of her library is 'the record of such fleeting moments in the lives of men, women and donkeys'.[14]

In the nineteenth century, Leah Price writes, 'bibliophilia took over the work of idolatry'.[15] Yet readers hardly abandoned the sensation that their books were physical. Mr Lydgate in George Eliot's *Middlemarch* (1871–2) is always deep in a book: 'something he must read, when he was not riding the pony'. By the age of ten, Lydgate knew instinctively that 'books were stuff', that is, made of matter, but also equivalent to rubbish.[16] Yet even as novels begin to privilege mental actions over manual ones, Price observes, books come to be haunted by a renewed sense of presence, whether of the author or the reader. This is the place where 'books are imagined to possess a self'.[17] Individual books on shelves have destinies of their own, Benjamin says.[18] W. E. Gladstone called his library a 'book-cemetery'. The

Fig. 72. 'The library as mausoleum'; Old Public Library, Cincinnati, OH

Old Public Library in Cincinnati (Fig. 72) was built in 1874 and brutally demolished in 1955.

It was a mausoleum of cast iron: shelf on shelf on shelf, linked by spiral staircases.[19] Unwanted novels or government information required more mundane disposal: in the 1880s, the Stationery Office intervened to help public libraries destroy old stock.[20] Anxieties transfer between owner and copy. Readers worry if a book has a fine enough binding, or too ostentatious; whether their books are too tidy or not clean enough. At the age of fifteen, Emma Bovary 'spent six months breathing the dust of old lending libraries'; she quivers as she handles the satin bindings.[21] Woolf complains that books 'need dusting for ever'.[22] For Foucault, 'the dust of books' is a sign of temporality and instability in human discourse.[23] Neurosis is a history of domestic enslavement and of the uncanny. Books are felt to be reinhabited by selves even as they disown their gods.

In this way, the revolutionary moment in France can be thought of not only in terms of liberation, but also as the presence of a ghost that has never yet been exorcized. Here, Jacques-Louis David's *The Death of Marat*, or *Marat assassiné*, now in the Musées royaux des Beaux-Arts in Brussels (Pl. 4), comes into focus as the image of the writer as martyr. It was commissioned by Deputy Guirault the very next day after Marat was assassinated on 13 July 1793 by the Girondiste Charlotte Corday. At the moment the Convention announced the death of the *montagnard*, Guirault turned to David and said, 'there is one more painting for you to do'.[24] He was referring to David's involvement in a previous memorial, to Louis-Michel Lepeletier, Marquis of Saint-Fargeau, who had been assassinated on the eve of the execution of Louis XVI while eating at a restaurant in the Palais Royal in Paris. Lepeletier, a member for the *noblesse* at the States-General in 1789, and later an educational reformer, was awarded a magnificent funeral by the National Convention in honour of one of its own star members. David designed the funeral tableau in which Lepeletier's fleshly remains were placed on top of a pedestal that had once supported the statue of Louis XV in the place Vendôme. He followed this with a painting, *Les derniers moments de Michel Lepeletier*, sometimes described as the first official painting of the French Revolution, now lost, and known only via a drawing.

A similar tableau was commissioned for the funeral of Marat, but in the hot July of 1793 the corpse deteriorated quickly; in addition, Marat suffered from a terrifying disease of the skin. To prevent the republican hero turning into a freak show, David suggested wrapping him in a cloth kept cool and humid, but it did not prevent further putrefaction. Perfumes and white painted make-up were insufficient. Press reports recorded Marat's head and torso as a vivid green. Metaphysical anxieties, too, lurked in representing martyrdom in the new Republic. Thomas Crow has shown how a depiction of the funeral of Marat in the disused chapel of the Cordeliers secularizes burial rites in a conscious pastiche of David's *Brutus* (now in the Louvre).[25] Classicism cannot quite cover over the cracks. Maximilien Robespierre worried about Marat's populist charisma. The instructions he gave David for the memorial were that he should commemorate but not incite a cult. David's masterwork is violent and oblique, Christian iconography twisted into republican modernity. Its proper title is *Marat à son dernier soupir*—'at his last breath'. Being still alive, he is not yet a saint. An upright tea chest suggests a sacrificial monument but bears the stark inscription 'À MARAT'. The iconographic register is of a *pietà*—Crow suggests the model is Anne-Louis Girodet's Christian revivalist version from just before the Revolution in 1789. Yet if the bottom half of David's painting is like Caravaggio's *Entombment of Christ* (1602–3) for the Oratory of St Philip Neri in Rome, the top half could be by Mark Rothko. Virtually half the canvas is dedicated to a thick, purple-brown, shrouded darkness, highlighted by miniature brushmarks of lighter pigment. One person to comment that the 'upper half is almost totally black' is Slavoj Žižek.[26] There is no description better than Charles Baudelaire's: 'a soul is flying in the cold air of this room, on these cold walls, around this cold funerary tub'.[27]

What fixes the painting within human life are marks of writing. Most obvious is the wooden box, the artist's name in a Roman epitaph, and a date in the republican calendar form of 'L'AN DEUX'. In the hero's hand is gripped the fatal letter which Corday gave to him requesting his help, the pretext for her visit. On top of the box another letter, by Marat in reply to Corday, lies folded, one half in the perspectival space of the room of the assassination, the other as if entering into the space of the viewer. Marat's *dernier soupir* is caught on paper, and now dangles, in suspension. Marat has been killed in the act of writing, the quill caught in his dying fingertips. Behind his hand, beneath the bath, as if at the foot of the viewer, is the murderer's weapon. The ancient corollaries of pen and knife, victim and assailant, are poised in exquisite balance. In a further visual signifier, another pen lies on the table, pointing back towards the martyr's wounds.

At one level, David's masterpiece, at such a turning point in modern history, signals the movement from sacred to secular writing. Citizen Marat lives and dies by the pen, freed from the yoke of Christian signification. At another level, he represents even the gradual disembodiment of writing. The shadowy blankness of half of the painting, as Baudelaire suggests, is like 'une âme voltige'. Another absence is Corday herself, although she reappears in Edvard Munch's equally extraordinary *Death of Marat* (1907).[28] The horizontal line is this time occupied by the naked bloody torso of the artist, spattered with blood. In the vertical plane, by contrast, the wood box is replaced by a statuesque erect nude of Charlotte, rendered as Munch's lover Tulla Larsen. While the signs of writing have been removed, the bloody hand of artist/author is iconic (and Freudian) enough.

Ernst Gombrich (in *The Story of Art*) called the *Death of Marat* the first modern painting.[29] Such statements are arbitrary, but Gombrich drew attention to important features of the painting: its fixture in the present, down to the details of the police records; its elimination of anything that is not true to Marat's career as a modern revolutionary. Modern writing, we might infer, is the absent presence of the text. Christ has left the painting, to be replaced by the author. Yet David's image is also haunted by what cannot be seen, carrying traces of ancient signification, whether of classical orator or martyred saint. In the 1780s, David painted important historical scenes of a series of classical figures, including not only Brutus and Horatius, but the *Death of Socrates*.[30] As Socrates takes the hemlock, raising his left hand, Plato sits brooding at the end of the bed, a written scroll at his feet. The spoken word of Socrates is poised, ready to be written down. Yet it is one of the formal oddities of the French Revolution that its heroes are only ambiguously literary figures. Danton left behind almost no writing at all. Robespierre, although more voluminous, is mainly known for pamphlets like *On the King's Flight* (1791) and *Justification for the Use of Terror* (1794). The revolution spread instead via new forms of journalism: Marat's own *L'ami du Peuple*,

Jacques Hébert's *Père Duchesne*, and most original of all, the mercurial Camille Desmoulins and his *Vieux Cordelier*. The genius of Desmoulins was his discovery of the power of irony and literary obliquity. What is not said is as important as what is.

T. J. Clark outreaches Gombrich: 'the beginning of modernism' can be dated to *25 vendémaire An deux* (16 October 1793), when David's painting was hastily released.[31] This has something to do with David's Jacobin politics but is also associated by Clark with Marat's role in the Republic's dechristianization. In death, Marat was compared with Christ—*Jésus le sans-culotte*—and not always to Christ's advantage.[32] 'Jesus was but a false prophet but Marat is a god.'[33] The purging of priests and the closing of monasteries began in 1789 and was well under way by 1791. The destruction of great monastic buildings (such as the abbey of Cluny in Burgundy) has long held a plangent place in the history of iconoclasm.[34] Churches in Paris and the regions were stripped of sacerdotal objects; bells melted to cannon; stained-glass windows smashed; altarpieces broken. Saints and images were smashed in the open road.[35] The 'black Holy Virgin' in Boulogne, having escaped the English in the Hundred Years' War, was publicly burned.[36] Meanwhile Reason trampled over hallowed ground. Liberty trees were planted all over France; in the church of Amplepuis, one replaced the crucifix in the rood.[37] Notre-Dame de Paris, unbaptized, hosted a Festival of Reason in November 1793. The tabernacle of the Mass was converted into a Graeco-Roman sculpture, while the Bishop of Paris (who had solemnly abjured his faith two days earlier) was replaced in ceremonial function by an actor playing Liberty, dressed in white and holding a pike while gesturing to the flame of Reason.[38] There were doubters in the new faith of the republic, of course: not least Robespierre, who demurred from anti-Christian sentiment as a descent into disorder, and who privately thought atheism a characteristically aristocratic affectation. Nonetheless, Clark sees in the Revolution more widely, and in David's painting in the precise sense, the 'disenchantment of the world'.[39]

The phrase is of course a translation of Max Weber's term *Entzauberung*.[40] The word commonly demonstrates a secularization of modernity, in an emergence of modernized, bureaucratic, societies, where scientific progress is valued above religious belief, and where culture is governed by rational goals. The 'Secular Age' applies also to literature: Proust, Charles Taylor tells us, 'gives us a sense of a higher time, built out of the sensibility of a modern living in the flow of secular time'.[41] Weber used the term in a less positivist way: he was sceptical about universalist claims for secularization, and found many of the arguments produced in its name either nihilistic or technocratic. Indeed, part of Weber's project was re-enchantment, motivated by a sense of the disempowerment of the modern self. Either way, however, the French Revolution is characteristically seen as a turning point. The artwork, as displayed by David's painting, or writing, as represented within its frame, are marked by this theory of desacralization.

Perhaps indeed we can see (in David) writing as a work of art, and the work of art as a form of writing. Yet it is also, Baudelaire says, 'le triomphe du spiritual-isme'. Marat's agony of the spirit catches something of the ambiguity of Hegel's theory of the apotheosis of modern art. The history of art, according to Hegel, involved increasing secularization and humanization. Among the ancient Greeks, and up to the Renaissance, art was closely allied to religion, its function being to make the divine visible. Luther's Protestant Reformation by contrast found God to be present in faith alone, simultaneously making God invisible and ridding the art object of divine presence:

> To Protestantism alone the important thing is to get a sure footing in the prose of life, to make it absolutely valid in itself independently of religious associations, and to let it develop in unrestricted freedom.[42]

Art, like religion or literature, turns inward. In that sense it makes itself belated, fleeting, more difficult to locate. Art in modernity 'falls apart' (*zerfällt*) into the exigencies of ordinary daily life. Paradoxically, therefore it also needs to do something more than imitate nature. In order to become philosophical again, art has to show us something nature does not know, the 'liveliness' (*Lebendigkeit*) of things: such as the 'vanishing glimpse of the moon or the sun, a smile, the expression of a swiftly passing emotion'.[43] Dutch seventeenth-century still lifes or interior paintings do this best, such as Johannes Vermeer's genre paintings of young women writing. *A Lady Writing a Letter* (1665) interrupts its subject turning to the viewer, quill in hand, caught in interior thought.[44]

If as a total theory of the history of art Hegel's argument now has its detractors, his writing in the early nineteenth century, in the wake of the French Revolution, gives voice to a yearning for something that is passing, as well as a drive towards the new. No word expresses this ambiguity in Hegel better than the German word that haunts his philosophy and has proved hardest to translate: *Geist*. 'Being' in Hegel is to be understood as a self-determining reason or 'Idea'. As such it depends on a form of life that is self-conscious, that exists in language and can exercise freedom. Hegel calls this self-conscious life (or 'ideal spectator') *Geist*, usually translated 'spirit', although it has English connotations of 'mind', 'intellect', and 'ghost'.[45] He was finishing his book, *Phänomenologie des Geistes* (*Phenomenology of Spirit*), just as Napoleon entered the city of Jena in October 1806, where Hegel was working as an unsalaried professor. Rather than a classic propositional exercise in philosophy it is structured more like a *Bildungsroman* in the style of Rousseau's *Émile* or Goethe's *Wilhelm Meisters Lehrjahre*.

In this work Hegel develops an early version of his theory of the relation between religion and art. Here he proposed an idea of *Kunstreligion*, the religion of art formed in ancient Greece, where *Geist* elevates its shape into the 'form of consciousness' itself.[46] It comes into being through a divorce from its durable existence. It therefore has a kind of double meaning, between durable existence and 'truth'. This indeed gives art its power. 'The first work of art exists as immediate, abstract and individual', he says.[47] In its elevation towards the self-consciousness which is a pre-condition of its success, it must give way to an *Aufhebung*, a kind of opposition to its own spirit.[48]

> By the elevation of the whole into the pure concept, this shape acquires its pure form, appropriate to the spirit.[49]

Hegel struggles here to find a metaphor that corresponds adequately to his theory. He begins with the image of a crystal containing a thing within itself; then switches to the house of the dead to which the soul is external; then moves again to a plant, and the relationship of its life form to the roots, branches, and leaves in which it is incorporated. Here, Hegel encounters an obstruction (or 'incommensurability') in his theory. What is the relation between the 'straight line and plane surface' of the art object and the 'abstract form of the understanding'? The only resolution lies in the idea of a dialectic.

Here we find the innate tension in Hegel's idea of art. Modern poetry, too, equivocates between heard sound and printed line, so that it loses its connection with 'the spiritual meaning'.[50] The work of art in the visual medium, by contrast, is immediate and abstract, he says. Yet it is not the 'ensouling' *of* something, or an 'imitation' *of* the thing ensouled. This would be to confuse art with the original appearance of the god within religion. The god has to have some other way of coming into light than in a descent into externality. Hegel expresses this thought through another dark metaphor:

> However, the indwelling god is the black stone removed from its animal covering and now pervaded with the light of consciousness.[51]

The reference is generally taken to be to *al-Ḥajaru al-Aswad* or 'the Black Stone' of the Ka'ba in Mecca; Inwood glosses that 'Hegel takes it to symbolize the human interior'.[52] Some see in this Hegel's characteristically dismissive attitude to Islam. Yet the mysterious place of it in his argument, without any anecdotal gloss, suggests a more serious intent. The Black Stone was only recently coming into view in Western travel accounts. The Swiss traveller Johann Ludwig Burckhardt visited Mecca in 1814:

> It is very difficult to determine accurately the quality of this stone which has been worn to its present surface by the millions of touches and kisses it has received. It appeared to me like a lava, containing several small extraneous particles of a whitish and of a yellow substance. Its colour is now a deep reddish brown approaching to black. It is surrounded on all sides by a border composed

of a substance which I took to be a close cement of pitch and gravel of a similar, but not quite the same, brownish colour.[53]

The nature of the stone has been much debated. It has been described as basalt, agate, natural glass, or even a meteorite. Originally a single piece of rock, it consists today of a number of fragments cemented together. It was already an object of veneration in pre-Islamic times. According to tradition, Muhammad set the stone within the Ka'ba before his elevation to prophethood.[54] After his conquest of Mecca in 630 CE, he rode by camel round the Ka'ba seven times, touching the stone with his stick in reverence. The stone is not an object of worship but plays a central part in the ritual of *istilam*, when pilgrims kiss the Black Stone, touch it with their hands, or raise their hands towards it. It is believed to occupy the place where Adam and Eve built an altar; originally bright white it became black through human sin; touching it takes sin away.

For Hegel, the black stone is a metaphor for internalization, 'Being-there in which the Self exists as Self'. Nature withdraws into essence, 'an inessential shell': Hegel calls it 'simple darkness, the motionless, the black, formless stone'.[55] In this process, the natural is turned into bare sign. Within it, the 'shape of the god' is stripped; in its stead is the '*essence* of the god' (*Das* Wesen *des Gottes*)—italicized for emphasis, but also in admission of the mystery of the process—the unity of 'self-conscious spirit' (*Geist*).[56] It is like 'an obscure memory within itself'. Spirit is eternal.[57] No wonder the metaphors become unclear—Hegel calls them 'muddied boundaries' – when Hegel's very subject is the process by which the imitation of nature takes place within art or language. Not that is, imitation in the sense of verisimilitude—Hegel is contemptuous of such things—but imitation as a theory of representationality. Even at this level of implied equivalence, Hegel doubles down on the idea of metaphorization, showing how the original 'religion of art' gives way to the level of the symbolic, twice over, once in the passage from the Greeks to the Renaissance, and again in the emergence of the modern.

The 'black stone' thus forms a powerful iconography of a renewed doubleness in the history of consciousness that can be located in the post-revolutionary moment. It is idealism reidealized. At the same time, for Hegel it is a troubling symbol. Spirit has been turned back to its starting point, back into a cycle of necessity all over again:

All these determinations have been shed in the loss experienced by the self in absolute freedom. Its negation is the meaningless death, the pure terror of the negative that contains nothing positive, nothing that fills it.[58]

While much prejudice and superstition have been banished, Hegel says, still the question comes: '*What next? What is the truth Enlightenment has propagated in their stead?*' (§557). However ambiguous Hegel's own view of the French

Revolution, it haunts these passages in the *Phenomenology of Spirit*. Here is Hegel's writing lesson: the spirit of freedom, or ghost in the machine, which offers a place for imagination and threatens it with violence. This leads (in Harris's striking phrase) to Hegel's 'manifest disparagement of the printed word'.[59] The writer is always potentially a fallen creature in Hegel, perhaps even a traitor on the inside, whether to the soul or to spirit itself. This reminds us of the volatile power of writing in David's painting, in the parallel positioning of pen and knife. The power of David's art lies in the simultaneous way that the *Death of Marat* represents both human suffering and a renewal of a call to revolutionary zeal.

'Terror is the order of the day', was the rallying cry of 1793. Simon Schama finds in David's painting a dangerous plea for emotion, calling it an instrument of terror.[60] And yet David also promised to 'Return Marat whole to us again'. Perhaps the dichotomy between violence and the purity of the Rights of Man suppresses the urgency of the philosophical questions contained in revolution. The quixotic career of Camille Desmoulins expresses this ambiguity perfectly. A schoolmate of Robespierre, at the outset of revolution he lived a precariously obscure life as a lawyer. He sprang to fame in the awful daring of a moment's surrender, leaping on a table on Sunday, 12 July 1789 outside the Café du Foy in the Palais Royal.[61] Delivering a quintessential revolutionary call to arms, he urged the crowd to don the tricolour as a badge. After the storming of the Bastille, he led the popular chorus in song, offering to string the aristocrats up from the lamppost at the Place de la Grève. In September followed the incendiary pamphlet *Discours de la lanterne*, with its ironic epigraph: *Qui male agit odit lucem.*[62]

Desmoulins was ambiguity itself. The stammerer turned tribune of public speaking; the dandy aristo-basher; the classicist and Biblicist who whipped up the mob. Above all he was a terrorist as archetypal victim of the Terror. Poor Robespierre, who longed to save him, became trapped by his own logic into condemning him to death; poor Camille, who assumed Robespierre would always forgive him, relentlessly goaded Maximilien into signing his death warrant. On 5 April 1794, Desmoulins, along with Hérault de Séchelles, Fabre L'Eglantine, and Danton himself, went to his death at the Place de la Concorde. From his prison in the Luxembourg palace he wrote to his wife Lucille:

> I rest my head calmly upon the pillow of my writings…I have dreamed of a Republic such as all the world would have adored. I could never have believed that men could be so ferocious and so unjust.[63]

At the tumbril, however, sang-froid departed Camille. Agonized by the news that his wife had been condemned to face the guillotine herself, he went mad himself with grief.

Dr Guillotin's marvellous machine of death has become a byword for violent terror, but in origin it was anything but. The first principles of the guillotine were democratic and humanitarian. The machine eliminated the distinction in capital punishment between aristocracy and the working class, Lepeletier declared; as also the calculated spectacle, humiliation, and degradation invested in the actions of hanging or breaking on the wheel.[64] In addition, Guillotin advertised the virtue of his invention as eliminating pain by making death instantaneous and surgical.[65] An engraving recommending its adoption in 1789 is like a scene from Rousseau, the victim passive, the executioner (who superintends rather than enacts the command of the state) sensitively averting his eyes.[66] France retained the use of the guillotine until capital punishment itself was abolished in 1981; in the United States, as recently as 1996 the state of Georgia proposed introducing it as more humane and less accident-prone than the electric chair.

The guillotine aspired, rather like the idea of *Geist* in Hegel, to efface the borderline of reason itself, so that there might be no interruption in the radical decree of the law. It was merely the visible form of justice.[67] Whether the machine acted with quite the instantaneous precision claimed for it in dividing body from soul remained a point of controversy. Observations at an execution conducted by a Dr Beaurieux as late as 1898 suggested that the eyes of the victim remained responsive for several seconds after decapitation, and the prisoner was at some level conscious of his name being called.[68] The ambiguity of the relationship between death and the machine was expressed almost immediately by humour, especially in dead-pan soubriquets such as the affectionate *la Louisette* (after the machine's original designer); *la veuve* ('the widow'); *le moulin à silence* (the 'silence mill'); *la raccourcisseuse patriotique* ('the patriotic shortener'); and *le rasoir national*. This last shows also the heuristic dimension of the guillotine as an Occam's razor for reason of state: the simplest solution is the best.

Meanwhile, the hope of Desmoulins that he might 'rest my head calmly upon the pillow of my writings' expresses not only irresistible wit (or insane courage), but a new ideal of writing. This is the writing of reason, produced in the moment, automatic, and with no physical motivation or obstruction.[69] Beginning on 5 December 1793, seven issues of *Le Vieux Cordelier* appeared, one every five days. The title spoke for 'old' members of the Club des Cordeliers but also on behalf of old Republican Rome, Cicero back from the dead to rail against the death of virtue, or Tacitus to enumerate the crimes of the Emperor Tiberius. In exchange for Hébert's overt literary populism, he offers simplicity: 'Liberty is happiness, reason, and equality'. Making writing equal to imagination and happiness placed Desmoulins in direct opposition to Robespierre and Saint-Just.[70] In a rebuke to Robespierre and the Committee of Public Safety, he asks, 'Do you want to exterminate all your enemies by the guillotine?'[71] In Number 4, he openly addressed his old schoolfriend, using the terms of Latin *amicitia*: 'Remember the lessons of history and philosophy: love is stronger, more lasting than fear.' Desmoulins calls for a new Committee of Public Clemency to defend the original values of the Declaration of Rights.

On 7 January 1794, the Jacobin Club voted to expel Desmoulins from its membership. Robespierre, still yearning to be Camille's saviour, suggested in alternative that the offending issues of the *Vieux Cordelier* be publicly burned. Desmoulins in response remarked *Brûler n'est pas répondre* ('Burning is not answering'), a pointed citation of Rousseau at the burning of *Émile* in Geneva.[72] As always, the burning of books attests to a quarrel over existential boundaries. Writing and revolution were intimately connected. Pierre Rétat insists that the printing press in 1789 cannot be seen merely as an informational source, ideology by other means. The press was 'a new management of time, speech, and political discourse'.[73] At the heart of this was the newspaper as revolutionary oracle if not yet mass medium.[74] Élysée Loustallot's *Révolutions de Paris* applied new rhetorical techniques of eyewitness report in using innovative mechanical techniques such as including prints alongside his written sources. Marat called Loustallot the ideal printer for 'the liberty of a new people'.[75] Schama argues for a direct relationship between 'blood and freedom' in Loustallot, whose journal lasted only until 1790. In this, Schama argues against the commonplace view of the Terror as aberration, instead seeing it as 'merely 1789 with a higher body count'.[76] The rule of violence is an inexorable law, he states, culminating in 26 executions a day in the hot summer of 1794.[77] By the time Robespierre received his *contrapasso* in the Thermidorean Reaction, the official figure for death by guillotine in France reached 16,594.

Schama regards violence as essential to Revolutionary zeal, but is it so simple? Jacobins fought for a radical realignment of reason and the body, in which writing and the book, are once again primary symptoms. Yet Kant had predicted how 'the nature of our thinking being and its conjunction with the corporeal world' leads only to dispute. These are the limits of experience, the 'Pillars of Hercules', beyond which 'the voyage of reason' cannot venture.[78] William Doyle proposes a cautionary analysis of 'terror'.[79] Robespierre admired those passages in Montesquieu's *Spirit of the Law* that carefully enumerated the fanaticism and violence of the *ancien régime*; the danger always existed that revolution might take bloody revenge.[80] As early as *Les Révolutions de France et de Brabant*, Desmoulins warned the aristocrats were plotting bloody counter-revolution.[81] A revolution of the press made violence abstract and existential. One difference was that ideology now targeted not one king, but every man.[82] This is akin to turning politics inside out, making the press an arm of Kant's idealist manifesto that science, morality, and religion rest on the one foundation of human autonomy. For Kant, *Autonomie* is 'the ground of the dignity of a human and of every rational creature'.[83]

Allied to the ideological plane of revolutionary writing is its basis in a new materialist economics.[84] Loustallot, financed by J. L. Prudhomme, wrote sixty issues of the *Révolutions de Paris* for a new society based on the Rights of Man.[85] By 1790, when he died of illness, 194 journals were produced in the capital, as royal censorship lapsed; followed soon by over 50,000 pamphlets and hundreds of thousands of handbills.[86] In 1793, Antoine-François Momoro published his *Traité élémentaire de l'imprimerie*, also known as 'the manual of the printer'.[87] When he began business in the rue de la Harpe in 1787, on admission to the Paris Book Guild, Momoro stocked just eleven titles.[88] The declaration of the freedom of the press in August 1789 transformed his fortunes. Within a year he owned four printing presses, ten cases of type, and a foundry for making his own type characters. On the publication of his *Traité* he was still a comparatively small player, but his book aspired to make printing a business within the ambition of anybody. Soon he was the official printer for the Cordeliers, producing pamphlets, minutes of meetings, handbills, and posters. Once an ally of Danton, he switched allegiance to the Hébertistes, and was guillotined with them in March 1794.

C'est affreux, mais il est nécessaire (Fig. 73) is an anonymous engraving published in the *Journal de l'autre monde* in 1794. It shows over twenty heads, male and female, young and old, bald and hirsute, in a bucolic circle of celebratory printed busts, surrounded by laurel fronds. In the centre is a black circular disk. This is of course an image of *la veuve* herself, the blade providing the vertical lynchpin of the image, top to bottom. Yet the decapitated heads are as ambiguous as the image's lapidary motto: 'it's dreadful, but necessary', with the extra note: *Tableau d'histoire naturelle du Diable*. The heads in the diabolic museum of natural history have entered a printed pantheon, drained of blood and brought back to life—a kind of immortality—in ink. They are anonymous but not entirely unhappy. Artistically, they belong in the tradition of Charles Le Brun, who attempted a formalist catalogue of all human passions, reduced to archetypal grimaces of fear or lust or terror.[89] These revolutionary faces, caught in the last breath of the guillotine, tongues sometimes sticking out, attest not only to horror but also to stoicism, puzzlement, inquiry, anger, resignation, and irony. They adopt, we may say, the spirit of the times. Yet as reason triumphs, their fate shows the return of the repressed body.

Another print of the same year (Fig. 74) shows Robespierre himself, 'having guillotined all of France', as the happy executioner of the executioner.[90] Robespierre is on the point of pulling the cord, at which point his will be the only head left in France. There are eighteen machines in operation in total, depicted with distorted perspective so as to fill the whole image, top to bottom, side to side. They are lettered *A* to *S* in an ironic printed key to the diagram, in truth needing no explication. One body lies in a basket; the executioner slides down to join him. A pyramid has been erected to commemorate 'All France Lies Here'. Robespierre, meantime, dressed in plumed hat as at the Festival of the Supreme Being, tramples on the Constitutions of 1791 and 1793.

The image invites Schama's deconstruction: terror over freedom. However, republican representation cannot part body from spirit, blood from ink. Ink

Fig. 73. 'Talking heads'; *Ce mélange est affreux, mais il est nécessaire*, engraving, 1794. Ville de Paris/ Bibliothèque historique

Fig. 74. 'Guillotining books'; *Robespierre guillotinant le boureau*, engraving 1794.
Paris, Bibliothèque nationale de France

production, like paper and typefounding, were still hand-made industries in the
late eighteenth century.[91] Gutenberg made oil-based lampblack ink for his press
using varnish and egg-white.[92] First made in China 3,000 years ago, ink never lost
its origin in animal stuff.[93] The Chinese created India ink by mixing glue (from
animal hide), burnt animal bones, and lampblack, dried in a ceramic dish. The
French Republic aspired to exchange blood for ink, rendering itself pure spirit.
This is modernity's idealistic promise to escape a ritual embodiment in the past.
Yet spirit cannot escape body. Robespierre's dedication to Rousseau's spirit was

genuine, even as he set fire to Desmoulins's Rousseauiste pamphlets. It is similar to how David's pictorial death hymn of a republican hero shows a pen next to the knife, which has cut into Marat's heart. Blood and ink sit side by side on canvas, in shared metonymy. *MARAT N'EST POINT MORT*.[94] His ghost, released from earthly prison, glides up and flies throughout France. Writing is not material but *always* dialectical, as in the poets exalted by Desmoulins. For Horace, the poet is never 'a body without soul'.[95] 'Do not, my soul, strive for immortal life', sings Pindar.[96]

Δοκεῖ μοι τότε ἡμῶν ἡ ψυχὴ βιβλίῳ τινὶ προσεοικέναι. 'It seems to me at such a time that the soul is like a book', Plato makes Socrates say in the *Philebus*.[97] Not, that is, that the book is like a soul, in the commonplace that it has meaningful content. Plato's idea is more counterintuitive, that a person's spirit is constructed like a book, bearing the imprint of permanent marks of language. Hans-Georg Gadamer's commentary on the *Philebus* calls this 'fixing through words', a process complemented in Plato by another form of 'holding fast to what is thought' – the production of inner images.[98] In Derrida's paraphrase, 'the book imitates the soul, or the soul imitates the book, because each is the image or *likeness* of the other'.[99] Indeed, writing is like a painting that is like a metaphor. Memory unites the senses, so that we seem (to Socrates) 'almost to write words in our souls'. Four kinds of being exist, Socrates says: those that are 'limitless'; things with measurement or number; 'mixed' being (the everyday manner in which human beings experience life); and finally, reason itself. The Enlightenment believed in a world of reason in which difference could disappear. Yet even as it eliminated every trace it was haunted by presence (or *Geist*), once disavowed. 'The guillotine takes life almost without touching the body', Foucault writes, but the key word, perhaps, is 'almost'.[100] In a similar way, law reduced itself to spirit, yet expressed itself in spilling ink, even when not blood. It is not coincidence that in the 1830s 'guillotine' became a vogue word for a machine to cut paper, especially in making printed books.

In 1937, Paul Klee was dying of scleroderma, a wasting disease. His work was exhibited in a Nazi show of 'degenerate art' in Munich. Back in Germany, his output flourished. Among works of that year (Fig. 75) is *Geist eines Briefes*, made of pigmented paste on newspaper, about the size of a sheet of paper in a printer's ream. The outer frame is flat grey, in which the shrinking paper, through absorption of glue, can still be seen, like wrinkles on a face. In the centre, Klee paints over newspaper in a fleshy pigment, under which lines of print are visible yet not legible. Onto the cream colour he draws by hand the outlines of an envelope, sealed with one lip firmly closing the other. The borders of the envelope are painted in starker black, as if the letter is a traditional mourning letter, of a kind commonplace in Bern in his Swiss childhood. This is the *Brief* of the title, the German word for a letter in the post. There is no sign of the letter's contents,

Fig. 75. 'Letter ghost'; Paul Klee, *Geist eines Briefes,* pigmented paste on newspaper, 1937. New York, MOMA

elegiac or not. Instead, into the frame of the envelope, Klee scribbled a childlike doodle of a human face, one line for the nose, two circles for eyes, and a thin downturned grimace of a mouth.

In 1949, Gilbert Ryle invented the concept of 'the ghost in the machine' to critique the idea that the mind is distinct from the body.[101] Koestler's book of that title in 1967 built on Descartes to suggest everything in nature is both a whole and a part. Every living thing (*holon*) has two contradictory tendencies: to express itself, and to disappear in some thing greater.[102] Every person senses herself, as it were, as a ghost. At the same time mankind as a whole yearns for self-destruction, as in the ultimate madness of nuclear war. Klee has created a *Geist* at many levels. The upper lip of the envelope metamorphoses into a face; the lower into a torso, black loops suggesting the meeting place of chest and arms. Another loop, in impenetrable symbolism, marks a chest below the chin. It is a human form, without human personhood. Are all letters like that, contents without hermeneutics? *Making sense*, Ryle says, mediates between seeing a picture and the 'ghost of a word'.[103] Human presence haunts Klee's painting without representation, in the outline of a death mask. In the process, he dismembers the physical features of the writing industry and reassembles them: pulp, paste, lampblack ink, newspaper, manuscript, envelope. Hermetic heuristic lies inside the 'letter ghost'.

22

The Smartphone Inside Our Heads

What is the status of writing in the age of the internet? Often this question is posed in terms of *how* people now write, or should write, or no longer write as they used to. On this question opinions differ. For many, especially older, observers, the effect of the internet, from email to Twitter, has appeared deleterious. Twitter has become synonymous with displays of ego or virtue-signalling, just as Snapchat has with trolling. Gretchen McCulloch in *Because Internet: Understanding the New Rules of Language* disagrees. We are using the internet, she says, to 'restore our bodies to our writing'.[1] Typographical short hands and abbreviations are now used, like emojis, to provide a sense of the tone of voice. It is like having a new form of grammatical inflection in a third dimension. We write what we feel, and our friends infer that feeling in reading.

Not every electronic communication feels like that. What McCulloch implies is that experience is now expressed freely; but this does not mean unambiguously. Everyone must have received a text (even or especially from someone whose feelings we know well, such as a partner or close family member) where they interpret a tone of voice but have imagined the wrong one entirely. SMS is the worst place in the world to negotiate such infelicities. Every attempt at correction only compounds the problem (especially with the involuntary mediation of autocorrection). We return in this way to the old problem with writing identified by Plato in the *Phaedrus*. Writing imperfectly represents the person by leaving out the voice.[2] McCulloch wishes to 'restore' the body, but she does not deny that somewhere it got lost in the first place.

Meanwhile, however, it is not so clear that we know *where* writing exists anymore. We feel like Tansley in *To the Lighthouse*: 'If only he could be alone in his room working, he thought, among his books. That was where he felt at his ease.'[3] Digital writing is at once closer and more distant from our bodies. A message appears at my thumb or fingertip, as I write it on my phone: and yet whether, how, or when it appears on the recipient's phone is to me something of a mystery. Its actual location is on the carrier's server, somewhere inside cyberspace. Even if I delete it from my phone, it still exists somewhere else. The news is full of stories of old deleted messages coming back to haunt their authors. The past lurks as a spectral phantom of future embarrassment, humiliation, dismissal, or litigation. 'Are text messages ever really deleted?' is an urgent question asked in search engines, and the answer is broadly in the negative.

About fifteen years ago I worried I had lost information on my computer. Someone from IT took me to a back office at the university, where she logged into her own computer, created a new login page, and entered my name. The screen divided into two, one a mirror of the other. Meanwhile she was able to manipulate my avatar as if I was at the desktop in my own office. The cursor moved in front of my eyes for all the world as if it was me. *Hocus pocus*, the information I needed was retrieved. At the same time, my eyes had been opened. Any illusion I had that my computer was *my* computer, or my self was *my* self, had disappeared. In future, I realized, I had better understand that not only were my emails legible by my employer (I had assumed that already) but every file, every note, every nuance of every memory, was present on the desktop of my avatar. In the decade since, such matters have become normalized and we are no longer surprised. When your computer has been hacked, and you ring security, they talk you through some protocols, and you watch the cursor dancing to the tune of another, a hundred or even three thousand miles away, your own fingers not moving a millimetre.

Zuboff calls this 'the problem of the two texts'.[4] Behind the surface text in which I am typing out this sentence, or the public-facing world of the web or of Gmail, through which I can send my script to you at the press of a button, or correct the footnotes within it by reference to a million databases in the wonderful world of connectivity, lies another 'shadow' text. This text is not visible to me or to you. When my mother used to write in Fortran at the kitchen table it was obvious that the computer thought in a different language. Now the distinction is occluded. The second text is an infinite mirror of the first text, which is disseminated, analysed, or consumed beyond our knowledge.

However, as well as two texts, we could also configure (via Zuboff's model) the problem of two writers and two readers. We agree with Mrs Ramsay now: 'Books, she thought, grew of themselves.'[5] Writing is no longer constituted by signs within a human semiology: it is like Thomas Jefferson's polygraph in which a machine copied his hand's movements as he wrote.[6] Writing becomes a duplicating automaton, in which what I appear to write using a keyboard, consisting of signs within a natural language such as German or Korean or Arabic, is in fact a numeric equivalent within an artificial language (or more properly a formal language) comprising a set of instructions whereby output is translated. An early standard within the computing industry was ASCII (American Standard Code for Information Interchange) which developed out of telegraph code in the early 1960s.[7] Originally based on the English language, ASCII encoded 128 (later 256) specified characters into seven-bit integers, 95 of which were printable (lower-case and upper-case alphabetic letters, digital numerals, and punctuation symbols). The other 33 characters covered features familiar from a typewriter such as carriage return or tabs.

In order to accommodate the many writing systems outside the English alphabet, a new international and multilingual system called Unicode began to be developed in the late 1980s, originally through a collaboration between Xerox and Apple. The original design by Joe Becker of Xerox outlined a 16-bit character model, on the basis that all of the characters used in all of the newspapers and magazines in the world in 1988 added up to at most 2^{14} (16,384, or over 100 times more than the 2^7 in ASCII).[8] Nonetheless this version of Unicode contained restrictions, reducing the variant glyphs in a complex written language such as Chinese to a unified system of graphemes. In the latest version (12.1) of Unicode in May 2019 the number of characters has therefore been expanded to 137,994 (including 165 format characters and 65 control characters). By this means the character set has mushroomed to include historic scripts as well as modern ones, along with a plethora of mathematical and scientific symbols and also emojis. For the World Wide Web, a version of Unicode called UTF-8 is used, with one byte dedicated to the original 128 characters in ASCII, supplemented with four bytes for all other characters, capable of encoding over a million code points in total. As of February 2020, UTF-8 accounts for the encoding of over 94 per cent of the world's websites.

In this way Unicode creates an additional problem in Zuboff's terms, a problem of 'two readers'. This is a far larger problem than 'two writers'. I can, perhaps, trust my computer to translate my thoughts via my keyboard from the signs imprinted onto it back into ASCII or Unicode and then forwards again onto my screen. The fact that I can read my text as it appears in front of me is a reassurance that the two-way reversible translation process is working, even if I have no idea how. Such a translation began in Gutenberg's printing shop, where compositors set type in reverse, using letter shapes that were mirrors of their originals.[9] However, the reading process on a computer is a far more arcane or even illegible mechanism. This is invisible to us when reading a Word document, but it does become apparent (or virtually so) as soon as we search the internet.

As of 20 February 2020, the current size of the web is 6.18 billion pages.[10] The size of the World Wide Web is itself an extrapolation, created by estimating the number of pages indexed in the three largest search engines, Google, Bing, and Yahoo. From this sum, an estimated overlap between the big three is then subtracted. The size of the index for each, in turn, is also an extrapolation. Every day, 50 words are sent to each search engine. These words are chosen to select evenly across logarithmic frequency intervals. The number of webpages found for each word is recorded, and then averaged out according to the word frequencies associated with these words in an independent corpus test.[11] It will be obvious, then, that such calculations are dependent on a gigantic hermeneutic search circle. We know how many words we can find by first searching for them in a search engine. It is the digital equivalent to estimating the population of live hedgehogs by counting the dead ones on the road.

The search engine now rules the world. In 2018, 3.7 million Google enquiries were made every minute.[12] Such is the power of searching that Google did not know what resources it possessed until after it had already become exceedingly good at doing it. When Google Search was invented in 1997, it joined a world becoming attuned to the idea that the key to knowledge was no longer an encyclopaedia or dictionary but an algorithm. An algorithm (named via a Latinization of the name of the ninth-century Persian astronomer Al-Khwārizmī) is a finite sequence of definable instructions used in order to solve problems. Arithmetical algorithms reach back to the Babylonian mathematicians of 2500 BCE.[13] Euclid's algorithm in his *Elements* (*c.*300 BCE) for finding the greatest common divisor of two numbers is one of the oldest in common use, and has been subjected to intense analysis in uncovering computational efficiency.[14] Even before the creation of a physical computer, Alan Turing used the concept of the algorithm to hypothesize a mathematical model of computation. He invented a theoretical 'Turing machine' in 1936, consisting of a mathematical description of a simple device capable of arbitrary computations, such that he was able to prove properties of computation in general. In the process he uncovered the philosophical limits of the *Entscheidungsproblem* ('decision problem') that originated in Leibniz's dream of a universal calculating machine.[15] While Leibniz thought of the problem as technical, and set himself the task of finding a formal language adequate to solving it, Turing answered the question in the negative, influenced by Kurt Gödel's incompleteness theorem, which shows that there is no set of axioms capable of solving all mathematical problems.[16]

By showing that some decision problems are undecidable, Turing paradoxically opened the way to real-world computers, although these are based on random access memory rather than Turing's concept of an infinite memory tape. In a later paper in 1950, Turing extended his problem to the classic humanist problem, 'Can machines think?'[17] Here he devised his brilliant concept of the 'imitation game', in which a man (A) and a woman (B) are asked questions by a third Interrogator (C) who may be of either sex and sits in a room apart from the other two. The aim of the game is to determine which of the two is the man and which is the woman; the kink in the question is created by Turing then asking, 'What will happen when a machine takes the part of A in this game?' Will a machine make mistakes as often as a man? In answering his question, Turing deduced the concept of a 'learning machine', playing havoc with a whole set of normatively human, gendered, ontological and theological assumptions about mind and matter.

For the purposes of an argument about the relationship of the 'two readers', one human and the other computational, it is important to bear in mind Turing's scepticism about privileging natural over artificial intelligence. Margaret Boden cites Turing's hypothesis of whether a computer program might eventually be able to appreciate, or even write, sonnets. Turing constructs a humorous but nevertheless serious set of algorithmic questions that a computer might ask Shakespeare:

In the first line of your sonnet which reads 'Shall I compare thee to a summer's day,' would not 'a spring day' do as well or better?

It wouldn't scan.

How about 'a winter's day.' That would scan all right.

Yes, but nobody wants to be compared to a winter's day.

Boden confesses that she does not believe such a program will ever be devised in practice; but that does not mean that it could never be in principle.[18]

Language-learning has become a key area in defining the nature of artificial intelligence. J. R. Searle's 'Chinese Room' argument, supposedly disproving it, is based on an imagined experiment in which a computer learns Chinese.[19] However, the question of whether a computer reads language in a different way from a human being is compounded by the problem that linguistic philosophers disagree about how humans understand their own languages. Noam Chomsky's theory of universal grammar proposed that human grammatical systems operate on general principles that are formal and computational, independent of the semantics or pragmatics of everyday life.[20] However, in cognitive and constructionist approaches to language, the linguistic forms humans use *constitute* their language capacity. We come to know a language by aggregating these different forms, and then combine them in a theoretically infinite set of possible utterances.[21] Whatever conclusion we make on the philosophical point, computer search engines like Google have followed the second theory. While eminently pragmatic, Google's choices are anything but arbitrary. Google Search introduces a series of stop words (small words like *and* and *the*) in order to isolate keywords in routine text mining. After that, it chooses not according to the principles we had in mind when we posed a question ('find me an answer to what I want to know') but according to its own principles of 'relevance': the quality of the links from one site to another.

Google works, that is, by indexing, crawling, and ranking. It creates bots to crawl through billions of websites, which are hence known popularly as 'spiders'. Yet the bot does not know where to travel without reference to the index that Google has already created. Nothing is more crucial for a savvy webmaster than to understand the protocols by which their site acquires a ranking on SERPs (Search Engine Results Pages). Yet only Google knows how its algorithm works or has access to its own index. Indeed, it only indexes sites that are friendly to its bots. All of us have experience of ways of navigating round its algorithm to find what we think we want; and then also of how Google superimposes its own ways of making us find what it wants. Increasingly, the answer to that conundrum is financial rather than epistemological. Indeed, Chinese researchers (funded by Microsoft) published findings in 2017 which showed that the revenue of search businesses is tied to estimating the click-through rate (CTR) of ads. Search is a means of increasing revenue through the reliability of predicting the success of advertisements, rather than the other way around.[22]

In other words, Google Search analyses and manipulates human language in ways that are structurally different from how human beings use language. Methods in Digital Humanities try to obviate the apparatus of Google Search. At its most simple level, which many of us have tried doing, this involves surrounding a search term within inverted commas. This function is a residue from when Search was still designed to find usable knowledge, yet buried so deep in Google's software that it is presumably too expensive to eliminate. It forces Search to ignore stop words, and to look for a fixed sequence of words rather than the co-occurrence of keywords. The search engine's desire for 'relevance' (or, as it might be, profitability) is diverted into what the reader might herself be looking for. At this point the laser accuracy of search comes spookily into view, as a small sequence of words within quotation marks yields perhaps a handful of results. Yet the same search terms *without* quotation marks might be hidden behind pages of results in a standard Search, thus becoming invisible, since nobody continues a search beyond about the tenth page. Other Boolean searches, such as the asterisk or 'wildcard', allow a sequence to include a *variable* word within its string; while 'near' allows proximity rather than sequence to rule the search. Sophisticated versions of searches within Digital Humanities have been dubbed 'cyberformalism'.[23] 'Regular expressions' (regex) is a pattern-matching process standard within digital text processing that identifies phrases in common use. Part-of-speech (POS) tags can be used to search for nouns, verbs, or adjectives, or for grammatical subcategories such as modal auxiliaries. This can be 'lemmatized' to include inflectional variants of a word.[24]

Not everyone in the humanities is happy with these phenomena, or with the proportion of grant funding that has accompanied them. Jonathan Culler complains that 'new electronic resources make it possible to do literary research without reading at all'.[25] Gayatri Spivak, more philosophically, objects that the search only ever finds what it was looking for in the first place: 'nothing is accidental anymore because the connections are all already made for you'.[26] Ted Underwood, an advocate of digital research, therefore calls for more neutral methodologies such as Bayesian statistics in humanist digital 'mining'.[27] At the heart of this is an argument as old as literature (and perhaps as writing) about whether meaning is strictly quantifiable. The modern benchmark is William Empson's revolutionary study, *Seven Types of Ambiguity* (1930): 'In a sufficiently extended sense any prose statement could be called ambiguous.'[28] Ambiguity is inherent to any notion of poetry, with the inevitable test-case of Shakespeare's *Sonnets*:

The barren tender of a poet's debt.[29]

As Empson points out, there is no pun, double syntax, or even uncertainty of feeling here. Yet simple words work in several ways at once. Nevertheless, Empson's whole book is dedicated to a principle that ambiguity can, after all, be analysed. At around the same time as Empson, the Russian linguist Roman Jakobson developed comparisons between Russian and Czech poetic forms, which eventually resulted in his seminal paper 'Linguistics and Poetics'. Poetry is nothing like arbitrary: 'the poetic function projects the principle of equivalence from the axis of selection onto the axis of combination'.[30]

Most accounts of language, or poetry, depend on a model of communication in which one person intends to mean something, and another attempts to grasp that intention. Jakobson rejects a communicative model in favour of a formalist one. While operating from a different philosophical standpoint, this is like Wittgenstein's rejection in *Philosophical Investigations* of the implications of theories of 'meaning' as 'intention':

> For a *large* class of cases of the employment of the word 'meaning'—though not for all—this word can be explained in this way: the meaning of a word is its use in the language.[31]

Yet the same scepticism about the term 'communication' can produce different analyses of the pertinence of linguistic forms. In one direction there is Empson's attentiveness to the indirections of every single word in an anatomy of 'ambiguity'; in the other there is Benjamin's insistence that all language is translatable into any other language:

> A real translation is transparent; it does not cover the original, does not block its light, but allows the pure language, as though reinforced by its own medium to shine upon the original all the more fully.[32]

Benjamin followed Mallarmé here in thinking all natural languages to be imperfect, precisely because they are pluralistic. In a revived myth of the Tower of Babel, Benjamin appealed to a concept of a 'pure language' in the sense of *thinking* itself: what Mallarmé called *penser étant écrire sans accessoires* ('thinking being writing without accessories').[33]

It is not as if Google has not already been thinking along such lines, however. Google Translate was launched in 2006. Initially it translated the required text into English before translating again into the selected language. Using predictive algorithms without independent checking, it became a byword for grammatical inaccuracy and clunkiness. In November 2016, however, the platform switched to a new engine—Google Neural Machine Translation, which translates whole sentences at a time, rather than clause by clause. It translates not only between languages but across them, using deep learning techniques so that, comparing

Japanese–English and English–Korean, it can generate Japanese-Korean translations without ever passing through English. This is called 'zero-shot' translation.[34] For James Bridle, it is the realization of Benjamin's dream: 'the meaningless metalanguage of the arcade'.[35] With poetic justice, one of only five languages (out of the 103 on Google Translate) still without the full 'zero-shot' capacity is Latin, perhaps the most successful bilingual language in history.[36]

Vox diuersa sonat populorum, tum tamen una est, said Martial of the Roman world.[37] The languages of the peoples of the world are many, yet somehow, they all speak in unison. What Martial said in praise of the Roman emperor Titus has come to pass in the age of Page and Brin. In advance of the long-awaited platform 'Google Irony', Martial's merciless critique of the day-to-day exigencies of Roman power will have to do. Google Brain is a deep learning artificial intelligence team founded in 2011. In October 2016 it invented a program involving three AIs.[38] Two of them, Alice and Bob, worked together to protect their communications from a third, Eve the eavesdropper (she always gets the blame, whatever the story). Alice and Bob succeeded in developing new encryption strategies as they went along, without any cryptographic algorithms being prescribed in advance. Google called this an amazing breakthrough in the protection of personal computer security, without admitting to the most significant lesson of the game: the machines had learned to keep their own secrets without telling anyone else.

The relevance of this to the real world, or what is left of it, is by now glaringly apparent. In June 2013, thousands of classified documents belonging to the National Security Agency (NSA) were published by the *Guardian* and the *Washington Post*. The source was Edward Snowden, who worked for the CIA from 2006, originally at Langley, Virginia, and then in the field, as a computer expert in Geneva.[39] From 2009 he was sub-contracted by the NSA to Dell, defending US military digital networks against Chinese hackers. In March 2012, Dell moved him from Tokyo to Hawaii as lead technologist (indeed, according to Snowden, sole member) of the NSA's Office of Information Sharing.[40] On 1 December 2012, Snowden made his first contact with the American security journalist Glenn Greenwald, who had recently moved to the UK to work for the *Guardian*. The email began: 'The security of people's communications is very important to me.'[41] He signed himself after a legendary defender of the early Republic, immortalized in Livy's *History of Rome*. Roman Cincinnatus assumed complete control over the state before relinquishing all his power and retiring to his farm.[42] Cincinnatus in Livy is the guardian of civic virtue, and in Cicero the epitome of the constitution.[43] American Cincinnatus concluded his email by warning Greenwald to use stronger PGP encryption.

Initially, the international media sensation concerned the magnitude and sensitivity of the documents released from the NSA. There was of course precedent: primarily WikiLeaks, under its founder Julian Assange and later under its editor-in chief Kristinn Hrafnsson, which claimed to release 10 million documents in its first ten years, beginning in 2006.[44] However, it was the extent of the exposure of the NSA which alarmed the *Guardian*'s editors and lawyers.[45] Indeed, within days, Snowden was issued by the US Department of Justice with charges on two counts covered by the Espionage Act of 1917. Greenwald had in fact warned Snowden in advance that Obama's administration had prosecuted more leakers under the 1917 Act than all previous US governments combined, even under its architect Woodrow Wilson in World War I.[46] By this time, Snowden had left his NSA job in Hawaii for Hong Kong; he then fled to Moscow, his US passport having been revoked. Russia granted him right of asylum, with extensions repeated to the present day.

Snowden's notoriety derived from his position as a sting for the world's largest military and intelligence power. Still nobody knows the extent of the leaks; the NSA at first believed between 50,000 and 200,000 of its files had been exposed; however, a US intelligence report declassified in June 2015 said Snowden took down 900,000 Department of Defense files, and some estimates have been higher.[47] Outside the US, Australian officials counted 15,000 leaked intelligence files, the British 58,000. The US Joint Chiefs of Staff were at pains to emphasize that Snowden compromised international security and endangered the lives of agents in the field. The personal reputation of Obama maintained a high moral tone, and up to leaving office Obama insisted that a presidential pardon could only be offered if Snowden first faced US courts to answer charges. For a moment, a winner of the Nobel Peace Prize sounded a little like Henry VIII. Snowden posed as a defender of freedoms. 'I do not want to live in a world where everything I do and say is recorded', he said. 'My sole motive is to inform the public as to that which is done in their name and that which is done against them.'[48] He styled himself a whistleblower not a leaker, in contrast to Assange. He claimed to have vetted every document to ensure it was safe and just to do so. As a result Assange accused him of self-censorship and toadying to the US government.[49] To Snowden, his stance was different: 'Nothing is harder than living with a secret that can't be spoken.'[50]

The reputation of the US Department of Defense as innocent injured party took a blow when Angela Merkel, German Federal Chancellor, discovered the NSA had eavesdropped on her personal cellphone for years. Ringing Obama to complain, she compared the NSA with the East German Stasi of her youth.[51] In truth the new methods were the stuff of dreams for secret service agents of Anne Funder's *Stasiland*: there, phone tapping was so useless that one citizen in fifty was instead employed to inform on their neighbours in a weird world of intimate personal invasion.[52] In Snowden's universe, the US government could get between your sheets or under your skin without meeting you:

> Any website: You can watch traffic to and from it. Any computer that an individual sits at: You can watch it. Any laptop that you're tracking: you can follow it as it moves from place to place throughout the world.[53]

This happened not because of over-zealous hacking, it was an instrument of state. Keith B. Alexander was appointed Director of the NSA by Donald Rumsfeld in 2005; in 2010 he rose to four-star general as chief of the US Cyber Command, a division of the Department of Defense. Alexander's doctrine of information was dizzyingly simple. Rather than look for a single needle in the haystack, he said: 'Let's collect the whole haystack. Collect it all, tag it, store it … And whatever it is you want you go searching for it.'[54]

Collection of metadata took place in cooperation with the governments of France (70 million files), Spain (60 million), Italy (47 million), the Netherlands (1.8 million), Norway (33 million), and Denmark (23 million). The relative modesty of the Dutch total only emphasizes the gluttony of the other figures, each equivalent to the respective national population.[55] In the UK, by 2012 GCHQ was able to survey about 1,500 out of 1,600 high-capacity cables in and out of the country. In theory, it accessed a flow of 21.6 petabytes of data per day, equivalent to 192 times the entire British Library book collection.[56]

The popular analogy for this universal reach is a technological species of phone-tapping. The inevitable literary comparison is the opening chapter of George Orwell's *Nineteen Eighty-Four* (1949), where the Telescreen can pick up anything Winston says, 'above the level of a very low whisper', and instantly transmit it. The comparison of the GCHQ's surveillance techniques with a megalibrary or universal book, however, is a reminder that Orwell's concept of the Thought Police is more totalizing than a James Bond bug:

> There was of course no way of knowing whether you were being watched at any given moment. How often, or on what system, the Thought Police plugged in on any individual wire was guesswork. It was even conceivable that they watched everybody all the time. But at any rate they could plug in your wire whenever they wanted to.[57]

The model for this is at least as old as the library. Ashurbanipal writes a colophon in Akkadian to one of the texts in his library: 'I wrote on tablets, checked and collated, and deposited within my palace for perusal and reading.'[58] The library gives him ultimate power, 'king of totality, king of Assyria', a power expressed symptomatically in the remedies his library owns in order to provide medicine or magic to control people's lives.[59] Ashurbanipal boasts of his capacity to possess the body, and to cure it, using the canonical expression 'from the top of the head to the toenails'. Writing invests the body with meaning and at the same time derives its power from this understanding.

What explains the astonishing success of the Egyptian and Chinese languages in ancient society, asks Nicholas Ostler? These languages, so different in inflection, word order, morphology, and grammar, have a common factor: the absolute power of an emperor, and unity under single rule.[60] In addition, Egyptian and Chinese idolized continuity in the writing system, a major drive of which was the bureaucracy of information systems. 'Behold their words remain in writing', boasts an instruction for King Merikare in mid-twentieth-century BCE Egypt: 'Open, that thou mayest read and copy wisdom.'[61] Standardization of systems of education and administration, and immunity to reform, gave these languages 'gross survivability' over millennia, power residing in a 'literate class.'[62]

Grammar and government go together, Ostler says in a resonant phrase, especially in the ability to explain past, present and future. In Egypt this power resided in the manic bureaucracy of the Nile: listing the time and extent of the annual flood year by year, and archiving it, so that it can be predicted in future. In Chinese, it is in the subtle discrimination of time throughout a vast empire: *guò-qu* (passing/go); *xiàn-zài* (appear/be-there); *wèi-lái* (not-yet/come). Sovereignty is passed through language into an abstraction of the continuous presence of the emperor. The Chinese Empire depended on a bureaucracy of writing supplemented by a vast courier system. During the plot against the Emperor Yongzheng in 1728, documents were sent from Beijing 750 miles southeast to Nanjing, 1,000 miles to Hangzhou, and 1,200 to the Hunan capital of Changsha.[63] In the last case it took two weeks for a missive to be received, and another two for a reply; the prerogative of Chinese power was this scriptural pattern.

The Roman Empire learned a similar lesson. The boundaries of the Roman world consisted not only in roads but epigraphy: a vast number of political, funereal, commemorative, and commercial signs, small and large, handwritten, painted or engraved.[64] The most important, however, were the *carved* letters that still make up the bulk of Europe's classical museums. Letters were built to last. Inscriptions carried the signifiers not only of *imperium*, but cultural memory and linguistic uniformity.[65] These concerns, as old as human language, came into acute presence in the late twentieth and early twenty-first centuries CE. Armando Petrucci has described how the Renaissance monumental city was founded on urban epigraphy, in conscious emulation of Roman models.[66] In modern times this was replaced by the ubiquity of advertising boards. Writing is everywhere. Michel de Certeau in 1980 commented on the hieratic status of writing in modernity, created by the fetishization of print technologies. 'Writing, this modern mythical practice', he says, has created 'a cybernetic society.'[67]

For three hundred years, writing in education has become the key to entry into capitalist society; while print technology submits the body to the articulation of this text through writing. Cybernetics as a concept is constructed as a closed signalling loop, in which action within the system generates a change in the environment, creating what is called 'feedback'. It is hardly surprising that the CIA should have become interested in cybernetic theory. Snowden's placement in the CIA station at the American Embassy in the United Nations in Geneva was no accident: Geneva was seen as the epitome of a meeting-place between old-world banking, Swiss secrecy, and the new cyberspace.[68]

Yet lurking within the power of the archive is a fear that it might miss something, that what Certeau calls the 'machinery of representation' may be incomplete.[69] 'Writing cannot express all words, words cannot express all ideas', is a Confucian saying from the fifth century BCE that lies at the heart of Chinese scepticism about power, especially power to resist change.[70] Snowden recounts how the Geneva station was saturated with knowing references to the fact that Geneva was home to Mary Shelley's *Frankenstein*. The 'Frankenstein effect' was intelligence-community shorthand for the idea of a monstrous technology out of step with normative moral thinking, and for the Murphy's Law of security policies producing effects opposite from intended. 'Blowback'—policy meant to advance American interests but that instead hopelessly compromised or contradicted them—was the CIA equivalent to the 'feedback' of cybernetics.

However, Snowden notes a stranger link between *Frankenstein* and the revolution in information that he was charged to put into effect. He calls the book 'an epistolary novel that reads like a thread of overwritten emails'.[71] Shelley's text opens with four letters written by Robert Walton, which set out his literary and emotional needs:

> I shall commit my thoughts to paper, it is true; but that is a poor medium for the communication of feeling. I desire the company of a man who could sympathize with me, whose eyes would reply to mine.[72]

Walton desires writing to be an exact replica of feeling, but finding writing wanting, he projects the idea onto an as yet non-existent friend. This friend will be his double. The remainder of the novel is an enactment of this fatal exercise of doubling. Walton finds his double in Victor Frankenstein, who finds *his* double in the sapient creature of his scientific experiment. We enter the territory of Otto Rank's *Der Doppelgänger* (1914). Art and myth are always purveyors of the double: the mirror-image, the guardian spirit, the immortal soul.[73] The 'modern Prometheus' is a *Doppelgänger*, like Zoroaster meeting 'his own image walking in the garden' in *Prometheus Unbound*, by Mary's husband Percy Bysshe Shelley.[74] The Prometheus myth could have been designed for the internet, of course. From the moment of his first arrival in Geneva, Snowden seems to foreknow his destiny as *Doppelgänger*, as in a memo of June 2008: 'Step forth and assume your name in the pantheon. It's always been there, your avatar's true name.'[75]

Did Snowden steal America's fire or give humanity back its freedom? It depends on your view of the hall of mirrors in computerized text. 'What have you got to hide?' we are asked, if we question why it is necessary to record and read every online conversation. Google's CEO stated in an interview with CNBC in 2008: 'If you have something that you don't want anyone to know, maybe you shouldn't be doing it in the first place.'[76]

In Auden's poem 'The Watchers' (1932), a man looks out from his window at the darkest blackness of the Fascist future:

> O Lords of Limit training dark and night
> And setting a tabu twixt left and right

The lords of the internet make no distinction between information and society. Facebook's three 'big company goals' are 1. Connecting Everyone. 2. Understanding the World. And 3. Building the Knowledge Economy.[77] These goals are blankly utopian rather than dystopian: futuristic, idealistic, and infantilist. Yet they depend on a model of language and of writing as totally transparent, against all available analysis and experience. From Nineveh's Ashurbanipal to Anderson at the NSA, the mantra has been 'collect the whole haystack'. But what does the haystack mean, once collected? Anderson's minions recognized minimally the problem of metaphor. Greenwald cites the 'BOUNDLESS INFORMANT program' which in a one-month period beginning 8 March 2013, collected data from more than 3 billion phone calls and emails passing through the US telecommunications system.[78] Does it make a difference that the name of this Big Data visualization tool sounds like Orwellian irony? The totalitarian ambition of the program is transparent: this tool rivalled the entire data collection of Russia or China. Yet BOUNDLESS INFORMANT acknowledges a gap between information and understanding, which Zuckerberg denies by reducing everything to 'content'.[79] Meanwhile the NSA created an extraordinary alliance with Google and Facebook. EGOTISTICAL GIRAFFE (Thomas Pynchon appears to have taken over narration) enabled anonymity in mining online browsing; MUSCULAR (Norman Mailer interposes) invaded the private networks of Google and *Yahoo!*; OLYMPIA (Margaret Atwood desires a hearing) spied on Brazilian energy by hacking Canada.[80] In case of misprision, it should be noted that all these codenames were created at random to avoid public scrutiny.

For a top secret order under the Foreign Intelligence Surveillance Act in April 2013, Swift is presiding muse, perhaps in the mode of *An Argument Against Abolishing Christianity* (1708): 'IT IS HEREBY ORDERED that, the Custodian of Records shall produce to the National Security Agency (NSA) upon service of this Order, and continue production on an ongoing daily basis thereafter for the duration of the Order, unless otherwise ordered by the Court, an electronic copy of the following tangible things'. These tangibles cover the trifling matter of 'all call detail records'; all electronic telephony between the USA and abroad; or for that matter, within the USA; and with a final bathos especially close to Swift, 'including local telephone calls'. Being 'very sensible what a Weakness and Presumption it is, to reason against the general Humour and Disposition of the World', the US government commits itself wearily to the paradox that in order to protect all its citizens, it must order Verizon to spy on all its citizens.[81]

As Snowden recounts, the gathering of electronic harvest is accompanied by a concealment of harvesters. This is called a 'Tor protocol': traffic is distributed and bounced around through randomly generated pathways from Tor server to Tor server, with the purpose of replacing the identity of the source of every communication with that of the last Tor server, in a 'constantly shifting chain'.[82] Yet the most significant aspect of Snowden's memoir is how he reveals that it is not *content*, in the ordinary sense, that the NSA is after. Most people still think that government agencies are interested in content in this sense: that the flow of conversation online is read as if from a book, scanning line by line, recording the thought processes in our heads. According to Snowden, government 'cares comparatively little about that content'; it conducts that kind of surveillance by traditional (if sometimes illegal or violent) human means. The algorithms are working instead on metadata. They analyse on a vast scale for patterns and discrepancies. As need arises, they home in, and at a microscopic level make 'perfect maps, chronologies and associative synopses of an individual person's life'.[83] Metadata tell the intelligence services 'virtually everything they'd ever want or need to know about you', without having any idea of (or interest in) what is going on in your head.

About a decade before the invention of the World Wide Web, Certeau dubbed the operation of the law *la machine à écrire*.[84] The law, he says, writes itself on bodies.

> If the skin were parchment, and the blows you gave were ink
> Your own handwriting would tell you what I think.

So states Dromio in Shakespeare's *Comedy of Errors*.[85] The law makes a book out of each person. It is a premonition of Kafka's seminal fable *In der Strafkolonie*, written late in 1914 and published in 1919. A traveller is shown a remarkable piece of apparatus by an officer at a penitentiary. By means of the machine, punishment is made to fit perfectly with crime, in that the name of the crime is inscribed onto the body while it lies on a shelf inside the machine. In the act of writing, the person dies. The elegance of the machine, the officer recounts, has been so perfected by the previous Commandant that nobody outside the machine knows what is taking place; and different parts of the machine act independently of each other. The machine has three essential components: *das Bett*, the Bed where the condemned person lies; *die Egge* ('the Harrow'), which cuts into the body, following the shape of the human form, with different blades for torso, limbs, and head; and *der Zeichner* ('the Designer') which contains the text.[86] 'In the Designer are all the cogwheels that control the movements of the Harrow, and the machinery is regulated according to the inscription demanded by the sentence', says the Officer.[87] However, the condemned man does not know his sentence in advance; he learns it 'on his body' (*auf seinem Leib*).[88] When the traveller asks about legal defence, the answer is there is no need, since the crime is pre-known.

Everything is presented as if there is transparency of process, with perfect fit between crime, sentence, and punishment. The knowledge economy has no boundaries; indeed, the law has taken on what Certeau calls 'the incarnation of knowledge'.[89] Nonetheless it becomes evident not all is well; that is why the traveller has been invited. Some problems are habitual; the execution process is disagreeably messy. The officer admits the moving parts are not all in good order, and co-ordinating them with a dying body's movements is tricky: 'This is a very complex machine, it can't be helped that things are breaking or giving way here and there.'[90] However, mechanical malfunctions conceal more fundamental issues. In order for the body to be inscribed a text has to be inserted into *der Zeichner*. When the traveller takes a look, however, he cannot read it: 'all he could see was a labyrinth of lines crossing and recrossing each other, which covered the paper so thickly that it was difficult to discern the blank spaces between them.'[91] In any case, the script used by *der Zeichner* is one he has never encountered before. Of course, replies the officer: 'it's no calligraphy for children.' The script kills a man over the course of twelve hours, becoming decipherable to the condemned only after six. The script therefore needs many flourishes and embellishments to fill space.

It turns out that there is no visible or legible correspondence between the original legal *Urteil* ('sentence'), and what is then inscribed on the Designer, and what the Harrow writes. Of special ambiguity is *der Zeichner*: a word in any case ambiguous in German between abstract and physical senses, so that its function is both to conceptualize and to draw the letters. It is hard now, a hundred years after Kafka, not to see *der Zeichner* as a metaphor for software, just as it is hard in the twenty-first century not to see software as a metaphor for what writing has been doing all through its history. Writing forecloses language, by giving it physical form. As it does so, it makes it appear that there is no gap between what we write and what we mean. However, it is only the assertion of the officer that the original sentence is being written onto the body of the condemned, or that the body of the condemned receives it in the same form. All the traveller sees is machinery and blood. *Der Zeichner* is indecipherable, and no indication is made of how one text is translated into the other. The process is steeped in metadata.

Josipovici calls 'In the Penal Colony' the 'most repulsive story Kafka ever wrote'; it is a compliment. With great perception, Josipovici comments that the story itself 'seems to have become a sort of malfunctioning machine'.[92] There is no point of view of narration to which we can escape in order to find redemption from the narrative. The machine carries on regardless. Is it here that the myth of mimetic perfection in the computer is exposed? Objective and subjective reading are held in artificial intelligence to intercalate and imitate each other's secret motivations. However, *In der Strafkolonie* shows a fundamental feedback loop. The machine claims to work with perfect symmetry between the interpretation of crime and punishment: 'now justice was being carried out'. Similarly, we are expected to confirm that in a perfect knowledge economy, there will never be any possibility of injustice, since the truth is always in sight. Truth, knowledge, language, are exactly equivalent. Nietzsche's 1873 essay 'On truth and lying' refutes this. 'Is language the full and adequate expression of all realities?'[93] Only by an illusion; in fact, words are forced arbitrarily to fit situations where they are not equal. *Der Begriff entsteht aus einem Gleichsetzen des Nichtgleichen:* 'Every concept comes into being by making equivalent that which is non-equivalent.'[94] A world of perfect legibility pretends things to be equal that are not. Language consists of a constant aggregation of countless processes of equation. Digital futures promise transparency, whereas human linguistic transaction is based instead on metaphor and transference.

However, while it is often thought that the information revolution changes everything, it has actualized something theoretically contained within writing all along. Writing is always technological: from clay tablet to papyrus roll to typewriter to laptop there is a territorial invasion of function into form. Indeed, Greenwald notes how the surveillance state copies ideas from the history of censorship, reaching back to Jeremy Bentham's Panopticon.[95] *A Plan for a Penitentiary Inspection-House* (Fig. 76), written in imperial Russia and published in Dublin in 1791, begins with a literary synopsis of an architectural model for a building with total surveillance. It reads in a straight line to Kafka:

Before you look at the plan, take in words the general idea of it.

The building is circular.

The apartments of the prisoners occupy the circumference. You may call them, if you please, the *cells*.

These *cells* are divided from one another, and the prisoners by that means secluded from all communication with each other, by *partitions* in the form of *radii* issuing from the circumference towards the centre, and extending as many feet as shall be thought necessary to form the largest dimension of the cell.

The apartment of the inspector occupies the centre: you may call if you please the *Inspector's lodge*.[96]

From the tower, a guard can see every cell and inmate and yet the inmates cannot see into the tower. Prisoners never know whether or not they are being watched. This is not a fable or even a fantasy: Bentham placed his ideas in the Library of the Patent Office, and they survive in a copy in the British Library. Several United States Penitentiaries were inspired by Bentham. The Koepelgevangenis in Haarlem is one of three panopticon prisons designed in the Netherlands by the architects Metzelaar, completed in 1901. It now houses a refuge for asylum seekers and a small museum of Bentham's idea.[97]

Fig. 76. 'The panoptic book'; Willey Reveley, Elevation, section and plan of Jeremy Bentham's Panopticon, 1791. London, UCL Special Collections, Bentham Papers Box 119, fos. 119–30

It is easy enough to see in Bentham an exemplary allegory of a culture of supervision: the outlines of a system not confined to modes of punishment, but applicable to knowledge in general. Bentham proposed extending it to a design for schools: it has the advantage, he says, of eliminating corporal punishment, since play, chatter, and distraction will disappear in front of an omnipresent teacher. Far from seeing his system as sinister, Bentham is neutral in tone, enlightened to the point of smugness. He recalls Psammetichus I, Pharaoh of Egypt, who 'contrived to breed up two children in a sequestered spot, secluded, from the hour of their birth, from all converse with the rest of humankind'. The Panoptical School could scale this up; indeed, he says, improving on the Pharaoh, you could separate for sixteen or eighteen years all the males from all the females, and 'at the end of that period see what the language of love would be'.[98] From this mass experiment in gender orientation, Bentham aspires towards something larger, what he calls 'A rare field for discovery in *metaphysics*'. Bentham's principle is not confined to the prison-house, instead it is a universal map of epistemology.

The story of Psammetichus originates in Herodotus, where it is said to be an experiment into the origin of language. Leaving two newborn children to be brought up by a shepherd, with instructions that no one was to speak with them, the shepherd was to record the first word each spoke for each thing, and thus uncover the root language underlying all others. Hearing the girl cry *bekos*, the Phrygian word for bread, the Pharaoh concluded that Phrygian was the first language of mankind.[99] It is not unlike Augustine's famous account in the *Confessions* of how he first learned language as an infant: 'when people gave a name to an object and when, following the sound, they moved their body towards that object, I would see and retain the fact that that object received from them this sound which they pronounced when they intended to draw attention to it'.[100] It is to this combined theory of language as referentiality and communication that Zuckerberg still appeals, when he assures us all that in the future, technology is going to 'free us up to spend more time on the things we all care about, like enjoying and interacting with each other and expressing ourselves in new ways'.[101]

It is worth paying attention to Wittgenstein's caveat on Augustine's account of language in the *Confessions*: 'But one can say also that it is the idea of a language more primitive than ours'.[102] We are so used to thinking of language as communication, he says, that we think 'the whole point lies in someone else grasping the sense of my words', and taking this as the content of my mind.[103] But what if I say, 'I am in pain!'? The theory of language as communication behaves as if everyone has a box with a beetle in it; no one can look into anyone else's box; everyone says they can only know what a beetle is by looking in their own box.[104] But that is not at all what happens when I cry out in pain.

Wittgenstein's boxes may be contrasted with a theory in science and computing. A 'black box' is a device, system, or object that can be viewed in terms of inputs and outputs, with no knowledge of its internal workings. The idea applies to an algorithm, to the human brain, to an engine or a government. Its implementation is opaque:

> The constitution and structure of the box are altogether irrelevant to the approach under consideration, which is purely external or phenomenological. In other words, only the behaviour of the system will be accounted for.[105]

The system has observable (and relatable) inputs and outputs, but the system is still 'black' to the observer (that is, non-openable). In contemporary society, surveillance capitalism collides with liberal concepts of freedom and privacy. This apparently irreconcilable problem may be explained by the fact that the mining of metadata is a classic example of the black box in action, while defence against it is posited using the model of beetle boxes. Neither is an adequate explanation of human language.

The Enlightenment dreamed also of an idea of human subjectivity as transparent. Facebook appears to agree, making every person into a page. *Tristram Shandy* illustrates the absurdity of the idea by imagining the hero's life in visual terms as perfectly linear. Attempting 'a tolerable straight line', Shandy resorts to a series of incomprehensible squiggles, audaciously reproduced in the first edition.[106] Sterne worked closely with John Hinxman at 35 Stonegate in York for the first two volumes, and with Robert Dodsley in London for the rest, to ensure his text was printed in all its deviance.[107]

No life is an algorithm. Narrowing the scope of the human subject, Foucault argues, was the first ideal of panopticism. To achieve the perfection of power:

> it is at once too much and too little that the prisoner should be constantly observed by an inspector: too little, for what matters is that he know himself to be observed; too much, because he has no need in fact of being so.[108]

With shocking accuracy, Foucault knew in advance what Snowden shows the NSA wants us to think. An inmate never knows for sure whether she *is* being looked upon at any one moment; but she is always sure that she *may* be being looked at. This is the point of the panopticon: 'a machine for dissociating the *see/being seen* dyad: in the peripheric ring, one is totally seen, without ever seeing; in the central tower, one sees everything without ever being seen'. Power is therefore visible and yet unverifiable.

Has the internet actualized Marx's terrifying prophecy in 'The Fragment on Machines'?

> The worker's activity, reduced to a mere abstraction of activity, is determined and regulated on all sides by the movement of the machinery, and not the opposite. The science which compels the inanimate limbs of the machinery, by their construction, to act purposefully, as an automaton, does not exist in the worker's consciousness, but rather acts upon him through the machine as an alien power, as the power of the machine itself.[109]

As a self-sufficient arrangement of knowledge, the book has been the most successful information system in history, from cuneiform cylinder to the paperback. As the physical form of the book extends into the smartphone, it becomes not only a practical solution to the problem of organizing, containing, or disseminating knowledge, but an ideal of knowledge *qua* knowledge. If Big Data corresponds to the world as a whole, an iPhone corresponds to the diminutive *studium generale* of an individual human subject. It contains an aspiration towards an encyclopaedia of the self, and yet an awareness of the limits of personal knowledge, of the mind's measure and finitude. Like human pathology, the book has become a reminder of mortality, of an innate tendency towards decay and decomposition. What is the internet if not the sublimation of a dream in which knowledge is never irretrievable, might even be immortal? And what is the iPhone if not the fragile fantasy machine of the human person, an object that fits in the palm of my hand and that contains all the things I ever thought?

23
Heresy and Modernity

With desire comes a commensurable fear. At the edge between the surface of the page, and what lies beneath or inside, lurks the mystery of personhood itself, of what identifies me as me. The Tyris, site of the old Police Station in Bradford, is one of the lost places of modernity: that world of the uncanny where significant things once took place in spaces which no longer exist. In January 1989, a crowd of 800 gathered outside the brutal concrete edifice, of mixed age, anywhere between 10 years old and 80, but every one of them male. The demonstration had a number of grievances against routine British racism, such as the failure to serve Halal meat in schools, and the Ray Hunniford case (who had declared that white children were held back by having to teach Asian children English). That something else was going on was shown by the presence of a small number of the national Press, including a photographer, tipped off in advance.[1]

The event was organized by the Bradford Council of Mosques. It was a cold winter's day in Yorkshire; the crowd was quiet, dour, even subdued. The older men wore traditional Muslim costume; the large number of teenagers and youths, on the other hand, were in jeans, anoraks, and other western clothes. There were some impromptu banners and boards, painted by hand. Some were straightforwardly insulting ('Rushdie stinks'), or crudely opinionated ('Penguin publishes rubbish'); others attempted a kind of surreal humour: 'Rushdie eat your words' or 'Rushdie has less imagination than a peeled balloon'. Several proclaimed censorship ('Ban the Satanic Verses'), but none violently.

The burning itself (Fig. 77) takes place on a platform high above so as to be visible to all. The novel is carried on a kind of bier. The spine is nailed to a stake, with another pole (designed for fireworks) alongside. The book when held aloft is open, the fore-edge visible and the paper flapping. There is an element of ritual; an imam and two other figures of authority perform the burning, with youths behind in affirmation. Attempts are made unsuccessfully to set it alight with old-fashioned Sadlers matches, using a piece of paper as a firelighter. This element seems low-key. Nonetheless, the book is set on fire, and once it takes light, the flames are fierce. The photographer winces at the heat from having to get close. Once lit, the show is deeply impressionable: the book is held aloft; the crowd shows its acclamation with hands aloft, and indeed some fists. Yet it is not a threatening or even intimidating event. It is rather solemn and intense.

The event made no headlines; *The Sunday Times* put a photograph on an inside page. While full of foreboding (by association with Nazi Germany), the Bradford

Fig. 77. 'The book at the stake'; Bradford, January 1989. Photo: Asadour Guzelian

book-fire found iconic status retrospectively, in the Ayatollah Khomeini's Valentine's Day fatwa:

> I am informing all brave Muslims of the world that the author of *The Satanic Verses*, a text written, edited, and published against Islam, the Prophet of Islam, and the Qur'an, along with all the editors and publishers aware of its contents, are condemned to death. I call on all valiant Muslims wherever they may be in the world to kill them without delay, so that no one will dare insult the sacred beliefs of Muslims henceforth. And whoever is killed in this cause will be a martyr, Allah Willing.[2]

These words still have a power to chill as strong as any from the godforsaken century that produced them. To commit a person to death, in arbitrary fashion, anywhere in the world, with no time limit, is unspeakable. As noted by Islamic scholars at the time, it bore no relation to a traditional idea of a fatwa as a non-binding legal opinion on a point of sharia law. Coming from the Arabic root *f-t-w* ('newness, clarification, explanation'), the word *fatwā* dates back to the Qur'an, in the characteristic formula, 'When they ask you, say' (for example, Q 2: 136). The ḥadīth contains sayings and deeds of companions of the prophet (*ṣaḥāba*) sometimes in anthologies known as *kutub* (or 'books').[3] Here, a three-way commentary between God, Prophet, and believer is replaced by question and answer catechism between Muhammad and his companions.[4]

From here it acquired a standard status in legal practice for clarification by a *mufti* of difficult points. In Twelver Shi'ism, the idea of the 'hidden imam' (derived from Q 18: 65–6) developed from its ninth and tenth century meanings to lend to *fatwā* a broad political impact.[5] Its political use became controversial when the Ottoman Sultan, encouraged by the Germans, declared jihad to mark the Ottoman Empire's entry into the First World War in November 1914.[6] This usage was widely condemned by Islamic scholars. In Iran, Ayatollah Khomeini used the term to inaugurate the Council of the Islamic Revolution and the Iranian National Parliament in 1979. However, he did not use it of his incitement to murder Rushdie; by contrast, when Osama bin Laden used the word to proclaim jihad 'against Jews and Crusaders' in 1998, it was pointed out by jurists that he was not a mufti and had no right to declare either a *fatwā* or jihad.[7]

The escalation of the word into an inviolable taboo or unpronounceable ban, bringing death with its utterance, mirrors the conception of Rushdie's novel as having a content so horrible it cannot be named. Khomeini never explained in one alif his interpretation of the novel or identified the part of the text found offensive.[8] The 'Satanic verses' of the title occur in early exegesis of the Qur'an and in the biography of Muhammad by al-Tabari (915 CE).[9] In Sura 53 ('An-Najm'), the divine voice reassures the prophet that he has not gone mad, nor does he speak out of personal desire. In the interpolated version at verse 20, mentioned in al-Tabari, Muhammad is tempted by Satan to utter a further line: 'These are the exalted *gharāniq*, whose intercession is hoped for'. The word occurs nowhere else in Arabic, although it is related to a word for a 'crane'. Commentators suggested that the prophet was making charitable allowance for idol-worshippers sometimes to become Muslims. By the thirteenth century the *gharāniq* verses had been decisively rejected, and in modern Islam they are thought of as heretical, since they make the prophet appear to make concessions on the status of pagan deities.[10]

By 1988, these verses were the stuff of footnotes. Some draw attention instead to details in the novel insulting to Islam: the use of the name Mahound, a derogatory Crusader nickname for the prophet; or of the Angel Gibreel (Gabriel) for a film star; or the prophet's wife Ayesha for a fanatical Indian girl; or of his other wives, for the prostitutes in a brothel in the city of Jahilia, which itself (meaning 'ignorance') is the standard term for the pre-Islamic period in Arabia. It is speculated Khomeini took personal offence to an account of an imam in Section IV ('Ayesha'), which Rushdie read out at a promotional event, presenting a satirical portrait of the Ayatollah during exile in Paris:

> grown monstrous, lying in the palace forecourt with his mouth yawning open at the gates; as the people march through the gates he swallows them whole.[11]

Beyond this lies a larger question about the nature of sacred texts or the meaning of blasphemy. While *The Satanic Verses* represent for Rushdie an idea of the limits of truth and fiction, for the Bradford imam who burned a book he had never read, the title took on a different identity, which called into question the very idea of a holy book. Into this aporia Khomeini rushed in with bloodthirsty vengeance. There were riots in Islamabad and Srinagar; Hezbollah in Lebanon offered to carry out the death sentence; a $6 m bounty was put on Rushdie's head; the artist escaped into hiding, moving from house to house every few days, desperate and fearful, with 24-hour protection from the British police. Two bookshops were bombed in the Charing Cross Road in London, along with the department store Liberty, which contained a Penguin bookstore.

Into this maelstrom jumped a host of Western critics, some determined to endorse an irrevocable culture war between East and West, some (in a strange act of doublethink), bent on finding ways of making Rushdie guilty of a crime that did not exist. The writers John Le Carré and Roald Dahl coruscated Rushdie for not applying self-censorship. The Labour MP Keith Vaz first announced his forthright support for Rushdie, and then joined a march in Leicester to ban the book. Margaret Thatcher, the Prime Minister, refused to contemplate a ban; but the Archbishop of Canterbury and Chief Rabbi, rather than defend the book against a charge of blasphemy, asked for the crime of blasphemy to be extended, in order to protect Christians and Jews.

'Blasfemie' is an old French word which also leads to the word 'blame'; it comes from ancient Greek, 'to speak injury', used in Athens to regulate slander. Blasphemy was part of canon law, and was used by Pope Gregory XI in 1377 in his bull distinguishing divine from civil dominion.[12] On this basis, Wyclif and the Lollards were condemned in 1382.[13] In 1401, the statute *De heretico comburendo* announced the death penalty for relapsed and impenitent heretics in England.[14] Between 1407 and 1409, Thomas Arundel, Archbishop of Canterbury, formalized this into more general linguistic laws. Preaching had to be licensed; preachers and schoolmasters could not discuss the sins of the clergy; matters of faith could not be discussed outside universities.[15] From here, and ominously, Arundel's Constitutions switched from supervision of speaking to writing, especially vernacular.[16] Tudor law after the Reformation switched attention from blasphemy to treason and sedition.[17] Only in 1697 did blasphemy enter statute, once again to clear up problems in general censorship following changes in book licensing. It was extended to His Majesty's province of the Massachusetts Bay the same year. Ever since, blasphemy has served a turn for any government wanting to get its way, or any lawyer employed by a client to limit what somebody wants to say of him.

What did Rushdie do to deserve disowning by the religious establishment? His epic novel *Midnight's Children* (1981), expiating British India from violent colonial past, opens with a quotation from the Qur'an: 'Recite in the name of the Lord thy Creator, who created man from clots of blood.'[18] Yet in the interests of toleration of religion, religious leaders urged the banning of a book. India joined with Muslim countries, along with apartheid South Africa, in the last major act of a distinguished history of censorship. The Council of South African Writers disinvited Rushdie from speaking at an anti-apartheid literary festival on security grounds; an action causing long-term embarrassment to Nadime Gordimer and J. M. Coetzee.[19] The ban only expired post-apartheid in 2002, alongside renewed complaints against the book that it was hurtful to Islam.[20] Meanwhile, spurred by controversy, sales took off, 750,000 copies purchased by May 1989. Figures took a downturn when major booksellers such as Barnes and Noble refused to stock it, out of threat and fear rather than sympathy with censorship.

The novelist Hanif Kureishi in a thirtieth anniversary article in 2019, suggests a deeper meaning: 'Touching the Untouchable'.[21] 'Untouchable' in two senses: first, the book touched questions of the sacred; second, as a result, book and author were treated as untouchable. While scathing of hypocrisies large and small that surrounded the case, Kureishi is convinced it marked a turning point in cultural and literary history. He (like Rushdie) is only too aware of how Western liberal values have often acted as a code for colonial assumptions; Rushdie was an early defender of the Iranian revolution. However, Kureishi sees through blasphemy to a deeper intellectual malaise. Islam has no monopoly on forbidden speech. This has produced contorted results. Some historically Christian countries have been embarrassed into repealing draconian blasphemy laws by silent sensitivity over the Rushdie case: England and Wales abolished blasphemy in 2008, the Netherlands in 2014, Denmark in 2017, Ireland by referendum in 2018, New Zealand in 2019. Yet meantime measures redescribing blasphemy as a 'hate crime' have sprung up, often in the same countries. What is this debate showing, or else concealing?

Rushdie himself responded to the terrifying fate befalling him with an astonishingly graceful and philosophical essay (*Is Nothing Sacred?*) published in February 1990, less than a year after the so-called fatwa. Given as the Herbert Read Lecture and read aloud by Harold Pinter with its author in hiding, Rushdie states that until recently his reply was negative: 'No, nothing is sacred in and of itself.'[22] Ideas, texts, and people have been made sacred in history (from the Latin *sacrare*, 'to set apart'); but this is an act of human naming. Nevertheless, Rushdie declares that it never occurred to him that his own secularism should be felt as in conflict with another person's belief. Now, he adds with understatement, 'I find my entire world-picture under fire.' Is he forced after all to find *something* sacred: consisting, perhaps, in the very freedom of the imagination to exist outside the tenets of another people's sense of the sacred? He apologizes for his absence from his audience, then redoubles this absence as an expression of his deeper presence *in words* rather than in person. He now asserts the significance of the novel as a peculiar type of language. If religion 'seeks to privilege one language above all others', he says, the novel has always asserted the simultaneous existence of different languages.[23] Indeed, he elevates the form of the novel above any other, because it creates a secure arena for 'conflicting discourses *right inside our heads*'. He calls this 'a secret identity': one that is *shared*, perhaps *merged*, between writer and reader.[24]

Is Rushdie the Michael Servetus of the twentieth century? The trial and death of Miguel Serveto is a traumatic event in the history of freedom of conscience. Mathematician, anatomist, astrologer, poet and theologian, he was accused of anti-trinitarianism and anti-paedobaptism. Condemned by the Catholic church in France, he was put to death on 27 October 1553 in Protestant Geneva. Sebastian Castellio, in *Contra libellum Calvini*, is the only contemporary voice who speaks in Servetus' favour, until retrospective biographies by Polish Socinians in the seventeenth century such as Benedykt Wiszowaty. Voltaire wrote that the arrest and execution of Servetus in Geneva was a barbaric act and an insult to the rights of Nations.[25] His execution by burning at the stake still reverberates.[26] At the 500th Anniversary of the birth of Calvin in Geneva in 2009, the trial of Servetus was an open wound, even among *aficionados*. Geneva's conscience has blushed for hundreds of years. A planned memorial to Servetus was fudged in 1903, resulting in a pusillanimous plaque off the beaten track, further redress refused.[27]

Finally, in 2011, a statue was erected for Servetus' 500th anniversary, at Champel, south-east of Plainpalais, a part of the city where it is easy to find oneself by getting lost.[28] For the occasion, a chocolate cake in the shape of Servetus' *Christianismi Restitutio* ('The Restoration of Christianity'), was baked. It is dubbed the 'fourth surviving copy': all others were destroyed, many of them in fires at public burnings.

Servetus, a native of Spain, settled in Vienne in the Dauphiné in the 1540s to work as personal physician to the archbishop, Pierre Palmier. It was here, at the behest of Jean Frellon the printer, that Servetus began a fatal correspondence with Calvin.[29] Servetus had experimented with heterodox ideas for years: he published *De Trinitatis Erroribus* ('On the Errors of the Trinity') in 1531 and the next year *Dialogorum de Trinitate libri duo* ('Dialogues on the Trinity'). If he expected a sympathetic ear from Calvin, arch-heretic of the Catholic world, Calvin believed himself to be nothing if not orthodox. Already in 1546 Calvin wrote to Guillaume Farel, 'Servetus has just sent me a long volume of his ravings', implying Servetus would not be safe if he came to Geneva in person.[30] From Lyon in 1553 came the *Christianismi Restitutio*. Here Servetus added predestination to his list of targets: God, he argued, cannot condemn arbitrarily a majority of his creation. Calvin sent him a copy of *Institutio Christianae Religionis* in admonishment. Servetus, scratching the itch, annotated this with critical observations.[31]

In the meantime, on 16 February 1553, Servetus was denounced as a heretic in Catholic Vienne, and with Balthasard Arnollet (printer of *Christianismi Restitutio*), he was questioned at Lyon by the inquisitor Matthieu d'Ory.[32] By April he was in prison. After escaping, he was condemned in his absence—partly on the testimony of the heretic Calvin (either by delicious irony, or in a malevolent interconfessional dance). Although Calvin denied stitching him up with the Catholics in Lyon, Servetus was sentenced to be burned with his books. He planned an escape to Italy but, perhaps believing too much in his own luck, or else planning to challenge Calvin directly, he turned up in Geneva, attended a sermon by Calvin in the church of St Pierre, and promptly got arrested again.

Neither Calvin nor the city authorities intended letting Servetus off lightly.[33] Calvin's personal animus corroborated a fear that anything less than full condemnation would expose Geneva politically; in any event he was convinced God wanted it. On 26 October 1553 the city council met and sentenced Servetus to a condemnation openly modelled on trials for heresy in the medieval church. It cited evidence even-handedly from Protestant and Catholic processes against the Spanish doctor, dating back to his treatises on the Trinity in Hagenau in Germany. That was from Servetus' Straßburg period, when he shocked Bucer and Capito, and was also cited by German Catholic authorities. Indeed, the Calvinists even freely quoted from Catholics in Vienne. The 'church of God', it seemed, reunified for a moment in common horror. The Genevan city fathers concluded in conscious imitation of the Lyon Inquisition:

we condemn you Michael Servetus to be bound and taken to Champel and there attached to a stake and burned alive together with your book written by your hands, as well as printed, until your body will be reduced to ashes.[34]

To modern eyes, Servetus is a natural intellectual hero. His *Christianismi Restitutio* contains not only theology, but the first correct description of the function of pulmonary circulation in Europe.[35] His *Syruporum universia ratio* ('Complete Explanation of the Syrups') is a landmark in the emerging science of pharmacology. He was enough of an astronomer to predict an occultation of Mars by the Moon. Who now crosses fields so effortlessly, from chemistry to philosophy to geography to anatomy? Also, Servetus' heterodoxy appeals to us for precisely the reasons it horrified his contemporaries. His ideas on the Trinity begin from a premise that the concept is not scriptural. Yet he also hoped that rejecting trinitarian dogma would make Christianity more appealing to Judaism and Islam. Servetus was questioned by the *procureur général* in Geneva about the Qur'an (and about his sexuality). He was also examined about his Jewish ancestry: Servetus declared his parents were 'Christians of ancient race'.[36] His Spanish homeland made him aware of the sensitivities of *converso* Jews and Muslims. The monotheism of Judaism and Islam was affronted by what Servetus called the 'tritheism' of the Trinity. According to Servetus, divine *logos* manifested itself in Christ; but only the *logos* was eternal. In *De trinitatis erroribus*, he stated that Christ is not the eternal son of God but 'the Son of the eternal God'. In that sense, he agreed with a central tenet of Arius in the fourth century: *there was a time when the son did not exist*, ἦν ποτε ὅτε οὐκ ἦν. Nonetheless, Servetus distanced himself from Arianism: 'The incomprehensible God is known through Christ, by faith, rather than by philosophical speculations. He manifests God to us, as the expression of his very being, and through him alone God is known'.[37] Servetus' theology, if tinged with mysticism, appeals to Enlightenment sensibility. He rejects philosophical speculation in favour of a simpler articulation of faith.

Servetus became a seminal figure in the Enlightenment argument for religious toleration, above all in Voltaire. Voltaire said that he could have liked Calvin, if he had not burned Servetus; with epigrammatic even-handedness, he says he could have agreed with the Council of Constance, without the burning of Jan Hus.[38] By 1757 the irony is still there but has become more ferocious: 'Calvin avait une âme atroce aussi bien qu'un esprit éclairé'.[39] The murder of Servetus, he says, today seems abominable. The idea of a fierce soul allied to an enlightened mind lingered long in the European imagination. In the *Philosophical Dictionary*, begun in 1752, Voltaire describes a bonfire of dogmas ('Les Dogmes'), in which character 'C' appears boasting of victories over the Pope, idolatry, and free will. As he is speaking, the ghost of a man called 'S' appears at a burning stake. 'S' condemns 'C' as a 'monster' for putting a man to death by the cruellest of tortures, at which point 'C' is himself thrown into the fiery abyss.[40]

Voltaire's argument gained piquancy from the fact that in the 1750s he sought refuge in Geneva from censorship elsewhere. Typically, he tormented his Calvinist hosts by arguing that they, too, would never condemn Servetus now. He contrasts a bloodthirsty Calvin with his gentle modern inheritors, egging them on to declare for toleration, or else inciting them to renewed intolerance. He embarrassed Enlightenment Geneva by claiming it is now empty of true Calvinists: 'je ne connais pas de ville où il y ait moins de calvinistes que dans cette ville de Calvin'.[41] However, he also attacked Servetus for being a fool (*un sot*)—and worse—a mad fool. In this, theology itself is the ultimate offender.[42] Goaded into foolishness, the Genevan Consistory responded to Voltaire's wit by banning Voltaire's works as contrary to religion and sound morals.[43]

Voltaire is now best known for a *bon mot* on tolerance which he never wrote: 'I disapprove of what you say, but I will defend to the death your right to say it'. It is not from *Candide* but instead was written by Evelyn Beatrice Hall in 1906.[44] Voltaire understands better than Hall what has come to be known as the 'paradox of toleration'.[45] If *sacrare* means to set something apart, *tolerare* means to put up with something, to accept on sufferance. Bernard Williams calls it 'the impossible virtue': simultaneously we are required to think something is terribly bad, but also that it is good for it to be allowed to flourish.[46] Is this liberal virtue of superiority so obviously better than the religious one? Yes, says Voltaire, because it does not involve killing anyone. No one put this more succinctly than Voltaire's fellow countryman Castellio, *hominem occidere non est doctrinam tueri sed hominem occidere* ('To kill a man does not mean to protect a doctrine, it means to kill a man').[47] The epigram is the stronger because it appears to contain a translingual pun on the Latin verb *tueri*, which is the ancestor of the French verb *tuer* ('to kill', perhaps originally with a mafia-style sense of 'protection'). And yet, Voltaire notes, it is tolerance that is said to be dangerous.[48]

Nonetheless, Voltaire insists, tolerance is a human right, while intolerance is the right of tigers.[49] In this he was building on Jean Bodin's perception that tolerance is the most prudent policy for a state in pursuing political equilibrium. In the seventeenth century, this argument reached its apogee in Spinoza's *Tractatus Theologico-Politicus* (1670), which maintained that while the state has the right to regulate the external exercise of religion, it cannot exercise authority over inner beliefs. In a free commonwealth, Spinoza states, every man may think as he pleases, and say what he thinks. This quotes a saying of Tacitus, *ubi sentire quae velis et quae sentias dicere licet*.[50] This does not, Spinoza says, infringe the right of the sovereign.[51] At the heart of Spinoza's argument, Jonathan Israel contends, is a questioning of the 'theological view of the universe'.[52]

At the end of the century a kind of consensus formed itself after two hundred years of internecine Christian wars of religion. The most radical position was adopted by Pierre Bayle, a French Protestant in exile in Holland. Bayle argued in his *Commentaire* that religion is based on personal faith, not on the apprehension of objective truth.[53] He therefore refuted Augustine's view, expressed in his famous Letter 93 against the heresies of the Donatists, that in certain circumstances force is an act of charitable necessity in order to save the soul of another.[54] On the contrary, compulsory faith is an offence to the deity.[55] Religion is a different form of knowledge than that acquired by reason alone, Bayle argues, and therefore is beyond politics. A less radical position was adopted by Locke in his *Letter Concerning Toleration*, published in Latin in the Netherlands (the only place in Europe where common sense was tolerated). Locke argued for a separation of the jurisdiction of church and state, in a fashion that has been profoundly influential in Western democracies. Religion, he says, consists in the 'inward persuasion of the mind'.[56] The state takes responsibility for the 'civic interests' of the people, but 'care of the soul' lies beyond it. Who can be judge between legislator and people? *Solus Deus*, 'God alone'. The free exercise of religion is therefore God-given. Having established this position, Locke then punched holes in it, in the balance between the internals and externals of religion: while allowing for outward freedom of worship, he rejects the right to atheism, since it is a public evil. Some forms of toleration are intolerable. More oddly, Locke's idea of toleration is founded on religious principles.[57]

Locke's illiberal liberalism stands behind a defence of freedom of speech down to the time of Rushdie. Yet it also allows a form of attack on Rushdie, for example, arguments for freedom of religion, or against religious hatred. Civil peace, it is argued, can only be maintained by banning the book; or alternatively, that the existence of the book is an offence against freedom to follow Islam. In the opposite direction, Martha Nussbaum advocates legal constraints 'when religious practice violates the rights of nonconsenting people'.[58] This is in spite of an expansion in the concept of toleration in modern liberalism, for instance in the political theory of John Rawls. Toleration is fundamental to modern democracy, Rawls says, and must 'cohere with equal justice' to all citizens.[59] To the older version of religious freedom, he responds with the widest view of 'public reason': 'Accounts of human nature we put aside and rely on a political conception of persons as citizens instead.'[60] For this purpose Rawls makes a curious alliance between 'public culture' and 'the internal life', in which the one supports and nurtures the other.

However, the Rushdie case reminds us that the alignment of external and internal definitions of freedom is exactly the problem. It was not Rushdie's inward opinions that came under threat, but the physical existence of his book. Until 1988, the imam in Bradford had hardly heard of him: Rushdie was part and parcel of an infidel liberal majority. Yet with the Ayatollah's so-called fatwa it was not the banning of a book that shocked but the extermination of the author. There is thus a double fetishization going on, first between an idea and a book, and secondly between the book and the human body. In the face of this, conventional pieties of freedom of speech and thought become hopelessly inadequate to the emotions embroiled. Rushdie's book is pinned to the stake and put to the fire. In this sense, the book marks the boundary between internal and external life. Once again, the parallels between Servetus and Rushdie are only too clear. Calvin owned a manuscript copy of the *Restitutio* which he refused to give over to the printer but instead supplied to the Geneva Council as 'an aid to burning the author'.[61] When Arnoullet was set to print Servetus in Lyon, he did so on condition that it be undertaken with the utmost secrecy, and that the author bear all the costs of production. Printing commenced on St Michael's Day, 29 September 1552: 'The manuscript was burned leaf by leaf as the printed text was set in type'.[62] Or recall Servetus' sentence in France before his final quietus in Geneva: he is to be burned in effigy since his body is missing. His picture was symbolically hanged, to deprive it of breath, and then burned; alongside (in an uncanny extra) five bales of blank paper.[63]

It needs to be remembered that however rational he sounds, Servetus nonetheless offended just about everyone. Offence is a necessary precondition of toleration as much as intolerance. Who else unites the Inquisition with the Calvinists, the Calvinists with the Lutherans, Strasbourg with Zurich? Even the usually benign Melanchthon endorsed the condemnation.[64] The self-styled 'libertines', the anti-Calvinist party in Geneva, approved burning as the means of death, even though Calvin himself suggested beheading as more humane.[65] What is it that makes Servetus so reviled? He is, of course, an anti-Trinitarian; and as Rowan Williams stated in his biography of Arius, 'Arianism has often been regarded as the archetypal Christian deviation, something aimed at the very heart of the Christian confession.'[66] Second, perhaps, there is a more atavistic prejudice: John Henry Newman called Arius 'judaizing' and 'humanitarian', neither of which he meant as compliments.[67] Underlying all these problems is a more profound issue of human embodiment.

In understanding the violence of the reaction against Servetus in the Protestant world, we need first of all to recognize that Trinitarianism, after the repudiation of Arius, became the benchmark of every kind of Christian orthodoxy. It is at the heart of the Nicene Creed, used by churches east *and* west, Catholic *and* Protestant. Nicene Christianity is the philosophical stratum used to claim unity whatever the division, to decorate the tent outside which Mormons or Jehovah's Witnesses congregate. Protestant groups in the early generations needed a sense of orthodoxy, not despite, but *because* Catholic theologians called them unorthodox. It is for this reason that in England, too, although much less celebrated, the last burnings for heresy, in 1612, were on charges principally of anti-Trinitarianism.[68] Bartholomew Legate was burned at the stake at Smithfield in March 1612, and three weeks later, Edward Wightman in Lichfield.

What connects these heresies at a visceral level is scepticism about incarnation, both in the sense of Christ's adoption of the godhead in human form, and in the incarnation of the human in general as a divine creation. Anti-Trinitarianism is the heresy, if you like, of disembodiment. No wonder it became the cardinal sin, or holy vice, of the Enlightenment. It dethrones the mystical body and replaces it with mere ideas, reducing Christianity to a great moral theory. It is this which also brings down upon it a peculiarly vicious form of bodily punishment. Here a detail of Servetus' trial and quietus is significant: in the sentence of death he should be 'burned alive together with your book written by your hands, as well as printed, until your body will be reduced to ashes'. Just so, Servetus went to his death, not only by burning but with green wood, still bearing leaves, to extend the torture. As a *coup de grâce*, he bore on his person his last, banned, book, chained to his leg.[69] This is Kafka's death written on the body.

It is Servetus' theory of body, in which the spark of divine spirit is found in human blood as much as it is within Christ's person, that so distressed Calvin. Calvin reported in *Defensio orthodoxae fidei*, published by Robert Estienne in 1554, that 'I begged him rather to think and ask God's mercy, whom he vilely blasphemed by wanting to abolish the three persons that are in his essence'.[70] Servetus in turn accused anyone distinguishing between God as Father, Son, and Holy Spirit of 'fabricating an infernal dog with three heads'.[71] Servetus called the Trinity a 'devil'; Calvin responded by calling *him* 'un démoniacle'.[72] Servetus, Calvin declared, disfigured human nature. Yet Calvin could not quite get rid of Servetus. In the last edition of the *Institutio* in 1559, a year before his own death, Calvin returned to the subject of the Trinity. Servetus held that God is made tripartite by being said to have three persons. Since God must possess unity, such a triad (according to Servetus) must be 'imaginary': *hanc esse imaginariam*.[73] Servetus makes persons equivalent to 'external ideas' – *externas quasdam ideas*. However, *logos* is not, Calvin insists, equivalent to an *idea*. Servetus has made belief in the Trinity into idolatry—as if a portion of God could be found in a person, as in wood or stone. But the word of God cannot be, Calvin says, 'an outward or figurative splendour' (*non potuit certe externus esse aut figurativus splendor*); it must have ὑπόστασις, existence or essence, 'that resided in God himself'.[74] What the word of God *is*, Calvin admits in a previous chapter, is not something human words (*aut cogitatio aut lingua*) can express. It is a mystery; or to use a word Calvin habitually uses when the going gets tough, a *labyrinthus*.[75] How can human mind, which can barely understand the body of the sun (*corpus Solis*), or even its own nature, comprehend the mystery of the nature of God?

What lies within one *corpus* or another? Calvin uses the same word of the sun, of humanity, and of Christ the son of God. In stretching the distance between his own conception and that of Servetus, Calvin puts language itself to the stake. Servetus calls representing the divine in words an *imago*, Calvin a *mysterium*. One man's imaginary is another's mystery. Calvin two chapters earlier in the *Institutes* states that every figurative representation of God contradicts his essence.[76] He cites Augustine in the *City of God* on a lost passage in Seneca, in which the Latin philosopher mocks popular belief in a material god, where god is given different sexes and diverse bodies or a living and breathing form.[77] All this is idolatry, making God become a monster. Yet in revisiting the problem of the Trinity after the trial of Servetus, Calvin comes close to contradicting his own discussion of the nature of the Word (and of words). God is known by words and the Word only. Every *figura* of God is therefore an *idolon*. Images can never stand in place of books (*imagines esse pro libris*).[78]

Strapping the book to the leg of Servetus as he burned was like a last vestige for the Calvinists of treating a book like a thing. The idea of the Trinity threatens what otherwise we could call a disincorporation of the world of the book within Calvin's theology, the word made disincarnate. Rousseau, child of Geneva, declared that Christianity is 'une religion toute spirituelle', a sentiment justly Calvinist.[79] Yet his conclusion, that the social contract requires of us a civic religion, might have appealed to Robespierre but would have horrified Calvin. The Word in Calvin is spirit, because only as spirit can the Word be universal and eternal. Is heresy a bodily crime or a mental one? In medieval theology heresy was defined (of course) as intellectual error, but the metaphors for understanding it are prevalently bodily.[80] Matthieu d'Ory, Servetus' accuser, was appointed 'l'inquisiteur de la foy' by François 1er at Lyon, on 30 May 1536. He transferred both the concept and the system of punishment for crimes such as blasphemy into ordinances against printers and booksellers. François set up a special court, 'La chambre ardente' ('the fiery chamber') to try such cases.[81] Ory examined Etienne Dolet, Rabelais' publisher; Dolet, perhaps anti-Trinitarian, was burned in 1546.

Punishment for blasphemy ranged from confiscation of property, to banishment, or (in extreme cases), strangling followed by burning. Banned books found in a person's possession were burned in their presence. For Pierre Bricquet in Moulins in 1547, 'seront les livres réprouvez et censurez trouvez en sa possession, bruslez en sa présence'.[82] Pierre watches his books burn with his feet and head bared, forced to hold a burning candle one pound in weight. In October 1548 in Paris, Léonard Dupré was condemned to be burned alive in the place Maubert, his books burned in his presence beforehand as part of the spectacle. In a curious appendix, commonplace in Spain as well as in France, an effigy of Léonard was also burned in Bar-sur-Seine, where his original crimes took place. If Dupré persists, his tongue will be cut out; but if he repents and shows a true conversion, after he has felt a little the heat of the flames (*ung peu senty le feu*), he will be strangled as a mercy.[83] A logic of bodily substitution takes place. Heresy is a falling away from reason rather than rational choice; it is behaviour that is compulsive, disordered, disruptive of bodily control. As a form of socialized disease, its punishment is therefore also a form of bodily purgation: the disease is burnt away to nothing so that the body of society that remains is free from further harm.

At the end of the century in the Campo de' Fiori in Rome, Giordano Bruno was burned at the stake, his tongue bound because of his wicked words. In the nineteenth century he was reinvented as a 'martyr for science', assuming (wrongly) that his heterodoxy consisted in the Copernican theory of the revolutions of the heavens.[84] Milton tarred the Inquisition with the same brush for the imprisonment of Galileo.[85] Voltaire declared that a Portuguese Isaac Newton would have suffered an auto-da-fé.[86] Whiggish and Protestant history forgets that Bruno was condemned not for astronomy, but for denying the Trinity and the divinity of Christ; and Galileo for sounding like Bruno.[87] Newton is anti-Trinitarian. The ultimate heresy is disincarnation. The conflict found in Rawls between external and 'internal life' reaches back from Locke to Calvin. Indeed, Servetus and Castellio were still banned books at the time of Locke. Calvin is caught in the act of reinventing heresy as mental rather than bodily crime. Calvinism discovers inwardness and immediately imprisons it. Rawls reinvents political liberty at the level of inwardness, but inwardness never exists in its own right. As Rushdie's life shows better than anybody, the 'internal life' is tested to its extreme only externally. His book acts as a bodily substitution, it is subjected to violence in a stupefyingly literal form of mimesis. What the Rushdie and the Servetus cases share is a sense of how a philosophy of the book is bound up in a material history, just as the material life of books is subject to a complex nexus of ideas about what the status of the book is felt to be. The book is characterized not so much by an objective reality, as by its status as a liminal object, marking *a boundary* between material object and human subject.

That boundary can be held to exist on a number of levels. In a fundamental sense, the book exists as a physical object consisting of marks on the page, and yet equally (and by contrast) as a repository of meanings abstracted from those marks. Yet the struggle lies deeper still, within language itself. An impossibility of maintaining a division between body and soul in writing, or text and meaning, is equivalent to an impossibility of driving a wedge between signifier and signified, because there is no wedge or bridge, only a series of metaphors failing to resolve the problem. At the heart of the controversy over *The Satanic Verses* lies a *horror vacui*, shared with Calvin's anxiety over the Trinity. This is the fury of monotheism, regulating the world of writing in all its aspects. *The Satanic Verses* casts doubt on a capacity of words to touch the sacred. What if words do not contain what is promised within them? Are they image, figure, or mystery?

In 1934, Stefan Zweig, the Viennese Jewish *littérateur*, left Austria for good. He stopped writing novels and embarked instead on a pair of polemical historical biographies, first *Erasmus von Rotterdam*, and then *Castellio gegen Calvin* (1936). A displacement activity in the face of Nazi persecution is barely repressed. Erasmus on the first page becomes *der erste streitbare Friedensfreund* ('the first peace-loving fighter').[88] A connection between Zweig's projects is found in Servetus' last words (in praise of Erasmus) on the scaffold: 'he had something'. What Erasmus had, was what Rushdie has called that most sacred of things, literary freedom, or what Castellio called *De arte dubitandi* (1561), the 'art of doubt'.[89] Zweig knew this from the inside: in 1924 his Viennese friend Freud gave him

Fig. 78. 'The relic of 1933'; *Lesen gegen das Vergessen*, Berlin, Bebelplatz, 2012

the manuscript of his lecture 'Der Dichter und das Phantasieren'—'the poet and fantasy'—where Freud argues that literature sets free repressed desires.[90] Zweig could see the threat coming: his novel *Amok* (1922) was torched in the book-burnings of 1933. In 2012, a political installation (Fig. 78) displayed a scorched copy of *Amok* in Berlin.

In 1933, Helmut Knochen, leader of the local National Socialist Students' Union, picked the half-burnt book out of the Göttingen bonfire as a souvenir for his French teacher. From 1940, Knochen worked for the SS in Paris, promoted in 1942 to direct the hunt for Jews and Communists in occupied France.[91] He employed his old teacher Jean-Philippe Larrose as an interpreter. After the war, Knochen escaped two sentences of death, later defending colleagues in war-crimes trials by claiming not to know the fate of deported Jews. Larrose, mean-while, in 1997 donated his book to the Museum of Resistance in Besançon, having kept it for sixty-four years.[92] From there, the Nazi-hunter Beate Klarsfeld bor-rowed it for the annual book festival of the German political party Die Linke.[93]

The event was called a 'reading against forgetting'. Reading, more than an act of remembrance, is an act of unforgetting. How much is Larrose forgetting in his letter of donation in 1997, where he reports meeting Knochen, one of his 'best students', for an innocent drink at a bar in Theaterplatz (already renamed Hitler-Platz) in Göttingen? What is he repressing when he calls the singed book 'un sou-venir de cet holocauste nationale-socialiste'? Or remembering, when he calls the book 'une relique', expresses his admiration for Zweig, and dedicates his gift 'au tabernacle', with the epigraph, 'Mémoire de mes Amis Juifs'?[94] Never underestimate the power of denial. Larrose is complicit in things he refuses to know. He had not forgotten: a shocking photo survives of the two sharing another drink in old age.[95] In 2001, he interviewed Knochen for a history of the Bordeaux occupation, where Larrose was professor of German from 1939 to 1945.[96] It is as if the burned *Amok* leads back to the unconscious of collaboration.

Amok (from an Indonesian word for a blind anger which results not only in the death of the enemy, but also self-destruction) is Zweig's novella telling the Freudian story of an obsession leading to inevitable death. A woman seeks an abortion from a physician, but when he offers to perform it, she refuses; she dies, but makes him promise that he will never reveal that she has been pregnant. He issues a false death certificate; leaves Indonesia for Europe; then dies at sea, throwing himself onto the woman's lead coffin.[97] *Amok* combines an odour of fever and blood with the manic folly of a pathological return of the repressed. It is perhaps also a reading of Freud's classic essay *Das Unheimliche*, which appeared three years earlier. The word *heimlich* in German, Freud says, contains two different ideas, which if not contradictory are inherently ambiguous: something 'familiar and comfortable', or else something 'concealed and kept hidden'.[98] Its opposite, *unheimlich* ('uncanny') thus struggles between contrary meanings, a thing which is disagreeable, but which as if by necessity comes to light. It is like seeing your back in the mirror, Lacan said, without being able to see your face.[99]

The uncanny in *Amok* is the strangely familiar process by which taboo is brought open by a desire to suppress it. The melodrama of the plot forces a reader to encounter the anxiety. In this way, Zweig presents in outline an analysis of the shibboleth. The Hebrew letter *shin* marks the entrance to traditional Jewish homes. *Shin* stands for ש, *Shaddai*, meaning the 'almighty'. It is written on the cover of a ritual object called a *mezuzah*, a scroll encased in a small ornamental box. The word itself translates as 'doorpost', which is where it is placed, and the scroll contains the verses from which the obligation to affix a *mezuzah* to the doorpost is derived. Judaism, Christianity and Islam share in common a shibboleth of the book. Montesquieu's *Persian Letters* (1721) dreams of a religious pluralism that is impossible because of this common literary ancestry. Is this the spirit of the uncanny in religion, its strangely familiar allure? Castellio was a friend of Calvin who learned to despise him, yet hoped nonetheless to achieve religious unity through natural reason.[100] *Errare non est maledicere*, he said in words almost written for Rushdie: to make a mistake is not to curse God.[101] 'The letter appears in flesh', Jerome said in his work on Leviticus.[102] Fragile as it is, 'the word is incarnate in scripture'.[103] Augustine, in a work read by Luther and Calvin, hovered between *littera* and *spiritus*.[104] Yet Origen, the Church Father who understood best the distinction, was *ex post facto* a heretic; Emperor Justinian I ordered his books to be burned.[105] Perhaps not inappositely, Peter Gay calls modernism 'the lure of heresy': in Freud, Joyce, or Beckett, the conflict of desire and the 'aura' of heresy meet in the transgression of language.[106]

If the original shibboleth was a Hebrew word the Ephraimites could not pronounce properly, in modernity it has transferred to something deep within culture: spirit, meaning, inwardness. Freud referred to the Oedipus complex as 'the shibboleth distinguishing the devotees of psychoanalysis from its opponents'.[107] Derrida wrote of the poem 'Schibboleth' by Paul Celan: 'le poème ne dévoile un secret que pour confirmer qu'il y a là du secret'.[108] ('The poem does not reveal a secret except to confirm that there is, there, a secret'.)

> Setz deine Fahne auf Halbmast,
> Erinnrung.
> Auf Halbmast
> für heute und immer.[109]

The poem is, of course, untranslatable: 'Set your flag at half-mast, | Memory. | At half-mast | today and for ever'.[110] It is a secret and yet not hermetic, Derrida says; the eradication of interpretation, or else the rendering of language as mere mark.

Future generations will wonder, Castellio wrote in *De arte dubitandi*, how after so splendid a dawn, humanity fell back to Cimmerian darkness. The saying is an epigraph to Zweig's *Castellio gegen Calvin*.[111] By now the optimism of his study of Erasmus had run out. Erasmus shot arrows of brilliant wit, but Castellio, Zweig lamented, was the only humanist of all 'to leave cover and wittingly to meet his fate'.[112] Montaigne deplored how Castellio died destitute, saying any friend of literature should have helped him out.[113] Zweig thought Montaigne too sanguine: 'No one spared a finger to save Castellio'.[114] The end of his book is a call to arms, to man the barricades of liberty and joy, but is tinged with despair. Zweig and his wife Lotte committed suicide by overdose of barbiturates in February 1942; they were discovered holding hands.[115] The same year, Celan's parents died in Romanian internment camps. In Cernăuți (now western Ukraine) in 1941, Celan himself was pressed into labour, first to clear debris from the demolished post office, then to gather and destroy Russian books. In 1970, Celan chose suicide by drowning in the Seine in Paris. He wrote of the concentration camps: 'Only one thing remained reachable, close, and secure amid all losses: language [*die Sprache*]. Yes, language. In spite of everything, it remained secure against loss'. Is language a remedy after all, after Servetus, after Rushdie? Celan falters on the edge of an elegy for lost words. Language has to work through its own lack of answers, he says. 'Language passed through it, and gave no words for what it was, that happened.'[116] *Sie ging hindurch und gab keine Worte her für das, was geschah.*[117]

24

Glyph

'Does that Aleph exist, within the heart of a stone? Did I see it when I saw all things, and then forget it?'[1] As everyone knows, writes Borges, 'aleph' is 'the name of the first letter of the alphabet of the sacred language'. Like all letters, the aleph is a mark made in matter. Yet what does the aleph contain? In the Kabbala, it represents the pure and unlimited godhead; 'it has also been said that its shape is that of a man pointing to the sky and the earth'. The earth below is a map and mirror of the sky above. Elsewhere in *The Aleph*, in 'The Writing of God', Borges imagines the first day of creation, when god foresees all the disasters that will befall mankind and earth. Yet there is hope. 'The god had written a magical phrase', one that will ward off all these calamities, a piece of writing to outlast all generations, that cannot be changed by fate. 'No one knows where it is written, or with what letters, but we do know that it endures, a secret text.'[2] At the end of time, there will be one who can read it, and he is ('I am') that last priest.

A model for Borges's imaginary Babel exists in several fragments throughout the world. All over Easter Island on 2 January 1864, in huts he stepped into, Eugène Eyraud, lay friar of the Congregation of the Sacred Hearts of Jesus and Mary, found wood artefacts, hundreds in all, bearing inscriptions.[3] Eyraud left in October, returning a while later to the island, where he died of tuberculosis. When in 1868 the Bishop of Tahiti received a gift of one of the boards, he was stunned by its beauty and strangeness; but by then only about two dozen could be discovered.[4] They are now scattered across museums and private collections in Rome, Paris, London, Vienna, Berlin, St Petersburg, New York, the Smithsonian in Washington, DC, Honolulu, Santiago, and Tahiti. None remains on the island of Rapa Nui itself.[5] Some are driftwood; one is a chieftain's staff; one is a statuette in the shape of a bird-man. The original name of the script was said to be *kohau motu mo rongorongo*, which means in Rapa Nui, 'lines incised for chanting out'. Yet none of the islanders could read them, the bishop was told; Peruvian slavers killed all the wise men in 1862, and now the boards were used for fishing or as firewood.[6]

This uncanny object of Pacific rosewood (Fig. 79), oblong, warped, fluted, with rounded edges and a single hole used for hanging, is covered on both sides with ten and twelve lines respectively of text making up about 1,200 marks in total. The artist, it is remarked, worked with flair, vigour, fluency, and a keen sense of proportion.[7] Many examples of Rongorongo survive on the same rosewood, grown in sacred groves throughout eastern Polynesia. Thomas Barthel, the German

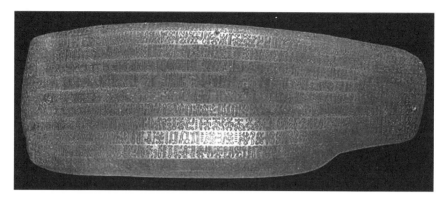

Fig. 79. 'Rongorongo'; Tablet B (*Aruku-Kurenga*): verso. Rosewood, 43 cm × 16 cm.
Rome, Congregation of the Sacred Hearts of Jesus and Mary

ethnologist who catalogued the inscriptions, believed scribes might originally have used banana leaves, which form a natural kind of fluting in their veins, of a size exactly corresponding to the surviving marks.[8] According to oral tradition, scribes used obsidian flakes or small shark teeth to make incisions, tools still used to carve wood in Polynesia. With this they made stylized shapes of plants, animals, humans, or geometric designs: palm trees, squid, frigate birds, sea turtles, centipedes, lozenges, chevrons, saltire crosses, men standing, sitting, eating, some with heads, sometimes with mouth open, sometimes with eyes or ears.

These are the interpretative descriptions given in Barthel, who made a comprehensive list of around 600 glyphs, grouped according to whether or not they have heads, on which side they have wings or arms and whether they point upwards or downwards, and so on. The texts are written in alternating directions, using the system of a reverse boustrophedon: beginning on the left at the bottom, a line of text is read left to right; then the object is turned upside down, and the next line is read again left to right; and repeated. In one case, Tablet C or Mamari, Barthel identified two lines of calendrical information based on a lunar cycle. But in no other example of the twenty-odd carved objects, using up to 2,000 glyphs, has any successful decipherment ever been made.

Undeciphered script is the forgotten scoria at the heart of human language. For the epigraphist, it is the holy grail. Barthel, before Easter Island, worked as a cryptographer for the Wehrmacht during the war, and then wrote his doctoral thesis on the Meso-American Mayan scripts.[9] Deciphering the Mayan scripts in the 1950s and 1960s followed the legendary legacy of the decipherment of Egyptian hieroglyphs by Champollion and others in the 1820s; of Babylonian cuneiform by Henry Rawlinson and others in the 1850s; and of Mycenaean Linear B by Michael Ventris in 1952–3. A majority of the Mayan codices, along with 5,000 images, were burned in an auto-da-fé on 12 July 1562 in south-eastern Mexico by the Franciscan Inquisitor Diego de Landa, declaring:

We found a great number of books in these letters, and since they contained nothing but superstitions and falsehoods of the devil we burned them all, which the Maya took most grievously, and which gave them great pain.[10]

Nevertheless, Landa's *Relación de las cosas de Yucatán* (1566) contained a detailed account of the Mayan books, with paper made from the roots of a tree, folded and written on both sides (p. 13). He also described the writing system, with a proposal of a one-to-one correspondence between the Mayan syllables and the Spanish alphabet (p. 83). This turned out to be nonsense, but his drawings of the symbols and record of the sounds of the Mayan language still proved useful when the Soviet linguist Yuri Knorosov created the theory (in his ground-breaking paper 'Ancient Writing of Central America' of 1952) that the Mayan system consisted of syllabic rather than alphabetic symbols. It is now believed that Mayan writing used logograms in combination with syllabic glyphs, somewhat like modern Japanese writing.

Cold War politics made the leading American scholar Eric Thompson sceptical about the syllabic theory, and Barthel and Knorosov also fell out over phonetic interpretations. Consensus only arrived in the 1970s, since when agreement has been reached on interpretation of 90 per cent of the Mayan script, although it is still not available in Unicode. There has been renewed debate about how much the script reveals about the people who wrote it. The epigraphists still quarrel with the 'dirt archaeologists' about whether writing speaks louder than stone.[11] A deeper uncertainty lies here about the very concept of decipherability. Landa's urge to destroy what he could not fathom within the Mayan characters was not entirely dispelled in Thompson's reverse assumptions about the scribes as gentlemen-scholars rather like himself. In any case there are even older Meso-American scripts which remain indecipherable. In September 2006, *Science* magazine reported a new discovery of a stone the size of a writing tablet. The Cascajal block is made of serpentine with 62 glyphs of a style unlike anything else. Dated to 900 BCE, the Olmec script appears to be the oldest in the Americas.[12] The Zapotec writing from a later period found in Oaxaca, in southern Mexico, survives extensively and includes some calendrical material. The Isthmian script found at the isthmus of Tehuantepec, the narrowest gap between the Gulf of Mexico and the Pacific Ocean, like Mayan mixes logograms with a syllabary. As with Rongorongo, arguments abound about whether these scripts are phonetic, or what their links are to other scripts (such as the later Mayan). Some even believe that Rongorongo was brought from elsewhere in Polynesia, or was even adapted from European practice.[13] At the heart of this is a profound myth of the origin of writing, the elusive story of what writing is: system of ideas, or representation of sound, or material object.

Melville writes: 'Champollion deciphered the wrinkled granite hieroglyphics. But there is no Champollion to decipher the Egypt of every man's and every being's face.'[14] A Cretan bowl in the Ashmolean Museum marks an exquisite case of the indecipherable. Made from dolomitic marble, mottled grey and white, much of the upper part damaged or lost, its circular rim is covered in the script now known as Linear A (1800 to 1450 BCE).[15] This is one of three types of script discovered by Arthur Evans in the 1890s.[16] Linear B (1450 to 1200 BCE) survived in larger numbers on tablets accidentally preserved by the fire at the palace at Knossos, in circumstances similar to the preservation of cuneiform at Nineveh. Its fame has eclipsed that of Linear A precisely because of the mythology of the cryptognostic magus, in this case Ventris, who (aged fourteen) heard Evans speak at Burlington House in London in 1936. Fifteen years and a World War later, Ventris compared the tablets with some unearthed at Pylos on mainland Greece, and eventually worked out that Linear B represented an early form of the Greek language, only syllabically, as opposed to the alphabetic script developed later from Phoenician text.[17] Yet Linear A, while sharing some of B's shapes, has eluded interpretation. Beyond the reach of decryption, A is a secret code, the chisel's enigma.

Writing can be undeciphered for different reasons. Etruscan writing using virtually the same alphabet as ancient Greek cannot be read because no one knows the language it is written in. Mayan scripts for long remained a mystery even though the language they were written in is still spoken today.[18] At the furthest remove, sealstones survive from the Indus valley from around 2500 BCE using an unknown script for an unknown language.[19] Linear A may involve the same unfathomable problem. Somehow in the passage of history we have entirely lost the art of reading the Cretan bowl. Yet it presents a paradox, since although we cannot read it, we can tell that it *is written*, in order to be read. It was this knowledge that drove Turing on at Bletchley, knowing that even the deepest Enigma is meant to be read, even if only by a computer yet to be built. Its inherent legibility is apparent to us even as we are baffled by it. By the same paradox, writing in our own language, although its meaning appears to be transparent, retains a sense that it could become indecipherable at some point yet to come. When creatures arrive from some unknown wormhole in the future to encounter our writing, frozen or else fired by heat in the climate catastrophe, what would they see?

All writing involves a transaction, and in that transaction retains an enigma. We become so familiar with our own signs that they no longer appear to us to be signs. Nothing shows us this ambiguity better than picture writing. Most theories of full writing assume that the symbols used in it were originally preceded by pictographic systems. Some people think Rongorongo is a kind of picture writing in this sense; or else a memory device of another kind. There is debate as to whether it is logographic or syllabic; or even that it mimics Western writing while having no real content. The interesting thing is that there is nothing in the signs themselves that can be used to prove this. Indeed, pictographic writing, despite its seeming basis in direct representation, say of a pot or a fish or a human head, is harder than anything to read. As Robinson writes, its 'iconicity soon became so abstract that it is barely perceptible to us'.[20] The oracle bones of ancient China, perhaps as old as the fifth millennium BCE, and thus 2,000 years older than cuneiform, are pictographic in this sense: pictures that tell no story at all.

What is the difference between a glyph and a letter? A glyph is defined as a symbolic element within an agreed system of symbols. Every letter is a glyph, just as every glyph was once a letter. The difference is that a letter carries with it a seeming guarantee of that symbolic agreement, merely by the fact that it can be read. As our eyes travel from side to side, the secret inside the letters appears to open itself out to us. Yet every letter is a secret, nevertheless. Without the key to open it, we do not know whether to read from right to left, or from bottom to top. We encounter this strange familiarity when we visit a new country: as a friend leaves us at the bus station, say in Cheongju in South Korea, and we find, surrounded by strange script, we do not know what bus to board. Writing has always played on a relationship between secret and key. Writing cannot lie, said its inventor Palamedes, only for Odysseus to deliver him to his death in writing.[21]

Hamlet, sleepless onboard ship from Denmark to England, discovers a secret letter bearing his own death warrant, to be executed on arrival.[22] He replaces it with another which passes the sentence on to Rosencrantz and Guildenstern, who are spying on him. Without knowing it, Shakespeare repeated a plot line familiar (more or less) from that of Sargon, king of Akkadia.[23] A 'letter' in English, as in French or Latin, puns between written mark and epistle. Hamlet's letter is found within a 'packet', the seal of which he has to break and then remake; and in a similar way, perhaps to our consternation, cuneiform letters were also placed inside envelopes.[24] A letter was inscribed onto a piece of clay shaped like a small pillow, and then baked hard. It was placed inside a thin receptacle also made of clay, with some clay powder to prevent sticking, which then was baked a second time.[25] One example of an envelope, 4,000 years old, from Anatolia, survives with its contents in the Metropolitan Museum.[26] The writer attempts to solve a family dispute over some slave girls; he covers the entire tablet on both sides, including the edge, with script; then adds a postscript on another smaller tablet, and puts both inside the same envelope. The letter, of course, could not be read without the envelope being broken, which acted as a protection of the secret inside. A seal might also be added before baking. The word *unku* meant both a seal, and a sealed letter.[27]

'Letterlocking' was an elaborate technology popular in the Renaissance for folding, cutting, and sewing letters so they could not be opened unknown.[28] In literature, the sealed letter has become a trope for the idea of meaning withheld. In Henry James's *The Aspern Papers* (1888) a nameless narrator seeks out Miss Bordereau (French for 'memorandum'), the former lover of a now dead American poet, who lives in a palazzo near the Rio Manin in Venice. The novella tells the story of the narrator's increasingly reckless search for the lost letters and papers of the poet. In the palazzo, he finds himself in a room where there is a 'tall old secretary'—a kind of bureau—in French Empire style. He becomes convinced—without any evidence—that the unassuming piece of furniture contains the secret he is after. He conspires to fake an excuse to find himself alone in the room, and then, having got there, finds himself transfixed by anxiety, as if caught *in flagrante delicto*. In a tremor lest anyone else come in, he looks at the secretary 'very idiotically':

> for what had it to say to me after all? In the first place it was locked, and in the second it almost surely contained nothing in which I was interested. Ten to one the papers had been destroyed; and even if they had not been destroyed the old woman would not have put them in such a place as that.[29]

On the point of testing if it will open without a key, Miss Bordereau enters. She chides him ('Ah, you publishing scoundrel!') and he leaves Venice the next morning; neither he, nor we, ever find out if there are any letters, or what if anything they contained.

Traditionally taken as an exemplary tale of authorial privacy, about which James had his own personal concerns, *The Aspern Papers* also describes ascribing contents to writing even when the writing has not been read. The infamous logical extreme of this is Edgar Allan Poe's *The Purloined Letter* (1844). A letter from the queen's lover has been stolen from her by one of the king's ministers, who has substituted for it another letter of no consequence. It has been deduced that the minister still has the letter, so keeps it near at hand, to be able to produce it at a moment's notice. His room has been rifled for the purpose, carpets and wallpaper removed and replaced, chairs probed with magnifying glasses, and cushions with needles. It is nowhere to be found. Dupin the amateur detective is commissioned to discover the letter, and does so almost immediately, handing it over in exchange for a large cheque. How on earth has he done it? By looking, he says, in plain sight. The minister has put a half-torn letter on a rack on the wall, a letter which has been written on the reverse of the stolen one, refolded the opposite way, and sealed with his own seal. Dupin makes an excuse to return the next day, and after surprising the minister with a ruse, substitutes yet another letter for it.

'Perhaps the mystery is a little too plain', Dupin jokes to the prefect of police.[30] Lacan's analysis in his 'Seminar' on Poe's story makes up for any reliance on the self-evident cleverness of Poe's perfect detective story, by arguing that the content of the queen's original letter is irrelevant. The letter stands instead for the signifier itself: for the process through which language signifies. This is a symbolic structure in which the place of the signifier never stays still, but is displaced from one person to another, just as the letter (as epistle) is continuously substituted for another in its place. The queen, her lover, the minister, the detective, the prefect, all keep making exchanges without the supposed 'contents' ever coming into view. Every linguistic exchange is like this, Lacan says, and yet (in a final *bon mot*, right at the end of the seminar): *une lettre arrive toujours à destination.*[31] 'A letter always arrives at its destination'.[32] The die is cast.

Purloined poems in the hands of policemen figured in real life in the Paris of Louis XV. In 1749, François Bonis, medical student at the Collège Louis-le-Grand, was interrogated whether he had composed a poem against the king. He replies that he is not a poet; that none of his poems attack anyone; that when he chanced to be in hospital, a priest (who was above average height) had pulled out a poem, which he had copied out, but without reading it properly. Asked what use he made of the poem, he recalled reciting it aloud at the Collège, and afterwards burning it, because he realized that it contained references to the Jansenist heresy. The police are not as yet interested in anything other than the name of the priest: and so, Jean Édouard is marched to the Bastille.[33]

In asserting that a letter can always be read, and yet that the meaning of the letter remains elusive, Lacan put in play one of the seminal moments in post-structuralist literary theory. Derrida added the rider that it is not that the letter *lacks* meaning, but that Lacan makes the lack into the meaning.[34] Hereafter, the phallus takes over.[35] Yet located just before his famous climax, Lacan alludes to a more ancient example of the dark secret within the letter, when Belshazzar looks at the writing on the wall:[36]

ופרסין תקל מנא מנא

Such is the blindness of man, Lacan remarks gnomically, when face to face with the letters that spell his destiny. Belshazzar's feast condemns the new Babylonian king's pride, in contrast to the humility of Nebuchadnezzar, who acknowledged God and was given back his throne. The point of the story is that while the Chaldean wise men cannot read the writing, Daniel the prophet can. Yet it is easy to miss an acute commentary here on the detail of the process of writing. Rembrandt's oil painting of 1635 makes the invisible writing hand visible, yet instead of inscribing right to left, the hand works in vertical lines downwards, starting at the top right corner.[37] The reading supplied by the prophet in the Book of Daniel, meanwhile, depends on subtle knowledge of the abjad form of Hebrew glyphs. Daniel supplies vowels to Hebrew consonants in two different ways. By this means, words are read first as nouns, then as verbs. The nouns are monetary weights; the verbs, acts of numbering. And so: 'That very night, Belshazzar the Chaldean king was killed, and Darius the Mede received the kingdom.'[38]

Decipherment takes place whenever we open a book. As we see in 1749, it is not just a literary device. In the summer of 1539, in the midst of the English Reformation, policy took another turn.[39] After a campaign against traditional religion in support of Henry VIII's Act of Supremacy in 1534, now the government was on the look-out for Protestant heretics. At the end of June, the Act of Six Articles renewed penalties for denying transubstantiation.[40] Books containing matter contrary to the Act are to be burned.[41] These religious tergiversations have been interpreted as the to-and-fro of Catholic and Protestant factions. In another sense, however, writing always labours under a risk of misapprehension. Meaning exists not according to fixed points of doctrine, but as a system of exchange ready to be redistributed. Even the authorities are subject to these vicissitudes. Thomas Cromwell, who was appointed 'vicegerent in spirituals' in 1535, and therefore the king's enforcer in religious matters, sent agents far and near to search for missals or lives of St Thomas Becket or any book with 'papa' in it not crossed out.[42] Yet in Parliament's Act of Attainder against him in 1540, he, too, was cited for distributing 'erroneous books', and approving a translation against the sacrament of the altar.[43]

The Archbishop of Canterbury himself was not immune from misconstruction. When a Member of Parliament accused Thomas Cranmer of breaking the law of the Six Articles, the king roundly defended his archbishop and turned on his attacker.[44] However, the king also jested to Cranmer: 'I knowe nowe who is the greatest heretique in Kente.'[45] When Henry VIII is joking you know you are in trouble. Indeed, dark comedy surrounds one of the oddest tales of writing and violence in the sixteenth century. Cranmer's secretary Ralph Morice, in a manuscript memoir, reports his master's habit of writing work-in-progress notes on religion 'moste dangerouslie' as he went along.[46] Foxe's *Actes and Monuments* records one such case, when Cranmer dictated to Morice a series of citations from Scripture and the Church Fathers in preparation for a meeting with the king to discuss his doubts about the Six Articles. Well aware of the scandalous potential of such a manuscript, he warns Morice 'to be circumspect thereof', and to keep the notebook on his person at all times; better still, to keep it under lock and key.[47]

Now the story of Cranmer's purloined letter gathers pace. Morice finds himself accidentally locked out of his own rooms. His father is coming up to London and wants to meet him in the city. The fastidious secretary, all of a fluster, decides in a panic to take the book with him as he makes the trip down river. Never, it appears, get into a boat with important papers. However, things get worse: he has to pass by the King at Paul's wharf on the Thames, near the stage of a bear-baiting.[48] The bear gardens are a notorious place of sometimes violent disorder.[49] The denouement is inevitable. They come too close, so that the bear catches sight of them and, chased by the dogs, comes aboard the boat and starts shaking it. As the boat takes in water, the secretary sits down in the prow. The bear is frightened and bewildered, so sits down on the secretary:

> The Beare seekyng as it were, aide and succour of hym, came backe with hys hynder partes vppon hym, and so rushyng vppon him, the booke was losed from hys gyrdle and fell into the Thamys out of hys reach

The notebook is now, as it were, a floating signifier. Cranmer's secret is lost on the water, sheets of paper scattering in the wind, which are then picked up by chance by one of the King's agents. He can make out enough of the letters, despite the smudging, to implicate the archbishop. He rushes off to Hampton Court to condemn Cranmer. Yet now he makes a crucial mistake: he hands the book to Cromwell, who switches books to turn the tables on him, and the agent is arrested instead. Slapstick lurks in equal parts with menace. The archbishop comes within a heartbeat of being exposed as a traitor.

No letter is free from suspicion in the Tudor world of books. The problem lies in locating meaning or authority within the teeming marks on the page. A strikingly similar pattern occurs in an incident from imperial China. In 1728, General Yue Zhongqi received a letter signed not with a name but with the peculiar soubriquet, 'Summer Calm, the Leaderless Wanderer of the Southern Seas'.[50] Yue's suspicions are further raised by the way that he himself is addressed in the letter, not by one of his official titles, but as 'the Commander-in-Chief deputed by Heaven'. He is correct: the letter teems with treason. Yet what is he to do? Even in uncovering the letter to the emperor he will open himself out to accusation. After two days of deliberation, on 30 October, Yue sends a top-secret report in his own handwriting for the eyes of the emperor only, thereby excluding the bureaucrats. He writes on white paper reserved for senior officials, ten inches high and two feet broad, folded in a concertina binding. The ink is black, and space is left for the emperor's annotation in red between the lines. Even here there is a similarity between the worlds of Manchu emperor and Tudor king: the 1539 'Act of abolishing diversity of opinion in religion' leaves room for Henry VIII's annotations and lemmas.[51] Even with these careful caveats, Yue does not risk sending the letter itself. Instead, he deposits it in a sealed packet with Governor Xiling. In another secret package he gives Xiling two apparently innocuous books which the original messenger had on his person. One is a guide to taking a degree in literature; the other an abridgement and commentary on Confucian classics.[52] The borderlines of orthodoxy and unorthodoxy are blurred.

Where, we may ask, is the boundary between body and mind? Like a border between verbal and visual, or text and meaning, writing draws attention to the boundary, redoubles its significance, then ambiguates the process of discriminating it. In medieval French (as in Latin), 'la question' is a synonym for torture: torture takes place to elicit the correct answer to a question.[53] Bernard Gui's manual of inquisition gives lists of the correct questions to ask. Ask the right interrogatory, he says, and people will confess 'everything, even those things that never occurred to them in their minds'.[54] Bernard enquired about anything: how to make fish pie; or a recipe for *ribollita*, a sauce mixing bread and cabbages.[55] Its equivalent in sixteenth-century England, minus the gastronomy, is the phenomenon known as 'the bloody question'.[56] This was a formula invented at the behest of William Cecil, Lord Burghley, to create unanswerable questions for prisoners suspected of being Catholic priests (or their supporters). The 'Act against Jesuits, seminary priests, and such other like disobedient persons' was passed in 1585, providing for questions in relation to oaths of obedience to queen or pope.[57] Just by making any answer to a question, a prisoner was condemned, either way. Torture is supererogatory, providing supplementary confirmation of what is already known. It is not, contrary to general sense, a search for information: a torturer hears what he wants. The technique works from Westminster to Beijing: the messenger Zhang is tortured so that Yue will have something—anything will do—to tell the emperor.[58] Before Cecil, Cromwell told his prisoners what was necessary for them to say, then punished them for it. For treason cases, Cromwell wrote out the interrogatories, then composed the indictments; it was but a short step for him also to add in advance the evidence needed to be offered.[59]

Sir Thomas More in 1535 was convicted for treason on the basis of mere words he had said, corroborated by the hearsay of a single person.[60] Tudor law increasingly equated writing with speech, and so on with intention, then with treasonable action. In January 1615, Edmond Peacham was arrested for treason in the reign of James I. Even the laconic synopsis of the case in Howell's *Collection of State Trials* is saturated with irony: 'Edmund Peacham was indicted of Treason for divers treasonable passages in a Sermon which was never preached, nor intended to be preached, but only set down in writings, and found in his study: he was tried and found guilty, but not executed.'[61] A further note speaks volumes: 'many of the Judges were of opinion, that it was not Treason'. Howell does not record the reason why Peacham was not executed. For seven months he lingered in jail. On 27 March 1616, John Chamberlain wrote to Dudley Carleton, the Ambassador to the United Provinces: 'Peacham, the condemned minister, is dead in the jail at Taunton, where, they say, he left behind him a most wicked and desperate writing, worse than that he was convicted for.'[62] But this paper, too, does not survive.

Peacham was charged with the writing of 'a booke or pamphlett conteining matters treasonable'.[63] The interrogatories by which he was examined set out a perfect legal fiction, and at the same time an almost insoluble legal paradox. For of course Peacham had not actually been caught trying to kill the king. Indeed, there was never any plot to kill the king that was discovered, even in imaginary form. Peacham was a minister of the church, rector of Hinton St George for the past thirty years, by now an old man. He had been a Puritan in sympathy since his youth; since at least 1603 he had been known for his sermons against king and bishops, in relation to policy in both church and state. James Montagu (his bishop) complained of his directness of speech; of a book written against the court circulated in manuscript; and fatally, of libels against Montagu's own person. In December 1614 Peacham was found guilty of libel and deprived of holy orders. But this was the beginning of his troubles. In the search of his house for writings against Montagu, the officers found what they claimed to be notes for a sermon. These notes were said to contain a litany of complaints about the corruption of the king's ministers, the king's own extravagance, the tyranny of the ecclesiastical courts; and lastly, in wording never revealed, a suggestion that a popular rebellion, resulting in the king's own death, was the inevitable consequence of the government's misdoings.

In other words, Peacham was referring to the intervention of divine providence. Since the notes are nowhere recorded, it can only be inferred from Peacham's own responses to questioning that the origins of his treasonable writing, described (in the language of the law of the time) as 'imagining the death of the king', consisted in the citation of biblical passages. In the Book of Judges and elsewhere, biblical kings are frequently subject to the sudden and irascible violence of God's mortal judgement.[64] The questions made of Peacham attempt to give some physical formation to these inferences of scriptural interpretation: 'What use mean you to make of the said writings? Was it by preaching of them in a sermon, or by publishing them in a treatise?' But in another direction, actions are employed to define Peacham in terms of mental states: 'What was the reason, and to what end did you first set down in scattered papers, and after knit up, in form of a treatise or sermon, such a mass of treasonable slanders against the king, his posterity, and the whole state?' What is at stake, however, can be gleaned from Secretary Winwood's annotation in the margin of the trial record: 'Upon these Interrogatories, Peacham this day was examined before torture, in torture, between torture, and after torture; notwithstanding, nothing could be drawn from him, he still persisting in his obstinate and insensible denials, and former answers.'[65]

In procedural terms, Peacham's case created a *locus classicus* in English law, in which Sir Edward Coke emerges as hero, and Sir Francis Bacon the dissimulating villain.[66] Bacon took the view that Peacham imagined the death of the king (*imaginatus est*) by saying that James was incapable; Coke that no 'words of scandal' can be equal to treason.[67] Bacon makes writing equivalent to mental process. King James's paranoid escalation of the import of words is recorded in his own handwriting. He concludes that Peacham is so old, so weak, and from such a remote part of the country, that implying the death of the king in a sermon is the closest he can come to killing the king in fact. James uses the imaginary status of his murder as proof of Peacham's villainy:

> it must be a quintessence of an alchemy, spirit without a body, or popish accidents without a substance; and then to what end would he have published such a ghost, or shadow without substance, *cui bono*?[68]

Behind this lurks the ultimate fear that all meaning is an alchemical spirit or an accident lacking a substance. Hence the king's overriding certainty that writing is an overt act, indeed that a purpose to be published is a *vouloir-dire* of manic proportions. In this proliferation of metaphors for meaning 'outside-the-text', meaning turns from ghost, to essence, to venom. Meaning has disappeared; the text empties itself out.

The medieval idea of 'la question' was revived in *ancien régime* France in cases of half-proof, such as where only one eyewitness came forward. The judge then accompanied the prisoner to the place of torture. Usually employing the *strappado*, the 'queen of torments', the judge listened to the answer to the question, making it the second half of the proof.[69] After the execution of Louis XVI in 1793, John Barrell observes, it became existentially impossible for anyone in England not to imagine a similar death for King George III.[70] It did not matter whether they thought of Louis mournfully or vengefully, they were imagining the death of a king all the time. As a result, treason becomes figurative, with implications reaching right to the age of Guantánamo Bay. Immediately following 9 September 2001, even the respectable pages of liberal journals began imagining the inconceivable: the reinvention of torture in ordinary modern times.[71] With no limits to fantasy, there are no limits, it appears, to the violence of the state.

What is at stake in any literary act is nothing less than the production of meaning itself. Torture, in Elaine Scarry's words, is part of the 'making and unmaking of the world': it is 'the fiction of power'.[72] This is the mystery that the physical medium of writing, whether in manuscript, printed type, or digital form, occludes. Such is the fate of nations. In 1894, the Dreyfus affair in France began with the discovery of an anonymous letter in a wastepaper basket at the German Embassy, apparently revealing the contents of a memorandum (bordereau) of military secrets. The letter was on thin notepaper, almost transparent, torn twice from top to bottom; the original documents were never found, or the envelope it came in. In 1948, Alger Hiss was accused of leaking secrets at the US State Department, a case which launched the career of Richard M. Nixon. The physical evidence against Hiss hinged on matching samples from different typewriters, one of which Hiss later claimed was forged. In 2020 the Chinese government was accused of using Huawei, the giant tech company, for espionage, by manipulating its 5G phone network infrastructure. Technology changes, the secrets within messages endure.

Located here is the treasury of human imagination locked within all of us, even as we face oblivion. This speaks also of the sacred transaction of writing itself, of the ghost in the machine, or the spirit of the letter: the miracle of human language. 'As my fancies present themselves, I pile them up': writing is Montaigne's room of the imaginary.[73] In Locke's *Essay Concerning Human Understanding*, mind is compared to a piece of paper awaiting the act of writing:

> Let us then suppose the Mind to be, as we say, white Paper, void of all Characters, without any *Ideas*.[74]

The store of the mind is then provided by experience. The fountains of its knowledge are sensible objects and the mental perceptions which capture them.

When Tristram Shandy expresses his incapacity to figure forth the beauty of Widow Wadman, he conjures an imaginary reader, one who is male (as elsewhere he imagines her female). Soliciting the 'concupiscible', he invites him to take pen and ink:

> paint her to your own mind—as like your mistress as you can—as unlike your wife as your conscience will let you—'tis all one to me—please but your own fancy in it.[75]

On the facing page is a blank piece of paper for imagination to run wild. In another place, asterisks supply the missing words for Uncle Toby's liaison with the Widow.[76] Locke's theory that human beings are born without prior mental content is one of the foundations of empiricism. Yet it is also notable that the mind without thought is imagined not as a vacuum but as a writing surface. The mind as it were waits to be written on. Aristotle in *De anima* expressed a puzzle as to how the mind is potentially whatever is thinkable but is actually nothing until it has thoughts. He goes on: 'What the mind thinks, must be in it, in the same sense as the letters are on a tablet which bears no actual writing.'[77] The Stoic Zeno of Citium is reported by Diogenes Laertius as saying that a mental perception is like an 'imprint on the soul' or the mark of a seal on wax.[78]

The Greeks from early times used folding wax-tablets formed like a diptych as a surface to be scratched with a stylus and then erased. Evidence of similar technology survives from Mesopotamia, Syria, and Palestine. In the Roman world it became a standard form of portable and transitory writing.[79] Examples are preserved in waterlogged deposits at Vindolanda on Hadrian's Wall. Claudia Severa's invitation to Lepidina to her birthday party is the earliest known example of writing in Latin by a woman.[80] Cicero used the *cera* or wax tablet as a standard figure for the process of human memory.[81] Martial in book 14 of the *Epigrams* spun a series of poems on tablets as metaphors for the variety of human experience: 'You will erase whenever you want to write afresh' (*scripta novare voles*).[82] From here it is a short step to the image of the *tabula rasa* or 'clean slate' as a dominant image in medieval philosophy. Avicenna in twelfth-century Persia used it to conceptualize pure human potentiality that is actualized through education.[83] Aquinas similarly followed Aristotle in describing the unformed mind as *sicut tabula rasa in qua nihil est scriptum*.[84] Once something is written on it, it takes physical form as *informatio materiae*.[85] Even in our own time the use of writing to describe the mind has not disappeared, but has transferred itself to the computer. Boden (in proposing such a model) cites Turing, still showing the influence of Locke: 'Presumably the child's brain is something like a notebook as one buys it from a stationer's.'[86]

Writing saturates human culture so deeply that since Aristotle we have found it difficult to imagine human thought without reference to it. Freud defines the Id as containing 'everything present at birth', the inherited conditions of the body; which the Ego then learns to read and interpret.[87] The grammatical nature of his thinking is clearer in the original German: the *Es* is a third person singular pronoun ('it') while the *Ich* ('I') is the first person subject position. The *Es* is a book, an especially turbulent and ambiguous one, waiting to be read. Looking for a model for human perception complex enough to incorporate both the retentiveness of memory and the improvisatory rush of new impressions, Freud chose a 'Magic Notepad', in which the mind 'can respond as a blank page to each fresh perception'.[88] The mind is writing with two hands at once: 'while one hand writes upon the surface of the magic pad', the other periodically lifts 'the covering sheet from the wax tablet' in order for it to be continually refreshed.[89]

If the mind is a page waiting to be written, the life of a person may be imagined as a book. In the Book of Job this is made into a symbol of permanence:

> Oh that my words were now written! Oh that they were printed in a book!
>   That they were graven with an iron pen and lead in the rock for ever![90]

Charmingly, the King James Version updates the technology of the ancient world by switching metaphors to words 'printed in a book'. In genetics, the metaphor switches again. The DNA molecule is made up of four nucleotides: adenine (A), thymine (T), guanine (G) and cytosine (C). In common parlance, genetic sequencing works as a language made of four letters, a 'code' that yields the identity of every living thing. Eric Lander, explaining the Human Genome Project to the lay observer in order to promote it more widely, took a volume off a library shelf and compared it to 'the Book of Life'.[91]

Human knowledge, meanwhile, is a library full of all the books that can be written.

> But here it is, all the writers that ever were, ancient and modern, good and bad alike, in both Latin and Greek and in every known subject—in short, it is the whole range of the written word.

So Erasmus writes in the *Adagia*.[92] Erasmus imagines here the world as encyclopaedia—a universal model of education forming a never-ending circle. He took the term from Quintilian's *The Orator's Education*.[93] He borrowed it in turn from Cicero, who thought of knowledge as a vast storehouse, or language as a river flowing through eternity.[94] The word entered print in the vernacular in Rabelais, where Thaumaste rhapsodizes the extent of Pantagruel's knowledge: 'il m'a ouvert le vray puys et abisme de Encyclopedie'.[95] Thaumaste promises to have it printed to the benefit of everyone. Writing is a well or an abyss, or else a *mise en abyme*, a story in a story, like in Poe.[96] For Diderot, the purpose of an encyclopaedia is 'to collect knowledge disseminated around the globe, to set forth its general system to the men with whom we live, and transmit it to those who will come after us'.[97] Diderot's article on 'Encyclopédie' (in his *Encyclopédie*) appears as an epigraph to the entry for 'Encyclopaedia' in Wikipedia.[98] Turn, and turn again.

The metaphors do not work, exactly. DNA is neither a language nor a code, neither can we 'read' it. In 1785, four years before revolution, Étienne-Louis Boullée proposed a new library for Louis XVI, which would be the largest in the world, an 'immense basilica' with a skylight in the vault. The Bibliothèque du Roy in Paris, the Bodleian in Oxford, the Augustiniana in Wolfenbüttel (which bought up huge numbers of books in Holland, housing them under an immense Rotunda in 1704), the Hofbibliothek in Berlin and that in Vienna, all aspired to be 'universal libraries'.[99] In 1728, the library of Elector Augustus II of Saxony, now also king of Poland, moved to the Zwinger in Dresden, next to the opera house, to accommodate the increase in stock. Leibniz, the librarian in Wolfenbüttel, was approached by Tsar Peter the Great to accomplish the same for Russia. In 1775, the new Ministry of Education under Stanislas II August, King of Poland and Grand Duke of Lithuania, joined all the libraries in Kraków into the Collegium Maius. In Paris a gigantic catalogue was published from 1739 to 1753, mirroring the collections.

However, it was never enough: Boullée desired what Chartier calls 'libraries without walls'.[100] The point of the metaphor of the encyclopaedia is to show the impossibility of the idea. Erasmus admits that a lifetime is not enough to span such knowledge, that he has had to make do, not with the world as library, but the library of one man, his friend Aldus Manutius. Diderot, in the article on the word 'Livre', confesses that there are too many books already, that books are too long, and that the best library in the world would contain only one book.[101] The irony does not escape his reader that his own *Encyclopédie* is composed of 17 enormous folio volumes. An ideal library might consist of just a Bible or a Qur'an, he says, two books he palpably despises. Perhaps Kant's 'all-crushing' book of 1781, *Critique of Pure Reason*, fulfilled Diderot's prophecy.[102] Writing is the inevitable metaphor for everything, and so becomes the metaphor for the failure of metaphor. In the well or abyss, language drops like a stone, never to find a true place.

At the other end of the scale, the book disappears into itself. In Auschwitz, Primo Levi recalls trying to explain Dante's *Divine Comedy* to Jean. But, 'Who is Dante? What is the Comedy?'[103] Out of nowhere he begins to recite from memory the Canto of Ulysses:

indi la cima qua e là menando,
come fosse la lingua che parlasse.[104]

He stops and tries to translate for Jean: *the shade of Ulysses is waving a flame at Dante as if it were a tongue that tried to speak.* Jean the Pikolo 'likes the bizarre simile', but the narrator's tongue is tied. What comes next? There is nothing, a hole in his memory: *Il nullo. Un buco nella memoria.*[105] Faced with the book that means more than anything to an Italian, he falls short. The lines disappear, like lemon ink. He recovers to deliver a rapturous rendition of Ulysses: 'As if I also was hearing it for the first time: like the blast of a trumpet, like the voice of God. For a moment I forget who I am and where I am.'[106] Only then he is back in the soup kitchen and the cacophony of the concentration camp, *Kraut und Rüben, Kaposzta és répak*, cabbages and turnips. Dante is left as a voiceover in the mind: *infin che 'l mar fu sovra noi richiuso*, 'until the sea again closed over us.'[107]

The book lies dormant between silence and the voice of God (*la voce di Dio*), Levi suggests. 'To write poetry after Auschwitz is barbaric.'[108] Adorno later regretted writing this, perhaps thinking of Levi and of Celan: a tortured man has the 'right to scream', he says, adding that the more pertinent question after Auschwitz is whether it is possible to go on living in the same light as before.[109] Adorno insists on a materialist transformation of Hegel's *Geist*. Rather than trusting in familiar meanings and habits of culture, Adorno suggests that atonement for modern history lies in fragments and dreams, as if we were 'no longer living at all'.

In Anselm Kiefer's *For Paul Celan: Ash Flower* (2006), piles of books lie like monuments (Fig. 80) in a frozen ploughed field. The title of the painting recalls Celan's poem 'Ich bin allein':

> I am alone, I put the ash flower
> in the glass full of ripe blackness

At the top of the image, like a half-hidden secret, lines from Celan appear out of the dark sky on the horizon, in long loops of Kiefer's handwriting. In an earlier work entitled *Die Aschenblume* (1983–97), in the Modern Art Museum of Fort Worth, Kiefer smothers the surface of paint and emulsion with ash, onto which a dried sunflower has been pasted. Books appear in collage in Kiefer's work since the 1960s, both in paintings and later as freestanding sculptures, such as *Book with Wings* (1992–4), a massive lead book with feathered wings made out of tin, supported on a steel lectern. It exists in two versions, one (in Los Angeles) with wings aloft, as if in triumph, the other (in Fort Worth) with feathers drooping in a dying fall. In *Osiris und Isis* (1985–7), a great pyramid or ziggurat dominates the whole canvas, made of giant bricks which on closer inspection turn out to be books and slabs of clay. At the apex of the building a motherboard of a computer sprouts upwards supported by copper wires. At the foot of the painting, seventeen pieces of porcelain have been embedded into the dense material surface. These represent, perhaps, the dismembered fragments of the corpse of Osiris which Isis is unable to reassemble. The pyramid is the tomb made for his sarcophagus. Between the clay bricks and the motherboard, Kiefer projects a history of writing from cuneiform into futurity. His violent cityscape is both archaic and apocalyptic, suggesting how the book (as an idea) is both fixed in time and yet timeless,

Fig. 80. 'Ash-flower'; Anselm Kiefer, *Für Paul Celan: Aschenblume* (2006), Oil, acrylic, emulsion, shellac, and burnt books on canvas, Private Collection

permanent and yet fragile. After the Holocaust, in the midst of Anthropocene ecological breakdown, what can survive of it?

Tout, au monde, existe pour aboutir à un livre, Stephane Mallarmé wrote: 'everything in the world exists in order to end up as a book'.[110] For the last thirty years of his life he embarked on a project called *Le livre*. Legendary, unfinished, it was published finally only in 1957, sixty years after he died. Fragmentary and yet in its way comprehensive, it consists of shards of verse painstakingly presented at precise points on the page, with blank paper prevailing on all sides of writing. The words are freed from context or association or authorial intention, left to their own devices. 'It happens on its own', Mallarmé said. In this respect, *Le livre* resembled his poem, 'Un coup de dés jamais n'abolira le hasard' (a throw of the dice will never abolish chance), written just before he died and published, according to his meticulous instructions, only in 1914.[111] Spread out over twenty pages, each pair of consecutive facing pages is to be read as a single panel. The text flows back and forth in both directions, along irregular lines. *Le livre*, like any book, bodies forth the mortality of writer and reader: it ends as it begins.

In an 1895 essay, Mallarmé calls the book 'un instrument spirituel'. Its closed leaves contain a secret, a silence which encloses 'des signes évocatoires' (evocative signs).[112] Underneath the furling of the paper, its black characters cast a shadow which barely reveals itself even as 'un bris de mystère' ('a fracture/rupture of mystery'). Every writing is an exterior treasure containing 'le mystère dans les lettres'. *VTOPOS HA BOCCAS PEULA CHAMA*.[113] So begins More's *Utopia*, in an imaginary language, using an alphabet of twenty-two letters (like Hebrew or Latin), invented by Pieter Gilles, friend of More and Erasmus.[114] He could be writing in Rongorongo, for all that we can decipher, except that Gilles supplies a Latin translation *ad verbum* (although we only have his word for it). It is always like this, at some level, as if interpreting dreams. In sleep, Freud says in *Die Traumdeutung*, dream-content 'is expressed as it were in a pictographic script'.[115] He compares this to the use of determinatives in hieroglyphic script, which 'serve merely to elucidate other signs'.[116] And yet the intention embodied in the production of dream-work is not, he insists, *verstanden* ('understanding'); rather, the symbols are translated, just as by Egyptologists, into another language.[117] The same content is rendered in two grammars, neither of which we know. As Lacan sardonically glosses Freud on this point, 'a cryptogram takes on its full dimension only when it is in a lost language'.[118]

Is writing whatever is left after the contents have been explained away? Adam Phillips says of Freud: 'Freud changes our reading habits. He makes us wonder, among many other things, what we may be doing when we are reading, what the desire to read is a desire for.'[119] Writing has an incalculable impact in the modern world: we suffer and enjoy more words than any other people in history; we are made of writing, informed by it, economically and politically as well as culturally. Even since Phillips wrote this in 2006, reading and being read have changed all over again, becoming all the more burdensome, yet all the more invisible, guided by algorithms we would not understand even if we had access to them. Language is automated and mass-produced, not just machine readable but machine writable. Text designs itself to be read, rather than is written for reading. The machine by my bed wakes me up in the morning and tells me when to sleep, what is and what isn't. Freud's desperate epigraph from Virgil's *Aeneid* on the title-page of his *Interpretation of Dreams* is more apt than ever: *Flectere si nequeo superos, Acheronta movebo*.[120] 'If I cannot move heaven, then I shall raise hell.'

Verba volant, scripta manent: words fly away, but writing remains. Yet script, too, will disappear, Lacan mockingly reflects.[121] 'I have finished with the English language', Joyce remarked when writing *Finnegans Wake*.[122] A work 'more talked about and written about during the period of its composition than any previous work of literature', Faber & Faber announced in 1939; adding, they will 'waste no words in describing the book'.[123] How could they put into other words, a work in a language not yet written by anyone else, yet containing fragments of over forty known human languages (including Latin, French, Japanese, Hebrew, and Greek on the first two pages).[124] And so it begins:

> riverrun, past Eve and Adam's, from swerve of shore to bend of bay, brings us by a commodius vicus of recirculation back to Howth Castle and Environs.[125]

Joyce draws attention to how writing conceals language in the act of displaying it, for all to see. He sees writing as geological strata or débris, shorn of capacity for information. A special joy of his was the Book of Kells (see Pl. 3), that Old Irish masterpiece of calligraphy, an illustrated edition of which he carried with him always. In *Finnegans Wake* the narrator marvels at 'a word as cunningly hidden in its maze of confused drapery as a field mouse in a nest of coloured ribbons'.[126] He treats the arcane warp and woof of an illuminator's work as a secret language or wild spectacle of emojis:

> all those red raddled obeli cayennepeppercast over the text, calling unnecessary attention to errors, omissions, repetitions and misalignments.[127]

'Ostrogothic kakography' makes order out of error, just as Thomas More complained that the written scriptures had been copied so often there was little true text left. This is why the law is written in the minds of men rather than the 'dede skynnes of bestes'.[128]

In all the 'whiplooplashes' who can tell what is the meaning of the 'baffling Chrismon trilithon sign'? Or, as Lacan said of Freud in the face of Egyptian script, 'which is an *aleph*' – or a chick, a bread bun, an owl, or a serpent?[129] *Finnegans Wake*, nonetheless, ends with what we might call Joyce's Aleph, the very last words of which are:

> A way a lone a last a loved a long the[130]

Joyce gleaned the idea from W. W. Skeat's *Etymological Dictionary*, one of his favourite books, where the first entry is for the unadorned glyph, 'A'. Skeat immediately deviates to the commonplace use of the prefix 'a-' in the English language: '(1) adown; (2) afoot; (3) along; (4) arise; (5) achieve; (6) avert; (7) amend; (8) alas; (9) abyss'.[131] A little below, Skeat writes: 'These prefixes are discussed at greater length under the headings **Of, On, Along, Arise** and then **Alas, Aware, Avast**'. From here Joyce dives into the abyss to find pieces of text to place within *Finnegans Wake*. He described this collage writing process brilliantly in a letter of 1921: 'I have not read a work of literature for several years. My head is full of pebbles and rubbish and broken matches and bits of glass picked up'.[132] Writing is the place where we keep things safe and then lose them.

'Where do you begin in this?', Stephen asks in *Ulysses*, while picking up another book.[133] *Finnegans Wake* begins where it ends, in a sentence which spirals in a circle, like Dante's *Divine Comedy*, to be read on repeat: 'A way a lone a last a loved a long the | riverrun, past Eve and Adam's'. Wonderfully, the manuscript includes the extra dicolon 'a lost', but this got mislaid in the printed edition.[134] Joyce echoes in the process one of his earliest published stories, 'The Dead' (1914): 'How pleasant it would be to walk out alone, first along by the river and then through the park!'[135] Also, Coleridge's mystic mantra of consciousness, *Kubla Khan, Or a Vision in a Dream. A Fragment* (1798):

> Where Alph, the sacred river, ran[136]

In ending the book with an uncompleted sentence, beginning with the indefinite article, 'a', and finishing with the definite article, 'the', Joyce compared the ending to *Ulysses*, where Molly Bloom finishes the final chapter-long sentence of the book and gives in to sleep saying, 'Yes'.[137] This was 'the least forceful word I could possibly find', Joyce says: denoting 'the end of all resistance'. For *Finnegans Wake* he tried to go one better, or else, fail better:

> This time I have found the word which is most slippery, the least accented, the weakest word in English, a word which is not even a word, which is scarcely sounded between the teeth, a breath, a nothing, the article the.[138]

This is what Beckett called Joyce's 'savage economy of hieroglyphics'.[139] Awake, aware, adrift, the reader wanders astray into blank space, awaiting absence. 'Till finally you hear how words are coming to an end', Beckett writes with his last breath in the late story *Company*. 'And you as you always were. Alone.'[140] Here is where the book ends.

Endnotes

Chapter 1

1. Eric Schmidt and Jared Cohen, *The New Digital Age: Reshaping the Future of People, Nations and Business* (New York: Jon Murray, 2013), 315.
2. John Browning, 'Libraries without Walls for Books without Pages', *Wired*, 1 (1 April 1993, 12.00 p.m.).
3. London Book Fair, April 2007.
4. Shoshana Zuboff, *The Age of Surveillance Capitalism: The Fight for a Human Future at the New Frontier of Power* (New York and London: Profile Books, 2019).
5. F. T. Marinetti, *Distruzione della sintassi/Immaginazione senza fili/Parole in libertà* (11 May 1913); tr. '*Destruction of Syntax – Radio Imagination – Words-in-Freedom*', in *Futurism: An Anthology*, ed. Lawrence Rainey, Christine Poggi and Laura Wittman (New Haven & London: Yale University Press, 2009), 143–51, see also 229.
6. Scott Fitzgerald, 'Pasting it Together', *Esquire* (April 1936), 78.
7. Benjamin 'Krisis des Romans: zu Döblin's *Berlin Alexanderplatz*', in *Gesammelte Schriften*, vol. iii. 230–36; Barthes, 'La mort de l'auteur', *Le bruissement de la langue: Essais critiques* (Paris: Seuil, 1984), iv. 63–9. The essay was first published in English in 1967 and in French in 1968.
8. Deuteronomy 13: 3.
9. Deborah Black, 'Psychology, Soul and Intellect', in P. Adamson and R. Taylor (eds.), *The Cambridge Companion to Arabic Philosophy* (Cambridge: Cambridge University Press, 2005), 187.
10. Bill Cope and Angus Phillips (eds.), *The Future of the Book in the Digital Age* (Oxford: Chandos Publishing, 2006).
11. Mark Perlman, 'If it Isn't on the Internet it Doesn't Exist'; *The Future of the Book in the Digital Age*, 19.
12. Stephan Füssel, *The Gutenberg Bible of 1454* (Cologne: Taschen, 2018), 9.
13. Luther, *Table Talk*, WA TR, no. 1038, i. 523; cf. no. 4697, iv. 436–7. For Luther's meaning, see Jean-François Gilmont, *The Reformation and the Book* (Aldershot: Ashgate, 1998), 1–3.
14. Alexandra Walsham, *Providence in Early Modern England* (Oxford: Oxford University Press, 1999), 54.
15. *Dr Martini Lutheri Colloquia Mensalia; or, Dr Martin Luther's Divine Discourses at his table* (London: William Dugard, 1652).
16. Little Hans's fear of horses appears in *Case Histories I: The Penguin Freud Library*, viii, tr. A. and J. Strachey (London: Pelican Books, 1977), 187–94. The term *Phobie* is discussed in outline theory in *Bruchstück einer Hysterie-Analyse* (1905) in Freud, *Gesammelte Werke*, vol. v; tr. in *Penguin Freud Library*, viii. 61–2.
17. Shakespeare, *Hamlet, Prince of Denmark*, 5. 1. 70, 104.

18. 'Je ravie le mort'; Jean de Franchières, *La fauconnerie* (Poitiers: Enguilbert de Marnef, Jacques Bouchet, et Guillaume Bouchet, 1567), printer's device. It is reproduced as the cover image in Ronald B. McKerrow, *An Introduction to Bibliography for Literary Students* (Oxford: Clarendon Press, 1960), and also on p. 45.

19. Sterne, *The Life and Opinions of Tristram Shandy, Gentleman*, 9 vols. (York and London: J. Hinxman, R. Dodsley, T. Becket, *et al.*, 1759–67), i. 72–4.

20. Naoko Inose, *Persona: A Biography of Yukio Mishima* (Berkeley, CA: Stone Bridge Press, 2013).

21. Proust, *Du côté de chez Swann* (1913); *À la recherche du temps perdu*, Éditions de la Pléiade, ed. Jean-Yves Tadié, 4 vols. (Paris: Gallimard, 1987–9), i. 3.

22. Proust, *The Way by Swann's*, tr. Lydia Davis (London: Penguin Classics, 2003), 7.

23. Joyce, *Ulysses: The 1922 Text*, ed. Jeri Johnson (Oxford: World's Classics, 1993), 793.

24. Stanislaus Joyce, *My Brother's Keeper: James Joyce's Early Years* (New York: Viking, 1969), 90–1.

25. Joyce, *Ulysses*, 67.

26. Aristotle, *Poetics*, 1451^{a}3–6.

27. Horace, *Ars poetica*, 6–9.

28. Foucault, 'Structuralism and Post-Structuralism', *Aesthetics: Essential Works of Foucault 1954–1984*, 3 vols. (London: Penguin Books, 1998–2000), ii. 455.

29. Lois Mai Chan, 'The Burning of the Books in China, 213 B.C.', *The Journal of Library History*, 7 (1972), 101–8.

30. Glen Dudbridge, *Lost Books of Medieval China*, Panizzi Lectures, 15 (London: British Library, 2000), 9–10.

31. Virginia Woolf, *To the Lighthouse* (London: Hogarth Press, 1963), 97.

32. Martin Hägglund, *Dying for Time: Proust, Woolf, Nabokov* (Cambridge, MA: Harvard University Press, 2012), 25.

33. Proust, *Time Regained*, tr. Stephen Hudson, 353.

34. Hobsbawm, 'The Avant Garde Dies', *The Age of Extremes: The Short Twentieth Century 1914–1991* (London: Abacus, 1998), 519.

35. Benjamin, *Illuminationen: ausgewählte Schriften I* (Frankfurt am Main: Suhrkamp, 1977), 145.

36. Benjamin, *The Work of Art in the Age of Mechanical Reproduction*, tr. J. A. Underwood (London: Penguin Books, 2008), 3.

37. Benjamin, *The Work of Art in the Age of Mechanical Reproduction*, 10.

38. Hegel, *Aesthetics: Lectures on Fine Art*, tr. T. M. Knox, 2 vols. (Oxford: Clarendon Press, 1975), i. 101.

39. Stephen Greenblatt, 'The Word of God in the Age of Mechanical Reproduction', *Renaissance Self-Fashioning* (Berkeley and Los Angeles: University of California Press, 1980).

40. J. S. Edgren, 'The History of the Book in China', in Michael F. Suarez and H. R. Woudhuysen (eds.), *Oxford Companion to the Book* (Oxford: Oxford University Press, 2010), i. 355–6.

41. Gabriella Pomara, 'Manuscript Tradition of the Commedia', in Richard Lansing (ed.), *The Dante Encyclopaedia* (London: Routledge, 2010), 198–9.

42. Woudhuysen and Suarez, *The Book: A Global History* (Oxford: Oxford University Press, 2013), p. xii.

43. Barthes, 'The Death of the Author', in *Image—Music—Text*, tr. Stephen Heath (London: Fontana, 1977), 142–8 at 142.

44. Roberta Binkley, *Rhetoric Before and Beyond the Greeks* (Albany, NY: SUNY Press, 2004), 47.

45. Derrida, 'La fin du livre et le commencement de l'écriture', *De la grammatologie* (Paris: Éditions de Minuit, 1967), 15; *Of Grammatology*, translated by Gyatri Chakravorty Spivak (Baltimore: Johns Hopkins University Press, 1976), 6.

46. McLuhan, *The Gutenberg Galaxy: The Making of Typographic Man* (Toronto: University of Toronto Press, 1962), 249.

47. McLuhan, *Gutenberg Galaxy*, 32.

48. Derrida, *De la grammatologie*, 208; 'a supplement to speech', Of Grammatology, 144.

49. Derrida, *Marges de la philosophie* (Paris: Éditions de Minuit, 1972), 382.

50. Derrida, 'La différance', in *Marges*, 6; see also the earlier essay on Levinas, 'Violence et métaphysique' (1964), tr. in *Writing and Difference*, tr. Alan Bass (Chicago: University of Chicago Press, 1978), 151.

51. For example, Petrarch, *Rime sparse*, RVF 194 line 1 ('L'aura gentil'), where 'the gentle breeze' puns on the name Laura.

52. Milton, 'Elegia tertia', *Poems of Mr John Milton, both English and Latin* (London: Ruth Raworth, 1634), 18.

53. Benjamin, *The Work of Art in the Age of Mechanical Reproduction*, 13.

54. 'Wissenschaft als Beruf' (originally given as a lecture in Munich, November 1919), in Max Weber, *Gesamtausgabe*, ed. Wolfgang J. Mommsen, vol. xvii: *Wissenschaft als Beruf* (Tübingen: Mohr Siebeck, 1992), 46.

55. Benjamin, *The Work of Art in the Age of Mechanical Reproduction*, 39.

56. Jacques Derrida, *Speech and Phenomena: And Other Essays on Husserl's Theory of Signs,* tr. David Allison (Evanston, IL: Northwestern University Press, 1973), 156.

57. Benjamin, in *Gesammelte Schriften*, ii/1. 476.

58. Nagel, *Medieval Modern: Art Out of Time* (London: Thames & Hudson, 2012).

59. Michelle O'Malley and Evelyn Welch, *The Material Renaissance* (Manchester: Manchester University Press, 2007), 72–3.

60. Laura Marcus, *The Tenth Muse: Writing About Cinema in the Modernist Period* (Oxford: Oxford University Press, 2008), 424–5.

61. Adorno, 'Form and Content', *Aesthetic Theory*, tr. Robert Hullot-Kentor (London: Athlone Press, 1997), 144.

62. 'Notiz über den "Wunderblock"', *Gesammelte Werke*, xiv (Frankfurt am Main: S. Fischer Verlag, 1991), 4–8, this ref. p. 4.

63. *Note on the 'Magic Notepad'*, in *The Penguin Freud Reader*, ed. Adam Phillips (London: Penguin Books, 2006), 101.

64. Derrida, 'Freud and the Scene of Writing', in *Writing and Difference*, 199.

65. Locke, *An Essay Concerning Human Understanding*, II§ii, ed. P.H. Nidditch (Oxford: Clarendon Press, 1975), 104.

66. Calvino, *If on a winter's night a traveller* (London: Picador, 1982), 43.

67. Irving Finkel and Jonathan Taylor, *Cuneiform* (London: The British Museum Press, 2015), 6.

68. Nicholas Ostler, *Empires of the Word: A Language History of the World* (London: Harper Collins, 2005), 110.

69. *The Literature of Ancient Sumer*, ed. and trans. J. Black, G. Cunningham, E. Robson, and G. Zólyomi (Oxford: Oxford University Press, 2004), 5.

70. Black et al, *Literature of Ancient Sumer*, 44.

71. Homer, *Iliad*, 6. 168–9; 2 Samuel 11: 14–15.

72. https://www.bbc.co.uk/programmes/p03f65py.

73. Plato, *Phaedrus*, 275a; Erasmus, *Lingua* (1525), in *Collected Works of Erasmus* [CWE] 29.262; Derrida, 'Plato's Pharmacy', *Dissemination*, 125–6.

74. The first known interstellar object is described by astronomer Avi Loeb, *Extraterrestrial: The First Sign of Intelligent Life Beyond Earth* (London: Hachette, 2021).

75. Martial, *Epigrams*, 1.2.

76. Martial, *Epigrams*, 8.3.

77. Harry Y. Gamble, *Books and Readers in the Early Church: A History of Early Christian Texts* (New Haven and London: Yale University Press, 1995), 49.

78. Georgios Boudalis, *The Codex and Crafts in Late Antiquity* (Chicago: University of Chicago Press, 2018), 1.

79. Gamble, *Books and Readers in the Early Church*, 66, 74.

80. Ashim Bhattacharyya, *Hindu Dharma: Introduction to Scriptures and Theology* (New York: iUniverse, 2006), 5.

81. M. Schwartz, 'The Religion of Achaemenian Iran', in Ilya Gershevitch (ed.), *The Cambridge History of Iran, Vol. 2: Median and Achaemenian Periods* (Cambridge: Cambridge University Press, 2008), 664–6. A Yasna fragment is Oxford, Bodleian Library, MS J2.

82. Lars Fogelin, *Archaeology of Early Buddhism* (London: Rowman & Littlefield, 2006), 13.

83. Peter Brown, *The World of Late Antiquity: From Marcus Aurelius to Muhammad* (London: Thames and Hudson, 1971), 164; the Cologne Mani-Codex, dated 5th c. CE, was found in the 1960s, adding substantially to a sparse literature.

84. Gurinder Singh Mann, 'Gurū Granth: The Scripture of the Sikhs', *Brill's Encyclopaedia of Sikhism Online*, https://brill.com/view/db/beso [accessed 18 December 2020].

85. Johann Sleidan, *Address to the Estates of the Empire* (1542).

86. Lotte Hellinga, 'Press and Text in the First Decades of Printing', *Libri tipografi biblioteche*, Biblioteca di bibliografia italiana, 148 (Florence: Olschki, 1997), 1–23.

87. Grafton, *Codex in Crisis* (New York: Crumpled Press, 2008).

88. Rabelais, *Gargantua*, I; *Oeuvres complètes*, ed. Mireille Huchon and François Moreau, Éditions de la Pléiade (Paris: Gallimard, 1994), 10; *Gargantua and Pantagruel*, tr. T. Urquhart (London: J. M. Dent, 1946), 8.

89. Stephanie Ann Frampton, *Empire of Letters: Writing in Roman Literature and Thought from Lucretius to Ovid* (Oxford: Oxford University Press, 2019), 16–17, 89.

90. London, British Library, MS Royal 13. D. iv.

91. Jennifer Summit, *Memory's Library: Medieval Books in Early Modern England* (Chicago: University of Chicago Press, 2008), 221.

92. Richard de Bury, *Philobiblon*, tr. E. C. Thomas (London: De la More Press, 1903), 9.

93. Virgil, *Aeneid*, 3. 286–8.

94. Maureen Carroll, *Spirits of the Dead: Roman Funerary Commemoration in Western Europe* (Oxford: Oxford University Press, 2006), 4.

95. J. M. C. Toynbee, *Death and Burial in the Roman World* (Ithaca: Cornell University Press, 1971), 35.

96. Penelope Wilson, *Hieroglyphs: A Very Short Introduction* (Oxford: Oxford University Press, 2004), 50–1.

97. *ΜΝΗΣΑΡΕΤΗ ΣΩΚΡΑΤΟΣ*; Munich, Glyptothek, Inv. 491.

98. Ovid, *Tristia*, 3. 2. 30.

99. Frampton, *Empire of Letters*, 153.

100. Richard de Bury, *Philobiblon*, 96.

101. Boethius, *Consolatio philosophiae* 1. 4. 1 (Homer); 3. 7. 6 (Euripides); 3. 4. 2 (Catullus).

102. On Boethius' library, see Peter Brown, *The Rise of Western Christendom: Triumph and Diversity, AD 200–1000*, 2nd edn. (Oxford: Wiley-Blackwell, 2013), 195–6.

103. Juliet Fleming, *Graffiti and the Writing Arts of Early Modern England* (London: Reaktion Books, 2011), 56.

104. Ruth Ahnert, *The Rise of Prison Literature in the Sixteenth Century* (Cambridge: Cambridge University Press, 2013), 47–8.

105. Eamon Duffy, *Marking the Hours: English People and their Prayers* (New Haven and London: Yale University Press, 2011), 108.

106. *Horae* (Paris: François Regnault, 1530), Yale University, Beinecke Library, MS Vault More, sig. C1r.

107. Bonhoeffer, *Letters and Papers from Prison* (Minneapolis, MN: Fortress Press, 2010), 320.

108. Rushdie, *Is Nothing Sacred?* (London: Granta Press, 1990), 2.

109. Rushdie, 'Book Burning', *New York Review of Books*, 36 (2 March 1989), 26.

110. Levi, *Se questo è un uomo*, ed. Alberto Cavaglion (Turin: Einaudi, 2012), 15; *If This is a Man* (London: Abacus Books, 1987), 28.

111. Levi, *If This is a Man*, 109.

112. Levi, *If This is a Man*, 113.

113. Levi, *Se questo è un uomo*, 15. Levi refers directly to the Malebolge of *Inferno* xxi in 'Esame di chimica', 93.

114. Susan Jacoby, *Strange Gods: A Secular History of Conversion* (London: Penguin Books, 2017), p. xvi.

115. Cassiodorus, *Institutiones divinarum et saecularium litterarum*, Praefatio, 5–7.

116. Hegel, *Aesthetics*, i. 103.

117. Obama, *Dreams from my Father: A Story of Race and Inheritance* (Edinburgh: Canongate Books, 2008), 29.

118. Talmud, Shabbat 14a.

119. Confucius, The *Analects (Lunyu)*, 2.3; tr. Annping Chin (London: Penguin Books, 2014), 13.

120. Confucius, *Analects* 6. 7; see Chin's note on p. 94.

121. Peter Kornicki, *The Book in Japan: A Cultural History from the Beginnings to the Nineteenth Century* (Leiden: Brill, 1998), 455.

122. Davis, *The Gift in Sixteenth-Century France* (Oxford: Oxford University Press, 2000), 78.

123. Leedham-Green, *Books in Cambridge Inventories: Book-Lists from Vice-Chancellor's Court Probate Inventories in the Tudor and Stuart Periods*, 2 vols. (Cambridge: Cambridge University Press, 1986).

124. Richard de Bury, *Philobiblon*, 46.

125. The story of Zeno comes from Diogenes Laertius, *Lives of Eminent Philosophers*, 9. 5.

126. Richard de Bury, *Philobiblon*, 52.

127. Kafka, *The Trial* (London: Penguin Books, 1976), 48, 61.

128. David Schalkwyck, *Hamlet's Dreams:The Robben Island Shakespeare* (London: Methuen, 2013), 64.

129. Shakespeare, *Julius Caesar*, 2. 2. 36–7.

130. G. H. Hardy, *A Mathematician's Apology* (Cambridge: Cambridge University Press, 1941). The inscription reads: 'To remind you of Maths | + of Moggy + perhaps of me'.

131. Samuel Beckett, *Company* (London: John Calder, 1980), 7.

132. Hoffmann, 'The Sandman', from *Die Nachtstücke* (1817); Freud's summary appears in 'The Uncanny' (1919), *The Uncanny*, ed. Hugh Haughton, New Penguin Freud (London: Penguin Books, 2003), 135–8.

133. Freud, *The Uncanny*, ed. Haughton, 139–40.

134. Erasmus, *Praise of Folly*, tr. Hoyt Hudson (Princeton: Princeton University Press, 2015), 36; citing the speech of Alcibiades in Plato, *Symposium*, 215b.

Chapter 2

1. http://blogs.bl.uk/thenewsroom/2015/01/into-the-void.html.

2. http://www.culture24.org.uk/history-and-heritage/historic-buildings/art73770.

3. https://www.loc.gov/about/fascinating-facts/.

4. https://www.loc.gov/about/general-information/#year-at-a-glance.

5. https://www.loc.gov/exhibits/jefferson/jefflib.html.

6. https://www.forbes.com/sites/andrewcave/2017/04/13/what-will-we-do-when-the-worlds-data-hits-163-zettabytes-in-2025/1.

7. http://searchstorage.techtarget.com/magazineContent/Dealing-with-big-data-The-storage-implications.

8. James Bridle, *New Dark Age; Technology and the End of the Future* (London: Verso, 2018), 7.

9. http://www.datacenterknowledge.com/archives/2016/06/27/heres-how-much-energy-all-us-data-centers-consume.

10. Melville, *Moby-Dick: or, the Whale*, in *The Writings of Herman Melville: The Northwestern-Newberry Edition, Vol. 6*, ed. Harrison Hayford, Hershel Parker, and G. Thomas Tanselle (Evanston, IL: Northwestern University Press, 1988), 433.

11. Bruno Chiavazzo, *Da Gutenberg a Zuckerberg: la rivoluzione della communicazione* (Milton Keynes: Lightning Source, 2018).

12. Thompson, 'The Future of Reading in a Digital World', *Wired*, 22 May 2007.

13. Carr, *The Shallows: How the Internet is Changing the Way we Think, Read and Remember* (London: W. W. Norton, 2010), 134.

14. Eco, 'From Internet to Gutenberg', http://www.umbertoeco.com/en/from-internet-to-gutenberg-1996.html.
15. Ovid, *Heroides*, 1. 1. 2.
16. Moses I. Finley, *The World of Odysseus* (London: Viking Press, 1954), 9.
17. Bede, *Abbots of Wearmouth and Jarrow*, ed. C. W. Grocock and I. N. Woods, Oxford Medieval Texts (Oxford: Oxford University Press, 2013), 124.
18. Heloïse to Abelard, Letters 2 and 4; *The Letters of Abelard and Heloise*, tr. Betty Radice (London: Penguin Books, 2003), 117, 130.
19. Dronke, *Women Writers of the Middle Ages* (Cambridge: Cambridge University Press, 1984), 107. Dronke provides a similar instance of a nun (Constance of Angers), reading the same passage of the *Heroides*, 90.
20. Clanchy, *Abelard: A Medieval Life* (Oxford: Blackwell, 1999), 169.
21. Paris, Bibliothèque nationale de France, ms. latin 2923; Petrarch acquired it between 1337 and 1343.
22. Charlotte Mews, *The Lost Love Letters of Heloise and Abelard: Perceptions of Dialogue in Twelfth-Century France* (New York: Springer, 2016), 41.
23. Walter Ong, *Ramus, Method, and the Decay of Dialogue* (Cambridge, MA: Harvard University Press, 1983), 194–5.
24. Gamble, *Books and Readers in the Early Church*, 66–7.
25. David McKitterick, *Print, Manuscript and the Search for Order, 1450–1830* (Cambridge: Cambridge University Press, 2003), 102.
26. Ramus, *Dialectique* (Paris: Wéchel, 1555); see Ong, *Ramus*, 310.
27. Ann M. Blair, *Too Much to Know: Managing Scholarly Information Before the Modern Age* (New Haven and London: Yale University Press, 2010), 46, 50, 137–44.
28. Adrian Johns, *The Nature of the Book: Print and Knowledge in the Making* (Chicago: University of Chicago Press, 1998), 435–7.
29. Anthony Grafton, *The Footnote: A Curious History* (Cambridge, MA: Harvard University Press, 1997), 24–5.
30. David Wootton, *The Invention of Science: A New History of the Scientific Revolution* (London: Penguin Books, 2015), ch. 5.
31. Steven Shapin, *A Social History of Truth: Civility and Science in Seventeenth-Century England* (Chicago: University of Chicago Press, 1998), 124–6.
32. Zuboff, *Age of Surveillance Capitalism*, 59.
33. Zuboff, *Age of Surveillance Capitalism*, 401.
34. Quintilian, *Institutio oratoria*, 11.2.1.
35. Hal R. Varian, 'Big Data: New Tricks for Econometrics', *Journal of Economic Perspectives*, 28 (2014), 113.
36. Zuboff, *Age of Surveillance Capitalism*, 87.
37. Aristotle, *Poetics*, 1447ª13–16.
38. Donald, *Origins of the Modern Mind: Three Stages in the Evolution of Culture and Cognition* (Cambridge, MA: Harvard University Press, 1991), 116.
39. Aristotle, *De interpretatione*, 16ª3–4.
40. Tai T'ung, *The Six Scripts, or the Principles of Chinese Writing*, tr. L. C. Hopkins (Cambridge: Cambridge University Press, 1954), 31.
41. *Dictionnaire philosophique portatif par Mr De Voltaire* (1764).
42. Christian Keysers, 'Mirror Neurons', *Current Biology*, 19 (2010), 271–3.

43. Sapir, *Language: An Introduction to the Study of Speech* (New York: Harcourt & Brace, 1921), 1.

44. Sapir, *Language*, 15.

45. Harris, *Rethinking Writing* (London: Athlone Press, 2000), 24.

46. Gelb, *A Study of Writing: The Foundations of Grammatology* (Chicago: University of Chicago Press, 1952), 11.

47. Gelb, *Study of Writing*, 24.

48. *The World's Writing Systems*, ed. Peter T. Daniels and William Bright (New York: Oxford University Press, 1996), 4.

49. Peter T. Daniels, 'Fundamentals of Grammatology', *Journal of the American Oriental Society*, 110 (1990), 727–31.

50. Daniels and Bright, *World's Writing Systems*, 489.

51. Daniels and Bright, *World's Writing Systems*, 561.

52. J. Weingreen, *A Practical Grammar for Classical Hebrew*, 2nd edn. (Oxford: Clarendon Press, 1959), 251.

53. Daniels and Bright, *World's Writing Systems*, 485.

54. Daniels and Bright, *World's Writing Systems*, 489–91.

55. Gelb, *Study of Writing*, 166.

56. Beth McKillop, 'The Book', *Buddhism: Origins, Traditions and Contemporary Life* ed. Jana Igunma and San San May (London: British Library, 2019), 134.

57. Ostler, *Empires of the Word*, 156.

58. Tacitus, *Annals*, 11. 13–14.

59. Rosanna Friggeri, *The Epigraphic Collection of the Museo Nazionale Romano at the Baths of Diocletian* (Rome: Electa, 2004), 26.

60. C. Williamson, 'Monuments of Bronze: Roman Legal Documents on Bronze Tablets', *Classical Antiquity*, 6 (1987), 160–83.

61. Horace, *Carmina*, 3. 30. 1.

62. Frampton, *Empire of Letters*, 155.

63. W. V. Harris, *Ancient Literacy* (Cambridge, MA: Harvard University Press, 1987), 34.

64. Erasmus, *Adagiorum chiliades* (Basel: Johannes Froben, 1515).

65. Blair, *Too Much to Know*, 121, 260.

66. Daniels and Bright, *World's Writing Systems*, 26–7.

67. Gelb, *Study of Writing*, 15.

68. Harris, *Rethinking Writing*, 170.

69. Zuboff, *Age of Surveillance Capitalism*, 188.

70. Hilbert, 'Big Data for Development: From Information to Knowledge Societies' (United Nations Report, Social Sciences Research Network, 2013).

71. Barthes, *Empire of Signs* (New York: Noonday Press, 1982), 9.

72. Freud, *The Uncanny*, ed. Haughton, 142.

73. Edward Champlin, 'Serenus Sammonicus', *Harvard Studies in Classical Philology*, 85 (1981), 189–212.

74. Hyginus, *Fabulae*, 183. Hyginus' authorship of this dubious work is itself dubious.

75. Irenaeus, *Adversus haereses*, 1. 24.

76. Hippolytus, *Refutatio omnium haeresium*, 7. 26; see Elaine Pagels, *The Gnostic Gospels* (London: Hachette, 2013), 88–9.

77. Lausanne, Musée cantonal d'archéologie et d'histoire, Inv. 30,969.

78. Boccaccio, *Decameron*, VI. 10, tr. Wayne A. Rebhorn (New York: Norton, 2013), 909; *Il decamerone di m. Giouanni Boccaccio nouamente corretto con tre nouelle aggiunte* (Venice: house of Aldus Manutius, 1522), fo. 178ᵛ.

79. Defoe, *A Journal of the Plague Year* (London: E. Nutt, 1722), 40.

80. Talmud, Berachot, 55a.

81. US Supreme Court Report, 333 U.S. at 765 (1948).

82. Rushdie, *Midnight's Children* (London: Picador, 1982), 454; 'bom' means Mumbai.

83. J. K. Rowling, *Harry Potter and the Goblet of Fire* (London: Bloomsbury, 2000), ch. 14. Most of the writings cited in this paragraph, from the Talmud to Potter, have been banned at some point.

84. Sharon Olds, *Odes* (London: Cape Poetry, 2016), 116.

Chapter 3

1. Wayne A. Wiegand and Donald G. Davis, Jr (eds.), *Encyclopedia of Library History* (New York: Garland Publishing, 1994), 26.

2. Michael H. Harris, *History of Libraries in the Western World*, 4th edn. (1st edn. by Elmer D. Johnson) (New York and London: Scarecrow Press, 1999), 18–19.

3. D. T. Potts, 'Libraries in the Ancient Near East', *The Library of Alexandria: Centre of Learning in the Ancient World*, ed. Roy McLeod (London: I. B. Tauris, 2005), 19–33.

4. S. Parpola, 'Assyrian Library Records', *Journal of Near Eastern Studies*, 42 (1983), 1–29.

5. The 'Celestial Emporium of Benevolent Knowledge' is described in the 1942 essay 'El idioma analítico de John Wilkins'; Borges, *Selected Nonfictions* (London: Penguin Books, 1999), 231.

6. Foucault, *Les mots et les choses: une archéologie des sciences humaines* (Paris: Gallimard, 1966), 7.

7. Foucault, *The Order of Things* (London: Vintage Books, 1994), 143.

8. H. Albert-Schulte, 'Leibniz and Library Classification', *Journal of Library History*, 6 (1971), 133–52.

9. Irving Finkel, 'Ashurbanipal's Library: Contents and Signficance', in Gareth Brereton (ed.), *I am Ashurbanipal, King of the World, King of Assyria* (London: British Museum, 2018), 83–4.

10. Grant Frame and A. R. George, 'The Royal Libraries of Nineveh: New Evidence for King Ashurbanipal's Tablet Collecting', *Iraq*, 47/1 (2005), 265–84.

11. V. Gregory, *Collection Development and Management for 21st Century Library Collections: An Introduction* (New York: Neal Schuman, 2011).

12. Finkel, 'Ashurbanipal's Library', 80.

13. A. H. Layard, *Discoveries in the Ruins of Nineveh and Babylon* (1853), rev. edn., 2 vols. (Cambridge: Cambridge University Press, 2011).

14. H. V. Hilprecht, *The Excavations in Assyria and Babylonia* (Philadelphia: University of Pennsylvania Press, 1904), 7–22.

15. Morris Jastrow, *The Civilization of Babylonia and Assyria* (London: J. B. Lippincott, 1915), 406.

16. Diodorus, *Library of History*, 2. 23–8.

17. Aristotle, *Nicomachean Ethics*, 1095^{b}20.

18. Martin Noth, *A History of Israel* (London: A. & C. Black, 1959), 269.

19. E. A. Parsons, *The Alexandrian Library: Glory of the Hellenic World* (New York: Elsevier, 1967), 5.

20. Mary Beard, 'Cleopatra's Books', *London Review of Books*, 12/3 (8 February 1990), 11.

21. https://www.britishmuseum.org/research/research_projects/all_current_projects/ashurbanipal_library_phase_1.aspx.

22. Tablet I, lines 7–10; *The Epic of Gilgamesh*, tr. Andrew George (London: Penguin Books, 1999), 1.

23. Jeremy Black, *Gods, Demons and Symbols of Ancient Mesopotamia* (London: British Museum, 1992), 137–8.

24. Paris, Musées du Louvre; D. O. Edzard, *Gudea and his Dynasty*, Royal Inscriptions of Mesopotamia: Early Periods (Toronto: University of Toronto Press, 1997), 68–101.

25. Black *et al.*, *Literature of Ancient Sumer*, 293.

26. George Hart, *Dictionary of Egyptian Gods and Goddesses* (London: Routledge, 2005), 141.

27. *Asiatic Researches*, Calcutta Edition (London: J. Sewell, 1799), 272–3.

28. Roberto Calasso, *Ka: Stories of the Mind and Gods of India* (London: Jonathan Cape, 1998), 14.

29. Jamie Novotny and Joshua Jeffers, 'Inscriptions on Prisms, Part 1 (text nos. 1–7)', *RINAP 5: The Royal Inscriptions of Ashurbanipal, Aššur-etel-ilāni, and Sîn-šarra-iškun*, http://oracc.museum.upenn.edu/rinap/rinap5/.

30. Jon Taylor, 'Knowledge: The Key to Assyrian Power', in Brereton (ed.), *I am Ashurbanipal*, 90.

31. Robert H. Pfeiffer, *State Letters of Assyria*, American Oriental Series, 6 (New Haven: Yale University Press, 1935), 180.

32. Finkel and Taylor, *Cuneiform*, 48.

33. Jeremy Black, 'Lost Libraries of Ancient Mesopotamia', in James Raven (ed.), *Lost Libraries: The Destruction of Great Book Collections since Antiquity* (London: Palgrave Macmillan, 2004), 51–5.

34. Robin Lane Fox, *Pagans and Christians* (London: Viking Books, 1986), 569.

35. Robin Lane Fox, *Augustine: Conversions and Confessions* (London: Penguin Books, 2015), 155–8.

36. Augustine, *Confessions* 5. 6. 11.

37. Augustine, *Confessions*, 5. 7. 12.

38. Augustine, *Confessions*, 6. 10. 16.

39. Darwin, *On the Origin of Species by Means of Natural Selection, or the Preservation of Favoured Races in the Struggle for Life* (London: John Murray, 1859).

40. Hawking, *A Brief History of Time: From the Big Bang to Black Holes* (London: Bantam Dell, 1988).

41. Arthur Koestler, *The Sleepwalkers: A History of Man's Changing Vision of the Universe* (London: Macmillan, 1968), 191.

42. Owen Gingerich, *The Book Nobody Read* (London: Heinemann, 2004) describes many early readers of Copernicus. For the record, I have read both Darwin and Hawking.

43. Freud, *Beyond the Pleasure Principle*, in *Penguin Freud Reader*, ed. Phillips, 166.

44. Bernhard Metz, 'Bibliomania and the Folly of Reading', *Comparative Critical Studies* 5/2–3 (2008), 249–69.

45. 'LIVRE', *Encyclopédie, ou dictionnaire raisonné des sciences, des arts et des métiers, etc.*, ed. Denis Diderot and Jean le Rond d'Alembert (University of Chicago: ARTFL Encyclopédie Project, 2011), ix. 610.

46. Pliny, *Epistles*, 1. 20. 4.

47. *The Fragments of Callimachus*, ed. R. Pfeiffer (Oxford: Clarendon Press, 1949), fr. 465.

48. *Mélanges de littérature, d'histoire et de philosophie*, 2 vols. (Berlin: n.p., 1753), ii. 3–4.

49. Diderot, *Lettres à Sophie Volland*, 3 vols. (Paris: NRF, 1930), i. 306–7.

50. Kant, 'Remarks', in *Observations on the Feeling of the Beautiful and Sublime and Other Writings*, ed. Patrick Frierson and Paul Gayer (Cambridge: Cambridge University Press, 2011), 94.

51. Nicolas de Caritat, marquis de Condorcet, *Œuvres* (Stuttgart : Friedrich Fromann Verlag, 1968), 534.

52. Freud, *Beyond the Pleasure Principle*, in *Penguin Freud Reader*, 183.

53. Woolf, *The Waves* (London: Hogarth Press, 1931), 322.

54. Rachel Whiteread, *British Pavilion XLVII Venice Biennale 1997* (London: British Council, 1997).

55. Benjamin, 'Unpacking my Library: A Talk about Book Collecting', *Illuminations*, tr. Harry Zohn with an introduction by Hannah Arendt (London: Fontana Press, 1973), 59.

56. McKitterick, 'Libraries and the Organisation of Knowledge', in Elisabeth Leedham-Green and Teresa Webber (eds.), *The Cambridge History of Libraries in Britain and Ireland, vol. 1: to 1640* (Cambridge: Cambridge University Press, 2006), 594.

57. *Bibliotheca Universalis, sive Catalogus omnium Scriptorum locupletissimus, in tribus linguis, Latina, Græca, & Hebraica; extantium & non extantium* (Zürich: Christoph Froschauer, 1545).

58. Doris Behrens-Abouseif, *The Book in Mamluk Egypt and Syria (1250–1517)*, Islamic History and Civilization, 162 (Leiden: Brill, 2019), 7.

59. Sebald, *Austerlitz*, tr. Anthea Bell (London: Penguin Books, 2002), 389.

60. Emmanuel de Roux, 'Rétrocontroverse: 1988, la Très Grande Bibliothèque', *Le Monde*, 31 July 2007.

61. John Naughton, *A Brief History of the Future: The Origins of the Internet* (London: Weidenfeld and Nicholson, 2000), part II.

62. Viktor Mayer-Schonberger and Kenneth Cukier, *Big Data: A Revolution that will Transform how We Live, Work, and Think* (Boston: Houghton Mifflin Harcourt, 2013), ch. 2 ('More').

63. Howard W. Winger and Richard Daniel Smith (eds.), *Deterioration and Preservation of Library Materials, 34th Annual Conference of the Graduate Library School, August 4–6, 1969* (Chicago: University of Chicago Press, [1970]), 6.

64. See Sharon Ringell and Angela Woodall's report for the Tow Center for Digital Journalism at Columbia's Graduate School of Journalism, March 2019: 'A Public Record at Risk: The Dire State of News Archiving in the Digital Age'; https://www.cjr.org/tow_center_reports/the-dire-state-of-news-archiving-in-the-digital-age.php.

65. https://www.bl.uk/collection-guides/uk-web-archive.

66. Xenophon, *Anabasis*, 3. 4. 10; he calls it 'Mespila'.

67. Edmund Bosworth, *Historic Cities of the Islamic World*. (Leiden: Brill, 2007), 414.

68. Jonathan N. Tubb, Falih Almutrb, and Sebastian Rey, 'The Future of Iraqi Cultural Heritage Under Threat', in Brereton (ed.), *I am Ashurbanipal*, 312–14.

69. https://www.newyorker.com/news/news-desk/mosuls-library-without-books.

70. https://en.unesco.org/news/unesco-alarmed-news-mass-destruction-books-mosul.

Chapter 4

1. Levi, *If This is a Man*, 44.

2. Levi, *Se questo è un uomo*, 25.

3. Levi, *If This is a Man*, 39.

4. Levi, *If This is a Man*, 79.

5. Gerhard von Rad, *Genesis: A Commentary* (London: SCM, 1972), 150.

6. See the survey by Ulrike Wegener, *Die Faszination des Masslosen: der Turmbau zu Babel von Pieter Bruegel bis Athanasius Kircher* (Hildesheim: Georg Olms Verlag, 1995).

7. Michael Seymour, 'The Tower of Babel in Art', in I. L. Finkel and M. J. Seymour (eds.), *Babylon: Myth and Reality* (London: British Museum, 2008), 132.

8. Walther Eichrodt, *Theology of the Old Testament*, 2 vols. (London: SCM, 1961), i. 464.

9. Josephus, *Jewish Antiquities*, 1. 113–19.

10. Walter S. Gibson, *Bruegel* (London: Thames and Hudson, 1993), 96.

11. Seymour, 'The Tower of Babel in Art', 134–5.

12. Roger Mols, SJ, *Introduction à la démographie historique des villes d'Europe du XIVᵉ au XVIIIᵉ siècle*, 3 vols. (Louvain: J. Duculot, 1955), ii. 520.

13. S. A. Mansbach, 'Pieter Bruegel's Towers of Babel', *Zeitschrift für Kunstgeschichte*, 45.1 (1982), 43–56 at 46–9.

14. Foucault, *The Order of Things*, 39.

15. Sandhedrin 109a.

16. Herodotus, *Histories*, i. 181; tr. A. D. Godley, 225.

17. *Enûma Eliš*, VI 63; see A. R. George, 'E-sangil and E-temen-anki, the Archetypal Cult-centre?', in J. Renger, *Babylon: Focus mesopotamischer Geschichte, Wiege früher Gelehrsamkeit, Mythos in der Moderne* (Saarbrücken: Harrassowitz, 1999), 301–2.

18. Stephen L. Harris, *Understanding the Bible*, 6th edn. (New York: McGraw-Hill, 2002), 51.

19. Margaret A. Sullivan, 'Bruegel's Misanthrope: Renaissance Art for a Humanist Audience', *Artibus et Historiae*, 13 (1992), 143–62.

20. K. C. Lindsay, 'Mystery in Bruegel's Proverbs', *Jahrbuch der Berliner Museen*, 38 (1996), 63–76.

21. 'Musée des Beaux Arts', *Another Time* (London: Faber and Faber, 1940), 47.

22. Diarmaid MacCulloch, *Reformation: Europe's House Divided, 1490–1700* (London: Penguin Books, 2004), 134–5, 211.

23. Andrew G. Johnston and Jean-François Gilmont, 'Printing and the Reformation in Antwerp', in Jean-François Gilmont (ed.), *The Reformation and the Book*, Eng. tr. (Aldershot: Ashgate, 1998), 189.

24. Albert van der Heide, *Hebraica Veritas: Christopher Plantin and the Christian Hebraists* (Antwerp: Plantin-Moretus Museum, 2008).

25. Marino Zorzi, *La libreria di san Marco: Libri, lettori, società nella Venezia dei dogi* (Milan: Mondadori, 1987).

26. Roger Jones and Nicholas Penny, *Raphael* (New Haven: Yale University Press, 1983), 58.

27. Vasari, *Vite*, iv. 333; *Lives of the Artists*, tr. J. and P. Bondanella (Oxford: Oxford World's Classics, 2008), 316.

28. Cellini, *Autobiography*, tr. George Bull (Harmondsworth: Penguin Books, 1978), 79.

29. Joëlle Rollo-Koster in Jonathan Davies (ed.), *Aspects of Violence in Renaissance Europe* (London: Routledge, 2016), 42.

30. McLuhan, *Gutenberg Galaxy*, 1.

31. McLuhan, *Gutenberg Galaxy*, 3.

32. Eisenstein, *The Printing Press as an Agent of Change: Communications and Cultural Transformations in Early Modern Europe* (Cambridge: Cambridge University Press, 1980), 71–159.

33. McLuhan, *Understanding Media: the Extensions of Man* (New York: McGraw-Hill, 1964), 23.

34. Marshall McLuhan and Quentin Fiore, co-ordinated by Jerome Agel, *The Medium Is the Massage* (Harmondsworth: Penguin Books, 1967).

35. Johns, *The Nature of the Book*, 10–19; McKitterick, *Print, Manuscript and the Search for Order*, 142.

36. McLuhan, *Understanding Media*, 36.

37. Francis Bacon, *The Advancement of Learning*, ed. Michael Kiernan, *The Oxford Francis Bacon, Vol. 4* (Oxford: Oxford University Press, 2000), 53.

38. Milton, *Areopagitica*, ed. Ernest Sirluck, *Complete Prose Works of John Milton*, ii: *1643–8* (New Haven: Yale University Press, 1959), 492.

39. David Norbrook, *Writing the English Republic: Poetry, Rhetoric and Politics 1627–1660* (Cambridge: Cambridge University Press, 2000), 119–20.

40. W. R. Parker, *Milton: A Biography*, 2 vols. (Oxford: Clarendon Press, 1968), i. 266.

41. Sharon Achinstein, *Milton and the Revolutionary Reader* (Princeton, NJ: Princeton University Press, 2014), 34.

42. Apollodorus, *Library*, 3. 4; Hyginus, *Fabulae*, 178.

43. Montaigne, *Essais*, ii. 10; 'Of Books', *Complete Works*, tr. Donald Frame (New York: Everyman, 2003), 359.

44. Steven Runciman, *The Medieval Manichee: A Study of the Dualist Heresy*, rev. edn. (Cambridge: Cambridge University Press, 2010), 31.

45. Peter Brown, *Rise of Western Christendom*, 82.

46. Desmond Durkin-Meisterernst, 'Manichean Script', *Encyclopaedia Iranica* (14 October 2005).

47. A variety of texts grouped as 'The Life of Mani', 'Scriptures', etc., are edited by I. Gardner and S. N. C. Lieu, *Manichaean Texts from the Roman Empire* (Cambridge: Cambridge University Press 2004), 46–108.

48. Lane Fox, *Augustine*, 95–7.

49. R. N. Frye, 'The Political History of Iran under the Sasanians', in E. Yar-Shater (ed.), *The Cambridge History of Iran, Vol. 3: Seleucid, Parthian and Sasanian Periods* (Cambridge: Cambridge University Press, 1983), i. 139.

50. Peter Brown, *World of Late Antiquity*, 86, 106.

51. Christine Caldwell Ames, *Medieval Heresies: Christianity, Judaism and Islam* (Cambridge: Cambridge University Press, 2015), 88.

52. Xinru Liu, *Silk and Religion: An Exploration of Material Life and the Thought of the People* (Oxford: Oxford University Press, 1997), 182.

53. S. N. C. Lieu, *Manichaeism in Central Asia and China* (Leiden: Brill, 1998), 129.

54. Brown, *World of Late Antiquity*, 56, 68, 160, 190.

55. Peter Brown, *Augustine of Hippo: A Biography*, rev. edn. (Berkeley and Los Angeles: University of California Press, 2000), 43–4.

56. Lane Fox, *Augustine*, 435–9.

57. Brown, *Augustine of Hippo*, 178.

58. Bernard Hamilton, 'Wisdom from the East', in Peter Biller and Anne Hudson (eds.), *Heresy and Literacy 1000–1530* (Cambridge: Cambridge University Press, 1994), 38–9.

59. Malcolm Lambert, *Medieval Heresy: Popular Movements from the Gregorian Reform to the Reformation* (Oxford: Blackwell, 1992), 20–2.

60. Augustine, *Confessions*, 8. 12. 80; tr. Chadwick, 153.

61. William James, *The Varieties of Religious Experience: A Study in Human Nature* (London: Longman, Green, 1905), 479.

62. Luther, 'Preface to Luther's Latin Writings' (1545); *Luther's Works*, 34. 337. Latin text in WA 1. 185. 16.

63. Bunyan, *Grace Abounding to the Chief of Sinners*, ed. Roger Sharrock (Oxford: Oxford University Press, 2013), 10.

64. Anna Trapnel, *A Legacy for Saints; Being Several Experiences of the Dealings of God* (London: T. Brewster, 1654), 2.

65. Brian Cummings, 'Autobiography and the History of Reading', in Brian Cummings and James Simpson (eds.), *Cultural Reformations: Medieval and Renaissance in Literary History* (Oxford: Oxford University Press, 2010), 635–57.

66. James, *Varieties of Religious Experience*, 199.

67. Journal of the priest Iakov Netsvetov, 1828–43; Washington, DC, Library of Congress, Alaskan Russian Church Archives, Manuscript Division, D45/(41a).

68. Brown, *The Rise of Western Christendom*, 284–5.

69. Seymour, 'The Tower of Babel in Art', 141.

70. Joscelyn Godwin, *Athanasius Kircher's Theatre of the World* (London: Thames & Hudson, 2009).

71. Alberto Manguel, *A History of Reading* (London: Flamingo, 1997), 198.

72. Borges, 'The Library of Babel', *Labyrinths: Selected Stories and Other Writings* (London: Penguin Books, 1970), 78.

73. Borges, *Ficciones* (Caracas: Fundación Biblioteca Ayacuch, 1986), 40.

74. Borges, 'The Library of Babel', *Labyrinths*, 85.

75. Bradbury, *Fahrenheit 451* (London: Flamingo, 1993), 11.

76. Bradbury, *Fahrenheit 451*, 68.

77. *Handbook of Physical Testing of Paper*, 2 vols. (Boca Raton: CRC Press, 2001), ii. 442–6.

Chapter 5

1. Guenter Lewy, *Harmful and Undesirable: Book Censorship in Nazi Germany* (Oxford: Oxford University Press, 2016), 10.
2. Gerhard Sauder (ed.), *Die Bücherverbrennung: zum 10. Mai 1933* (Munich: Carl Hanser, 1983), 173–218.
3. Leonidas E. Hill, 'The Nazi Attack on "Un-German" Literature, 1933–1945', in Jonathan Rose (ed.), *The Holocaust and the Book: Destruction and Preservation* (Amherst: University of Massachusetts Press, 2001), 16.
4. Lewy, *Book Censorship in Nazi Germany*, 11.
5. Hobsbawm, *Age of Extremes*, 149.
6. Pamela Spence Richards, 'Deutschlands wissenschaftliche Verbindungen mit dem Ausland 1933–1945', in Peter Vodosek and Manfred Komorowski (eds.), *Bibliotheken während des Nationalsozialismus*, 2 vols., Wolfenbütteler Schriften zur Geschichte des Buchwesens, 16 (Wiesbaden: Harrassowitz, 1989–92), ii. 1129.
7. Richard J. Evans, *The Third Reich in Power, 1933–1939* (London: Penguin Books, 2006), 16.
8. Heine, *Tragödien, nebst einem lyrischen Intermezzo* (Berlin: Dümmler, 1823).
9. Hill, in *The Holocaust and the Book*, 16.
10. Lewy, *Book Censorship in Nazi Germany*, 11.
11. 'Against class conflict and materialism: for people, community, and idealistic living standards: Marx, Kautsky', in Sauder (ed.), *Die Bücherverbrennung*, 77.
12. https://www.aclu.org/issues/free-speech/artistic-expression/banned-books.
13. Myron Sharaf, *Fury on Earth: A Biography of Wilhelm Reich* (Boston, MA: Da Capo, 1994), 461.
14. Mark Rose, 'Copyright, Authors and Censorship', in Michael F. Suarez and Michael L. Turner (eds.), *Cambridge History of the Book in Britain, Vol. 5, 1695–1830* (Cambridge: Cambridge University Press, 2009), 118.
15. Annabel Patterson, *Censorship and Interpretation: The Conditions of Writing and Reading in Early Modern England* (Madison, WI: University of Wisconsin Press, 1984), 54.
16. Nigel Smith, *Literature and Revolution in England 1640–1660* (New Haven and London: Yale University Press, 1997), 23.
17. At first for 21 years; or 14 for new books; in the latter case renewable if an author lived: in most countries today, it is the lifetime of the author plus 50 to 70 years.
18. Habermas, *The Structural Transformation of the Public Sphere: An Inquiry into a Category of Bourgeois Society* (Cambridge, MA: MIT Press, 1991), 95.
19. Rose, 'Copyright, Authors and Censorship', 127–8.
20. Peter Lake and Steven Pincus, 'Introduction', *The Politics of the Public Sphere in Early Modern England* (Manchester: Manchester University Press, 2007), 12; see also Rachel Wil in the same volume, p. 241.
21. Jefferson to Abigail Adams, *The Adams–Jefferson Letters: The Complete Correspondence Between Thomas Jefferson and Abigail and John Adams*, ed. Lester J. Capon (Chapel Hill: University of North Carolina Press, 1987), 35.

22. 'Appeal to the Inhabitants of Quebec', 26 October 1774, in Charles S. Hyneman and Donald S. Lutz (eds.); *American Political Writing During the Founding Era, 1760–1805* (Indianapolis: Liberty Press, 1983), 233–4.

23. Jean-Baptiste Alphonse Karr, quoted in John George Wood, *A Tour Round My Garden* (London: G. Routledge, 1855), 313.

24. Richard D. Brown, 'The Revolution's Legacy for the History of the Book', in Robert A. Gross and Mary Kelley (eds.), *An Extensive Republic: Print, Culture, and Society in the New Nation, 1790–1840*, History of the Book in America, 2 (Chapel Hill: University of North Carolina Press, 2010), 63.

25. Jonathan I. Israel, *Radical Enlightenment: Philosophy and the Making of Modernity 1650–1750* (Oxford: Oxford University Press, 2002), 39.

26. Desmond M. Clarke, *Descartes: A Biography* (Cambridge: Cambridge University Press, 2006), 411.

27. Israel, *Radical Enlightenment*, 39.

28. Edward Peters, *Inquisition* (Berkeley and Los Angeles: University of California Press, 1989), 247.

29. Israel, *Radical Enlightenment*, 43.

30. J. G. A. Pocock, *The Machiavellian Moment: Florentine Political Thought and the Atlantic Republican Tradition* (Princeton, NJ: Princeton University Press, 2003), 98.

31. Israel, *Radical Enlightenment*, 44.

32. Anthony Grafton, *Defenders of the Text: Traditions of Scholarship in an Age of Science 1450–1800* (Cambridge, MA: Harvard University Press, 1994), 179–81.

33. Israel, *Radical Enlightenment*, 101–2.

34. Freya Sierhuis, *The Literature of the Arminian Controversy* (Oxford: Oxford University Press, 2015), 84.

35. Israel, *Radical Enlightenment*, 292.

36. Richard H. Popkin, 'Spinoza's Excommunication', in H. M. Raven and L. E. Goodman (eds.), *Jewish Themes in Spinoza's Philosophy* (Albany, NY: SUNY Press, 2012), 263–80.

37. Peters, *Inquisition*, 196.

38. Israel, *Radical Enlightenment*, 276.

39. Israel, *Radical Enlightenment*, 276.

40. Ohad Nachtomy, 'On Living Mirrors and Mites: Leibniz's Encounter with Pascal on Infinity', *Oxford Studies in Early Modern Philosophy*, 8 (2019), 159.

41. Kant, 'Remarks', in *Observations on the Feeling of the Beautiful and Sublime*, 137.

42. Susan James, *Spinoza on Philosophy, Religion and Politics* (Oxford: Oxford University Press, 2012), 294.

43. Spinoza, *Tractatus Theologico-Politicus*, ed. Carl Gebhart, *Opera*, iii. 239.

44. John Marshall, *John Locke, Toleration, and Early Enlightenment Culture* (Cambridge: Cambridge University Press, 2006), 337.

45. *Hugo Grotius's Remonstrantie of 1615*, ed. David Kromhout and Adri K. Offenberg (Leiden: Brill, 2019), 211.

46. Sierhuis, *Literature of the Arminian Controversy*, 145.

47. Charles S. Edwards, *Hugo Grotius, Miracle of Holland* (Chicago: Nelson Hall, 1981), 7.

48. Hill, in *The Holocaust and the Book*, 20.

49. The figure is the estimate of Jan-Pieter Barbian and Frank Simon Ritz, in a survey undertaken for the Deutsche Nationalbibliothek in Leipzig.

50. Hill, in *The Holocaust and the Book*, 12.

51. Joseph Hilgers, *Der Index der verbotenen Bücher in seiner neuen Fassung dargelegt und rechtlich-historisch gewürdigt* (Freiburg in Breisgau: Herder, 1904), 480–2.

52. H. J. Schroeder, *Disciplinary Decrees of the General Councils: Text, Translation and Commentary* (St. Louis, MI: B. Herder, 1937), 504–5.

53. Paul F. Grendler, 'Printing and Censorship', in Charles B. Schmitt and Quentin Skinner (eds.), *The Cambridge History of Renaissance Philosophy* (Cambridge: Cambridge University Press, 1988), 45–6.

54. Richard Bonney, *Confronting the Nazi War on Christianity: The Kulturkampf Newsletters, 1936–1939* (London: Peter Lang, 2009), 17.

55. Hill, in *The Holocaust and the Book*, 13.

56. Lewy, *Book Censorship in Nazi Germany*, 11.

57. Lewy, *Book Censorship in Nazi Germany*, 109.

58. Volker Dahm, *Das jüdische Buch im Dritten Reich*, 2 vols. (Munich: C. H. Beck, 1979); i: *Die Ausschaltung der jüdischen Autoren, Verleger und Buchhändler*), 197.

59. Christoph Zuschlag, 'Censorship in the Visual Arts in Nazi Germany', in Elizabeth C. Childs (ed.), *Suspended License: Censorship and the Visual Arts* (Seattle: University of Washington Press, 1997), 213–14.

60. Evans, *The Third Reich in Power*, 159.

61. Livy, *History of Rome*, 11. 45.

62. Cicero, *Ad familiares*, 3. 11 (*Letters to Friends*, 74. 5).

63. Erasmus, *Travels of the Apostles* (LB 6. 426); CWE 41. 954 (see also Robert Sider's footnote on Erasmus' annotation to Acts 15: 19 in his New Testament of 1516).

64. Freud, *The Interpretation of Dreams*, tr. James Strachey (Harmondsworth: Penguin Books, 1980), 567.

65. Lewy, *Book Censorship in Nazi Germany*, 12.

66. Hill, in *The Holocaust and the Book*, 14.

67. *Völkischer Beobachter*, 14 April 1933.

68. Freud, *The Uncanny*, ed. Haughton, 139.

69. Dietrich Aigner, 'Die Indizierung schädlichen und unerwünschten Schrifttums im Dritten Reich', *Archiv für Geschichte des Buchwesens*, 11 (1971), 948–9.

Chapter 6

1. In Sauder (ed.), *Die Bücherverbrennung*, 71–5.

2. *Cahiers juifs* (Paris, No. 5/6, September/November 1933, 161–9).

3. Joseph Roth, 'The Auto-da-Fé of the Mind', *What I Saw: Reports from Berlin, 1920–1933*, tr. Michael Hoffman (London: Granta, 2004), 207–217 at 207, 208.

4. Zweig, *Triumph und Tragik des Erasmus von Rotterdam* (Vienna: Herbert Reichner, 1934), 168.

5. Johannes Evelein, *Literary Exiles from Nazi Germany: Exemplarity and the Search for Meaning* (London: Boydell & Brewer, 2014), 150.

6. Ernst Robert Curtius, *European Literature and the Latin Middle Ages* (New York: Bollingen, 1953), 248.

7. *Letter of Aristeas to Philocrates*, 9.

8. Roy MacLeod, 'Alexandria in History and Myth', in MacLeod (ed.), *The Library of Alexandria*, 2.

9. Athenaeus, *Deipnosophistae*, 1. 3.

10. Parsons, *Alexandrian Library*, 84–7.

11. Robert Barnes, 'Cloistered Bookworms in the Chicken-Coop of the Muses: The Ancient Library of Alexandria', in MacLeod (ed.), *The Library of Alexandria*, 62–3.

12. Mostafa El-Abbadi, *The Life and Fate of the Ancient Library of Alexandria* (Paris: UNESCO, 1996).

13. *Oxyrhynchus Papyri*, 1241.

14. Rudolf Blum, *Kallimachos: The Alexandrian Library and the Origins of Bibliography*, tr. Hans H. Wellisch (Madison, WI: University of Wisconsin Press, 1991), 182.

15. Listed in Parsons, *Alexandrian Library*, 138–53.

16. Parsons, *Alexandrian Library*, 110.

17. Aulus Gellius, *Attic Nights*, 7. 17. 3, tr. Rolfe, ii.138–9; see also Ammianus Marcellinus, *History* 22. 16. 13.

18. James Raven, 'The Resonances of Loss', in Raven (ed.), *Lost Libraries*, 1–40.

19. William Blades, *The Enemies of Books*, rev. edn. (London: E. Stock, 1902).

20. Parsons devotes an Appendix to the various sources: *Alexandrian Library*, 188–90.

21. Plutarch, *Life of Caesar*, 49.

22. Dio Cassius, *Historiae Romanae*, 42. 38. 2.

23. Aulus Gellius, *Attic Nights*, 7. 17.

24. Parsons, *Alexandrian Library*, 333–9.

25. Barnes, 'The Ancient Library of Alexandria', 73.

26. Orosius, *Historiae adversum paganos*, 6. 15. 31.

27. Lane Fox, *Pagans and Christians* (London: Viking Books, 1986), 301.

28. Anthony Grafton and Megan Williams, *Christianity and the Transformation of the Book: Origen, Eusebius and the Library of Caesarea* (Cambridge, MA: Harvard University Press, 2009), 70.

29. *Letter of Aristeas to Philocrates*, 11.

30. Augustine, Letter to Jerome *c.*394; *Letters*, No. 28; see also *City of God*, 18 42–3.

31. Jerome, *Letter* 112 to Augustine, justifying his new translation based on the Hebrew.

32. Metzger, *The Bible in Translation* (Grand Rapids: Baker Academic, 2001), 15.

33. *Etymologiae*, 6. 3. 3; *The Etymologies of Isidore of Seville*, ed. Stephen A. Barney, W. J. Lewis, J. A. Beach, and Oliver Berghof (Cambridge: Cambridge University Press, 2006), 139.

34. Alfred J. Butler, *The Arab Conquest of Egypt* (Oxford: Clarendon Press, 1902) created the classic Orientalist account of the Caliphate.

35. Chase Robinson, 'The Rise of Islam, 600-705', in Chase Robinson (ed.), *New Cambridge History of Islam, Vol. 1: The Formation of the Islamic World, Sixth to Eleventh Centuries* (Cambridge: Cambridge University Press, 2010), 196.

36. Barnes, 'The Ancient Library of Alexandria', 74.

37. ʿAlī ibn Yūsuf Qifṭī, *Taʾrīḫ al-Ḥukamāʾ*, ed. August Müller and Julius Lippert (Leipzig: Dieterich, 1903), 354–7.

38. Gibbon, *Decline and Fall of the Roman Empire*, Everyman Edition, 6 vols. (London: J. M. Dent, 1910), iii. 131.

39. Butler, *Return to Alexandria: An Ethnography of Cultural Heritage Revivalism and Museum Memory* (London: Routledge, 2016), 148.

40. Luciano Canfora, *The Vanished Library: A Wonder of the Ancient World* (Berkeley and Los Angeles: University of California Press, 1990), 84.

41. Richard Sorabji, *Philoponus and the Rejection of Aristotelian Science* (London: Duckworth, 1987), 45.

42. Uwe Michael Lang, *John Philoponus and the Controversies over Chalcedon in the Sixth Century* (Leuven: Peeters, 2001), 6.

43. Canfora, *The Vanished Library*, 99.

44. Tacitus, *Germania*, 39. 3–4.

45. Augustine, *Retractiones*, 2.69.

46. Augustine, *City of God*, 3. 29.

47. Patrick J. Geary, *Language and Power in the Early Middle Ages* (Waltham, MA: Brandeis University Press, 2013), 45.

48. Janet L. Nelson, *King and Emperor: A New Life of Charlemagne* (London: Allen Lane, 2019), 68.

49. Alcuin, *Carmen*, line 1535; ed. Peter Godman, *Alcuin: The Bishops, Kings and Saints of York* (Oxford: Clarendon Press, 1982), 120.

50. Mary Garrison, 'The Library of Alcuin's York', in Richard Gameson (ed.), *The Cambridge History of the Book in Britain*, vol. 1, *c.400–1100* (Cambridge: Cambridge University Press, 2011), 633–64.

51. Alcuin, *Ep.* 20; Nelson, *King and Emperor*, 301.

52. Michael Gullick, 'Bookbinding', in Gameson (ed.), *Cambridge History of the Book in Britain*, i. 294.

53. Bede, *Life of Cuthbert*, Prologue; *The Age of Bede*, ed. D. H. Farmer (London: Penguin Books, 2004), 44.

54. *Alfred the Great: Asser's Life of King Alfred and Other Contemporary Sources*, ed. Simon Keynes and Michael Lapidge (Harmondsworth: Penguin Books, 1983), 123.

55. Jane Bately, '"Those books that are most necessary for all men to know": The Classics and Late Ninth-Century England: A Reappraisal', in Aldo Bernardo and Saul Levin (eds.), *The Classics in the Middle Ages* (Binghamton, NY: MRTS, 1990), 45–78.

56. Snorri Sturluson, *The Prose Edda*, tr. Jesse L. Byock (London: Penguin Books, 2005), 1.

57. John Lindow, 'Mythology and Mythography', *Old Norse-Icelandic Literature*, ed. Carol Clover and John Lindow (Toronto: University of Toronto Press, 2005), 22.

58. Elizabeth M. Tyler, *England in Europe: English Royal Women and Literary Patronage, c.1000-c.1150* (Toronto: University of Toronto Press, 2017), 59–61.

59. Bede, *Ecclesiastical History of the English People*, 'Praefatio'; ed. Bertram Colgrave and R. A. B. Mynors (Oxford: Clarendon Press, 1969), 6; see Virgil, *Aeneid*, 12. 608.

60. Michael Lapidge, *The Anglo-Saxon Library* (Oxford: Oxford University Press, 2006), 106.

61. Kathy Eden, *The Renaissance Rediscovery of Intimacy* (Chicago: University of Chicago Press, 2012), 6–9.

62. Petrarch, *Familiares*, 24. 8.

63. Berlin, Staatsbibliothek, MS Hamilton 166; Christopher De Hamel, *A History of Illuminated Manuscripts* (London: Phaidon Press, 1997), 238.

64. R. R. Bolgar, *The Classical Heritage and its Beneficiaries* (Cambridge: Cambridge University Press, 1977), 263.

65. Pocock, *Machiavellian Moment*, 52.

66. Martin Davies, *Aldus Manutius: Printer and Publisher of Renaissance Venice* (London: British Library, 1997), 18.

67. Peter Godman, 'Poggio Bracciolini and Niccolò Niccoli', *Neulateinisches Jahrbuch*, 21 (2019), 78.

68. Poggio, Letter III (18 May 1416; *Ep.* 46 in Harth's edition); *Two Renaissance Book Hunters: The Letters of Poggius Bracciolini to Nicolaus de Niccolis*, tr. Phyllis Walter Goodhart Gordan (New York: Columbia University Press, 1991), 24.

69. Virgil, *Aeneid* 6. 306–8.

70. Poggio, Letter III, *Two Renaissance Book Hunters*, 26.

71. Godman comments at length on Poggio's Latin neologist term *Caesarstoul*, from German *Stühl*; 'Poggio Bracciolini and Niccolò Niccoli', 80.

72. Ovid, *Metamorphoses*, 4. 607.

73. Poggio, Letter III, *Two Renaissance Book Hunters*, 27.

74. Poggio, Letter III, *Two Renaissance Book Hunters*, 29.

75. Dante, *Purgatorio*, 28. 64–6.

76. Bolgar, *Classical Heritage*, 275.

77. Lodi Nauta, *In Defense of Common Sense: Lorenzo Valla's Critique of Scholastic Philosophy* (Cambridge, MA: Harvard University Press, 2009), 232.

78. Erasmus, *De copia*, in CWE 24: 297.

79. Luther, letter to Georg Spalatin, 29 November 1519, WA Br 1. 563.

80. Jacques Chomarat, 'Les Annotations de Valla, celles d'Érasme et la grammaire', in O. Fatio and P. Fraenkel (eds.), *Histoire de l'exégèse au XVIᵉ siècle* (Geneva: Droz, 1978), 202–28.

81. Poggio, *Orationes in L. Vallam* (1452–3); Angelo Mazzocco, *Linguistic Theories in Dante and the Humanists: Studies of Language and Intellectual History in Late Medieval and Early Renaissance Italy* (Leiden: Brill, 1993), 70–2.

82. Greenblatt, *The Swerve: How the World Became Modern* (New York: W. W. Norton, 2011).

83. Erasmus, *Colloquies*, vol. 2, CWE 40. 1075.

84. *Montaigne's Annotated Copy of Lucretius: A Transcription and Study of the Manuscript, Notes and Pen-marks*, ed. M. A. Screech (Geneva: Droz, 1998).

85. More, *Utopia, Complete Works*, iv. 160–70, 220–4.

86. *Two Renaissance Book Hunters*, Appendix 1, 188.

87. Poggio, Letter XV (13 November 1421), *Two Renaissance Book Hunters*, 59.

88. Poggio, Letter X (29 October 1420), *Two Renaissance Book Hunters*, 46.

89. Daniel Wakelin, *Humanism, Reading, and English Literature 1430–1530* (Oxford: University Press, 2007), 49.

90. David Rundle, 'English Books and the Continent', in Alexandra Gillespie and Daniel Wakelin (eds.), *The Production of Books in England 1350–1500* (Cambridge: Cambridge University Press, 2011), 276–91 at 284.

91. Rundle, 'British Barbarians in Italy and Scotland's First Humanist', *The Renaissance Reform of the Book and Britain* (Cambridge: Cambridge University Press, 2019), 89–120.

92. Behrens-Abouseif, *The Book in Mamluk Egypt and Syria*, 12.

93. Amalia Levanoni, 'The Mamlūks in Egypt and Syria: The Turkish Mamlūk sultanate', in Maribel Fierro (ed.), *New Cambridge History of Islam, Vol. 2: The Western Islamic World, Eleventh to Eighteenth Centuries* (Cambridge: Cambridge University Press, 2010), 237.

94. Behrens-Abouseif, *The Book in Mamluk Egypt and Syria*, 15–16.

95. Behrens-Abouseif, *The Book in Mamluk Egypt and Syria*, 46–8.

96. Elisabeth Leedham-Green, 'University Libraries and Booksellers', in Lotte Hellinga and J. B. Trapp (eds.), *Cambridge History of the Book in Britain, vol. 3: 1400–1557* (Cambridge: Cambridge University Press, 1999), 322.

97. De Hamel, *History of Illuminated Manuscripts*, 232. The condition was that the books would belong to Venice after his death. Petrarch reneged on the deal; only 44 have been identified to date (de Hamel, 234).

98. James P. Carley, 'The Dispersal of the Monastic Libraries', in Leedham-Green and Webber (eds.), *Cambridge History of Libraries in Britain and Ireland, vol. 1: to 1640*, 266.

99. MacCulloch, *Reformation*, 200–1.

100. Leland, *De viris illustribus/On Famous Men*, ed. and tr. James P. Carley (Toronto: Pontifical Institute of Medieval Studies, 2010).

101. *Joannis Lelandi antiquarii de rebus Britannicis collectanea*, 6 vols. in 7 (Oxford: Thomas Hearne, 1715), iii. 36–7.

102. Bale, *Illustrium majoris Britanniae scriptorum, hoc est, Angliae, Cambriae, ac Scotiae Summarium* (Wesel: John Overton, 1548).

103. Machiavelli, *Lettere*, ed. F. Gaeta (Milan: Feltrinelli, 1961), 304.

104. Pocock, *Machiavellian Moment*, 62.

105. Auden, 'Spain, 1937', *Another Time*, 103.

106. Brown, *Rise of Christendom*, 357, commenting on the eighth century.

107. De Hamel, *History of Illuminated Manuscripts*, 18.

108. James Carley, 'The libraries of Archbishops Whitgift and Bancroft', *The Book Collector*, 62 (2013), 209–27.

109. Julian Roberts, 'Scholar Collectors', in Leedham-Green and Webber (eds.), *Cambridge History of Libraries in Britain and Ireland*, 307.

110. Bede, *Ecclesiastical History of the English People*, ed. Colgrave and Mynors, xxvii.

111. Joshua Hammer, *The Bad-Ass Librarians of Timbuktu: And Their Race to Save the World's Most Precious Manuscripts* (New York: Simon and Schuster, 2016), 71–2.

112. Hammer, *The Bad-Ass Librarians of Timbuktu*, 211.

113. Dalrymple, *From the Holy Mountain* (London: Flamingo Books, 2000), 141.

114. Leo Africanus, *A Geographical Historie of Africa, Written in Arabicke and Latin* (London: George Bishop, 1600), 287.

115. Elias N. Saad, *Social History of Timbuktu: The Role of Muslim Scholars and Notables* (Cambridge: Cambridge University Press, 1983), 79–80.

116. Natalie Zemon Davis, *Trickster Travels: The Search for Leo Africanus* (London: Faber & Faber, 2008), 32–3, 69–70, 85.

117. Hammer, *The Bad-Ass Librarians of Timbuktu*, 25.

118. Canetti, *Auto-da-Fé* (London: Jonathan Cape, 1971), 11.

119. Canetti, *Auto-da-Fé* (London: Jonathan Cape, 1971), 67.
120. William Collins Donahue, *The End of Modernism: Canetti's Auto da fé* (Chapel Hill, NC: University of North Carolina Press, 2001).
121. John Tzetzes, Letter 52; *Epistolae*, ed. Theodore Pressel (Tübingen: Franciscus Fues, 1851), 60.

Chapter 7

1. Pliny the Elder, *Natural History*, 7. 30. 114.
2. Harold Love, 'Introduction', *The Works of John Wilmot Earl of Rochester* (Oxford: Oxford University Press, 1999), p. xxx.
3. Dickinson, *Complete Poems*, ed. Thomas H. Johnson (London: Faber, 1970), p. ix.
4. 'Postscript to the First Edition', Kafka, *The Trial* (New York: Schocken, 1984), 265–6.
5. Kafka, *Letters to Friends, Family, & Editors*, ed. Richard and Clara Winston (New York: Schocken, 1977), 289.
6. Kafka to Oscar Pollak, 27 January 1904; *Letters to Friends, Family, & Editors*, 16.
7. Adam Smyth, *Material Texts in Early Modern England* (Cambridge: Cambridge University Press, 2018), 59.
8. *Deterioration and Preservation of Library Materials*, 3.
9. Henry Hallam, *The Constitutional History of England from the Accession of Henry VII to the Death of George II*, 2 vols. (London: John Murray, 1827), ii. 517.
10. John Stuart Mill, *On Liberty* (London: Longmans, Green, and Company, 1867), 10.
11. Sima Qian, *The First Emperor: Selections from the Historical Records*, tr. Raymond Dawson, Oxford World's Classics (Oxford: Oxford University Press, 2007), 74.
12. Matthew Battles, *Library: An Unquiet History* (London: William Heinemann, 2003), 35.
13. Mark Edward Lewis, *Writing and Authority in Early China* (New York: SUNY Press, 1999), 308.
14. Borges, *Labyrinths*, 221.
15. Battles, *Library*, 36.
16. Martin Kern, *The Stele Inscriptions of Ch'in Shih-huang: Text and Ritual in Early Chinese Imperial Representation* (New Haven: American Oriental Society, 2000), 132.
17. Kin Haines-Eitzen, 'Engendering Palimpsests: Reading the Textual Tradition of the Acts of Paul and Thecla', in W. E. Klingshirn and L. Safran (eds.), *The Early Christian Book* (Washington, DC: Catholic University of America Press, 2007), 187–9.
18. Tacitus, *Agricola*, 2.
19. Ann Chrystys, *Christians in Al-Andalus, 711–1000* (London: Routledge, 2002), 142.
20. Karina Galperín, 'The Passion According to Berruguete: Painting the Auto-de-Fé and the Establishment of the Inquisition in Early Modern Spain', *Journal of Spanish Cultural Studies,* 14 (2013), 315–47.
21. Arnold, 'Inquisition, Texts and Discourse', *Texts and the Repression of Medieval Heresy*, ed. Caterina Bruschi and Peter Biller (Woodbridge: York Medieval Press, 2003), 63–4.
22. Chartier, *The Order of Books: Readers, Authors, and Libraries in Europe between the Fourteenth and Eighteenth Centuries*, tr. Lydia G. Cochrane (Cambridge: Polity Press, 1994), 3.

23. Gui, *Practica inquisitionis*, 5. 5; *Manuel de l'inquisiteur*, ed. C. Douais, 2 vols., Les classiques de l'histoire de France au moyen âge, 8–9 (Paris: Les Belles Lettres, 1926).

24. Peter Biller, 'The Cathars of Languedoc and written materials', in *Heresy and Literacy*, 71.

25. Emmanuel Le Roy Ladurie, *Montaillou: The World-Famous Portrait of Life in a Medieval Village* (London: Penguin Books, 1980), 236.

26. Ginzburg, *The Cheese and the Worms: The Cosmos of a Sixteenth-Century Miller* (London: Penguin Books, 1992), 51.

27. Ginzburg, *The Cheese and the Worms*, 29.

28. Ladurie, *Montaillou*, 147.

29. McKillop, 'The Book', in Igunma and San San May (eds.) *Buddhism: Origins, Traditions and Contemporary Life*, 115.

30. Talya Fishman, *Becoming the People of the Talmud: Oral Torah as Written Tradition in Medieval Jewish Cultures* (Philadelphia: University of Pennsylvania Press, 2013), 173.

31. Hyam Maccoby, *Judaism on Trial: Jewish-Christian Disputations in the Middle Ages* (Plainsboro: Associated University Presses, 1982), 37.

32. Joseph Isaac Lifshitz, *Rabbi Meir of Rothenburg and the Foundation of Jewish Political Thought* (Cambridge: Cambridge University Press, 2016), 43.

33. Martyn Rady, 'The Corvina Library and the Lost Royal Hungarian Archive', in Raven, *Lost Libraries*, 91.

34. Eco, *Il nome della rosa* (Milan: Bompiani, 1980), 499.

35. https://www.dw.com/en/library-goes-up-in-flames-destroying-literary-legacy/a-1317151.

36. I. Bukreeva *et al.*, 'Virtual Unrolling and Deciphering of Herculaneum Papyri by X-ray Phase-Contrast Tomography', *Scientific Reports* 6, Article number: 27227 (2016).

37. *nomenque erit indelebile nostrum*; Ovid, *Metamorphoses*, 15. 876.

38. Ovid, *Tristia*, 3. 3. 81–2.

39. Frampton, *Empire of Letters*, 147.

40. 'Extract from the Annals of Tiglath-Pileser I', quoted from A. H. Sayce, *An Elementary Grammar of the Assyrian Language in the Cuneiform Type*, orig. publ. 1875 (Cambridge: Cambridge University Press, 2014), 109–10.

41. Steven Michael Press, 'False Fire: The Wartburg Book-Burning of 1817', *Central European History*, 42 (2009), 621–46 at 621.

42. Heiko A. Oberman, *Luther: Man between God and Devil* (New Haven: Yale University Press, 1982), 13.

43. Martin Brecht, *Martin Luther: His Road to Reformation* (Minneapolis: Fortress Press, 1985), 390–1.

44. Brecht, *Road to Reformation* 404.

45. WA Br. 2. 137. 25.

46. 'Epistolae Reformatorum', *Zeitschrift für Kirchengeschichte*, 2 (1878), 122.

47. WA 7. 183.

48. WA Br. 2. 234. 4; in Luther, *Letters*, 3 vols., i. 186–7, in *Luther's Works*, vol. 48; see also the report on the book-burning in WA 7. 184–6.

49. *Letters*, 3 vols., i. 192, in *Luther's Works*, vol. 48.

50. Brecht, *Road to Reformation*, 424.

51. WA 7.161–82.

52. *Luther's Works*, 31. 383.

53. Crouzet, *Les guerriers de Dieu: la violence au temps des troubles de religion, vers 1525 – vers 1610*, 2 vols. (Seyssel: Champ Vallon, 1990), i. 584.

54. Hermann Rafetseder, *Bücherverbrennungen: die öffentliche Hinrichtung von Schriften im historischen Wandel* (Vienna: Böhlau Verlag, 1988), 135.

55. Brecht, *Road to Reformation*, 395.

56. Wrede, Adolf, *Deutsche Reichstagsakten unter Kaiser Karl V.*, in *Deutsche Reichstagsakten*, 4 vols. (Gotha: Friedrich Andreas Perthes, 1893–1905), ii. 455.

57. M. E. Kronenberg, *Verboden boeken en opstandige drukkers in de hervormingstijd* (Amsterdam: P. N. van Kampen, 1948), 28.

58. Erasmus, *Opus epistolarum*, ed. Allen, iv. 375. 5–6, 398. 53–9.

59. *Acta Academiae Lovaniensis contra Lutherum*; in *Erasmi opuscula*, ed. W. K. Ferguson (The Hague: Martinus Nijhoff, 1933), 328.

60. *Deutsche Reichstagsakten*, ii. 471.

61. Brecht, *Road to Reformation*, 419.

62. Craig Harline, *A World Ablaze: The Rise of Martin Luther and the Birth of the Reformation* (Oxford: Oxford University Press, 2017), 186.

63. Luther, *Letters*, i. 194.

64. Brecht, *Road to Reformation*, 426.

65. Lyndal Roper, *Martin Luther: Renegade and Prophet* (London: Vintage Books, 2017), 178.

66. *Deutsche Reichstagsakten*, ii. 655; the Latin, Dutch and French texts of this are in *Corpus documentorum inquisitionis inquisitionis haereticae pravitatis neerlandicae*, ed. Paul Fredericq, 5 vols. (s'Gravenhage: Martinus Nijhoff, 1889–1902), iv. 47–76.

67. *Corpus documentorum*, v. 404.

68. *The Reformation and the Book*, 189–90.

69. *Corpus documentorum inquisitionis*, v. 405.

70. Margaret Aston, 'Rites of Destruction by Fire', in *Faith and Fire* (London: Hambledon Press, 1993), 300.

71. Peter W. M. Blayney, *The Stationers' Company and the Printers of London, 1501–1557*, 2 vols. (Cambridge: Cambridge University Press, 2013), i. 243.

72. Lodovico Spinelli, Secretary to the Venetian Ambassador in England to his brother Gasparo; *CSPV*, iii. 213 (see also 210).

73. Paul F. Grendler, *The Roman Inquisition and the Venetian Press, 1540–1605* (Princeton: Princeton University Press, 1977), 74, 82.

74. Felipe Fernández-Armesto, *Reformation* (London: Bantam Books, 1996), 189–91.

75. Jeanne Nuechterlein, *Translating Nature into Art: Holbein, the Reformation, and Renaissance Rhetoric* (University Park: Pennsylvania State University Press, 2011), 30–2.

Chapter 8

1. Lévi-Strauss, *Tristes Tropiques*, tr. John and Doreen Weightman (London: Jonathan Cape, 1973), 298; French text *Tristes tropiques* (Paris: Librairie Plon, 1955), 352.

2. *Tristes Tropiques*, 299.

3. Douglas, *Leviticus as Literature* (Oxford: Oxford University Press, 1999), 57.

4. 2 Chronicles 35: 12, citing Leviticus 3: 3; 3: 5; 3: 9–11; 3: 14–16.

5. Kafka, 'Before the Law', *Collected Stories*, ed. Gabriel Josipovici (London: Everyman, 1993), 173.

6. Kafka, *Der Proceß* (Frankfurt am Main: Fischer Verlag, 1994), 226.

7. Mauss, *The Gift: The Form and Reason for Exchange in Archaic Societies* (London: Routledge, 1990), 69; 'no gift is free' is Mary Douglas's epigram in her foreword, ix.

8. Rousseau, *Du contrat social*, I.iv ('De l'esclavage'); *Œuvres complètes*, Bibliothèque de la Pléiade, 5 vols. (Paris: Gallimard, 1959–95), iii. 355.

9. Rousseau, *Du contrat social*, iii. 358.

10. Lévi-Strauss, *Tristes tropiques*, 276.

11. Harris, *Ancient Literacy*, 110–11.

12. Plato, *Theaetetus*, 143b–c.

13. 'Look after yourself, my dear Tiro, do', 7 November 50 BCE; Cicero, *Ad familiares*, 16. 6. 2 (*Letters to Friends*, 125. 2).

14. Elizabeth Rawson, *Cicero: A Portrait* (London: Allen Lane, 1975), 143–4.

15. Harris, *Ancient Literacy*, 160.

16. Plutarch, *Aemilius Paullus*, 20. 8–10.

17. Greenblatt, *Marvelous Possessions: The Wonder of the New World*, Oxford Clarendon Lectures (Chicago: University of Chicago Press, 1991), 57.

18. *Requerimiento* (1513); Robert A. Williams, *The American Indian in Western Legal Thought* (Oxford: Oxford University Press, 1992), 91–3.

19. Davis, *Trickster Tales*, 85.

20. *Novísima recopilación de leyes de España*, 12 vols. (Madrid: Iusticia, 1805), 1. VIII.

21. J. M. de Bujanda, 'Literary Censorship in Sixteenth-Century Spain', *Canadian Catholic Historical Association*, 38 (1971), 51–63 at 53–4.

22. Bernal Díaz del Castillo, *The Conquest of New Spain* (Harmondsworth: Penguin Books, 1973), 214.

23. Anthony Pagden, *European Encounters with the New World: from Renaissance to Romanticism* (New Haven and London: Yale University Press, 1993), 62.

24. *Histoire d'un voyage faict en la terre du Brésil*, ed. Frank Lestringant with an introduction by Claude Lévi-Strauss (Paris: Livres de Poche, 1994), 380.

25. Bernabé Cobo, *Inca Religion and Customs*, tr. Roland Hamilton (Austin: University of Texas Press, 2010), 103.

26. Derrida, *De la grammatologie*, 184; tr. Spivak, *Of Grammatology*, 126.

27. Rousseau, *On the Origin of Language*, tr. John H. Moran and Alexander Gode (New York: Frederick Ungar, 1966), 16.

28. Rousseau, *Confessions*, tr. Angela Scholar, Oxford World's Classics (2000), 7.

29. Proverbs 13: 24.

30. Quintilian, *The Orator's Education* 1. 3. 13–17.

31. Erasmus, *On Education for Children*, CWE 26. 332.

32. Locke, *Some Thoughts Concerning Education* (London: A. J. Churchill, 1693), 85.

33. Richard H. Brodhead, 'Sparing the Rod: Discipline and Fiction in Antebellum America', *Representations*, 21 (1988), 67–96.

34. Patricia Lopes Don, *Bonfires of Culture: Franciscans, Indigenous Leaders, and Inquisition in Early Mexico, 1524–1540* (Norman, OK: University of Oklahoma Press, 2010), 113, 200.

35. Michiel van Groesen, *The Representation of the Overseas World in the De Bry Collection of Voyages 1590–1634* (Leiden: Brill, 2008), 293.

36. Janet Duitsman Cornelius, *When I Can Read My Title Clear: Literacy, Slavery, and Religion in the Antebellum South* (Columbia, SC: University of South Carolina Press, 1991).

37. Offences against Public Policy, 54. 198; *The Code of Virginia* (Richmond, VA: William F. Ritchie, 1849), §31, 747.

38. Colson Whitehead, *The Underground Railroad* (New York: Doubleday, 2016), 95.

39. Pierre Bourdieu, 'The Forms of Capital', *Handbook of Theory of Research for the Sociology of Education*, ed. John Richardson (Westport, CT: Greenwood Press, 1986), 46–58.

40. Whitehead, *The Underground Railroad*, 96.

41. Adams to Jefferson, 22 May 1785; *Adams–Jefferson Letters*, ed. Cappon, 21.

42. Jefferson, *Notes on the State of Virginia*, 2nd edn. (London: John Stockdale, 1787), 264.

43. Jefferson, *Notes on the State of Virginia*, 227.

44. Jefferson to Adams, 21 January 1821; *Adams–Jefferson Letters*, ed. Cappon, 570.

45. Milton, *Paradise Lost*, 1. 201.

46. Melville, *Moby-Dick*, 137.

47. Melville, *Moby-Dick*, 145.

48. Johns, *Nature of the Book*, 248.

49. Kant, 'Remarks' in *Observations on the Feeling of the Beautiful*, 187–8.

50. Kant, *Groundwork of the Metaphysics of Morals*, 4. 456; German–English Edition, ed. Mary Gregor and Jens Timmermann (Cambridge: Cambridge University Press, 2010), 141.

51. Kant, *Observations on the Feeling of the Beautiful and Sublime*, 58; repeated in 'On the Use of Teleological Principles in Philosophy' in 1788.

52. Hegel, *Phänomenologie des Geistes,* §189; *The Phenomenology of Spirit*, tr. Michael Inwood (Oxford: Oxford University Press, 2018), 79.

53. Hegel, *Phänomenologie des Geistes,* ed. Eva Moldenhauer and Karl Markus Michel, *Werke,* 20 vols. (Frankfurt am Main: Suhrkamp, 1970–79), iii. 145.

54. Luther, *Von der Freiheit eines Christenmenschen* (Wittenberg: Johann Rhau-Grunenberg, 1520), sig. A2ʳ.

55. *Freedom of a Christian*, tr. Henrike Lähnemann, Taylor Online Editions, https://editions.mml.ox.ac.uk/editions/freiheit-1520/ [accessed 8 December 2020]. Note that the translation in *Luther's Works*, vol. 31 is from the Latin edition not the German.

56. Heermann-Sinai, 'Luther and Hegel on Lordship and Bondage', November 2020, The Reformation at the Taylor Institution Library, https://blogs.bodleian.ox.ac.uk/taylor-reformation/2020/11/27/luther-and-hegel-on-lordship-and-bondage/ [accessed 8 December2020].

57. Susan Buck-Morss, 'Hegel and Haiti', *Critical Inquiry*, 26 (2000), 821–65.

58. Jonathan Israel, *Revolutionary Ideas: An Intellectual History of the French Revolution from The Rights of Man to Robespierre* (Princeton, NJ: Princeton University Press, 2014), 362.

59. Hegel, *Phänomenologie des Geistes,* §178; tr. Inwood, 76.

60. Kant, *Critique of Pure Reason*, 1st edn. (A99); ed Paul Guyer and Allen W. Wood (Cambridge: Cambridge University Press, 1997), 228.

61. M. J. Inwood, *Hegel* (London: Routledge, 2002), 101.
62. Derrida, *De la grammatologie*, 41.
63. Derrida, *Of Grammatology*, 26.
64. Hegel, *Phänomenologie des Geistes*, §§316; tr. Inwood, 127.
65. Hegel, *Phänomenologie des Geistes*, §484; tr. Inwood, 194.
66. Lacan, 'Aggressivity in Psychoanalysis', *Écrits: A Selection*, tr. Alan Sheridan (London: Routledge, 1977), 26.
67. Lacan, *Écrits*, tr. Sheridan, 28; referring (without citation) to Dante, *Inferno*, 5. 136.
68. Derrida, *Glas* (Paris: Galilée, 1974), 114.
69. Brown, *Augustine of Hippo*, 542.
70. Gamble, *Books and Readers in the Early Church*, 134.
71. Pettegree, *Brand Luther* (London: Penguin Books, 2015), 114.
72. Euan Cameron, 'The Luther Bible', *New Cambridge History of the Bible, Vol. 3: From 1450 to 1750*, ed. Cameron (Cambridge: Cambridge University Press, 2016), 219–20.
73. Ginzburg, *The Cheese and the Worms*, 46.
74. Montaigne, 'Des cannibales', *Essais*, 1. 31; *Complete Works*, 185.
75. Lévi-Strauss, *La pensée sauvage* (Paris: Plon, 1962), 5–15.
76. Ginzburg, *The Cheese and the Worms*, 47.
77. Boccaccio, *Decameron*, tr. Guido Waldmann (Oxford: Oxford World's Classics, 1998), 40–1.
78. Gordon Leff, *Heresy in the Later Middle Ages: The Relation of Heterodoxy to Dissent*, 2 vols. (Manchester: Manchester University Press, 1967), i. 657.
79. Crouzet, *Les guerriers de Dieu*, ii. 112.
80. William Monter, *Judging the French Reformation: Heresy Trials by Sixteenth-Century Parlements* (Cambridge, MA: Harvard University Press, 1999), 58.
81. J. M. de Bujanda, Francis K. Higman, and James K. Farge, *Index de l'Université de Paris, 1544, 1545, 1547, 1549, 1551,1556*, Index des Livres Interdits, 1 (Geneva: Droz, 1985).
82. Paris, Archives Nationales, MM.248: register of conclusions of the Sorbonne from November 1533 to August 1549. The *arrêts criminels* are contained in a separate register: Paris, Archives Nationales, X2a 93.
83. N. Weiss, 'Arrêt inédit du Parlement de Paris contre l'Institution chrétienne (1ᵉʳ juillet 1542)', *Bulletin de la Société de l'histoire du protestantisme français*, 33 (1884), 15–21.
84. Gigliola Fragnito (ed.), *Church, Censorship and Culture in Early Modern Italy*, tr. Adrian Belton (Cambridge: Cambridge University Press, 2001), 3.
85. Blair, *Too Much to Know*, 248–9.
86. Peter Godman, *Die geheime Inquisition: aus den verbotenen Archiven des Vatikan* (Wiesbaden: Marix Verlag, 2005).
87. Fragnito, *Church, Censorship and Culture*, 35.
88. 'Fountain of sorrow, home of wrath, school of errors, heresy's own temple: once Rome, now false and wicked Babylon, cause of sighing and so much weeping'; *Rime sparse*, RVF 138: 1–4, ed. R. M. Durling, *Petrarch's Lyric Poems* (Cambridge MA: Harvard University Press, 1976).
89. Yale University, Beinecke Library MS 706 has ink frames round the sonnets.
90. Peter Stallybrass, 'Petrarch and Babylon: Censoring and Uncensoring the *Rime*, 1559-1651', in Ann Blair and Anja-Silvia Goeing (ed.), *For the Sake of Learning: Essays in Honor of Anthony Grafton* (Leiden: Brill, 2016), 581–601 at. 590.

91. 'Here are missing three sonnets'; *Il Petrarca con nuove spositioni* (Venice: G. Angelieri, 1595), 207–9, Beinecke Library.

92. University of Toronto, Centre for Renaissance and Reformation Studies Erasmus Library, shelf mark BR 65.J4 1524a.

93. Freud to Fliess, 22 December 1897; *The Complete Letters of Sigmund Freud to Wilhelm Fliess 1887–1904*, ed. and trans. Jeffrey Masson (Cambridge, MA: Harvard University Press, 1985), 289.

94. Freud, *Die Traumdeutung* (Frankfurt am Main: S. Fischer Verlag, 1972), 507; *Interpretation of Dreams*, 676.

95. Lacan, *Écrits*, tr. Sheridan, 67.

96. Malcolm Bowie, *Lacan* (London: Fontana Press, 1991), 108.

97. Lacan, *The Four Fundamental Concepts of Psychoanalysis* (Séminaire XI), tr. Alan Sheridan (London: Penguin Books, 1994), 20.

98. Lacan, *Écrits*, tr. Sheridan, 147.

99. Lacan, *Écrits*, tr. Sheridan, 153.

100. Hegel, *Phänomenologie des Geistes,* §§189–90; tr. Inwood, 79.

101. Hegel, *Phänomenologie des Geistes,* §§179; tr. Inwood, 76.

102. Gill Partington, 'Dust Jackets', in Dennis Duncan and Adam Smyth (eds.), *Book Parts* (Oxford: Oxford University Press, 2019), 18.

103. Coleridge, *Biographia Literaria*, ed. J. Shawcross, 2 vols. (Oxford: Oxford University Press, 1907), ii. 116.

104. Girard, *Violence and the Sacred*, tr. Patrick Gregory (Baltimore: Johns Hopkins University Press, 1977), 99–100.

105. Lévinas, *Du sacré au saint: cinq nouvelles lectures talmudiques* (Paris: Minuit, 1977).

106. Derrida, *Of Grammatology*, 203.

107. Derrida, *Of Grammatology*, 254.

108. Rousseau, *Confessions*, 238.

109. Proust, *Time Regained*, 348.

110. Samuel Beckett, *Malone Dies* (New York: Grove Press, 1991), 209.

111. Arendt, *On Violence* (San Diego: Harcourt Brace & Co., 1970), 51.

112. Hill, in *The Holocaust and the Book*, 13.

Chapter 9

1. Michael Greenhalgh, *Marble Past, Monumental Present: Building with Antiquities in the Medieval Mediterranean* (Leiden: Brill, 2008), 309.

2. Eduardo Moreno, 'The Iberian Peninsula and Northern Africa', in Robinson (ed.), *New Cambridge History of Islam, Vol. 1* 602.

3. Manuel Nieto Cumplido, *La Mezquita-Catedral de Córdoba* (Granada: Edilux, 2005), 15.

4. Robert Hillenbrand, *Islamic Art and Architecture* (London: Thames & Hudson, 1999), 172.

5. Finbarr Barry Flood, *The Great Mosque of Damascus: Studies on the Makings of an Umayyad Visual Culture*, Islamic History and Civilization, 33 (Leiden: Brill, 2001), 52.

6. Flood, *The Great Mosque of Damascus*, 47.

7. Hillenbrand, *Islamic Art and Architecture*, 172.

8. Robert Hillenbrand, *Islamic Architecture: Form, Function and Meaning* (Edinburgh: Edinburgh University Press, 1994), 31.

9. Jonathan M. Bloom, 'Mosque', *Encyclopaedia of the Qur'an*, ed. Jane Dammen McAuliffe, Brill Online (accessed 4 December 2020).

10. Richard Kimber, 'Qibla', *Encyclopaedia of the Qur'an*, Brill Online (accessed 4 December 2020).

11. Robinson, 'The Rise of Islam, 600–705', *New Cambridge History of Islam, Vol. 1*, 174.

12. Jonathan Bloom and Sheila Blair, *Islamic Arts* (London: Phaidon Press, 1997), 23.

13. K. A. C. Creswell, rev. James W. Allan, *A Short Account of Early Muslim Architecture* (Aldershot: Scolar Press, 1989), 46.

14. Bloom and Blair, *Islamic Arts*, 33.

15. Hillenbrand, *Islamic Architecture: Form, Function and Meaning*, 31.

16. Bloom and Blair, *Islamic Arts*, 28.

17. Sheila S. Blair, *Islamic Inscriptions* (Edinburgh: Edinburgh University Press, 1998), 10.

18. Gerald R. Hawting, 'Idols and Images', *Encyclopaedia of the Qur'an*, Brill Online (accessed 4 December 2020).

19. J. R. Osborn, *Letters of Light: Arabic Script in Calligraphy, Print and Digital Design* (Cambridge, MA: Harvard University Press, 2017), 73–4.

20. Bloom and Blair, *Islamic Arts*, 30–1.

21. Sheila S. Blair, *Islamic Calligraphy* (Edinburgh: Edinburgh University Press, 2006), 3.

22. Qur'an, Q 96: 1–5; tr. Arthur Arberry (Oxford: Oxford World's Classics, 2008), 651.

23. Blair, *Islamic Calligraphy*, 10.

24. Blair, *Islamic Calligraphy*, 11.

25. Bloom and Blair, *Islamic Arts*, 71.

26. Alain Fouad George, 'The Geometry of the Qur'an of Amajur', *Muqarnas*, 20 (2003), 1–15 at 3–4.

27. Blair, *Islamic Calligraphy*, 105–6.

28. Helen Loveday, *Islamic Paper: A Study of the Ancient Craft* (London: Archetype, 2001).

29. Jonathan Bloom, *Paper before Print: The History and Impact of Paper in the Islamic Word* (New Haven and London: Yale University Press, 2001).

30. Blair, *Islamic Calligraphy*, 171–3.

31. Beatrice Gruendler, 'Arabic Script', *Encyclopaedia of the Qur'an*, Brill Online (accessed 4 December 2020).

32. Behrens-Abouseif, *The Book in Mamluk Egypt and Syria*, 29–30.

33. Behrens-Abouseif, *The Book in Mamluk Egypt and Syria*, 104.

34. Dublin, Chester Beatty Library, MS 1431; Bloom and Blair, *Islamic Arts*, 195–7.

35. Beatrice Manz, 'The Rule of the Infidels: The Mongols and the Islamic World', in David O. Morgan and Anthony Reid (eds.), *New Cambridge History of Islam, Vol. 3: The Eastern Islamic World, Eleventh to Eighteenth Centuries* (Cambridge: Cambridge University Press, 2010), 143.

36. David James, *Qur'ans of the Mamluks* (London: Alexandria Press, 1989), Cat. 39, 235. The surviving fragments are dispersed over three continents.

37. James, *Qur'ans of the Mamluks*, 89–92.

38. Blair, *Islamic Calligraphy*, 250. This MS is also scattered between libraries in Germany, Denmark and Turkey; it is Cat. 40 in James, *Qur'ans of the Mamluks*.
39. James, *Qur'ans of the Mamluks*, 113; Cat. 45 (Cairo, National Museum, MS 72).
40. Bloom and Blair, *Islamic Arts*, 206–7.
41. James, *Qur'ans of the Mamluks*, 115.
42. James, *Qur'ans of the Mamluks*, 103. This MS (Cat. 42) is also widely scattered.
43. Cairo, National Library, MS 72; James, *Qur'ans of the Mamluks*, 112.
44. Behrens-Abouseif, *The Book in Mamluk Egypt*, 107.
45. Levanoni, 'The Mamlūks in Egypt and Syria', in Fierro (ed.), *New Cambridge History of Islam, Vol. 2*, 240.
46. James, *Qur'ans of the Mamluks*, 30.
47. James, *Qur'ans of the Mamluks*, 32–3.
48. Behrens-Abouseif, *The Book in Mamluk Egypt*, 108.
49. London, British Library, Add. MSS 22406–22412; James, *Qur'ans of the Mamluks*, Cat. 1.
50. Behrens-Abouseif, *The Book in Mamluk Egypt*, 120.
51. James, *Qur'ans of the Mamluks*, 38–9.
52. James, *Qur'ans of the Mamluks*, 45 (Cat. 4).
53. James, *Qur'ans of the Mamluks*, 182–8.
54. Cairo, National Museum MS 10 (James Cat. 32); described in James, *Qur'ans of the Mamluks*, 1982–1.
55. Blair, *Islamic Calligraphy*, 322–3.
56. Blair, *Islamic Calligraphy*, 260.
57. A. M. Gowing, *Empire and Memory: The Representation of the Roman Republic in Imperial Culture* (Cambridge: Cambridge University Press, 2005), 144.
58. Friggeri, *Epigraphic Collection of the Museo Nazionale Romano*, 169.
59. I. M. Diakonoff, 'Media', in Gershevitch (ed.), *Cambridge History of Iran, Vol. 2*, 38–9.
60. Ann Farkas, 'The Behistun Relief', in Gershevitch (ed.), *Cambridge History of Iran, Vol. 2*, 828–9.
61. Wilhelm Eilers, 'Iran and Mesopotamia', in Yar-Shater (ed.), *Cambridge History of Iran, Vol. 3*, 485.
62. Blair, *Islamic Inscriptions*, 10–11.
63. *Reading the Alhambra: A Visual Guide to the Alhambra through its Inscriptions* (Granada: Patronato de la Alhambra y Generalife, 2010), 13.
64. Maribel Fierro, 'The Almohads and the Hafsids', in Fierro (ed.), *New Cambridge History of Islam, Vol. 2*, 132.
65. Huizinga in *Herfsttij der Middeleeuwen* (Haarlem: Tjeenk Willink, 1919), ch. 12: 'De kunst in het leven'.
66. Oleg Grabar, *The Alhambra*, 2nd edn. (Sebastopol: Solipsist Press, 1992), 76.
67. *Reading the Alhambra*, 13.
68. A. R. Nykl, 'Inscripciones árabes de la Alhambra y del Generalife', *Al-Andalus*, 4 (1936), 174–94.
69. Derived from Q 3: 126; *Reading the Alhambra*, 127.
70. Puerta Vilchez, *Reading the Alhambra*, 128–9.
71. Grabar, *The Alhambra*, 113.

Chapter 10

1. 'According to the Rabbis, those scrolls are not read in public, but they are still sacred and require burial'; Talmud, Shabbat 115a.

2. Adina Hoffman and Peter Cole, *Sacred Trash: The Lost and Found World of the Cairo Geniza*, Jewish Encounters (New York: Schocken Books, 2011), 12.

3. Alexandra Walsham, 'Introduction', *The Social History of the Archive: Record-Keeping in Early Modern Europe*, Supplementary issue, *Past and Present*, 230 (2016), 10–11.

4. Behrens-Abouseif, *The Book in Mamluk Egypt*, 71, 74; the market moved to Cairo under Sultan Qalawun (1279–90).

5. Igunma and San May (eds.), *Buddhism: Origins, Traditions and Contemporary Life*, 112.

6. Michael Cook, *The Koran: A Very Short Introduction* (Oxford: Oxford University Press, 2000), 61.

7. Ribhi Mustafa Ellayan, 'The History of the Arabic-Islamic Libraries, 7th–14th Centuries', *International Library Review*, 22 (1990), 119–35.

8. Hoffman and Cole, *Sacred Trash*, 6.

9. Marina Rustow, *The Lost Archive: Traces of a Caliphate in a Cairo Synagogue* (Princeton: Princeton University Press, 2020), 451.

10. Hoffman and Cole, *Sacred Trash*, 16–17.

11. Peter Gentry, 'Origen's Hexapla', in A. Salvesen and T. M. Law (eds.), *The Oxford Handbook of the Septuagint* (Oxford: Oxford University Press, 2020).

12. R. G. Jenkins, 'The First Column of the Hexapla: The Evidence of the Milan Codex and the Cairo Genizah Fragment', in Alison Salvesen (ed.), *Origen's Hexapla and Fragments* (Tübingen: Mohr Siebeck, 1998), 88–102.

13. Codex Nitriensis, British Library, Add. MS 17211.

14. Rawson, *Cicero*, 143.

15. Cicero, *Ad familiares*, 7. 18 (*Letters to his Friends*, 37).

16. Cicero, *De partitione oratoria*, 26.

17. Genette, *Palimpsests: Literature in the Second Degree* (Lincoln: University of Nebraska Press, 1997), 400.

18. Jane Dammen McAuliffe, 'Bible', *Encyclopaedia of the Qur'an*, Brill Online (accessed 4 December 2020).

19. M. Ben-Dov, *Synagogues in Spain* (Tel Aviv, 1989).

20. Sarah Stroumsa, *Maimonides in his World: Portrait of a Mediterranean Thinker* (Princeton: Princeton University Press, 2009), 8.

21. Stroumsa, *Maimonides in his World*, 60.

22. Hoffman and Cole, *Sacred Trash*, 234.

23. Davis, *Trickster Travels*, 85–6.

24. Uppsala, University Library, MS O BJ. 48.

25. Istanbul University Library, MS A 6755; J. D. Dodds (ed.), *Al-Andalus: The Art of Islamic Spain* (New York, 1992), fig. 1.

26. Katrin Kogman-Appel, *Jewish Book Art Between Islam and Christianity: The Decoration of Hebrew Bibles in Medieval Spain*, tr. Judith Davidson, *The Medieval and Early Modern World* (Leiden and Boston: Brill, 2004), 38.

27. Signed in 1232 by Israel ben Moses ibn Casares; Paris, Bibliothèque nationale de France, cod. hébr. 25.

28. Marseille, Bibliothèque municipale, cod. 1626.

29. Katrin Kogman-Appel, *Jewish Book Art Between Islam and Christianity: The Decoration of Hebrew Bibles in Medieval Spain*, tr. Davidson, *The Medieval and Early Modern World*, 4–5.

30. Parma, Biblioteca Palatina, MS Parm 2668, fo. 7^v.

31. Madrid, Biblioteca Nacional, cod. vit. 13–11.

32. O. K. Werckmeister, 'Art of the Frontier: Mozarabic Monasticism', in Jerrilynn D. Dodds (ed.), *The Art of Medieval Spain, 500–1200* (New York: Metropolitan Museum of Art, 1993), 121–33.

33. Rafael López Guzmán, *Arquitectura Mudéjar* (Madrid: Ediciones Cátedra, 2016).

34. Dodds, 'Mudéjar Tradition and the Synagogues of Medieval Spain', in Vivian B. Mann, Thomas F. Glick, and Jerrilynn D. Dodds (eds.), *Convivencia: Jews, Muslims, and Christians in Spain* (New York: G. Braziller, 1992).

35. Davis, *Trickster Travels*, 65.

36. *Epistles of Maimonides*, ed. A. Halkin (New York: Jewish Publication Society, 1993), 15–45.

37. Fierro, 'The Almohads and the Hafsids', in Fierro (ed.), *New Cambridge History of Islam, Vol. 2*, 136.

38. I. C. Levy, R. George-Tvrtković, and D. F. Duclow (eds.), *Nicholas of Cusa and Islam: Polemic and Dialogue in the Late Middle Ages* (Leiden: Brill, 2016).

39. Robin Lane Fox, *Pagans and Christians*, 520.

40. Eusebius, *Ecclesiastical History*, 6. 8.

41. Peter Brown, *The Body and Society: Men, Women, and Sexual Renunciation in Early Christianity* (London: Faber & Faber, 1988), 168.

42. Henry Chadwick, *The Early Church* (London: Penguin Books, 1993), 108–9.

43. Graphic examples are a *Roman de la Rose* (France, 15th c.): Oxford, Bodleian MS Douce 195, fo. 122^v; and a *Cybele* (15th c.): The Hague, Museum Meermanno-Westreenianum, MS 10 A 11, fo. 341^v.

44. Villon, *Ballades*, in Étienne Gilson, *Les idées et les lettres* (Paris: Vrin, 1932), 49.

45. On Abelard's castration, Clanchy, *Abelard*, 198–9.

46. Beryl Smalley, *The Study of the Bible in the Middle Ages* (Notre Dame, IN: University of Notre Dame Press, 1978), 6; the citation is from 1 Corinthians 10: 11 and forms the basis of Origen's theory of typology.

47. Elizabeth Drayson, *The Lead Books of Granada* (Houndsmill: Palgrave Macmillan, 2013).

48. A. Katie Harris, *From Muslim to Christian Granada: Inventing a City's Past in Early Modern Spain* (Baltimore, MD: The Johns Hopkins University Press, 2010), p. xx.

49. M. Barrios Aguilera and M. García-Arenal, *The Orient in Spain: Converted Muslims, the Forged Lead Books of Granada, and the Rise of Orientalism*, Studies in the History of Religions, 142 (Leiden: Brill, 2013), 153.

50. *Los plomos del Sacromonte. Invención y tesoro*, ed. M. Barrios Aguilera and M. García-Arenal (València: Universitat de València, 2006).

51. Curtius, 'The Book as Symbol', *European Literature and the Latin Middle Ages*, 303–4.

52. William M. Schniedewind, 'Writing and Book Production in the Ancient Near East', in James Carleton Paget and Joachim Schaper (eds.), *New Cambridge History of the Bible, Vol. 1: From the Beginnings to 600* (Cambridge: Cambridge University Press, 2013), 57.

53. Schniedewind, 'Writing and Book Production in the Ancient Near East', 58.

54. David C. Parker, 'The New Testament Text and Versions', in James Carleton Paget and Joachim Schaper (eds.), *New Cambridge History of the Bible, Vol. 1*, 413–14.

55. C. T. R. Hayward, 'Scripture in the Jewish Temple', in Carleton Paget and Schaper (eds.), *New Cambridge History of the Bible, Vol. 1*, 328, 336.

56. Josephus, *Jewish Antiquities*, 11. 154–5.

57. Mishnah, Sotah 7: 8.

58. Judith Olszowy-Schlanger, 'The Hebrew Bible', in Richard Marsden and Ann Matter (eds.), *New Cambridge History of the Bible, Vol. 2: From 600 to 1450* (Cambridge: Cambridge University Press, 2012), 24.

59. Olszowy-Schlanger, 'The Hebrew Bible', 39.

60. John Reeve (ed.), *Sacred: Books of the Three Faiths: Judaism, Christianity, Islam* (London: British Library, 2007), 164.

61. Rachel Wischnitzer, *The Architecture of the European Synagogue* (Philadelphia: Jewish Publication Society of America, 1964), 32.

62. Olszowy-Schlanger, 'The Hebrew Bible', 39.

63. Moses Maimonides, *The Guide for the Perplexed* (New York: Dover Books, 2012), 325.

64. Jewish Museum London, Barnett 613; see *Sacred*, 181.

65. Pavlos D. Vasileiadis, 'Aspects of Rendering the Sacred Tetragrammaton in Greek', *Open Theology*, 1 (2014), 56–88 at 59.

66. Eugene Ulrich, 'The Old Testament Text and its Transmission', in Carleton Paget and Schaper (eds.), *New Cambridge History of the Bible, Vol. 1*, 93.

67. Vasileiadis, 'Aspects of Rendering the Sacred Tetragrammaton in Greek', 60.

68. John Barton, 'The Old Testament Canons', in Carleton Paget and Schaper (eds.), *New Cambridge History of the Bible, Vol. 1*, 161.

69. G. Stroumsa, 'A Nameless God: Judaeo-Christian and Gnostic Theologies of the Name', *Hidden Wisdom* (Leiden: Brill, 2005), 185–6.

70. Vasileiadis, 'Aspects of Rendering the Sacred Tetragrammaton in Greek', 59.

71. E. Tov, 'Some Thoughts at the Close of the Discoveries in the Judaean Desert Publication project', in A. Roitman, L. Schiffmann and S. Tzoref (eds.), *The Dead Sea Scrolls and Contemporary Culture* (Leiden: Brill, 2011), 1–13.

72. Olszowy-Schlanger, 'The Hebrew Bible', 22–3.

73. W. O. E. Oesterley, *The Religion and Worship of the Synagogue: An Introduction to the Study of Judaism from the New Testament Period* (London: Isaac Pitman, 1907), 28.

74. Hoffman and Cole, *Sacred Trash*, 11.

75. W. G. Day, 'Recirculated Material in an Eighteenth-Century Library', in A. Fenneteaux, A. Junqua, and S. Vasset (eds.), *The Afterlife of Used Things* (London: Routledge, 2014), 169–83; Anna Reynolds, 'Early Modern Encounters with Binding Waste', *Journal of the Northern Renaissance*, 8 (2017), 1–43.

76. Jonson, *The Staple of News*, in *Works* (London: Richard Meighen, 1640), 43.

77. Ricks, 'Tennyson's Methods of Composition', *Proceedings of the British Academy*, 52 (1968), 210; see also his British Academy Shakespeare Lecture, *Proceedings of the British Academy*, 121 (2003), 145.

78. Treason Act (26 Henry VIII, c. 13), November 1534.

79. G. R. Elton, 'The Law of Treason', *Policy and Police: The Enforcement of the Reformation in the Age of Thomas Cromwell* (Cambridge: Cambridge University Press, 1985), 276–8.

80. Cummings, *Mortal Thoughts*, 137–41.

81. Hudson, *Lollards and their Books* (London: Hambledon Press, 1985), 188.

82. Hudson, *The Premature Reformation: Wycliffite Texts and Lollard History* (Oxford: Clarendon Press, 1988), 482–3.

83. Hudson, *Premature Reformation*, 491–4.

84. Zuboff, *Age of Surveillance Capitalism*, 59.

85. Zuboff, *Age of Surveillance Capitalism*, 190.

86. Richard Marius, *Thomas More* (London: Weidenfeld, 1993), 505.

87. Margaret Roper to Alice Alington, [August 1534]; *The Correspondence of Sir Thomas More*, ed. Elizabeth Frances Rogers (Princeton: Princeton University Press, 1947), 519. The letter was said in the 16th c. to be possibly of the hand of More himself.

88. More to Margaret Roper, 2 or 3 May 1535; *Correspondence*, 552.

89. More to Margaret Roper, [3 June 1535]; *Correspondence*, 557.

90. More to Margaret Roper, [3 June 1535]; *Correspondence*, 558.

91. Samuel Beckett, *L'innommable* (Paris: Éditions de Minuit, 1953), 195.

92. Solomon Schechter, 'A Hoard of Hebrew MSS.' *The Times*, 3 August 1897.

Chapter 11

1. Plato, *Phaedrus*, 230d5.

2. *Phaedrus*, 242d2.

3. Plato, *Philebus*, 18b6.

4. *Phaedrus*, 274e4.

5. *Phaedrus*, 275c5–9.

6. Harvey Yunis, *Written Texts and the Rise of Literate Culture in Ancient Greece* (Cambridge: Cambridge University Press, 2003).

7. Yunis, *Plato: Phaedrus* (Cambridge: Cambridge University Press, 2011), 223.

8. Harvey Yunis, *Taming Democracy: Models of Political Rhetoric in Classical Athens* (Ithaca: Cornell University Press, 1996), 173.

9. Derrida, *The Post Card: From Socrates to Freud and Beyond*, tr. Alan Bass (Chicago: University of Chicago Press, 1987), 12 (originally published as *La carte postale*, 1980).

10. Nicholas Carr, 'Is Google Making us Stupid?', *The Atlantic*, July/August 2008; https://www.theatlantic.com/magazine/archive/2008/07/is-google-making-us-stupid/306868/.

11. *The Shallows: How the Internet Is Changing the Way We Think, Read and Remember* (London: W. W. Norton, 2010), 122–34.

12. *Phaedrus*, 275a5.

13. Diogenes Laertius, *Lives of Eminent Philosophers* 3 (Plato). 6.

14. Derrida, *La dissémination* (Paris: Éditions du Seuil, 1972), 94.

15. *Dissemination*, tr. Barbara Johnson (London: Athlone Press, 1981), 76.

16. 'il n'y a là nulle métaphore', *La dissémination*, 95.

17. *Phaedrus*, 276a6.
18. Derrida, *Dissemination*, tr. Johnson, 93.
19. Penelope Wilson, *Sacred Signs: Hieroglyphs in Ancient Egypt* (Oxford: Oxford University Press, 2003), 103.
20. *Dissemination*, tr. Johnson, 91.
21. Clement of Alexandria, *Stromata*, 5. 4. 20–1; on the Egyptian transliteration, see Wilson, *Sacred Signs*, 22.
22. Herodotus, *Histories*, 2. 36.
23. Robert K. Ritner, 'Egyptian Writing', *The World's Writing Systems*, ed. Daniels and Bright, 73.
24. Wilson, *Sacred Signs*, 104.
25. B. J. Kemp, *Ancient Egypt: Anatomy of a Civilization* (Cambridge: Cambridge University Press, 1989), 40–1.
26. Wilson, *Hieroglyphs*, 9–10.
27. Plutarch, *De Iside et Osiride*, 56.
28. See Ritner, 'Egyptian Writing', tables 4.1, 4.2, 4.3.
29. Ritner, 'Egyptian Writing', 76.
30. Wilson, *Sacred Signs*, 28.
31. Wilson, *Hieroglyphs*, 89.
32. Champollion, *Précis du système hiéroglyphique des anciens Égyptiens, ou, Recherches sur les élémens premiers de cette écriture sacrée*, rev. ed. (Paris: Imprimerie Royale, 1827), 49.
33. Champollion, *Journey to Egypt* (London: Gibson Square, 2019), 29.
34. Champollion, *Journey to Egypt*, 39.
35. Champollion, *Lettres et journaux écrits pendant le voyage d'Égypte*, ed. H. Hartleben (Paris: Christian Bourgeois, 1986), 118.
36. Champollion to Champollion-Figeac, 5 October 1828 (from his camp at Saqqara), *Lettres et journaux*, 117.
37. Wolfgang Schenkel, *Lexicon der Ägyptologie*, 717–18.
38. Gelb, *Study of Writing*, 78.
39. https://www.york.ac.uk/news-and-events/news/2020/research/mummy-nesyamun-sound/. The sound in question is a repeated horrified groan, perhaps understandably.
40. Wilson, *Sacred Signs*, 23.
41. *European Literature and the Latin Middle Ages*, 304.
42. Martial, *Epigrams*, 14.6–7.
43. Herodotus, *Histories*, 5. 58.
44. Barry B. Powell, *Homer and the Origin of the Greek Alphabet* (Cambridge: Cambridge University Press, 1996), 9–10.
45. Yves Gerhard, 'La "coupe de Nestor": reconstitution du vers 1', *Zeitschrift für Papyrologie und Epigraphik*, 176 (2011), 7–9.
46. Friggeri, *Epigraphic Collection of the Museo Nazionale Romano*, 17.
47. *World's Writing Systems*, 265.
48. Powell, *Homer and the Origin of the Greek Alphabet*, 227.
49. A. B. Lord, *The Singer of Tales* (Cambridge, MA: Harvard University Press, 1960), 124.
50. Powell, *Homer and the Origin of the Greek Alphabet*, 211.
51. Gelb, *Study of Writing*, 184.

52. Powell, *Homer and the Origin of the Greek Alphabet*, 233–6.

53. *Aeneid* 2. 82: *Belidae nomen Palamedis*.

54. Apollodorus, *Epitome*, E3. 7; a lost play of Sophocles, *Mad Odysseus*, is based on this myth.

55. Hyginus, *Fabulae*, 105.

56. 'On my own I established remedies for forgetfulness, which are without speech and yet speak, by creating syllables; I invented writing for men's knowledge, so a man absent over the ocean might know what was happening back at home'; Euripides, Fragment 578 (*Palamedes*), from Stobaeus 2. 4. 8; tr. Christopher Collard and Martin Cropp in Euripides, *Dramatic Fragments* (Loeb Classical Library), p 53.

57. Pausanias, *Description of Greece*, 31.1.

58. Hyginus, *Fabulae*, 277.

59. Philostratus, *Heroicus*, 33.11.

60. *Odyssey*, 8.570–3, tr. Fagles.

61. Davies, *Aldus Manutius*, 10.

62. Nigel Wilson, *From Byzantium to Italy: Greek Studies in the Italian Renaissance* , 2nd. edn. (London: Bloomsbury, 2017), 143.

63. Davies, *Aldus Manutius*, 10.

64. Wilson, *From Byzantium to Italy*, 64, 147.

65. Uelli Dill and Petra Schierli, *Das bessere Bild Christi: Das Neue Testament in der Ausgabe des Erasmus von Rotterdam* (Basel: Schwabe Verlag, 2016), 70.

66. K. Staikos, *The Greek Editions of Aldus Manutius and his Greek Collaborators* (New York: Oak Knoll Press, 2016), 59–64.

67. Gelb, *Study of Writing*, 246.

68. Zuboff, *Age of Surveillance Capitalism*, 187.

69. Erasmus, *Adagia*, III. iii. 1; tr. Barker, 243.

70. Plato, *Symposium*, 215b2.

71. Erasmus, *Adagia*, II. i. 1; tr. Barker, 137.

72. Maurizio Campanelli, 'Marsilio Ficino's Portrait of Hermes Trismegistus and its Afterlife', *Intellectual History Review*, 29 (2019), 53–71.

73. Q 19: 56–7; see Yorem Erder, 'Idrīs', *Encyclopaedia of the Qur'an*, Brill Online (accessed 4 December 2020).

74. Charles Burnett, 'The Legend of the Three Hermes and Abū Ma'shar's *Kitāb al-Ulf* in the Latin Middle Ages', *Journal of the Warburg and Courtauld Institutes*, 39 (1976), 231.

75. Cicero, *De natura deorum*, 3. 56.

76. Lactantius, *Divinae Institutiones*, 1. 6. 3.

77. Ficino, *Philebus Commentary*, 273 (bk 1, ch. 29); see Campanelli, 'Marsilio Ficino's portrait of Hermes Trismegistus', 55.

78. *La rivelazione segreta di Ermete Trismegisto*, ed. Paolo Scarpi, Fondazione Lorenzo Valla/Scrittori Greci e Latini, 2 vols. (Milan: Arnoldo Mondadori, 2011), ii. 12–13.

Chapter 12

1. Jinwung Kim, *A History of Korea: From 'Land of the Morning Calm' to States in Conflict* (Bloomington: Indiana University Press, 2012), 189.

2. Young-Key Kim-Renaud, *The Korean Alphabet: Its History and Structure* (Honolulu: University of Hawaii Press, 1997), 15–16.
3. The work was long lost and only rediscovered in 1940; the single copy is in the Gansong Art Museum, National Treasure, No. 70.
4. Ross King, 'Korean Writing', *World's Writing Systems*, 220 (where diagrams are given).
5. Ro Myounggu and Park Suhee, *The King at the Palace: Joseon Royal Court Culture* (Seoul: Designintro, 2016), 23.
6. Kim, *A History of Korea*, 189.
7. Kang Jae-eun, *The Land of Scholars: Two Thousand Years of Korean Confucianism* (Paramus: Homa & Sekey Books, 2006), 219–22.
8. Kim, *A History of Korea*, 194–5.
9. *National Palace Museum of Korea* (Seoul: National Museum, 2007), 13.
10. Ro and Park, *Joseon Royal Court Culture*, 70.
11. Beth McKillop, 'The History of the Book in Korea', in Suarez and Woudhuysen (eds.), *Oxford Companion to the Book*, i. 368.
12. Edward Shultz, *Generals and Scholars: Military Rule in Medieval Korea* (Honolulu: University of Hawaii Press, 2000), 78.
13. Kim, *A History of Korea*, 199.
14. McKillop, 'History of the Book in Korea', i. 371.
15. *National Palace Museum of Korea*, 22–3.
16. Kim, *A History of Korea*, 273.
17. Finkel and Taylor, *Cuneiform*, 37–8.
18. Wilson, *Sacred Signs*, 19.
19. Sohn Pow-Key, *Early Korean Typography*, Korean Library Science Research Institute (Seoul: Po Chin Chai, 1982), provides facsimiles from the *Jikji* alongside other examples of Korean printing.
20. McKillop, 'The Book', in Igunma and San May (eds.), *Buddhism*, 145.
21. Victor Mair, 'Modern Chinese Writing', *World's Writing Systems*, 200.
22. Craig Clunas, *Art in China* (Oxford: Oxford University Press, 1997), 109.
23. J. S. Edgren, 'The History of the Book in China', *Oxford Companion to the Book*, i. 355.
24. British Library MS Oriental 8210; see Igunma and San May (eds.), *Buddhism*, 22–3.
25. Sohn Pow-Key, 'Early Korean Printing', *Journal of the American Oriental Society*, 79: 2 (April–June, 1959), 96–103 at 99.
26. McKillop, 'History of the Book in Korea', i. 370.
27. Michael Sullivan, *The Arts of China* (London: Thames & Hudson, 1973), 81.
28. Igunma and San May (eds.), *Buddhism*, 21–2.
29. Edgren, 'History of the Book in China', i. 355–7.
30. Kornicki, *The Book in Japan*, 43.
31. Kornicki, *The Book in Japan*, 44.
32. Kōjirō Ikegami, *Japanese Bookbinding: Instructions from a Master Craftsman* (Tokyo: Weatherhill Books, 1986), 4.
33. Kornicki, *The Book in Japan*, 178.
34. Gelb, *Study of Writing*, 85.
35. William G. Boltz, in Feng Li and David Prager Branner (eds.), *Writing and Literacy in Early China* (Seattle: University of Washington Press, 2011), 65.

36. *World's Writing Systems*, 191.

37. 'Imagisme', from *Poetry* (March, 1913): attributed to F. S. Flint on first publication but written by Pound; quoted from 'A Retrospect', in *Literary Essays of Ezra Pound*, ed. T. S. Eliot (London: Faber & Faber, 1960), 3.

38. From *Lustra*, in *Collected Shorter Poems*, 2nd edn. (London: Faber & Faber, 1968), 118.

39. Phrase from 'The Teacher's Mission', in *Literary Essays of Ezra Pound*, ed. T. S. Eliot, 61.

40. *Writing and Literacy in Early China*, 72.

41. 'Chinese Ideographs and Western Ideas', *The Journal of Asian Studies*, 52.2 (May, 1993), 373–99.

42. Michael Loewe, 'The First Emperor and the Qin Empire', in Jane Portal (ed.), *The First Emperor: China's Terracotta Army* (London: British Museum, 2007), 75–6.

43. Clunas, *Art in China*, 166–7.

44. Raymond Dawson, introduction to *The First Emperor*, Oxford World's Classics, xxiii.

45. *World's Writing Systems*, 196.

46. Loewe, 'The First Emperor', 67–8.

47. Lewis, *Writing and Authority in Early China*, 10.

48. *Writing and Authority in Early China*, 317.

49. Jessica Rawson, 'The First Emperor's Tomb', in Portal (ed.), *The First Emperor*, 115.

50. Rawson, 'The First Emperor's Tomb', 120.

51. Rawson, 'The First Emperor's Tomb', 145.

52. *Shiji* (Beijing: Zhonghua shuju, 1985), 6. 280.

53. Nylan, 'The Art of Persuasion from 100 BCE to 100 CE', in *China's Early Empires: A Re-Appraisal* (Cambridge: Cambridge University Press, 2010), 503.

54. Clunas, *Art in China*, 135–7.

55. Loewe, Michael, 'The Former Han Dynasty', in Denis Twitchett and Michael Loewe (eds.), *The Cambridge History of China: Volume I: The Ch'in and Han Empires, 221 B.C.–A.D 220* (Cambridge: Cambridge University Press, 1986), 189.

56. Nylan, 'The Art of Persuasion', 498–501.

57. *Writing and Authority in Early China*, 208.

58. Robert E. Harrist, *The Landscape of Words: Stone Inscriptions from Early and Medieval China* (Seattle: University of Washington Press, 2008), 219–20.

59. Harrist, *The Landscape of Words*, 211.

60. Harrist, *The Landscape of Words*, 287–8.

61. Richard Curt Kraus, *Brushes with Power: Modern Politics and the Chinese Art of Calligraphy* (Berkeley: University of California Press, 1991).

62. Alexander C. Cook (ed.), *Mao's Little Red Book: A Global History*, (Cambridge: Cambridge University Press, 2014). David Leese provides detailed statistics on 36; the term 'Mao Bible' is discussed by Quinn Slobodian, 216.

63. Oliver Lei Han, *Sources and Early Printing History of Chairman Mao's 'Quotations'*, Bibliographical Society of America, Bibsite (2004), 2–4 (https://bibsocamer.org/BibSite/Han/index.html).

64. Han, *Sources and Early Printing History*, 4–5.

65. Daniel Leese, *Mao Cult: Rhetoric and Ritual in China's Cultural Revolution*, (Cambridge: Cambridge University Press 2013), 108.

66. Lanjun Xu, 'Translations and Internationalism', in Cook (ed.), *Mao's Little Red Book* 86–7.

67. Zhengyuan Fu, *Autocratic Tradition and Chinese Politics* (Cambridge: Cambridge University Press 1994), 186.

68. http://news.bbc.co.uk/1/hi/world/asia-pacific/7163445.stm.

69. Confucius, *Analects*, 1. 12; tr. Chin, 9.

70. Andrea Bachner, *Beyond Sinology: Chinese Writing and the Scripts of Culture* (New York: Columbia University Press, 2014), 1–2.

71. *Lectures on the Philosophy of History*, I. i. 141.

72. Victor H. Mair, 'Script Reform in China', *The World and I* (October, 1989), 635–43; see also John DeFrancis, *Nationalism and Language Reform in China* (Princeton: Princeton University Press, 1950).

73. *World's Writing Systems*, 204.

74. *World's Writing Systems*, 204–5.

75. *Characters and Computers*, ed. Victor H. Mair and Yongquan Liu (Amsterdam: IOS Press, 1991).

76. Bachner, *Beyond Sinology*, 39.

Chapter 13

1. René Magritte, 'Les mots et les images', *La Révolution surréaliste*, 12 (15 December 1929), 32–3.

2. Drawing in Brussels, Musée Magritte; Michel Draguet, *Magritte: son œuvre, son musée* (Paris: Hazan, 2009), 70.

3. Bruxelles, Musées royaux des Beaux-Arts de Belgique, Inv. 11675.

4. W. J. T. Mitchell, *Picture Theory: Essays on Verbal and Visual Representation* (Chicago: University of Chicago Press, 1995), 15.

5. Carr, *Shallows*, 30.

6. Leonard Shlain, *The Alphabet Versus the Goddess: The Conflict Between Word and Image* (New York: Viking, 1998).

7. *Viṣṇudharmottara Purāṇa*, Part III, ch. 108.

8. Julius J. Lipner, 'Ancient Banyan: An Inquiry into the Meaning of "Hinduness"', *Religious Studies*, 32. 1 (1996), 109–26 at 117–18.

9. Timothy Lubin, 'Vratá Divine and Human in the Early Veda', *Journal of the American Oriental Society*, 121. 4 (2001), 565–79 at 566.

10. Quoted in Lipner, 'Ancient Banyan', 117.

11. Melville, *Moby-Dick*, 363.

12. British Library MS Or. 8210/P.2; *Diamond Sūtra* (London: British Library, 2004).

13. McKillop, 'The Book', in Igunma and San May (eds.), *Buddhism*, 139.

14. *Understanding Media: The Extensions of Man* (New York: Mentor Books, 1964), 3.

15. 'A poem is like a picture'; Horace, *Ars poetica*, 361.

16. *Laocoon: An Essay on the Limits of Painting and Poetry* (London: Longman, Brown, etc., 1853), 101.

17. *Pädogogische Schriften*, ed. C. Patz (Langensalza, 1876), 580.

18. Schleiermacher, 'The Hermeneutics: Outline of the 1819 Lectures', *New Literary History*, 10/1 (Autumn, 1978), 2–3.

19. 'The Reformation Critique of the Image', in Bob Scribner (ed.), *Bilder und Bildersturm im Spätmittelalter und in der frühen Neuzeit*, Wolfenbütteler Forschungen, 46 (Wiesbaden: Harrassowitz, 1990), 50–67 at 53.

20. Exodus 20: 4.

21. *War Against the Idols: The Reformation of Worship from Erasmus to Calvin* (Cambridge: Cambridge University Press, 1986), 151.

22. 'The word of God is spiritual, and it alone is useful to believers'; Karlstadt, *Von abtuhung der Bylder* (Wittenberg: Nyckell Schyrlentz, 1522), fo. 5ʳ.

23. 'Newe ordnung der Stat Wittenberg', *Evangelische Kirchenordnung* [EKO], Art. 160, i. 697.

24. MacCulloch, *Reformation*, 558–63.

25. Margaret Aston, *Broken Idols of the English Reformation* (Cambridge: Cambridge University Press, 2016), 19.

26. Natalie Zemon Davis, *Society and Culture in Early Modern France* (Stanford, CA: Stanford University Press, 1975), 166.

27. Aston, *Broken Idols*, 21.

28. Crouzet, *Les guerriers de Dieu*, ii. 510.

29. Davis, *Society and Culture in Early Modern France*, 173.

30. Koerner, *The Reformation of the Image* (Chicago: University of Chicago Press; London: Reaktion Books, 2004).

31. Cameron, 'The Luther Bible', 218.

32. Alister E. McGrath, *Luther's Theology of the Cross* (Oxford: Blackwell, 1991), 2.

33. Koerner, *Reformation of the Image*, 10.

34. First expressed in Luther, *Heidelberg Disputation* (*Luther's Works*, 31. 40–1); the most extended expression is in *The Bondage of the Will* (1525), WA 18. 684–6.

35. Gregory, *Registrum Epistolarum*, ed. P. Ewald and L.M. Hartmann, 2 vols., Monumenta Germaniae Historica (Berlin: Hahn, 1887–95), ii. 270.

36. Margaret Aston, *Lollards and Reformers: Images and Literacy in Late Medieval Religion* (London: Hambledon Press, 1984), 119.

37. *On Religion*, ed. Richard Crouter (Cambridge: Cambridge University Press, 1988), 60.

38. Greenberg, *Collected Essays and Criticism*, ed. J. O'Brian, 4 vols. (Chicago: University of Chicago Press, 1993), iv. 62.

39. 'On the Question of Form', *The Blue Rider Almanac*, tr. H. Falkenstein (New York: Viking, 1974), 165.

40. Morley, *Writing on the Wall: Word and Image in Modern Art* (London: Thames & Hudson, 2003), 16.

41. *Au Bon Marché* (1913), collage: oil and pasted paper on cardboard, Aachen: Suermondt Ludwig Museum.

42. Morley, *Writing on the Wall*, 40–1.

43. Vallier and Braque, 'Braque, la peinture et nous', *Cahiers d'Art*, 29, no. 1 (Paris, October 1954), 13–24.

44. Braque, *Fruit, Dish and Glass* (1912), Charcoal and cut-and-pasted printed wallpaper with gouache on white laid paper; subsequently mounted on paperboard, Metropolitan Museum of Art, 2016.237.33.

45. Magritte, *La trahison des images* (1929), Oil on canvas, Los Angeles County Museum of Art, 78.7.

46. Pliny the Elder, *Natural History* 35. 66.

47. Erasmus, *Parabolae*, CWE 23. 276.

48. Juan Gris, *Cartes à jouer avec siphon* (1916), Oil on panel, Kröller-Müller Museum, Otterlo (Veluwe, Netherlands), KM 102.219.

49. Dullaert, *Wandstilleven* (1653–84?), Oil on panel, KM 102.698.

50. Mitchell, 'The Politics of Genre: Space and Time in Lessing's *Laocoon*', *Representations*, 6 (Spring 1984), 98–115.

51. Mitchell, *Iconology: Image, Text, Ideology* (Chicago: University of Chicago Press, 1986), 43.

52. Saussure, *Course in General Linguistics*, tr. Roy Harris (London: Duckworth, 1983), 112–13.

53. James Simpson, *Under the Hammer: Iconoclasm in the Anglo-American Tradition*, Claredon Lectures (Oxford: Oxford University Press, 2010), 1–5.

54. Brown, *Rise of Christendom*, 392–3.

55. Cyril Mango, 'Byzantium: A Historical Introduction', *Byzantium 330–1453*, ed. Robin Cormack and Maria Vassilaki (London: Royal Academy of Arts, 2008), 28–9.

56. Brown, *Rise of Christendom*, 388–9.

57. Brown, *Rise of Christendom*, 405–6.

58. Bernhard Bischoff, *Manuscripts and Libraries in the Age of Charlemagne*, tr. Michael Gorman (Cambridge: Cambridge University Press, 1994), 16–17.

59. Marcia L. Colish, *Medieval Foundations of the Western Intellectual Tradition, 400–1400* (New Haven and London: Yale University Press, 1999), 67.

60. Edward M. Thompson, *An Introduction to Greek and Latin Palaeography* (Oxford: Clarendon Press, 1911), 191–4.

61. Brown, *Rise of Christendom*, 387.

62. Thomas F. Matthews, *The Early Churches of Constantinople: Architecture and Liturgy* (Philadelphia: Pennsylvania State University Press, 1971), 149.

63. Moscow, Historical Museum, MS. D. 129.

64. Henry Maguire, 'From Constantine to Iconoclasm', in *Byzantium 330–1453*, 69–70.

65. Oleg Tarasov, *Icon and Devotion: Sacred Spaces in Imperial Russia*, tr. Robin Milner-Gulland (London: Reaktion Books, 2004), 119.

66. Matthews, *Early Churches of Constantinople*, 168.

67. Tarasov, *Icon and Devotion*, 120.

68. Vladimir Ivanov, *Russian Icons* (New York: Rizzoli, 1988), 160.

69. Oleg Tarasov, *Framing Russian Art: From Early Icons to Malevich* (London: Reaktion Books, 2012), 349.

70. Robin Cormack and Maria Vassilaki, 'The Art of Byzantium 330–1453', in *Byzantium 330–1453*, 41.

71. Tarasov, *Icon and Devotion*, 123.

72. Aston, *England's Iconoclasts: Laws Against Images* (Oxford: Clarendon Press, 1988), 61.

73. Cambridge, Corpus Christi College, MS 128, 14.

74. Aston, *Broken Idols*, 21.

75. *Martin Bucer and the Book of Common Prayer*, ed. E. C. Whitaker (Great Wakering: Alcuin Club, 1974), 54–5.

76. Aquinas, *Summa theologiae*, 2a2ae. 84. 1; see Augustine, *De civitate Dei*, 6 (Preface).

77. Aston, *Lollards and Reformers*, 141.

78. *From Iconoclasm to Iconophobia: The Cultural Impact of the Second English Reformation,* Stenton Lecture (Reading: Reading University Press, 1986).

79. Tara Hamling, *Decorating the Godly Household: Religious Art in Post-Reformation Britain* (New Haven and London: Yale University Press, 2011).

80. 'Fleetwood Cabinet', National Museum of Ireland, Collins Barracks.

81. Melville, *Moby-Dick*, 260 ('Of the Monstrous Pictures of Whales').

82. Koerner, *Reformation of the Image*, 11.

83. J. David Bolter, *Writing Space: A Hypertext* (Hillsdale: Laurence Erlbaum, 1991), 11.

84. Harris, *Rethinking Writing*, 238.

85. Morley, *Writing on the Wall*, 112–13.

86. Friggeri, *Epigraphic Collection of the Museo Nazionale Romano*, 66.

87. Alison E. Cooley, *The Cambridge Manual of Latin Epigraphy* (Cambridge: Cambridge University Press, 2012), 424.

88. Lyon, Musée gallo-romain.

Chapter 14

1. Rushdie, *Is Nothing Sacred?*, 2.

2. Melville, *Moby-Dick*, 259.

3. Thoreau, *Walden and Other Writings* (New York: Modern Library, 2000), 93.

4. Dickinson, *Complete Poems*, 176–7.

5. Pliny the Elder, *Natural History*, 7.29.

6. Luke 2: 28.

7. Thomas à Kempis, *Doctrinale juvenum*, 5; *Opera* (Paris: Badius Ascensius, 1523), f. xlvii.

8. More, *Correspondence*, 558.

9. Price, *How to Do Things with Books in Victorian Britain* (Princeton: Princeton University Press, 2012), 39–40.

10. *British Medical Journal*, 4 February 1893, i.267.

11. *British Medical Journal*, 1901, i.726.

12. Mary Douglas, *Natural Symbols*, 2nd edn. (London: Routledge, 1996), 2.

13. James Gillray, *Evidence to Character; – Being a Portrait of a Traitor, by his Friends & by Himself* (1798), British Museum, 1981,U.320.

14. Eliot, *The Mill on the Floss*, ed. A. S. Byatt (London: Penguin Books, 2003), 285.

15. *A Christian Directory, or, A Summ of Practical Theologie and Cases of Conscience Directing Christians How to Use their Knowledge and Faith* (London: Robert White, 1673), 416.

16. Peter Brown, *The Cult of the Saints: Its Rise and Function in Latin Christianity* (London: SCM Press, 1981), 88.

17. Paulinus, Poem 27; for his ownership of the relic, see Cynthia Jean Hahn, *Strange Beauty: Issues in the Making and Meaning of Reliquaries, 400-1204* (University Park, PA: Pennsylvania State University Press, 2012), 22.

18. Martina Bagnoli, 'The Stuff of Heaven: Materials and Craftsmanship in Medieval Reliquaries', *Treasures of Heaven: Saints, Relics and Devotion in Medieval Europe*, ed. M. Bagnoli, H. Klein, C. Mann, and J. Robinson (London: British Museum, 2010), 137–48.

19. Brown, *Society and the Holy in Late Antiquity* (London: Faber and Faber, 1982), 224.

20. Gregory the Great, *Epistolae*, 2.30.

21. Hahn, *Strange Beauty*, 158.

22. Duffy, *Stripping of the Altars: Traditional Religion in England, 1400-1580*, 2nd edn. (New Haven and London: Yale University Press, 2005), 154.

23. Winnicott's ground-breaking paper, 'Transitional Objects and Transitional Phenomena' was published in the *International Journal of Psycho-Analysis*, 34 (1953); and is reprinted in *Playing and Reality* (London: Routledge Classics, 2005), 1–34.

24. Belting, *Bild und Kult: eine Geschichte des Bildes vor dem Zeitalter der Kunst* (Munich: C.H. Beck, 1990).

25. Hahn, *Strange Beauty*, 127.

26. Winnicott, *Playing and Reality*, 8.

27. Duffy, *Stripping of the Altars*, 112.

28. Douglas, *Natural Symbols*, 8.

29. *Praise of Folly* tr. Hudson, 56.

30. Erasmus, *Colloquies*, tr. Craig Thompson, *Collected Works of Erasmus*, 40: 631.

31. 'A Pilgrimage for Religion's Sake', *Collected Works of Erasmus*, 40: 635.

32. *Collected Works of Erasmus*, 61: 24.

33. G. R. Potter, *Zwingli* (Cambridge: Cambridge University Press, 1984), 141.

34. *Collected Works of Erasmus*, 39: 194.

35. Euan Cameron, *Enchanted Europe: Superstition, Reason and Religion, 1250-1750* (Oxford: Oxford University Press, 2010), 68.

36. Augustine, *Confessions*, 8.12.29; see Cummings, *Grammar and Grace*, 61.

37. *Institutiones*, I.xxx.1; on Cassiodorus and books, see Brown, *Rise of Western Christendom*, 196–7.

38. Gamble, *Books and Readers in the Early Church*, 36.

39. Rosamond McKitterick, *The Carolingians and the Written Word* (Cambridge: Cambridge University Press, 1989), 150.

40. Peter Godman, *Poetry of the Carolingian Renaissance* (London: Duckworth, 1985), No. 11, 139.

41. *Anglo-Saxon Kingdoms: Art, Word, War*, ed. Claire Breay and Joanna Story (London: British Library, 2018), 110.

42. Dorothy Shepard, 'The Latin Gospel-Book, c.600-1200', *New Cambridge History of the Bible, Vol. 2*, 353.

43. De Hamel, *History of Illuminated Manuscripts*, 32 and 40.

44. Shepard, 'The Latin Gospel-Book', 346.

45. Michelle P. Brown, *The Lindisfarne Gospels: Society, Spirituality & the Scribe* (London: The British Library, 2003), 200.

46. Brown, *The Lindisfarne Gospels*, 95.

47. Janet Backhouse, *The Lindisfarne Gospels* (Ithaca, NY: Cornell University Press, 1981), 28.

48. Brown, *The Lindisfarne Gospels*, 281.

49. Brown, *The Lindisfarne Gospels*, 205.

50. *Anglo-Saxon Kingdoms*, 120.

51. Backhouse, *The Lindisfarne Gospels*, 31.

52. Brown, *The Lindisfarne Gospels*, 288.

53. Carol Farr, *The Book of Kells: its Function and Audience* (London: British Library, 1997), 25–6.

54. Shepard, 'The Latin Gospel-Book', 351–2.

55. Robert G. Calkins, *Illuminated Books of the Middle Ages* (Ithaca, NY: Cornell University Press, 1983), 82–5.

56. Brown, *Society and the Holy*, 218.

57. Farr, *The Book of Kells*, 44.

58. Shepard, 'The Latin Gospel-Book', 351.

59. Brown, *The Lindisfarne Gospels*, 359–61.

60. Christopher de Hamel, *The Book: A History of the Bible* (London: Phaidon Press, 2001), 34.

61. *Treasures of Heaven*, ed. Bagnoli et al., 128–9.

62. Clanchy, *From Memory to Written Record*, 3rd edn. (Oxford: Blackwell, 2012), 323–7.

63. Brown, *The Lindisfarne Gospels*, 209.

64. Shepard, 'The Latin Gospel-Book', 340.

65. *Thesaurus sacrorum rituum auctore Bartholomaeo Gavanto* (Rome: Merati, 1738), 200.

66. *Missale Nidrosiense* (Copenhagen: Paul Reff, 1519), authorized by Archbishop Erik Vankendorf.

67. Duffy, *Stripping of the Altars*, 126.

68. Sappho, *Fragment* 58a (from the 3rd century BCE Papyrus Oxyrhynchus 1787, found in Cologne University archives in 1922).

69. Catullus, *Carmina*, 5. 7; he is greedy: he asks for 2,300 more in the next few lines.

70. Catullus, *Carmina*, 7. 1–3.

71. Paul Murgatroyd, *The Amatory Elegies of Johannes Secundus* (Leiden: Brill, 2000), 5.

72. Montaigne, 'Of Books', *Complete Essays*, 361.

73. *Greek Anthology*, 5.78.

74. Donne, 'To Sir Henry Wotton', lines 1–2; *Satires, Epigrams, and Verse Letters*, ed. Walter Milgate (Oxford: Clarendon Press, 1967), 71.

75. Baldassare Castiglione, *Il cortegiano* (1528); *The Book of the Courtier*, tr. Sir Thomas Hoby (London: Everyman Books, 1903), 315.

76. Thomas à Kempis, *The Imitation of Christ* (London: Macmillan, 1874), 281.

77. Freud, *Three Essays on Sexual Theory*, in *The Psychology of Love*, The New Penguin Freud (London: Penguin Books, 2006), 129.

78. Freud, *Three Essays on Sexual Theory*, 160.

79. Freud, 'Analysis Terminable and Interminable', *Wild Analysis*, tr. Alan Bance, The New Penguin Freud (London: Penguin Books, 2002), 189.

80. Karen Harvey, *The Kiss in History* (Manchester: Manchester University Press, 2005), 21.

81. Duffy, *Stripping of the Altars*, 127.

82. Duffy, *Stripping of the Altars*, 136 and 143–4.

83. Erasmus, *A Playne and Godly Exposytion or Declaration of the Commune* (London: Robert Redman, 1534), sig. T8r.

84. Phillips, *On Kissing, Tickling and Being Bored* (London: Faber and Faber, 1994), 107.

85. Aston, *Lollards and Reformers*, 109.

86. John Fitzherbert, *Here Begynneth a Ryght Frutefull Mater: and Hath to Name the Boke of Surueyeng and Improumentes* (London: Rycharde Pynson, 1523), sig. C1ᵛ.

87. *Institutions in the lawes of Englande* (London: J. Byddell, 1538), sig. E2v-E3r.

88. Aston, *Lollards and Reformers*, 112.

89. Hudson, *Lollards and their Books*, 236.

90. 'The Testimony of William Thorpe', *Two Wycliffite Texts*, ed. Anne Hudson (Oxford: Early English Text Society, 1993), 30.

91. *The Examinacion of Master William Thorpe Preste Accused of Heresye before Thomas Arundell* (Antwerp: Merten de Keyser, 1530).

92. J. M. Gray, 'Conscience and the Word of God: Religious Arguments against the Ex Officio Oath', *Journal of Ecclesiastical History*, 64.3 (2013), 494–512.

93. Aston, *Lollards and Reformers*, 110.

94. 'The Testimony of William Thorpe', 60.

95. 'The Testimony of William Thorpe', 74.

96. Jerome, Epistle *Ad Paulinam*, PL 22.543.

97. John Frith, *A Boke Made by Iohn Frith Prisoner in the Tower of London* (Antwerp: H. Peetersen, 1533), sig. K8r.

98. Edward Bonner, *A Profitable and Necessarye Doctrine with Certayne Homelyes Adioyned Therunto* (London: John Cawoode, 1555), sig. 2I3r.

99. Brian Cummings, *The Book of Common Prayer: A Very Short Introduction* (Oxford: Oxford University Press, 2018), 47–51.

100. *The Book of Common Prayer: The Texts of 1549, 1559, and 1662*, ed. Brian Cummings (Oxford: Oxford World's Classics, 2013), 706 and 736.

101. Bucer, *Censura* on the 1549 book; *Martin Bucer and the Book of Common Prayer*, ed. E. C. Whitaker (Great Wakering: Alcuin Club, 1974), 138–9.

102. Thomas Becon, *The Displaying of the Popish Masse*, repr. edn. (London: Stationers' Company, 1637), 55.

103. *Book of Common Prayer*, ed. Cummings, 776.

104. *Directory for the Publique Worship of God, Throughout the Three Kingdoms of England, Scotland, and Ireland* (London: Ralph Smith and John Field, 1644), 62–3.

105. 'Of Ceremonies', *Book of Common Prayer*, ed. Cummings, 215.

106. *Christian Directory*, 418.

107. London, Lambeth Palace Library, MS 2550, fo.180.

108. Calvin, *Institutes*, 4, 15, 1.

109. James Simpson, *Permanent Revolution: The Reformation and the Illiberal Roots of Liberalism* (Cambridge, MA: Harvard University Press, 2019), 299–301.

110. Sir Thomas Aston, *A Remonstrance, against Presbytery. Exhibited by Divers of the Nobilitie, Gentrie, Ministers and Inhabitants of the County Palatine of Chester* (London: John Aston, 1641), sig. I4ᵛ.

111. 'When Adam delved and Eve span | Who was then the gentleman'; cited famously in Christopher Hill, 'The Norman Yoke', *Puritanism and Revolution* (London: Secker & Warburg, 1958), 50 and 121–2.

112. More, *Dialogue Concerning Heresies*, in *Complete Works of Thomas More*, vi, 46.

113. *Answer to More*, ed. Anne O'Donnell, 60.

114. Aston, *England's Iconoclasts*, 181.

115. 'Skeletons in the Cupboard: Relics after the English Reformation', in *Relics and Remains*, ed. Alexandra Walsham, *Past and Present, Supplement* (Oxford: Oxford University Press, 2010), 138.

116. David Cressy, 'Books as Totems in Seventeenth-century England and New England', *Journal of Library History*, 21 (1986), 92–106.

117. Cressy, 'Books as Totems', 99.

118. Adam of Eynsham, *Magna vita sancti Hugonis*, i.169–70; see Hahn, *Strange Beauty*, 233–4.

119. Ezekiel, 3: 1–4.

120. Augustine, *Confessions*, 6.3.3.

121. Mary Carruthers, *The Book of Memory: A Study of Memory in Medieval Culture* (Cambridge: Cambridge University Press, 1990), 165.

122. Revelation 10: 10.

123. Erasmus, *CWE* 61.6.

124. Nürnberg, Germanisches Nationalmuseum, Codex Aureus of Echternach.

125. Dalrymple, *From the Holy Mountain*, 189–90.

126. Matthew Champion, *Medieval Graffiti: The Lost Voices of England's Churches* (New York: Random House, 2015).

127. Mishnah, Avot 3: 3.

128. Thomas à Kempis, *The Imitation of Christ*, i. 4.

129. De Hamel, *History of Illuminated Manuscripts*, 231; see also his Pl. 208.

130. 'the moment before orgasm, the same in that way as the one after death'; Proust, *Le Côté de Guermantes*, II. ii (1921); *À la recherche du temps perdu*, ed. Tadié, ii. 662.

Chapter 15

1. *Missale ad vsum celeberrime ecclesie Eboracensis* (Rouen: P. Olivier, 1516), York Minster Library, shelf mark: Stainton 12 (Stainton Collection).

2. *Missale*, York Minster Library, Stainton 12, sig. A5ᵛ.

3. York Minster Library, Stainton 12, sig. N3ʳ.

4. *Tudor Royal Proclamations*, ed. Paul L. Hughes and James F. Larkin, 3 vols. (New Haven: Yale University Press, 1965–9), i. 231 (No.158).

5. Westminster, 16 November [1538]; *Tudor Royal Proclamations*, i. 276 (No.186).

6. Aston, *Broken Idols*, 367–78.
7. Injunctions in *Visitation Articles and Injunctions*, II. 34–43; see Elton, *Policy and Police*, 255–6 and Duffy, *The Stripping of the Altars*, 406–12.
8. Bible Society Collection, Cambridge University Library, shelf mark: BSS.201.B37.6.
9. *Tudor Royal Proclamations*, No.191, i. 284–6.
10. London, British Library, MS Cotton Cleopatra E. V, fo. 311.
11. William Camden, *Annales rerum Anglicarum et Hibernicarum*, 3 vols. (Oxford: Thomas Hearne, 1717), i, p. xxx.
12. Duffy, *The Stripping of the Altars*, 418–19.
13. Book of Hours, Sarum Use (Netherlands, *c*1500), London, British Library, MS Kings 9, fos. 38ᵛ–39ʳ. See James Carley, *The Books of Henry VIII and his Wives* (London: British Library, 2004), 105.
14. Aston, *Broken Idols*, Part III, ch. 9, 'Word Against Image'.
15. William Fulke, *Stapleton and Martiall (Two Popish Heretikes) Confuted, and of their Particular Heresies Detected* (London: Henry Middleton, 1580), sig. N5ᵛ.
16. Duffy, *The Stripping of the Altars*, 349.
17. Ethan H. Shagan, *Popular Politics and the English Reformation* (Cambridge: Cambridge University Press, 2003), 218.
18. Calvin, *Traité des reliques*, in *Three French Treatises*, ed. Higman, 94–5.
19. Alexandra Walsham, 'The Art of Iconoclasm', in Antonina Bevan Zlatar and Olga Timofeeva (eds.), *What is an Image in Medieval and Early Modern England* (Tübingen: Narr Francke, 2017), 83–4.
20. Shagan, *Popular Politics and the English Reformation*, 165, 171.
21. Charles Wriothesley, *A Chronicle of England during the Reigns of the Tudors*, ed. W. D. Hamilton, 2 vols. (New York: Camden Society, 1965), i. 90.
22. Richard W. Pfaff, *The Liturgy in Medieval England: A History* (Cambridge: Cambridge University Press, 2009), 458.
23. London, British Library MS Stowe 10, fos. 113ᵛ–114ʳ.
24. New York, Pierpont Morgan Library MS M.331 fo. 186ᵛ.
25. London, British Library MS Harley 2985, fo. 37ᵛ.
26. London, British Library Egerton 1821, fos. 1ᵛ–2ʳ. See Lowden's comments in the online Catalogue of Illuminated Manuscripts.
27. *Thys [prymer in En]glyshe and in La[ten]* (London: R. Redman, 1537?), Lambeth Palace Library: shelf mark 1537.4 (STC 15997).
28. *Thys prymer in Englyshe and in Laten: Is Newly Translated after the Laten Texte* (London: R. Redman, 1537?), Canterbury Cathedral Library: shelf mark W/S-10-3 (from the Templeman Library).
29. Arendt, *Eichmann in Jerusalem: A Report on the Banality of Evil* (London: Penguin Books, 2006), 252.
30. *Areopagitica, in Complete Prose Works*, ii. 492.
31. Parker, *Milton*, 268.
32. Sir Sidney Lee, 'Shakespeare And The Inquisition. A Spanish Second Folio. How The Plays Were Expurgated. Politics And Drama', *The Times*, Monday, 10 April 1922, 15.
33. *Mr William Shakespeares Comedies, Histories, & Tragedies* (London: Thomas Cotes, 1632), Folger Library, Washington, DC, shelf mark: STC 22274 Fo.2 no.07, title-page (*A2ʳ).

34. *The Washington Post*, 18 October 2004. www.washingtonpost.com/wp-dyn/articles/ A40960–2004Oct17 3.html, accessed 19 September 2017.

35. Anthony James West, *The Shakespeare First Folio: A New Worldwide Census of First Folios* (Oxford: Oxford University Press, 2001), 9–12.

36. 'Letters to the Editor', *The Times*, Wednesday, 12 April 1922, 13.

37. Henry Foley, *Records of the English Province of the Society of Jesus*, 7 vols. in 8 parts (London: Burns and Oates, 1877–83), vii. 685–6.

38. Edwin Henson, *Registers of the English College at Valladolid*, Catholic Record Society (London, 1930), xxviii.

39. Edwin Henson, *Registers of the English College at Madrid 1611–1767*, Publications of the Catholic Record Society, 29 (London: Catholic Record Society, 1929), ix.

40. For a full account, see Brian Cummings, 'Shakespeare and the Inquisition', *Shakespeare Survey*, 65 (2012), 306–22.

41. 'sous rature' is Derrida's phrase from *De la grammatologie* (Paris: Éditions de Minuit, 1967), 80; tr. *Of Grammatology*, 2nd edn., 60.

42. The missing text is sig. F1^r–G6^v.

43. Edward M. Wilson, 'Shakespeare and Christian Doctrine: Some Qualifications', *Shakespeare Survey*, 23 (1970), 79–89.

44. Fragnito, *Church, Censorship and Culture*, 4.

45. Fragnito, *Church, Censorship and Culture*, 40.

46. Cardinal Valier to the inquisitor of Ferrara, 10 October 1600, cited in Fragnito, 44.

47. Fragnito, *Church, Censorship and Culture*, 46.

48. *The Fundamental Concepts of Metaphysics*, tr. William McNeill and Nicholas Walker (Bloomington, IN: Indiana University Press, 1995), 60–1.

49. Heidegger, *The Question of Being*, tr. William Kluback and Jean T. Wilde (New York: Twayne, 1958), 80–1.

50. Shakespeare, *Measure for Measure*, 3. 1. 96–8; F2, F6^r.

51. *Measure for Measure*, 3. 1. 105; F2, F6^r.

Chapter 16

1. Shakespeare, *The Tempest*, n 5. 1. 50–7.

2. James Kearney, 'The Book and the Fetish: the Materiality of Prospero's Text', *Journal of Medieval and Early Modern Studies*, 32 (2002), 433–68 at 439.

3. Wu Hung, *Making History: Wu Hung on Contemporary Art* (Hong Kong: Timezone 8, 2008), 69.

4. *Shakespearean Negotiations: The Circulation of Social Energy in Renaissance England* (Berkeley and Los Angeles: University of California Press, 1988), 159.

5. Henry M. Stanley, *Through the Dark Continent*, 2 vols. (New York: Harper and Bros, 1878), ii. 385.

6. *Shakespearean Negotiations*, 163.

7. On books as gifts in relation to Shakespeare, see Jason Scott-Warren, *Sir John Harington and the Book as Gift* (Oxford: Oxford University Press, 2001), 33.

8. Marx, *Capital*, Vol. I, I. 1.§1 and I. 1.§3.

9. *1 Henry IV*, 3. 3. 125.

10. *Capital*, Vol. I, I. 1§3.

11. *Capital*, Vol. I, I. 1 §4.

12. *A Companion to Marx's Capital* (London: Verso, 2010), 38.

13. 'From *Capital* to Marx's Philosophy', in Louis Althusser and Étienne Balibar, *Reading Capital*, tr. Ben Brewster (London: Verso, 2009), 17.

14. Lacan, 'Agency of the Letter in the Unconscious', *Écrits*, tr. Sheridan, 174.

15. *Reading Capital*, 16.

16. Jardine, *Worldly Goods: A New History of the Renaissance* (London: Macmillan, 1996), 171.

17. Goldthwaite, *Wealth and the Demand for Art in Italy, 1300–1600* (Baltimore, MD: Johns Hopkins University Press, 1993), 64.

18. McKenzie, *Bibliography and the Sociology of Texts*, The Panizzi Lectures, 1985, repr. edn. (Cambridge: Cambridge University Press, 1999), 95.

19. Clunas, *Art in China*, 220.

20. Wu Hung, *Making History*, 69.

21. Xu Bing in Wu Hung (ed.), *Reinventing Books in Contemporary Chinese Art* (New York: China Institute Gallery, 2006).

22. Wu Hung, *Making History*, 81.

23. Hong Hao, in Wu Hung (ed.), *Reinventing Books*.

24. Wu Hung, *Making History*, 87.

25. Qin Chong, in Wu Hung (ed.), *Reinventing Books*.

26. Marjorie Garber, 'Shakespeare as Fetish', *Shakespeare Quarterly*, 41 (1990), 242–50; on Greenblatt specifically, 244.

27. Qi-Xin He, 'China's Shakespeare', *Shakespeare Quarterly*, 37 (1986), 149–59.

28. Price, *How to do Things with Books in Victorian Britain*, 40.

29. Melville, *Moby-Dick*, 50.

30. Edward Douwers Dekker, *Max Havelaar, of de koffi-veilingen der Nederlandsche Handel-Maatschappy* (Amsterdam: J. de Ruyter, 1860). Dekker's Latin pseudonym *Multatuli* = 'I have suffered much'; the subtitle translates as 'The Coffee Auctions of the Dutch Trading Company'.

31. Toer, *The Fugitive* (Hong Kong: Heinemann International, 1975).

32. Marvin Spevack, *James Orchard Halliwell-Phillipps: The Life and Works of the Shakespearean Scholar and Bookman* (New Castle, DE: Oak Knoll Press, 2001), 141. Spevack argues that the father never owned the *Hamlet*.

33. 'Marx's Coat', in Daniel Miller (eds.), *Consumption: Theory and Issues in the Study of Consumption* (London: Taylor & Francis, 2001), 312. First published in *Border Fetishisms*, ed. P. Spyer (1998).

34. 'The Problem of the Fetish, II', *RES: Anthropology and Aesthetics*, 13 (Spring 1987), 23–45 at 23. The four conditions are summarized in the preliminaries to this article, having first been outlined in 'The Problem of the Fetish, I', 7–9.

35. *Beschrijvinghe ende Historische verhael vant Gout Koninckrijck van Gunea* (Amsterdam: Cornelis Claesz, 1602), 240.

36. 'Problem of the Fetish, I', 7.

37. 'A token of triumph over the threat of castration *and* a safeguard against it'; 'Fetishism' (1927), in *On Sexuality*, Penguin Freud Library, vii. 351–7.

38. Simon Eliot, Andrew Nash and Ian Willison (eds.), *Literary Cultures and the Material Book* (London: British Library, 2007); Gillespie and Lynch (eds.), *The Unfinished Book*.

39. *Mr William Shakespeares Comedies, Histories, & Tragedies* (London: Isaac Jaggard and Edward Blount, 1623), sig. A1ᵛ.

40. *The Tempest*, 3. 2. 87–95.

41. Shakespeare, *Macbeth*, 1. 3. 2–4; Kerrigan, *Archipelagic English: Literature, History, and Politics 1603–1707* (Oxford: Oxford University Press, 2008), 104.

42. *Doctor Faustus* (A Text), 5. 2. 106–15. OWC, ed. Bevington, 182.

43. James Kearney, *Incarnate Text*, 177.

44. 'Marx's Coat', 313.

45. *The Controversy of Renaissance Art* (Chicago: University of Chicago Press, 2011), 120.

46. 'Traces of the Holy: The Contemporary Art Work as *"crypto-relic"*', *TLS*, 4 October 2015.

47. Andy Clark and David J. Chalmers, 'The Extended Mind', *Analysis* 58 (1998), 7–19.

48. Jobs, 'Stanford University Commencement Address', June 2005.

49. H. R. Woudhuysen, 'The Foundations of Shakespeare's Text', *Proceedings of the British Academy*, 125 (2004), 69–100.

50. Anthony J. West, *The Shakespeare First Folio: The History of the Book*, i: *An Account of the First Folio Based on its Sales and Prices, 1623–2000* (Oxford: Oxford University Press, 2001).

51. Charlton Hinman, *The Printing and Proof-Reading of the First Folio* (Oxford: Clarendon Press, 1963); Peter W. M. Blayney, *The First Folio of Shakespeare* (Washington, DC: Folger Shakespeare Library, 1991).

52. The 'Hinman Collator'; S. E. Smith, ' "The Eternal Verities Verified": Charlton Hinman and the Roots of Mechanical Collation', *Studies in Bibliography*, 53 (2000), 129–61.

53. Joshua Simon, *Neomaterialism* (Berlin: Sternberg Press, 2013), 1.

54. Bhabha, 'Of Mimicry and Man', *The Location of Culture* (London: Routledge, 1994), 91.

55. *The Tempest*, 2. 2. 119–37.

Chapter 17

1. Smalley, *Study of the Bible in the Middle Ages*, 1.

2. Commentary on Mark. ch. 6; PL 30. 608.

3. Geoffrey Parker, *The Thirty Years' War* (London: Routledge, 1997), 159.

4. H. Medick and P. Selwyn, 'Historical Event and Contemporary Experience: The Capture and Destruction of Magdeburg in 1631', *History Workshop Journal*, 52 (2001), 23–48.

5. Peter H. Wilson, *Europe's Tragedy: A New History of the Thirty Years War* (London: Penguin Books, 2010), 470.

6. Otto von Guericke, *Die Belagerung, Eroberung und Zerstörung der Stadt Magdeburg am 10./20. Mai 1631*, tr. in T. Helfferich, *The Thirty Years War: A Documentary History* (Indianapolis: Hackett, 2009), 108–9.

7. Medick and Selwyn, 'Historical Event and Contemporary Experience'.

8. Jan Lorenzen, *Die großen Schlachten: Mythen, Menschen, Schicksale* (Frankfurt am Main: Campus Verlag, 2006), 158–60.

9. Jonsson Calmar, *Der Vertraute Gustav Adolphs des Großen* (Nuremberg: Korn, 1838), 217.

10. Heinrich Bornkamm, *Luther in Mid-Career 1521–1530* (London: Dartman, Longman and Todd, 1983), 602.

11. Pettegree, *Brand Luther*, 316.

12. Gregory B. Lyon, 'Baudouin, Flacius, and the Plan for the Magdeburg Centuries', *Journal of the History of Ideas*, 64 (2003), 253–72.

13. Anthony Grafton, 'Church History in Early Modern Europe: Tradition and Innovation', in Katherine van Liere, Simon Ditchfield, and Howard Louthan (eds.), *Sacred History: Uses of the Christian Past in the Renaissance World* (Oxford: Oxford University Press, 2012), 3–26.

14. McKerrow, *Introduction to Bibliography*, 6–7.

15. Brown, *Rise of Christendom*, 199.

16. François Rigolot, 'Curiosity, Contingency, and Cultural Diversity: Montaigne's Readings at the Vatican Library', *Renaissance Quarterly*, 64 (2011), 847–74 at 848.

17. Montaigne, 'Journal de Voyage en Italie', *Œuvres complètes*, 1221.

18. Vatican Library, MS Vat. lat. 3867; see Jan Ziolkowski and Michael Putnam, *The Virgilian Tradition: The First Fifteen Hundred Years* (New Haven and London: Yale University Press, 2008), 434.

19. Montaigne, 'Journal de Voyage en Italie', *Œuvres complètes*, 1223.

20. Montaigne, *Travel Journal*, tr. Donald M. Frame, *Complete Works*, 1158.

21. Rome, Vatican Library, MS Vat. lat. 3777; see Rigolot, 'Montaigne's Readings at the Vatican Library', 857–8.

22. Montaigne, 'Journal de Voyage en Italie', *Œuvres complètes*, 1222.

23. Rome, Vatican Library, MS Vat. lat. 3806; see Rigolot, 'Montaigne's Readings at the Vatican Library', 858.

24. Rome, Vatican Library, MS Vat. lat. 3804; see Rigolot, 'Montaigne's Readings at the Vatican Library', 859.

25. Montaigne, 'Journal de Voyage en Italie', *Œuvres complètes*, 1224.

26. Warren Boutcher, *The School of Montaigne*, 2 vols. (Oxford: Oxford University Press, 2017), i.281.

27. Montaigne, *Complete Works*, 1169–71.

28. Montaigne, *Essais*, 'Au lecteur', *Œuvres complètes*, 9; Barthes, *Roland Barthes by Roland Barthes*, 119.

29. Barthes, *Roland Barthes by Roland Barthes*, 139.

30. Martin, *The History and Power of Writing* (Chicago: University of Chicago Press, 1994), 131.

31. Nelson, *King and Emperor*, 37–41.

32. Lucien Febvre and Henri-Jean Martin, *The Coming of the Book: The Impact of Printing* (London: Verso, 1997), 74–5.

33. Martin, *History and Power of Writing*, 371.

34. Charles Ripley Gillett, *Burned Books: Neglected Chapters in British History and Literature*, 2 vols. (New York: Columbia University Press, 1932), 15.

35. Boccaccio, *Vite di Dante* (Milan: Mondadori, 2002), 54.

36. Anne Hudson, *Premature Reformation*, 84–5.

37. Thomas A. Fudge, *Jan Hus: Religious Reform and Social Revolution in Bohemia* (London: I.B.Tauris, 2017), 102.

38. Anne Hudson, *Lollards and their Books,* 159.

39. Pecock: 'I here openly assent, that my said books . . . be deputed unto the fire, and openly be burnt, unto the example and terror of all other'; David Wilkins, *Concilia magnae Britanniae et Hiberniae*, 4 vols. (London: R. Gosling, 1737), iii. 576.

40. Aquinas, *Summa theologiae*, 2a2ae. 11. 1.

41. Hudson, *Premature Reformation*, 166.

42. Fudge, *Jan Hus*, 204.

43. Foxe, *Actes and Monuments* (1563), 452.

44. Daniel Wakelin, 'Writing the Words', in Gillespie and Wakelin (eds.), *The Production of Books in England 1350–1500*, 34–58.

45. Johns, *The Nature of the Book*, 373–4.

46. McKitterick, *Print, Manuscript and the Search for Order,* 123.

47. Gillespie, 'Books', in Paul Strohm (ed.), *Middle English*, Twenty-First Approaches to Literature (Oxford: Oxford University Press, 2009), 89.

48. Orietta da Rold, 'Materials', *Production of Books in England*, ed. Gillespie and Wakelin, 12–33, this ref. 21.

49. De Hamel, *History of Illuminated Manuscripts*, 9.

50. McKenzie, *Bibliography and the Sociology of Texts*, 19.

51. Kristian Jensen, *Incunabula and their Readers: Printing, Selling and Using Books in the Fifteenth Century* (London: British Library, 2003), 83.

52. Andrew Pettegree, *The Book in the Renaissance* (New Haven and London: Yale University Press, 2010), 22, 25.

53. Martin Davies, *The Gutenberg Bible* (London: British Library, 1997), 28.

54. Antony Griffiths, *Prints and Printmaking: An Introduction to the History and Techniques* (Berkeley and Los Angeles: University of California Press, 1996), 16.

55. Stephen Colclough, 'Distribution', in David McKitterick (ed.), *The Cambridge History of the Book in Britain, 1830–1914* (Cambridge: Cambridge University Press, 2009), 238–80.

56. Davies, *Aldus Manutius*, 4.

57. Brian Cummings, 'What is a Book?', in Alexandra Gillespie and Deidre Lynch (eds.), *The Unfinished Book*, Twenty-First Century Approaches to Literature (Oxford: Oxford University Press, 2020), 31.

58. Cummings, *Grammar and Grace*, 30–8.

59. Pettegree, *Brand Luther*, 308.

60. Erasmus, *Novum instrumentum omne* (Basel: Johannes Froben, 1516).

61. Blair, *Too Much to Know*, 55.

62. Peters, *Inquisition*, 71.

63. Peter McNiven, *Heresy and Politics in the Reign of Henry IV: The Burning of John Badby* (Woodbridge: Boydell Press, 1987), 204.

64. *Great Chronicle of London*, ed. A. H. Thomas and I. D. Thornley (London: Library of the Corporation of the City, 1938), 87.

65. McNiven, *Heresy and Politics*, 215–16.

66. Foxe, *Actes and Monuments* (1563), 224.

67. William Monter, *Frontiers of Heresy: The Spanish Inquisition from the Basque Lands to Sicily* (Cambridge: Cambridge University Press, 2003), 22.

68. Grendler, *Roman Inquisition*, 71.

69. Grendler, *Roman Inquisition*, 67.

70. Antwerp, Stadsarchief, PK 93 ('*Het Registerboeck der stadt van Antwerpen inhoudende criminele geextendeerde vonnissen*'); see also PK 914, fo. 129^r.

71. Blayney, *The Stationers' Company*, i. 246–7.

72. John Bossy, *The English Catholic Community, 1570–1850* (London: Darton, Longman and Todd, 1975), 89, 102.

73. Allison and Rogers, 135.1; A. F. Allison and D. M. Rogers, *The Contemporary Printed Literature of the English Counter-Reformation Between 1558 and 1640: An Annotated Catalogue*, 2 vols. (Aldershot: Scolar Press, 1989), 24.

74. H. R. Woudhuysen, *Sir Philip Sidney and the Circulation of Manuscripts 1558–1640* (Oxford: Clarendon Press, 1996), 15.

75. M. Graves, 'Campion, Edmund', *Oxford Dictionary of National Biography*, online edition [Acccessed 11 December 2020].

76. A. C. Southern, *Elizabethan Recusant Prose, 1559–1582* (London: Sands & Co., 1950), 399.

77. Louise Imogen Guiney, *Recusant Poets* (London: Sheed & Ward, 1938), 178.

78. Gerard Kilroy, *Edmund Campion: A Scholarly Life* (Farnham: Ashgate, 2015), 79.

79. San Marino, Huntington Library MS 904.

80. Oxford, Bodleian MS Eng. Poet. b .5.

81. Barthes, *A Lover's Discourse* (London: Penguin Books, 1990), 73.

82. Brown, 'Paperchase: The Dissemination of Catholic Texts in Elizabethan England, in Peter Beal and Jeremy Griffiths (eds.), *English Manuscript Studies* (New York: Blackwell, 1989-), i. 120–44.

83. Southwell, *Collected Poems*, ed. Peter Davidson and Anne Sweeney (Manchester: Carcanet, 2007), 147.

84. *The Poems of Robert Southwell*, ed. James H. McDonald and Nancy Pollard Brown (Oxford: Clarendon Press, 1967), pp. xxxvii f.

85. Peter Beal, *Index of English Literary Manuscripts*, 2 vols. (London: Mansell, 1980), 499.

86. *The Martin Marprelate Tracts*, ed. Joseph L. Black (Cambridge: Cambridge University Press, 2008), pp. l–liii.

87. San Marino, Huntington Library, shelf mark 60,619 (the Earl of Bridgewater's copy).

88. San Marino, Huntington Library MS Ellesmere 2156, fo. 1^r.

89. San Marino, Huntington Library MS Ellesmere 483, fo. 29^v.

90. Donald J. McGinn, *John Penry and the Marprelate Controversy* (New Brunswick, NJ: Rutgers University Press, 1966), 169.

91. David Cressy, 'Book Burning in Tudor and Stuart England', *The Sixteenth Century Journal*, 36 (2005), 359–74 at 361.

92. Blayney, *The Stationers' Company*, i. 561.

93. James McConica, *History of the University of Oxford. Volume III: The Collegiate University* (Oxford: Oxford University Press, 1986).

94. Blayney, *The Stationers' Company*, ii. 738.

95. H. C. Porter, *Reformation and Reaction in Tudor Cambridge* (Cambridge: Cambridge University Press, 1958), 73.

96. Blayney, *The Stationers' Company*, ii. 925–6.

97. *Records of the Court of the Stationers' Company: 1576–1602*, ed. W. W. Greg and E. Boswell (London: Bibliographical Society, 1930), p. lx.

98. Anthony Grafton, *Inky Fingers: The Making of Books in Early Modern Europe* (Cambridge, MA: Harvard University Press, 2020), 227.

99. Stationers' Register, Court Book B; *Records of the Court*, ed. Greg and Boswell, 79. See W. W. Greg, *Some Aspects and Problems of London Publishing between 1550 and 1650*, Lyell Lectures (Oxford: Clarendon Press, 1956), 20.

100. Cyndia Clegg, 'Burning Books in Jacobean England, *Literature and Censorship in Renaissance England*, ed. Andrew Hadfield (London: Palgrave, 2001), 165–86.

101. David R. Como, 'Secret Printing, the Crisis of 1640, and the Origins of Civil War Radicalism', *Past and Present*, 196 (2007), 37–82 at 48.

102. Cressy, 'Book Burning in Tudor and Stuart England', 370.

103. Smyth, *Material Texts in Early Modern England*, 68.

104. Rabelais, *Œuvres complètes*, 7; *Gargantua and Pantagruel*, 5.

105. Swift, *An Account of a Battel between the Antient and Modern Books*, ed. Herbert Davis, *A Tale of a Tub with Other Early Works* (Oxford: Basil Blackwell, 1965), 223.

106. McKerrow, *Introduction to Bibliography*, 44.

107. Sterne, *The Life and Opinions of Tristram Shandy, Gentleman*, Book 1, ch. 40, 79.

108. 'Homie the Clown', *The Simpsons*, 12 February 1995.

109. *New York Tribune*, 8 February 1856.

110. Susan Brigden, *London and the Reformation* (Oxford: Clarendon Press, 1989), 109–10.

111. Thomas R. Gray, *The Confessions of Nat Turner* (Baltimore: T. R. Gray, 1831), 11.

112. Morrison, *Beloved* (New York: Random House, 2014), 246.

113. P. S. Bassett, 'A Visit to the Slave Mother who Killed her Child', *American Baptist*, 12 February 1856.

114. Kristen Oertel, *Harriet Tubman: Slavery, the Civil War, and Civil Rights in the Nineteenth Century* (London: Routledge, 2015), 98–100.

115. *Select Parts of the Holy Bible, for the Use of the Negro Slaves, in the British West-India Islands* (London: Law and Gilbert, 1807).

116. Galatians 3: 28.

117. Colson Whitehead, *The Underground Railroad*, 8.

118. Thoreau, 'A Plea for Captain John Brown', *Walden and Other Writings*, 738.

119. Thoreau, 'A Plea for Captain John Brown', 720.

120. Bunyan, *Grace Abounding*, 8.

121. Baxter, *The Certainty of the Worlds of Spirits and, Consequently, of the Immortality of Souls of the Malice and Misery of the Devils and the Damned* (London: T. Parkhurst and J. Salisbury, 1691), 162–3.

122. *The Souldiers Pocket Bible: Containing the Most (if not all) those Places Contained in Holy Scripture, Which doe Shew the Qualifications of his Inner Man, that is a Fit Souldier to Fight the Lords Battels, Both Before he Fight, in the Fight, and after the Fight* (London: G.B. and R.W., 1643), 7.

123. David Daniell, *The Bible in English* (New Haven and London: Yale University Press, 2003), 471.

124. Joyce, *Ulysses* ('Scylla and Charybdis').

125. Jason McElligott, 'In the Line of Fire', *History Ireland*, 20 (2012), 42–3.

126. Johann Eduard Hess, *Gottfried Heinrich, Graf zu Pappenheim* (Leipzig: T. D. Weigel, 1855), 308.

127. Benjamin, *The Work of Art in the Age of Mechanical Reproduction*, 32.

128. Wilhelm Levison, *England and the Continent in the Eighth Century*, The Ford Lectures, 1943 (Oxford: Clarendon Press, 1946), 70–2.

129. Theodor Schieffer, *Winfrid-Bonifatius und die christliche Grundlegung Europas*, 2nd edn. (Darmstadt: Wissenschaftliche Buchgesellschaft, 1972), 272–3.

130. Levison, *England and the Continent*, 90.

131. John J. Contreni, *Carolingian Learning, Masters and Manuscripts* (Brookfield, VT: Variorum, 1992), 61.

132. Ludwig Pralle, *Gaude Fulda! Das Bonifatiusjahr 1954* (Fulda: Parzeller, 1954), 59.

133. Bischoff, *Manuscripts and Libraries*, 102.

134. Bischoff, *Manuscripts and Libraries*, 104.

135. Fulda Sacramentary; Göttingen, Staats- und Universitätsbibliothek, 2° Cod. MS theol. 231, fo. 126v.

136. C. H. Talbot, *The Anglo-Saxon Missionaries in Germany* (London and New York: Sheed and Ward, 1954), §8.

137. *Vitae Sancti Bonifatii archiepiscopi moguntini*, ed. W. Levison, Monumenta Germaniae historica, 57 (Hanover: Hahn, 1905), 78.

138. Levison, *England and the Continent*, 294.

139. Bischoff, *Manuscripts and Libraries*, 16.

140. McKitterick, *The Carolingians and the Written Word*, 170.

141. McKitterick, *The Carolingians and the Written Word*, 259.

142. Geary, *Furta Sacra: Thefts of Relics in the Central Middle Ages*, rev. edn. (Princeton: Princeton University Press, 2011), 46–7.

143. Brown, *The Cult of the Saints*, 90.

144. Aaij, 'Boniface's Booklife: How the Ragyndrudis Codex Came to be a *Vita Bonifatii*', *The Heroic Age: A Journal of Early Medieval Northwestern Europe*, 10 (2007); https://www.heroicage.org/issues/10/aaij.html.

145. Barthes, *Roland Barthes by Roland Barthes*, 150.

146. Borges, 'Mis libros', in *La rosa profunda* (Buenos Aires: Emecé, 1975).

147. Barthes, *Lover's Discourse*, 98.

148. Mostert, *754, Bonifatius bij Dokkum vermoord* (Hilversum: Uitgeverij Verloren, 1999), 80.

Chapter 18

1. Petrarch, *Familiares*, 6. 1; *Selected Letters*, ed. Elaine Fantham, 2 vols., I Tatti Renaissance Library 76–7 (Cambridge: Harvard University Press, 2017), i. 57.

2. Petrarch, *Selected Letters*, i. 53.

3. Augustine, *Confessions*, 10. 8. 15; quoted in Petrarch, *Selected Letters*, i.57.
4. The troubled etymology of *Buch* ('book') is discussed by M. Pierce in *Historische Sprachforschung*, 119 (2006), 273–82.
5. Cassiodorus, *Introduction to Divine and Human Readings*, tr. L. W. Jones (New York: Columbia University Press, 1946), 144.
6. Vasari, *Lives of the Artists*, tr. Bondanella, 434.
7. Petrarch, *Selected Letters*, i. 57.
8. Rome, Vatican Library, MS Vat. gr. 1209.
9. https://www.bl.uk/collection-items/codex-sinaiticus.
10. British Museum 38303, 47589.
11. Finkel and Taylor, *Cuneiform*, 16–17.
12. Eileen Gardner and Ronald G. Musto, in Suarez and Woudhuysen (eds.), 'The Electronic Book', *The Book: A Global History*, 273.
13. Roger Chartier, *Forms and Meanings: Texts, Performances, and Audiences from Codex to Computer* (Philadelphia: University of Pennsylvania Press, 1995), 20.
14. Augustine, *City of God*, 19. 5.
15. Horace, *Ars Poetica* 269; Gillian Clark, 'City of Books: Augustine and the World as Text', *Early Christian Book*, ed. Klingshirn and Safran, 120.
16. De Hamel, *History of Illuminated Manuscripts*, 6.
17. De Hamel, *History of Illuminated Manuscripts*, 159.
18. Pfaff, *Liturgy in Medieval England*, 7.
19. Duffy, *Marking the Hours*, 4.
20. Alexandra Walsham, 'Jewels for Gentlewomen: Religious Books as Artefacts in Late Medieval and Early Modern England', *Studies in Church History*, 38 (2004), 123–42.
21. Duffy, *Marking the Hours*, 23.
22. *St John Altarpiece*, Bruges, Sint-Jans Hospitaal (Memlingmuseum); *Virgin and Child between St James and St Dominic*, Paris, Musées du Louvre; *Donne Triptych* (London, National Gallery).
23. Chantilly, Musée de Condé, MS 65.
24. Thomas Kren and Scott McKendrick, *Illuminating the Renaissance: The Triumph of Flemish Manuscript Painting in Europe* (Los Angeles, CA: J. Paul Getty Museum, 2003), 104.
25. San Marino, CA, Huntington Library, MS HM 1173.
26. Kren and McKendrick, *Illuminating the Renaissance*, 354.
27. San Marino, CA, Huntington Library, MS HM 1131.
28. Kren and McKendrick, *Illuminating the Renaissance*, 467 (Hennessy Hours).
29. San Marino, CA, Huntington Library, MS HM 1162, fo. 86^v.
30. Heather Coffey, 'Between Amulet and Devotion', in Christiane J. Gruber (ed.), *The Islamic Manuscript Tradition* (Bloomington, IN: Indiana University Press, 2010), 114.
31. https://www.bl.uk/collection-items/the-infants-library.
32. Stuart Gillespie, *Shakespeare's Books* (London: Continuum, 2004), 245, citing the work of Matthew Black in the 1940s.
33. Michelle Brown, 'The Triumph of the Codex: The Manuscript Book before 1100', in Simon Eliot and Jonathan Rose (eds.), *A Companion to the History of the Book* (Malden, MA: Wiley, 2007), 182.

34. Sterne, *The Life and Opinions of Tristram Shandy, Gentleman*, III. 33, 255.

35. Ian Campbell Ross, *Laurence Sterne: A Life* (Oxford: Oxford University Press, 2001), 341.

36. Leader, *Hands: What we Do with them and Why* (London: Penguin Books, 2017), 9.

37. Leader, *Hands*, 90.

38. Rousseau, *Confessions*, I; *Œuvres complètes*, i. 40 ('les lire que d'une main'); see also 109.

39. William H. Sherman, *Used Books: Marking Readers in Renaissance England* (Philadelphia: University of Pennsylvania Press, 2010), 41.

40. Montaigne, 'Of Books'; *Complete Essays*, 361.

41. Heidegger, *Sein und Zeit* (Tübingen: Max Niemeyer Verlag, 2006), 69.

42. Heidegger, *Being and Time*, tr. John Macquarrie and Edward Robinson (Oxford: Blackwell, 1962), 98.

43. Michael Inman, *A Heidegger Dictionary* (Oxford: Blackwell, 1999), 129.

44. Heidegger, 'The Question concerning Technology', *Basic Writings*, ed. David Farrell Krell (London: Routledge, 1993), 339.

45. Leader, *Hands*, 91.

46. Augustine, *Confessions*, 6. 3. 3; tr. Chadwick 93.

47. Carruthers, *The Book of Memory*, 171.

48. Nietzsche, *Beyond Good and Evil*, ed. Horstmann and Norman, §247.

49. Nietzsche, *Ecce Homo*, ed. Ridley and Norman, 95–6.

50. Josef Balogh, '*Voces Paginarum*: Beiträge zur Geschichte des lauten Lesens und Schreibens', *Philologus*, 82 (1927), 84–109, 202–40.

51. Bernard M. W. Knox, 'Silent Reading in Antiquity', *Greek, Roman and Byzantine Studies*, 9 (1968), 421–35.

52. Malcolm Parkes, *Pause and Effect: An Introduction to the History of Punctuation in the West* (Berkeley and Los Angeles: University of California Press, 1993), 20–9; and 'Reading, Copying, and Interpreting in the Early Middle Ages', *A History of Reading in the West*, ed. Guglielmo Cavallo and Roger Chartier (Amherst: University of Massachusetts Press, 1999), 90–102.

53. Saenger, *Space between Words: The Origins of Silent Reading* (Stanford: Stanford University Press, 1997), 8.

54. Harris, *Rethinking Writing*, 235.

55. Manguel, *A History of Reading*, 51.

56. Chartier, 'The Practical Impact of Writing', *The Book History Reader*, ed. David Finkelstein and Alistair McCleery, 2nd edn. (London: Routledge, 2006), 164.

57. A. K. Gavrilov, 'Techniques of Reading in Classical Antiquity', *Classical Quarterly*, NS 47 (1997), 56–73; M. F. Burnyeat, 'Postscript on Silent Reading', *Classical Quarterly*, NS 47 (1997), 74–6.

58. R. W. McCutcheon, 'Silent Reading in Antiquity and the Future History of the Book', *Book History*, 18 (2015), 1–32 at 7.

59. Quintilian, *Institutio oratoriae* (*The Orator's Education*), 1. 1. 34; tr. Donald A Russell, Loeb Classical Library, i .81.

60. Lucian, *Adversus indoctum*, 2; tr. A. M. Harmon, 177.

61. Quintilian, *Institutio*, 1. pr. 2; tr. Donald A. Russell, i. 51.

62. Euripides, *Hippolytus*, 865–6; tr. David Kovacs, 208–9.

63. Ovid, *Heroides* 21. 1; tr. Grant Showerman, 292–3.

64. Plutarch, *Cato the Younger*, 24; tr. B. Perrin, 290–1.

65. Cicero, *Tusculan Disputations*, 5; tr. J. E. King, 542–3.

66. Nalini Balbir, 'Polysémies: d'une langue à l'autre en Inde ancienne', *Études romanes de Brno*, 35 (2014), 53–79.

67. Daniel Donoghue, *How the Anglo-Saxons Read Their Poems* (Philadelphia: University of Pennsylvania Press, 2018), 51, 55.

68. This influential term was coined by Brian Stock, *The Implications of Literacy* (Princeton: Princeton University Press, 1983), 90–2.

69. Plutarch, *Cicero*, 48; tr. B. Perrin, 206–7. See Rawson, *Cicero*, 295–6.

70. Plutarch, *Antony*, 20; tr. B. Perrin, 180–1.

71. Shane Butler, *The Hand of Cicero* (London: Routledge, 2002), 2.

72. Ong, *The Presence of the Word: Some Prolegomena for Cultural and Religious History* (New Haven: Yale University Press, 1967).

73. Butler, *The Hand of Cicero*, 35–60.

74. M. Tullius Tiro; Rawson, *Cicero*, 144.

75. Rawson, *Cicero*, 42.

76. Euan Cameron, *The European Reformation* (Oxford: Oxford University Press, 1991), 138–44.

77. *Luther's Works*, 32. 189.

78. *Epistolae*, 82.

79. Wyclif, *De veritate sacrae scripturae*, 114, ed. Ian Christopher Levy (Kalamazoo, Mich.: Medieval Institute Publications, 2001).

80. Peter Marshall, 'The Debate over "Unwritten Verities" in Early Reformation England', in Bruce Gordon (ed.), *Protestant History and Identity in Sixteenth-Century Europe*, 2 vols. (Aldershot: Scolar Press, 1996), i. 60–77.

81. *Responsio ad Lutherum*, in *Collected Works*, v.240–2.

82. *Responsio ad Lutherum*, in *Collected Works*, v.99–101.

83. William Tyndale, *The obedience of a Christen man and how Christen rulers ought to governe* ([Antwerp]: [Merten de Keyser], [1528]], H7^r).

84. *CWTM* vi. 144.

85. 2 Corinthians 3: 6.

86. Clanchy, *From Memory to Written Record*, ch. 9 ('Trusting Writing').

87. Price, 'Reading: The State of the Discipline', *Book History*, 7 (2004), 309.

88. Augustine, *Confessions* 6. 3. 3; Tr. Chadwick, 92.

89. Chartier, 'Leisure and Sociability: Reading Aloud in Early Modern Europe', in Susan Zimmermann and Ronald F. E. Weissman (eds.), *Urban Life in the Renaissance* (Toronto: University of Toronto Press, 1989), 103–20.

90. Carruthers, *Book of Memory*, 171.

91. *In ruminatione*; Augustine, *Sermones*, 352, 1; PL 39. 1550.

92. Jerome, *Commentarium in Ezekiel*, 3. 5; P., 25. 35.

93. Hugh of St Victor, *Didascalion*, 5, 5.

94. Rabelais, *Gargantua*, V; *Œuvres complètes*, 19; *Gargantua and Pantagruel*, 17.

95. *Epistulae*, 84. 3; Loeb Classical Library, 278–9.

96. Virgil, *Aeneid*, 1. 432.

97. Petrarch, *Familiares* 22, 2.
98. Petrarch, *My Secret Book*, 18.
99. Petrarch, *Secretum*, 2; *My Secret Book*, 51.
100. Virgil, *Aeneid*, 1. 52–7.
101. Carruthers, *Book of Memory*, 164.
102. E. K. Waterhouse, 'The Fresco by Foppa in the Wallace Collection', *Burlington Magazine*, 92 (1950), 177.
103. Plutarch, *Cicero* 2; Loeb Classical Library, 84–5.
104. Bolgar, *The Classical Heritage and its Beneficiaries*, 53, 133, 266, 340, 365.
105. Chartier, *Order of Books*, 22.
106. Jerome, *Epistolae*, 22, 36.
107. Plutarch, *Cicero* 49; Loeb Classical Library, 208–9.
108. Leader, *Hands*, 15.
109. Freud, *Three Essays on Sexual Theory*, 159.
110. Burton White, *The First Three Years of Life* (Madison, WI: Prentice-Hall, 1975), 39.
111. Fraiberg, *Insights from the Blind* (New York: Basic Books, 1977), 10.
112. Milton, *Paradise Lost*, 9. 795.
113. Piaget, *Origins of Intelligence in Children* (New York: International Universities Press, 1952), 194.
114. The 'clutching drive'; Freud, *Three Essays on Sexuality*, 159.
115. Dante, *Inferno*, 5. 127.
116. Dante, *Inferno*, 5. 136–8.

Chapter 19

1. Shira Neshat, interview in Linda Weintraub, *In the Making: Creative Options for Contemporary Art* (New York: Distributed Art Publishers, 2003), 214.
2. Farokhzad, 'The Window', *Escrito sobre el corpo: Shirin Neshat* (Madrid: Fundación Telefónica, 2013), 16.
3. Dick Davis, *Shahnameh: The Persian Book of Kings* (New York: Viking, 2006), p. xx.
4. *Shahnameh*, tr. Davis, 5.
5. Shahram Karini, 'El Arte de Shirin Neshat', *Escrito sobre el corpo*, 66.
6. Robert Hillenbrand (ed.), *Shahnama: The Visual Language of the Persian Book of Kings*, ed. (London: Ashgate, 2004).
7. Sheila S. Blair, *Text and Image in Medieval Persian Art* (Edinburgh: Edinburgh University Press, 2019).
8. Karini, 'El Arte de Shirin Neshat', 62.
9. Melville, *Typee: A Peep at Polynesian Life*, in ed. Harrison Hayford, Hershel Parker and G. Thomas Tanselle, *The Writings of Herman Melville: The Northwestern-Newberry Edition, Vol. 1*, ed. Harrison Hayford, Hershel Parker and G. Thomas Tanselle, p. 219.
10. *Captain Cook's Journal during his First Voyage round the World*, ed. W. Wharton (London: Elliot Stock, *1893*), p. 93.
11. Harriet Guest, 'Curiously Marked: Tattooing, Masculinity and Nationality in British Perceptions of the South Pacific', in John Barrell (ed.), *Painting and the Politics of Culture: New Essays on British Art 1700-1850* (Oxford: Oxford University Press, 1992), 101–34.

12. Marco Samadelli *et al.*, 'Complete Mapping of the Tattoos of the 5300-Year-)ld Tyrolean Iceman', *Journal of Cultural Heritage*, 16: 5 (2015), 753–8.

13. Richard S. Bianchi, 'Tätowierung', *Lexicon der Ägyptologie*, vi. 145–6.

14. Herodotus, *Histories*, 5. 6. 2.

15. Herodotus, *Histories*, 2. 113. 2.

16. Herodotus, *Histories*, 7. 233; tr. A. D. Godley, 548–9, where the translation is 'the king's marks'.

17. Pierre Briant, *From Cyrus to Alexander: A History of the Persian Empire* (Winona Lake, IN: Eisenbrauns, 2002), 458.

18. Jones, 'Stigma: Tattooing and Branding in Graeco-Roman Antiquity', *Journal of Roman Studies*, 72 (1987), 139–55.

19. Herodas, *Mimes*, No. 5.

20. C. P. Jones, 'Stigma and Tattoo', in Jane Caplan (ed.), *Written on the Body: The Tattoo in European and American History* (London: Reaktion Books, 2000), 9.

21. Aristophanes, *Wasps*, 1296.

22. Petronius, *Satyricon*, 103.

23. Pontius, *Life of Cyprian*, 7 (PL, 3: 1488).

24. Mark Gustafson, 'The Tattoo in the Later Roman Empire and Beyond', in Caplan (ed.), *Written on the Body*, 18.

25. Hilary, *Against Constantius*, 11. 4–7.

26. *Theodosian Code*, 9. 40. 2.

27. Gustafson, 'The Tattoo in the Later Roman Empire', 29.

28. Procopius of Gaza, *Commentary on Isaiah*, 44. 5.

29. Jones, 'Stigma and Tattoo', 10.

30. Thoreau, *Walden and Other Writings*, 25.

31. Melville, *Typee*, 221.

32. Cook, *A Voyage to the Pacific Ocean*, 4 vols. (London: Champante and Whitrow, 1793), iii. 348.

33. Melville, *Typee*, 220. Cook thought that both words used the prefix *ta-* meaning 'mark', but it is now thought that *tapu* is a non-compound word.

34. Freud, *Totem and Taboo* (New York: Cosimo, 2009), 27.

35. Mauss (with Henri Hubert), 'Essai sur la nature et la fonction du sacrifice', *L'Année sociologique* (1898); tr. in *Sacrifice: Its Nature and Function* (London: Cohen & West, 1964), 14; Durkheim, *Les formes élémentaires de la vie religieuse* (Paris: Félix Alcan, 1912), 448. For Giorgio Agamben's critique in *Homo Sacer*, see *The Omnibus Homo Sacer* (Stanford: Stanford University Press, 2017), 68.

36. Talmud, Yoma 72b.

37. Freud, *Totem and Taboo*, 76.

38. Melville, *Moby-Dick*, 89.

39. Foucault, *Discipline and Punish*, 102.

40. Levi, *If this is a Man*, 33.

41. Foucault, *Discipline and Punish*, 111.

42. Lévi-Strauss, *Structural Anthropology*, i. 257.

43. Gell, *Wrapping in Images: Tattooing in Polynesia* (Oxford: Clarendon Press, 1993), 30.

44. Butler, 'Foucault and the Paradox of Bodily Inscriptions', *The Journal of Philosophy*, 86 (1989), 601–7 at 607.

45. W. R. van Gulik, *Irezumi: The Pattern of Dermatography in Japan* (Leiden: Brill, 1982), 13.

46. Juliet Fleming, 'The Renaissance Tattoo', in Caplan (ed.), *Written on the Body*, 79.

47. Lithgow, *Total Discourse of the Rare Adventures* (London: J. Oakes, 1640), 269.

48. Hamish Maxwell-Stewart and Ian Duffield, 'Skin Deep Devotions', in Caplan (ed.), *Written on the Body*, 125.

49. M. Thévoz, *The Painted Body* (New York: Skira, 1984), 70.

50. Nietzsche, *The Genealogy of Morality* (Indianapolis, IN: Hackett, 1998), 57.

51. Freud, *Totem and Taboo*, 143.

52. Foucault, *Discipline and Punish*, 55.

53. Foucault, *Discipline and Punish*, 113.

54. Elton, *Policy and Police*, 219–20.

55. *Tudor Royal Proclamations*, No. 122; ed. Hughes, i. 181–. Blayney, *Stationers' Company*, i. 326–9, carefully reviews the evidence to show Hughes's text is inaccurately drawn from Foxe and Wilkins, and thus includes a later list of books from 1532.

56. *Tudor Royal Proclamations*, ed. Hughes, No. 129; see Blayney, i, 329–30.

57. British Library, Ellesmere MS 2652, fo. 15.

58. John Guy, *The Public Career of Sir Thomas More* (New Haven: Yale University Press, 1980), p. 173.

59. British Library, Harleian MS 425, fo. 15.

60. Foxe, *Actes and Monuments* (1570), ii. 1381.

61. Foxe, *Actes and Monuments* (1570), ii. 1365.

62. Foxe, *Actes and Monuments* (1570), ii. 1381.

63. Hudson, *Premature Reformation*, 43.

64. Foxe, *Actes and Monuments* (1570), i. 571.

65. Hudson, *Premature Reformation*, 84.

66. Aston, *Lollards and Reformers*, 262–3.

67. *Ein ware histori vom leben, sterben, begrebnuss, anklagung der ketzerey, verdammung, ausgraben, verbrennen und letstlich ehlicher wider ynsetzung der säligen und hochgelehrten Theologen D. Martini Buceri vnd Pauli Fagii* (Strasbourg: Paul Messerschmidt, 1562).

68. Ceri Law, *Contested Reformations in the University of Cambridge, 1535–84*, Royal Historical Society Studies in History (Woodbridge: Boydell & Brewer, 2018), 76.

69. Foxe, *Actes and Monuments* (1570), ii. 2186.

70. Ruth Luborsky and Elizabeth M. Ingram, *A Guide to English Illustrated Books 1536–1603*, 2 vols (Tempe, Arizona: MRTS, 1998), i. 407–8.

71. Reginaldus Gonsalvius Montanus, *Sanctae inquisitionis hispanicae artes aliquot detectae, ac palam traductae* (Heidelberg: n.p., 1567).

72. *A Discovery and Playne Declaration of Sundry Subtill Practises of the Holy Inquisition of Spayne* (London: John Day, 1569), endpiece.

73. Francisco Bethencourt, 'The Auto da Fe: Ritual and Imagery', *Journal of the Warburg and Courtauld Institutes*, 55 (1992), 155–68.

74. Peters, *Inquisition*, 235.

75. Francisco Bethencourt, *The Spanish Inquisition: A Global History, 1478–1834* (Cambridge: Cambridge University Press, 2009), 421–2.

76. Foucault, 'Verité et pouvoir', *L'Arc*, 70 (1978), 18.

77. Album C85, Madrid, Museo Nacional del Prado; C88, London, British Museum 1862,0712.187.

78. Juliet Wilson Bareau, *Goya: Drawings from His Private Albums* (London: Hayward Gallery, 2001), 22.

79. Helen Rawlings, 'Goya's Inquisition: From Black Legend to Liberal Legend', *Vida Hispanica*, 46 (2012), 15–21 at 19.

80. Bareau, *Goya: Drawings from His Private Albums*, 86.

Chapter 20

1. *Mahāparinibbāna Sutta*, i DN 16.

2. Akira Hirakawa, *A History of Indian Buddhism: From Śākyamuni to Early Mahāyāna* (Delhi: Motilal Banarsidass, 1993), 101.

3. John C. Huntington, 'Sowing the Seeds of the Lotus', *Orientations*, 17 (September 1986), 47.

4. Frederick Asher, 'From Place to Sight: Locations of the Buddha's Life', *Artibus Asiae*, 69 (2009), 244.

5. John S. Strong, *Relics of the Buddha* (Delhi: Motilal Banarsidass, 2007), 136–7.

6. Donald S. Lopez, Jr, *The Lotus Sutra*, Lives of Great Religious Books (Princeton: Princeton University Press, 2016), 17.

7. Dan Martin, 'Pearls from Bones: Relics, Chortens, Tertons and the Signs of Saintly Death in Tibet', *Numen*, 41/3 (1994), 274.

8. Hsueh-Man Shen, 'Realizing the Buddha's "Dharma" Body during the Mofa Period: A Study of Liao Buddhist Relic Deposits', *Artibus Asiae*, 61 (2001), 263–303.

9. Hamish Todd, 'The Lotus Sutra', in Igunma and San May (eds.), *Buddhism*, ed. 72–3.

10. Lopez, *The Lotus Sutra*, 45.

11. Lopez, *The Lotus Sutra*, 60–1.

12. Lotus Sūtra, 31c (ch. 10); tr. Tsugunari Kubo and Akiro Yuyama (Berkeley, CA: Numata Center for Buddhist Translation and Research, 2007), 161.

13. Lopez, *The Lotus Sutra*, 70.

14. D. Max Moerman, 'The Death of the Dharma: Buddhist Sutra Burials in Early Medieval Japan', *The Death of Sacred Texts: Ritual Disposal and Renovation of Texts in World Religions*, ed. Kristina Myrvold (Aldershot: Ashgate, 2010), 71–90 at 71.

15. Lopez, *The Lotus Sutra*, 76.

16. Moerman, 'Buddhist Sutra Burials', 74.

17. Tokyo National Museum, 'Ancient Sutra Mounds of Kyushu'.

18. Moerman, 'Buddhist Sutra Burials', 75–6.

19. Lopez, *The Lotus Sutra*, 83.

20. *Kanjin Honzon-shō*, quoted in Lopez, *The Lotus Sutra*, 93.

21. Lopez, *The Lotus Sutra*, 96.

22. Eusebius, *Life of Constantine*, tr. Averil Cameron and S. G. Hunt (Oxford: Oxford University Press, 1999), 79.

23. Paul the Silentiary, *Descriptio ambonis*, lines 244–51, ed. Claudio De Stefani, Bibliotheca Teubneriana (Berlin: de Gruyter, 2011); see Matthews, *Early Churches of Constantinople*, 124–5.

24. John Lowden, 'The Word Made Visible: The Exterior of the Early Christian Book as Visual Argument', in Klingshirn and Safran (eds.), *Early Christian Book*, 28.

25. Jelena Bogdanović, 'The Proclamation of the New Covenant: the Pre-Iconoclastic Altar Ciboria in Rome and Constantinople', *Athanor*, 20 (2002), 7–19 at 13.

26. Timothy Thibodeau, 'Western Christendom', in Geoffrey Wainwright (ed.), *The Oxford History of Christian Worship* (Oxford: Oxford University Press, 2006), 226.

27. Vanessa L. Ochs, *Inventing Jewish Ritual* (Philadelphia: Jewish Publication Society, 2010), 5–6, and 31.

28. Vanessa L. Ochs, *The Passover Haggadah: A Biography* (Princeton, NJ: Princeton University Press, 2020), 11.

29. Kristina Nelson, *The Art of Reciting the Qur'an* (Cairo: American University Press, 2001), 62.

30. John Lowden, 'The Word Made Visible', *Early Christian Books*, 23.

31. Hahn, *Strange Beauty*, 169.

32. London, British Library, MS 89,000, fo. 1^r. formerly known as the 'Stonyhurst Gospel'.

33. Gameson, 'Materials, Text, Layout and Script', in Claire Breay and Bernard Meehan (eds.), *The St Cuthbert Gospel: Studies on the Insular Manuscript of the Gospel of John* (London: British Library, 2015), 33.

34. Symeon of Durham, *Opera et collectanea*, Surtees Society, 190.

35. Gamble, *Books and Readers in the Early Church*, 101–3.

36. Bernard Meehan, *The St Cuthbert Gospel*, 83.

37. Claire Breay and Bernard Meehan, 'Introduction', *The St Cuthbert Gospel*, 7.

38. Symeon of Durham, *Opera*, 198–9.

39. Hunt, 'Post-Medieval Movements of the Manuscript', *The St Cuthbert Gospel*, 142.

40. Bede, *Vita Cuthberti, Age of Bede*, 99.

41. *Reginaldi Libellus*, ed. Raine, Surtees Society, 197–201.

42. Hunt, 'Post-Medieval Movements of the Manuscript', 139.

43. Richard Ovenden, 'The Libraries of the Antiquaries', in Leedham-Green and Webber (eds.), *Libraries in Britain and Ireland*, 560.

44. *Rites of Durham*, ed. J. T. Fowler, Surtees Society, 107 (Durham: Andrews & Co., 1903), 102.

45. This is from the work's title in the Cosin MS in Durham; *Rites of Durham*, 1.

46. Shakespeare, Sonnet 73, line 4.

47. *Rites of Durham*, 7.

48. *Rites of Durham*, 8.

49. *Rites of Durham*, 4.

50. *Rites of Durham*, 70.

51. Hegel, *Philosophy of History*, 377.

52. Dupront, 'Pèlerinage et lieux sacrés', *Mélanges F. Braudel*, 191

53. Brown, *Cult of the Saints*, 87.

54. Josipovici, *Touch* (New Haven and London: Yale University Press, 1996), 68.

55. Marianne Schleicher, 'Accounts of a Dying Scroll: On Jewish Handling of Sacred Texts', *Death of Sacred Texts*, 23.

56. François Deroche, *Qur'ans of the Umayyads: A First Overview*, Leiden Studies in Islam and Society (Leiden: Brill, 2013), 76.

57. Yemen, Dār al-Makhṭūṭāt ('House of Manuscripts'), Ṣanʿāʾ 1 or DAM 01–27.1.

58. Deroche, *Qur'ans of the Umayyads*, 70.

59. Jomier, *L'Islam vécu en Égypte: 1945–1975*, Études Musulmanes, 35 (Paris: Vrin, 1994), 279.

60. Måns Broo, 'Rites of Burial and Immersion: Hindu Ritual Practices', *Death of Sacred Texts*, 91.

61. Douglas, *Purity and Danger: An Analysis of Concepts of Pollution and Taboo* (London: Routledge & Kegan Paul, 1966), 44.

62. Gethin Rees, 'Stupas', in Igunma and San May (eds.), *Buddhism*, 198–9.

63. Måns Broo, 'Hindu Ritual Practices', 98.

64. Gay Daly, *The Pre-Raphaelites in Love*, 363.

65. Browne, *Hydrotaphia, Urne Buriall, or, a discourse of the sepulchrall urnes late found in Norfolk* (London: Henry Brome, 1658), sig. A2^r.

66. Matthews, *Poetical Remains: Poets' Graves, Bodies, and Books in the Nineteenth Century* (Oxford: Oxford University Press, 2004), 192.

67. Kristina Myrvold, 'Making the Scripture a Person: Reinventing Death Rituals of Guru Granth Sahib in Sikhism', *Death of Sacred Texts*, 128–9.

Chapter 21

1. Chartier, *The Cultural Origins of the French Revolution* (Durham, NC: Duke University Press, 1991), 67.

2. Hobsbawm, *The Age of Revolution 1789–1848* (New York: Mentor Books, 1962), 143–4.

3. Popper, *Unended Quest: An Intellectual Autobiography* (London: Routledge, 2005), 213.

4. Ginzburg, 'Morelli, Freud, and Sherlock Holmes: Clues and Scientific Method', in Umberto Eco and Thomas Sebeok (eds.), *The Sign of Three: Dupin, Holmes, Peirce* (Bloomington, IN: Indiana University Press, 1984), 81–118.

5. Darnton, *The Forbidden Best-Sellers of Pre-Revolutionary France* (New York: W. W. Norton, 1996).

6. Darnton, *A Literary Tour de France: The World of Books on the Eve of the French Revolution* (Oxford: Oxford University Press, 2018); on Montpellier, 131; Besançon, 247.

7. McKenzie, 'Printers of the Mind: Some Notes on Bibliographical Theories and Printing-House Practices', *Studies in Bibliography*, 22 (1969), 1–75.

8. Darnton, *The Business of Enlightenment: A Publishing History of the Encyclopédie, 1775–1800* (Cambridge, MA: Harvard University Press, 1987).

9. Raven, *The Business of Books: Booksellers and the English Book Trade 1450–1850* (New Haven and London: Yale University Press, 2007), 329, 343.

10. St Clair, *The Reading Nation in the Romantic Period* (Cambridge: Cambridge University Press, 2004), 98.

11. Lyman Ray Patterson, *Copyright in Historical Perspective* (Nashville, TN: Vanderbilt University Press, 1968), 151.

12. Patterson, *The Nature of Copyright: A Law of Users' Rights* (Athens, GA: University of Georgia Press, 1991), 48.

13. 'Are Too Many Books Written & Published?', Leonard and Virginia Woolf, Wireless Broadcast, 1927; *Essays of Virginia Woolf: Vol. 6, 1933–1941*, ed. Stuart N. Clarke (London: Hogarth Press, 2011), 610–16.

14. 'How Should One Read a Book?', Woolf, *The Common Reader*, Second Series (London: Hogarth Press, 1932), 263.

15. Price, *How to Do Things with Books in Victorian Britain*, 41.

16. Eliot, *Middlemarch*, ed. Rosemary Ashton (London: Penguin Books, 1994), 143.

17. Price, *How to Do Things with Books in Victorian Britain*, 120.

18. Benjamin, 'Unpacking my Library', *Illuminations*, 61.

19. John Fleischmann, *Free & Public: 150 Years at the Public Library of Cincinnati* (Cincinnati: Public Library, 2002).

20. McKitterick, 'Organizing Knowledge in Print', in McKitterick (ed.), *The Cambridge History of the Book in Britain, 1830–1914*, 557.

21. Flaubert, *Madame Bovary: Provincial Manners*, tr. Margaret Mauldon (Oxford: Oxford World's Classics, 2004), 34–5.

22. 'Are Too Many Books Written & Published?', *Essays of Virginia Woolf*, 613.

23. Foucault, *The Archaeology of Knowledge* (London: Pantheon Books, 1972), 25.

24. Daniel and Guy Wildenstein, *Documents complémentaires au catalogue de l'oeuvre de Louis David* (Paris: Wildenstein Foundation, 1973), 55.

25. Crow, *Emulation: Making Artists for Revolutionary France* (New Haven: Yale University Press, 1995), 165.

26. Slavoj Žižek, *Less Than Nothing: Hegel and the Shadow of Dialectical Materialism* (London: Verso Books, 2012), 710.

27. 'dans l'air froid de cette chambre, sur ces murs froids, autour de cette froide et funèbre baignoire, une âme voltige'; Baudelaire, *Salon de 1846*, ed. David Kelley (Oxford: Oxford University Press, 1974).

28. Oslo, Munch Museet.

29. Gombrich, *The Story of Art*, 16th edn. (London: Phaidon Books, 1995), 485.

30. New York, Metropolitan Museum of Art.

31. Clark, 'Painting in the Year Two', *Representations*, 47, Special Issue: *National Cultures before Nationalism* (Summer, 1994), 13–63 at 13.

32. Clark, 'Painting in the Year Two', 31.

33. F. P. Bowman, 'Le Sacré Cœur de Marat', *Annales historiques de la Révolution française*, 221 (July–September 1974).

34. Janet T. Marquadt, *From Martyr to Monument: The Abbey of Cluny as Cultural Patrimony* (Newcastle: Cambridge Scholars, 2009), 15.

35. Schama, *Citizens: A Chronicle of the French Revolution* (London: Penguin Books, 1989), 777.

36. Jonathan Israel, *Revolutionary Ideas*, 495.

37. Colin Lucas, *Annales historiques de la Révolution française*, 194 (October–December 1968), 489–533.

38. Clark, 'Painting in the Year Two', 32.

39. Clark, 'Painting in the Year Two', 54.

40. Weber, 'Science as a Vocation', *From Max Weber: Essays in Sociology*, ed. H. H. Geerth and C. Wright Mills (London: Routledge, 2009), 155; for the German term see Weber, *Gesammelte Aufsätze zur Wissenschaftslehre*, ed. J. Winckelmann (Tübingen: J. C. B. Mohr, 1985), 594.

41. Charles Taylor: *A Secular Age* (Cambridge, MA: Harvard University Press, 2007), 720.

42. Hegel, *Aesthetics*, i. 598.

43. Hegel, *Aesthetics*, i. 599.

44. Washington, DC, National Gallery of Art; Adriaan Waiboer, Arthur K. Wheelock, and Blaise Ducos (eds.), *Vermeer and the Masters of Genre Painting* (New Haven and London: Yale University Press, 2017).

45. Inwood, *Hegel*, 532.

46. Hegel, *Phänomenologie des Geistes*, §699; *Phenomenology of Spirit*, tr. Inwood, 277.

47. *Phänomenologie des Geistes*, §705 (*Das abstrakte Kunstwerk*).

48. Inwood, *Hegel*, 240, suggests 'elimination' as a translation of Hegel's word.

49. *Phänomenologie des Geistes*, §706 (tr. Inwood, 279).

50. Hegel, *Aesthetics*, ii. 1036.

51. *Phänomenologie des Geistes*, §707 (tr. Inwood, 279).

52. *The Phenomenology of Spirit*, tr. Inwood, 479.

53. *Travels in Arabia* (London: Henry Colburn, 1829), 250.

54. Robinson, 'The Rise of Islam, 600–705', in Robinson (ed.), *New Cambridge History of Islam, Vol. 1*, 184.

55. *Phänomenologie des Geistes*, §696 (tr. Inwood, 276).

56. *Phänomenologie des Geistes*, §707 (tr. Inwood, 279).

57. Inwood, *Hegel*, 443.

58. *Phänomenologie des Geistes*, §594 (tr. Inwood, 237).

59. Roy Harris, *Rethinking Writing*, 226.

60. *Power of Art*, BBC TV, 2006; https://www.bbc.co.uk/arts/powerofart/david.shtml.

61. Israel, *Revolutionary Ideas*, 60.

62. 'He who does evil hates the light'; John 3: 20.

63. Jules Claretie, *Camille Desmoulins and His Wife: Passages from the History of the Dantonists* (London: Smith, Elder, & Co., 1876), 303.

64. Foucault, *Discipline and Punish*, 12–13.

65. Daniel Arasse, *The Guillotine and the Terror* (London: Penguin Books, 1989), 13.

66. Schama, *Citizens*, 621.

67. Arasse, *The Guillotine*, 75.

68. *Clinical Journal*, 12 (1898), 436.

69. Georges Benrekassa, 'Camille Desmoulins: écrivain révolutionnaire', in Thierry Bonnet (ed.), *La Carmagnole des Muses* (Paris: Armand Colin, 1988), 223–41.

70. Israel, *Revolutionary Ideas*, 553.

71. *Le Vieux Cordelier*, ed. Henri Calvet (Paris, 1936).

72. Caroline Weber, *Terror and Its Discontents: Suspect Words in Revolutionary France* (Minneapolis, MN: University of Minnesota Press, 2003), 152.

73. Rétat, *La Révolution du journal, 1788–1794* (Paris: CNRS, 1989), 8.

74. Jeremy D. Popkin, 'Journals: the New Face of News', in Robert Darnton and Daniel Roche (eds.), *Revolution in Print: The Press in France, 1775–1800* (Berkeley and Los Angeles, CA: University of California Press, 1989), 141–64.

75. J. Gilchrist, *The Press in the French Revolution: A Selection of Documents from the Press of the Revolution for the Years 1789–1794* (London: St Martin's Press, 1971), 15.

76. Schama, *Citizens*, 447.

77. Schama, *Citizens*, 837.

78. Kant, *Critique of Pure Reason*, A395; ed Guyer and Wood, 439.

79. Doyle, *The Oxford History of the French Revolution* (Oxford: Oxford University Press, 1990), 292.

80. Melvyn Richter, *The Political Theory of Montesquieu* (Cambridge: Cambridge University Press, 1977), 6.

81. Israel, *Revolutionary Ideas*, 207.

82. Max Hulliung, *Montesquieu and the Old Regime* (Berkeley and Los Angeles: University of California Press, 1977), 222.

83. Kant, *Groundwork of the Metaphysics of Morals,* 101.

84. Popkin, 'Journals: the New Face of News', 154.

85. Israel, *Revolutionary Ideas*, 26–7.

86. Carla Hesse, 'Print Culture in the Enlightenment', in Martin Fitzpatrick, Peter Jones, Christa Knellwolf, and Iain MacCalman (eds.), *The Enlightenment World* (London: Routledge, 2004), 366–80 at 378.

87. Philippe Minard, *Typographes des Lumières* (Seyssel: Champ Vallon, 1989), 47–8.

88. Hesse, 'Print Culture in the Enlightenment', 376.

89. Charles le Brun, *Expressions des passions de l'Âme* (1730).

90. 'Robespierre guillotinant le boureau après avoir fait guillot<ine>r. tous les Français: cy gyt toute la France', Paris, Bibliothèque Nationale de France.

91. Raven, *Business of Books*, 136.

92. Martyn Lyons, *Books: A Living History* (Los Angeles: Getty Museum, 2011).

93. Tsien Tsuen-Hsuin, 'Paper and Printing', in Joseph Needham, *Science and Civilization in China, Vol. 5: Chemistry and Chemical Technology* (Cambridge: Cambridge University Press, 1985), 234.

94. Jacques Roux, *L'ombre de Marat au peuple français* (Paris, 1793).

95. Horace, *Epistles*, 1. 4. 5.

96. Pindar, *Pythian Odes*, 3. 61–2.

97. *Philebus* 38e.

98. Hans-Georg Gadamer, *Plato's Dialectical Ethics: Phenomenological Interpretations Relating to the* Philebus (New Haven and London: Yale University Press, 1991), 168.

99. Derrida, *Dissemination*, tr. Barbara Johnson, 188.

100. Foucault, *Discipline and Punish*, 13.

101. Ryle, *The Concept of Mind* (London: Hutchinson, 1949), 32.

102. Koestler, *The Ghost in the Machine* (London: Hutchinson, 1967), 56.

103. Ryle, *Concept of Mind*, 253–4.

Chapter 22

1. McCulloch, *Because Internet: Understanding the New Rules of Language* (London: Penguin Books, 2019), 14.
2. Plato, *Phaedrus*, 274e.
3. Woolf, *To the Lighthouse*, 135.
4. Zuboff, *Age of Surveillance Capitalism*, 186.
5. Woolf, *To the Lighthouse*, 46.
6. Silvio A. Bedini, *Thomas Jefferson's Copying Machines* (Charlottesville, VA: University of Virginia Press, 1988).
7. Gardiner and Musto, 'The Electronic Book', 278.
8. Thomas Petzold, *Global Knowledge Dynamics and Social Technology* (New York: Springer, 2017), 27.
9. Pettegree, *The Book in the Renaissance*, 25–6.
10. https://www.worldwidewebsize.com.
11. The methodology is explained by Maurice de Kunder and others in *Scientometrics* (9 February, 2016).
12. World Economic Forum, cited in Ewan Clayton (ed.), *Writing: Making Your Mark* (London: British Library, 2019), 10.
13. Jean-Luc Chabert, *A History of Algorithms: From the Pebble to the Microchip* (New York: Springer, 2012), 7.
14. Donald Knuth, *The Art of Computer Programming*, 4 vols. (Reading, MA: Addison-Wesley, 2011), ii. 339–64.
15. Matthew L. Jones, *Reckoning with Matter: Calculating Machines, Innovation, and Thinking about Thinking from Pascal to Babbage* (Chicago: University of Chicago Press, 2016), 67–70.
16. A. M. Turing, 'On Computable Numbers, with an Application to the *Entscheidungsproblem*', *Proceedings of the London Mathematical Society*, 42/1 (1936), 230–65.
17. A. M. Turing, 'Computing Machinery and Intelligence', *Mind*, 49 (1950), 433–60.
18. Boden, *The Creative Mind*, 2nd edn. (London: Routledge, 2003), 20.
19. Searle, 'Minds, Brains and Programs', *Behavioural and Brain Sciences*, 3 (1980), 417–57; Turing in fact anticipated Searle's main line of argument in his 1950 paper and discounted it.
20. Chomsky, *Syntactic Structures* (Berlin: de Gruyter, 1957), 17.
21. William Croft and Alan Cruse, *Cognitive Linguistics* (Cambridge: Cambridge University Press, 2004), 223.
22. Zuboff, *Age of Surveillance Capitalism*, 95.
23. Daniel Shore, *Cyberformalism: Histories of Linguistic Forms in the Digital Archive* (Baltimore: Johns Hopkins University Press, 2018), p. xii.
24. Shore, *Cyberformalism*, 41.
25. Culler, 'The Closeness of Close Reading', *ADE Bulletin*, 149 (2010), 24.
26. Spivak, 'Interview with Gayatri Spivak', *PMLA* 125 (2010), 2010.
27. Underwood, 'Theorizing Research Practices we Forgot to Theorize Twenty Years Ago', *Representations*, 127/ 1 (2014), 66.

28. Empson, *Seven Types of Ambiguity* (Harmondsworth: Pelican Books, 1977), 19.

29. *Sonnets*, 83 line 4; Empson, *Seven Types of Ambiguity*, 162–3.

30. Jakobson, 'Linguistics and Poetics', in Krystyna Pomorska and Stephen Rudy (eds.), *Language in Literature* (Cambridge MA: Harvard University Press, 1987) 71.

31. *Philosophical Investigations*, § 3.

32. Benjamin, 'The Task of the Translator', *Illuminations*, 79.

33. Mallarmé, *Crise de vers*.

34. Melvin Johnson *et al.*, 'Google's Multilingual Neural Machine Translation System: Enabling Zero-Shot Translation', *ARXIV*, 14 November 2016, www.arxiv.org.

35. Bridle, *New Dark Age*, 156.

36. J. N. Adams, *Bilingualism and the Latin Language* (Cambridge: Cambridge University Press, 2003), 111. Adams compares the inter-relation of 16 languages (other than Greek) with Latin; for a full account of the pluralism of the Roman world see G. Neumann and W. Untermann, *Die Sprachen im römischen Reich der Kaiserzeit* (Cologne: Habelt, 1980).

37. Martial, *Liber spectaculorum*, 3. 11–12.

38. Martín Abadi and David G. Andersen, 'Learning to Protect Communications with Adversarial Neural Cryptography', *ARXIV*, 2016; www.arxiv.org.

39. Edward Snowden, *Permanent Record* (London: Macmillan, 2019), 150.

40. Snowden, *Permanent Record*, 214.

41. Glenn Greenwald, *No Place to Hide: Edward Snowden, the NSA & the Surveillance State* (London: Penguin Books, 2015), 7.

42. Livy, *Histories*, 3. 29.

43. Cicero, *Post reditum in senatu*, 12.

44. https://wikileaks.org/10years/.

45. Greenwald, *No Place to Hide*, 59.

46. Greenwald, *No Place to Hide*, 50.

47. Jason Leopold, *Vice News*, 4 June 2015.

48. Snowden, interviewed in *The Guardian*, 9 June 2013.

49. Nirak Chokshi, 'Snowden and WikiLeaks Clash', *New York Times*, 29 July 2016, https://www.nytimes.com/2016/07/30/us/snowden-wikileaks.html.

50. Snowden, *Permanent Record*, 241.

51. Greenwald, *No Place to Hide*, 176.

52. Funder, *Stasiland: Stories from Behind the Berlin Wall* (London: Granta Books, 2003), 74.

53. 'Snowden Interview: Transcript', NDR, 26 January 2014; www.ndr.de.

54. Ellen Nakashima and Joby Warrick, *The Washington Post*, 14 July 2013.

55. Greenwald, *No Place to Hide*, 93.

56. Ewan MacAskill *et al.*, 'How does GCHQ's internet surveillance work?', *The Guardian*, 21 June 2013, theguardian.com/uk/2013/jun/21/how-does-gchq-internet-surveillance-work.

57. Orwell, *Nineteen Eighty-Four* (London: Penguin Classics, 2013), 4.

58. Assur Medical Catalogue, cited in Ulrike Steinert, *Assyrian and Babylonian Scholarly Text Catalogues: Medicine, Magic and Divination* (Berlin: de Gruyter, 2018), 60. Over 50 instances of this phrase survive; see Fischer, *A History of Reading*.

59. The title 'king of 'totality/the universe' was first used in around 1700 BCE; it is unique to Assyria and not found in Persia; Jonathan E. Dyck, *The Theocratic Ideology of the Chronicler* (Leiden: Brill, 1998), 98.
60. Ostler, *Empires of the Word*, 151.
61. *Ancient Near-Eastern Texts Relating to the Old Testament*, ed. James B. Pritchard (Princeton: Princeton University Press, 1969), 415.
62. Ostler, *Empires of the Word*, 158.
63. Jonathan Spence, *Treason by the Book: Traitors, Conspirators and Guardians of the Emperor* (London: Penguin Books, 2001), 36–7.
64. Armando Petrucci, *Public Lettering: Script, Power, and Culture* (Chicago: University of Chicago Press, 1993), 1.
65. Giancarlo Susini, *Epigrafia Romana* (Rome: Jouvence, 1997), 116–17.
66. Petrucci, *Public Lettering*, 34.
67. Certeau, *The Practice of Everyday Life* (Berkeley and Los Angeles, 2011), 136.
68. Snowden, *Permanent Record*, 150.
69. Certeau, *Practice of Everyday Life*, 149.
70. *Yi Jing*, Appendix, i. 12; *Book of Changes*, tr. Richard Wilhelm and Cary F. Baynes, 2 vols (New York: Pantheon Books, 1950), i. 374, 378.
71. Snowden, *Permanent Record*, 149.
72. Shelley, *Frankenstein: or, The Modern Prometheus*, ch. 2.
73. Freud, *The Uncanny*, ed. Haughton, 142.
74. Shelley, *Prometheus Unbound*, lines 191–9.
75. Edward Jay Epstein, *How America Lost Its Secrets: Edward Snowden, the Man and the Theft* (New York: Alfred A. Knopf, 2017), 14.
76. Eric Schmidt quoted in Greenwald, *No Place to Hide*, 170.
77. Zuboff, *Age of Surveillance Capitalism*, 402.
78. Greenwald, *No Place to Hide*, 92.
79. Zuboff, *Age of Surveillance Capitalism*, 403.
80. Greenwald, *No Place to Hide*, 94.
81. Swift, *An Argument to Prove, That the Abolishing of Christianity in England, May, as Things Now Stand, be attended with some Inconveniences*, in *Bickerstaff Papers and Pamphlets on the Church*, ed. Herbert Davis (Oxford: Basil Blackwell, 1957), Prose Writings of Jonathan Swift, ii. 26.
82. Snowden, *Permanent Record*, 156.
83. Snowden, *Permanent Record*, 180.
84. *L'invention du quotidien. 1 Arts de faire*, new edn. (Paris: Gallimard, 1990), 209.
85. Shakespeare, *Comedy of Errors* 3. 1. 13–14.
86. Kafka, 'In der Strafkolonie', *Die Erzählungen* (Frankfurt am Main: Fischer Verlag, 1996), 167.
87. 'In the Penal Colony'; Kafka, *Collected Stories*, 140.
88. *Die Erzählungen*, 170; *Collected Stories*, 136.
89. Certeau, *Practice of Everyday Life*, 143.
90. Kafka, *Collected Stories*, 142.
91. Kafka, *Collected Stories*, 140.
92. Introduction to *Collected Stories*, p. xxix.

93. Nietzsche, 'On Truth and Lying in a Non-Moral Sense', *The Birth of Tragedy and Other Writings*, ed. Raymond Geuss and Ronald Spiers (Cambridge: Cambridge University Press, 1999), 143.

94. Nietzsche, 'Über Wahrheit und Lüge im außermoralischen Sinne', eKGWB/ NF-1872,23[11]—Nachgelassene Fragmente Winter 1872–3; 'On Truth and Lying', 145.

95. Greenwald, *No Place to Hide*, 175.

96. Bentham, 'Letter II', in *The Works of Jeremy Bentham,* ed. John Bowring, 11 vols. (Edinburgh: William Tait, 1838–43), 4.

97. BBC News, 18 May 2016; https://www.bbc.co.uk/news/in-pictures-36314536.

98. *Works of Jeremy Bentham,* iv. 115.

99. Herodotus, *Persian Wars*, 2. 2.

100. Augustine, *Confessions*, 1. 8. 13; tr. Chadwick, 10–11.

101. Zuboff, *Age of Surveillance Capitalism*, 403.

102. Wittgenstein, *Philosophical Investigations*, §2.

103. Wittgenstein, *Philosophical Investigations*, §363.

104. Wittgenstein, *Philosophical Investigations*, §293.

105. Mario Bunge, 'A General Black-Box Theory', *Philosophy of Science*, 30 (1963), 346–58.

106. Sterne, *Tristram Shandy*, vi. 152.

107. Campbell Ross, *Laurence Sterne*, 201–2.

108. Foucault, *Discipline and Punish*, 201.

109. Marx, *Grundrisse*, 693.

Chapter 23

1. The eyewitness account that follows is based on an interview in December 2019 with the photographer Asadour Guzelian, whose photographs of the day, syndicated for the *Sunday Times*, are the only surviving record.

2. BBC News, 14 February 1989; http://news.bbc.co.uk/onthisday/hi/dates/stories/ february/14/newsid_2541000/2541149.stm.

3. Linda L. Kern, 'Companions of the Prophet', *Encyclopaedia of the Qur'an*, Brill Online, accessed 7 December 2020.

4. David S. Powers, 'Fatwā, premodern', in Kate Fleet *et al.* (eds.), *Encyclopaedia of Islam*, 3rd edn. (Leiden: Brill, 2017).

5. Ahmad S. Dallal and Jocelyn Hendrickson, 'Fatwā, modern', *Encyclopaedia of Islam*.

6. Erik Jan Zürcher, *Jihad and Islam in World War I* (Leiden: Leiden University Press, 2016), 14.

7. Knut S. Vikør, *Between God and the Sultan: A History of Islamic Law* (Oxford: Oxford University Press, 2005), 142.

8. Nikki Keddie, 'Culture and Politics in Iran since the 1979 Revolution', in Robert W. Hefner (ed.), *New Cambridge History of Islam, Vol. 6: Muslims and Modernity: Culture and Society since 1800* (Cambridge: Cambridge University Press, 2010), 443.

9. Shahab Ahmed, 'Ibn Taymiyyah and the Satanic Verses', *Studia Islamica*, 87 (1998), 67–124.

10. John D. Erickson, *Islam and Postcolonial Narrative* (Cambridge: Cambridge University Press, 1990), 140.

11. Rushdie, *The Satanic Verses* (London: Vintage Books, 1988), 215.

12. Hudson, *Premature Reformation*, 359.

13. Lambert, *Medieval Heresy*, 299.

14. Aston, *Lollards and Reformers*, 41.

15. Nicholas Watson, 'Censorship and Cultural Change in Late Medieval England', *Speculum*, 70 (1995), 822–64 at 827.

16. Hudson, *Premature Reformation*, 430–1.

17. MacCulloch, *Reformation*, 691.

18. Rushdie, *Midnight's Children*, 10, quoting Sura 96 (al-Alaq).

19. Peter D. McDonald, *The Literature Police: Apartheid Censorship and Its Cultural Consequences* (Oxford: Oxford University Press, 2009), 213.

20. McDonald, *Literature Police*, 350.

21. Kureishi, 'Touching the Untouchable', *Times Literary Supplement*, 1 March 2019.

22. Rushdie, *Is Nothing Sacred?*, 3.

23. Rushdie, *Is Nothing Sacred?*, 7.

24. Rushdie, *Is Nothing Sacred?*, 13.

25. Voltaire, *Essai sur les moeurs*, ed. René Pomeau, 2 vols. (Paris: Garnier, 1963), ii. 244–50.

26. Bruce Gordon, *Calvin* (New Haven and London: Yale University Press, 2009), 217–32.

27. Philip Benedict and Sarah Scholl, 'Religious Heritage and Civic Identity in Geneva', in Brian Cummings, Ceri Law, Karis Riley, and Alexandra Walsham (eds.), *Remembering the Reformation* (London: Routledge, 2020), 275.

28. *Tribune de Genève*, 4 October 2011, 23.

29. Henry Kamen, *The Rise of Toleration* (London: Weidenfeld and Nicolson, 1967), 75–6.

30. Gordon, *Calvin*, 218.

31. Roland Bainton, *Hunted Heretic: The Life and Death of Michael Servetus, 1511–1553* (Boston: Beacon Books, 1960), 144.

32. Bainton, *Hunted Heretic*, 154.

33. Gordon, *Calvin*, 219.

34. Bainton, *Hunted Heretic*, 209.

35. Bainton, *Hunted Heretic*, 118.

36. Gordon, *Calvin*, 220.

37. *The Restoration of Christianity*, tr. Christopher Hofmann and Marian Hiller, 72.

38. Voltaire, Letter to Vernet, 14 September 1733; *Correspondance*, ed. Théodore Besterman, 13 vols., Bibliothèque de la Pléiade (Paris: Gallimard, 1963–93), i. 421.

39. Voltaire, Letter to Nicolas-Claude Thieriot, 26 March 1757; *Correspondance*, iv. 979 (No. 4738 [D7213]).

40. Voltaire, *Philosophical Dictionary*, tr. Peter Gay 2 vols. (New York: Basic Books, 1962), i.243.

41. Voltaire, Letter to d'Alembert, 26 June [1766]; *Correspondance*, viii. 516 (No. 9482 [D13374]).

42. Graham Gargett, *Voltaire and Protestantism* (Oxford: Voltaire Foundation, 1980), 63.

43. Jennifer Powell McNutt, *Calvin Meets Voltaire: The Clergy of Geneva in the Age of Enlightenment, 1685–1798* (Farnham: Ashgate, 2014), 154.

44. Hall, *The Friends of Voltaire* (London: Smith Elder, 1906), 199.

45. Rainer Forst, *Toleration in Conflict: Past and Present* (Cambridge: Cambridge University Press, 2013), 20.

46. Williams, 'Toleration: An Impossible Virtue?', in D. Heyd (ed.), *Toleration: An Elusive Virtue* (Princeton: Princeton University Press, 1996), 18–27 at 25.

47. Castellio, *Contra libellum Calvini*, art. 116.

48. Voltaire, *Traité sur la tolerance* (1763); *Mélanges*, Bibliothèque de la Pléiade (Paris: Gallimard, 1963–93), 575.

49. Voltaire, *Traité sur la tolerance*, 584.

50. Tacitus, *Histories*, 1. 1. .4.

51. Spinoza, *Theological-Political Treatise*, tr. Samuel Shirley (Indianapolis: Hackett, 1998), 233.

52. Jonathan Israel, *Enlightenment Contested: Philosophy, Modernity, and the Emancipation of Man, 1670–1752* (Oxford: Oxford University Press, 2006), 65.

53. Bayle, *Philosophical Commentary*, I. ii; ed. Knud Haakonssen (Indianapolis: Liberty Fund, 2005), 76.

54. Augustine, Letter, 93.

55. Elisabeth Labrousse, *Bayle* (Oxford: Oxford University Press, 1983), 84.

56. Locke, *A Letter Concerning Toleration*, in *Selected Political Writings*, ed. Paul E. Sigmund (New York: W. W. Norton, 2005), 130.

57. John Dunn, *The Political Theory of John Locke* (Cambridge: Cambridge University Press, 1969), xi.

58. Nussbaum, *The New Religious Intolerance: Overcoming the Politics of Fear in an Anxious Age* (Cambridge, MA: Harvard University Press, 2012), 118.

59. John Rawls, *Political Liberalism: Expanded Edition* (New York: Columbia University Press, 2005), 461.

60. Rawls, *Political Liberalism*, 482.

61. Bainton, *Hunted Heretic*, 182.

62. Bainton, *Hunted Heretic*, 150.

63. Bainton, *Hunted Heretic*, 164.

64. Kamen, *Rise of Toleration*, 76.

65. Gordon, *Calvin*, 223.

66. Williams, *Arius: Heresy and Tradition* (London: SCM, 2001), 1.

67. Newman, *The Arians of the Fourth Century* (London: Longman, Green and Co., 1891), 22.

68. John Coffey, *Persecution and Toleration in Protestant England 1558–1689* (London: Routledge, 2014), 16.

69. Nancy and Lawrence Goldstone, *Out of the Flames* (New York: Broadway Books, 2003), 199.

70. Calvin, *Defensio Orthodoxae Fidei de Sacra Trinitate*, ed. Joy Kleinstuber (Geneva: Droz, 2009).

71. Quoted in Calvin, *Opera omnia*, viii. 460.

72. Calvin, *Déclaration pour maintenir la vraye foy que tiennent tous Chrestiens de la Trinité des persones en un seul Dieu* (Geneva: Robert Estienne, 1554), 826.

73. Calvin, *Institutio*, 1. 13. 22; *Opera selecta*, ed. Barth and Niesel, iii. 137.

74. Calvin, *Institutes*, 1. 13. 22; tr. Battles, i. 148.

75. Calvin, *Institutio*, 1. 13. 21; *Opera selecta*, iii. 136.

76. Calvin, *Institutio*, 1. 11.2 ; *Opera selecta*, iii. 89.

77. Augustine, *City of God*, 6 .10; PL 41. 190.

78. Calvin, *Institutio*, 1. 11. 5; *Opera selecta*, iii. 93.

79. Rousseau, *Du contrat social*, IV. viii ('La religion civile'); *Œuvres complètes*, iii. 466.

80. Lambert, *Medieval Heresy*, 4–5.

81. L. J. Taylor, *Heresy and Orthodoxy in Sixteenth Century Paris* (Leiden: Brill, 1999), 77.

82. N. Weiss, *La chambre ardente* (Geneva: Slatkine, 1970), 20.

83. Weiss, *La chambre ardente*, 249.

84. Peters, *Inquisition*, 243.

85. Milton, *Areopagitica*, in *Complete Prose Works*, ii.538.

86. Voltaire, *Dictionnaire philosophique*.

87. Peters, *Inquisition*, 245.

88. Zweig, *Triumph und Tragik des Erasmus von Rotterdam*, 9; *Erasmus and The Right to Heresy* (London: Souvenir Books, 1979), 1.

89. Castellio, *De arte dubitandi et confidendi, ignorandi et sciendi*, ed. Elisabeth Feist-Hirsch (Leiden: E. J. Brill, 1981).

90. British Library, Zweig MS 150 (1907); see Freud, *Gesammelte Werke* (1941), vii. 213–23; *The Uncanny*, ed. Haughton, 23–34.

91. David Cesarini, *Final Solution: The Fate of the Jews, 1933–49* (London: Pan Macmillan, 2016), 594.

92. Besançon, Musée de la Résistance et de la Déportation, Inv. 2001.1324.01.

93. https://www.linksfraktion.de/themen/nachrichten/detail/verbrannte-seele-auf-dem-bebelplatz/.

94. 'Lettre de Mr Jean-Philippe Larrose, agrégé de l'Université de Besançon, faite à Paris en juin 1997'; Besançon, Musée de la Résistance et de la Déportation.

95. https://resistancerepublicaine.com/2017/06/17/certains-disaient-deja-vous-naurez-pas-ma-haine-aux-nazis/.

96. Hubert de Beaufort, *Le livre blanc: Une étude exhaustive de l'histoire de l'occupation de Bordeaux* (Paris, 2001); http://livreblanc.maurice-papon.net/interv-knochen.htm.

97. Zweig, *Amok: Novellen einer Leidenschaft* (Frankfurt am Main: Fischer Verlag, 1966).

98. Freud, *The Uncanny*, ed. Haughton, 132.

99. Lacan, *Anxiety: The Seminar of Jacques Lacan, Book X*, ed. Jean-Alain Miller (London: Polity Press, 2016).

100. Castellio, *De arte dubitandi*, 15.

101. Castellio, *Contra libellum Calvini*, art. 116.

102. Jerome, *In libros informationum litterae et spiritus super Leviticum*, preface; PL 104 616.

103. Smalley, *Study of the Bible in the Middle Ages*, 1.

104. Augustine, *De spiritu et littera*; a work read by Luther in 1516 and Calvin in 1531.

105. Rowan Williams, 'Origen: Between Orthodoxy and Heresy', in W.A. Bienert and U. Kuhneweg (eds.), *Origeniana Septima* (Leuven: Leuven University Press, 1999), 3–14.

106. Gay, *Modernism: The Lure of Heresy from Baudelaire to Beckett and Beyond* (New York: Random House, 2007), 10.

107. *Three Essays on Sexual Theory*, 208 (in a footnote added in 1920).

108. Derrida, *Schibolleth: pour Paul Celan* (Paris: Galilée, 1986), 50.

109. Celan, *Gedichte*, 2 vols. (Frankfurt am Main: Suhrkamp, 1981), i.131.

110. Celan, *Selected Poems*, tr. Michael Hamburger (London: Penguin Books, 1996), 99.

111. Zweig, *Castellio gegen Calvin: oder Ein Gewissen gegen die Gewalt* (Frankfurt am Main: Fischer Verlag, 1936), 1.

112. Zweig, *The Right to Heresy*, 181.

113. Montaigne, 'D'un defaut de nos polices', *Essais*, i. 35; *Complete Works*, 200.

114. Zweig, *The Right to Heresy*, 252.

115. 'Stefan Zweig, Wife End Lives in Brazil', *New York Times*, 23 February 1942.

116. 'Speech on the Occasion of Receiving the Literature Prize of the Free Hanseatic City of Bremen'; Celan, *Collected Prose*, tr. Rosemarie Waldrop (New York: Sheep Meadow Press, 1986), 34 (corrected).

117. Celan, *Gesammelte Werke*, ed. Beda Allemann and Stefan Reichert, 7 vols. (Frankfurt am Main: Surhrkamp, 1986), iii. 186.

Chapter 24

1. Borges, *The Aleph*, tr. Andrew Hurley (London: Penguin Books, 1998), 133.

2. Borges, *The Aleph*, 90.

3. 'Lettre du Fr. Eugène Eyraud, au T. R. P. Supérieur général (1864)', *Annales de la Propagation de la Foi* (Lyon, 1866), 36: 52–71, 124–38.

4. Steven Roger Fischer, *RongoRongo, the Easter Island Script: History, Traditions, Texts* (Oxford: Oxford University Press, 1997), 21–4.

5. Full list in Thomas Barthel, *Grundlagen zur Entzifferung der Osterinselschrift* (Hamburg: de Gruyter, 1958), 83–4.

6. S.-C. Chauvet, *l'île de Pâcques et ses mystères* (Paris: Éditions Tel, 1935), 381–2.

7. Alfred Métraux, *Ethnology of Easter Island* (Honolulu: Bishop Museum, 1940), 393–4.

8. Barthel, 'Pre-contact Writing in Oceania', *Current Trends in Linguistics*, 8 (1971), 1165–86; this ref. 1169.

9. Michael D. Coe, *Breaking the Mayan Code* (London: Thames & Hudson, 1992), 153.

10. Diego de Landa, *Yucatan Before and After the Conquest*, tr. William Gates (New York: Dover, 1978), 82; see Inga Clendinnen, *Ambivalent Conquests: Maya and Spaniard in Yucatan, 1517–1570*, 2nd edn. (Cambridge: Cambridge University Press, 2003), 70.

11. Coe, *Breaking the Mayan Code*, 268.

12. M. del Carmen Rodríguez Martínez *et al.*, 'Oldest Writing in the New World', *Science*, 313, issue 5793 (15 September 2006), 1610–14.

13. Andrew Robinson, 'The Origins of Writing', in Clayon (ed.), *Writing: Making Your Mark*, 26.

14. Melville, *Moby-Dick*, 347.

15. Peter Warren, *Minoan Stone Vases*, Cambridge Classical Studies, 23 (Cambridge: Cambridge University Press, 1969), 67.

16. Evans, *Scripta Minoa* (Oxford: Clarendon Press, 1909).

17. Dennis Duncan, 'Languages Lost in Time', in Duncan *et al.*, *Babel: Adventures in Translation* (Oxford: Bodleian Library, 2019), 158.

18. Robinson, *Writing: Making Your Mark*, 29.

19. For example, New York, Metropolitan Museum of Art, 49.40.1.

20. Robinson, *Writing: Making Your Mark*, 25.

21. Hyginus, *Fabulae*, 105.

22. Shakespeare, *Hamlet*, 5. 2. 13–26.

23. Black, *Literature of Ancient Sumer*, 44.

24. Alan Stewart, *Shakespeare's Letters* (Oxford: Oxford University Press, 2008), 267–8.

25. C. H. W. Johns, *Babylonian and Assyrian Laws, Contracts and Letters* (London: T. & T. Clark, 1904), 262.

26. New York, Metropolitan Museum of Art, 1983.135.4a–c.

27. Johns, *Babylonian and Assyrian Laws*, 262.

28. Helen Smith, 'The Proliferating Surfaces of Early Modern Paper', *Journal of the Northern Renaissance*, 8 (2017), 2–37.

29. James, *The Aspern Papers* (London and New York: Longman and Co., 1888), ch. VIII.

30. 'The Purloined Letter', *The Gift* (Philadelphia: Carey and Hart, 1845), 56.

31. 'Le séminaire sur la lettre volée', *La Psychanalyse*, 2 (1956), 1–44 at 44.

32. Lacan, 'Seminar on 'The Purloined Letter', *Seminar, II: The Ego in Freud's Theory and in the Technique of Psychoanalysis, 1954–1955* (Cambridge: Cambridge University Press, 1988), 205.

33. Robert Darnton, *Poetry and the Police: Communication Networks in Eighteenth-Century France* (Cambridge, MA: Harvard University Press, 2010), 8–10.

34. Derrida, 'Le facteur de la verité' (1975), translated in *The Post Card: from Socrates to Freud*.

35. Barbara Johnson, 'The Frame of Reference: Poe, Lacan, Derrida', in John P. Muller and William J. Richardson (eds.), *The Purloined Poe* (Baltimore: Johns Hopkins University Press, 1988).

36. 'And this is the writing that was written, MENE, MENE, TEKEL, UPHARSIN' (Daniel 5: 25).

37. London, National Gallery, NG 6350.

38. Daniel 5: 30–1.

39. MacCulloch, *Reformation*, 201.

40. Brigden, *London and the Reformation*, 305.

41. Stanford E. Lehmberg, *The Later Parliaments of Henry VIII, 1536–1547* (Cambridge: Cambridge University Press, 1977), 72.

42. *Letters and Papers* (1540), xv. 395.

43. *Letters and Papers*, xv. 498; see Brigden, *London and the Reformation*, 314.

44. MacCulloch, *Thomas Cranmer: A Life* (New Haven and London: Yale University Press, 1996), 252.

45. J. G. Nichols, *Narratives of the Days of the Reformation*, Camden Society, 77 (London, 1859), 252.

46. Cambridge, Corpus Christi College, MS 128, p. 405.

47. Foxe, *Actes and monuments* (1570), ii. 1355.

48. John Stow, *A Survey of London*, ed. C. L. Kingsford, 2 vols. (Oxford: Clarendon Press, 1971), ii.54.

49. *The Diary of Henry Machyn*, ed. J. G. Nichols, Camden Society, 42 (London, 1848), 78.

50. Spence, *Treason by the Book*, 2.

51. London, British Library, MS Cotton Cleopatra. E V, fo. 313.

52. Spence, *Treason by the Book*, 14.

53. Edward Peters, *Torture* (Philadelphia: University of Pennsylvania Press, 1996), 54.

54. *Omnia, etiam quae nunquam ipsis in mentem venerunt*; Philip van Limborch, *Historia inquisitionis*, (Amsterdam: Henrik Wetstein, 1692), 276.

55. Peter Biller, 'Why no food? Waldensian Followers in Bernard Gui's *Practica inquisitionis* and *culpe*', *Texts and the Repression of Medieval Heresy*, ed. Bruschi and Biller, 127.

56. John Bellamy, *The Tudor Law of Treason* (London: Routledge & Kegan Paul, 1979), 108.

57. G. R. Elton, *The Tudor Constitution: Documents and Commentary* (Cambridge: Cambridge University Press, 1975), 424–7.

58. Spence, *Treason by the Book*, 11.

59. Bellamy, *Tudor Law of Treason*, 145.

60. Bellamy, *Tudor Law of Treason*, 152.

61. Thomas Bayly Howell, *Complete Collection of State Trials and Proceedings for High Treason*, 21 vols. (London: Longman etc., 1816), ii. 870.

62. *Letters of John Chamberlain*, ed. N. E. McClure, 2 vols. (Philadelphia: American Philosophical Society, 1939), i. 616.

63. Letter of Sir Ralph Winwood, 18 January 1615; *Acts of the Privy Council*, 34 (1542–1631), 17.

64. Christopher Hill, *The English Bible and the Seventeenth-century Revolution* (London: Penguin Books, 1993), 67.

65. Howell, *State Trials*, ii. 871.

66. Todd Butler, 'The Cognitive Politics of Writing in Jacobean England: Bacon, Coke, and the Case of Edmund Peacham', *Huntington Library Quarterly*, 78 (2015), 21–39.

67. Lisa Jardine and Alan Stewart, *Hostage to Fortune: the Troubled Life of Francis Bacon 1561–1626* (London: Phoenix Books, 1999), 357.

68. Howell, *State Trials*, ii. 878.

69. Peters, *Torture*, 67–8.

70. Barrell, *Imagining the King's Death: Figurative Treason, Fantasies of Regicide, 1793–1796* (Oxford: Oxford University Press, 2000), 68–9.

71. 'An awkward case', *The Economist*, 29 November, 2001.

72. Scarry, *The Body in Pain: the Making and Unmaking of the World* (Oxford: Oxford University Press, 1987), 27.

73. Montaigne, 'Of Books'; *Complete Essays*, 360.

74. Locke, *Essay Concerning Human Understanding*, II. i§2; ed. Nidditch, 104.

75. Sterne, *Tristram Shandy*, vi. 146.

76. Sterne, *Tristram Shandy*, vi. 71.

77. Aristotle, *De anima*, 429^{b}30–30^{a}2.

78. Diogenes Laertius, *Lives of Eminent Philosophers*, 7. 46.

79. Frampton, *Empire of Letters*, 85–6.

80. 'For the day of the celebration of my birthday, I give you a warm invitation to make sure that you come to us'; http://vindolanda.csad.ox.ac.uk/.

81. Cicero, *De oratore*, 2. 86.

82. Martial, *Epigrams*, 14. 7.

83. Avicenna, *Kitāb al-Šifāʾ, Avicenna's De anima*, ed. F. Rahman (New York: Oxford University Press, 1959), 249.

84. 'like a clean slate on which nothing is written'; Aquinas, *Summa theologiae*, 1a. 101. 1.

85. Aquinas, *Summa theologiae*, 1a. 110. 2.

86. Margaret A. Boden, *Computer Models of Mind: Computational Approaches in Theoretical Psychology* (Cambridge: Cambridge University Press, 1988), 187.

87. Freud, *An Outline of Psychoanalysis*, New Penguin Freud, 176.

88. 'Note on the "Magic Notepad"', *Penguin Freud Reader*, ed. Phillips, 102.

89. 'Note on the "Magic Notepad"', *Penguin Freud Reader*, ed. Phillips, 105.

90. Job 19: 24.

91. Lily E. Kay, 'A Book of Life? How the Genome Became an Information System and DNA a Language', *Perspectives in Biology and Medicine*, 41(1998), 504–28.

92. Erasmus, *Adagia*, III. i. 1; CWE 34. 172.

93. 'the course of learning which the Greeks call *enkyklios paideia*; Quintilian, *Institutio oratoria* 1. 10. 1.

94. *universum flumen*; Cicero, *De oratore*, 2. 39.

95. Rabelais, *Pantagruel*, XX; *Oeuvres complètes*, 290.

96. Poe, 'The Fall of the House of Usher', *Burton's Gentleman's Magazine* (September 1839).

97. *The Encyclopedia of Diderot & d'Alembert Collaborative Translation Project*, tr. Philip Stewart (Ann Arbor: University of Michigan Library, 2002); https://quod.lib.umich.edu/cgi/t/text/.

98. https://en.wikipedia.org/wiki/Encyclopedia#cite_note-7.

99. Israel, *Radical Enlightenment*, 124–5.

100. Chartier, *The Order of Books*, 62.

101. Diderot and D'Alembert, *Encyclopédie, ou dictionnaire raisonné des sciences, des arts et des métiers*, ed. Robert Morrissey (University of Chicago: ARTFL Encyclopédie Project, 2011), ix. 609; http://encyclopedie.uchicago.edu.

102. Frierson and Guyer, Introduction to Kant's *Observations*, p. vii; the phrase *alles zermalmender Kant* originates with Moses Mendelssohn in 1785.

103. Levi, *If This is a Man*, 118.

104. Dante, *Inferno*, 26. 88–9.

105. Levi, *Se questo è un uomo*, 98.

106. Levi, *If This is a Man*, 119.

107. Dante, *Inferno*, 26. 142.

108. Adorno, 'Cultural Criticism and Society', *Prisms*, 34.

109. Adorno, *Negative Dialectics*, 362.

110. Mallarmé, *Quant au livre* (Périgueux: Art et Arts, 2010), 16.

111. Mallarmé, *Oeuvres complètes*, ed. Bernard Marchal, 2 vols., Bibliothèque de la Pléiade (Paris: Gallimard, 1998), i. 369–87.

112. Mallarmé, *Quant au livre*, 18; see also Oeuvres complètes, ii.225.

113. More, *Utopia, Complete Works*, iv. 18–19.

114. Weingreen, *Grammar for Classical Hebrew*, 1; Benjamin Hall Kennedy, *Revised Latin Primer* (London: Longman, 1962), 2.

115. Freud, *Interpretation of Dreams*, 381.

116. Freud, *Interpretation of Dreams*, 433.

117. Freud, *Traumdeutung*, 337; *Interpretation of Dreams*, 457.

118. Lacan, 'The agency of the letter in the unconscious', *Écrits*, 160.

119. Phillips, 'Introduction' to *Penguin Freud Reader*, p. vii.

120. Virgil, *Aeneid*, 7. 312; cited in *Traumdeutung*, 11. Freud reports his intention to use it as a 'motto' to the book in a letter to Fliess, 17 July 1899; *Complete Letters*, 361.

121. Lacan, 'Seminar on the Purloined Letter', *Seminar of Jacques Lacan*, ii. 198.

122. Letter to August Suter, cited in Richard Ellmann, *James Joyce*, 546.

123. Joyce, *Finnegans Wake*, repr. edn. (London: Faber & Faber, 1946), dust jacket.

124. Joyce made a list on the verso of the last page of his manuscript; British Library Additional MS 47488, fo. 180v.

125. Joyce, *Finnegans Wake*, 3.

126. James Joyce, *Finnegans Wake*, 120.

127. James Joyce, *Finnegans Wake*, 120.

128. More, *Dialogue Concerning Heresies*, Collected Works, vi. 144.

129. Lacan, *Écrits*, 159.

130. Joyce, *Finnegans Wake*, 628.

131. Skeat, *An Etymological Dictionary of the English Language*, 4th edn. (Oxford: Clarendon Press, 1910), 1.

132. Joyce to Harriet Shaw Weaver, 21 June 1921; British Library Additional MS 57346.

133. Joyce, *Ulysses*, 25 ('Nestor').

134. The MS variant reads: 'A way a lone \ a lost / a last a loved a long the'; British Library Additional MS 47488, fo. 160r.

135. Joyce, 'The Dead', *Dubliners* (Harmondsworth: Penguin Books, 1974), 189.

136. Coleridge, *Complete Poetical Works*, ed. E. H. Coleridge, 2 vols. (Oxford: Oxford University Press, 1912), i. 297.

137. Joyce, *Ulysses*, 732 ('Penelope').

138. Joyce to Louis Gillet, cited in Gillet, Stèle pour James Joyce (Marseille: Sagittaire, 1941), 164-5; trans. Ellmann, *James Joyce*, 712.

139. Beckett, 'Dante…Bruno. Vico…Joyce', in Our Exagmination Round His Factification for Incamination of Work in Progress (London: Faber & Faber, 1929), 1–22 at 15.

140. Beckett, *Company* (London: James Calder, 1980), 88-9.

Bibliography

Aaij, Michael, 'Boniface's Booklife: How the Ragyndrudis Codex Came to be a *Vita Bonifatii*', *The Heroic Age: A Journal of Early Medieval Northwestern Europe*, 10 (2007), online journal.

Abadi, Martín, and Andersen, David G., 'Learning to Protect Communications with Adversarial Neural Cryptography', *ARXIV*, 2016; www.arxiv.org.

Achinstein, Sharon, *Milton and the Revolutionary Reader* (Princeton, NJ: Princeton University Press, 2014).

Acts of the Privy Council of England, ed. J. R. Dasent (London: HMSO, 1890–1907). [APC]

Adams, J. N., *Bilingualism and the Latin Language* (Cambridge: Cambridge University Press, 2003).

Adams–Jefferson Letters, The: The Complete Correspondence Between Thomas Jefferson and Abigail and John Adams, ed. Lester J. Cappon (Chapel Hill: University of North Carolina Press, 1987).

Adamson, P., and Taylor, R. (eds.), *The Cambridge Companion to Arabic Philosophy* (Cambridge: Cambridge University Press, 2005).

Adorno, Theodor W., *Aesthetic Theory*, tr. Robert Hullot-Kentor (London: Athlone Press, 1997).

Adorno, Theodor W., *Negative Dialectics* (London: Continuum, 2001).

Adorno, Theodor W., *Prisms* (Cambridge, MA: MIT Press, 1983).

Agamben, Giorgio, *The Omnibus Homo Sacer* (Stanford: Stanford University Press, 2017).

Aguilera, M., and Barrios, M., *The Orient in Spain: Converted Muslims, the Forged Lead Books of Granada, and the Rise of Orientalism*, Studies in the History of Religions, 142 (Leiden: Brill, 2013).

Aguilera, M. Barrios, and García-Arenal, M., *Los plomos del Sacromonte. Invención y tesoro* (València: Universidad de València, 2006).

Ahnert, Ruth, *The Rise of Prison Literature in the Sixteenth Century* (Cambridge: Cambridge University Press, 2013).

Aigner, Dietrich, *Die Indizierung schädlichen und unerwünschten Schrifttums im Dritten Reich*, Archiv für Geschichte des Buchwesens, 11 (Frankfurt am Main: Buchhändler Vereinigung, 1971).

Albert-Schulte, H., 'Leibniz and Library Classification', *Journal of Library History*, 6 (1971), 133–52.

Allison, A. F., and Rogers, D. M., *The Contemporary Printed Literature of the English Counter-Reformation Between 1558 and 1640: An Annotated Catalogue*, 2 vols. (Aldershot: Scolar Press, 1989).

Althusser, Louis, and Balibar, Étienne, *Reading Capital*, tr. Ben Brewster (London: Verso, 2009).

Ames, Christine Caldwell, *Medieval Heresies: Christianity, Judaism and Islam* (Cambridge: Cambridge University Press, 2015).

Arasse, Daniel, *The Guillotine and the Terror* (London: Penguin Books, 1989).

Arendt, Hannah, *Eichmann in Jerusalem: A Report on the Banality of Evil* (London: Penguin Books, 2006).

Arendt, Hannah, *On Violence* (San Diego: Harcourt Brace & Co., 1970).

Asher, Frederick, 'From Place to Sight: Locations of the Buddha's Life', *Artibus Asiae*, 69 (2009), 244.

Aston, Margaret, *Broken Idols of the English Reformation* (Cambridge: Cambridge University Press, 2016).

Aston, Margaret, *England's Iconoclasts: Laws Against Images* (Oxford: Clarendon Press, 1988).

Aston, Margaret, *Faith and Fire* (London: Hambledon Press, 1993).

Aston, Margaret, *Lollards and Reformers: Images and Literacy in Late Medieval Religion* (London: Hambledon Press, 1984).

Aston, Sir Thomas, *A remonstrance, against presbytery. Exhibited by divers of the nobilitie, gentrie, ministers and inhabitants of the county Palatine of Chester* (London: John Aston, 1641).

Auden, W. H., *Another Time* (London: Faber and Faber, 1940).

Augustine, *Confessions*, tr. Henry Chadwick (Oxford: Oxford University Press, 1991).

Avicenna, *Kitāb al-Šifāʾ*, *Avicenna's De anima*, ed. F. Rahman (New York: Oxford University Press, 1959).

Bachner, Andrea, *Beyond Sinology: Chinese Writing and the Scripts of Culture* (New York: Columbia University Press, 2014).

Backhouse, Janet, *The Lindisfarne Gospels* (Ithaca, NY: Cornell University Press, 1981).

Bacon, Francis, *The Advancement of Learning*, ed. Michael Kiernan, *The Oxford Francis Bacon, Vol. 4* (Oxford: Oxford University Press, 2000).

Bagnoli, M., Klein, H., Mann C., and Robinson, J. (eds.), *Treasures of Heaven: Saints, Relics and Devotion in Medieval Europe* (London: British Museum, 2010).

Bainton, Roland, *Hunted Heretic: The Life and Death of Michael Servetus, 1511–1553* (Boston: Beacon Books, 1960).

Balbir, Nalini, 'Polysémies: d'une langue à l'autre en Inde ancienne', *Études romanes de Brno*, 35 (2014), 53–79.

Bale, John, *Illustrium majoris Britanniae scriptorum, hoc est, Angliae, Cambriae, ac Scotiae Summarium* (Wesel: John Overton, 1548).

Balogh, Josef, '*Voces Paginarum*: Beiträge zur Geschichte des lauten Lesens und Schreibens', *Philologus*, 82 (1927), 84–109, 202–40.

Bareau, Juliet Wilson, *Goya: Drawings from His Private Albums* (London: Hayward Gallery, 2001).

Barrell, John *Imagining the King's Death: Figurative Treason, Fantasies of Regicide, 1793–1796* (Oxford: Oxford University Press, 2000).

Barrell, John (ed.), *Painting and the Politics of Culture: New Essays on British Art 1700–1850* (Oxford: Oxford University Press, 1992).

Barthel, Thomas, *Grundlagen zur Entzifferung der Osterinselschrift* (Hamburg: de Gruyter, 1958).

Barthel, Thomas, 'Pre-Contact Writing in Oceania', *Current Trends in Linguistics*, 8 (1971), 1165–86.

Barthes, Roland, *Le bruissement de la langue: Essais critiques*, 4 vols. (Paris: Seuil, 1984).

Barthes, Roland, *A Lover's Discourse* (London: Penguin Books, 1990).

Barthes, Roland, *Empire of Signs* (New York: Noonday Press, 1982).

Barthes, Roland, *Image—Music—Text*, tr. Stephen Heath (London: Fontana, 1977).

Barthes, Roland, *Roland Barthes by Roland Barthes* (London: Macmillan, 1977).

Battles, Matthew, *Library: An Unquiet History* (London: William Heinemann, 2003).

Baudelaire, Charles, *Salon de 1846*, ed. David Kelley (Oxford: Oxford University Press, 1974).

Baxter, Richard, *A Christian Directory, or, A Summ of Practical Theologie and Cases of Conscience Directing Christians How to Use their Knowledge and Faith* (London: Robert White, 1673).

Baxter, Richard, *The Certainty of the Worlds of Spirits and, Consequently, of the Immortality of Souls of the Malice and Misery of the Devils and the Damned* (London: T. Parkhurst and J. Salisbury, 1691).

Bayle, Pierre, *Philosophical Commentary*, ed. Knud Haakonssen (Indianapolis: Liberty Fund, 2005).

Beal, Peter, and Griffiths, Jeremy (eds.), *English Manuscript Studies* (New York: Blackwell, 1989–).

Beal, Peter, *Index of English Literary Manuscripts*, 2 vols. (London: Mansell, 1980).

Beard, Mary, 'Cleopatra's Books', *London Review of Books*, 12.3 (8 February 1990), 11.

Beaufort, Hubert de, *Le livre blanc: Une étude exhaustive de l'histoire de l'occupation de Bordeaux* (Paris, 2001).

Beckett, Samuel, *Company* (London: John Calder, 1980).

Beckett, Samuel, 'Dante…Bruno. Vico…Joyce', in *Our Exagmination Round His Factification of Work in Progress* (London: Faber & Faber, 1929), 3–22.

Beckett, Samuel, *L'innommable* (Paris: Éditions de Minuit, 1953).

Beckett, Samuel, *Malone Dies* (New York: Grove Press, 1991).

Becon, Thomas, *The Displaying of the Popish Masse*, repr. edn. (London: Stationers' Company, 1637).

Bede, *Abbots of Wearmouth and Jarrow*, ed. C. W. Grocock and I. N. Woods, Oxford Medieval Texts (Oxford: Oxford University Press, 2013).

Bede, *Ecclesiastical History of the English People*, ed. Bertram Colgrave and R. A. B. Mynors (Oxford: Clarendon Press, 1969).

Bedini, Silvio A., *Thomas Jefferson's Copying Machines* (Charlottesville, VA: University of Virginia Press, 1988).

Behrens-Abouseif, Doris, *The Book in Mamluk Egypt and Syria (1250–1517)*, Islamic History and Civilization, 162 (Leiden: Brill, 2019).

Bellamy, John, *The Tudor Law of Treason* (London: Routledge & Kegan Paul, 1979).

Belting, Hans, *Bild und Kult: eine Geschichte des Bildes vor dem Zeitalter der Kunst* (Munch: C. H. Beck, 1990).

Ben-Dov, M., *Synagogues in Spain* (Tel Aviv: Devir, 1989).

Benedict, Philip, and Scholl, Sarah, 'Religious Heritage and Civic Identity in Geneva', in Brian Cummings, Ceri Law, Karis Riley, and Alexandra Walsham (eds.), *Remembering the Reformation* (London: Routledge, 2020).

Benjamin, Walter, *Gesammelte Schriften*, ed. Rudolf Tiedemann and Hermann Schweppenhäuser, 7 vols. (Frankfurt am Main: Suhrkamp, 1972–99).

Benjamin, Walter, *Illuminations*, tr. Harry Zohn with an intro. by Hannah Arendt (London: Fontana Press, 1973).

Benjamin, Walter, *The Work of Art in the Age of Mechanical Reproduction*, tr. J. A. Underwood (London: Penguin Books, 2008).

Bentham, Jeremy, *The Works of Jeremy Bentham*, ed. John Bowring, 11 vols. (Edinburgh: William Tait, 1838–43).

Bernardo, Aldo, and Levin, Saul, *The Classics in the Middle Ages* (Binghamton, NY: MRTS, 1990).

Bethencourt, Francisco, 'The Auto da Fe: Ritual and Imagery', *Journal of the Warburg and Courtauld Institutes*, 55 (1992), 155–68.

Bethencourt, Francisco, *The Spanish Inquisition: A Global history, 1478–1834* (Cambridge: Cambridge University Press, 2009).

Bevan Zlatar, Antonina, and Timofeeva, Olga (eds.), *What is an Image in Medieval and Early Modern England?* (Tübingen: Narr Francke, 2017).

Bhabha, Homi, *The Location of Culture* (London: Routledge, 1994).

Bhattacharyya, Ashim, *Hindu Dharma: Introduction to Scriptures and Theology* (New York: iUniverse, 2006).

Biller, Peter, and Hudson, Anne (eds.), *Heresy and Literacy 1000–1530* (Cambridge: Cambridge University Press, 1994).

Binkley, Roberta, *Rhetoric Before and Beyond the Greeks* (Albany, NY: SUNY Press, 2004).

Bischoff, Bernhard, *Manuscripts and Libraries in the Age of Charlemagne*, tr. Michael Gorman (Cambridge: Cambridge University Press, 1994).

Black, J., Cunningham, G., Robson, E., and Zólyomi, G. (ed. and tr.), *The Literature of Ancient Sumer* (Oxford: Oxford University Press, 2004).

Black, Jeremy, *Gods, Demons and Symbols of Ancient Mesopotamia* (London: British Museum, 1992).

Black, Joseph L. (ed.), *The Martin Marprelate Tracts* (Cambridge: Cambridge University Press, 2008).

Blades, William, *The Enemies of Books*, rev. edn. (London: E. Stock, 1902).

Blair, Ann M., *Too Much to Know: Managing Scholarly Information Before the Modern Age* (New Haven and London: Yale University Press, 2010).

Blair, Sheila S., *Islamic Calligraphy* (Edinburgh: Edinburgh University Press, 2006).

Blair, Sheila S., *Islamic Inscriptions* (Edinburgh: Edinburgh University Press, 1998).

Blair, Sheila S., *Text and Image in Medieval Persian Art* (Edinburgh: Edinburgh University Press, 2019).

Blayney, Peter W. M., *The First Folio of Shakespeare* (Washington, DC: Folger Shakespeare Library, 1991).

Blayney, Peter W. M., *The Stationers' Company and the Printers of London, 1501–1557*, 2 vols. (Cambridge: Cambridge University Press, 2013).

Bloom, Jonathan, *Paper before Print: The History and Impact of Paper in the Islamic Word* (New Haven and London: Yale University Press, 2001).

Bloom, Jonathan, and Blair. Sheila, *Islamic Arts* (London: Phaidon Press, 1997).

Blum, Rudolf, *Kallimachos: The Alexandrian Library and the Origins of Bibliography*, tr. Hans H. Wellisch (Madison, WI: University of Wisconsin Press, 1991).

Boccaccio, Giovanni, *Il Decamerone di m. Giouanni Boccaccio nouamente corretto con tre nouelle aggiunte* (Venice: house of Aldus Manutius and Andreas Torresanus, 1522).

Boccaccio, Giovanni, *Vite di Dante* (Milan: Mondadori, 2002).

Boccaccio, Giovanni, *Decameron*, tr. Guido Waldmann (Oxford: Oxford World's Classics, 1998).

Boden, Margaret A., *Computer Models of Mind: Computational Approaches in Theoretical Psychology* (Cambridge: Cambridge University Press, 1988).

Boden, Margaret A., *The Creative Mind*, 2nd edn. (London: Routledge, 2003).

Bogdanović, Jelena, 'The Proclamation of the New Covenant: The Pre-Iconoclastic Altar Ciboria in Rome and Constantinople', *Athanor*, 20 (2002), 7–19.

Bolgar, R. R., *The Classical Heritage and its Beneficiaries* (Cambridge: Cambridge University Press, 1977).

Bolter, J. David, *Writing Space: A Hypertext* (Hillsdale: Laurence Erlbaum, 1991).

Bonhoeffer, Dietrich, *Letters and Papers from Prison* (Minneapolis, MN: Fortress Press, 2010).

Bonner, Edward, *A Profitable and Necessarye Doctrine with Certayne Homelyes Adioyned Therunto* (London: John Cawoode, 1555).

Bonnet, Thierry (ed.), *La Carmagnole des muses: l'homme de lettres et l'artiste dans la Révolution* (Paris: Armand Colin, 1988).

Bonney, Richard, *Confronting the Nazi War on Christianity: The Kulturkampf Newsletters, 1936–1939* (London: Peter Lang, 2009).

Book of Changes, tr. Richard Wilhelm and Cary F. Baynes, 2 vols (New York: Pantheon Books, 1950),

Book of Common Prayer: The Texts of 1549, 1559, and 1662, ed. Brian Cummings (Oxford: Oxford University Press, 2010).

Borges, Jorge Luis, *Ficciones* (Caracas: Fundación Biblioteca Ayacuch, 1986).

Borges, Jorge Luis, *La rosa profunda* (Buenos Aires: Emecé, 1975).

Borges, Jorge Luis, *Labyrinths: Selected Stories and Other Writings* (London: Penguin Books, 1970).

Borges, Jorge Luis, *Selected Nonfictions* (London: Penguin Books, 1999).

Borges, Jorge Luis, *The Aleph*, tr. Andrew Hurley (London: Penguin Books, 1998).

Bornkamm, Heinrich, *Luther in Mid-Career 1521–1530* (London: Darton, Longman and Todd, 1983).

Bossy, John, *The English Catholic Community, 1570–1850* (London: Darton, Longman and Todd, 1975).

Bosworth, Edmund, *Historic Cities of the Islamic World* (Leiden: Brill 2007).

Boudalis, Georgios, *The Codex and Crafts in Late Antiquity* (Chicago: University of Chicago Press, 2018).

Bourdieu, Pierre, 'The Forms of Capital', *Handbook of Theory of Research for the Sociology of Education*, ed. John Richardson (Westport, CT: Greenwood Press, 1986), 46–58.

Boutcher, Warren, *The School of Montaigne*, 2 vols. (Oxford: Oxford University Press, 2017).

Bowie, Malcolm, *Lacan* (London: Fontana Press, 1991).

Bowman, F. P., 'Le Sacré Cœur de Marat', *Annales historiques de la Révolution française*, 221 (July–September 1974).

Bown, Matthew, 'Traces of the Holy: The Contemporary Art Work as "*crypto-relic*"', *TLS*, 4 October 2015.

Bracciolini, Poggio, *Two Renaissance Book Hunters: The Letters of Poggius Bracciolini to Nicolaus de Niccolis*, tr. Phyllis Walter Goodhart Gordan (New York: Columbia University Press, 1991).

Bradbury, Ray, *Fahrenheit 451* (London: Flamingo, 1993).

Breay, Claire, and Meehan, Bernard (eds.), *The St Cuthbert Gospel: Studies on the Insular Manuscript of the Gospel of John* (London: British Library, 2015).

Breay, Claire, and Story, Joanna (eds.), *Anglo-Saxon Kingdoms: Art, Word, War* (London: British Library, 2018).

Brecht, Martin, *Martin Luther: His Road to Reformation* (Minneapolis: Fortress Press, 1985).

Brereton, Gareth (ed.), *I am Ashurbanipal, King of the World, King of Assyria* (London: British Museum, 2018).

Briant, Pierre, *From Cyrus to Alexander: A History of the Persian Empire* (Winona Lake, IN: Eisenbrauns, 2002).

Bridle, James, *New Dark Age; Technology and the End of the Future* (London: Verso, 2018).

Brigden, Susan, *London and the Reformation* (Oxford: Clarendon Press, 1989).

Brodhead, Richard H., 'Sparing the Rod: Discipline and Fiction in Antebellum America', *Representations*, 21 (1988), 67–96.

Brown, Michelle P., *The Lindisfarne Gospels: Society, Spirituality & the Scribe* (London: The British Library, 2003).

Brown, Peter, *Augustine of Hippo: A Biography*, rev. edn. (Berkeley and Los Angeles: University of California Press, 2000).

Brown, Peter, *Society and the Holy in Late Antiquity* (London: Faber and Faber, 1982).

Brown, Peter, *The Body and Society: Men, Women, and Sexual Renunciation in Early Christianity* (London: Faber & Faber, 1988).

Brown, Peter, *The Cult of the Saints: Its Rise and Function in Latin Christianity* (London: SCM Press, 1981).

Brown, Peter, *The Rise of Western Christendom: Triumph and Diversity, A.D. 200–1000*, 2nd edn. (Oxford: Wiley-Blackwell, 2013).

Brown, Peter, *The World of Late Antiquity: From Marcus Aurelius to Muhammad* (London: Thames and Hudson, 1971).

Browne, Thomas, *Hydriotaphia, Urne Buriall, or, a Discourse of the Sepulchrall Urnes Late Found in Norfolk* (London: Henry Brome, 1658).

Browning, John, 'Libraries without Walls for Books without Pages', *Wired*, 1 (1 April 1993).

Bruschi, Caterina, and Biller, Peter (eds.), *Texts and the Repression of Medieval Heresy* (Woodbridge: York Medieval Press, 2003).

Bucer, Martin, *Martin Bucer and the Book of Common Prayer*, ed. E. C. Whitaker (Great Wakering: Alcuin Club, 1974).

Buck-Morss, Susan, 'Hegel and Haiti', *Critical Inquiry*, 26 (2000), 821–65.

Bujanda, J. M. de, 'Literary Censorship in Sixteenth-Century Spain', *Canadian Catholic Historical Association*, 38 (1971), 51–63.

Bujanda, J. M. de, Higman, Francis K., and Farge, James K., *Index de l'Université de Paris, 1544, 1545, 1547, 1549, 1551, 1556*, Index des Livres Interdits, 1 (Geneva: Droz, 1985).

Bukreeva, I., *et al.*, 'Virtual Unrolling and Deciphering of Herculaneum Papyri by X-ray phase-contrast tomography', *Scientific Reports*, 6, Article number: 27227 (2016).

Bunge, Mario, 'A General Black-Box Theory', *Philosophy of Science*, 30 (1963), 346–58.

Bunyan, John, *Grace Abounding to the Chief of Sinners*, ed. Roger Sharrock (Oxford: Oxford University Press, 2013).

Burckhardt, Johann Ludwig, *Travels in Arabia* (London: Henry Colburn, 1829).

Burnett, Charles, 'The Legend of the Three Hermes and Abū Maʿshar's *Kitāb al-Ulūf* in the Latin Middle Ages', *Journal of the Warburg and Courtauld Institutes*, 39 (1976), 231–4.

Burnyeat, M. F., 'Postscript on Silent Reading', *Classical Quarterly*, NS 47 (1997), 74–6.

Butler, Alfred J., *The Arab Conquest of Egypt* (Oxford: Clarendon Press, 1902).

Butler, Beverley, *Return to Alexandria: An Ethnography of Cultural Heritage Revivalism and Museum Memory* (London: Routledge, 2016).

Butler, Judith, 'Foucault and the Paradox of Bodily Inscriptions', *The Journal of Philosophy*, 86 (1989), 601–607.

Butler, Shane, *The Hand of Cicero* (London: Routledge, 2002).

Butler, Todd, 'The Cognitive Politics of Writing in Jacobean England: Bacon, Coke, and the Case of Edmund Peacham', *Huntington Library Quarterly*, 78 (2015), 21–39.

Calasso, Roberto, *Ka: Stories of the Mind and Gods of India* (London: Jonathan Cape, 1998).

Calendar of State Papers, Domestic Series, of the Reigns of Edward VI, Mary, Elizabeth and James I, ed. R. Lemon and M. A. E. Green (London: HMSO, 1856–72). [CSPD]

Calendar of State Papers and Manuscripts, Relating to English Affairs, Existing in the Archives and Collections of Venice ed. R. Brown *et al.*Click here to enter text. (London: Public Record Office, 1865–1947). [CSPV]

Calkins, Robert G., *Illuminated Books of the Middle Ages* (Ithaca, NY: Cornell University Press, 1983).

Callimachus, *The Fragments of Callimachus*, ed. R. Pfeiffer (Oxford: Clarendon Press, 1949).

Calmar, Jonsson, *Der Vertraute Gustav Adolphs des Großen* (Nuremberg: Korn, 1838).

Calvin, Jean, *Déclaration pour maintenir la vraye foy que tiennent tous Chrestiens de la Trinité des persones en un seul Dieu* (Geneva: Robert Estienne, 1554).

Calvin, Jean, *Defensio Orthodoxae Fidei de Sacra Trinitate*, ed. Joy Kleinstuber (Geneva: Droz, 2009).

Calvin, Jean, *Opera selecta*, ed. P. Barth and W. Niesel, 2nd edn., 5 vols. (Munich: C. Kaiser, 1957–9).

Calvin, Jean, *Three French Treatises*, ed. Francis M. Higman (London: The Athlone Press, 1970).

Calvin, Jean, *Institutes of the Christian Religion*, ed. J. T. McNeil, tr. F. L. Battles, 2 vols. (Philadelphia: Westminster Press, 1960).

Calvino, Italo, *If on a winter's night a traveller* (London: Picador, 1982).

Camden, William, *Annales rerum Anglicarum et Hibernicarum*, 3 vols. (Oxford: Thomas Hearne, 1717).

Cameron, Euan, *Enchanted Europe: Superstition, Reason and Religion, 1250–1750* (Oxford: Oxford University Press, 2010).

Cameron, Euan, *The European Reformation* (Oxford: Oxford University Press, 1991).

Cameron, Euan, (ed.), *New Cambridge History of the Bible, Vol. 3: From 1450 to 1750* (Cambridge: Cambridge University Press, 2016).

Campanelli, Maurizio, 'Marsilio Ficino's Portrait of Hermes Trismegistus and its Afterlife', *Intellectual History Review*, 29 (2019), 53–71.

Canetti, Elias, *Auto-da-Fé* (London: Jonathan Cape, 1971).

Canfora, Luciano, *The Vanished Library: A Wonder of the Ancient World* (Berkeley and Los Angeles: University of California Press, 1990).

Caplan, Jane (ed.), *Written on the Body: The Tattoo in European and American History* (London: Reaktion Books, 2000).

Carleton Paget, James, and Schaper, Joachim (eds.), *New Cambridge History of the Bible, Vol. 1: From the Beginnings to 600* (Cambridge: Cambridge University Press, 2013).

Carley, James, *The Books of Henry VIII and his Wives* (London: British Library, 2004).

Carley, James, 'The Libraries of Archbishops Whitgift and Bancroft', *The Book Collector*, 62 (2013), 209–27.

Carr, Nicholas, *The Shallows: How the Internet is Changing the Way we Think, Read and Remember* (London: W. W. Norton, 2010).

Carroll, Maureen, *Spirits of the Dead: Roman Funerary Commemoration in Western Europe* (Oxford: Oxford University Press, 2006).

Carruthers, Mary, *The Book of Memory: A Study of Memory in Medieval Culture* (Cambridge: Cambridge University Press, 1990).

Caruth, Cathy, 'Interview with Gayatri Spivak', *PMLA*, 125 (2010), 1020–25.

Cassiodorus, *Institutiones*, ed. R. A. B. Mynors (Oxford: Clarendon Press, 1937).

Cassiodorus, *Introduction to Divine and Human Readings*, tr. L. W. Jones (New York: Columbia University Press, 1946).

Castellio, Sebastian, *Contra libellum Calvini*, ed. Uwe Plath (Geneva: Droz, 2019).

Castellio, Sebastian, *De arte dubitandi et confidendi, ignorandi et sciendi*, ed. Elisabeth Feist-Hirsch (Leiden: Brill, 1981).

Castiglione, Baldassare, *The Book of the Courtier*, tr. Sir Thomas Hoby (London: Everyman Books, 1903).

Cavallo, Guglielmo, and Chartier, Roger (eds.), *A History of Reading in the West* (Amherst: University of Massachusetts Press, 1999).

Celan, Paul, *Gedichte*, 2 vols. (Frankfurt am Main: Suhrkamp, 1981).

Celan, Paul, *Gesammelte Werke*, ed. Beda Allemann and Stefan Reichert, 7 vols. (Frankfurt am Main: Surhrkamp, 1986).

Celan, Paul, *Collected Prose*, tr. Rosemarie Waldrop (New York: Sheep Meadow Press, 1986).

Celan, Paul, *Selected Poems*, tr. Michael Hamburger (London: Penguin Books, 1996).

Cellini, Benvenuto, *Autobiography*, tr. George Bull (Harmondsworth: Penguin Books, 1978).

Certeau, Michel de, *L'invention du quotidien. 1 Arts de faire*, 2nd edn. (Paris: Gallimard, 1990).

Certeau, Michel de, *The Practice of Everyday Life* (Berkeley and Los Angeles, 2011).

Cesarini, David, *Final Solution: The Fate of the Jews, 1933–49* (London: Pan Macmillan, 2016).

Chabert, Jean-Luc, *A History of Algorithms: From the Pebble to the Microchip* (New York: Springer, 2012).

Chadwick, Henry, *The Early Church* (London: Penguin Books, 1993).

Chamberlain, John, *Letters*, ed. N. E. McClure, 2 vols. (Philadelphia: American Philosophical Society, 1939).

Champion, Matthew, *Medieval Graffiti: The Lost Voices of England's Churches* (New York: Random House, 2015).

Champlin, Edward, 'Serenus Sammonicus', *Harvard Studies in Classical Philology*, 85 (1981), 189–212.

Champollion, Jean-François, *Lettres et journaux écrits pendant le voyage d'Égypte*, ed. H. Hartleben (Paris: Christian Bourgeois, 1986).

Champollion, Jean-François, *Précis du système hiéroglyphique des anciens Égyptiens, ou, Recherches sur les élémens premiers de cette écriture sacrée*, rev. edn. (Paris: Imprimerie Royale, 1827).

Champollion, Jean-François, *Journey to Egypt* (London: Gibson Square, 2019).

Chan, Lois Mai, 'The Burning of the Books in China, 213 B.C.', *The Journal of Library History*, 7 (1972), 101–8.

Chartier, Roger, *Forms and Meanings: Texts, Performances, and Audiences from Codex to Computer* (Philadelphia: University of Pennsylvania Press, 1995).

Chartier, Roger, 'Leisure and Sociability: Reading Aloud in Early Modern Europe', *Urban Life in the Renaissance*, ed. Susan Zimmermann and Ronald F. E. Weissman (Toronto: University of Toronto Press, 1989), 103–20.

Chartier, Roger, *The Cultural Origins of the French Revolution* (Durham, NC: Duke University Press, 1991).

Chartier, Roger, *The Order of Books: Readers, Authors, and Libraries in Europe between the Fourteenth and Eighteenth Centuries* (Cambridge: Polity Press, 1994).

Chauvet, S.-C., *L'île de Pâques et ses mystères* (Paris: Éditions Tel, 1935).

Chiavazzo, Bruno, *Da Gutenberg a Zuckerberg: la rivoluzione della communicazione* (Milton Keynes: Lightning Source, 2018).

Childs, Elizabeth C. (ed.), *Suspended License: Censorship and the Visual Arts* (Seattle: University of Washington Press, 1997).

Chomarat, Jacques, 'Les Annotations de Valla, celles d'Érasme et la grammaire', in O. Fatio and P. Fraenkel (eds.), *Histoire de l'exégèse au XVIe siècle* (Geneva: Droz, 1978), 202–28.

Chomsky, Noam, *Syntactic Structures* (Berlin: de Gruyter, 1957).

Chrystys, Ann, *Christians in Al-Andalus, 711–1000* (London: Routledge, 2002).

Clanchy, Michael, *Abelard: A Medieval Life* (Oxford: Blackwell, 1999).

Clanchy, Michael, *From Memory to Written Record*, 3rd edn. (Oxford: Blackwell, 2012).

Claretie, Jules, *Camille Desmoulins and His Wife: Passages from the History of the Dantonists* (London: Smith, Elder, & Co., 1876).

Clark, Andy, and Chalmers, David J., 'The Extended Mind', *Analysis*, 58 (1998), 7–19.

Clark, T. J., 'Painting in the Year Two', *Representations*, 47, Special Issue: *National Cultures before Nationalism* (Summer, 1994), 13–63.

Clarke, Desmond M., *Descartes: A Biography* (Cambridge: Cambridge University Press, 2006).

Clayton, Ewan (ed.), *Writing: Making Your Mark* (London: British Library, 2019).

Clendinnen, Inga, *Ambivalent Conquests: Maya and Spaniard in Yucatan, 1517–1570*, 2nd edn. (Cambridge: Cambridge University Press, 2003).

Clover, Carol, and Lindow, John (eds.), *Old Norse-Icelandic Literature* (Toronto: University of Toronto Press, 2005).

Clunas, Craig, *Art in China* (Oxford: Oxford University Press, 1997).

Cobo, Bernabé, *Inca Religion and Customs*, tr. Roland Hamilton (Austin: University of Texas Press, 2010).

Coe, Michael D., *Breaking the Mayan Code* (London: Thames & Hudson, 1992).

Coffey, John, *Persecution and Toleration in Protestant England 1558–1689* (London: Routledge, 2014).

Coleridge, Samuel Taylor, *Biographia Literaria*, ed. J. Shawcross, 2 vols. (Oxford: Oxford University Press, 1907).

Coleridge, Samuel Taylor, *Complete Poetical Works*, ed. E. H. Coleridge, 2 vols. (Oxford: Oxford University Press, 1912).

Colish, Marcia L., *Medieval Foundations of the Western Intellectual Tradition, 400–1400* (New Haven and London: Yale University Press, 1999).

Collinson, Patrick, *From Iconoclasm to Iconophobia: The Cultural Impact of the Second English Reformation,* Stenton Lectures, 19 (Reading: Reading University Press, 1986).

Como, David R., 'Secret Printing, the Crisis of 1640, and the Origins of Civil War Radicalism', *Past and Present*, 196 (2007), 37–82.

Condorcet, Nicolas de Caritat, marquis de, *Œuvres* (Stuttgart: Friedrich Fromann Verlag, 1968).

Confucius, *The Analects*, tr. Annping Chin (London: Penguin Books, 2014).

Contreni, John J., *Carolingian Learning, Masters and Manuscripts* (Brookfield, VT: Variorum, 1992).

Cook, Alexander C., *Mao's Little Red Book: A Global History* (Cambridge: Cambridge University Press, 2014).

Cook, James, *A Voyage to the Pacific Ocean*, 4 vols. (London: Champante and Whitrow, 1793).

Cook, Michael, *The Koran: A Very Short Introduction* (Oxford: Oxford University Press, 2000).

Cooley, Alison E., *The Cambridge Manual of Latin Epigraphy* (Cambridge: Cambridge University Press, 2012).

Cope, Bill, and Phillips, Angus (eds.), *The Future of the Book in the Digital Age* (Oxford: Chandos Publishing, 2006).

Cormack, Robin, and Vassilaki, Maria (eds.), *Byzantium 330–1453* (London: Royal Academy of Arts, 2008).

Cornelius, Janet Duitsman, *When I Can Read My Title Clear: Literacy, Slavery, and Religion in the Antebellum South* (Columbia, SC: University of South Carolina Press, 1991).

Cressy, David, 'Book Burning in Tudor and Stuart England', *The Sixteenth Century Journal*, 36 (2005), 359–74.

Cressy, David, 'Books as Totems in Seventeenth-Century England and New England', *Journal of Library History*, 21 (1986), 92–106.

Creswell, K. A. C., *A Short Account of Early Muslim Architecture*, rev. James W. Allan (Aldershot: Scolar Press, 1989).

Croft, William, and Cruse, Alan, *Cognitive Linguistics* (Cambridge: Cambridge University Press, 2004).

Crouzet, Denis, *Les guerriers de Dieu: la violence au temps des troubles de religion, vers 1525 – vers 1610*, 2 vols. (Seyssel: Champ Vallon, 1990).

Crow, Thomas, *Emulation: Making Artists for Revolutionary France* (New Haven: Yale University Press, 1995).

Culler, Jonathan, 'The Closeness of Close Reading', *ADE Bulletin*, 149 (2010), 20–5.

Cummings, Brian, 'Autobiography and the History of Reading', *Cultural Reformations: Medieval and Renaissance in Literary History*, ed. Brian Cummings and James Simpson (Oxford: Oxford University Press, 2010).

Cummings, Brian, *The Book of Common Prayer: A Very Short Introduction* (Oxford: Oxford University Press, 2018).

Cummings, Brian, *The Literary Culture of the Reformation: Grammar and Grace* (Oxford: Oxford University Press, 2002).

Cummings, Brian, *Mortal Thoughts* (Oxford: Oxford University Press, 2013).

Cummings, Brian, 'Shakespeare and the Inquisition', *Shakespeare Survey*, 65 (2012), 306–22.

Curtius, Ernst Robert, *European Literature and the Latin Middle Ages* (New York: Bollingen, 1953).

Dahm, Volker, *Das jüdische Buch im Dritten Reich*, 2 vols. (Frankfurt am Main: C. H. Beck, 1979).

Dalrymple, William, *From the Holy Mountain* (London: Flamingo Books, 2000).

Daly, Gay, *The Pre-Raphaelites in Love* (London: Orion, 1988).

Daniell, David, *The Bible in English* (New Haven and London: Yale University Press, 2003).

Daniels, Peter T., 'Fundamentals of Grammatology', *Journal of the American Oriental Society*, 110 (1990), 727–31.

Daniels, Peter T., and Bright, William (eds.), *The World's Writing Systems* (New York: Oxford University Press, 1996).

Dante, *Divina Commedia*, ed. Natalino Sapegno, 3 vols. (Florence: Nuova Italia, 1956–7).

Darnton, Robert, and Roche, Daniel (eds.), *Revolution in Print: The Press in France, 1775–1800* (Berkeley and Los Angeles, CA: University of California Press, 1989).

Darnton, Robert, *A Literary Tour de France: The World of Books on the Eve of the French Revolution* (Oxford: Oxford University Press, 2018).

Darnton, Robert, *Poetry and the Police: Communication Networks in Eighteenth-Century France* (Cambridge, MA: Harvard University Press, 2010).

Darnton, Robert, *The Business of Enlightenment: A Publishing History of the Encyclopédie, 1775–1800* (Cambridge, MA: Harvard University Press, 1987).

Darnton, Robert, *The Forbidden Best-Sellers of Pre-Revolutionary France* (New York: W. W. Norton, 1996).

Darwin, Charles, *On the Origin of Species by Means of Natural Selection, or the Preservation of Favoured Races in the Struggle for Life* (London: John Murray, 1859).

Davies, Jonathan (ed.), *Aspects of Violence in Renaissance Europe* (London: Routledge, 2016).

Davies, Martin, *Aldus Manutius: Printer and Publisher of Renaissance Venice* (London: British Library, 1997).

Davies, Martin, *The Gutenberg Bible* (London: British Library, 1997).

Davis, Dick (ed.), *Shahnameh: The Persian Book of Kings* (New York: Viking, 2006).

Davis, Natalie Zemon, *Society and Culture in Early Modern France* (Stanford, CA: Stanford University Press, 1975).

Davis, Natalie Zemon, *The Gift in Sixteenth-Century France* (Oxford: Oxford University Press, 2000).

Davis, Natalie Zemon, *Trickster Travels: The Search for Leo Africanus* (London: Faber & Faber, 2008).

Day, W. G., 'Recirculated Material in an Eighteenth-Century Library', in A. Fenneteaux, A. Junqua, and S. Vasset (eds.), *The Afterlife of Used Things* (London: Routledge, 2014), 169–83.

Defoe, Daniel, *A Journal of the Plague Year* (London: E. Nutt, 1722).

DeFrancis, John, *Nationalism and Language Reform in China* (Princeton: Princeton University Press, 1950).

Deroche, François, *Qur'ans of the Umayyads: A First Overview*, Leiden Studies in Islam and Society (Leiden: Brill, 2013).

Derrida, Jacques, *De la grammatologie* (Paris: Éditions de Minuit, 1967).

Derrida, Jacques, *Glas* (Paris: Galilée, 1974).

Derrida, Jacques, *La dissémination* (Paris: Éditions du Seuil, 1972).

Derrida, Jacques, *Marges de la philosophie* (Paris: Éditions de Minuit, 1972).

Derrida, Jacques, *Schibolleth: pour Paul Celan* (Paris: Galilée, 1986).

Derrida, Jacques, *Dissemination*, tr. Barbara Johnson (Chicago: University of Chicago Press, 1981).

Derrida, Jacques, *Of Grammatology*, tr. Gyatri Chakravorty Spivak (Baltimore: Johns Hopkins University Press, 1976).

Derrida, Jacques, *Speech and Phenomena: And Other Essays on Husserl's Theory of Signs*, tr. David Allison (Evanston, IL: Northwestern University Press, 1973).

Derrida, Jacques, *The Post Card: From Socrates to Freud and Beyond*, tr. Alan Bass (Chicago: University of Chicago Press, 1987).

Derrida, Jacques, *Writing and Difference*, tr. Alan Bass (Chicago: University of Chicago Press, 1978).

Desmoulins, Camille, *Le Vieux Cordelier*, ed. Henri Calvet (Paris: Armand Colin, 1936).

Díaz del Castillo, Bernal, *The Conquest of New Spain* (Harmondsworth: Penguin Books, 1973).

Dickinson, Emily, *Complete Poems*, ed. Thomas H. Johnson (London: Faber, 1970).

Diderot, Denis, *Lettres à Sophie Volland*, 3 vols. (Paris: NRF, 1930).

Diderot, Denis, and Alembert, Jean le Rond d' (ed.), *Encyclopédie, ou dictionnaire raisonné des sciences, des arts et des métiers* (University of Chicago: ARTFL Encyclopédie Project, 2011).

Dill, Uelli, and Schierli, Petra, *Das bessere Bild Christi: Das Neue Testament in der Ausgabe des Erasmus von Rotterdam* (Basel: Schwabe Verlag, 2016).

Directory for the publique worship of God, throughout the three kingdoms of England, Scotland, and Ireland (London: Ralph Smith and John Field, 1644).

Dodds, Jerrilynn D. (ed.), *Al-Andalus: the Art of Islamic Spain* (New York, 1992).

Dodds, Jerrilynn D. (ed.), *The Art of Medieval Spain, 500–1200* (New York: Metropolitan Museum of Art, 1993).

Dodds, Jerrilynn D., Mann, Vivian B., and Glick, Thomas F. (eds.), *Convivencia: Jews, Muslims, and Christians in Spain* (New York: G. Braziller, 1992).

Don, Patricia Lopes, *Bonfires of Culture: Franciscans, Indigenous Leaders, and Inquisition in Early Mexico, 1524–1540* (Norman, OK: University of Oklahoma Press, 2010).

Donahue, William Collins, *The End of Modernism: Canetti's Auto da fé* (Chapel Hill, NC: University of North Carolina Press, 2001).

Donald, Merlin, *Origins of the Modern Mind: Three Stages in the Evolution of Culture and Cognition* (Cambridge, MA: Harvard University Press, 1991).

Donne, John, *Satires, Epigrams, and Verse Letters*, ed. Walter Milgate (Oxford: Clarendon Press, 1967).

Donoghue, Daniel, *How the Anglo-Saxons Read Their Poems* (Philadelphia: University of Pennsylvania Press, 2018).

Douglas, Mary, *Leviticus as Literature* (Oxford: Oxford University Press, 1999).

Douglas, Mary, *Natural Symbols*, 2nd edn. (London: Routledge, 1996).

Douglas, Mary, *Purity and Danger: An Analysis of Concepts of Pollution and Taboo* (London: Routledge & Kegan Paul, 1966).

Douwers Dekker, Eduard [Multatuli], *Max Havelaar, of de koffi-veilingen der Nederlandsche Handel-Maatschappy* (Amsterdam: J. de Ruyter, 1860).

Doyle, William, *The Oxford History of the French Revolution* (Oxford: Oxford University Press, 1990).

Draguet, Michel, *Magritte: son œuvre, son musée* (Paris: Hazan, 2009).

Drayson, Elizabeth, *The Lead Books of Granada* (Houndsmill: Palgrave Macmillan, 2013).

Dronke, Peter, *Women Writers of the Middle Ages* (Cambridge: Cambridge University Press, 1984).

Dudbridge, Glen, *Lost Books of Medieval China*, Panizzi Lectures, 15 (London: British Library, 2000).

Duffy, Eamon, *Marking the Hours: English People and their Prayers* (New Haven and London: Yale University Press, 2011).

Duffy, Eamon, *The Stripping of the Altars: Traditional Religion in England, 1400–1580*, 2nd edn. (New Haven and London: Yale University Press, 2005).

Duncan, Dennis, *et al.*, *Babel: Adventures in Translation* (Oxford: Bodleian Library, 2019).

Duncan, Dennis, and Smyth, Adam (eds.), *Book Parts* (Oxford: Oxford University Press, 2019).

Dunn, John, *The Political Theory of John Locke* (Cambridge: Cambridge University Press, 1969).

Dupront, A., 'Pèlerinage et lieux sacrés', *Mélanges offerts à Fernand Braudel*, 2 vols. (Toulouse: Privat, 1973), 189–206.

Durkheim, Émile, *Les formes élémentaires de la vie religieuse* (Paris: Félix Alcan, 1912).

Durkin-Meisterernst, Desmond, 'Manichean Script', *Encyclopaedia Iranica* (14 October 2005).

Dyck, Jonathan E., *The Theocratic Ideology of the Chronicler* (Leiden: Brill, 1998).

Eco, Umberto, *Il nome della rosa* (Milan: Bompiani, 1980).

Eden, Kathy, *The Renaissance Rediscovery of Intimacy* (Chicago: University of Chicago Press, 2012).

Edwards, Charles S., *Hugo Grotius, Miracle of Holland* (Chicago: Nelson Hall, 1981).

Edzard, D. O., *Gudea and his Dynasty*, Royal Inscriptions of Mesopotamia: Early Periods (Toronto: University of Toronto Press, 1997).

Eichrodt, Walther, *Theology of the Old Testament*, 2 vols. (London: SCM, 1961).

Eire, Carlos, 'The Reformation Critique of the Image', in Bob Scribner (ed.), *Bilder und Bildersturm im Spätmittelalter und in der frühen Neuzeit*, Wolfenbütteler Forschungen, 46 (Wiesbaden: Harrassowitz, 1990), 50–67.

Eire, Carlos, *War Against the Idols: The Reformation of Worship from Erasmus to Calvin* (Cambridge: Cambridge University Press, 1986).

Eisenstein, Elizabeth, *The Printing Press as an Agent of Change: Communications and Cultural Transformations in Early Modern Europe*, 2 vols. (Cambridge: Cambridge University Press, 1980).

El-Abbadi, Mostafa, *The Life and Fate of the Ancient Library of Alexandria* (Paris: UNESCO, 1996).

Eliot, George, *Middlemarch*, ed. Rosemary Ashton (London: Penguin Books, 1994).

Eliot, George, *The Mill on the Floss*, ed. A. S. Byatt (London: Penguin Books, 2003).

Eliot, Simon, and Rose, Jonathan (eds.), *A Companion to the History of the Book* (Malden, MA: Wiley, 2007).

Eliot, Simon, Nash, Andrew, and Willison, Ian (eds.), *Literary Cultures and the Material Book* (London: British Library, 2007).

Ellayan, Ribhi Mustafa, 'The History of the Arabic–Islamic Libraries, 7th–14th Centuries', *International Library Review*, 22 (1990), 119–35.

Ellmann, Richard, *James Joyce* (Oxford: Oxford University Press, 1992).

Elton, G. R., *Policy and Police: The Enforcement of the Reformation in the Age of Thomas Cromwell* (Cambridge: Cambridge University Press, 1985).

Elton, G. R., *The Tudor Constitution: Documents and Commentary* (Cambridge: Cambridge University Press, 1975).

Empson, Wiliam, *Seven Types of Ambiguity* (Harmondsworth: Pelican Books, 1977).

Epic of Gilgamesh, The, tr. Andrew George (London: Penguin Books, 1999).

Epstein, Edward Jay, *How America Lost Its Secrets: Edward Snowden, the Man and the Theft* (New York: Alfred A. Knopf, 2017).

Erasmus, Desiderius, *Adagiorum chiliades* (Basel: Johannes Froben, 1515).

Erasmus, Desiderius, *Opus Epistolarum*, ed. P. S. Allen, 12 vols. (Oxford: Clarendon Press, 1906–58).

Erasmus, Desiderius, *Erasmi opuscula*, ed. W. K. Ferguson (The Hague: Martinus Nijhoff, 1933).

Erasmus, Desiderius, *Novum instrumentum omne* (Basel: Johannes Froben, 1516).

Erasmus, Desiderius, *A playne and godly exposytion or declaration of the commune crede* (London: Robert Redman, 1534).

Erasmus, Desiderius, *Adages*, tr. William Barker (Toronto: University of Toronto Press, 2001).

Erasmus, Desiderius, *Collected Works of Erasmus*, 89 vols. (Toronto: University of Toronto Press, 1974–). [CWE]

Erasmus, Desiderius, *Praise of Folly*, tr. Hoyt Hudson (Princeton: Princeton University Press, 2015).

Erickson, John D., *Islam and Postcolonial Narrative* (Cambridge: Cambridge University Press, 1990).

Eusebius, *Life of Constantine*, tr. Averil Cameron and S. G. Hunt (Oxford: Oxford University Press, 1999).

Evans, Arthur J., *Scripta Minoa* (Oxford: Clarendon Press, 1909).

Evans, Richard J., *The Third Reich in Power, 1933–1939* (London: Penguin Books, 2006).

Evelein, Johannes, *Literary Exiles from Nazi Germany: Exemplarity and the Search for Meaning* (London: Boydell & Brewer, 2014).

Farmer, D. H. (ed.), *The Age of Bede* (London: Penguin Books, 2004).

Farr, Carol, *The Book of Kells: Its Function and Audience* (London: British Library, 1997).

Febvre, Lucien, and Martin, Henri-Jean, *The Coming of the Book: The Impact of Printing* (London: Verso, 1997).

Fernández-Armesto, Felipe, *Reformation* (London: Bantam Books, 1996).

Fierro, Maribel (ed.), *New Cambridge History of Islam, Vol. 2: The Western Islamic World, Eleventh to Eighteenth Centuries* (Cambridge: Cambridge University Press, 2010).

Finkel, I. L., and Seymour, M. J. (eds.), *Babylon: Myth and Reality* (London: British Museum, 2008).

Finkel, Irving, and Taylor, Jonathan, *Cuneiform* (London: The British Museum Press, 2015).

Finkelstein, David, and McCleery, Alistair (eds.), *The Book History Reader*, 2nd edn. (London: Routledge, 2006).

Finley, Moses I., *The World of Odysseus* (London: Viking Press, 1954).

Fischer, Steven Roger, *A History of Reading* (London: Reaktion Books, 2004).

Fischer, Steven Roger, *RongoRongo, the Easter Island Script: History, Traditions, Texts* (Oxford: Oxford University Press, 1997).

Fishman, Talya, *Becoming the People of the Talmud: Oral Torah as Written Tradition in Medieval Jewish Cultures* (Philadelphia: University of Pennsylvania Press, 2013).

Fitzgerald, F. Scott, 'Pasting it Together', *Esquire* (April 1936), 78.

Fitzherbert, John, *Here begynneth a ryght frutefull mater: and hath to name the boke of surueyeng and improumentes* (London: Rycharde Pynson, 1523).

Flaubert, Gustave, *Madame Bovary: Provincial Manners*, tr. Margaret Mauldon (Oxford: Oxford World's Classics, 2004).

Fleet, Kate, *et al.* (eds.), *Encyclopaedia of Islam*, 3rd edn. (Leiden: Brill, 2017).

Fleischmann, John, *Free & Public: 150 Years at the Public Library of Cincinnati* (Cincinnati: Public Library, 2002).

Fleming, Juliet, *Graffiti and the Writing Arts of Early Modern England* (London: Reaktion Books, 2011).

Flood, Finbarr Barry, *The Great Mosque of Damascus: Studies on the Makings of an Umayyad Visual Culture*, Islamic History and Civilization, 33 (Leiden: Brill, 2001).

Fogelin, Lars, *Archaeology of Early Buddhism* (London: Rowman & Littlefield, 2006).

Foley, Henry, *Records of the English Province of the Society of Jesus*, 7 vols. in 8 parts (London: Burns and Oates, 1877–83).

Forst, Rainer, *Toleration in Conflict: Past and Present* (Cambridge: Cambridge University Press, 2013).

Foucault, Michel, *Les mots et les choses: une archéologie des sciences humaines* (Paris: Gallimard, 1966).

Foucault, Michel, *Surveiller et punir: Naissance de la prison* (Paris: Gallimard, 1975).

Foucault, Michel 'Verité et pouvoir', *L'Arc*, 70 (1978), 16–26.

Foucault, Michel, *Aesthetics: Essential Works of Foucault 1954–1984*, 3 vols. (London: Penguin Books, 1998–2000).

Foucault, Michel, *Discipline and Punish: The Birth of the Prison* (London: Allen Lane, 1977).

Foucault, Michel, *The Archaeology of Knowledge* (London: Pantheon Books, 1972).

Foucault, Michel, *The Order of Things* (London: Vintage Books, 1994).

Foxe, John, *The Unabridged Acts and Monuments Online* (The Digital Humanities Institute, Sheffield, 2011) [TAMO].

Fragnito, Gigliola (ed.), *Church, Censorship and Culture in Early Modern Italy*, tr. Adrian Belton (Cambridge: Cambridge University Press, 2001).

Fraiberg, Selma, *Insights from the Blind* (New York: Basic Books, 1977).

Frame, Grant, and George, A. R., 'The Royal Libraries of Nineveh: New Evidence for King Ashurbanipal's Tablet Collecting', *Iraq*, 47 (2005), 265–84.

Frampton, Stephanie Ann, *Empire of Letters: Writing in Roman Literature and Thought from Lucretius to Ovid* (Oxford: Oxford University Press, 2019).

Fredericq, Paul (ed.), *Corpus documentorum inquisitionis haereticae pravitatis neerlandicae*, 5 vols. (The Hague: Martinus Nijhoff, 1889–1902).

Frere, Walter Howard, and Kennedy, W. P. M. (eds.), *Visitation Articles and Injunctions of the Period of the Reformation*, 3 vols. (London: Longman, Geeen and Co., 1863–1938).

Freud, Sigmund, *Die Traumdeutung* (Frankfurt am Main: S. Fischer Verlag, 1972).

Freud, Sigmund, *Gesammelte Werke*, 18 vols. (Frankfurt am Main: S. Fischer Verlag, 1991).

Freud, Sigmund, *An Outline of Psychoanalysis*, New Penguin Freud (London: Penguin Books, 2003).

Freud, Sigmund, *Case Histories* I, tr. A. and J. Strachey, The Penguin Freud Library, vol. 8 (London: Pelican Books, 1977).

Freud, Sigmund, *The Complete Letters of Sigmund Freud to Wilhelm Fliess 1887--1904*, ed. and trans. Jeffrey Masson (Cambridge, MA: Harvard University Press, 1985).

Freud, Sigmund, *The Interpretation of Dreams*, tr. James Strachey (Harmondsworth: Penguin Books, 1980).

Freud, Sigmund, *The Penguin Freud Reader*, ed. Adam Phillips (London: Penguin Books, 2006).

Freud, Sigmund, *The Uncanny*, ed. Hugh Haughton, New Penguin Freud (London: Penguin Books, 2003).

Freud, Sigmund, *Three Essays on Sexual Theory*, in *The Psychology of Love*, The New Penguin Freud (London: Penguin Books, 2006).

Freud, Sigmund, *Totem and Taboo* (New York: Cosimo, 2009).

Freud, Sigmund, *Wild Analysis*, tr. Alan Bance, The New Penguin Freud (London: Penguin Books, 2002).

Friggeri, Rosanna, *Epigraphic Collection of the Museo Nazionale Romano at the Baths of Diocletian* (Rome: Electa, 2004).

Frith, John, *A boke made by Iohn Frith prisoner in the tower of London* (Antwerp: H. Peetersen, 1533).

Fudge, Thomas A., *Jan Hus: Religious Reform and Social Revolution in Bohemia* (London: I. B.Tauris, 2017).

Fulke, William, *Stapleton and Martiall (two popish heretikes) confuted, and of their particular heresies detected* (London: Henry Middleton, 1580).

Funder, Anna, *Stasiland: Stories from Behind the Berlin Wall* (London: Granta Books, 2003).

Füssel, Stephan, *The Gutenberg Bible of 1454* (Cologne: Taschen, 2018).

Gadamer, Hans-Georg, *Plato's Dialectical Ethics: Phenomenological Interpretations Relating to the* Philebus (New Haven and London: Yale University Press, 1991).

Galperín, Karina, 'The Passion According to Berruguete: Painting the Auto-de-Fé and the Establishment of the Inquisition in Early Modern Spain', *Journal of Spanish Cultural Studies,* 14 (2013), 315–347.

Gamble, Harry Y., *Books and Readers in the Early Church: A History of Early Christian Texts* (New Haven and London: Yale University Press, 1995).

Gameson, Richard (ed.), *The Cambridge History of the Book in Britain*, vol. 1, *c.400–1100* (Cambridge: Cambridge University Press, 2011).

Garber, Marjorie, 'Shakespeare as Fetish', *Shakespeare Quarterly*, 41 (1990), 242–50.

Gardner, I., and Lieu, S. N. C. (eds.), *Manichaean Texts from the Roman Empire* (Cambridge: Cambridge University Press, 2004).

Gargett, Graham, *Voltaire and Protestantism* (Oxford: Voltaire Foundation 1980).

Gavanto, Bartolomeo, *Thesaurus sacrorum rituum auctore Bartholomaeo Gavanto* (Rome: Merati, 1738).

Gavrilov, A. K., 'Techniques of Reading in Classical Antiquity', *Classical Quarterly*, NS 47 (1997), 56–73.

Gay, Peter, *Modernism: The Lure of Heresy from Baudelaire to Beckett and Beyond* (New York: Random House, 2007).

Geary, Patrick J., *Furta Sacra: Thefts of Relics in the Central Middle Ages*, rev. edn. (Princeton: Princeton University Press, 2011).

Geary, Patrick J., *Language and Power in the Early Middle Ages* (Waltham, MA: Brandeis University Press, 2013).

Gelb, I. J., *A Study of Writing: The Foundations of Grammatology* (Chicago: University of Chicago Press, 1952).

Gell, Alfred, *Wrapping in Images: Tattooing in Polynesia* (Oxford: Clarendon Press, 1993).

Genette, Gérard, *Palimpsests: Literature in the Second Degree* (Lincoln: University of Nebraska Press, 1997).

George, Alain Fouad, 'The Geometry of the Qur'an of Amajur', *Muqarnas*, 20 (2003), 1–15.

Gerhard, Yves, 'La "coupe de Nestor": reconstitution du vers 1', *Zeitschrift für Papyrologie und Epigraphik*, 176 (2011), 7–9.

Gershevitch, Ilya (ed.), *The Cambridge History of Iran, Vol. 2: Median and Achaemenian Periods* (Cambridge: Cambridge University Press, 2008),

Gesner, Conrad, *Bibliotheca Universalis, sive Catalogus omnium Scriptorum locupletissimus, in tribus linguis, Latina, Græca, & Hebraica; extantium & non extantium* (Zürich: Christoph Froschauer, 1545).

Gibbon, Edward, *Decline and Fall of the Roman Empire*, Everyman Edition, 6 vols. (London: J. M. Dent, 1910).

Gibson, Walter S., *Bruegel* (London: Thames and Hudson, 1993).

Gilchrist, J., *The Press in the French Revolution: A Selection of Documents from the Press of the Revolution for the Years 1789–1794* (London: St Martin's Press, 1971).

Gillespie, Alexandra, and Lynch, Deidre (eds.), *The Unfinished Book,* Twenty-First Century Approaches to Literature (Oxford: Oxford University Press, 2021).

Gillespie, Alexandra, and Wakelin, Daniel (eds.), *The Production of Books in England 1350–1500* (Cambridge: Cambridge University Press, 2011).

Gillespie, Stuart, *Shakespeare's Books* (London: Continuum, 2004).

Gillet, Louis, *Stèle pour James Joyce* (Marseille: Sagittaire, 1941).

Gillett, Charles Ripley, *Burned Books: Neglected Chapters in British History and Literature*, 2 vols. (New York: Columbia University Press, 1932).

Gilmont, Jean-François, *The Reformation and the Book* (Aldershot: Ashgate, 1998).

Gilson, Étienne, *Les idées et les lettres* (Paris: Vrin, 1932).

Gingerich, Owen, *The Book Nobody Read* (London: Heinemann, 2004).

Ginzburg, Carlo, 'Morelli, Freud, and Sherlock Holmes: Clues and Scientific Method', in Umberto Eco and Thomas Sebeok (eds.), *The Sign of Three: Dupin, Holmes, Peirce* (Bloomington, IN: Indiana University Press, 1984), pp. 81–118.

Ginzburg, Carlo, *The Cheese and the Worms: The Cosmos of a Sixteenth-Century Miller* (London: Penguin Books, 1992).

Girard, René, *Violence and the Sacred*, tr. Patrick Gregory (Baltimore: Johns Hopkins University Press, 1977).

Godman, Peter, *Die geheime Inquisition: aus den verbotenen Archiven des Vatikan* (Wiesbaden: Marix Verlag, 2005).

Godman, Peter, *Poetry of the Carolingian Renaissance* (London: Duckworth, 1985).

Godman, Peter, 'Poggio Bracciolini and Niccolò Niccoli', *Neulateinisches Jahrbuch*, 21 (2019), 69–94.

Godman, Peter (ed.), *Alcuin: The Bishops, Kings and Saints of York* (Oxford: Clarendon Press, 1982).

Godwin, Joscelyn, *Athanasius Kircher's Theatre of the World* (London: Thames & Hudson, 2009).

Goldstone, Nancy and Lawrence, *Out of the Flames* (New York: Broadway Books, 2003).

Goldthwaite, Richard A., *Wealth and the Demand for Art in Italy, 1300–1600* (Baltimore, MD: Johns Hopkins University Press, 1993).

Gombrich, Eric, *The Story of Art*, 16th edn. (London: Phaidon Books, 1995).

González de Montes, Raimundo, *Sanctae inquisitionis hispanicae artes aliquot detectae, ac palam traductae* (Heidelberg: n.p., 1567).

González de Montes, Raimundo, *A Discovery and Playne Declaration of Sundry Subtill Practises of the Holy Inquisition of Spayne* (London: John Day, 1569).

Gordon, Bruce, *Calvin* (New Haven and London: Yale University Press, 2009).

Gordon, Bruce, ed.,(ed.), *Protestant History and Identity in Sixteenth-Century Europe*, 2 vols. (Aldershot: Scolar Press, 1996).

Gowing, A. M., *Empire and Memory: The Representation of the Roman Republic in Imperial Culture* (Cambridge: Cambridge University Press, 2005).

Grabar, Oleg, *The Alhambra*, 2nd edn. (Sebastopol: Solipsist Press, 1992).

Grafton, Anthony, *Codex in Crisis* (New York: Crumpled Press, 2008).

Grafton, Anthony, *Defenders of the Text: Traditions of Scholarship in an Age of Science 1450–1800* (Cambridge, MA: Harvard University Press, 1994).

Grafton, Anthony, *Inky Fingers: The Making of Books in Early Modern Europe* (Cambridge, MA: Harvard University Press, 2020).

Grafton, Anthony, *The Footnote: A Curious History* (Cambridge MA: Harvard University Press, 1997).

Grafton, Anthony, and Williams, Megan, *Christianity and the Transformation of the Book: Origen, Eusebius and the Library of Caesarea* (Cambridge, MA: Harvard University Press, 2009).

Gray, J. M., 'Conscience and the Word of God: Religious Arguments against the Ex Officio Oath', *Journal of Ecclesiastical History,* 64 (2013), 494–512.

Gray, Thomas R., *The Confessions of Nat Turner* (Baltimore: T. R. Gray, 1831).

Great Chronicle of London, The, ed. A. H. Thomas and I. D. Thornley (London: Library of the Corporation of the City, 1938).

Greenberg, Clement, *Collected Essays and Criticism*, ed. J. O'Brian, 4 vols. (Chicago: University of Chicago Press, 1993).

Greenblatt, Stephen, *Marvelous Possessions: The Wonder of the New World*, Oxford Clarendon Lectures (Chicago: University of Chicago Press, 1991).

Greenblatt, Stephen, *Renaissance Self-Fashioning* (Berkeley and Los Angeles: University of California Press, 1980).

Greenblatt, Stephen, *Shakespearean Negotiations: The Circulation of Social Energy in Renaissance England* (Berkeley and Los Angeles: University of California Press, 1988).

Greenblatt, Stephen, *The Swerve: How the World Became Modern* (New York: W. W. Norton, 2011).

Greenhalgh, Michael, *Marble Past, Monumental Present: Building with Antiquities in the Medieval Mediterranean* (Leiden: Brill, 2008).

Greenwald, Glenn, *No Place to Hide: Edward Snowden, the NSA & the Surveillance State* (London: Penguin Books, 2015).

Greg, W. W., *Some Aspects and Problems of London Publishing between 1550 and 1650*, Lyell Lectures (Oxford: Clarendon Press, 1956).

Greg, W. W., and Boswell E. (eds.), *Records of the Court of the Stationers' Company: 1576–1602* (London: Bibliographical Society, 1930).

Gregory, V., *Collection Development and Management for 21st Century Library Collections: An Introduction* (New York: Neal Schuman, 2011).

Gregory the Great, *Registrum Epistolarum*, ed. P. Ewald and L.M. Hartmann, 2 vols., Monumenta Germaniae Historica (Berlin: Hahn, 1887–95).

Grendler, Paul F., *The Roman Inquisition and the Venetian Press, 1540–1605* (Princeton: Princeton University Press, 1977).

Griffiths, Antony, *Prints and Printmaking: An Introduction to the History and Techniques* (Berkeley and Los Angeles: University of California Press, 1996).

Groesen, Michiel van, *The Representation of the Overseas World in the De Bry Collection of Voyages 1590–1634* (Leiden: Brill, 2008).

Gross, Robert A., and Kelley, Mary (eds.), *An Extensive Republic: Print, Culture, and Society in the New Nation, 1790–1840*, History of the Book in America, 2 (Chapel Hill, NC: University of North Carolina Press, 2010).

Grotius, Hugo, *Hugo Grotius's Remonstrantie of 1615*, ed. David Kromhout and Adri K. Offenberg (Leiden: Brill, 2019).

Gruber, Christiane J. (ed.), *The Islamic Manuscript Tradition* (Bloomington, IN: Indiana University Press, 2010).

Gui, Bernard, *Practica inquisitionis*, ed. C. Douais, 2 vols., Les classiques de l'histoire de France au moyen âge, 8–9 (Paris: Les Belles Lettres, 1926).

Guiney, Louise Imogen, *Recusant Poets* (London: Sheed & Ward, 1938).

Gulik, W. R. van, *Irezumi: the Pattern of Dermatography in Japan* (Leiden: Brill, 1982).

Guy, John, *The Public Career of Sir Thomas More* (New Haven: Yale University Press, 1980).

Habermas, Jürgen, *The Structural Transformation of the Public Sphere: An Inquiry into a Category of Bourgeois Society* (Cambridge, MA: MIT Press, 1991).

Hadfield, Andrew (ed.), *Literature and Censorship in Renaissance England* (London: Palgrave, 2001).

Hadsen, Chad, 'Chinese Ideographs and Western Ideas', *The Journal of Asian Studies*, 52: 2 (May, 1993), 373–99.

Hägglund, Martin, *Dying for Time: Proust, Woolf, Nabokov* (Cambridge, MA: Harvard University Press, 2012).

Hahn, Cynthia Jean, *Strange Beauty: Issues in the Making and Meaning of Reliquaries, 400–1204* (University Park, PA: Pennsylvania State University Press, 2012).

Hall, Evelyn Beatrice, *The Friends of Voltaire* (London: Smith Elder, 1906).

Hallam, Henry, *The Constitutional History of England from the Accession of Henry VII to the Death of George II*, 2 vols. (London: John Murray, 1827).

Hamel, Christopher de, *A History of Illuminated Manuscripts* (London: Phaidon Press, 1997).

Hamel, Christopher de, *The Book: A History of the Bible* (London: Phaidon Press, 2001).

Hamling, Tara, *Decorating the Godly Household: Religious Art in Post-Reformation Britain* (New Haven and London: Yale University Press, 2011).

Hammer, Joshua, *The Bad-Ass Librarians of Timbuktu* (New York: Simon and Schuster, 2016).

Hardy, G. H., *A Mathematician's Apology* (Cambridge: Cambridge University Press, 1941).

Harline, Craig, *A World Ablaze: The Rise of Martin Luther and the Birth of the Reformation* (Oxford: Oxford University Press, 2017).

Harris, A. Katie, *From Muslim to Christian Granada: Inventing a City's Past in Early Modern Spain* (Baltimore, MD: The Johns Hopkins University Press, 2010).

Harris, Michael H., *History of Libraries in the Western World*, 4th edn. (New York and London: Scarecrow Press, 1999).

Harris, Roy, *Rethinking Writing* (London: Athlone Press, 2000).

Harris, Stephen L., *Understanding the Bible*, 6th edn. (New York: McGraw-Hill, 2002).

Harris, W. V., *Ancient Literacy* (Cambridge, MA: Harvard University Press, 1987).

Harrist, Robert E., *The Landscape of Words: Stone Inscriptions from Early and Medieval China* (Seattle: University of Washington Press, 2008).

Hart, George, *Dictionary of Egyptian Gods and Goddesses* (London: Routledge, 2005).

Harvey, David, *A Companion to Marx's Capital* (London: Verso, 2010).

Harvey, Karen, *The Kiss in History* (Manchester: Manchester University Press, 2005).

Hawking, Stephen J., *A Brief History of Time: From the Big Bang to Black Holes* (London: Bantam Dell, 1988).

He, Qi-Xin, 'China's Shakespeare', *Shakespeare Quarterly*, 37 (1986), 149–59.

Hefner, Robert W. (ed.), *New Cambridge History of Islam, Vol. 6: Muslims and Modernity: Culture and Society since 1800* (Cambridge: Cambridge University Press, 2010).

Hegel, Georg Wilhelm Friedrich, *Werke*, ed. Eva Moldenhauer and Karl Markus Michel, 20 vols. (Frankfurt am Main: Suhrkamp, 1970–79).

Hegel, Georg Wilhelm Friedrich, *Aesthetics: Lectures on Fine Art*, tr. T. M. Knox, 2 vols. (Oxford: Clarendon Press, 1975).

Hegel, Georg Wilhelm Friedrich, *Lectures on the Philosophy of History*, tr. J. Sibree (New York: Dover, 2001).

Hegel, Georg Wilhelm Friedrich, *The Phenomenology of Spirit*, tr. Michael Inwood (Oxford: Oxford University Press, 2018).

Heide, Albert van der, *Hebraica Veritas: Christopher Plantin and the Christian Hebraists* (Antwerp: Plantin-Moretus Museum, 2008).

Heidegger, Martin, *Sein und Zeit* (Tübingen: Max Niemeyer Verlag, 2006).

Heidegger, Martin, *Basic Writings*, ed. David Farrell Krell (London: Routledge, 1993).

Heidegger, Martin, *Being and Time*, tr. John Macquarrie and Edward Robinson (Oxford: Blackwell, 1962).

Heidegger, Martin, *The Fundamental Concepts of Metaphysics*, tr. William McNeill and Nicholas Walker (Bloomington, IN: Indiana University Press, 1995).

Heidegger, Martin, *The Question of Being*, tr. William Kluback and Jean T. Wilde (New York: Twayne, 1958).

Heine, Heinrich, *Tragödien, nebst einem lyrischen Intermezzo* (Berlin: Dümmler, 1823).

Helck, Wolfgang, Otto, Eberhard, and Westendorf, Wolfhart (eds.), *Lexikon der Ägyptologie*, 7 vols. (Wiesbaden: O. Harrassowitz, 1972–92).

Helfferich, T., *The Thirty Years War: A Documentary History* (Indianapolis: Hackett, 2009).

Hellinga, Lotte, 'Press and Text in the First Decades of Printing', in A. Ganda, E. Grignani, and A. Petrucciani (eds.), *Libri tipografi biblioteche*, Biblioteca di bibliografia italiana, 148 (Florence: Olschki, 1997), 1–23.

Hellinga, Lotte, and Trapp J. B. (eds.), *Cambridge History of the Book in Britain, vol. 3: 1400–1557* (Cambridge: Cambridge University Press, 1999).

Henson, Edwin, *Registers of the English College at Madrid 1611–1767* (London: Catholic Record Society, 1929).

Henson, Edwin, *Registers of the English College at Valladolid* (London: Catholic Record Society, 1930).

Hess, Johann Eduard, *Gottfried Heinrich, Graf zu Pappenheim* (Leipzig: T. D. Weigel, 1855).

Hesse, Carla, 'Print Culture in the Enlightenment', in Martin Fitzpatrick, Peter Jones, Christa Knellwolf, and Iain MacCalman (eds.), *The Enlightenment World* (London: Routledge, 2004), 366–80.

Hilgers, Joseph, *Der Index der verbotenen Bücher in seiner neuen Fassung dargelegt und rechtlich-historisch gewürdigt* (Freiburg in Breisgau: Herder, 1904).

Hill, Christopher, *Puritanism and Revolution* (London: Secker & Warburg, 1958).

Hill, Christopher, *The English Bible and the Seventeenth-Century Revolution* (London: Penguin Books, 1993).

Hillenbrand, Robert, *Islamic Architecture: Form, Function and Meaning* (Edinburgh: Edinburgh University Press, 1994).

Hillenbrand, Robert, *Islamic Art and Architecture* (London: Thames & Hudson, 1999).

Hillenbrand, Robert (ed.), *Shahnama: The Visual Language of the Persian Book of Kings* (London: Ashgate, 2004).

Hilprecht, H. V., *The Excavations in Assyria and Babylonia* (Philadelphia: University of Pennsylvania Press, 1904).

Hinman, Charlton, *The Printing and Proof-Reading of the First Folio* (Oxford: Clarendon Press, 1963).

Hirakawa, Akira, *A History of Indian Buddhism: From Śākyamuni to Early Mahāyāna* (Delhi: Motilal Banarsidass, 1993).

Hobsbawm, Eric, *The Age of Extremes: The Short Twentieth Century 1914–1991* (London: Abacus, 1998).

Hobsbawm, Eric, *The Age of Revolution 1789–1848* (New York: Mentor Books, 1962).

Hoffman, Adina, and Cole, Peter, *Sacred Trash: The Lost and Found World of the Cairo Geniza* (New York: Schocken Books, 2011).

Homer, *Odyssey*, tr. Robert Fagles (London: Penguin Books, 1997).

Howell, Thomas Bayly, *Complete Collection of State Trials and Proceedings for High Treason*, 21 vols. (London: Longman etc., 1816).

Hubert, Conrad, *Ein ware histori vom leben, sterben, begrebnuss, anklagung der ketzerey, verdammung, ausgraben, verbrennen und letstlich ehlicher wider ynsetzung der säligen und hochgelehrten Theologen D. Martini Buceri vnd Pauli Fagii* (Strasbourg: Paul Messerschmidt, 1562).

Hudson, Anne, *Lollards and their Books* (London: Hambledon Press, 1985).

Hudson, Anne, *The Premature Reformation: Wycliffite Texts and Lollard History* (Oxford: Clarendon Press 1988).

Hudson, Anne (ed.), *Two Wycliffite Texts* (Oxford: Early English Text Society, 1993).

Hughes, Paul L., and Larkin, James F. (eds.), *Tudor Royal Proclamations*, 3 vols. (New Haven: Yale University Press, 1965–9).

Huizinga, Johan, *Herfsttij der Middeleeuwen* (Haarlem: Tjeenk Willink, 1919).

Hulliung, Max, *Montesquieu and the Old Regime* (Berkeley and Los Angeles: University of California Press, 1977).

Huntington, John C., 'Sowing the Seeds of the Lotus, I–V', *Orientations*, 16/11 (1985), 46–61; 17/2 (1986), 28–43; 17/3 (1986), 32–46; 17/7 (1986), 28–40; 17/9 (1986), 46–58.

Hyneman, Charles S., and Lutz, Donald S. (eds.), *American Political Writing During the Founding Era, 1760–1805* (Indianapolis: Liberty Press, 1983).

Igunma, Jana, and May, San San (eds.), *Buddhism: Origins, Traditions and Contemporary Life* (London: British Library, 2019).

Ikegami, Kōjirō, *Japanese Bookbinding: Instructions from a Master Craftsman* (Tokyo: Weatherhill Books, 1986).

Inose, Naoko, *Persona: A Biography of Yukio Mishima* (Berkeley, CA: Stone Bridge Press, 2013).

Inwood, Michael, *A Heidegger Dictionary* (Oxford: Blackwell, 1999).

Inwood, M. J., *Hegel* (London: Routledge, 2002).

Isidore of Seville, *The Etymologies*, ed. Stephen A. Barney, W. J. Lewis, J. A. Beach, and Oliver Berghof (Cambridge: Cambridge University Press, 2006).

Israel, Jonathan I., *Radical Enlightenment: Philosophy and the Making of Modernity 1650–1750* (Oxford: Oxford University Press, 2002).

Israel, Jonathan I., *Enlightenment Contested: Philosophy, Modernity, and the Emancipation of Man, 1670–1752* (Oxford: Oxford University Press, 2006).

Israel, Jonathan I., *Revolutionary Ideas: An Intellectual History of the French Revolution from The Rights of Man to Robespierre* (Princeton, NJ: Princeton University Press, 2014).

Ivanov, Vladimir, *Russian Icons* (New York: Rizzoli, 1988).

Jacoby, Susan, *Strange Gods: A Secular History of Conversion* (London: Penguin Books, 2017).

Jacobsen, Knut A., Mann Singh, Gurinder, and Myrvold, Kristina, *Brill's Encyclopedia of Sikhism* [online].

Jakobson, Roman, *Language in Literature*, ed. Krystyna Pomorska and Stephen Rudy (Cambridge MA: Harvard University Press, 1987).

James, David, *Qur'ans of the Mamluks* (London: Alexandria Press, 1989).

James, Henry, *The Aspern Papers* (London and New York: Longman and Co., 1888).

James, Susan, *Spinoza on Philosophy, Religion and Politics* (Oxford: Oxford University Press, 2012).

James, William, *The Varieties of Religious Experience: A Study in Human Nature* (London: Longman, Green, 1905).

Jardine, Lisa, *Worldly Goods: A New History of the Renaissance* (London: Macmillan, 1996), p. 171.

Jardine, Lisa, and Stewart, Alan, *Hostage to Fortune: The Troubled Life of Francis Bacon 1561–1626* (London: Phoenix Books, 1999).

Jastrow, Morris, *The Civilization of Babylonia and Assyria* (London: J. B. Lippincott, 1915).

Jefferson, Thomas, *Notes on the State of Virginia*, 2nd edn. (London: John Stockdale, 1787).

Jensen, Kristian, *Incunabula and their Readers: Printing, Selling and Using Books in the Fifteenth Century* (London: British Library, 2003).

Johns, Adrian, *The Nature of the Book: Print and Knowledge in the Making* (Chicago: University of Chicago Press, 1998).

Johns, C. H. W., *Babylonian and Assyrian Laws, Contracts and Letters* (London: T. & T. Clark, 1904).

Johnson, Melvin, *et al.*, 'Google's Multilingual Neural Machine Translation System: Enabling Zero-Shot Translation', *ARXIV*, 14 November, 2016, www.arxiv.org.

Jomier, Jacques, *L'Islam vécu en Égypte: 1945–1975*, Études Musulmanes, 35 (Paris: Vrin, 1994).

Jones, C. P., 'Stigma: Tattooing and Branding in Graeco-Roman Antiquity', *Journal of Roman Studies*, 72 (1987), 139–55.

Jones, Matthew L., *Reckoning with Matter: Calculating Machines, Innovation, and Thinking about Thinking from Pascal to Babbage* (Chicago: University of Chicago Press, 2016).

Jones, Roger, and Penny, Nicholas, *Raphael* (New Haven: Yale University Press, 1983).

Jonson, Ben, *Works* (London: Richard Meighen, 1640).

Josipovici, Gabriel, *Touch* (New Haven and London: Yale University Press, 1996).

Joyce, James, *Dubliners* (London: Penguin Books, 1976).

Joyce, James, *Finnegans Wake*, repr. edn. (London: Faber & Faber, 1946).

Joyce, James, *Ulysses: The 1922 Text*, ed. Jeri Johnson (Oxford: World's Classics, 1993).

Joyce, Stanislaus, *My Brother's Keeper: James Joyce's Early Years* (New York: Viking, 1969).

Kafka, Franz, *Die Erzählungen* (Frankfurt am Main: Fischer Verlag, 1996).

Kafka, Franz, *Der Proceß* (Frankfurt am Main: Fischer Verlag, 1994).

Kafka, Franz, *Collected Stories*, ed. Gabriel Josipovici (London: Everyman, 1993).

Kafka, Franz, *Letters to Friends, Family, & Editors*, ed. Richard and Clara Winston (New York: Schocken, 1977).

Kafka, Franz, *The Trial* (London: Penguin Books, 1976).

Kamen, Henry, *The Rise of Toleration* (London: Weidenfeld and Nicolson, 1967).

Kandinsky, Wassily, 'On the Question of Form', *The Blue Rider Almanac*, tr. H. Falkenstein (New York: Viking, 1974).

Kang, Jae-eun, *The Land of Scholars: Two Thousand Years of Korean Confucianism* (Paramus, NJ: Homa & Sekey Books, 2006).

Kant, Immanuel, *Critique of Pure Reason*, ed Paul Guyer and Allen W. Wood (Cambridge: Cambridge University Press, 1997).

Kant, Immanuel, *Groundwork of the Metaphysics of Morals*, German—English Edition, ed. Mary Gregor and Jens Timmermann (Cambridge: Cambridge University Press, 2010).

Kant, Immanuel, *Observations on the Feeling of the Beautiful and Sublime and Other Writings*, ed. Patrick Frierson and Paul Guyer (Cambridge: Cambridge University Press, 2011).

Karlstadt, Andreas, *Von abtuhung der Bylder* (Wittenberg: Nyckell Schyrlentz, 1522).

Kay, Lily E., 'A Book of Life? How the Genome Became an Information System and DNA a Language', *Perspectives in Biology and Medicine*, 41(1998), 504–28.

Kearney, James, 'The Book and the Fetish: the Materiality of Prospero's Text', *Journal of Medieval and Early Modern Studies*, 32 (2002), 433–468.

Kearney, James, *The Incarnate Text: Imagining the Book in Reformation England* (Philadelphia: University of Pennsylvania Press, 2009).

Kemp, B. J., *Ancient Egypt: Anatomy of a Civilization* (Cambridge: Cambridge University Press, 1989).

Kennedy, Benjamin Hall, *Revised Latin Primer* (London: Longman, 1962).

Kern, Martin, *The Stele Inscriptions of Ch'in Shih-huang: Text and Ritual in Early Chinese Imperial Representation* (New Haven: American Oriental Society, 2000).

Kerrigan, John, *Archipelagic English: Literature, History, and Politics 1603–1707* (Oxford: Oxford University Press, 2008).

Keynes, Simon, and Lapidge, Michael (eds.), *Alfred the Great: Asser's Life of King Alfred and Other Contemporary Sources* (Harmondsworth: Penguin Books, 1983).

Keysers, Christian, 'Mirror Neurons', *Current Biology*, 19 (2010), 271–3.

Kilroy, Gerard , *Edmund Campion: A Scholarly Life* (Farnham: Ashgate, 2015).

Kim, Jinwung, *A History of Korea: From 'Land of the Morning Calm' to States in Conflict* (Bloomington: Indiana University Press, 2012).

Kim-Renaud, Young-Key, *The Korean Alphabet: Its History and Structure* (Honolulu: University of Hawaii Press, 1997).

Klingshirn, W. E., and Safran, L. (eds.), *The Early Christian Book* (Washington, DC: Catholic University of America Press, 2007).

Knox, Bernard M. W., 'Silent Reading in Antiquity', *Greek, Roman and Byzantine Studies*, 9 (1968), 421–35.

Knuth, Donald, *The Art of Computer Programming*, 4 vols. (Reading, MA: Addison-Wesley, 2011).

Koerner, Joseph Leo, *The Reformation of the Image* (Chicago: University of Chicago Press; London: Reaktion Books, 2004).

Koestler, Arthur, *The Ghost in the Machine* (London: Hutchinson, 1967).

Koestler, Arthur, *The Sleepwalkers: A History of Man's Changing Vision of the Universe* (London: Macmillan, 1968).

Kogman-Appel, Katrin, *Jewish Book Art Between Islam and Christianity: The Decoration of Hebrew Bibles in Medieval Spain*, The Medieval and Early Modern World (Leiden and Boston: Brill, 2004).

Kornicki, Peter, *The Book in Japan: A Cultural History from the Beginnings to the Nineteenth Century* (Leiden: Brill, 1998).

Kraus, Richard Curt, *Brushes with Power: Modern Politics and the Chinese Art of Calligraphy* (Berkeley: University of California Press, 1991).

Kren, Thomas, and McKendrick, Scott, *Illuminating the Renaissance: the Triumph of Flemish Manuscript Painting in Europe* (Los Angeles, CA: J. Paul Getty Museum, 2003).

Kronenberg, M. E., *Verboden boeken en opstandige drukkers in de hervormingstijd* (Amsterdam: P. N. van Kampen, 1948).

Kureishi, Hanif, 'Touching the Untouchable', *Times Literary Supplement*, 1 March 2019.

Labrousse, Elisabeth, *Bayle* (Oxford: Oxford University Press, 1983).

Lacan, Jacques, *Écrits*, Texte intégral, 2 vols. (Paris: Éditions du Seuil, 1966).

Lacan, Jacques, 'Le séminaire sur la lettre volée', *La Psychanalyse*, 2 (1956), 1–44.

Lacan, Jacques, *Anxiety: The Seminar of Jacques Lacan, Book X*, ed. Jean-Alain Miller (London: Polity Press, 2016).

Lacan, Jacques, *Écrits: A Selection*, tr. Alan Sheridan (London: Routledge, 1977).

Lacan, Jacques, *Seminar, II: The Ego in Freud's Theory and in the Technique of Psychoanalysis, 1954–1955* (Cambridge: Cambridge University Press, 1991).

Lacan, Jacques, *The Four Fundamental Concepts of Psychoanalysis* (Séminaire XI), tr. Alan Sheridan (London: Penguin Books, 1994).

Ladurie, Emmanuel Le Roy, *Montaillou: The World-Famous Portrait of Life in a Medieval Village* (London: Penguin Books, 1980).

Lake, Peter, and Pincus, Steven (eds.), *The Politics of the Public Sphere in Early Modern England* (Manchester: Manchester University Press, 2007).

Lambert, Malcolm, *Medieval Heresy: Popular Movements from the Gregorian Reform to the Reformation* (Oxford: Blackwell, 1992).

Landa, Diego de, *Yucatan Before and After the Conquest*, tr. William Gates (New York: Dover Publications, 1978).

Lane Fox, Robin, *Augustine: Conversions and Confessions* (London: Penguin Books, 2015).

Lane Fox, Robin, *Pagans and Christians* (London: Viking Books, 1986).

Lang, Uwe Michael, *John Philoponus and the Controversies Over Chalcedon in the Sixth Century* (Leuven: Peeters, 2001).

Lansing, Richard (ed.), *The Dante Encyclopaedia* (London: Routledge, 2010).

Lapidge, Michael, *The Anglo-Saxon Library* (Oxford: Oxford University Press, 2006).

Law, Ceri, *Contested Reformations in the University of Cambridge, 1535–84*, Royal Historical Society Studies in History (Woodbridge: Boydell & Brewer, 2018).

Layard, A. H., *Discoveries in the Ruins of Nineveh and Babylon*, rev. edn., 2 vols. (Cambridge: Cambridge University Press, 2011).

Le Brun, Charles, *Expressions des passions de l'Âme* (Paris: Jean Audran, 1727).

Leader, Darian, *Hands: what we do with them and why* (London: Penguin Books, 2017).

Lee, Sir Sidney, 'Shakespeare And The Inquisition. A Spanish Second Folio. How The Plays Were Expurgated. Politics And Drama', *The Times*, Monday, 10 April 1922, 15.

Leedham-Green, Elisabeth, *Books in Cambridge Inventories: Book-Lists from Vice-Chancellor's Court Probate Inventories in the Tudor and Stuart Periods*, 2 vols (Cambridge: Cambridge University Press, 1986).

Leedham-Green, Elisabeth, and Webber, Teresa (eds.), *The Cambridge History of Libraries in Britain and Ireland, vol. 1: to 1640* (Cambridge: Cambridge University Press, 2006).

Leese, Daniel, *Mao Cult: Rhetoric and Ritual in China's Cultural Revolution* (Cambridge: Cambridge University Press 2013).

Leff, Gordon, *Heresy in the Later Middle Ages: The Relation of Heterodoxy to Dissent*, 2 vols. (Manchester: Manchester University Press, 1967).

Lehmberg, Stanford E., *The Later Parliaments of Henry VIII, 1536–1547* (Cambridge: Cambridge University Press, 1977).

Lei Han, Oliver, 'Sources and Early Printing History of Chairman Mao's "Quotations"', *Bibliographical Society of America*, Bibsite (2004), 2–4. (https://bibsocamer.org/BibSite/Han/index.html).

Leland, John, *De viris illustribus/On Famous Men*, ed. and tr. James P. Carley (Toronto: Pontifical Institute of Medieval Studies, 2010).

Leland, John, *Joannis Lelandi antiquarii de rebus Britannicis collectanea*, 6 vols. in 7 (Oxford: Thomas Hearne, 1715).

Leo Africanus, *A Geographical Historie of Africa, written in Arabicke and Latin* (London: George Bishop, 1600).

Léry, Jean de, *Histoire d'un voyage faict en la terre du Brésil*, ed. Frank Lestringant (Paris: Lives de Poche, 1994).

Lessing, Gotthold Ephraim, *Laocoon: An Essay on the Limits of Painting and Poetry* (London: Longman, Brown, etc., 1853).

Letters and Papers, Foreign and Domestic, of the Reign of Henry VIII, ed. J. S. Brewer, J. Gairdner, and R. H. Brodie (London: HMSO, 1862–1932).

Letters of Abelard and Heloise, The, tr. Betty Radice (London: Penguin Books, 2003).

Lévi-Strauss, Claude, *La pensée sauvage* (Paris: Librairie Plon, 1962).

Lévi-Strauss, Claude, *Tristes tropiques* (Paris: Librairie Plon, 1955).

Lévi-Strauss, Claude, *Structural Anthropology*, 2 vols. (Harmondsworth: Penguin Books, 1972).

Lévi-Strauss, Claude, *Tristes Tropiques*, tr. John and Doreen Weightman (London: Jonathan Cape, 1973).

Levi, Primo, *Se questo è un uomo*, ed. Alberto Cavaglion (Turin: Einaudi, 2012).

Levi, Primo, *If This is a Man* (London: Abacus Books, 1987).

Lévinas, Emmanuel, *Du sacré au saint: cinq nouvelles lectures talmudiques* (Paris: Minuit, 1977).

Levison, Wilhelm, *England and the Continent in the Eighth Century*, The Ford Lectures, 1943 (Oxford: Clarendon Press, 1946).

Levison, Wilhelm (ed.), *Vitae Sancti Bonifatii archiepiscopi moguntini*, Monumenta Germaniae historica, 57 (Hanover: Hahn, 1905).

Levy, I. C., George-Tvrtković, R., and Duclow, D. F. (eds.), *Nicholas of Cusa and Islam: Polemic and Dialogue in the Late Middle Ages* (Leiden: Brill, 2016).

Lewis, Mark Edward, *Writing and Authority in Early China* (New York: SUNY Press, 1999).

Lewy, Guenter, *Harmful and Undesirable: Book Censorship in Nazi Germany* (Oxford: Oxford University Press, 2016).

Li Feng and Branner, David Prager (eds.), *Writing and Literacy in Early China* (Seattle: University of Washington Press, 2011).

Liere, Katherine van, Ditchfield, Simon, and Louthan, Howard (eds.), *Sacred History: Uses of the Christian Past in the Renaissance World* (Oxford: Oxford University Press, 2012).

Lieu, S. N. C., *Manichaeism in Central Asia and China* (Leiden: Brill, 1998).

Lifshitz, Joseph Isaac, *Rabbi Meir of Rothenburg and the Foundation of Jewish Political Thought* (Cambridge: Cambridge University Press, 2016).

Limborch, Philip van, *Historia inquisitionis* (Amsterdam: Henrik Wetsteijn, 1692).

Lindsay, K. C., 'Mystery in Bruegel's Proverbs', *Jahrbuch der Berliner Museen,* 38 (1996), 63–76.

Lipner, Julius J., 'Ancient Banyan: An Inquiry into the Meaning of "Hinduness"', *Religious Studies*, 32. 1 (1996), 109–126.

Lithgow, John, *Total Discourse of the Rare Adventures* (London: J. Oakes, 1640).

Liu, Xinru, *Silk and Religion: An Exploration of Material Life and the Thought of the People* (Oxford: Oxford University Press, 1997).

Locke, John, *An Essay Concerning Human Understanding*, ed. P. H. Nidditch (Oxford: Clarendon Press, 1975).

Locke, John, *Selected Political Writings*, ed. Paul E. Sigmund (New York: W. W. Norton, 2005).

Locke, John, *Some Thoughts Concerning Education* (London: A. J. Churchill, 1693).

Lopez, Jr., Donald S., *The Lotus Sutra*, Lives of Great Religious Books (Princeton: Princeton University Press, 2016).

López Guzmán, Rafael, *Arquitectura Mudéjar* (Madrid: Ediciones Cátedra, 2016).

Lord, A. B., *The Singer of Tales* (Cambridge, MA: Harvard University Press, 1960).

Lorenzen, Jan, *Die großen Schlachten: Mythen, Menschen, Schicksale* (Frankfurt am Main: Campus Verlag, 2006).

Lotus Sūtra, tr. Tsugunari Kubo and Akiro Yuyama (Berkeley, CA: Numata Center for Buddhist Translation and Research, 2007).

Loveday, Helen, *Islamic Paper: A Study of the Ancient Craft* (London: Archetype, 2001).

Lubin, Timothy, 'Vratá Divine and Human in the Early Veda', *Journal of the American Oriental Society*, 121.: 4 (2001), 565–79.

Luborsky, Ruth, and Ingram, Elizabeth M., *A Guide to English Illustrated Books 1536–1603*, 2 vols. (Tempe, AZ: MRTS, 1998).

Lucas, Colin, *Annales historiques de la Révolution française*, 194 (October–December 1968), 489–533.

Luther, Martin, *D. Martin Luthers Werke: kritische Gesamtausgabe*, 68 vols. (Weimar: Hermann Böhlau, 1883–1999) [WA].

Luther, Martin, *D. Martin Luthers Werke: Briefwechsel*, 18 vols. (Weimar: Hermann Böhlau, 1930–85). [WA Br.]

Luther, Martin, *D. Martin Luthers Werke: Tischreden*, 6 vols. (Weimar: Hermann Böhlau, 1912–21). [WA TR]

Luther, Martin, *Von der Freiheit eines Christenmenschen* (Wittenberg: Johann Rhau-Grunenberg, 1520).

Luther, Martin, *Dr. Martini Lutheri Colloquia Mensalia; or, Dr. Martin Luther's Divine Discourses at his table* (London: William Dugard, 1652).

Luther, Martin, *Luther's Works*, ed. J. Pelikan and H. T. Lehmann, 56 vols. (Philadelphia: Fortress, 1955–86).

Lyon, Gregory B., 'Baudouin, Flacius, and the Plan for the Magdeburg Centuries', *Journal of the History of Ideas*, 64 (2003), 253–72.

Lyons, Martyn, *Books: A Living History* (Los Angeles: Getty Museum, 2011).

Maccoby, Hyam, *Judaism on Trial: Jewish–Christian Disputations in the Middle Ages* (Plainsboro: Associated University Presses, 1982).

MacCulloch, Diarmaid, *Reformation: Europe's House Divided, 1490–1700* (London: Penguin Books, 2004).

MacCulloch, Diarmaid, *Thomas Cranmer: A Life* (New Haven and London: Yale University Press, 1996).

Machiavelli, Niccolò, *Lettere*, ed. F. Gaeta (Milan: Feltrinelli, 1961).

Machyn, Henry, *The Diary of Henry Machyn*, ed. J. G. Nichols, Camden Society, 42 (London, 1848).

Magritte, René, 'Les mots et les images', *La Révolution surréaliste*,12 (15 December 1929), 32–33.

Maimonides, Moses, *Epistles of Maimonides*, ed. A. Halkin (New York: Jewish Publication Society, 1993).

Maimonides, Moses, *The Guide for the Perplexed* (New York: Dover Books, 2012).

Mair Victor H., and Liu, Yongquan (eds.), *Characters and Computers* (Amsterdam: IOS Press, 1991).

Mallarmé, Stéphane, *Crise de vers|Divagations* (Paris: Eugène Fasquelle, 1897).

Mallarmé, Stéphane, *Quant au livre* (Périgueux: Art et Arts, 2010).

Mallarmé, Stéphane, *Œuvres complètes*, ed. Bernard Marchal, 2 vols., Bibliothèque de la Pléiade (Paris: Gallimard, 1998).

Manguel, Alberto, *A History of Reading* (London: Flamingo, 1997).

Mansbach, S. A., 'Pieter Bruegel's Towers of Babel', *Zeitschrift für Kunstgeschichte*, 45 (1982), 43–56.

Marcus, Laura, *The Tenth Muse: Writing About Cinema in the Modernist Period* (Oxford: Oxford University Press, 2008).

Marees, Pieter de, *Beschrijvinghe ende Historische verhael vant Gout Koninckrijck van Gunea* (Amsterdam: Cornelis Claesz, 1602).

Marinetti, F. T., 'Distruzione della sintassi/Immaginazione senza fili/Parole in libertà', *Lacerba* (11 May 1913).

Marius, Richard, *Thomas More* (London: Weidenfeld, 1993).

Marlowe, Christopher, *Doctor Faustus and Other Plays*, ed. David Bevington (Oxford: Oxford University Press, 2001).

Marquadt, Janet T., *From Martyr to Monument: The Abbey of Cluny as Cultural Patrimony* (Newcastle: Cambridge Scholars, 2009).

Marsden, Richard, and Matter Ann (eds.), *New Cambridge History of the Bible, Vol. 2: From 600 to 1450* (Cambridge: Cambridge University Press, 2012).

Marshall, John, *John Locke, Toleration, and Early Enlightenment Culture* (Cambridge: Cambridge University Press, 2006).

Martin, Dan, 'Pearls from Bones: Relics, Chortens, Tertons and the Signs of Saintly Death in Tibet', *Numen* 41/3 (1994), 273–324.

Martin, Henri-Jean, *The History and Power of Writing* (Chicago: University of Chicago Press, 1994).

Marx, Karl, *Das Kapital: Kritik der politischen Ökonomie*, vol. 1, ed. F. Engels, *Karl Marx. Friedrich Engels. Werke*, Band 23 (Berlin: Dietz Verlag, 1962).

Marx, Karl, *Capital: A Critique of Political Economy*, Vol. 1, tr. Ben Fowkes (London: Penguin/New Left Review, 1990).

Marx, Karl, *Grundrisse: Foundations of the Critique of Political Economy (Rough Draft)* (London: Penguin Books, 1993).

Matthews, Samantha, *Poetical Remains: Poets' Graves, Bodies, and Books in the Nineteenth Century* (Oxford: Oxford University Press, 2004).

Matthews, Thomas F., *The Early Churches of Constantinople: Architecture and Liturgy* (Philadelphia: Pennsylvania State University Press, 1971).

Mauss, Marcel, *The Gift: The Form and Reason for Exchange in Archaic Societies* (London: Routledge, 1990).

Mauss, Marcel, and Hubert, Henri, *Sacrifice: Its Nature and Function* (London: Cohen & West, 1964).

Mayer-Schonberger, Viktor, and Cukier, Kenneth, *Big Data: A Revolution that will Transform how we Live, Work, and Think* (Boston: Houghton Mifflin Harcourt, 2013).

Mazzocco, Angelo, *Linguistic Theories in Dante and the Humanists: Studies of Language and Intellectual History in Late Medieval and Early Renaissance Italy* (Leiden: Brill, 1993).

McAuliffe, Jane Dammen (ed.), *Encyclopaedia of the Qur'an*, Brill Online.

McConica, James, *History of the University of Oxford. Volume III: The Collegiate University* (Oxford: Oxford University Press, 1986).

McCulloch, Gretchen, *Because Internet: Understanding the New Rules of Language* (London: Penguin Books, 2019).

McCutcheon, R. W., 'Silent Reading in Antiquity and the Future History of the Book', *Book History*, 18 (2015), 1–32.

McDonald, Peter D., *The Literature Police: Apartheid Censorship and Its Cultural Consequences* (Oxford: Oxford University Press, 2009).

McElligott, Jason, 'In the Line of Fire', *History Ireland*, 20 (2012), 42–3.

McGinn, Donald J., *John Penry and the Marprelate Controversy* (New Brunswick, NJ: Rutgers University Press, 1966).

McGrath, Alister E., *Luther's Theology of the Cross* (Oxford: Blackwell, 1991).

McKenzie, Donald F., *Bibliography and the Sociology of Texts*, Panizzi Lectures (Cambridge: Cambridge University Press, 1999).

McKenzie, Donald F., 'Printers of the Mind: Some Notes on Bibliographical Theories and Printing-House Practices', *Studies in Bibliography*, 22 (1969), 1–75.

McKerrow, Ronald B., *An Introduction to Bibliography for Literary Students* (Oxford: Clarendon Press, 1960).

McKitterick, David, *Print, Manuscript and the Search for Order, 1450–1830* (Cambridge: Cambridgc University Press, 2003).

McKitterick, David (ed.), *The Cambridge History of the Book in Britain, 1830–1914* (Cambridge: Cambridge University Press, 2009).

McKitterick, Rosamond, *The Carolingians and the Written Word* (Cambridge: Cambridge University Press, 1989).

McLeod, Roy (ed.), *The Library of Alexandria: Centre of Learning in the Ancient World* (London: I.B. Tauris, 2005).

McLuhan, Marshall, *The Gutenberg Galaxy: The Making of Typographic Man* (Toronto: University of Toronto Press, 1962).

McLuhan, Marshall, *Understanding Media: the Extensions of Man* (New York: McGraw-Hill, 1964).

McLuhan, Marshall, and Fiore, Quentin, with Jerome Agel, *The Medium Is the Massage* (Harmondsworth: Penguin Books, 1967).

McNiven, Peter, *Heresy and Politics in the Reign of Henry IV: The Burning of John Badby* (Woodbridge: Boydell Press, 1987).

McNutt, Jennifer Powell, *Calvin Meets Voltaire: The Clergy of Geneva in the Age of Enlightenment, 1685–1798* (Farnham: Ashgate 2014).

Medick, H., and Selwyn, P., 'Historical Event and Contemporary Experience: the Capture and Destruction of Magdeburg in 1631', *History Workshop Journal*, 52 (2001), 23–48.

Melville, Herman, *The Writings of Herman Melville: The Northwestern–Newberry Edition*, gen. ed. G. Thomas Tanselle, 9 vols. (Evanston, IL: Northwestern University Press, 1988).

Métraux, Alfred, *Ethnology of Easter Island* (Honolulu: Bishop Museum, 1940).

Metz, Bernhard, 'Bibliomania and the Folly of Reading', *Comparative Critical Studies*, 5/2–3 (2008), 249–29.

Metzger, Bruce M., *The Bible in Translation* (Grand Rapids: Baker Academic, 2001).

Mews, Charlotte, *The Lost Love Letters of Heloise and Abelard: Perceptions of Dialogue in Twelfth-Century France* (New York: Springer, 2016).

Mill, John Stuart, *On Liberty* (London: Longmans, Green, and Company, 1867).

Milton, John, *Complete Prose Works of John Milton*, 8 vols. (New Haven: Yale University Press, 1953–82).

Milton, John, *Poems*, ed. Alastair Fowler and John Carey (London: Longman, 1980).

Milton, John, *Poems of Mr John Milton, both English and Latin* (London: Ruth Raworth, 1634).

Minard, Philippe, *Typographes des Lumières* (Seyssel: Champ Vallon, 1989).

Missale ad vsum celeberrime ecclesie Eboracensis (Rouen: P. Olivier, 1516).

Mitchell, W. J. T., *Iconology: Image, Text, Ideology* (Chicago: University of Chicago Press, 1986).

Mitchell, W. J. T., *Picture Theory: Essays on Verbal and Visual Representation* (Chicago: University of Chicago Press, 1995).

Mitchell, W. J. T., 'The Politics of Genre: Space and Time in Lessing's *Laocoon*', *Representations*, 6 (Spring 1984), 98–115.

Mols, Roger, S J, *Introduction à la démographie historique des villes d'Europe du XIVe au XVIIIe siècle*, 3 vols. (Louvain: J. Duculot, 1955).

Montaigne, Michel de *Les Essais*, ed. Jean Balsamo, Catherine Magnien-Simonin, and Michel Magnien, Bibliothèque de la Pléiade (Paris: Librairie Gallimard, 2007).

Montaigne, Michel de, *Œuvres complètes*, ed. Maurice Rat and Albert Thibaudet, Bibliothèque de la Pléiade (Paris: Librairie Gallimard, 1963).

Montaigne, Michel de, *Complete Works*, tr. Donald Frame (New York: Everyman, 2003).

Monter, William, *Frontiers of Heresy: The Spanish Inquisition from the Basque Lands to Sicily* (Cambridge: Cambridge University Press, 2003).

Monter, William, *Judging the French Reformation: Heresy Trials by Sixteenth-Century Parlements* (Cambridge, MA.: Harvard University Press, 1999).

More, Thomas, *Correspondence*, ed. Elizabeth Rogers (Princeton: Princeton University Press, 1947).

More, Thomas, *The Complete Works*, ed. Louis L. Martz, Richard S. Sylvester, and Clarence H. Miller, 15 vols. (New Haven: Yale UP, 1963–97). [CWTM]

Morgan, David O., and Reid, Anthony (eds.), *New Cambridge History of Islam, Vol. 3: The Eastern Islamic World, Eleventh to Eighteenth Centuries* (Cambridge: Cambridge University Press, 2010),

Morley, Simon, *Writing on the Wall: Word and Image in Modern Art* (London: Thames & Hudson, 2003).

Morrison, Toni, *Beloved* (New York: Random House, 2014).

Mostert, M., *754, Bonifatius bij Dokkum vermoord* (Hilversum: Uitgeverij Verloren, 1999).

Muller, John P., and Richardson, William J. (eds.), *The Purloined Poe* (Baltimore: Johns Hopkins University Press, 1988).

Murgatroyd, Paul, *The Amatory Elegies of Johannes Secundus* (Leiden: Brill, 2000).

Myounggu, Ro, and Park, Suhee, *The King at the Palace: Joseon Royal Court Culture* (Seoul: Designintro, 2016).

Myrvold, Kristina (ed.), *The Death of Sacred Texts: Ritual Disposal and Renovation of Texts in World Religions* (Aldershot: Ashgate, 2010).

Nachtomy, Ohad, 'On Living Mirrors and Mites: Leibniz's Encounter with Pascal on Infinity', *Oxford Studies in Early Modern Philosophy*, 8 (2019), 191–225.

Nagel, Alexander, *Medieval Modern: Art Out of Time* (London: Thames & Hudson, 2012).

Nagel, Alexander, *The Controversy of Renaissance Art* (Chicago: University of Chicago Press, 2011).

Naughton, John, *A Brief History of the Future: The Origins of the Internet* (London: Weidenfeld and Nicholson, 2000).

Nauta, Lodi, *In Defense of Common Sense: Lorenzo Valla's Critique of Scholastic Philosophy* (Cambridge, MA: Harvard University Press, 2009).

Nelson, Janet L., *King and Emperor: A New Life of Charlemagne* (London: Allen Lane, 2019).

Nelson, Kristina, *The Art of Reciting the Qur'an* (Cairo: American University Press, 2001).

Neshat, Shirin, *Escrito sobre el corpo: Shirin Neshat* (Madrid: Fundación Telefónica, 2013).

Neumann, G., and Untermann, W., *Die Sprachen im römischen Reich der Kaiserzeit* (Cologne: Habelt, 1980).

Newman, John Henry, *The Arians of the Fourth Century* (London: Longman, Green and Co., 1891).

Nichols, J. G., *Narratives of the Days of the Reformation*, Camden Society, 77 (London, 1859).

Nieto Cumplido, Manuel, *La Mezquita-Catedral de Córdoba* (Granada: Edilux, 2005).

Nietzsche, Friedrich, *Kritische Gesamtausgabe*, ed. Giorgio Colli and Mazzino Montinari (Berlin/New York: de Gruyter, 1967–), eKGWB, online edition.

Nietzsche, Friedrich, *Beyond Good and Evil*, ed. Rolf-Peter Horstmann and Judith Norman (Cambridge: Cambridge University Press, 2012).

Nietzsche, Friedrich, *The Anti-Christ, Ecce Homo, Twilight of the Idols: And Other Writings*, ed. Aaron Ridley and Judith Norman (Cambridge: Cambridge University Press, 2011).

Nietzsche, Friedrich, *The Birth of Tragedy and Other Writings*, ed. Raymond Geuss and Ronald Spiers (Cambridge: Cambridge University Press, 1999).

Nietzsche, Friedrich, *The Genealogy of Morality* (Indianapolis, IN: Hackett, 1998).

Norbrook, David, *Writing the English Republic: Poetry, Rhetoric and Politics 1627–1660* (Cambridge: Cambridge University Press, 2000).

Noth, Martin, *A History of Israel* (London: A. & C. Black, 1959).

Nuechterlein, Jeanne, *Translating Nature into Art: Holbein, the Reformation, and Renaissance Rhetoric* (University Park: Pennsylvania State University Press, 2011).

Nussbaum, Martha, *The New Religious Intolerance: Overcoming the Politics of Fear in an Anxious Age* (Cambridge, MA: Harvard University Press, 2012).

Nykl, A. R., 'Inscripciones árabes de la Alhambra y del Generalife', *Al-Andalus*, 4 (1936), 174–94.

Nylan, Michael, and Loewe, Michael (eds.), *China's Early Empires: A Re-Appraisal* (Cambridge: Cambridge University Press, 2010).

O'Malley, Michelle, and Welch, Evelyn, *The Material Renaissance* (Manchester: Manchester University Press, 2007).

Obama, Barack, *Dreams from my Father: A Story of Race and Inheritance* (Edinburgh: Canongate Books, 2008).

Oberman, Heiko A., *Luther: Man between God and Devil* (New Haven: Yale University Press, 1982).

Ochs, Vanessa L., *Inventing Jewish Ritual* (Philadelphia: Jewish Publication Society, 2010).

Ochs, Vanessa L., *The Passover Haggadah: A Biography* (Princeton, NJ: Princeton University Press, 2020).

Oertel, Kristen, *Harriet Tubman: Slavery, the Civil War, and Civil Rights in the Nineteenth Century* (London: Routledge, 2015).

Oesterley, W. O. E., *The Religion and Worship of the Synagogue: An Introduction to the Study of Judaism from the New Testament Period* (London: Isaac Pitman, 1907).

Olds, Sharon, *Odes* (London: Cape Poetry, 2016).

Ong, Walter J., *The Presence of the Word: Some Prolegomena for Cultural and Religious History* (New Haven: Yale University Press, 1967).

Ong, Walter J., *Ramus, Method, and the Decay of Dialogue* (Cambridge MA: Harvard University Press, 1983).

Orwell, George, *Nineteen Eighty-Four* (London: Penguin Classics, 2013).

Osborn, J. R., *Letters of Light: Arabic Script in Calligraphy, Print and Digital Design* (Cambridge, MA: Harvard University Press, 2017).

Ostler, Nicholas, *Empires of the Word: A Language History of the World* (London: Harper Collins, 2005).

Pagden, Anthony, *European Encounters with the New World: From Renaissance to Romanticism* (New Haven and London: Yale University Press, 1993).

Pagels, Elaine, *The Gnostic Gospels* (London: Hachette, 2013).

Parker, Geoffrey, *The Thirty Years' War* (London: Routledge, 1997).

Parker, W. R., *Milton: A Biography*, 2 vols. (Oxford: Clarendon Press, 1968).

Parkes, Malcolm, *Pause and Effect: An Introduction to the History of Punctuation in the West* (Berkeley and Los Angeles: University of California Press, 1993).

Parpola, S., 'Assyrian Library Records', *Journal of Near Eastern Studies*, 42 (1983), 1–29.

Parsons, E. A., *The Alexandrian Library: Glory of the Hellenic World* (New York: Elsevier, 1967).

Patterson, Annabel, *Censorship and Interpretation: The Conditions of Writing and Reading in Early Modern England* (Madison, WI: University of Wisconsin Press, 1984).

Patterson, Lyman Ray, *Copyright in Historical Perspective* (Nashville, TN: Vanderbilt University Press, 1968).

Patterson, Lyman Ray, *The Nature of Copyright: A Law of Users' Rights* (Athens, GA: University of Georgia Press, 1991).

Paul the Silentiary, *Descriptio ambonis*, ed. Claudio De Stefani, Bibliotheca Teubneriana (Berlin: de Gruyter, 2011).

Peters, Edward, *Inquisition* (Berkeley and Los Angeles: University of California Press, 1989).

Peters, Edward, *Torture* (Philadelphia: University of Pennsylvania Press, 1996).

Petrarca, Francesco, *Canzoniere: Rerum vulgarium fragmenta*, ed. Rosanna Bettarini (Turin: Einaudi, 2005).

Petrarca, Francesco, *Il Petrarca con nuove spositioni* (Venice: G. Angelieri, 1595).

Petrarca, Francesco, *Le Familiari*, ed. Vittorio Rossi and Ugo Bosco, 4 vols. (Florence: G. C. Sansoni, 1933–42).

Petrarca, Francesco, *My Secret Book*, ed. Nicholas Mann, I Tatti Renaissance Library 72 (Cambridge: Harvard University Press, 2016).

Petrarca, Francesco, *Petrarch's Lyric Poems*, ed. R. M. Durling (Cambridge, MA: Harvard University Press, 1976).

Petrarca, Francesco, *Selected Letters*, ed. Elaine Fantham, 2 vols., I Tatti Renaissance Library 76–7 (Cambridge: Harvard University Press, 2017).

Petrucci, Armando, *Public Lettering: Script, Power, and Culture* (Chicago: University of Chicago Press, 1993).

Pettegree, Andrew, *Brand Luther* (London: Penguin Books, 2015).

Pettegree, Andrew, *The Book in the Renaissance* (New Haven and London: Yale University Press, 2010).

Petzold, Thomas, *Global Knowledge Dynamics and Social Technology* (New York: Springer, 2017).

Pfaff, Richard W., *The Liturgy in Medieval England: A History* (Cambridge: Cambridge University Press, 2009).

Pfeiffer, Robert H., *State Letters of Assyria*, American Oriental Series, 6 (New Haven: Yale University Press, 1935).

Phillips, Adam, *On Kissing, Tickling and Being Bored* (London: Faber and Faber, 1994).

Piaget, Jean, *Origins of Intelligence in Children* (New York: International Universities Press, 1952).

Pierce, M., 'The Book and the Beech Tree Revisited: The Life Cycle of a Germanic Etymology', *Historische Sprachforschung*, 119 (2006), 273–82.

Pietz, William, 'The Problem of the Fetish, I', *RES: Anthropology and Aesthetics*, 9 (Spring 1985), 5–17.

Pietz, William, 'The Problem of the Fetish, II', *RES: Anthropology and Aesthetics,* 13 (Spring 1987), 23–45.

Plato, *Phaedrus*, ed. Harvey Yunis (Cambridge: Cambridge University Press, 2011).

Pocock, J. G. A., *The Machiavellian Moment: Florentine Political Thought and the Atlantic Republican Tradition* (Princeton, NJ: Princeton University Press, 2003).

Poe, Edgar Allan, 'The Fall of the House of Usher', *Burton's Gentleman's Magazine* (September, 1839).

Poe, Edgar Allan, *The Gift* (Philadelphia: Carey and Hart, 1845).

Popper, Karl, *Unended Quest: An Intellectual Autobiography* (London: Routledge, 2005).

Portal, Jane (ed.), *The First Emperor: China's Terracotta Army* (London: British Museum, 2007).

Porter, H. C., *Reformation and Reaction in Tudor Cambridge* (Cambridge: Cambridge University Press, 1958).

Potter, G. R., *Zwingli* (Cambridge: Cambridge University Press, 1984).

Pound, Ezra, *Collected Shorter Poems*, 2nd ed. (London: Faber & Faber, 1968).

Pound, Ezra, *Literary Essays of Ezra Pound*, ed. T. S. Eliot (London: Faber & Faber, 1960).

Powell, Barry B., *Homer and the Origin of the Greek Alphabet* (Cambridge: Cambridge University Press, 1996).

Pralle, Ludwig, *Gaude Fulda! Das Bonifatiusjahr 1954* (Fulda: Parzeller, 1954).

Press, Steven Michael, 'False Fire: The Wartburg Book-Burning of 1817', *Central European History*, 42 (2009), 621–46.

Price, Leah, *How to Do Things with Books in Victorian Britain* (Princeton: Princeton University Press, 2012).

Price, Leah, 'Reading: The State of the Discipline', *Book History*, 7 (2004), 303–20.

Pritchard, James B. (ed.), *Ancient Near-Eastern Texts Relating to the Old Testament* (Princeton: Preinceton University Press, 1969).

Proust, Marcel, *À la recherche du temps perdu*, ed. Jean-Yves Tadié, 4 vols., Éditions de la Pléiade (Paris: Gallimard, 1987–9).

Proust, Marcel, *The Way by Swann's*, tr. Lydia Davis (London: Penguin Classics, 2003).

Proust, Marcel, *Time Regained*, tr. Stephen Hudson (London: Penguin Classics, 2000).

Puerta Vílchez, José Miguel, *Reading the Alhambra: A Visual Guide to the Alhambra through its Inscriptions* (Granada: Patronato de la Alhambra y Generalife, 2010).

Qiftī, 'Alī ibn Yūsuf, *Ta'rīḫ al-Ḥukamā'*, ed. August Müller and Julius Lippert (Leipzig: Dieterich, 1903).

Rabelais, François, *Œuvres complètes*, ed. Mireille Huchon and François Moreau, Éditions de la Pléiade (Paris: Gallimard, 1994).

Rabelais, François. *Gargantua and Pantagruel*, tr. T. Urquhart (London: J. M. Dent, 1946).

Rad, Gerhard von, *Genesis: A Commentary* (London: SCM, 1972).

Rafetseder, Hermann, *Bücherverbrennungen: die öffentliche Hinrichtung von Schriften im historischen Wandel* (Vienna: Böhlau Verlag, 1988).

Rainey, Lawrence, Poggi, Christine and Wittman, Laura, Futurism: An Anthology, ed. (New Haven & London: Yale University Press, 2009).

Ramus, Peter, *Dialectique* (Paris: Wéchel, 1555).

Raven, H. M., and Goodman L. E. (eds.), *Jewish Themes in Spinoza's Philosophy* (Albany, NY: SUNY Press, 2012).

Raven, James, *The Business of Books: Booksellers and the English Book Trade 1450–1850* (New Haven and London: Yale University Press, 2007).

Raven, James (ed.), *Lost Libraries: The Destruction of Great Book Collections since Antiquity* (London: Palgrave Macmillan, 2004).

Rawlings, Helen, 'Goya's Inquisition: From Black Legend to Liberal Legend', *Vida Hispanica*, 46 (2012), 15–21.

Rawls, John, *Political Liberalism: Expanded Edition* (New York: Columbia University Press, 2005).

Rawson, Elizabeth, *Cicero: A Portrait* (London: Allen Lane, 1975).

Reeve, John (ed.), *Sacred: Books of the Three Faiths: Judaism, Christianity, Islam* (London: British Library, 2007).

Renger, J., *Babylon: Focus mesopotamischer Geschichte, Wiege früher Gelehrsamkeit, Mythos in der Moderne* (Saarbrücken: Harrassowitz, 1999).

Rétat, Pierre, *La Révolution du journal, 1788–1794* (Paris: CNRS, 1989).

Reynolds, Anna, 'Early Modern Encounters with Binding Waste', *Journal of the Northern Renaissance*, 8 (2017), 1–43.

Richard de Bury, *Philobiblon*, tr. E. C. Thomas (London: De la More Press, 1903).

Richter, Melvyn, *The Political Theory of Montesquieu* (Cambridge: Cambridge University Press, 1977).

Ricks, Christopher, 'Tennyson's Methods of Composition', *Proceedings of the British Academy*, 52 (1968), 209–30.

Rigolot, François, 'Curiosity, Contingency, and Cultural Diversity: Montaigne's Readings at the Vatican Library', *Renaissance Quarterly*, 64 (2011), 847–874.

Rites of Durham, ed. J. T. Fowler, Surtees Society, 107 (Durham: Andrews & Co., 1903).

Robinson, Chase (ed.), *New Cambridge History of Islam, Vol. 1: The Formation of the Islamic World, Sixth to Eleventh Centuries* (Cambridge: Cambridge University Press, 2010).

Rochester, John Wilmot, Earl of, *The Works of John Wilmot Earl of Rochester*, ed. Harold Love (Oxford: Oxford University Press, 1999).

Rodríguez Martínez, M. del Carmen, *et al.*, 'Oldest Writing in the New World', *Science*, 313, issue 5793 (15 September 2006), 1610–14.

Roitman, A., Schiffmann, L., and Tzoref, S. (eds.), *The Dead Sea Scrolls and Contemporary Culture* (Leiden: Brill, 2011).

Roper, Lyndal, *Martin Luther: Renegade and Prophet* (London: Vintage Books, 2017).

Rose, Jonathan (ed.), *The Holocaust and the Book: Destruction and Preservation* (Amherst: University of Massachusetts Press, 2001).

Ross, Ian Campbell, *Laurence Sterne: A Life* (Oxford: Oxford University Press, 2001).

Roth, Joseph, *What I Saw: Reports from Berlin, 1920–1933*, tr. Michael Hoffman (London: Granta, 2004).

Rousseau, Jean-Jacques, *Œuvres complètes*, Bibliothèque de la Pléiade, 5 vols. (Paris: Gallimard, 1959–95).

Rousseau, Jean-Jacques, *Confessions*, tr. Angela Scholar (Oxford: Oxford World's Classics, 2000).

Rousseau, Jean-Jacques, *On the Origin of Language*, tr. John H. Moran and Alexander Gode (New York: Frederick Ungar, 1966).

Roux, Emmanuel de, 'Rétrocontroverse: 1988, la Très Grande Bibliothèque', *Le Monde*, 31 July 2007.

Roux, Jacques, *L'ombre de Marat au peuple français* (Paris: n.p., 1793).

Rowling, J. K., *Harry Potter and the Goblet of Fire* (London: Bloomsbury, 2000).

Runciman, Steven, *The Medieval Manichee: A Study of the Dualist Heresy*, rev. edn. (Cambridge: Cambridge University Press, 2010).

Rundle, David, *The Renaissance Reform of the Book and Britain* (Cambridge: Cambridge University Press, 2019).

Rushdie, Salman, 'Book Burning', *New York Review of Books*, 36 (2 March 1989), 26.

Rushdie, Salman, *Is Nothing Sacred?* (London: Granta Press, 1990).

Rushdie, Salman, *Midnight's Children* (London: Picador, 1982).

Rushdie, Salman, *The Satanic Verses* (London: Vintage Books, 1988).

Rustow, Marina, *The Lost Archive: Traces of a Caliphate in a Cairo Synagogue* (Princeton: Princeton University Press, 2020).

Ryle, Gilbert, *The Concept of Mind* (London: Hutchinson, 1949).

Saad, Elias N., *Social History of Timbuktu: The Role of Muslim Scholars and Notables* (Cambridge: Cambridge University Press, 1983).

Saenger, Paul, *Space between Words: The Origins of Silent Reading* (Stanford: Stanford University Press, 1997).

Salvesen, Alison (ed.), *Origen's Hexapla and Fragments*, Texte und Studien zum antiken Judentum, 58 (Tübingen: Mohr Siebeck, 1998).

Salvesen, Alison and Law T. M. (eds.), *The Oxford Handbook of the Septuagint* (Oxford: Oxford University Press, 2020).

Samadelli, Marco, *et al.*, 'Complete Mapping of the Tattoos of the 5300-Year-Old Tyrolean Iceman', *Journal of Cultural Heritage*, 16: 5 (2015), 753–58.

Sapir, Edward, *Language: An Introduction to the Study of Speech* (New York: Harcourt & Brace, 1921).

Sauder, Gerhard (ed.), *Die Bücherverbrennung: zum 10. Mai 1933* (Munich: Carl Hanser, 1983).

Saussure, Ferdinand de, *Course in General Linguistics*, tr. Roy Harris (London: Duckworth, 1983).

Sayce, A. H., *An Elementary Grammar of the Assyrian Language in the Cuneiform Type* (Cambridge: Cambridge University Press, 2014).

Scarpi, Paolo (ed.), *La rivelazione segreta di Ermete Trismegisto*, Fondazione Lorenzo Valla, 2 vols. (Milan: Arnoldo Mondadori, 2011).

Scarry, Elaine, *The Body in Pain: The Making and Unmaking of the World* (Oxford: Oxford University Press, 1987).

Schalkwyck, David, *Hamlet's Dreams: The Robben Island Shakespeare* (London: Methuen, 2013).

Schama, Simon, *Citizens: A Chronicle of the French Revolution* (London: Penguin Books, 1989).

Schechter, Solomon, 'A Hoard of Hebrew MSS', *The Times*, 3 August 1897.

Schieffer, Theodor, *Winfrid-Bonifatius und die christliche Grundlegung Europas*, 2nd edn. (Darmstadt: Wissenschaftliche Buchgesellschaft, 1972).

Schleiermacher, Friedrich, *Pädagogische Schriften*, ed. C. Patz (Langensalza: Hermann Beyer, 1876).

Schleiermacher, Friedrich, *On Religion*, ed. Richard Crouter (Cambridge: Cambridge University Press, 1988).

Schleiermacher, Friedrich, 'The Hermeneutics: Outline of the 1819 Lectures', *New Literary History*, 10 (1978), 1–6.

Schmidt, Eric, and Cohen, Jared, *The New Digital Age: Reshaping the Future of People, Nations and Business* (New York: Jon Murray, 2013).

Schmitt, Charles B., and Skinner, Quentin (eds.), *The Cambridge History of Renaissance Philosophy* (Cambridge: Cambridge University Press, 1988).

Schroeder, H. J., *Disciplinary Decrees of the General Councils: Text, Translation and Commentary* (St. Louis, MI: B. Herder, 1937).

Scott-Warren, Jason, *Sir John Harington and the Book as Gift* (Oxford: Oxford University Press, 2001).

Screech, M. A. (ed.), *Montaigne's Annotated Copy of Lucretius: A Transcription and Study of the Manuscript, Notes and Pen-Marks* (Geneva: Droz, 1998).

Searle, John R., 'Minds, Brains and Programs', *Behavioural and Brain Sciences*, 3 (1980), 417–57.

Sebald, W. G., *Austerlitz*, tr. Anthea Bell (London: Penguin Books, 2002).

Select Parts of the Holy Bible, for the Use of the Negro Slaves, in the British West-India Islands (London: Law and Gilbert, 1807).

Servetus, Michael, *The Restoration of Christianity*, tr. Christopher Hofmann and Marian Hiller (London: Edwin Mellen, 2006).

Shagan, Ethan H., *Popular Politics and the English Reformation* (Cambridge: Cambridge University Press, 2003).

Shahab Ahmed, 'Ibn Taymiyyah and the Satanic Verses', *Studia Islamica*, 87 (1998), 67–124.

Shakespeare, William, *Mr. William Shakespeares comedies, histories, & tragedies* (London: Isaac Jaggard and Edward Blount, 1623).

Shakespeare, William, *Mr. William Shakespeares comedies, histories, & tragedies* (London: Thomas Cotes, 1632).

Shapin, Steven, *A Social History of Truth: Civility and Science in Seventeenth-Century England* (Chicago: University of Chicago Press, 1998).

Sharaf, Myron, *Fury on Earth: A Biography of Wilhelm Reich* (Boston, MA: Da Capo, 1994).

Shelley, Mary, *Frankenstein: or, The Modern Prometheus*, The 1818 Text, ed. Nick Groom, Oxford World's Classics (Oxford: Oxford University Press, 2019).

Shelley, Percy Bysshe, *Poems Published in 1820*, ed. A. M. Hughes (Oxford: Oxford University Press, 1910).

Sherman, William H., *Used Books: Marking Readers in Renaissance England* (Philadelphia: University of Pennsylvania Press, 2010).

Shiji (Beijing: Zhonghua shuju, 1985).

Shlain, Leonard, *The Alphabet Versus the Goddess: The Conflict Between Word and Image* (New York: Viking, 1998).

Shore, Daniel, *Cyberformalism: Histories of Linguistic Forms in the Digital Archive* (Baltimore: Johns Hopkins University Press, 2018).

Shen, Hsueh-Man, 'Realizing the Buddha's "Dharma" Body during the Mofa Period: A Study of Liao Buddhist Relic Deposits', *Artibus Asiae*, 61 (2001), 263–303.

Shultz, Edward, *Generals and Scholars: Military Rule in Medieval Korea* (Honolulu: University of Hawaii Press, 2000).

Sierhuis, Freya, *The Literature of the Arminian Controversy* (Oxford: Oxford University Press, 2015).

Sima Qian, *The First Emperor: Selections from the Historical Records*, tr. Raymond Dawson, Oxford World's Classics (Oxford: Oxford University Press, 2007).

Simon, Joshua, *Neomaterialism* (Berlin: Sternberg Press, 2013).

Simpson, James, *Permanent Revolution: The Reformation and the Illiberal Roots of Liberalism* (Cambridge, MA: Harvard University Press, 2019).

Simpson, James, *Under the Hammer: Iconoclasm in the Anglo-American Tradition*, Clarendon Lectures (Oxford: Oxford University Press, 2010).

Skeat, W. W., *An Etymological Dictionary of the English Language*, 4th edn. (Oxford: Clarendon Press, 1910).

Smalley, Beryl, *The Study of the Bible in the Middle Ages* (Notre Dame, IN: University of Notre Dame Press, 1978).

Smith, Helen, 'The Proliferating Surfaces of Early Modern Paper', *Journal of the Northern Renaissance*, 8 (2017), 2–37.

Smith, Nigel, *Literature and Revolution in England 1640–1660* (New Haven and London: Yale University Press, 1997).

Smith, S. E., '"The Eternal Verities Verified": Charlton Hinman and the Roots of Mechanical Collation', *Studies in Bibliography*, 53 (2000), 129–61.

Smyth, Adam, *Material Texts in Early Modern England* (Cambridge: Cambridge University Press, 2018).

Snorri Sturluson, *The Prose Edda*, tr. Jesse L. Byock (London: Penguin Books, 2005).

Snowden, Edward, *Permanent Record* (London: Macmillan, 2019).

Sohn, Pow-Key, 'Early Korean Printing', *Journal of the American Oriental Society*, 79 (1959), 96–103.

Sohn, Pow-Key, *Early Korean Typography* (Seoul: Korean Library Science Research Institute, 1982).

Sorabji, Richard, *Philoponus and the Rejection of Aristotelian Science* (London: Duckworth, 1987).

Souldiers Pocket Bible, The: containing the most (if not all) those places contained in holy Scripture, which doe shew the qualifications of his inner man, that is a fit Souldier to fight the Lords Battels, both before the fight, in the fight, and after the fight (London: G.B. and R.W., 1643).

Southern, A. C., *Elizabethan Recusant Prose, 1559–1582* (London: Sands & Co., 1950).

Southwell, Robert, *Collected Poems*, ed. Peter Davidson and Anne Sweeney (Manchester: Carcanet, 2007).

Southwell, Robert, *The Poems of Robert Southwell*, ed. James H. McDonald and Nancy Pollard Brown (Oxford: Clarendon Press, 1967).

Spence, Jonathan, *Treason by the Book: Traitors, Conspirators and Guardians of the Emperor* (London: Penguin Books, 2001).

Spevack, Marvin, *James Orchard Halliwell-Phillipps: The Life and Works of the Shakespearean Scholar and Bookman* (New Castle, DE: Oak Knoll Press, 2001).

Spinoza, Baruch, *Opera*, ed. Carl Gebhart, 4 vols., im Auftrag der Heidelberger Akademie der Wissenschaften (Heidelberg: C. Winter, 1925).

Spinoza, Baruch, *Theological-Political Treatise*, tr. Samuel Shirley (Indianapolis: Hackett, 1998).

St Clair, William, *The Reading Nation in the Romantic Period* (Cambridge: Cambridge University Press, 2004).

Staikos, K., *The Greek Editions of Aldus Manutius and his Greek Collaborators* (New York: Oak Knoll Press, 2016).

Stallybrass, Peter, 'Marx's Coat', in *Consumption: Theory and Issues in the Study of Consumption*, ed. Daniel Miller (London: Taylor & Francis, 2001), 311–34.

Stallybrass, Peter, 'Petrarch and Babylon: Censoring and Uncensoring the *Rime*, 1559–1651', in Ann Blair and Anja-Silvia Goeing (eds.), *For the Sake of Learning: Essays in Honor of Anthony Grafton* (Leiden: Brill, 2016), 581–601.

Stanley, Henry M., *Through the Dark Continent*, 2 vols. (New York: Harper and Bros, 1878).

Steinert, Ulrike, *Assyrian and Babylonian Scholarly Text Catalogues: Medicine, Magic and Divination* (Berlin: de Gruyter, 2018).

Sterne, Laurence, *The Life and Opinions of Tristram Shandy, Gentleman*, 9 vols. (York and London: J. Hinxman, R. Dodsley, T. Becket, *et al.*, 1759–67).

Stewart, Alan, *Shakespeare's Letters* (Oxford: Oxford University Press, 2008).

Stock, Brian, *The Implications of Literacy* (Princeton: Princeton University Press, 1983).

Stow, John, *A Survey of London*, ed. C. L. Kingsford, 2 vols. (Oxford: Clarendon Press, 1971).

Strohm, Paul (ed.), *Middle English*, Twenty-First Approaches to Literature (Oxford: Oxford University Press, 2009).

Strong, John S., *Relics of the Buddha* (Delhi: Motilal Banarsidass, 2007).

Stroumsa, Guy, *Hidden Wisdom: Esoteric Traditions and the Roots of Christian Mysticism* (Leiden: Brill, 2005), pp. 185–6.

Stroumsa, Sarah, *Maimonides in his World: Portrait of a Mediterranean Thinker* (Princeton: Princeton University Press, 2009).

Suarez, Michael F., and Turner, Michael L. (eds.), *Cambridge History of the Book in Britain, Vol. 5, 1695–1830* (Cambridge: Cambridge University Press, 2009).

Suarez, Michael F., and Woudhuysen H. R. (eds.), *Oxford Companion to the Book*, 2 vols. (Oxford: Oxford University Press, 2010).

Sullivan, Margaret A., 'Bruegel's Misanthrope: Renaissance Art for a Humanist Audience', *Artibus et Historiae*, 13 (1992), 143–62.

Sullivan, Michael, *The Arts of China* (London: Thames & Hudson, 1973).

Summit, Jennifer, *Memory's Library: Medieval Books in Early Modern England* (Chicago: University of Chicago Press, 2008).

Susini, Giancarlo, *Epigrafia Romana* (Rome: Jouvence, 1997).

Swift, Jonathan, *A Tale of a Tub with Other Early Works*, ed. Herbert Davis, Prose Writings of Jonathan Swift, 1 (Oxford: Basil Blackwell, 1965).

Swift, Jonathan, *Bickerstaff Papers and Pamphlets on the Church*, ed. Herbert Davis, 2 vols., Prose Writings of Jonathan Swift, 2 (Oxford: Basil Blackwell, 1957).

T'ung, Tai, *The Six Scripts, or the Principles of Chinese Writing*, tr. L. C. Hopkins (Cambridge: Cambridge University Press, 1954).

Talbot, C. H., *The Anglo-Saxon Missionaries in Germany* (London and New York: Sheed and Ward, 1954).

Tarasov, Oleg, *Framing Russian Art: From Early Icons to Malevich* (London: Reaktion Books, 2012).

Tarasov, Oleg, *Icon and Devotion: Sacred Spaces in Imperial Russia*, tr. Robin Milner-Gulland (London: Reaktion Books, 2004).

Taylor, Charles, *A Secular Age* (Cambridge, MA: Harvard University Press, 2007).

Taylor, L. J., *Heresy and Orthodoxy in Sixteenth Century Paris* (Leiden: Brill, 1999).

Thévoz, M., *The Painted Body* (New York: Skira, 1984).

Thomas à Kempis, *Doctrinale juvenum*, 5; *Opera* (Paris: Badius Ascensius, 1523).

Thomas à Kempis, *The Imitation of Christ* (London: Macmillan, 1874).

Thomas Aquinas, *Summa theologiae*, Leonine Edition, 9 vols. (Rome: Typographia Polyglotta S. C. de Propaganda Fide, 1888–1906).

Thompson, Clive, 'The Future of Reading in a Digital World', *Wired*, 22 May, 2007.

Thompson, Edward M, *An Introduction to Greek and Latin Palaeography* (Oxford: Clarendon Press, 1911).

Thoreau, Henry David, *Walden and Other Writings* (New York: Modern Library, 2000).

Thorpe, William, *The examinacion of Master William Thorpe preste accused of heresye before Thomas Arundell* (Antwerp: Merten de Keyser, 1530).

Toer, Parmoedya Ananta, *The Fugitive* (Hong Kong: Heinemann International, 1975).

Toynbee, J. M. C., *Death and Burial in the Roman World* (Ithaca: Cornell University Press, 1971).

Trapnel, Anna, *A Legacy for Saints; being several experiences of the dealings of God* (London: T. Brewster, 1654).

Tsien Tsuen-Hsuin, 'Paper and Printing', in Joseph Needham (ed.), *Science and Civilization in China, Vol. 5: Chemistry and Chemical Technology* (Cambridge: Cambridge University Press, 1985).

Turing, A. M., 'Computing Machinery and Intelligence', *Mind*, 49 (1950), 433–460.

Turing, A. M., 'On Computable Numbers, with an Application to the *Entscheidungsproblem*', *Proceedings of the London Mathematical Society*, 42/: 1 (1936), 230–65.

Twitchett, Denis, and Loewe Michael (eds.), *The Cambridge History of China: Volume I: The Ch'in and Han Empires, 221 B.C.–A.D 220* (Cambridge: Cambridge University Press, 1986).

Tyler, Elizabeth M., *England in Europe: English Royal Women and Literary Patronage, c.1000-c.1150* (Toronto: University of Toronto Press, 2017).

Tyndale, William, *Answer to More*, ed. Anne O'Donnell and Jared Wicks (Washington, DC: Catholic University of America Press, 2000).

Tyndale, William, *The obedience of a Christen man and how Christen rulers ought to governe* ([Antwerp]: [Merten de Keyser], [1528]).

Tzetzes John, *Epistolae*, ed. Theodore Pressel (Tübingen: Franciscus Fues, 1851).

Underwood, Ted, 'Theorizing Research Practices we Forgot to Theorize Twenty Years Ago', *Representations*, 127 (2014), 64–72.

Vallier, Dora, and Georges Braque, 'Braque, la peinture et nous', *Cahiers d'Art*, 29, no. 1 (Paris, October 1954), 13–24.

Varian, Hal R., 'Big Data: New Tricks for Econometrics', *Journal of Economic Perspectives*, 28 (2014), 3–28.

Vasari, Giorgio, *The Lives of the Artists*, tr. J. and P. Bondanella (Oxford: Oxford World's Classics, 2008).

Vasileiadis, Pavlos D., 'Aspects of Rendering the Sacred Tetragrammaton in Greek', *Open Theology*, 1 (2014), 56–88.

Vikør, Knut S., *Between God and the Sultan: A History of Islamic Law* (Oxford: Oxford University Press, 2005).

Vodosek, Peter, and Komorowski, Manfred (eds.), *Bibliotheken während des Nationalsozialismus*, 2 vols., Wolfenbütteler Schriften zur Geschichte des Buchwesens, 16 (Wiesbaden: Harrassowitz, 1989–92).

Voltaire, *Correspondance*, ed. Théodore Besterman, 13 vols., Bibliothèque de la Pléiade (Paris: Gallimard, 1963–93).

Voltaire, *Dictionnaire philosophique portatif par Mr. de Voltaire* (Nancy: J. B. H. Leclerc, 1764).

Voltaire, *Essai sur les mœurs*, ed. René Pomeau, 2 vols. (Paris: Garnier, 1963).

Voltaire, *Mélanges*, Bibliothèque de la Pléiade (Paris: Gallimard, 1963–93).

Voltaire, *Philosophical Dictionary*, tr. Peter Gay 2 vols. (New York: Basic Books, 1962).

Waiboer, Adriaan, Wheelock, Arthur K., and Ducos, Blaise (eds.), *Vermeer and the Masters of Genre Painting* (New Haven and London: Yale University Press, 2017).

Wainwright, Geoffrey (ed.), *The Oxford History of Christian Worship* (Oxford: Oxford University Press, 2006).

Wakelin, Daniel, *Humanism, Reading, and English Literature 1430–1530* (Oxford: Oxford University Press, 2007).

Walsham, Alexandra, 'Jewels for Gentlewomen: Religious Books as Artefacts in Late Medieval and Early Modern England', *Studies in Church History*, 38 (2004), 123–42.

Walsham, Alexandra, *Providence in Early Modern England* (Oxford: Oxford University Press, 1999).

Walsham, Alexandra, *The Social History of the Archive: Record-Keeping in Early Modern Europe*, Supplementary issue, *Past and Present*, 230 (2016).

Walsham, Alexandra (ed.), *Relics and Remains*, Past and Present, Supplement (Oxford: Oxford University Press, 2010).

Warren, Peter, *Minoan Stone Vases*, Cambridge Classical Studies, 23 (Cambridge: Cambridge University Press, 1969).

Waterhouse, E. K., 'The Fresco by Foppa in the Wallace Collection', *Burlington Magazine* 92 (1950), 177.

Watson, Nicholas, 'Censorship and Cultural Change in Late Medieval England', *Speculum*, 70 (1995), 822–64.

Weber, Caroline, *Terror and Its Discontents: Suspect Words in Revolutionary France* (Minneapolis, MN: University of Minnesota Press, 2003).

Weber, Max, *Gesammelte Aufsätze zur Wissenschaftslehre*, ed. J. Winckelmann (Tübingen: J. C. B. Mohr, 1985).

Weber, Max, *Gesamtausgabe, I: Schriften und Reden*, ed. Wolfgang J. Mommsen *et al.* 25 vols. (Tübingen: Mohr Siebeck, 1988–2016).

Weber, Max, *From Max Weber: Essays in Sociology*, ed. H. H. Geerth and C. Wright Mills (London: Routledge, 2009).

Wegener, Ulrike, *Die Faszination des Masslosen: der Turmbau zu Babel von Pieter Bruegel bis Athanasius Kircher* (Hildesheim: Georg Olms Verlag, 1995).

Weingreen, J., *A Practical Grammar for Classical Hebrew*, 2nd edn. (Oxford: Clarendon Press, 1959).

Weintraub, Linda, *In the Making: Creative Options for Contemporary Art* (New York: Distributed Art Publishers, 2003).

Weiss, N., 'Arrêt inédit du Parlement de Paris contre l'Institution chrétienne (1er juillet 1542)', *Bulletin de la Société de l'histoire du protestantisme français*, 33 (1884), 15–21.

Weiss, N., *La chambre ardente* (Geneva: Slatkine, 1970).

West, Anthony J., *The Shakespeare First Folio: A New Worldwide Census of First Folios* (Oxford: Oxford University Press, 2001).

West, Anthony J., *The Shakespeare First Folio: The History of the Book*, vol. 1: *An Account of the First Folio Based on its Sales and Prices, 1623–2000* (Oxford: Oxford University Press, 2001).

Wharton, W. (ed.), *Captain Cook's Journal during his First Voyage round the World* (London: Elliot Stock, 1893).

White, Burton, *The First Three Years of Life* (Madison, WI: Prentice Hall, 1975).

Whitehead, Colson, *The Underground Railroad* (New York: Doubleday, 2016).

Whiteread, Rachel, *British Pavilion XLVII Venice Biennale 1997* (London: British Council, 1997).

Wiegand, Wayne A., and Davis, Jr., Donald G. (eds.), *Encyclopedia of Library History* (New York: Garland Publishing, 1994).

Wildenstein, Daniel and Guy, *Documents complémentaires au catalogue de l'œuvre de Louis David* (Paris: Wildenstein Foundation, 1973).

Wilkins, David, *Concilia magnae Britanniae et Hiberniae*, 4 vols. (London: R. Gosling, 1737).

Williams, Bernard, 'Toleration: An Impossible Virtue?', in D. Heyd (ed.), *Toleration: An Elusive Virtue* (Princeton: Princeton University Press, 1996).

Williams, Robert A., *The American Indian in Western Legal Thought* (Oxford: Oxford University Press, 1992).

Williams, Rowan, *Arius: Heresy and Tradition* (London: SCM, 2001).

Williams, Rowan, 'Origen: Between Orthodoxy and Heresy', in W. A. Bienert and U. Kuhneweg (eds.), *Origeniana Septima* (Leuven: Leuven University Press, 1999).

Williamson, C., 'Monuments of Bronze: Roman Legal Documents on Bronze Tablets', *Classical Antiquity*, 6 (1987), 160–83.

Wilson, Edward M., 'Shakespeare and Christian Doctrine: Some Qualifications', *Shakespeare Survey*, 23 (1970), 79–89.

Wilson, Nigel, *From Byzantium to Italy: Greek Studies in the Italian Renaissance*, 2nd. edn. (London: Bloomsbury, 2017).

Wilson, Penelope, *Hieroglyphs: A Very Short Introduction* (Oxford: Oxford University Press, 2004).

Wilson, Penelope, *Sacred Signs: Hieroglyphs in Ancient Egypt* (Oxford: Oxford University Press, 2003).

Wilson, Peter H., *Europe's Tragedy: A New History of the Thirty Years War* (London: Penguin Books, 2010).

Winger, Howard W., and Smith, Richard Daniel (eds.), *Deterioration and Preservation of Library Materials* (Chicago: University of Chicago Press, [1970]).

Winnicott, Donald, *Playing and Reality* (London: Routledge Classics, 2005).

Wischnitzer, Rachel, *The Architecture of the European Synagogue* (Philadelphia: Jewish Publication Society of America, 1964).

Wittgenstein, Ludwig, *Philosophical Investigations*, tr. G. E. M. Anscombe, 2nd edn. (Oxford: Blackwell, 1958).

Wood, John George, *A Tour Round My Garden* (London: G. Routledge, 1855).

Woolf, Virginia, *Essays of Virginia Woolf: Vol. 6, 1933–1941*, ed. Stuart N. Clarke (London: Hogarth Press, 2011).

Woolf, Virginia, *The Common Reader*, Second Series (London: Hogarth Press, 1932).

Woolf, Virginia, *The Waves* (London: Hogarth Press, 1931).

Woolf, Virginia, *To the Lighthouse* (London: Hogarth Press, 1963).

Wootton, David, *The Invention of Science: A New History of the Scientific Revolution* (London: Penguin Books, 2015).

Woudhuysen, H. R., *Sir Philip Sidney and the Circulation of Manuscripts 1558–1640* (Oxford: Clarendon Press, 1996).

Woudhuysen, H. R., 'The Foundations of Shakespeare's Text', *Proceedings of the British Academy*, 125 (2004), 69–100.

Woudhuysen, H. R., and Suarez Michael F. (eds.), *The Book: A Global History* (Oxford: Oxford University Press, 2013).

Wrede, Adolf (ed.), *Deutsche Reichstagsakten*, 4 vols. (Gotha: Friedrich Andreas Perthes, 1893–1905).

Wriothesley, Charles, *A Chronicle of England during the Reigns of the Tudors*, ed. W. D. Hamilton, 2 vols. (New York: Camden Society, 1965).

Wu Hung, *Making History: Wu Hung on Contemporary Art* (Hong Kong: Timezone 8, 2008).

Wu Hung (ed.), *Reinventing Books in Contemporary Chinese Art* (New York: China Institute Gallery, 2006).

Wyclif, John, *De veritate sacrae scripturae*, ed. Ian Christopher Levy (Kalamazoo, MI: Medieval Institute Publications, 2001).

Yar-Shater, E. (ed.), *The Cambridge History of Iran, Vol. 3.1: Seleucid, Parthian and Sasanian Periods* (Cambridge: Cambridge University Press, 1983).

Yunis, Harvey, *Taming Democracy: Models of Political Rhetoric in Classical Athens* (Ithaca: Cornell University Press, 1996).

Yunis, Harvey (ed.), *Written Texts and the Rise of Literate Culture in Ancient Greece* (Cambridge: Cambridge University Press, 2003).

Zhengyuan Fu, *Autocratic Tradition and Chinese Politics* (Cambridge: Cambridge University Press 1994).

Ziolkowski, Jan, and Putnam, Michael, *The Virgilian Tradition: The First Fifteen Hundred Years* (New Haven and London: Yale University Press, 2008).

Žižek, Slavoj, *Less Than Nothing: Hegel and the Shadow of Dialectical Materialism* (London: Verso Books, 2012).

Zorzi, Marino, *La libreria di san Marco: Libri, lettori, società nella Venezia dei dogi* (Milan: Mondadori, 1987).

Zuboff, Shoshana, *The Age of Surveillance Capitalism: The Fight for a Human Future at the New Frontier of Power* (New York and London: Profile Books, 2019).

Zürcher, Erik Jan, *Jihad and Islam in World War I* (Leiden: Leiden University Press, 2016).

Zweig, Stefan, *Amok: Novellen einer Leidenschaft* (Frankfurt am Main: Fischer Verlag, 1966).

Zweig, Stefan, *Castellio gegen Calvin: oder Ein Gewissen gegen die Gewalt* (Frankfurt am Main: Fischer Verlag, 1936).

Zweig, Stefan, *Erasmus and The Right to Heresy* (London: Souvenir Books, 1979).

Zweig, Stefan, *Triumph und Tragik des Erasmus von Rotterdam* (Vienna: Herbert Reichner, 1934).

Index of Manuscripts

Belgium
Antwerp, Stadsarchief, PK 93
Antwerp, Stadsarchief, PK 914

Canada
University of Toronto, Centre for Renaissance
  and Reformation Studies BR 65.J4 1524a

Egypt
Cairo, National Museum MS 10
Cairo, National Museum, MS 72

France
Besançon, Musée de la Résistance et de la
  Déportation, Inv. 2001.1324.01
Chantilly, Musée de Condé, MS 65
Marseille, Bibliothèque municipale, cod. 1626
Paris, Archives Nationales, MM.248
Paris, Archives Nationales, X2a 88
Paris, Archives Nationales, X2a 89
Paris, Archives Nationales, X2a 93
Paris, Bibliothèque nationale de France,
  MS Coréen 109
Paris, Bibliothèque nationale de France,
  cod. hébr. 25
Paris, Bibliothèque nationale de France,
  MS latin, 2079
Paris, Bibliothèque nationale de France,
  MS. latin 2923
Paris, Bibliothèque nationale de France,
  MS. latin 9389

Germany
Berlin, Staatsbibliothek, MS Hamilton 166
Fulda, Landesbibliothek, Codex Bonifatianus 2
Göttingen, Staats- und Universitätsbibliothek, 2°
  Cod. MS theol. 231
Nürnberg Germanisches Nationalmuseum, MS
  Hs 156142
Würzburg, Staatsarchiv, I 21 C 14/I

Ireland
Dublin, Chester Beatty Library, MS 1431
Dublin, Chester Beatty Library, MS Is 1457.1
Dublin, Trinity College Library, MS A. I. [58]

Italy
Florence, Biblioteca Medicea Laurenziana,
  MS Amiatino 1
Parma, Biblioteca Palatina, MS Parm 2668

Netherlands
The Hague, Museum Meermanno-
  Westreenianum, MS 10 A 11

Russia
Moscow, Historical Museum, MS 129

South Korea
Seoul, Gansong Art Museum, National
  Treasure No. 70

Spain
Madrid, Biblioteca Nacional, cod. vit. 13–11

Sweden
Uppsala, University Library, MS O BJ. 48

Switzerland
Zürich, Zentralbibliothek MS A 2

Turkey
Istanbul University Library, MS A 6755

United Kingdom
Cambridge, Corpus Christi College, MS 128
Cambridge University Library, Taylor-Schechter
  Genizah Collection T-S 12.182.
Cambridge University Library, BSS. 201. B37.6
Canterbury Cathedral Library W/S-10–3
Durham, University Library, Cosin MS B.ii.11
London, British Library, MS Cotton
  Cleopatra. E V
London, British Library Cotton MS Nero D.IV
London, British Library, MS Egerton 1821
London, British Library, MS Harley 425
London, British Library, MS Harley 2985
London, British Library, MS Kings 9
London, British Library, MS Royal 13. D. iv
London, British Library, MS Royal 18. A. lxvi
London, British Library, MS Stowe 10

Index